Communications
in Computer and Information Science   1294

More information about this series at http://www.springer.com/series/7899

Constantine Stephanidis ·
Margherita Antona · Stavroula Ntoa (Eds.)

HCI International 2020 – Late Breaking Posters

22nd International Conference, HCII 2020
Copenhagen, Denmark, July 19–24, 2020
Proceedings, Part II

 Springer

Editors
Constantine Stephanidis
University of Crete and Foundation
for Research and Technology – Hellas
(FORTH)
Heraklion, Crete, Greece

Margherita Antona
Foundation for Research and Technology –
Hellas (FORTH)
Heraklion, Crete, Greece

Stavroula Ntoa
Foundation for Research and Technology –
Hellas (FORTH)
Heraklion, Crete, Greece

ISSN 1865-0929   ISSN 1865-0937 (electronic)
Communications in Computer and Information Science
ISBN 978-3-030-60702-9   ISBN 978-3-030-60703-6 (eBook)
https://doi.org/10.1007/978-3-030-60703-6

This Springer imprint is published by the registered company Springer Nature Switzerland AG
The registered company address is: Gewerbestrasse 11, 6330 Cham, Switzerland

Foreword

The 22nd International Conference on Human-Computer Interaction, HCI International 2020 (HCII 2020), was planned to be held at the AC Bella Sky Hotel and Bella Center, Copenhagen, Denmark, during July 19–24, 2020. Due to the COVID-19 pandemic and the resolution of the Danish government not to allow events larger than 500 people to be hosted until September 1, 2020, HCII 2020 had to be held virtually. It incorporated the 21 thematic areas and affiliated conferences listed on the following page.

A total of 6,326 individuals from academia, research institutes, industry, and governmental agencies from 97 countries submitted contributions, and 1,439 papers and 238 posters were included in the volumes of the proceedings published before the conference. Additionally, 333 papers and 144 posters are included in the volumes of the proceedings published after the conference, as "Late Breaking Work" (papers and posters). These contributions address the latest research and development efforts in the field and highlight the human aspects of design and use of computing systems.

The volumes comprising the full set of the HCII 2020 conference proceedings are listed in the following pages and together they broadly cover the entire field of human-computer interaction, addressing major advances in knowledge and effective use of computers in a variety of application areas.

I would like to thank the Program Board Chairs and the members of the Program Boards of all Thematic Areas and Affiliated Conferences for their valuable contributions towards the highest scientific quality and the overall success of the HCI International 2020 conference.

This conference would not have been possible without the continuous and unwavering support and advice of the founder, conference general chair emeritus and conference scientific advisor, Prof. Gavriel Salvendy. For his outstanding efforts, I would like to express my appreciation to the communications chair and editor of HCI International News, Dr. Abbas Moallem.

July 2020   Constantine Stephanidis

HCI International 2020 Thematic Areas and Affiliated Conferences

Thematic Areas:

- HCI 2020: Human-Computer Interaction
- HIMI 2020: Human Interface and the Management of Information

Affiliated Conferences:

- EPCE: 17th International Conference on Engineering Psychology and Cognitive Ergonomics
- UAHCI: 14th International Conference on Universal Access in Human-Computer Interaction
- VAMR: 12th International Conference on Virtual, Augmented and Mixed Reality
- CCD: 12th International Conference on Cross-Cultural Design
- SCSM: 12th International Conference on Social Computing and Social Media
- AC: 14th International Conference on Augmented Cognition
- DHM: 11th International Conference on Digital Human Modeling & Applications in Health, Safety, Ergonomics & Risk Management
- DUXU: 9th International Conference on Design, User Experience and Usability
- DAPI: 8th International Conference on Distributed, Ambient and Pervasive Interactions
- HCIBGO: 7th International Conference on HCI in Business, Government and Organizations
- LCT: 7th International Conference on Learning and Collaboration Technologies
- ITAP: 6th International Conference on Human Aspects of IT for the Aged Population
- HCI-CPT: Second International Conference on HCI for Cybersecurity, Privacy and Trust
- HCI-Games: Second International Conference on HCI in Games
- MobiTAS: Second International Conference on HCI in Mobility, Transport and Automotive Systems
- AIS: Second International Conference on Adaptive Instructional Systems
- C&C: 8th International Conference on Culture and Computing
- MOBILE: First International Conference on Design, Operation and Evaluation of Mobile Communications
- AI-HCI: First International Conference on Artificial Intelligence in HCI

Conference Proceedings – Full List of Volumes

http://2020.hci.international/proceedings

40. CCIS 1226, HCI International 2020 Posters [Part III], edited by Constantine Stephanidis and Margherita Antona.

41. LNCS 12321, HCI International 2020 – Late Breaking Papers: User Experience Design and Case Studies. Edited by Constantine Stephanidis, Aaron Marcus, Elizabeth Rosenzweig, P.L. Patrick Rau, Abbas Moallem, and Matthias Rauterberg.

42. LNCS 12424, HCI International 2020 – Late Breaking Papers: Multimodality and Intelligence, edited by Constantine Stephanidis, Masaaki Kurosu, Helmut Degen, and Lauren Reinerman-Jones.

43. LNCS 12425, HCI International 2020 – Late Breaking Papers: Cognition, Learning and Games, edited by Constantine Stephanidis, Don Harris, Wen-Chin Li, Dylan D. Schmorrow, Cali M. Fidopiastis, Panayiotis Zaphiris, Andri Ioannou, Xiaowei Fang, Robert Sottilare, and Jessica Schwarz.

44. LNCS 12426, HCI International 2020 – Late Breaking Papers: Interaction Technology and Accessibility, edited by Constantine Stephanidis, Margherita Antona, and Qin Gao.

45. LNCS 12427, HCI International 2020 – Late Breaking Papers: Interaction, Knowledge and Social Media, edited by Constantine Stephanidis, Gavriel Salvendy, June Wei, Sakae Yamamoto, Hirohiko Mori, Gabriele Meiselwitz, Fiona Fui-Hoon Nan, and Keng Siau.

46. LNCS 12428, HCI International 2020 – Late Breaking Papers: Virtual and Augmented Reality, edited by Constantine Stephanidis, Jessie Y.C. Chen, and Gino Fragomeni.

47. LNCS 12429, HCI International 2020 – Late Breaking Posters, edited by Constantine Stephanidis, Margherita Antona, and Stavroula Ntoa.

48. CCIS 1293, HCI International 2020 – Late Breaking Posters, edited by Constantine Stephanidis, Margherita Antona, and Stavroula Ntoa.

49. CCIS 1294, HCI International 2020 – Late Breaking Posters [Part II], edited by Constantine Stephanidis, Margherita Antona, and Stavroula Ntoa.

http://2020.hci.international/proceedings

HCI International 2020 (HCII 2020)

The full list with the Program Board Chairs and the members of the Program Boards of all thematic areas and affiliated conferences is available online at:

http://www.hci.international/board-members-2020.php

HCI International 2021

The 23rd International Conference on Human-Computer Interaction, HCI International 2021 (HCII 2021), will be held jointly with the affiliated conferences in Washington DC, USA, at the Washington Hilton Hotel, July 24–29, 2021. It will cover a broad spectrum of themes related to human-computer interaction (HCI), including theoretical issues, methods, tools, processes, and case studies in HCI design, as well as novel interaction techniques, interfaces, and applications. The proceedings will be published by Springer. More information will be available on the conference website: http://2021.hci.international/

General Chair
Prof. Constantine Stephanidis
University of Crete and ICS-FORTH
Heraklion, Crete, Greece
Email: general_chair@hcii2021.org

http://2021.hci.international/

Contents – Part II

Virtual, Augmented and Mixed Reality

Learning

HCI, Culture and Art

Health and Wellbeing Applications

HCI in Mobility, Automotive and Aviation

Contents – Part I

Mobile and Multimodal Interaction

Interacting with Data, Information and Knowledge

Interaction and Intelligence

User Experience, Emotions and Psychophisiological Computing

Design for all and Assistive Technologies

Designing a Writing Grip for Children with Down Syndrome that Can Enhance Learning Process, Reduce Writing Exhaustion and Improve Quality of Life

Aalya AlBeeshi[1,3]([⊠]), Elham Almahmoud[1], Elaf Almahmoud[1],
Nawara Alosaimi[2], and Hind Alshammari[3]

[1] King Saud University, Riyadh, Saudi Arabia
aalbeeshi@acm.org
[2] General Assembly, Riyadh, Saudi Arabia
[3] Human-Computer Interaction (HCI) Design Lab, Riyadh, Saudi Arabia

Abstract. Currently, there is a major lack of funding for research regarding Down syndrome (DS) cases compared with other conditions. As a result, it is clear that in today's world, the development expectations of individuals with DS have been underestimated. A common problem in this environment occurs because many children with DS have dexterity issues that make manipulating small objects and grasping a pen particularly difficult. In an attempt to provide DS children with the ability to write longer with no discomfort, our proposed solution is a novel attachable pen grip that quantifies forces applied by the human hand while grasping the pen to write. Initially, data from a comprehensive questionnaire was collected on grip styles, writing speed, and how many words are written. Several other research methodologies were used, such as surveys, observations and interviews. Participants included experts, specialists, individuals with DS and families of children with DS. In executing this work, we gained a better understanding of the difficulties the child is facing and we were able to refine the design to best accommodate their needs. The market gap and limited writing tools for children with DS motivated this study to create the suitable product to reduce cramping, improve handwriting practice and to fulfil the physical and emotional need for children with DS. The overall potential benefit of the envisioned product is to improve the quality of life for these children and ease the minds of their caregivers.

Keywords: Design · User experience · Usability

1 Introduction

Down Syndrome (DS) is a genetic disorder caused when an abnormal cell division results in an extra copy of chromosome 21. According to the world health organization, the estimated incidence of DS is between 1 in 1,000 to 1 in 1,100 live births worldwide [1]. There is a major lack of funding for research in this area compared with other disorders. As a result, it is clear in today's world that the development expectations of individuals with DS have been underestimated. It is now encouraged to enroll children

© Springer Nature Switzerland AG 2020
C. Stephanidis et al. (Eds.): HCII 2020, CCIS 1294, pp. 3–9, 2020.
https://doi.org/10.1007/978-3-030-60703-6_1

with DS in regular schools with regularly developing children, because it is shown that the task-rich environment of general population classrooms pushes them to achieve more especially with writing and reading tasks [2, 3].

A common problem in this environment occurs because many children with DS have dexterity issues that make manipulating small objects and grasping a pen particularly difficult. These dexterity issues are related to multiple factors including loosened joints and ligaments. The thumb joint can be particularly lax causing additional difficulties when manipulating small objects and developing pencil control [4]. Abnormal hand formation also contributes to this difficulty, as they have shorter fingers and smaller hands and some of them may even lack some of the wrist bones. [5]. In addition, hypotonia is present with low muscle tone that leads to reduced muscle strength [6].

Learning any motor skill requires practice. As the neural pathway gets exposed to the same movement over and over again, it gets comfortable and better at performing it. Moreover, active practice of motor skills helps with strengthening the muscles used to perform that particular task [7]. Children with DS have inefficient motor-neural pathways, they need more practice than typically developed children. However, hypotonia and loosened joints in children with DS make the learning process of writing particularly difficult leading them to feel discouraged and have shorter practice time. In an attempt to provide DS children with the ability to write longer and with no discomfort, we propose a writing-aid that was co-designed with the target user population. The purpose of this paper is to bring awareness to the barriers that children with DS have during handwriting practice. This paper also promotes human centered design and shows how working with the user as a co-designer via interviews and feedback can lead to the development of usable and useful solutions.

2 Background

2.1 Problem Background

Currently, there are a number of grips and new tools that are available in the market that aim to ease the writing process for children with disabilities, however, they are not effective with DS [8]. In fact, a research study carried out in Mumbai to examine the difference between grip strength in children with DS and children without DS proved that those that have it exhibit 60% less grip strength than those without it [9]. Therefore, the grips that are currently available in the market are not considering the difference of muscle strength. This market gap and limited writing tools for children with DS motivated this study to create the suitable product to reduce cramping, improve handwriting practice and to fulfil the physical and emotional need for children with DS. This is achieved by choosing the right grip design and the right user interface.

Potential Grip Design. Our grip has a triangular shape which helps with achieving a tripod grip which is accomplished by grasping the pen or pencil by the thumb, index, and middle fingers. That is unique to the triangular shape because unlike the regular round pen grip, it has an indentation that aids in the adoption of a tripod grip. We aim for a tripod grip because experts and occupational therapists encourage it as it provides the hand with a wide range of motion while minimizing strain and pressure on the hand muscles and joints [10].

User Interface. The grip will be able to communicate inclusively by notifying the user about the strength of the grip through an intuitive and simple interface. It's simply a face that changes expressions depending on the pressure applied. For example, a happy face when the right amount of pressure is applied.

In an attempt to provide DS children with the ability to write longer and with no discomfort, our proposed solution is a novel attachable pen grip that quantifies forces applied by the human hand while grasping the pen to write. Measuring exerted pressure is done through a Force Sensing Resistor (FSR) which is "a device that allows measuring static and dynamic forces applied to a contact surface" [11]. It is a sensor that measures physical pressure, squeezing, and weight. The grip has a light-up feature to assist in inadequate pressure, the light is activated when the right amount of pressure is applied and deactivated when too much or too little pressure is applied. Studies show that writing pressure in a normal writing speed is 1.4–1.5 Newton (N). We will use this as a target pressure range.

3 Methods

The design method for the grip was an integrated design model aligned with IDC's Design Innovation (DI) approach [12]. The DI approach addresses design challenges in the creation of writing aids and integrates the creative, technical, and analytical methods that emerged from four schools of thought: Design Thinking, Business Design, Design Engineering and Systems Engineering.

Through our work with our co-designer, we developed the initial requirements. We have since created a comprehensive questionnaire, to collect data on grip styles, writing speed, and how many words are written by our users. This is done after obtaining the informed consent of a parent. By doing so, we gain a better understanding of the difficulties the child is facing and we are able to refine our design to best accommodate their needs.

3.1 Humanistic Co-design for Access Technology

Initial tools of assistive and access technologies developed for people with disabilities were mostly manual, while later tools incorporated automatic technologies or human involvement. The co-design process in developing assistive technology uses a human-centered approach for a more accurate design to address user needs [13]. The Humanistic Co-Design Program, Co-Create, adopts the design innovation (DI) process in its co-design practices by focusing on the users' needs via building empathy between designers, stakeholders and PWDs in the design process.

4 Results

Design Innovation modules is a human centered and interdisciplinary approach to innovate on and address complex challenges in our world. According to the design process, DI module is categorized into four phases: discover, design, develop and deliver (Fig. 1).

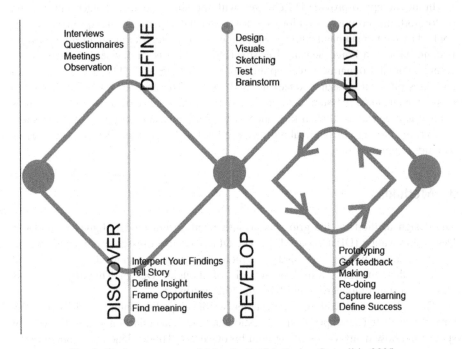

Interviews
Questionnaires
Meetings
Observation

DEFINE

Design
Visuals
Sketching
Test
Brainstorm

DELIVER

DISCOVER

Interpert Your Findings
Tell Story
Define Insight
Frame Opportunites
Find meaning

DEVELOP

Prototyping
Get feedback
Making
Re-doing
Capture learning
Define Success

Fig. 1. Design process model by the British Design Council in 2005

In the Discover phase, we conducted interviews. The interviews we conducted in the Humanistic Co-design workshop were used to extract deep qualitative insights, foresights and latent needs from users. By asking questions, the design team was able to uncover users' intentions, motivations and emotions when they use writing aids.

We then used a journey map to visualize the user's journey and identify the specific area for innovation. The journey map allowed us to experience a typical day of our user's life, this method helped us identify that the most important problem that the caregiver of the user wants to solve is to alleviate the cramping the user experiences during handwriting practice in order to be able to practice for a longer period of time (Fig. 2).

In the **Define phase** we used personas to help us further define our user. based on our interviews and observations and other discovering methodologies, we created a fictional depiction of our typical or extreme users in order to develop a solution that is inclusive and suitable to all our stages (Fig. 3).

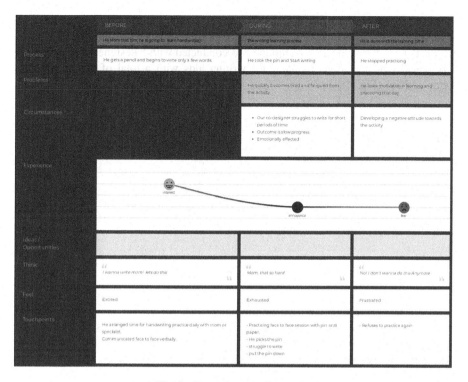

Fig. 2. Journey map of our user

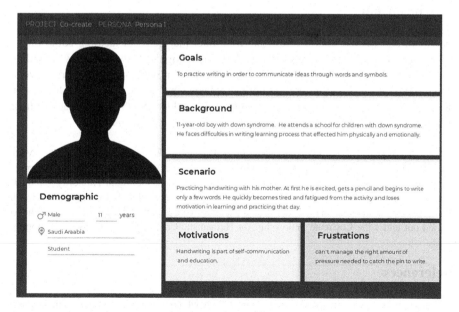

Fig. 3. Defined persona

In the **Develop phase** we used collaborative sketching (C-sketch) to generate and build upon the ideas that designers and co-designers have for writing aids. This graphical, team based ideation technique was conducted with 5 designers and generated 3 graphical representations of ideas for writing aids with a total of 4 passes of the sketch activity (Fig. 4).

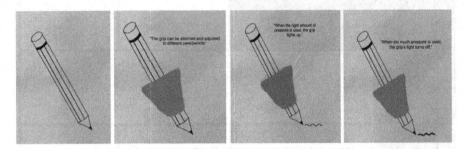

Fig. 4. Progressive sketch of writing aid

In the **Deliver phase** we used prototyping canvas to deliver our project strategically. This canvas helped us define important components like the stakeholders, the communication strategy for prototype, the prototyping approach, and the testing plans etc. Using a human-centered approach helped us innovate and use an interdisciplinary method to design our grip.

5 Conclusion

Our main aim in this study is to create a product that helps in tackling some of the common problems that children with DS face, including dexterity issues, by providing a solution that gives them the ability to write longer with no discomfort. Several possibilities can be explored in the future to enhance the product's impact. One can be developing an application for the caregivers of the child with DS to keep track of their progress.

Acknowledgment. Special thanks to Dr. Shiroq Almegren, Dr. Areej Al-wabil and Dr. Mark Oleksak. We thank the Humanistic Co-Design Initiative at MIT and the Human-Computer Interaction (HCI) Lab for supporting this work. We also thank the Saudi Authority for Intellectual Property (SAIP) and the Saudi Health Council's National Lab for Emerging Health Technologies for hosting and mentoring this work. This work is part of the authors' project that is carried out under the CoCreate Fellowship for Humanistic Co-Design of Access Technologies.

References

1. Genes and human diseases. (2020). https://www.who.int/genomics/public/geneticdiseases/en/index1.html. Accessed 1 June 2020

2. de Graaf, G., Van Hove, G., Haveman, M.: More academics in regular schools? The effect of regular versus special school placement on academic skills in Dutch primary school students with Down syndrome. J. Intellect. Disabil. Res. **57**(1), 21–38 (2013)

3. Cornhill, H., Case-Smith, J.: Factors that relate to good and poor handwriting. Am. J. Occup. Ther. **50**(9), 732–739 (1996)

4. Block, M.E.: Motor development in children with Down syndrome: a review of the literature. Adapt. Phys. Act. Q. **8**(3), 179–209 (1991)

5. Jacobsen, F.S., Hansson, G.: Orthopaedic disorders in Down's syndrome. Curr. Orthop. **14**(3), 215–222 (2000)

6. Morris, A.F., Vaughan, S.E., Vaccaro, P.: Measurements of neuromuscular tone and strength in Down's syndrome children. J. Ment. Defic. Res. **26**, 41–46 (1982)

7. Willingham, D.B.: A neuropsychological theory of motor skill learning. Psychol. Rev. **105**(3), 558 (1998)

8. Felix, V.G., Mena, L.J., Ostos, R., Maestre, G.E.: A pilot study of the use of emerging computer technologies to improve the effectiveness of reading and writing therapies in children with Down syndrome. Br. J. Educ. Technol. **48**, 611–624 (2017). https://doi.org/10.1111/bjet.12426

9. John, R., Dhanve, A., Mullerpatan, R.P.: Grip and pinch strength in children with Down syndrome. Hand Ther. **21**(3), 85–89 (2016). https://doi.org/10.1177/1758998316649102

10. Seng, M.H.: Development of pencil grip position in preschool children. Occup. Ther. J. Res. **18**(4), 207–224 (1998)

11. Sadun, A.S., Jalani, J., Sukor, J.A.: Force Sensing Resistor (FSR): a brief overview and the low-cost sensor for active compliance control. In: First International Workshop on Pattern Recognition (2016)

12. Camburn, B., et al.: Design innovation: a study of integrated practice. In: ASME 2017 International Design Engineering Technical Conferences and Computers and Information in Engineering Conference (2017)

13. Brady, E., Bigham, J.P.: Crowdsourcing accessibility: human-powered access technologies (2015)

Crowdsourcing Accessibility: A Review of Platforms, Mobile Applications and Tools

Reem Alqadi[1]($\boxtimes$), Maryam Alhowaiti[2], Fatimah Almohaimeed[3], Mawaddah Alsabban[4], and Sujithra Raviselvam[5]

[1] Qassim University, Qassim, Saudi Arabia
re.alqadi@qu.edu.sa
[2] RMIT University, VIC, Australia
maryam-musalam@hotmail.com
[3] King Saud University, Riyadh, Saudi Arabia
fnmohaimeed@gmail.com
[4] Saudi Authority for Intellectual Property (SAIP), Riyadh, Saudi Arabia
msabban@saip.gov.sa
[5] Singapore University of Technology and Design, Changi, Singapore
sujithra_raviselvam@mymail.sutd.edu.sg

Abstract. Crowdsourcing has the potential to become a preferred tool to rate the accessibility of the built environment and appeal preferences of users who are persons with disabilities (PwDs). Nevertheless, some reliability issues still exist, partially due to the subjectivity of ratings of accessibility features of places that might vary from one PwD to another or their caregivers. In this paper, we present a descriptive overview of existing crowdsourcing applications and the accessibility features that are included in such platforms as well as the diffusion, and popularity of these platforms. We also present several use cases and scenarios of use for these platforms via user populations.

Keywords: Accessibility · Platforms · Crowdsourcing

1 Introduction

Collaborative rating sites for the accessibility of places have become essential resources that many users consult to learn about the accessibility of a place before visiting the site. However, the utilization of such platforms has not grown due to different reasons ranging from technical challenges, aligned with variability in the perceived value of subjective ratings, as noted in [2], to the limitation in the scope of people who are willing to participate in evaluating and rating the accessibility of places [1].

In this paper, we aim to review the existing crowdsourcing applications and the accessibility features that are included in such platforms and identify the geographic coverage, reach and popularity of the in se platforms in the community of persons with disabilities (PwDs). Therefore, we investigate two main research questions: "What are the features offered by the existing crowdsourcing platforms for accessibility?" and "How the selected platforms motivated a large population to participate in evaluating the accessibility of a place?"

C. Stephanidis et al. (Eds.): HCII 2020, CCIS 1294, pp. 10–17, 2020.
https://doi.org/10.1007/978-3-030-60703-6_2

The remainder of this paper is organized as follows. Section 2 describes related work on crowdsourcing accessibility for the built environment, followed by a technical review of existing crowdsourcing applications in Sect. 3. Following that, Sect. 4 describes the use cases and scenarios described in the scenario-based persona method. We conclude in Sect. 5 with key contributions and future directions for research.

2 Related Work on Crowdsourcing Accessibility

In this section, we describe crowdsourcing as a concept, and we zoom into the scope of crowdsourcing for accessibility as a specific area of interest. As noted by Qui et al. in [3], "Crowdsourcing leverages the diverse skill sets of large collections of individual contributors to solve problems". Figure 1 illustrates how crowdsourcing platforms systematically account for the different goals of information seekers, information contributors (content contributors), and platforms, and their interactions.

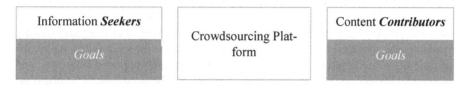

Fig. 1. Crowdsourcing models and interaction design for different users

We start in Sect. 2.1 with a focus on human-computer interaction HCI design consideration for crowdsourcing platforms, then we present a brief overview of the crowdsourcing technology designed specifically for PwDs to make the design of complex tasks easier and more efficient in Sect. 2.2.

2.1 HCI Design Consideration for Crowdsourcing Platforms

Since HCI is an essential aspect of crowdsourcing platforms, designers should consider motivating principles to encourage and retain user engagement, whether they are PwDs or beyond their scope. Moreover, it is important to ensure that the design is technically and functionally usable by people with disabilities. From the user experience perspective, the platform interface should be easily navigated and interacted with. Also, platform designers should consider that the interface can attract large users and meet the needs of different types of users; for example, visually impaired users need a non-visual interface. From the system design perspective, the outputs produced by the crowd of people must be meaningful and reliable since these platforms may depend on unknown users with novice backgrounds, which in turn makes low-quality outputs. Moreover, most of the crowdsourcing platforms lack high-quality outputs and are ineffective against data manipulation and cheating [4]. Besides, crowdsourcing platforms encounter challenges in sustaining the participation of the crowd [5].

Therefore, research has explored different methods to engage with the target user populations, filter out bad contributors, and produce high-quality output in crowd-sourcing platforms [5, 6]. Examples include using specific, measurable physical properties to identify the accessibility of a place instead of using 5-stars rating schemes to highlight issues such as the reliability of the gathered data for quality control [4].

2.2   Crowdsourcing Accessibility for PwDs

Collaborative rating platforms for accessibility of places drive a large number of decisions for PwDs. For example, caregivers rely on accessibility information and ratings to ensure a place is accessible before selecting a restaurant or cafe when they go out with a PwD. Typically, these platforms offer discrete information ranging from the accessibility of a specific part of a place, such as its entrance or seating to facilities and services or subjective ratings of accessibility posted via visitors.

3   Accessibility Platforms and Apps

In this section, we describe the technical features and services of existing accessibility crowdsourcing applications. For each platform, we describe the main functionality, the compatibility of the applications with different platforms, the supported languages, and the geographical coverage of the platforms. Besides, we focus on how these platforms utilize the power of the "crowd" to facilitate large scale review tasks that are costly or time consuming with traditional methods. Moreover, we describe the accessibility ratings that are embedded in popular applications (e.g. Foursquare, Google Map). Table 1 compares the main features offered by the crowdsourcing platforms for accessibility.

3.1   Crowdsourcing Accessibility Applications

Jaccede [7] is a collaborative platform launched in 2006 aimed to help people with reduced mobility to search accessible places and allow them to share information about accessibility anywhere. Users can contribute by describing the accessibility of public places as a place entrance, indoor, outdoor, and additional information about services and facilities.

Recently, Jaccede's founders launched a new mobile application called Jaccede Challenge works with the crowdsourcing app Jaccede. They employ gamification in the app in order to attract people to enrich the maps with accessibility information to places. The application allows users to play a game of exploration and challenges, where users can form teams and get points by adding information about the accessibility of places.

Apart from its platform, Jaccede also aims to raise awareness of the social inclusion of PwD. They are regularly organizing activities and events on accessibility to raise awareness and to get new members. It can be considered an important step to increase the popularity of such platforms and encourage the community to contribute to it.

WheelMap [8] is an online map for finding wheelchair accessible places, launched in 2010. The platform uses a traffic light system to rate the wheelchair accessibility of a place. Accordingly, it shows the venue colors on the map based on their level of accessibility. In addition, they provide descriptive text under each color to help users assess accessibility more accurately. As green means that the entrance and all rooms are reachable without steps, and orange means that the entrance contains one step with 3 inches high. This description can help in avoiding the subjectivity in evaluation. On the other hand, the platform has a news page to get the community engaged. It opens volunteers to help in enhancing the content to support multiple languages.

WheelMate [9] was launched in 2012. It allows users who use wheelchairs to find, rate, review, and add accessible restrooms or parking around the world. However, users cannot edit or report the inaccuracy of the existing entries. Thus, if a place or an establishment improved its accessibility or someone entered incomplete or false information, there is no way to edit it by the users.

AXS Map [10] is a crowdsourcing platform for accessible places powered by Google Maps API. It was founded in 2012 by Jason DaSilva, who had been diagnosed with multiple sclerosis [11]. The main motivation behind creating this app is to help PwDs after the increasing difficulties that Jason DaSilva faced when navigating through his daily life. AXS Map uses a 5-star schema to rate the accessibility of the entry and toilet of a place. In order to engage more community members and enrich the platforms with places' accessibility information, AXS Map founded AXS Marathons. Which are events that are held regularly in which community members come together using AXS Map to map the accessibility of the places and it has been held in over 50 US cities.

Ability App [12] is a web platform launched in 2015. It is mainly based on community reviews to help people with mobility, vision, hearing, and cognitive impairments to find and rate accessible places all around the world. The platform allows users to browse accessible places through a list of categories, explore the map, or search by place name. A list of place names with an accessibility rating score appears based on the 5-score schema. For each place, four primary disability categories appear: mobility, vision, hearing, and cognitive, each of them has its unique number of features to rate 36, 31, 19, and 31, respectively. Users can assess the accessibility features of a place using a smiley face system: a happy, neutral, and sad face which indicates a specific accommodation in place. Although the application is comprehensive for all types of disability, too much information is requested in an evaluation which could be a time-consuming task and people might be discouraged to complete them.

AccessNow [5] was launched in 2017. It provides an interactive map for people with different disabilities to rate, review, find, and add accessible places and establishments using the traffic light system —A green pin: fully accessible, yellow pin: partially accessible, and red pin: not accessible—. Besides, the AccessNow users can specify the accessibility features that are provided by the rated place (e.g., accessible parking, braille, and accessible restroom). However, this application does not offer a way to edit or report the inaccuracy of the existing entries. Thus, if a place or an establishment improved its accessibility or someone entered incomplete or false information, there is no way to edit it by AcessNow users.

Access Earth [13] is a platform founded by Matt Macan in 2017, who has a physical disability himself. The application shows the nearest places and tells the users whether it is rated by others or simply asking them to rate the accessibility of the place. To assess the accessibility of a place, the app displays a number of yes or no questions. For example, "Are the doors wide enough for wheelchair access? − 32 in. wide". This type of question is inflexible and may be confusing to users when rating a place.

iAccess Life [14] was launched in 2019. It allows users who use wheelchairs to find accessible places and establishments that accommodate their needs. Users can rate, review, and find places around the world based on the accessibility of the place's entrance, restroom, interior, and parking. Users can assess the accessibility of a specific place using the 5-star rating schema. In order to encourage people to contribute, this application provides users with a referral code to share it with their friends. It also allows users to gain insights on the total referrals and places that a user has rated using the lifetime activity dashboard.

Sociability App [15] is a free app that was developed in 2019. The application main feature is to help people with physical disabilities to get information about "venues accessibility" in three main areas which are entrance (i.e. ramp access, door width and stairs), toilets and space (i.e. interior space and pathways) by showing the nearest venues around the area and which accessibilities it support or by searching for the desired venue and get the accessibility info based on that. The application uses great color-coded icons to help easily understand the level of accessibility the venue supports. The user can contribute to enhancing the content by adding access info for the places they are visiting. This app is still on a beta stage and it is expected to be officially launched at the end of 2020.

Table 1. The table summarizes the main functionality of the platforms.

Application	Compatible platforms	Supported languages	Rating and comments feature	Diffusion	Target Disabilities
Jaccede	Web and Android	French, English, Italian, Germany, and Spanish	Yes	France, some European cities, and 11 cities around the world	Mobility
WheelMap	Web, iOS, and Android	25 Languages	No	Worldwide	Mobility
WheelMate	iOS, and Android	English, Danish, French, Swedish, and Germany	Yes	Worldwide	Mobility
AXS Map	Web	English	Yes	US	Mobility
Ability App	Web	English	Yes	Worldwide	For all
AccessNow	Web, iOS, and Android	English	Yes	Worldwide	For all
Access Earth	Web, iOS, and Android	English	No	Worldwide	Mobility
iAccess Life	iOS, and Android	English	Yes	Worldwide	Mobility
Sociability App	Web, iOS, and Android	English	No	UK	Mobility

3.2   Accessibility Rating in Popular Applications

Some travel apps and restaurant rating apps include accessibility information in their rating platforms, albeit in a limited way which falls short from conveying the important details for PwDs (e.g. parking, ramps, entrances, accessible routes, toilets, elevators). For example, Foursquare and Yelp have recently added the wheelchair accessibility feature to their apps. It allows adding information about the wheelchair accessibility to the venues, but without mentioning any other details. Also, they did not set specific standards on which wheelchair accessibility was assessed. This could cause a reliability problem with this information because the evaluation may be subject to personal opinions. Recently, Google has added a wheelchair accessibility feature to Google Maps, allowing users and business owners to contribute by adding accessibility information of entrance, toilets, seating, parking, and elevator. This, in turn, is a major contribution, in order to overcome the limitations of previous applications, by adding more details about places.

4   Use Cases for Crowdsourcing Platforms

Research has shown that putting the wisdom of the crowd 'to good use' in the context of accessibility platforms is feasible, desirable, and viable. These platforms facilitate leveraging the potential and resources of today's digitally connected, diverse, and distributed community of PwDs, their caregivers, and assistive technology (AT) enthusiasts. Although there are existing crowdsourcing platforms that enable a collaborative space to share information on accessibility, it is still challenging to realize a variety of scenarios a user might encounter while using application software. Personas and scenarios are considered to gather insights on the features that could enhance the accessibility of an accessibility crowdsourcing platform. In this section, we leverage personas and scenarios as one of the potential ways to capture such user experiences aligned with the approach in [16, 17] and depicted in Fig. 2, which describes several use cases and scenarios of use for these platforms via target user populations. A set of personas and a variety of scenarios associated with each persona are built and categorized to capture the common themes that arise during the identified scenarios. These personas are later used to derive the user-based feature requirements for the application software. Table 2 shows some of the built personas. The scenario-based personas combine the concepts of personas and scenarios in user-centered design [17]. Including persons with disabilities in large participatory innovation projects together with professional innovators such as developers, designers, engineers or clinicians often puts a strain on the person with disabilities who might not like to be the focus of attention. The artefacts depicted in Fig. 2 encapsulate the synthesized findings from user research and provide a communication tool for developers and stakeholders throughout the product design process from ideation to design, development and deployment. PwDs were part of knowledge gathering, idea generation, and concept development for this platform and the designers gave form to the ideas that emerged from the co-design process.

Fig. 2. Tangible scenario-based personas for crowdsourcing users and content contributors

Table 2. Persona description in different scenarios

Scenario's Context	Description
Restaurant or cafe	Ahmad is a 21-year-old college student who is wheelchair-bound. He often spends his evenings in local cafes or restaurants to meet with his startup co-founders. He likes to check the accessibility of places before he visits the place and currently the only information he finds is from direct contact (phone call) or by word of mouth
	Sarah is a 20-year-old college student who is wheelchair-bound. She often spends her afternoons in campus cafes to do homework and meet with friends. She likes to check the accessibility of places before she visits the place and currently the only information she finds is from direct contact (phone call) or by word of mouth
Entertainment	Nouf is an eighteen-year-old with motor disability and she uses a wheelchair to move around. Nouf loves movies and loves to watch the latest movies released in the cinema. Nouf often calls the cinema operator to inquire about cinema accessibility and provides special seats for wheelchairs
	May is a 35-year-old mother of 2 children. May is wheelchair-bound and she often spends her afternoons in local playgrounds with her children during their free play hours before homework. She likes to check the accessibility of public parks before she visits the place and currently the only information she finds is from direct contact (phone call) or by word of mouth

5   Conclusion

This study sheds light on how accessibility crowdsourcing platforms and mobile applications offer intriguing new opportunities for accomplishing different kinds of tasks or achieving broader participation from the PwD communities than previously possible. Moreover, it described different use cases through the lens of scenario-based personas. For future work, we will investigate the limitations of these applications, and how to motivate people beyond the scope of PwDs to participate in such platforms. In addition, we will conduct a usability study and investigate more in the limitations and weaknesses of the existing platforms.

Acknowledgment. We thank the Humanistic Co-Design Initiative at MIT and the Human-Computer Interaction (HCI) Lab for supporting this work. We also thank the Saudi Authority for Intellectual Property (SAIP) and the Saudi Health Council's National Lab for Emerging Health Technologies for hosting and mentoring this work. This work is part of the authors' project that is carried out under the CoCreate Fellowship for Humanistic Co-Design of Access Technologies.

References

1. Mazayev, A., Martins, J.A., Correia, N.: Improving accessibility through semantic crowdsourcing. In: Proceedings of the 7th International Conference on Software Development and Technologies for Enhancing Accessibility and Fighting Info-exclusion, pp. 408–413. Association for Computing Machinery, Vila Real, Portugal (2016). https://doi.org/10.1145/3019943.3020001
2. Salomoni, P., Prandi, C., Roccetti, M., Nisi, V., Nunes, N.J.: Crowdsourcing urban accessibility: some preliminary experiences with results. In: Proceedings of the 11th Biannual Conference on Italian SIGCHI Chapter, pp. 130–133. Association for Computing Machinery, Rome, Italy (2015). https://doi.org/10.1145/2808435.2808443
3. Qiu, C., Squicciarini, A., Rajtmajer, S.: Rating mechanisms for sustainability of crowdsourcing platforms. In: Proceedings of the 28th ACM International Conference on Information and Knowledge Management, pp. 2003–2012. Association for Computing Machinery, Beijing, China (2019). https://doi.org/10.1145/3357384.3357933
4. Challenges and solutions to crowdsourcing accessibility evaluations - Paper for Accessible Way-Finding Using Web Technologies. https://www.w3.org/WAI/RD/2014/way-finding/paper5/#ableroad
5. Access Now - pin-pointing accessibility worldwide. https://accessnow.com/
6. Vijayalakshmi, A., Hota, C.: Reputation-based reinforcement algorithm for motivation in crowdsourcing platform. In: Sahana, S.K., Bhattacharjee, V. (eds.) Advances in Computational Intelligence. AISC, vol. 988, pp. 175–186. Springer, Singapore (2020). https://doi.org/10.1007/978-981-13-8222-2_15
7. Jaccede - the guide to accessibility. https://www.jaccede.com/en
8. Wheelmap. https://wheelmap.org
9. WheelMate – Corporate. https://www.coloplast.com/products/bladder-bowel/wheelmate/
10. AXS Map. https://www.axsmap.com/
11. AXSMap (2020). https://en.wikipedia.org/w/index.php?title=AXS_Map&oldid=957719028
12. Ability App. https://theabilityapp.com/
13. Access Earth. https://access.earth/
14. AccessLife. https://www.iaccess.life/
15. Sociability. https://www.sociability.app/
16. Moser, C., Fuchsberger, V., Neureiter, K., Sellner, W., Tscheligi, M.: Revisiting personas: the making-of for special user groups. CHI '12 Extended Abstracts on Human Factors in Computing Systems, pp. 453–468. Association for Computing Machinery, Austin (2012). https://doi.org/10.1145/2212776.2212822
17. Saez, A.V., Garreta Domingo, M.G.: Scenario-based persona: introducing personas through their main contexts. CHI 2011 Extended Abstracts on Human Factors in Computing Systems, pp. 505–505. Association for Computing Machinery, Vancouver (2011). https://doi.org/10.1145/1979742.1979563

Human Factors in the Design of Wheelchair Tray Tables: User Research in the Co-design Process

Abdullah Alshangiti[1,2](✉), Mohammad Alhudaithi[1,2], and Abdullah Alghamdi[1]

[1] Human-Computer Interaction (HCI) Design Lab, Riyadh, Saudi Arabia
abdullah.alshangiti@kaust.edu.sa
[2] King Abdullah University for Science and Technology (KAUST), Thawal, Saudi Arabia

Abstract. Wheelchair tray tables offer a convenient way for wheelchair users to carry out daily tasks such as eating, reading, and using mobile devices. However, most tray tables are made to serve the majority of wheelchair users and are inaccessible to some with a limited range of motion. In our work, we address this issue by exploring the ergonomic problems and possible solutions. In this paper, we describe the human factors in the design and development of powered wheelchair tray tables. The process of humanistic co-design relies on the direct involvement of the targeted demographic in the design process. This ensures the outcome is centered around the specific needs of the individual. Our approach employs user research studies (e.g., interviews, questionnaires, and actively working with a wheelchair using co-designer) as a means towards gleaning valuable insight into the needs of wheelchair users. In these studies, we sought to explore their experiences with using tables made for wheelchairs. We also collected data about whether the tray tables required external assistance to stow and use, and the problems they faced using existing solutions. We then highlighted the various specific needs presented by the co-designers and questionnaire respondents. These needs are embodied into scenario-based personas in which they may find themselves in need of a table for use with their wheelchairs. Deriving these personas from our survey results provides an effective method of keeping the insight gathered present throughout the design process. Implications for design are discussed.

Keywords: Personas · Humanistic co-design · Accessibility · Wheelchair peripherals · Tray tables

1 Introduction

Individuals with spinal cord injuries, arthritis, balance disorders, and other conditions or diseases are typical users of wheelchairs. Research is underway to advance wheelchair design to prevent fatigue, reduce dependencies on caregivers or accommodate improved comfort related to stable surfaces for placing items while improving safety, functional performance and accessibility to the community of wheelchair users

© Springer Nature Switzerland AG 2020
C. Stephanidis et al. (Eds.): HCII 2020, CCIS 1294, pp. 18–24, 2020.
https://doi.org/10.1007/978-3-030-60703-6_3

[1]. Wheelchair tables are designed with the majority of users in mind. However, some wheelchair-using individuals find their specific needs unfulfilled by what is currently available [2].

Human factors is defined as the science concerned with the application of what we know about people, their abilities, characteristics, and limitations to the design of equipment they use, environments in which they function, and jobs they perform [3]. Our approach is a human-centered and interdisciplinary co-design process that aims to innovate on and address complex challenges facing persons with disabilities (PwDs). It involves the use of scenarios and personas to highlight the human factors in the design process. Scenario-based personas are used in user-centered design to cater to the specific needs and frustrations of the end-user [4, 5]. In our case, the main purpose of using personas is to provide a way to display the information gathered from the user research segment of our project in a useful way for the design process. Our approach consists of a text description of the user and situation as well as a visual illustration of the user and location. These provide a description of the predicted behaviors and desires of the end-users and allow us to effectively cater to their desires and frustrations, which will ensure their comfort.

The remainder of this paper is structured as follows: Sect. 2 presents an overview of background and literature in the scope of user-centered design for wheelchairs. Section 3 describes the user research methods that we used, and results are presented in Sect. 4. We conclude in Sect. 5 with a summary of human factors in the design of wheelchair tray tables and an overview of directions for future research.

2   Background Information

2.1   Uses of Personas

Personas can take the form of a photo of a person and a text description. There are also instances where they take the form of a silhouette superimposed onto a stock photo of the persona's location and a brief text description [5]. These representations could also be printed on tangible models, as shown in Fig. 1.

Previous research into the use of scenario-based personas as a means for presenting user analysis studies has established their use within the humanistic co-design community [5, 6]. Personas can be used to present user information that may otherwise be misinterpreted if presented as statistical figures. The use of fictitious personas in the design process is outlined within the work of Aquino et al. where they are used as a user modelling tool to simplify communication and aid in project decision making [6].

2.2   The Development of Wheelchair Designs

Power wheelchairs are used to increase the physical capabilities of a person with disabilities. However, certain commercial products do not completely address the needs of their user base, such as navigating narrow passages and servicing their broken wheelchairs [2]. Participatory design for the production of power wheelchairs has been used to provide comprehensive input in conjunction with subject matter experts such as doctors and accessibility researchers [2].

Fig. 1. Tangible scenario-based personas for wheelchair users in different use cases with tray tables; taking into account user preferences, socio-cultural factors and contexts of use.

3 Materials and Methods

Wheelchair trays are specially designed platforms or surfaces that attach to wheelchairs, providing a firm table for eating, working, reading, and other activities. In the process of requirements gathering, we sought to understand the ergonomics of existing wheelchair trays, and the challenges users encounter in their use of such devices. In this study, existing co-design methods and design principles were aligned with the Humanistic Co-Design model for assistive technology and tailored through a Design Innovation (DI) process to develop solutions with co-designers (i.e. Users of wheelchairs). Specifically, this study involved exploratory studies with co-designers and requirements elicitation from the community of wheelchair users through surveys. These studies were within the Design Innovation framework that is built, in part, on the UK Council's '4D' (Discover, Define, Develop, Deliver) model of design [7].

An online questionnaire was distributed to communities of PwDs via our co-designer, to gather data for our personas. The survey yielded 10 responses in a time-frame of 2 weeks. Basic demographic information about our respondents like age, gender, and place of residence was gathered. Following that, participants were asked about information relating to their experience with wheelchairs and wheelchair tray tables, and the problems they faced using them. The respondents were asked about their main uses for wheelchair tables and the heaviest items they place on them. We also conducted an interview with our co-designer, a wheelchair user. This gave us more insight into how specifically he used wheelchair tables. It also allowed us to deepen our understanding of the specific frustrations that wheelchair users face while using different tray table solutions. We were also able to develop a user journey map from his insights and comments. Using the responses gathered as a basis for the use cases, we constructed our personas in the form of a piece of text describing fictional characters aligned with PwDs in our target user population and outlining the contexts of use [3].

Above the text is a silhouette in the image of the individual placed on a photo of a scene to describe the context of use Fig. 1.

4 Results and Discussion

Understanding relationships between people, objects and their environments is important when considering human factors in designing assistive and accessible technologies. There is limited information on the difficulties PwDs experience in mounting objects on wheelchair tray tables and maneuvering their wheelchairs during daily activities. Insights from our user research studies were distilled into design implications for the shape, form, and function of mounting tray tables to wheelchair frames.

After sending out the questionnaire to various online wheelchair user communities, we received responses about different problems they faced while using current wheelchair tray tables. The main aim of the survey was gathering useful qualitative data, including a significant portion of what is in Table 1. The demographic information was as follows: 10% of our respondents were female, and 90% were male. 10% were under 15 years of age, 70% were between 15 and 35 years old, and 20% were above the age of 35.

Fig. 2. Scenario-based Persona comprised of a brief text outlining a design consideration and a relevant illustration to communicate the setting of the situation.

The main takeaway from our results were the key features our respondents outlined. For example, one answered that the heaviest item they wish to place on a tray table would be a large Qur'an (approximate weight 3 kg), so one of the personas we designed had this as a primary use case as depicted in Fig. 2.

Respondents also described their main uses for such a table which influenced our design considerations in Table 1. The human factors in the design of wheelchair tray tables are listed in the left column of Table 1, and the corresponding design considerations for tray tables are described in columns 2 and 3. Findings from the above-mentioned user studies shed light on usability and accessibility issues as well as layout design limitations in wheelchair tray tables.

The use of human factors to characterize the design considerations provides the reasoning and justification behind the design options [8–10]. It provides a factual basis to prioritize certain aspects of the user experience over others. For example, the ability to angle the table may be omitted if it interferes with the design of the folding mechanism and if the need for a folding table exceeds that of an angled one from the perspective of the user. It ultimately provides a way to relate the issues the users face to the potential solutions, as noted in [11, 12]. In future work, the factors will all be evaluated when developing and implementing the final design of the table.

Table 1. Human factors in the design of wheelchair tray tables

Human factors	Design considerations	
	Shape, form, or function	Tray table feature(s)
Vision: Maneuvering Visibility	Transparency for visibility	Polycarbonate Tray
Vision: Control Visibility	Salient visibility for components and ergonomic design for the controls	Controlled by a button near the other wheelchair controls
Physical Factor: Lack of Dexterity	Electrically folding without large movements from the user	Folding feature
Physical Factor: Muscle Fatigue	The ability to hold books and tablets at an angle that is comfortable to the user	Angled table
Motivational Factor: Not being burdensome as not to disincentivize use	Activated by a button	Flip Tray
Physical factor: Keeping cups stable during use	Depression within the surface to prevent cups from sliding	Cup Holder
Social factor: not relying on caregivers	Independent folding without caregiver's assistance	Folding feature
Physical Factor: Facilitating easy maintenance and cleaning	Locks for tray table mounting	Unlockable mounting clamps
Physical Factor: keeping items from falling off	Rough table surface to prevent items from sliding	Rough table surface

5   Conclusion

In this study, we were able to establish an initial connection between the users requirements and the physical design by utilizing scenario-based personas. We also gained a wealth of information from our co-designer through an initial interview and further correspondence. Going forward, we plan on conducting semi-structured interviews with a selected sample from our survey respondents to gain a deeper insight into their day to day needs regarding the use of tray tables and peripherals mounted on wheelchairs.

This study furthers our understanding of the difficulties and pain points that wheelchair-using PwDs experience during daily activities that might be alleviated by the ergonomic design of wheelchairs' tray tables. This knowledge will assist clinicians, technologists and researchers in two areas: in choosing design features that are ecologically valid for wheelchair users; and, in identifying areas for further development specific to the use of tray tables for wheelchairs.

Acknowledgement.   We thank the Humanistic Co-Design Initiative and the Human-Computer Interaction (HCI) Lab for supporting this work. We also thank the Saudi Authority for Intellectual Property (SAIP) and the Saudi Health Council's National Lab for Emerging Health Technologies for hosting and mentoring this work. We also thank Mawaddah AlSabban for her graphics in the design of scenario-based personas. The authors would also like to acknowledge the contribution of Ali Alnasser who was key during the initial stages of the co-design process, and the mentorship of Dr. Mark Oleksak and Dr. Ragad Allwihan. This work is part of the authors' project that is carried out under the CoCreate Fellowship for Humanistic Co-Design of Access Technologies.

References

1. Cooper, R.A., et al.: Engineering better wheelchairs to enhance community participation. IEEE Trans. Neural Syst. Rehabil. Eng. **14**(4), 438–455 (2006)
2. Torres, I.G., Parmar, G., Aggarwal, S., Mansur, N., Guthrie, A.: Affordable smart wheelchair. In: Extended Abstracts of the 2019 CHI Conference on Human Factors in Computing Systems (CHI EA 2019), pp. 1–6. Association for Computing Machinery, New York (2019). Paper SRC07, https://doi.org/10.1145/3290607.3308463
3. Wickens, C.D., Gordon, S.E., Liu, Y.: An Introduction to Human Factors Engineering. Pearson Prentice Hall, Upper Saddle River (2004)
4. Moser, C., Fuchsberger, V., Neureiter, K., Sellner, W., Tscheligi, M.: Revisiting personas: the making-of for special user groups. In: CHI 2012 Extended Abstracts on Human Factors in Computing Systems (CHI EA 2012), pp. 453–468. Association for Computing Machinery, New York (2012). https://doi.org/10.1145/2212776.2212822
5. Saez, A.V., Garreta Domingo, M.G.: Scenario-based persona: introducing personas through their main contexts. In: CHI 2011 Extended Abstracts on Human Factors in Computing Systems (CHI EA 2011), p. 505. Association for Computing Machinery, New York (2011). https://doi.org/10.1145/1979742.1979563

6. Junior, P.T.A., Filgueiras, L.V.L.: User modeling with personas. In: Proceedings of the 2005 Latin American Conference on Human-Computer Interaction (CLIHC 2005), pp. 277–282. Association for Computing Machinery, New York (2005). https://doi.org/10.1145/1111360. 1111388

7. "Design Innovation Learning Modules - What is Design Innovation?" Dimodules. www. dimodules.com/whatisdi

8. Paciello, M.G.: Designing for people with disabilities. Interactions 3(1), 15–16 (1996)

9. Bennett, C.L., Rosner, D.K.: The promise of empathy: design, disability, and knowing the "other". In: Proceedings of the 2019 CHI Conference on Human Factors in Computing Systems, pp. 1–13, May 2019

10. Van der Woude, L.H., Veeger, D.J.E., Rozendal, R.H.: Ergonomics of wheelchair design: a prerequisite for optimum wheeling conditions. Adapt. Phys. Act. Q. 6(2), 109–132 (1989)

11. Rajapakse, R., Brereton, M., Sitbon, L., Roe, P.: A collaborative approach to design individualized technologies with people with a disability. In: Proceedings of the Annual Meeting of the Australian Special Interest Group for Computer Human Interaction, pp. 29–33, December 2015

12. De Couvreur, L., Goossens, R.: Design for (every) one: co-creation as a bridge between universal design and rehabilitation engineering. CoDesign 7(2), 107–121 (2011)

Open Architecture for the Control of a Neuroprosthesis by Means of a Mobile Device

Adrián Contreras-Martínez[1] , Blanca E. Carvajal-Gámez[1,2(✉)] ,
J. Luis Rosas-Trigueros[1] , Josefina Gutiérrez-Martínez[3] ,
and Jorge A. Mercado-Gutiérrez[3]

[1] Instituto Politécnico Nacional, SEPI-ESCOM, Av. Juan de Dios Bátiz S/N, Nueva Industrial Vallejo, Gustavo A. Madero, 07738 Ciudad de México, CDMX, Mexico
{acontrerasm, becarvajal}@ipn.mx
[2] Instituto Politécnico Nacional, Unidad Profesional Interdisciplinaria de Ingeniería y Tecnologías Avanzadas, Av Instituto Politécnico Nacional 2580, La Laguna Ticomán, Gustavo A. Madero, 07340 Ciudad de México, CDMX, Mexico
[3] Instituto Nacional de Rehabilitación, Calz México-Xochimilco 289, Coapa, Arenal Tepepan, Tlalpan, 14389 Ciudad de México, CDMX, Mexico

Abstract. The Brain-Computer Interfaces (BCI) based on Electroencephalography (EEG), allow that through the processing of impulses or electrical signals generated by the human brain, people who have some type of severe motor disability or suffer from neurological conditions or neurodegenerative diseases, can establish communication with electronic devices. This paper proposes the development of an expert system that generates the control sequences for a neuroprosthesis that will be used in the rehabilitation of patients who cannot control their own muscles through neuronal pathways. This proposal is based on the EGG record during the operation of a BCI under the rare event paradigm and the presence or not of the P300 wave of the Event-Related Potential (ERP). Feature extraction and classification will be implemented on a mobile device using Python as a platform. The processing of the EEG records will allow obtaining the information so that an Expert System implemented in the mobile device, is responsible for determining the control sequences that will be executed by a neuroprosthesis. The tests will be performed by controlling a neuroprosthesis developed by the Instituto Nacional de Rehabilitación in México, which aims to stimulate the movement of a person's upper limb.

Keywords: Brain-Computer Interface · Neuroprosthesis · Mobile devices · EEG · Motor imagination

© Springer Nature Switzerland AG 2020
C. Stephanidis et al. (Eds.): HCII 2020, CCIS 1294, pp. 25–31, 2020.
https://doi.org/10.1007/978-3-030-60703-6_4

1 Introduction

According to the World Report on Disability issued by the World Health Organization (WHO) [1], it is estimated that more than 1 billion people in the world live with some form of disability; of these people, almost 200 million have considerable difficulties executing actions or tasks that are considered normal for a human being. In the medical area, physical rehabilitation has been used for the retraining of people affected by lesions to the nervous system, and it is through functional electrical stimulation (FES) that the motor nerves are artificially activated, causing muscle contractions that generate functional movement by applying electrical current pulses. On the other hand, the brain-computer interfaces (BCI), based on electroencephalography (EEG) provide an alternative for humans to establish communication with external devices, and are helpful for people who have some type of severe motor disability, suffer from neurological conditions or neurodegenerative diseases; This is currently possible because EEG-based BCIs record brain signals in order to create a non-muscular communication channel between mental intentions and electronic devices.

The main noninvasive methods of BCIs include Slow Cortical Potentials (SCPs), evoked potential of the P300 wave, Visual Steady State Potentials (SSVEPs) and Motor Imagination (MI) [2]. This change attracts the subject's attention, forcing him to use working memory to compare the rare or infrequent stimulus with frequent previous stimuli [3]. In this work we propose the development of a system that generates the control sequences through the P300 component for a neuroprosthesis that will be used in the rehabilitation of patients who cannot control their own muscles.

2 Methods and Materials

The general form of the methodology considered in this work is made up of the following steps:

Step 1 Acquisition of signals: The signal acquisition stage aims to record the electrical activity of the brain, which reflects the user's intentions, is carried out through an EEG using electrodes. In this first stage, the registered signal is prepared for further processing.

Step 2 EEG registration: Hardware and Software: A 16-channel biopotential amplifier, model g.USBamp™ from the company g.tec ™, was used, with which the EEG was registered in 10 positions of the International 10–20 System (Fz, C4, Cz, C3, P4, Pz, P3, PO8, Oz and P07) during the operation of the P300 Speller application of the experimental platform for the BCI2000 ™ [4], based on the original Donchin Speller [5].

Step 3 Feature Extraction: The methods to extract features such as Principal Component Analysis (PCA), Independent Component Analysis (ICA) and Common Spatial Pattern (CSP). For the analysis of the data in time-frequency, we find the Fourier Transform by Intervals (STFT), Wavelet Transform (WT), Autoregressive Models (AR) and Adaptive Filter (MF) with the same objective.

Step 4 Classifiers: In this stage, the parameters that classify the signal between different patterns or classes are established. Which can be: neural networks, deep neural networks, the support vector machine (SVM), etc.

Step 5 Control: Finally, the control stage corresponds to direct interaction with the end user. Once the features have been detected and they have been classified as control signals, the implemented application must perform the corresponding actions.

3 Results

To validate the advances in this research, from the EEG record database [6], the following test considerations were taken. A set of test subjects underwent 4 registration sessions organized as follows:....

Session 1. Directed Spelling. Number of sequences per symbol: 15. Record: 1. Target word: HEAT. Record 2: Target word: CARIÑO. Record 3: Target word: SUSHI.

Session 2. Directed Spelling with classification matrix. Number of sequences per symbol: 15. Record 1: Target word: SUSHI.

Session 3. Free Spelling with classification matrix. Number of sequences per symbol: 15. From 1 to 4 registers. Target words chosen by the subject.

Session 4. Free Spelling with fewer intensification sequences. Number of sequences: variable (1 to 15). From 1 to 10 records. Target words chosen by the subject.

3.1 Considerations

In directed spelling registers (sessions 1 and 2), the target words are predefined and the symbols that make them up are indicated one by one, performing 15 stimulation sequences per symbol. A stimulation sequence consists of the random intensification (the symbols contained in a row or column light up in white) of each of the 6 rows and the 6 columns of the symbol matrix. In the records of the free spelling sessions (3 and 4), the target words are freely chosen by the subject and the number of stimulation sequences per symbol in each record varies between 1 and 15, also by choice of the subject. For each of the 10 test subjects considered, each of the 4 EEG (directed spelling) records can be expressed as $x_{i,ch}$ (n), where i $\in$ {1, 2, 3, 4} represents the record number, ch $\in$ {1,2,..., 10} the channel number, n = 1, 2,..., N are the instants of the EEG signal sampling time, and N is the total number of samples from register i, which depends on the number of spelled symbols (5 or 6). Figure 2 shows the EGG signals.

With the EEG raw signal from each of the 10 channels, for each record $x_{i,ch}$ (n), the following is done:

- An EEG epoch is expressed as $x_{i,ch}^{k,y}$ (n), with n = {1, 2, ..., 257}, it is defined as a window with 257 samples (after the moment of stimulation) from register i and class k $\in$ {a, u} where k = a indicates an epoch of the attended class and k = u, an epoch of the unattended class.

- The super index k = a corresponds to the synchronized time with the intensification of a row or column of the matrix of the Speller P300, containing a target symbol (infrequent event), and k = u corresponds to a time of EEG associated with a intensification that does not include a target symbol (frequent event). The superscript indicates the type of epoch: the rows (y = f) or columns (y = c).

- In each of the 4 EEG records of each subject, all available times are extracted and divided into 4 groups, Fig. 1. Times attended by rows: $x_{i,ch}^{a,f}$ (n), times attended by columns: $x_{i,ch}^{a,c}$ (n), unattended times of rows: $x_{i,ch}^{u,f}$ (n), unattended times of columns: $x_{i,ch}^{u,c}$ (n).

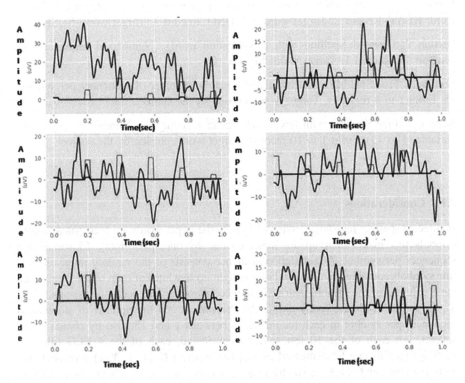

Fig. 1. Signal recording EEG in the target times.

The information from Record 1 of the Directed Spelling of Session 1 that has been specified in the previous section, was processed using Python tools and a total of 890 epochs were identified, of which 149 correspond to epochs attended and 741 to epochs not catered for. From said grouping, what is specified in Table 1 is obtained.

Table 1. Number of times for record 1 of Directed Spelling.

Letter	Attended	Not attended
C	29	140
A	29	139
L	29	142
O	29	147
R	29	140

From the extracted signals, the average of the records of the times attended and not attended by letter is calculated, through Directed Spelling and the registration channel, obtaining the information records shown in Figs. 2, 3 and 4.

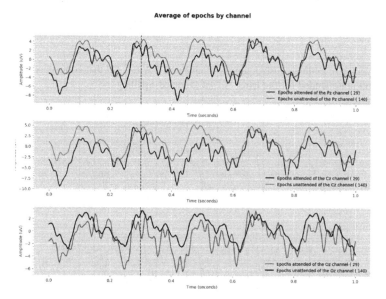

Fig. 2. Average recording of EEG signals of channels *Pz, Cz, Oz* that correspond to the times attended and not attended for the letter "C" of Directed Spelling.

As can be seen in Figs. 2, 3 and 4, the information that corresponds to the average of the times attended and not attended by the recording channel are very similar, this corresponds to the measurement of the signal power content versus the frequency of the channels that are of interest Pz, Cz and Oz.

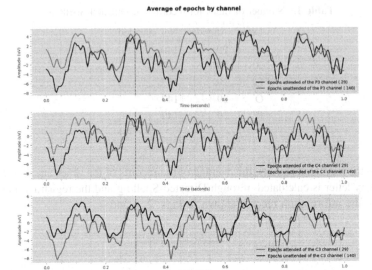

Fig. 3. Average recording of EEG signals of channels *P3, C4, C3* that correspond to the times attended and not attended for the letter "C" of Directed Spelling.

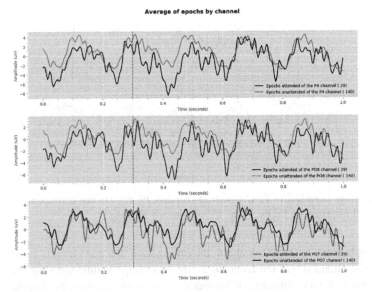

Fig. 4. Average recording of EEG signals of channels P4, PO8, PO7 that correspond to the times attended and not attended for the letter "C" of Directed Spelling.

4 Conclusions

In the course of this research, the registration of the EEG signals is obtained for a population of 10 individuals with different abilities, who were presented with the test board to start the acquisition of the signals. The acquired signals were subjected to the corresponding filtering as well as the extraction of the signal spectrum to detect the frequency in which it presents the greatest energy, this point being considered as the center of attention of the individual in the letter they wish to express. From the previous process already established, the corresponding acquisitions will be made to extract the pertinent characteristics and continue with the selection of the training and classification algorithm on mobile devices.

Acknowledgments. The team work thanks the Instituto Politécnico Nacional, the Instituto Nacional de Rehabilitación y a la Secretaria de Educación, Ciencia, Tecnología e Innovación de la Ciudad de México for the support, resources and facilities provided for the development of this research.

References

1. Organización Mundial de la Salud and Banco Mundial, Informe mundial sobre la discapacidad (2011)
2. Ortner, R., Allison, B.Z., Pichler, G., Heilinger, A., Sabathiel, N., Guger, C.: Assessment and communication for people with disorders of consciousness. JoVE **126**, 1–8 (2017). https://doi.org/10.3791/53639
3. Mercado, J.: Implementación de una nueva estrategia de identificación del potencial P300 para interfaces cerebro-computadora utilizando información espectral del eeg. Master's thesis, Universidad Autónoma Metropolitana Iztapalapa, August 2016
4. Schalk, G., McFarland, D., Hinterberger, T., Birbaumer, N., Wolpaw, J.: BCI2000: a general-purpose brain-computer interface (BCI) system. IEEE Trans. Biomed. Eng. **51**(6), 1034–1043 (2004). https://doi.org/10.1109/tbme.2004.827072
5. Farwell, L., Donchin, E.: Talking off the top of your head: toward a mental prosthesis utilizing event-related brain potentials. Electroencephalogr. Clin. Neurophysiol. **70**(6), 510–523 (1988). https://doi.org/10.1016/0013-4694(88)90149-6
6. Ledesma-Ramirez, C., Bojorges-Valdez, E., Yanez-Suarez, O., Saavedra, C., Bougrain, L.: An open-access P300 speller database. In: Fourth International Brain-Computer Interface Meeting, May 2010

Investigating Smart Home Needs for Elderly Women Who Live Alone. An Interview Study

Nana Kesewaa Dankwa[✉]

Research Centre for Information Systems Design, University of Kassel,
Pfannkuchstrasse 1, 34121 Kassel, Germany
nkdankwa@uni-kassel.de

Abstract. Identity aspects such as gender, race, culture, and socio-economic status should be considered when technologies are designed with and for persons [9]. HCI research in ageing populations can benefit from considering the complexity of identity, use and context of older persons. This short paper draws attention to gender as an aspect of identity in working with ageing populations. It presents results from an interview study with elderly women who live alone in Germany. This study is part of a larger research project dedicated to innovating smart home technologies with and for elderly women who live alone. The research project has comprised of an "exploratory getting-to know each other" session, use experience of a smart speaker and interview studies. This paper presents insights from semi-structured interviews with 7 elderly women who live alone. These insights are also presented as design considerations for smart home technology for elderly women living alone. The study is the basis for further work with the elderly women, which are co-creation sessions to design smart home devices and develop prototypes.

Keywords: Interviews · Ageing · Smart homes · Ageing-in-place · Gender

1 Introduction

Past HCI research in ageing populations is criticized as deficit oriented, not incorporating the holism of ageing [4, 11]. Recent HCI research has gravitated towards positive models of ageing like Successful Ageing, Active Ageing, and Ageing in Place. These models accentuate a comprehensive outlook on ageing based on the pillars of health, participation, and security of the elderly [10]. Moving forward, HCI research for ageing populations can harness overlooked opportunities by considering the complex identity and use contexts of older persons. Instead of a focus on a disability, design can consider how identity aspects intersect, and identity is situated in design [3].

Gender, an aspect of an individual's identity intersecting with age, is overlooked in technology design for older people even though gender influences participation, health, and financial status [8, 12]. This paper highlights these interactions. This study is part of ongoing research to design smart home devices with elderly women who live alone. It has till now engaged the women in an "exploratory getting to know each other" session, use experience of a smart speaker and interview studies.

© Springer Nature Switzerland AG 2020
C. Stephanidis et al. (Eds.): HCII 2020, CCIS 1294, pp. 32–38, 2020.
https://doi.org/10.1007/978-3-030-60703-6_5

This paper presents the interview study with 7 elderly women (65+) who live alone in a suburb of Kassel, Germany. The goal was understanding the women's lives, even as children and younger adults. The research questions were: How do elderly women manage their lives alone? What are the elderly women's perceptions towards (smart) technology? The findings show how gender, birth year, and living situation influence older adults' quality of life [12]. It shows their values and factors to wellbeing. This work paves way for future co-design of smart home technology.

This paper's contribution is three-fold. First, it presents an empirical study of elderly women living alone, adding to the scarce research corpus of this group. Second, it brings attention to the need to consider an individual's identity as an intersection of varying factors. Third, it presents design considerations for smart home technology for the elderly.

2   Method

Seven (7) elderly women (mean age = 79.9, SD = 2.61, age range = 75–83) were recruited for face-to-face semi-structured interviews. Semi-structured interviews are key in gaining in-depth insights into the ageing experiences of older persons [1, 2]. The questions were in four categories: 1. personal information, 2. life in past years, childhood, as young adults, family and hobbies, 3. present life, daily routines, social activities, relationships, and skills and 4. technology use and ownership. The interviews (avg. 53 min) were in German, audio recorded with a smart phone and in the women's homes. They lived alone with no support for daily chores. All women but two lived in their houses, two in rented and owned apartments. They were recruited through snowballing sampling. For the women, the interviews were a follow-up to the "exploratory getting to know each other" session (Table 1).

Table 1. Demographics of women. All names have been anonymized.

PID	Age	Years in current home	Years living alone	Education/training	Years worked
Anna	81	51	10	Pharmacy	–
Heike	83	50	7.5	Nursing (Pediatric)	6/7
Emma	82	50	3	Sales + Cosmetology	10
Beate	80	38	3	Home Economics	24
Eva	79	45	11	Tax Office	30+
Hanna	75	19	19	Bachelor (Education)	30+
Barbara	79	55	1.5	Wholesales	45

The interviews were analysed using conventional content analysis [6]. Some themes that rose out of the categories are reported. This study is limited to the geographic location and cultural contexts of the women. They are white with no migration backgrounds. They have no financial or health constraints which is not reflective of all elderly women. Gender is based on societal structures and not self-defined.

3   Findings

3.1   Building on Life Experiences

Nationality, age group, and gender impact the quality of life older persons. Belonging to the Silent Generation, all participants' parents experienced The Great Depression and World War II, influencing their lives as children, teenagers, and women. The choices for hobbies, education and jobs were marginal, making the best of what was available. For example, Eva said they *"would have loved to study if there had been money"* but did an apprenticeship. For this age group, family and childcare were definitive women roles. In the west of Germany, for example, where this study takes place, public nurseries for children below 3 years was non-existent and admission competitive. Mothers were not expected to be a primary part of the working class as fathers.

All women were married relatively early (mean age = 22). Anna and Heike were housewives, raised 4 and 3 children, respectively. Emma, Eva and Beate worked dependent on child-care options, raising 2, 2 and 1 child(ren), respectively. Hannah and Barbara had no children and worked fulltime. The women were financially reliant on their or their husband's pension. Elderly women may suffer more from pension deficiencies due to family and childcare roles or spousal separation.

The factors detailed above can influence women's lives especially if their pension benefits are minimal. They may be unable to afford sophisticated smart home technology that could help them live alone independently.

3.2   Living Alone but not Lonely

The participants were positive on ageing. They described aging as a stage of life, to be embraced and the most made of. 'Old' was reflective of how one felt. For Heike, *"I am as old as I feel"* *"sometimes I feel like I am 60 and sometimes I think that is not possible, I cannot do that anymore....but overall I do not feel like 83, no no"*. Barbara said, *"everything has its time....and now when one is older, really old at 79, it is also a beautiful time...one can undertake several things, do a lot and have many friends"*.

Loneliness as a subjective measure of the quality of relationships one has is dependent on age, financial situation, and health [5]. Though the study did not measure states of loneliness, it noted the variance between being lonely and living alone. The women lived alone due to the demise of their spouse. They valued living alone and did not see themselves as lonely. Anna said *"...being alone is enjoyable and when not, I go out to meet others"*. Heike said *"I do well living alone. I enjoy it as well"*. The social environment and activities contributed to them not being lonely and a reluctance to move away as this could lead to loneliness. Emma said that *„If I ever moved out of this neighborhood to a new place then I would be lonely"*. Anna said, *"When you keep busy, you do not fall into a hole. You keep a balance and have a feeling of self-worth"*.

All women did not wish to move to new environments even their children's. Emma said she could not imagine *"making new connections at 82 years"*.

The values of independence and freedom influenced their choice to live alone. For Beate: *„As long as I am independent and can still take care of everything by myself, I do not wish to live in a [care] home"*. Heike noted the freedom *„to do what I want to do when and how I want to do"*. Elderly men in the US shared similar values of freedom and satisfaction living alone [13] which contradict stereotypes of loneliness for the elderly living alone.

After the loss of spouse, over time, they picked up new hobbies, habits (e.g. cooking habits) and friendships were discovered while some hobbies, activities, and friendships were stopped.

3.3   Engaging in and with the Community

The study underscored the value of proximate friends, family, neighbors, and groups to the women's wellbeing. Each woman was a member of at least one club of a sort. For example, Anna, Emma, Beate, Hanna and Barbara were in a garden club, and Heike in a board game club. The clubs arranged periodic meetings for games, travel, Sunday lunches, dinner, or visits. Group membership and activities metamorphosed over the years. For example, Hanna goes out to eat every fortnight with a group she has been part of for 40+ years. They met for bowling, but due to health restrictions, the oldest now 99 years, now meet to eat out.

Heike, Eva, and Emma were enrolled in courses at the Adult School. Eva in an english course, Heike, and Emma in a novel reading course. Beate and Heike were part of regular meetings at the Community Center for crafting, and painting. They said it kept their minds active and they met others. They used telephones mostly to keep in touch with their community and preferred face-to-face interactions. Anna said, *"I prefer personal contact to talking on the phone."* They prioritized the nurturing of relationships over longer spans, meeting regularly, checking up on each other and running errands for each other. Korporaal et al. say this is a unique trait of women in guaranteeing the ongoing contact of kin and non-kin relationships [7].

3.4   Living with Technology

Persons born between 1924–1945 are identified as having traits (e.g. frugal, demand quality and simplicity) formed due to living situations in the years. On technology purchase, the women believed technology should be purchased when needed. And if it met its function, it need not be replaced. Hanna said: *"If a technology needs to be upgraded often with software or parts, then what was the essence of it"*, In addition, if new technology could not play a substantial role in their lives, make it better, it was not needed. For example, Anna said when computers became popular, they did not get one because, *"we never understood how a computer could make our lives better than it was"*. And for Heike, Emma, Beate, Eva and Hannah who had computers, they used them rarely, for 'administrative' tasks such as online banking, printing, scanning, email etc. Play or leisure was with the television and radio. However, Eva played Mahjong on her smart phone, Beate liked taking photos with her smart phone. Anna read books and news on her iPad. Heike and Emma like exchanging messages with family, neighbours, and friends on WhatsApp. Hanna and Barbara had mobile phones but no smart phones.

The use of a device did not imply emotional affinity, they did not need to have an attachment to technology regularly used. Also, a technology use skill could be acquired but not used. The acquired skill did not translate into affinity or desire to use the technology. For example, Anna and Hanna took computer and smart phone courses but did not have the devices. The use of smart phones was motivated by the desire to stay in contact with younger family generations. Their smart phone habits differed from younger persons. They did like to constantly carry or have conversations in public spaces with their mobile phones. Mobile phones were for emergency situations especially when travelling.

On smart homes, the women were familiar with the basic concept. But Anna thought *"it was for people who needed to do a lot at once"*. They wondered if it were something that would fit into their lives. Beate asked *"is there really a need to remotely control my blinds?"*. From an earlier study with the women, where they received a smart speaker (Amazon Echo Dot) and a diary to document how they adopted the new technology into their lives. Heike used it for two days and plugged it out due to the discomfort of being listened to. Eva attempted to use the device (asked others how to use, installed the app but unsuccessful in use). The others did not use the device. Beate and Hanna did not have wireless internet and Barbara did not have a smart phone. They generally commented that the device did not fit into their lives with concerns for privacy and security.

4   Discussion

4.1   Design Considerations

Alternative Interfaces
The design of alternative interfaces for smart homes that are ubiquitous, assimilating into the current habits, activities and spaces of the women could allow for the easy adoption of smart home technologies. The use of smart textiles, surfaces (e.g. mirrors, kitchen counters) as interfaces allow for easy integration into the women's homes. It avoids the introduction of entirely new elements, making the presence of smart home technology not intrusive as new technology can often be daunting for elderly women. However, adoption may be easier if the technology stems from a place of familiarity.

As smart home interfaces are often smart phones and with elderly women having different phone use habits, design could look at novel interfaces that do not require phones. Interactions can be based on switching knobs, pressing buttons or simple "on and off" buttons. In addition, this opens the opportunity for investigating diverse materials for designing smart home devices such as smart textiles and sustainable materials.

The women preferred face-to-face interactions, but as most digital technology minimises personal contact, smart home design can compensate with face in this need by facilitating convention with interconnected visually appealing interfaces that allow one to know

Designing with Elderly Women Living Alone

Co-design sessions should align with positive aspects of the lives of the elderly women. This means identifying the inherent skills and creative activities the women enjoy. This should inform material and toolkits choices, which may not entirely be foreign to the women. But if the material or toolkit must be electronic, then the women may first be eased into 'making' with activities they are familiar with. In addition, tech design should embrace the women's lives as valid as it is and not situated as a redeemer. If design is driven by the women, there may in the end be no need for new smart home tech, but a variation of current tech use.

Varying forms of sharing knowledge may be needed as the elderly women preferred oral interactions when they received new technology. Each woman shared similar experiences, on receipt of new tech, the installer orally explained how to use the tech and they wrote notes for future use. Design sessions could explore ways of designing easy to use manuals with interactive oral knowledge forms for the elderly.

Designing for Privacy and Security

All women were concerned with smart home devices recording their data and being stored somewhere they did not know. How can design assure them their data will be used only for what the permit and not against them in future? Also, they were not comfortable using Amazon devices due to data sale for marketing controversies. They feared that having these devices always on, meant being listened to almost like a spy. How can privacy be designed as transparent for elderly persons? Design could position privacy as a central purpose of the device. Therefore, the device works in maintaining privacy and everything else is secondary. Thus, for example by visually communicating data sources being streamed from or to, one always knows when errors occurs.

5 Conclusion

Elderly women may face additional barriers to wellbeing in living alone as compared to their peers and couples in other living conditions. The present case study contributes new understandings of the lives of elderly women, their values and their attitudes to technology use and ownership. It highlights the need to consider alternative interfaces, privacy & security and material choices to when designing considerations for smart home technology design which are

Acknowledgements. This work was supported by the INTeGER (Innovation through Gender in Computing) research project. The author thanks all the women who participated in this study and Claude Draude for her supervision of the project.

References

1. Bernard, H.R.: Research Methods in Anthropology, 5th edn. AltaMira, Blue Ridge Summit (2011)
2. Brandt, E., Binder, T., Malmborg, L., Sokoler, T.: Communities of everyday practice and situated elderliness as an approach to co-design for senior interaction. In: Proceedings of the 22nd Conference of the Computer-Human Interaction Special Interest Group of Australia on Computer-Human Interaction, pp. 400–403, November 2010
3. Brewer, R.N., Piper, A.M.: XPress: rethinking design for aging and accessibility through a voice-based online blogging community. Proc. ACM Hum.-Comput. Interact. 1(CSCW), 26 (2017)
4. Carroll, J.M., Convertino, G., Farooq, U., Rosson, M.B.: The firekeepers: aging considered as a resource. Univ. Access Inf. Soc. 11(1), 7–15 (2012). https://doi.org/10.1007/s10209-011-0229-9
5. Gierveld, J.D.J., Van Tilburg, T.: The De Jong Gierveld short scales for emotional and social loneliness: tested on data from 7 countries in the UN generations and gender surveys. Eur. J. Ageing 7(2), 121–130 (2010). https://doi.org/10.1007/s10433-010-0144-6
6. Hsieh, H.F., Shannon, S.E.: Three approaches to qualitative content analysis. Qual. Health Res. 15(9), 1277–1288 (2005)
7. Korporaal, M., Broese van Groenou, M.I., Van Tilburg, T.G.: Effects of own and spousal disability on loneliness among older adults. J. Aging Health 20(3), 306–325 (2008)
8. Schiebinger, L., Klinge, I., Paik, H.Y., Sánchez de Madariaga, I., Schraudner, M., Stefanick, M. (eds.): Gendered Innovations in Science, Health & Medicine, Engineering, and Environment (genderedinnovations.stanford.edu) 2011–2018
9. Schlesinger, A., Edwards, W.K., Grinter, R.E.: Intersectional HCI: engaging identity through gender, race, and class. In: Proceedings of the 2017 CHI Conference on Human Factors in Computing Systems, pp. 5412–5427, May 2017
10. Nassir, S., Leong, T.W., Robertson, T.: Positive ageing: elements and factors for design. In: Proceedings of the Annual Meeting of the Australian Special Interest Group for Computer Human Interaction, pp. 264–268, December 2015
11. Vines, J., Pritchard, G., Wright, P., Olivier, P., Brittain, K.: An age-old problem: examining the discourses of ageing in HCI and strategies for future research. ACM Trans. Comput.-Hum. Interact. (TOCHI) 22(1), 1–27 (2015)
12. WHO: Active Ageing: A policy framework, Madrid, Spain, pp. 1–59 (2002)
13. Yetter, S.L.: The experience of older men living alone. Geriatr. Nurs. 31(6), 412–418 (2010)

Communication Support Utilizing AAC for Verbally Challenged Children in Developing Countries During COVID-19 Pandemic

Walia Farzana[1], Farhana Sarker[2], Ravi Vaidyanathan[3], Tom Chau[4],
and Khondaker A. Mamun[1(✉)]

[1] Advanced Intelligent Multidisciplinary Systems Lab, Department of Computer Science and Engineering, United International University, Dhaka, Bangladesh
mamun@cse.uiu.ac.bd
[2] Department of Computer Science and Engineering, University of Liberal Arts Bangladesh, Dhaka, Bangladesh
[3] Department of Mechanical Engineering, Imperial College London, London, UK
[4] Institute of Biomaterials and Biomedical Engineering, University of Toronto, Toronto, Canada

Abstract. Functional communication is indispensable for child development at all times but during this COVID-19, non-verbal children become more anxious about social distancing and self-quarantine due to sudden aberration on daily designed practices and professional support. These verbally challenged children require the support of Augmentative and Alternative Communication (AAC) for intercommunication. Therefore, during COVID-19, assistance must be provided remotely to these users by a AAC team involving caregivers, teachers, Speech Language Therapist (SLT) to ensure collaborative learning and development of non-verbal child communication skills. However, most of the advanced AAC, such as Speech Generating Devices (SGD), Picture Exchange Communication System (PECS) based mobile applications (Android & iOS) are designed considering the scenario of developed countries and less accessible in developing countries. Therefore, in this study, we are focusing on representing feasible short term strategies, prospective challenges and as long term strategy, a cloud based framework entitled as "Bolte Chai+", which is an intelligent integrated collaborative learning platform for non-verbal children, parents, caregivers, teachers and SLT. The intelligent analytics within the platform monitors child overall progress by tracking child activity in mobile application and conversely support parents and AAC team to concentrate on individual child ubiquitous abilities. We believe, the proposed framework and strategies will empower non-verbal children and assist researchers, policy makers to acknowledge a definitive solution to implement AAC as communication support in developing countries during COVID-19 pandemic.

© Springer Nature Switzerland AG 2020
C. Stephanidis et al. (Eds.): HCII 2020, CCIS 1294, pp. 39–50, 2020.
https://doi.org/10.1007/978-3-030-60703-6_6

Keywords: Augmentative and Alternative Communication (AAC) ·
Intelligent system · Picture Exchange Communication System
(PECS) · Developing countries

1   Introduction

According to the International Society of Augmentative and Alternative Communication (ISAAC), AAC refers to a group of tools and procedures (sign, gesture,
speech generating devices) to mitigate challenges of regular communication of
non-verbal children [1]. AAC is employed when the development of communication does not follow conventional manner, substantial delay is observed and
to augment (not replace) communication process AAC is introduced [2]. Due to
COVID-19 pandemic situation, there is alternations in daily routines of verbally
challenged children that might create distress and anxiety in verbally challenged
children which can negatively influence family relationships and making parents empathetic during this pandemic time [3]. It is imperative for everyone to
apprehend the ongoing pandemic situation, exhibit individual needs, and obtain
significant information. These non-verbal children utilize AAC as a communication support and such assistance must be ensured remotely by parents, teachers, SLT to these AAC users. One of the feasible choice is to provide remote
support via telepractice. Telepractice indicates to services arranged at distance
utilizing video conference or other technologies [4]. To quote Kairy, Lehoux and
Vincent [5], the World Health Organization (WHO) endorsed that telepractice
leads to clinical equivalence or even better performance compare to traditional
approaches and substantially improve access to service. In this study, we put forward certain short term strategies for developing countries to aid communication
support with AAC for verbally challenged children during COVID-19 which are;
telepractice with SLT, parent training and coaching via Tele-AAC, online classroom learning and multi-modal application and adaptation of accessible AAC
system. However, some observable challenges which restrain communication support utilizing AAC in developing countries are; dearth of adequate budget and
technical infrastructure for telepractice, bandwidth limitation in certain areas,
lack of policy, skilled personnel and governmental support to ensure confiden-
tiality in telecommunication service, non-cooperation of parents, teacher, SLT
who have limited knowledge of technology.

Considering the COVID-19 pandemic situation, as a long term strategy, we
are proposing an integrated intelligent platform titled as "Bolte Chai+", which
is at present a framework under design process. This "Bolte Chai+" framework embeds all the features of "Bolte Chai" [6] along with integrated platform
which enables monitoring of child progress while utilizing mobile application and
the interactive dashboard provide opportunity of collaboration among parents,
teachers and SLT. The intelligent algorithm within system will monitor child
progress that will assist parents, teachers and SLT to acknowledge child development scope in communication skills. The nobility of this proposed framework is

that it will enable collaboration among child, parents, teachers, SLT, administrative personnel through one single platform and will provide directions regarding child substantial improvement in communication skills.

In this pandemic situation of COVID-19, we are delineating short term strategies, challenges and a framework "Bolte Chai+" as an aid to support communication with AAC for non-verbal children in developing countries. The following paper is organized as follows, Sect. 2 present short term strategies for communication support with AAC, Sect. 3 illustrate the challenges in developing countries. Finally, a demonstration of the framework, discussion and conclusion.

2 Strategies to Support Communication with AAC During COVID-19 in Developing Countries

2.1 Mutli-Modal AAC Adaptation

Multimodal communication refers to utilization of one or more method during intercommunication. It might consists of manual signs, gestures (pointing), approximate vocalization, facial manifestation as well as aided AAC technology (PECS, SGD) [2]. Primarily, it includes anything that individuals apply for communication. Multimodal communication provide flexibility. For instance, parents can motivate the child to utilize PECS whereas SLT provide speech therapy via online applications. Moreover, if a child use mobile apps, picture with relevant vocabularies can be personalized to support their understanding regarding COVID-19. For example, mobile apps like Bolte Chai [6] and Avaz [7] provide customization option to caregivers or parents.

2.2 Telepractice with SLT

Student with language impairment often receive speech language therapy from Speech Language Therapists (SLT) as a part of their educational program [8]. Considering the COVID-19 situation, where in person service delivery should be limited, remote training or telepractice is a plausible solution. In order to execute telepractice service, structural planning is required which involves prioritizing need of individual child to determine learning targets, gleaning information from family members regarding available resources at home, implementing action plans via online video-conferencing, such as Zoom, Google Meeting, document sharing platform, for instance, Google Drive and parents training and coaching is required to ensure the implementation of home learning for non-verbal children [9].

2.3 Online Classroom Learning

Considering the unusual situation of COVID-19, schools can facilitate classroom learning via internet, considering online or blended learning, which involves both elements of traditional education and online learning. A complete team is involved in school based online learning which comprises school administrators, teacher, technical support providers, parents, children and facilitator [10]. An effective collaborative approach is required for initiating learning opportunities, managing and distributing materials and gleaning information regarding student progress.

2.4   Blended Learning Network (BLN) via Tele-AAC

Blended Learning Network (BLN) refers to a method that facilitate knowledge exchange and learning about communication and AAC between parents and professionals of individuals with complex communication need [11]. Tele-AAC is a team based approach which call for appropriate technical structure, numerous practices and strategies [12]. While Speech-Language Professionals (SLP) train and coach parents, there will be a certain framework with different stages. The stages are identifying target skills that need to be improved in a child, strategies and parent friendly procedures developed by SLP to enhance targeted communication skills in child. Parent training and coaching has effective positive results for both parents and child, parents gain confidence in supporting their child and improvement in child expressive and initiation of communication [13].

3   Challenges in Disseminating Communication Support with AAC in Developing Countries

3.1   Ensuring Privacy and Confidentiality

For successful telepractice it is imperative to guarantee confidentially, privacy of data and security of recorded data. Educational institutions should be prohibited to share student's or non-verbal child information without parental consent. The pros and corns as well as prospective outcomes need to be disclosed to parents before offering telepractice services. However, the administrative system in developing country like Bangladesh is not yet reformed to meet the need of electronic world [14].

3.2   Lack of Technical Infrastructure and Funding

Technical infrastructure is critical for success of telepractice. There are key things that should be available to both the provider and the client places which includes computer/laptop, internet access, video-conferencing or screen sharing software. Additional items that are required consists of internet usage policy and bandwidth allocation, administrative and technical support. According to World Health Organization(WHO), one of the constraint is funding in case of telepractice service in developing countries [15].

3.3 Dearth of Quality Service

Regardless of the facilities, resources or services provided, interventions and assessment of services provided via telepractice need to be assessed for therapeutic effectiveness and might include feedback from client, caregivers to maintain quality assurance [16]. Ingrained communication between service providers and receivers improve the overall quality of service via telepractice or active consultation.

3.4 Absence of Skilled Personnel

Most of the people in developing countries like Bangladesh do not have enough understanding of utilizing computer, internet or electronic delivery services [17]. Therefore, on site Information Technology (IT) support is required while introducing telepractice project, as the professional are aware of the technical infrastructure that can be used in the premises [18].

4 Proposed Theoretical Framework: Bolte Chai+

Considering the COVID-19 pandemic situation, it is imperative that parents, teachers and SLT work altogether to monitor child progress and apply AAC interventions to enhance their communication skills. Therefore, we are proposing a cloud based intelligent integrated platform with mobile application and the framework is titled as "Bolte Chai+". The framework embeds all the features of Bolte Chai [6]. Basically, "Bolte Chai" application is based on PECS technology where parent mode and child mode is present and the parent mode enable customization of activities according to child preference. In addition, voice output through mobile microphone enable non-verbal child to express their needs and the help option within the application ensure that child could seek help from their relatives only by selecting pictures which enable sending immediate SMS. All the aforementioned features are incorporated with intelligent analytics in "Bolte Chai+" to monitor the progress of child through mobile application utilization and generated progress report can be viewed through interactive dashboard (Fig. 1).

4.1 Description of Proposed Framework

The diagram in Fig. 2 depicts the basic framework of Bolte Chai+ which integrates different users to cloud service.

4.2 User Role or Stakeholders of Bolte Chai+

In the proposed "Bolte Chai+" framework, there are in total six categories of users.

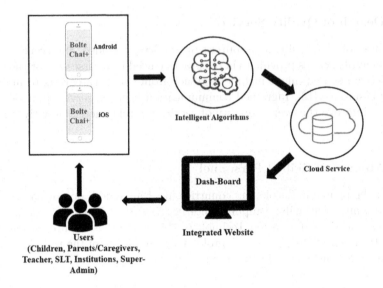

Fig. 1. Proposed architecture of Bolte Chai+

Child. Non-verbal child of developing countries will utilize the pictogram based mobile application. Each individual child will be registered will a unique user id at home or respective institutions.

Parents/Caregivers. Parents will have access to mobile application and integrated dashboard. In the mobile application they will able to customize help contacts; add/delete activities with picture, text and voice from cloud database or manually for child and in the website they will able to monitor child overall progress along with relevant information.

Teachers. Teachers will be able to edit activities for child utilizing the mobile application. While the dash-board in the website will enable teachers monitoring child progress and providing respective feedback.

Speech Language Therapists (SLT). SLT will recommend activities for child and will monitor child overall progress in interactive dashboard.

Institutions. Institutions refer to school or special organizations that work for non-verbal children. Access to website will enable them to integrate sub-institutions or all relevant information of child in one single platform.

Super-Admin. Super-Admin is responsible for user management, authentication and monitoring of the whole system with technical assistance from admin.

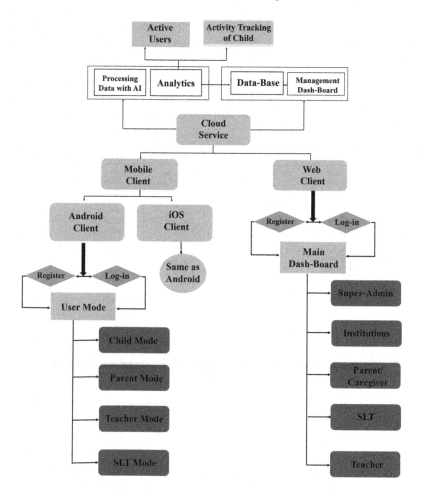

Fig. 2. Proposed framework of Bolte Chai+

Basically, through interactive dashboard it will be possible to get an overview of the present status and progress report of all child users.

4.3   Bolte Chai+ System

Bolte Chai+ System encompasses mobile application, user defined dashboard and cloud service. The dashboard have distinct functionality on the basis of user role.

Mobile Application. The application will have numerous activities with categories and sub-categories for both the android and iOS version. One example of activity is Food, under Food it will category that is breakfast, lunch and dinner. Therefore, under breakfast category, the sub-categories will be bread, jam, vegetables etc.

User Defined Dashboard. The integrated website will have dashboard that will enable different functions according to user role. The functions of dashboard for parents will be different from the functions of dashboard for teachers (Fig. 3).

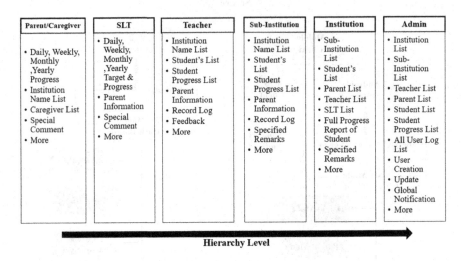

Parent/Caregiver	SLT	Teacher	Sub-Institution	Institution	Admin
• Daily, Weekly, Monthly ,Yearly Progress • Institution Name List • Caregiver List • Special Comment • More	• Daily, Weekly, Monthly ,Yearly Target & Progress • Parent Information • Special Comment • More	• Institution Name List • Student's List • Student Progress List • Parent Information • Record Log • Feedback • More	• Institution Name List • Student's List • Student Progress List • Parent Information • Record Log • Specified Remarks • More	• Sub-Institution List • Student's List • Parent List • Teacher List • SLT List • Full Progress Report of Student • Specified Remarks • More	• Institution List • Sub-Institution List • Teacher List • Parent List • Student List • Student Progress List • All User Log List • User Creation • Update • Global Notification • More

Hierarchy Level

Fig. 3. Management dash-board function according to user role in Bolte Chai+

Cloud Service. It will be responsible for all kind of user management and controlling operations with the mobile application and integrated website. Registration and authentication of registered users will be done in cloud via internet. Moreover, cloud management will store database of 1000+ activities and integrates Data-base information with dashboard. The Fig. 2 depicts the user function options based on the hierarchy level. For instance, Parent UI of dashboard provide functional option to monitor child progress via daily, weekly, monthly and yearly report, institution list, caregiver list and related feedback from teacher, SLT to enhance child communication skills. Respectively, there are definitive functional option in dashboard according to user role in the framework and one of the notable factor is with increment in user hierarchy there are substantial increase in the functionality of the user.

4.4   Main Objectives of Bolte Chai+

The main objectives of Bolte Chai+ includes product development, user centric analysis for further modification in the framework and user adaptability in order to address user feedback.

Product Development. We focused on the need of non-verbal children and their family to develop "Bolte Chai+". In collaboration with families, teachers, SLTs and concerned organizations we have analyzed users characteristics, workflow. On the basis of the analysis, an integrated intelligent platform with mobile application is under development process to monitor child activities and assist parents, teachers, SLT to acknowledge child progress at any place at any time. The mobile application will have interactive User Interface (UI), login function, backend database and analytics, privacy and language settings. In the long run, Natural Language Processing (NLP) will be integrated to remotely detect the progress the non-verbal child in utterance of certain words.

User Centric Analysis. After development and successful integration of "Bolte Chai+" in cloud server, user centric analysis (user experience, performance and security) will be conducted to analysis the efficacy of the android and iOS mobile application along with web service. Evaluation study of user experience will be conducted in schools, related organizations to gain feedback form the users and on the basis of feedback from parents, teacher, SLT and other stakeholders further development will be done in the application. All the critical findings will be considered for integration with the system and the application will be launched for public.

User Adaptability. The integrated platform "Bolte Chai+" provide opportunity of collaboration among non-verbal children, parents, teacher, caregivers and SLT. The development of the platform will address user feedback and will iterate the development process based on user acquisition. Initially, the evaluation of "Bolte Chai+" platform will be focused on Bangladeshi non-verbal children. Moreover, traditional and digital media will be utilized along with the support of concerned organizations to promote the applications to distinct communities and countrywide. In future, additional support will be added in different languages to ensure global exposure and sustainability of the platform.

5   Outcome

The "Bolte Chai+" will provide an opportunity to non-verbal child to exhibit their desire in a innovative manner and gain communication skills with assistance from teacher, parents and SLT. Moreover, parents, teacher, SLTs and other stakeholders will be able to collaborate in one single platform and monitor child progress. One of the encouraging outcome during evaluation sessions of our previous version "Bolte Chai" application is that it assist in developing communication skills in non-verbal children and relatively less expensive in context of developing countries, like Bangladesh [6]. It is expected that incorporating intelligent analytics and advanced features of "Bolte Chai+" will be beneficial for non-verbal children.

6 Discussion

The proposed framework "Bolte Chai+" possess the probability to become an optimal solution to support communication in non-verbal children during this COVID-19 pandemic and afterwards. Integration of machine learning and artificial intelligence in AAC systems has created a new dimension. For instance, application titled as LIVOX is a machine learning based android mobile application that recommend pictograms on the basis of time and location of user device [19]. Another example is Case Based Reasoning (CBR) machine learning approach that assist parent, caregiver and therapist to co-operate among themselves and closely monitor ASD children [20]. However, availability of these intelligent system is limited to developed countries. "Bolte Chai+" creates a premises of communication opportunity for non-verbal children in developing countries as well as for parents, teachers, SLTs and administrative authorities. A single platform integrates a complete team of concerned personnel in order to enhance the scope of communication skills for non-verbal children.

Regarding the proposed intelligent integrated framework "Bolte Chai+" we have outlined the following beneficial effects-

1. Through the smart mobile application, personalization of activities can be done according to individual child preference.
2. With user defined account, activities of individual child will be stored in the cloud and in case if the mobile phone utilized by child is lost, it will be possible to retrieve all the information of that child just by logging into personalized account from any device.
3. Parents, teacher and SLTs can monitor the progress of their child and on that basis they can decide on next target skills that can be developed in child.
4. Administrative authorities and policy makers can visualize the overall information of non-verbal children or students in one place through the dashboard of the proposed integrated platform. For instance, the number of non-verbal children utilizing "Bolte Chai+" application, their age group, institution, respective teacher, speech language professionals etc.
5. Collection of all information in one single platform will reduce the additional effort to gain information regarding child progress from different personnel.
6. With the integration of cloud service, it will reduce the dependency on direct/in-person therapy for non-verbal children.
7. Utilization of the app and integrated platform will assist in reducing workload of concerned organization by digitizing relevant information collection process regarding non-verbal children and their progress.

An intelligent integrated platform with mobile application, "Bolte Chai+", through which the development in non-verbal child communication skills can be monitored by parents, teacher, SLTs and with the utilization of mobile application it is possible to have personalized account, customized activities according to child preference and access to cloud based database of activities.

7   Conclusion and Future Work

In this study, we have focused on telepractice service and online education for non-verbal children as a short period strategy and underscored the significance of collaboration among parents, teacher, SLT and administrative personnel to support communication with AAC and illustrated a framework "Bolte Chai+" to provide an integrated platform. It is expected that with "Bolte Chai+" platform, we will be able to support development of communication skills in non-verbal and in the long run, with integration of Natural Language Processing(NLP)in the platform, we will be able to evaluate time frame of language development in individual non-verbal child. We believe that the proposed strategies, challenges and framework will direct researchers, developers, policy makers to acknowledge and initiate communication support with AAC for non-verbal children of developing countries during this unprecedented time of COVID-19.

Acknowledgment. We are thankful towards "Touri Foundation"-school for gifted children and the ICT Division, Ministry of Posts, Telecommunications and Information Technology, People's Republic of Bangladesh, for their financial and continuous support in research and development of this project.

References

1. ISAAC: International Society for Augmentative and Alternative Communication (ISAAC). Event (London) (2015)
2. Hill, K., Romich, B., Vanderheiden, G.: Augmentative and alternative communication. In: Med. Devices Hum. Eng. 47-1-47-10 (2014). https://doi.org/10.4324/9781315745152-5
3. Kathryn Asbury, L.F., Deniz, E., Code, A., Toseeb, U.: PsyArXiv Preprints — How is COVID-19 affecting the mental health of children with Special Educational Needs and Disabilities and their families? https://psyarxiv.com/sevyd/. Accessed 09 June 2020
4. ASHA: roles and responsibilities of speech-language pathologists in early intervention: guidelines (2008). https://doi.org/10.1044/policy.GL2008-00293
5. Kairy, D., Lehoux, P., Vincent, C., Visintin, M.: A systematic review of clinical outcomes, clinical process, healthcare utilization and costs associated with telerehabilitation (2009). https://doi.org/10.1080/09638280802062553
6. Khan, M.N.R., Sonet, H.H., Yasmin, F., Yesmin, S., Sarker, F., Mamun, K.A.: "Bolte Chai" - an Android application for verbally challenged children. In: 4th International Conference on Advances in Electrical Engineering, ICAEE 2017 (2017). https://doi.org/10.1109/ICAEE.2017.8255415
7. Avaz Full-featured AAC app - Features — Avaz Inc. https://www.avazapp.com/features/. Accessed 01 June 2020
8. COVID-19 response plan for speech-language professionals: what to do if school gets shut down for coronavirus-the SLP solution. https://www.slpsolution.com/covid-19-response-plan-for-speech-language-professionals/. Accessed 09 June 2020
9. COVID-19: Speech Language Therapy Services. http://www.fecisd.net/UserFiles/Servers/Server_1268391/File/Required%20Documents/Speech_Language%20Therapy%20Services%204.16.20.pdf

10. Crutchley, S., Campbell, M., Christiana, D.: Implementing a school-based telepractice program. Perspect. Telepract. **2**, 31–41 (2012). https://doi.org/10.1044/tele2. 1.31
11. Wilder, J., Magnusson, L., Hanson, E.: Professionals' and parents' shared learning in blended learning networks related to communication and augmentative and alternative communication for people with severe disabilities. Eur. J. Spec. Needs Educ. **30**, 367–383 (2015). https://doi.org/10.1080/08856257.2015.1023002
12. Anderson, K., et al.: Tele-AAC Resolution, vol. 4, pp. 79–82 (2012)
13. Barton, E.E., Fettig, A.: Parent-implemented interventions for young children with disabilities. J. Early Interv. (2013). https://doi.org/10.1177/1053815113504625
14. Hoque, M.R., Mazmum, M.F.A., Bao, Y.: e-health in Bangladesh: current status, challenges, and future direction. Int. Technol. Manag. Rev. **4**, 87 (2014). https:// doi.org/10.2991/itmr.2014.4.2.3
15. Word Health Organization: Global Observatory for eHealth: Atlas: eHealth country profiles. Atlhas eHealth Ctry. profiles Glob. Obs. eHealth Ser. 1, 230 (2011)
16. Professional Issues in Telepractice for Speech-Language Pathologists.https://www. asha.org/policy/PI2010-00315.htm. Accessed 09 June 2020
17. Khan, S.Z., Shahid, Z., Hedstrom, K., Andersson, A.: Hopes and fears in implementation of electronic health records in Bangladesh, In: Electron. J. Inf. Syst. Dev. Ctries. **54** (2012). https://doi.org/10.1002/j.1681-4835.2012.tb00387.x
18. Boisvert, M., Hall, N., Andrianopoulos, M., Chaclas, J.: The multi-faceted implementation of telepractice to service individuals with autism. Int. J. Telerehabilitation **4**, 11–24 (2012). https://doi.org/10.5195/ijt.2012.6104
19. Neamtu, R., Camara, A., Pereira, C., Ferreira, R.: Using artificial intelligence for augmentative alternative communication for children with disabilities. In: Lamas, D., Loizides, F., Nacke, L., Petrie, H., Winckler, M., Zaphiris, P. (eds.) INTERACT 2019. LNCS, vol. 11746, pp. 234–243. Springer, Cham (2019). https://doi.org/10. 1007/978-3-030-29381-9_15
20. Costa, M., Costa, A., Julián, V., Novais, P.: A task recommendation system for children and youth with autism spectrum disorder. In: De Paz, J.F., Julián, V., Villarrubia, G., Marreiros, G., Novais, P. (eds.) ISAmI 2017. AISC, vol. 615, pp. 87–94. Springer, Cham (2017). https://doi.org/10.1007/978-3-319-61118-1_12

An Evaluation of Augmentative and Alternative Communication Research for ASD Children in Developing Countries: Benefits and Barriers

Walia Farzana[1], Farhana Sarker[2], Quazi Delwar Hossain[3], Tom Chau[4],
and Khondaker A. Mamun[1(✉)]

[1] Advanced Intelligent Multidisciplinary Systems Lab, Department of Computer
Science and Engineering, United International University, Dhaka, Bangladesh
mamun@cse.uiu.ac.bd
[2] Department of Computer Science and Engineering, University of Liberal Arts
Bangladesh, Dhaka, Bangladesh
[3] Department of Electrical & Electronic Engineering, Chittagong University
of Engineering & Technology, Chittagong, Bangladesh
[4] Institute of Biomaterials and Biomedical Engineering, University of Toronto,
Toronto, Canada

Abstract. Augmentative and Alternative Communication (AAC) technology research not only enhance communication but also communal skills in verbally challenged children with Autism Spectrum Disorder (ASD). However, the research on AAC technology is mainly concentrated in developed countries and less explored in developing countries. In this study, we utilized evaluation method to analyze the prospects, existing practices and future possibilities, benefits and barriers of AAC research in developing countries. It is found that Speech Generating Devices (SGD) are mostly preferred by children and in future artificial intelligence (AI) based mobile application will augment communication skills among verbally challenged children. We conclude with general recommendation on succeeding research, collaborative approach and implementation with funding opportunities for substantial growth of AAC technology research in developing countries. This study will facilitate directions for initiating AAC research in developing countries and will accommodate researchers, developers and stakeholders to acknowledge opportunities, barriers, probable and current state of AAC research.

Keywords: Augmentative and Alternative Communication (AAC) · Developing countries · Autism Spectrum Disorder (ASD) · Picture Exchange Communication System (PECS) · Speech Generating Device (SGD)

1 Introduction

Augmentative and Alternative Communication (AAC) can be regarded as an approach that integrates tools and strategies (gestures, symbols, speech gener-

© Springer Nature Switzerland AG 2020
C. Stephanidis et al. (Eds.): HCII 2020, CCIS 1294, pp. 51–62, 2020.
https://doi.org/10.1007/978-3-030-60703-6_7

ating devices) to cope with daily communication challenges. AAC was devised with a view to making communication tools available to individuals with limited functional skills or verbal skills. According to World Health Organization (WHO), epidemiological data indicate that global frequency of Autism Spectrum Disorder (ASD) is one person in 160, which demonstrate 0.3% of the global burden of disease. On top of that, the ubiquity of ASD is unknown in many low and middle income countries [1]. Around 25% of individuals with autism are absent natural language as their simple means of contact as stated by the National Institute on Deafness and Other Communication Disorders [2]. It has been found that in 76% cases people diagnosed with autism will not strengthen eloquent communication and in case 30% cases no advancement to vocal output [3].

AAC system can be a feasible provisional or permanent communication resource for 30% ASD individuals who persist being non verbal throughout their life. According to H. C. Shane [4], there is alteration in nature and severity of communication techniques in individuals with ASD and distinguished collection of individuals fails to satisfy their day-to-day communication needs. There is a potential possibility in individuals to understand to handle picture exchange, speech generating device and manual sign but there emerge a noteworthy clinical question that which AAC mode will be appropriate for individual child with ASD [5]. Inspite of the upgrade in AAC, it can be burdensome, pricey and time consuming and can confound the user. In such cases, user level hardware (personal or tablet computer) can be employed to minimize the cost. The handheld devices available along with applications make a consumer-oriented distribution platform that allows for drastic transition in AAC for individuals with ASD. Furthermore, emerging technologies such as: Brain Computer Interface (BC1) and Machine Learning (ML) are also integrated in AAC research to overcome potential barriers for individuals with complex physical and verbal impairment.

Augmentative and Alternative Communication (AAC) can be commonly graded as aided and unaided AAC. Unaided AAC specifies certain modes not involving additional materials and examples are gesture, body language, sign language, facial expression etc. Aided AAC requires external materials and includes the low-tech, mid-tech and high-tech system. Low-tech systems don't require battery service and uses paper, pencil and alphabet boards. Examples of low technology AAC are Visual schedules and Picture Exchange Communication System. Medium Technology AAC devices involve pre-recorded message, which ranges from single message to multi-level message to numerous messages in distinct stages. Examples of such mid-tech system are; BIGmack^{TM}, LITTLE Step-by-Step^{TM}, and GoTalk^{TM}. High technology AAC systems involve dynamic display speech generating devices.

Most progress in the field of AAC is carried out in developed countries, which involves availability of resources and which are quite expensive in prospects of developing countries. However, in developing countries the research in AAC is limited even though it has the potential to enhance communication, communal interaction in non-verbal individuals. In this paper, we focus on evaluating opportunities and barriers of AAC technology research in developing countries.

2 Research on AAC, Practices and Future Prospects

2.1 Multi-Modal AAC System

Young non-verbal ASD children utilize variety of AAC systems based on their physical skills and communication impairments which ranges from sign language, Picture Exchange Communication System (PECS), Speech Generating Devices (SGD) to Mobile Apps. In order to ensure effective communicative means for non-verbal child, it is imperative to focus on their preference for AAC modes. Picture Exchange Communication System depends on picture symbols and provide visual reminder of objects for requesting. A smaller motor movement is required for requesting variety of elements. But the classical PECS has some demerits. At first, restricted capacity in the binder to accumulate cards and complexities to manage it out of convenient place, secondly, the paper cards containing picture decay after several use, Thirdly, the process to generate pictogram cards is rigorous. SGD is an electronic tool with speech-generating effects such as Proloquo2GoTM software and capable of incorporating considerable volume of vocabulary for the user and synthesized voice output is generated by tapping on the icons [6]. However, installation of app on commercial mobile device enhance the accessibility of AAC solution to families or care providers of individuals with autism spectrum disorder. Parents or caretaker can assess an app on the basis of rating and this grant a perceiving of authority and participation to the family in order to recognize voice for their child [7]. The purpose to adopt AAC device should not be limited to particularly requesting preferred items, in addition AAC instrument must assist students with ASD to express needs, exchange information and participation in social communication.

2.2 Comparative Usability of AAC Systems

AAC strategies begin with manual sign or hand gesture and advance to low-tech which includes communication boards and graphical symbols, which are nonelectric devices. With improvement in technology, mobile applications are becoming a major enthusiasm for the user because of low cost, portability and social acknowledgment. According to Department of Health and Human Services (DHHS), Interagency Autism Coordinating Committee's Strategic Plan for Autism Spectrum Disorder Research (DHHS, 2011) [8], there is a necessity for comparative study as it is significant in facilitating informed decision making on the basis of " head –to-head analyzes of interventions. In most cases participant preferred one of the AAC systems to others. Three AAC systems: PECS, SGD and Manual Signing (MS) were utilized among the participants in the study by McLay et al. [9,10]; where most of the participants exhibit preference and more frequently choose SGD system followed Picture Exchange Based System but almost all the participants maintained low preference for MS scheme. The reason behind preference can be related to some factors which are portability, demand of prerequisite skills, and advantages of SGD which are: variation in speech and local language according to the need of the user, minimal damage due to moisture, accidental falls, wears and tears and ease of maintenance, low demand of motor and linguistic skills due to simplistic design. Therefore, the AAC system which is suitable for individuals depends on multiple factors which are: learning priorities, existing physical and cognitive skills, families and individual's preference, the environment where communal interaction is considered. On the other hand, the new mobile technology offers low cost solution. The apps can be updated regularly and wirelessly, customization of additional factors require little effort from the user end. The studies of mobile based application by Tulshan [11]; Soomro and Soomro [12]; Signore [13] have a common focus which is personalization according to the user need in order to stimulate communication, social and functional skills of verbally challenged children with ASD. With these available applications, parents/caregivers can teach their children at anywhere at anytime and low cost of such applications provide more accessibility.

2.3   Innovative Technologies in AAC Research

Mobile Applications. Mobile applications incorporate multiple levels of function to interact with users. The implicit and explicit features of mobile applications can be categorized into functionality, appearance, shape/color, analytics and customization, all of which are involved to approach broad area of functions by users. In the following Table 1, the features of mobile application that assist in improvement of communication and social skills are delineated.

Table 1. Enhanced features in mobile application to Augment Skills in ASD children

Feature Type	Existing Features in Mobile Application
Functionality	– User centric design on the basis of feedback from guardians [11] – Provide support in decision making for educators, parents, caregivers by monitoring [12] – Motivating factors by including game section, loud output from device [13] – Access to multiple innovate functions (e.g. visual representation of emotions [14], daily routine and progress analysis [11]
Appearance	– Utilization of menu page and different modules [11] – Visualization of progress chart [12] – Using emoji to express emotions or feelings [14]
Shape/Color	– Utilization of multi-color PECS symbols [13] – Incorporation of variety shapes of characters [14]
Analytics	– Automated progress report within defined timeframe [11] – Behavioral and neurophysiological data analysis [15]
Customization	– User function for addition of images [12] – User based evaluation, design and availability [13] – Provide additional options to personalize images, voice according to cultural norm [14]

Brain-Computer Interface (BCI). With widespread utilization of touch-screen technology, there are interactive user interface (UI) through which selection of desired items is made but for individuals with severe physical impairment, this selection process becomes burdensome. In that case, utilization of user brain signal [Electroencephalogram, (EEG)] is employed for user selection which is independent of neuromuscular activity.The utilization of BCI technology requires support to set up technology and support from trained caregivers for management of system [16].

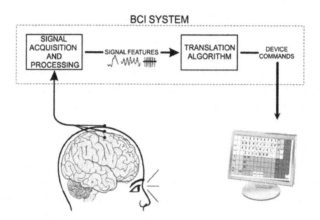

Fig. 1. A basic diagram of Brain-Computer Interface in AAC. The brain signal acquired from scalp, form cortical surface or from within the brain, are examined for features of signals (EEG) to illustrate user preference. Those features are transformed into commands for operation user interface of AAC [16].

The aforementioned figure depicts the basic integration of Brain-Computer Interface in AAC. However, different standardized metrics need to be considered from performance assessment of BCI based AAC system [17].

Machine Learning and Artificial Intelligence. The individuals with physical, cognitive and cognitive impairments utilize AAC system for ease of communication and such system should not become challenging and demanding. An application named LIVOX is a machine learning based android mobile application to recommend pictograms based on location and time of the user device. The notable features of LIVOX is artificial intelligence based recommendation system by analyzing past user data (used item, utilization time, touch time, GPS data, X and Y co-ordinates in touch screen) and another feature is Natural Language Processing (NLP) for speech recognition and enabling individuals to engage in conversation [18]. Moreover, a feedback framework which apply Case Based Reasoning (CBR) machine learning approach provide opportunity of close monitoring by therapists, parents or caregivers [19]. However, all these intelligent systems are available in developed countries. Even though there are research on detection on ASD children with machine learning methods, using home videos of Bangladeshi Children [20].

3   Opportunities and Benefits

3.1   Enhancement in Research Interest

Research in the domain of Augmentative and Alternative Communication (AAC) has developed over years. In beginning, gestures and sign language was utilized, later Picture Exchange Communication System (PECS) and Speech Generating Device (SGD) acquire preference among non-verbal children. With the advancement of mobile technology, mobile applications become more productive and portable solution. Recently, with the progress in the field of Brain-Computer Interface and Machine Learning, there are integrated researches within the mentioned one and AAC. Analytics are employed for task recommendation to ASD children and monitoring of child progress by parents and educators [19]. Machine-Learning approach is utilized to distinguish ASD and Typical Developed (TD) child through voice analysis and it performed better than experienced Speech Language Therapists (SLP) [21]. Moreover, Brain-Computer Interface promises to banish potential functional obstacles to AAC interventions for those with substantial physical and linguistic disorders. But all the aforementioned progress happened in developed countries. However, collaboration among multidisciplinary researchers and stakeholders are required for developing AAC system in prospects of developing country.

3.2   Mobilization of Existing Resources

The collaborative approach between researchers and organizations can successfully utilize the limited resources in order to propose a possible AAC solution to individuals with complex communication need. One such example is "Bolte Chai" which is an AAC device to augment communication in non-verbal children, the developmental cost of such device is less than other devices available in Bangladesh [22]. Moreover, later an android application was developed which can be personalized according to the child or user need and the application was productive to support verbal communication for students in Touri Foundation-school for gifted children as well as Bangladeshi Children [23]. In addition, there are organizations like Neuro-Developmental Disability Protection Trust under Ministry of Social Welfare in Bangladesh where the aim is to disseminate knowledge and empower people with neuro-development disabilities. With the support and limited resources from such organizations researchers can develop AAC system and ensure AAC system opportunities even in the rural area of Bangladesh.

3.3 Collaborative Approach Among Stakeholders

As the condition of individual ASD child is idiosyncratic and so does their challenges in case of utilization of AAC. To alleviate these challenges and proposing innovative technical solution, it is vital to have a direct collaboration with users and their respective families at each stage which ranges from problem identification, user testing, clinical evaluation to communal corroboration [23]. In terms of research and development it is imperative to have collaboration among service providers, technical developers, researchers from diverse discipline, special educators, speech language therapists, engineering knowledge in the field of computer science, cognitive science, performance evaluation of motor development, psychology and language development. Such multi-disciplinary intersection will maximize the technical development in the field of AAC. One of such example of virtual platform for collaborative approach is Rehabilitation Engineering Research Centre (RERC) on Augmentative and Alternative Communication (AAC) [24]. The RERC on AAC enrich research and disseminate knowledge in AAC. One of the significant information shared by RERC is how to support communication in individuals with complex communication need during the COVID-19 pandemic. Above all, related government organizations need to provide research and resource support to advance AAC research.

3.4 Widespread Utilization of Mobile Application

Recently, the communication scope provided by AAC system not only limited to expressing needs of children but also need to support social communication skills, interaction with others and knowledge transfer. Communication need not to be confined into face-to-face, rather they can be in written form or telecommunication. AAC system need to comprise all sorts of daily diverse communication needs which includes texting, mobile, internet access, social interaction. With the advancement in mobile technologies, there are numerous available apps which serve as a communication means for individuals with dynamic need for communication. The number of mobile subscriber in Bangladesh has extended to 165.337 million at the end of March 2020 [25]. The mobile application can not be only regarded as speech prosthesis, rather it serve multi-modal functions which are accessibility to information, entertainment, gaming activities and social interaction [26]. Families need not to be solely dependent on the recommendation of professionals and wait for funding from agency, they can become active decision make while availing mobile technology and app. In addition, they can customize the applications according to the need of their children.

3.5 Improvement in Quality of Life

There has been substantial transition in the utilization of AAC technology from single function to multi-function mobile applications and AAC systems. The advancement of Speech Generating Device (SDG) and mobile applications has created new opportunities for interaction. This offers expansion in the horizon of communication function and social inter-connectivity. Current technologies offer organization, social networking, overcoming architectural barriers, online education for individuals with dynamic need for communication [27]. Beyond the increased opportunities in communication, education and employment facility, AAC mobile application technology enhanced public awareness and acceptance [28]. The technological progress in AAC now can serve those who were previously unserved due to severe motor, cognitive and language impairments. For instance, the application of brain-computer interface ease communication and access to computer to those who are suffering from severe motor impairments. Communication encompasses all sphere of life ranges from enhanced educational success, communal inclusion, employment facilities and overall improved quality of life.

3.6   Policy and Advocacy

Collective efforts are required to ensure disseminate knowledge of AAC to medical professionals, Speech Language Therapists (SLT) so that they acknowledge children who require AAC system in order to improve communication skills. Public awareness is required to facilitate AAC utilization and increase acceptance of AAC system so that there is no such social or cultural barrier in terms of AAC use by ASD children. In addition, government funding is required to allocate AAC technologies to children which will provide greater communication and social skills.

4   Barriers and Challenges

4.1   Gap Between Research and Implementation

For effective technical solution it is imperative to have interaction between technical companies and multi-disciplinary regulation experts [24]. Industrial management team need to address the demand of individual ASD children and transfer such knowledge to technical developer and researchers so that they can focus on those field in terms of designing AAC systems. Collective effort is paramount to respond to the needs in case of low income and low resource country. In addition, technical companies need to place the demand of AAC technology that not only confined to individuals with slight impairments but also those with serious impairments. As research-driven technologies that are adequate for those with serious impairments can aid communities and make mainstream technology more effective [28]. Therefore, there is a crucial need for research that translates rapidly into daily practice and applicable to industrial stakeholders.

4.2   Lack of Research Driven Development

The traditional AAC systems were developed to augment the communication of individual with complex communication need but these systems were not designed according to the individual need of ASD children. According to research, when the technology is driven by practice (not by research), it might not appreciate underlying beliefs or values. As a consequence, AAC technology becomes demanding for utilization or learning [27, 29]. In such case, research is imperative to apprehend the cognitive, motor skills, speech development, receptive perception of each ASD children and on that basis AAC system should be developed to meet the need of individual. Therefore, expanded research in AAC technology is required to truly response to the demand of each ASD children, their respective families and cultural and social acceptance. If AAC systems are research-driven, user centric and appropriate for individual then it become more effective in case of supporting and participation of individuals with complex communication need [28, 30].

4.3 Ensuring Professional Training

There is considerable differences between the possibilities of AAC intervention in research and the extent of practices in daily practice [29]. AAC team generally comprised of special educators, medical professionals and speech language therapists. For instance, speech language therapist requires the knowledge how to asses the physical, cognitive and perceptual abilities or limitations of individual ASD child and suggest the implementation of AAC system. Special educators should have the basic knowledge of troubleshooting and handling AAC system as well as motivating ASD child or student to utilize AAC system in day-to-day practice. Therefore, it is imperative to organize training and efficacious dissemination of knowledge for effective transition of practice from research to practice and promoting awareness among the general public [30].

4.4 Absence of Acknowledgement and Acceptance

In order to ensure success in AAC implementation, it is prerequisite to acknowledge the preference and perception of families, clinical professionals and cultural, language diversity. In order to AAC system to be effective for ASD children, it needs to be ensured that they not only get access to their preferred AAC mode but also receiving accurate instructions to enhance their social and communication skills, literacy, strategic skills for communication purpose, support from family and assistance from communicative partner. There are erroneous beliefs among many clinicians that certain criteria of cognitive skills need to be fulfilled in order to implement AAC system and for such reason some of the children are deprived of the opportunity to utilize AAC. In addition some parents believe that utilization of AAC system will impede natural language development of their children. However, research evidenced that AAC does not affect negatively in speech development. Moreover, the positive result supported by research evidence that AAC system enhance awareness and acceptance [31].

5   Recommendations

After the investigation on barriers and benefits of AAC research in context of developing countries, we recommend few immediate actions to be taken. At first, it is imperative to develop government policy and support for AAC research in developing countries. Secondly, in order to bridge the gap of research and implementation as well as developing intelligent AAC systems, collaboration is required among researchers, developers, educators, speech language therapists and related government organizations. Finally, disseminating knowledge of AAC for verbally challenged children to gain public awareness and acceptance.

6   Conclusions

In this study, we concentrate on investigating benefits and barriers of Augmentative and Alternative Communication technology research in the context of developing countries. We have underscored the state-of- art research in AAC field in developed and developing countries, illuminating opportunities and barriers of AAC research on prospects of developing countries and elucidated the benefits of research in AAC. We believe that this study will assist researchers, technical developers, policy makers, stakeholders to have an overview of AAC research, benefits and challenges associated with AAC research and taking potential steps to bridge the gap between present and future applications and prospective impact of AAC technology research on community.

References

1. World Health Organization: Autism spectrum disorders & other developmental disorders: from raising awareness to building capacity. In: World Health Organization, Geneva, Switz, pp. 1–36 (2013)
2. National Institute of Deafness and Other Communication Disorders "NIDCD": Communication problems in children with Autism spectrum disorder. In: NIDCD Fact Sheet (2012)
3. Wodka, E.L., Mathy, P., Kalb, L.: Predictors of phrase and fluent speech in children with Autism and severe language delay. Pediatrics **131**, e1128 (2013). https://doi.org/10.1542/peds.2012-2221
4. Shane, H.C., Laubscher, E.H., Schlosser, R.W.: Applying technology to visually support language and communication in individuals with autism spectrum disorders. J. Autism Dev. Disord. **42**, 1228–1235 (2012). https://doi.org/10.1007/s10803-011-1304-z
5. Achmadi, D., et al.: Acquisition, preference, and follow-up data on the use of three AAC options by four boys with developmental disability/delay. J. Dev. Phys. Disabil. **26**(5), 565–583 (2014). https://doi.org/10.1007/s10882-014-9379-z
6. Waddington, H., Sigafoos, J., Lancioni, G.E.: Three children with autism spectrum disorder learn to perform a three-step communication sequence using an iPad®-based speech-generating device. Int. J. Dev. Neurosci. **39**, 59–67 (2014). https://doi.org/10.1016/j.ijdevneu.2014.05.001

7. Hershberger, D.: Mobile technology and AAC apps from an AAC developer's perspective. Perspect. Augment. Altern. Commun. **28**, 20 (2011). https://doi.org/10.1044/aac20.1.28
8. Interagency Autism Coordinating Committee (IACC).: Strategic Plan for Autism Spectrum Disorder Research. In: U.S. Department Health Human Service Interagration Autism Coordination Communication (2017)
9. McLay, L., van der Meer, L., Schäfer, M.C.M.: Comparing acquisition, generalization, maintenance, and preference across three AAC options in four children with Autism spectrum disorder. J. Dev. Phys. Disabil. **27**, 323–339 (2015). https://doi.org/10.1007/s10882-014-9417-x
10. McLay, L., Schäfer, M.C.M., van der Meer, L.: Acquisition, preference and follow-up comparison across three AAC modalities taught to two children with Autism spectrum disorder. Int. J. Disabil. Dev. Educ. **64**, 117–130 (2017). https://doi.org/10.1080/1034912X.2016.1188892
11. Gilroy, S.P., Leader, G., McCleery, J.P.: A pilot community-based randomized comparison of speech generating devices and the picture exchange communication system for children diagnosed with autism spectrum disorder. Austim Res. **11**, 1701–1711 (2018). https://doi.org/10.1002/aur.2025
12. Tulshan, A., Raul, N.: Krisha: an interactive mobile application for Autism children. In: Singh, M., Gupta, P.K., Tyagi, V., Flusser, J., Ören, T., Kashyap, R. (eds.) ICACDS 2019. CCIS, vol. 1046, pp. 207–218. Springer, Singapore (2019). https://doi.org/10.1007/978-981-13-9942-8_20
13. Soomro N., Soomro S.: Autism children's app using PECS. In: Annals of Emerging Technologies in Computing (AETiC), vol 2, pp. 7–16 (2018).https://doi.org/10.33166/aetic.2018.01.002
14. Signore, A.P.B.T.Y.: You Talk!-YOU vs AUTISM. In: 14th International Conference, ICCHP 2014 (2014).https://doi.org/10.1007/978-3-540-70540-6
15. Sharma, P., Upadhaya, M.D., Twanabasu, A., Barroso, J., Khanal, S.R., Paredes, H.: "Express your feelings": an interactive application for Autistic patients. In: Antona, M., Stephanidis, C. (eds.) HCII 2019. LNCS, vol. 11573, pp. 160–171. Springer, Cham (2019). https://doi.org/10.1007/978-3-030-23563-5_14
16. Wendt, O., Bishop, G., Thakar, A.: Design and evaluation of mobile applications for augmentative and alternative communication in minimally-verbal learners with severe Autism. In: Antona, M., Stephanidis, C. (eds.) HCII 2019. LNCS, vol. 11573, pp. 193–205. Springer, Cham (2019). https://doi.org/10.1007/978-3-030-23563-5_17
17. Hill, K.: Advances in augmentative and alternative communication as quality-of-life technology. Phys. Med. Rehabil. Clin. N. Am. **21**, 43–58 (2010). https://doi.org/10.1016/j.pmr.2009.07.007
18. Thompson, D.E., Blain-Moraes, S., Huggins, J.E.: Performance assessment in brain-computer interface-based augmentative and alternative communication. Biomed. Eng. Online **12**, 43 (2013). https://doi.org/10.1186/1475-925X-12-43
19. Neamtu, R., Camara, A., Pereira, C., Ferreira, R.: Using artificial intelligence for augmentative alternative communication for children with disabilities. In: Lamas, D., Loizides, F., Nacke, L., Petrie, H., Winckler, M., Zaphiris, P. (eds.) INTERACT 2019. LNCS, vol. 11746, pp. 234–243. Springer, Cham (2019). https://doi.org/10.1007/978-3-030-29381-9_15
20. Costa M., Costa A., Novais P.: A task recommendation system for children and youth with autism spectrum disorder. In: Advances in Intelligent Systems and Computing (2017).https://doi.org/10.1007/978-3-319-61118-1

21. Tariq, Q., Fleming, S.L.: Detecting developmental delay and autism through machine learning models using home videos of Bangladeshi children: development and validation study. J. Med. Internet Res. **21**, 1–15 (2019). https://doi.org/10.2196/13822

22. Nakai, Y., Takiguchi, T.: Detecting abnormal word utterances in children with Autism spectrum disorders: machine-learning-based voice analysis versus speech therapists. Percept. Mot. Skills **124**, 961 (2017). https://doi.org/10.1177/0031512517716855

23. Khan, M.N.R., Pias, M.N.H., Habib, K.: "Bolte Chai": an augmentative and alternative communication device for enhancing communication for nonverbal children. In: 1st International Conference on Medical Engineering, Health Informatics and Technology, MediTec 2016 (2017).https://doi.org/10.1109/MEDITEC.2016.7835391

24. Khan, M.N.R., Sonet, H.H.: "Bolte Chai"-an android application for verbally challenged children. In: 4th International Conference on Advances in Electrical Engineering, ICAEE 2017 (2017).https://doi.org/10.1109/ICAEE.2017.8255415

25. Frontera, W.R.: Rehabilitation research at the national institutes of health: moving the field forward (executive summary). Phys. Therapy **31**, 304 (2017). https://doi.org/10.1093/ptj/pzx027

26. McNaughton, D., Light, J.: The iPad and mobile technology revolution: benefits and challenges for individuals who require augmentative and alternative communication. AAC Augment. Altern. Commun. **29**, 107–116 (2013). https://doi.org/10.3109/07434618.2013.784930

27. Light, J., McNaughton, D.: Putting people first: re-thinking the role of technology in augmentative and alternative communication intervention. AAC Augment. Altern. Commun. **29**, 299 (2013). https://doi.org/10.3109/07434618.2013.848935

28. Light, J., Wilkinson, K.M.: Designing effective AAC displays for individuals with developmental or acquired disabilities: state of the science and future research directions. AAC Augment. Altern. Commun. **35**, 42 (2019). https://doi.org/10.1080/07434618.2018.1558283

29. Kent-Walsh, J., Binger, C.: Methodological advances, opportunities, and challenges in AAC research (2018).https://doi.org/10.1080/07434618.2018.1456560

30. McNaughton, D., Light, J.: Building capacity in AAC: a person-centred approach to supporting participation by people with complex communication needs. AAC Augment. Altern. Commun. **35**, 56 (2019). https://doi.org/10.1080/07434618.2018.1556731

31. Light, J., McNaughton, D.: The changing face of augmentative and alternative communication: past, present, and future challenges. AAC Augment. Altern. Commun. **28**, 197–204 (2012). https://doi.org/10.3109/07434618.2012.737024

Basic Study on Measuring Brain Activity for Evaluation Method of Visually Impaired Person's Orientation and Mobility Skills

Hiroaki Inoue[1]([✉]), Masaya Hori[2], Yu Kikuchi[3], Mayu Maeda[2],
Yusuke Kobayashi[3], Takuya Kiryu[3], Toshiya Tsubota[3],
and Shunji Shimizu[1]

[1] Department of Applied Information Engineering,
Suwa University of Science, Chino, Japan
{hiroaki-inoue,shun}@rs.sus.ac.jp
[2] Graduate School of Engineering and Management,
Suwa University of Science, Chino, Japan
{gh19701,gh18504}@ed.sus.ac.jp
[3] Shimizu Laboratory, Suwa University of Science, Chino, Japan
SRL@ed.sus.ac.jp

Abstract. Visually impaired persons recognize their surrounding with a white cane or a guide dog while walking. This skill called "Orientation and Mobility" is difficult to learn. The training of the "Orientation and Mobility Skills" is performed at the school for visually impaired person. However, the evaluation of this skill is limited to subjective evaluation by teacher. We have proposed that quantitative evaluation of the "Orientation and Mobility Skills" is required. In this paper, we tried to execute the quantitative evaluation of the "Orientation and Mobility Skills" using brain activity measurements. In this experiment, brain activity was measured when subjects are walking in the corridor alone or with guide helper. Experimental subjects were sighted person who was blocked visual information during walking. The blood flow of prefrontal cortex was increased as the movement distance of the subject increased when subjects walk alone. From this result, it can be considered that the feeling of fear and the attention relayed to "Orientation and Mobility Skills" could be measured quantitatively by measuring human brain activities.

Keywords: Visually impaired person · Brain activity · Orientation and Mobility Skills

1 Introduction

The visually impaired person recognizes the surrounding situation using a white cane and a guide dog while they walk. White canes and guide dogs are tactile information stimuli. At the same time as the tactile sensation, visually impaired people judge the surrounding situation by the environmental sound. It is very important to hear the environmental sound for recognition of their own position and surrounding situations in details. This means, they need "Orientation and Mobility Skills" [1, 2] to recognize the surrounding

© Springer Nature Switzerland AG 2020
C. Stephanidis et al. (Eds.): HCII 2020, CCIS 1294, pp. 63–70, 2020.
https://doi.org/10.1007/978-3-030-60703-6_8

situation by using sound information. [3, 4] "Orientation and Mobility Skills" is necessary to move in an unfamiliar place. The training of the "Orientation and Mobility Skills" is carried out a person with the visual impaired at school. However, the evaluation of the education effect is subjective method by teachers belonging to the school for visually impaired person. It is difficult for the teacher to understand all recognition action of the student even if a student achieves the problem of the walk under strong uneasiness. We think that the subjective evaluation of "Orientation and Mobility Skills" has lowered the understanding of the importance of gait training to society.

There is also a method of estimating the stress state during exercise from HF/LF. However, HF/LF is affected by heart rate variability due to exercise [5]. Therefore, we have proposed that quantitative evaluation of the "Orientation and Mobility Skills" is required.

NIRS is an apparatus that was possible to easily measure brain activity compared to other measurement apparatus of brain activity such as PET (Positron Emission Tomography) and fMRI (functional Magnetic Resonance Imaging). In these other brain activities measuring apparatuses, the subject's posture needs to be fixed in a supine position. Obviously, brain activity measurement during walking is impossible with these apparatuses. NIRS is possible to measure brain activity during while subjects exercise. However, NIRS measurement data is influenced by the artifact of various factors. For example, there are the artifact due to heartbeat and body movement. It is also difficult to separate multiple information stimuli into individual elements. In this paper, we measured the brain activity data for the quantitative evaluation of the "Orientation and Mobility Skills".

In the Sect. 2, we described the method of experiments conducted in this paper. In Sect. 3, we described brain activity data obtained by these experiments. In Sect. 4, we described the relationship between brain activity data and the stimulation by experimental tasks. In Sect. 5, we described the summary of this paper and future works (Fig. 1).

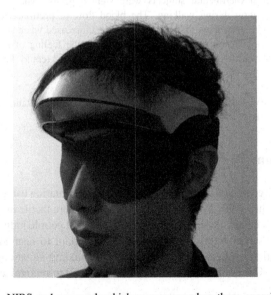

Fig. 1. NIRS and eye mask which were wear when these experiments.

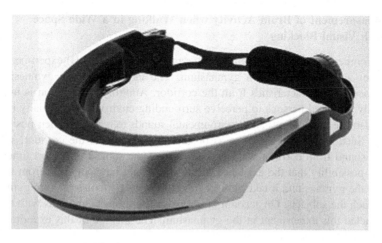

Fig. 2. NIRS used in these experiments.

2 Experimental Method

2.1 Measurement of Brain Activity when Walking Alone in the Corridor Without Visual Information

In this experiment, the brain activity that the subjects walked alone was measured. Walking distance is approximately 20 m. Subjects were blocked visual information by the eye mask. The resting time for stabilizing the brain activity of the subjects was set before and after walking. This resting time was more than 10 s. The experimental place is the corridor that the subject walks on a daily. These experiments were performed with no other pedestrians.

The experiment task setting was set as shown in the upper part of Fig. 3. The corridor which subjects walked through all experiments is the same. The subject was instructed to walk at a constant speed as much as possible. Subjects were orally instructed the timing to start walking and stop walking. The measurement equipment of brain activity used for the experiment is "Pocket NIRS", which was produced by DynaSense Inc in Japan (Fig. 2). This NIRS is lightweight and could measure brain activity in two channels in the prefrontal cortex. Measurement can be performed at a sampling rate of 100 Hz.

2.2 Measurement of Brain Activity when Subjects Walk with Guide Helper in the Corridor

In the above experiment, subjects walked alone in the corridor. In this experiment, the subjects walked with the pedestrians who simulated the guide helper. The experiment method was the same as the previous experiment. The experimental method is shown in the lower part of Fig. 3.

2.3 Measurement of Brain Activity when Walking in a Wide Space with Visual Blocking

The environment of this experiment is different from the A) and B) experiments. This experiment was performed in a gymnasium. The large space like gymnasium has different acoustic characteristics from the corridor. Auditory information is important for visually impaired persons to perceive surrounding environment. Visually impaired persons also use their echoes and environmental sounds to recognize their position and situation. Such ability is referred to as obstacle perception. In the corridor, subject's footsteps sound from corridor wall reach the ear of the subject in a short time. Thus, there is a possibility that the existence of the wall could be recognized from the echo sound. In the gymnasium, it takes longer time for subject's footsteps from gymnasium wall to reach the subjects. On account of not make the subject conscious with the wall, we conducted this experiment in the gymnasium. The method of this experiment was the same as the previous two experiments.

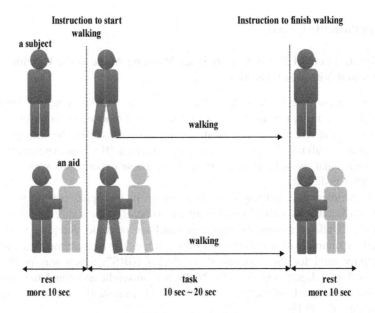

Fig. 3. Flow of experiments.

3 Experimental Result

3.1 Measurement of Brain Activity when Walking Alone in the Corridor

Figure 4 shows an example of brain activity data when one subject walked alone. The red line shows the change in oxygenated hemoglobin. The blue line shows the change in deoxygenated hemoglobin. As a result of this experiment, the cerebral blood flow did not increase when the subject started walking according to the instructions. When the movement distance of the subject increased to some extent, a large increase in oxygenated hemoglobin could be confirmed on right and left prefrontal cortex. After subjects were instructed to stop walking, blood flow on right and left prefrontal cortex gradually decreased. This tendency was seen from most subjects.

3.2   Measurement of Brain Activity when Subjects Walk with Guide Helper in the Corridor

Figure 5 shows the brain activity result of the subject when walking with a pedestrian who simulated a guide helper. In this experiment, the subject's cerebral blood flow decreased slightly after the onset of the gait task. Even when the migration distance increased, the concentration of oxygenated hemoglobin in the blood did not increase greatly. In listening survey after the experiment, subjects said that they were able to concentrate on walking without feeling uneasy in this experiment.

3.3   Measurement of Brain Activity when Walking in a Wide Space with Visual Blocking

Figure 6 shows the measurement results when walking alone. Figure 7 shows the result of brain activity when accompanied by a pedestrian simulated the guide helper. An increase of blood flow on the prefrontal cortex was seen when the subject received instructions to walk. However, an increase oxygenated hemoglobin that continued was not confirmed during walking. When subjects walk with guide helper, there was no change in oxygenated hemoglobin similar to previous experiment in the corridors.

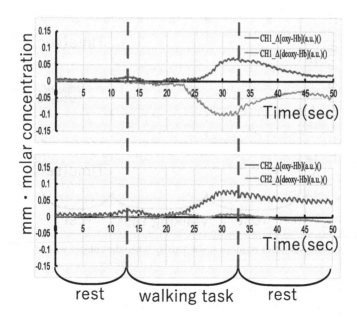

Fig. 4. Measurement result of brain activity when the subject walked alone.

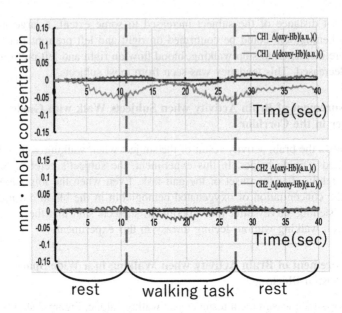

Fig. 5. Measurement results of brain activity when subjects walked with guide helper.

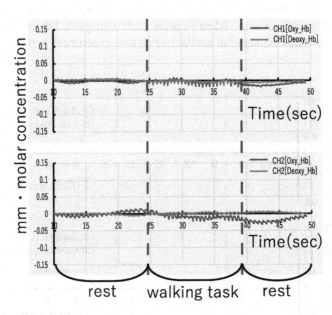

Fig. 6. Measurement result of brain activity when the subject walked alone.

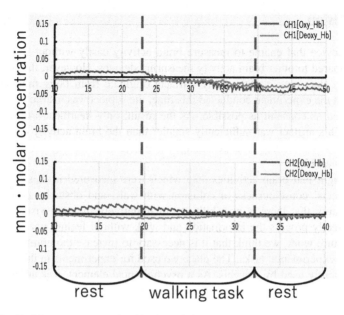

Fig. 7. Measurement result of brain activity when the subject walked alone.

4 Discussion

In these experiments, measuring brain activity were performed when subjects walk with guide helper and subjects walked alone. When subjects walked alone, it could be considered that subjects were in the state of mental strain. When subjects walked with a pedestrian who simulated a guide helper, subjects could rely on a pedestrian for safety confirmation and were able to walk in concentrating on walking. When subjects walked alone, most subject's oxygenated hemoglobin on prefrontal cortex was not showed an increase after instruction to start walking. As subject's walking distance increased, most subject's oxygenated hemoglobin on prefrontal cortex was increased. Such a change in oxygenated hemoglobin is considered that subjects strongly conscious the collision with the wall and obstacles.

When subjects stopped to walk, the oxygenated hemoglobin in prefrontal cortex decrease gradually. In the case of accompanying the pedestrian who simulated with guide helper, an increase of oxygenated hemoglobin in prefrontal cortex as compared with the case of walking alone could not be confirmed. Oxygenated hemoglobin in the prefrontal cortex of the subjects decreased slightly during walking. In addition, when subjects walked alone in the large space such as a gymnasium, no increase oxygenated hemoglobin was observed by the increase walking distance. Therefore, it is considered that the subject was able to walk without being conscious of a collision with a wall or an obstacle.

5 Conclusion

NIRS is a device that enable to measure brain activity easily without restraining the subject compared to other brain activity measuring devices. However, the obtained the brain activity data may contain many artifacts originate from body movements and heartbeats. In the experiment conducted this time, the subject was instructed to keep the walking speed as constant as possible. As the result, only heartbeat artifact could be confirmed. This artifact was sufficiently smaller than the brain activity data. Previous studies have not observed a large change in oxygenated hemoglobin during slow walking as well [6].

It is thought that brain activities data which were measured in these experiments include subjects' consciousness of collision with walls and obstacles could be measured. We think that there is possibility to quantitatively measure visually impaired persons correctly process the information and walk without feeling uneasy.

In the future work, we think that it is necessary to increase the number of subjects and types of experimental tasks. The place we used for experiments in this paper was a facility frequently used by subjects. As a psychological element, it is an experimental task that does not include brand newness or interest.

References

1. Cuturi, L.F., Aggius-Vella, E., Campus, C., Parmiggiani, A., Gori, M.: From science to technology: orientation and mobility in blind children and adults. Neurosci. Biobehav. Rev. **71**, 240–251 (2016)
2. Lahav, O., Schloerb, D.W., Srinivasan, M.A.: Rehabilitation program integrating virtual environment to improve orientation and mobility skills for people who are blind. Comput. Educ. **80**, 1–14 (2015)
3. Seki, Y., Sato, T.: A training system of orientation and mobility for blind people using acoustic virtual reality. IEEE Trans. Neural Syst. Rehabil. Eng. **19**(1), 95–104 (2011)
4. Bluaert, J.: Spatial Hearing. MIT Press, Cambridge (1996)
5. Pichon, A., Bisschop, C., Roulaud, M., Denjean, A.: Spectral analysis of heart rate variability during exercise in trained subjects. Med. Sci. Sports Exerc. **36**, 1702–1708 (2004)
6. Suzuki, M., et al.: Prefrontal and premotor cortices are involved in adapting walking and running speed on the treadmill: an optical imaging study. NeuroImage **23**, 1020–1026 (2004)

Turning Ideas into Reality for mHealth Technology Users with Disabilities

Hyung Nam Kim$^{(\boxtimes)}$ (iD)

Department of Industrial and Systems Engineering, North Carolina A&T State
University, Greensboro, NC 27411, USA
hnkim@ncat.edu

Abstract. Various technology transfer models have been introduced in the
literature, and those models have the potential to facilitate the design, development, evaluation, and dissemination of emerging technology. Yet, those
models are less likely to be suitable to mobile health (mHealth) technology
consumers who have disabilities due to lack of user-centered approach to
technology transfer. To address the gap, this paper introduced an innovative
framework for mHealth technology transfer to those with disabilities. The
framework consists of technology concept, technology engineering, technology
embedding, and ongoing participatory design. The framework is expected to
contribute to usability, accessibility, and safety of consumer mHealth technology for users with disabilities, ultimately leading to enhancement of health-
related quality of life and equity.

Keywords: Users with disabilities · Technology transfer · Mobile health ·
Human factors

1 Technology Transfer Models

Technology transfer is a process of conveying a technology (or knowledge) from one
party to another party, which is observed between countries, companies, and individuals [1]. Various technology transfer models (e.g., linear models, non-linear parallel-
sequential models, and non-linear back-feed models) have been introduced to facilitate
the transition. For example, the linear models include the appropriability model, the
dissemination model, and the knowledge utilization model [2–4]. The non-linear
parallel-sequential model uses a cyclical process that functions in a similar way as for a
linear model, yet different stages in multiple cycles are presented to enable non-linear
parallel-sequential interactions within the model. Thus, the non-linear parallel-
sequential model can provide an opportunity to perform different stages simultaneously [5], decreasing the total time of the process. The non-linear back-feed model is to
transform a parallel-sequential model into a back-feed model as the non-linear back-
feed model is similar to the parallel processes with connections between stages. Each
stage in the non-linear back-feed model collects and uses inputs from relevant organizations for the successful technology transfer.

© Springer Nature Switzerland AG 2020
C. Stephanidis et al. (Eds.): HCII 2020, CCIS 1294, pp. 71–78, 2020.
https://doi.org/10.1007/978-3-030-60703-6_9

2 Limitations of Existing Technology Transfer Models

In the following sections, we appraise the existing technology transfer models and discuss a way to improve them further, especially for mobile health (mHealth) technology users with disabilities.

2.1 Lack of Consideration for the Post-phase After Delivering Technology

Most technology transfer models tend to overlook the post-phase after disseminating new technology and merely emphasize the delivery process itself of new technology [6]. The technology transfer models are less likely to take into consideration whether the distributed technology is successfully adopted and continuously used by users. The technology transfer models merely focused on the relations between technology developments and outcomes; thus, the adoption stage was given less attention [7]. There is a need for a new technology transfer model that can continuously monitor the implementation and ongoing-use of technology in the end-user contexts.

2.2 Lack of Two-Way Iterative Process Approach

Although few studies took into account the post-phase after distributing technology, most of them paid less attention to updating their technology applications by adequately reflecting users' needs and concerns. Technology transfer should be dynamic because technology can be innovative "today" but will be conventional "tomorrow." Therefore, there is a need for a technology transfer model that contains a systematic means to continuously monitor and also update technology based on feedback from users in the field. Shahnavaz [8] conceptualized a utilization phase in the technology transfer model that facilitates interactions between technology suppliers and receivers, possibly leading to effective use of the transferred technology in the long run. Yet, the model did not elaborate sufficiently on how the utilization phase should be incorporated in the technology transfer model. Although the technology transfer model developed by Malik (2002) was set to reflect feedback from technology receivers, the model was designed to transfer technology only within a single organization. Thus, it would be inapplicable when technology is intended to be transferred from one domain (e.g., developers in the lab) to another domain (e.g., consumers in the field).

2.3 Exclusion of Consumers with Disabilities

Today, a great number of mHealth technology applications (apps) are developed and introduced in the consumer market to help people take care of their health conditions (e.g., disease prevention, chronic condition management, and so on) [9]. There is accumulating evidence that mHealth technologies have been used by all people regardless of their abilities and disabilities [10, 11]. Therefore, people with disabilities should also be viewed as major consumers of mHealth technology, and mHealth technology transfer models should not exclude those with disabilities.

2.4   Less User-Centered Designs of mHealth Technology

Lack of attention has been paid to user interface designs of mHealth technology applications for healthcare consumers with disabilities [9]. Today, a great number of people with visual disabilities use health apps for self-care, it is essential to develop the health apps accessible to those with such special needs; otherwise, the health technology applications are likely to be abandoned by those users. In addition to low adoption issues, the poorly designed "health" technology has a potential for users to ill-advisedly change their self-care regimens and ultimately encounter adverse health outcomes. People with disabilities frequently use the self-care apps that are available for free of charge in the app market and often they selected those apps without consulting their healthcare providers, ultimately transferring much of responsibility to the end users for any errors or adverse outcomes. Thus, a technology transfer model should take care of design, development, and dissemination phases comprehensively by ensuring good usability, accessibility, and safety for users regardless of their ability and disability. The standard ISO 9241-210:2010 [12] briefly mentioned the importance of system designs that accommodate people with the widest range of capabilities in intended user populations including people with disabilities; however, there is still a need for more concrete. practical guidelines for professionals and researchers.

3   An Innovative Framework of Transferring mHealth Technology to Users with Disabilities

As pointed out above, there is a need to develop a systematic guide for researchers and professionals in designing, developing, evaluating, and implementing mHealth technology to be usable, safe, and accessible to users with disabilities. We argue that human factors engineering can contribute to developing the systematic guide. Human factors engineering is a discipline that helps to discover and apply information about human behavior, abilities, limitations and other characteristics to the design of tools, machines, systems, tasks, jobs and environments for productive, safe, comfortable and effective human use. Thus, incorporating human factors in the system development life cycle can lead to multiple benefits [13] as humans are the most important system component, the most complex system component, the least understood system component, and the most vulnerable to failure [14]. As conventional models for technology transfer tend to pay less attention to human factors, we propose a new model that integrates human aspects especially for mHealth technology used by people with disabilities. The proposed model consists of several iterative phases: technology concept, technology engineering, technology embedding, and ongoing participatory design (See Fig. 1).

3.1   Technology Concept

Concepts for a new technology can arise from a wide range of sources such as personal experience, professional experience, theories, media, and other research studies (e.g., published articles and pilot empirical studies). As this paper focuses on transferring the mHealth technology (e.g., self-care smartphone apps) from a research lab to consumers,

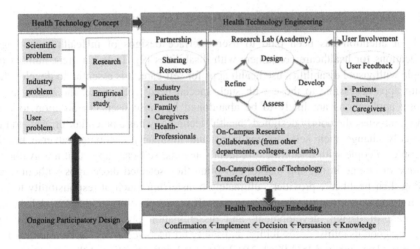

Fig. 1. Framework for health technology transfer to consumers with disabilities

especially people with disabilities, mHealth technology concepts can be brought by healthcare service providers, healthcare service consumers, scientific research teams, industry, or any combination of them. The scientific research teams can consist of students, faculty, and other researchers and conduct an exploratory research study to seek and address a problem associated with mHealth technology applications. The mHealth technology industry can also bring a new technology concept to address their target consumers' needs and concerns. Healthcare providers have a close relationship with healthcare service consumers (e.g., patients, caregivers, and family) in the healthcare field and have direct observations on how the consumers struggle with health problems and what they want. Thus, healthcare providers can contribute to developing ideas for a technology-based intervention. In addition, consumers can be active to inform those researchers and professionals about their needs and ideas of future mHealth technology to accommodate their needs. Ideally, they all should work together as a team.

3.2 Technology Engineering

In general, a research team in a lab can design and develop mHealth technology applications via collaborative partnerships along with industry, healthcare providers, users (e.g., those with disabilities and their family), and other research teams (e.g., other departments and colleges). Yet, in existing technology design and development approaches, users with disabilities are less likely to get deeply involved in design and development processes. Furthermore, even some prior studies that included users with disabilities merely focused on summative evaluation at the end of design and development processes or tended to conduct a study with participants who are not representative of the target user group [15]; for example, blindfolded sighted participants are instructed to pretend to be visually impaired for user experience testing. By inviting intended users, a deeper user involvement throughout the whole design and development processes is necessary.

To facilitate the technology engineering phase, a research team can use a user-centered design method [16]. In the user-centered design (e.g., co-design [17]), users can serve as a co-designer to work with designers and developers, which will empower users to be deeply involved in the design and development process [18]. For instance, empathic design is one of the user-centered design approaches that can contribute to moving designers closer to users' environments instead of bringing users to design-controlled environments [19], which helps to build creative understanding of users and their everyday lives [20]. Creative understanding is viewed as the combination of rich, cognitive, and affective understanding of users, contributing to translating this understanding into user-centered product or service designs [21]. Users with disabilities will thus be able to deeply engage in the technology engineering phase and contribute to usability, accessibility, and safety-related user interface designs and testing via the user-centered design approach. Multiple benefits are expected; for example, the research team can obtain more accurate information about the target users and tasks, provide more opportunities for the users to influence directly design decisions, generate more or better design ideas than a designer alone, and receive immediate feedback on design ideas. After a prototype is ready for evaluation, various assessment methods can be considered, such as lab-based user performance testing and a field observation for a short or long period of time. When a high-fidelity prototype is ready, a feasibility test can be performed to examine the technology prototype in terms of effectiveness, efficiency, and overall satisfaction of the target user group.

3.3   Technology Embedding

In the phase of technology embedding, the newly developed technology will be implemented into the users' contexts. A research team should develop a plan on how to introduce a new technology application to the intended user group and how to offer user trainings if needed. The mHealth technology application can be distributed for free but also commercialized or patented with supports from a university's office of technology transfer. The Diffusion of Innovation Theory [22] can further contribute to facilitating technology adoption, which will process a series of steps: (a) knowledge (b) persuasion (c) decision (d) implementation, and (e) confirmation. In the knowledge stage, a new technology will first be introduced to users although users may not be much inspired to actively seek information about the new technology yet. In the persuasion stage, users would become interested enough to be more active in seeking detailed information about the technology. Technology introduction should be provided in a variety of alternative formats for users with disabilities (e.g., audio, haptic/tactile, large print and Braille for users with blindness). In the decision stage, users would weight and compare the advantages and disadvantages of using the technology, which helps users to make a decision whether they adopt or reject it. If users decide to adopt it, the implementation and confirmation stages will follow for a long-term use. If users decide to reject it, they may be encouraged to provide feedback to the developers such that an updated version would be prepared and introduced to the user group.

Users in the decision stage would typically compare different mHealth apps to choose one that is believed to be best for their self-care without consulting their healthcare service providers. Therefore, the user's evaluation could be further facilitated with adequate evaluation instruments. Although there are a variety of evaluation instruments available (e.g., questionnaires, surveys, guidelines, and checklists) to examine a system, they are not applicable to the contexts of this study (e.g., users with disabilities, mHealth apps, self-evaluation, usability, accessibility, and safety). For example, a research team by Stonyanov [23] developed a rating scale for measuring the quality of a mobile app that can be administered by users without engagement of professional evaluators, which is named User Version of the Mobile Application Rating Scale (uMARS). It includes a 20-items measure to examine a system's quality associated with the following four components: functionality, aesthetics, engagement, and information. Yet, the uMARS is designed for general mobile apps such that it is not applicable to evaluating safety-relevant designs of mHealth apps. In addition, the uMARS is not applicable to users who have disabilities as it does not evaluate accessibility. Evaluation instruments for mobile apps used by people with disabilities should consider accessibility guidelines, such as Web Content Accessibility Guidelines (WCAG) of World Wide Web Consortium (W3C) [24]. The Word Health Organization (WHO) mHealth Technical and Evidence Review Group (mTERG) developed a Mobile Health Evidence Reporting and Assessment (mERA) checklist [25]. The checklist covers 16 items comprehensively associated with mHealth technology, which helps to identify a set of information needed to define what the mHealth technology is (i.e., content), where it is being implemented (i.e., context), and how it is implemented (i.e., technical features). However, the mERA is expected to be used by expert reviewers, professionals, and researchers, but not by end users. Another research team has recently introduced an Interactive Mobile App Review Toolkit - IMART [26], i.e., a technology-assisted system for managing verifiable app reviews. The IMART provides a set of systematized reviews via a searchable library in which clinicians can find and compare reviews about apps that are used for patient treatments. Thus, the IMART does not serve as an app "evaluation" tool, but simply collects user reviews that already exist. Further, the IMART's intended users are not patients (i.e., healthcare service consumers), but merely healthcare professionals. Another toolkit [27] is a Statement of Consolidated Standard of Reporting Trials (CONSRT) that contributes to the assessment and reporting of validity and applicability of mHealth technology. Yet, the CONSORT is also merely designed to support experts, but not end-users. There is a need to develop a user-friendly self-evaluation toolkit or checklist.

3.4 Ongoing Participatory Design

After dissemination of the technology application, users can still be engaged in improving further the technology application by providing feedback (e.g., user experience, error reports). The technology transfer model proposed by this study is an open, continuous loop to keep evolving to accommodate user needs. Thus, the proposed technology transfer model is anticipated to contribute to strong sustainability of the technology application.

4   Conclusion

In this paper, we argued that conventional technology transfer models are not suitable to mHealth technology applications for users with disabilities. Thus, we have discussed a new framework of transferring mHealth technology in which a new technology application is designed, developed, evaluated, and disseminated in collaboration with various stakeholders in different domains (industry, academy, and community) via a series of user-centered, system development life cycles: technology concept, technology engineering, technology embedding, and ongoing participatory design. The newly proposed framework of mHealth technology transfer would contribute to usability, accessibility, and safety of consumer mHealth technology for people with disabilities, ultimately leading to enhancement of health-related quality of life and equity.

Acknowledgements. This material is based upon work supported by the National Science Foundation under Grant No. 1831969.

References

1. Bozeman, B., Rimes, H., Youtie, J.: The evolving state-of-the-art in technology transfer research: revisiting the contingent effectiveness model. Res. Policy **44**(1), 34–49 (2015)
2. Hilkevics, S., Hilkevics, A.: The comparative analysis of technology transfer models. Entrepreneurship Sustain. Issues **4**(4), 540–558 (2017)
3. Sung, T.K., Gibson, D.V.: Knowledge and technology transfer: levels and key factors. International Conference on Technology Policy and Innovation (ICTPI) (2000)
4. Bradley, S.R., Hayter, C.S., Link, A.N.: Models and methods of university technology transfer. Found. Trends® Entrepreneurship **9**(6), 571–650 (2013)
5. Song, X., Balamuralikrishna, R.: JOTS v27n1-The process and curriculum of techonology transfer (2001). https://scholar.lib.vt.edu/ejournals/JOTS/Winter-Spring-2001/song.html
6. Choi, H.J.: Technology transfer issues and a new technology transfer model. J. Technol. Stud. **35**(1), 49–57 (2009)
7. Autio, E., Laamanen, T.: Measurement and evaluation of technology transfer: review of technology transfer mechanisms and indicators. Int. J. Technol. Manag. **10**(7-8), 643–664 (1995)
8. Shahnavaz, H.: Role of ergonomics in the transfer of technology to industrially developing countries. Ergonomics **43**(7), 903–907 (2000)
9. Jones, M., Morris, J., Deruyter, F.: Mobile healthcare and people with disabilities: current state and future needs. Int. J. Environ. Res. Public Health **15**(3), 515 (2018)
10. Pew Research Center. Device Ownership over Time (2016). Accessed 9 May 2016, http://www.pewinternet.org/data-trend/mobile/device-ownership
11. DeRuyter, F., Jones, M.L., Morris, J.T.: Mobile health apps and needs of people with disabilities: a national survey (2018)
12. International Organization for Standardization. ISO 9241–210: 2010-Ergonomics of human-system interaction-Part 210: Human-centred design for interactive systems (2010). https://www.iso.org/standard/77520.html
13. Ohnemus, K.R.: Incorporating human factors in the system development life cycle: marketing and management approaches. In: Proceedings of IPCC 1996 (1996)

14. Wenner, C.A.: What is Human Factors and Why is it Important? (No. SAND2013–7748C), Sandia National Lab. (SNL-NM), Albuquerque, NM (United States) (2013)
15. Sears, A., Hanson, V.: Representing users in accessibility research. In: Proceedings of the SIGCHI Conference on Human Factors in Computing Systems (2011)
16. Abras, C., Maloney-Krichmar, D., Preece, J.: User-centered design. In: Bainbridge, W. (ed.) Encyclopedia of Human-Computer Interaction, vol. 37, no. 4, pp. 445–456. Sage Publications, Thousand Oaks (2004)
17. Metatla, O., et al.: Voice user interfaces in schools: co-designing for inclusion with visually-impaired and sighted pupils. In: Proceedings of the 2019 CHI Conference on Human Factors in Computing Systems (2019)
18. Buhler, C.: Empowered participation of users with disabilities in R&D projects. Int. J. Hum. Comput. Stud. **55**(4), 645–659 (2001)
19. Steen, M.: The fragility of human-centred design (2008)
20. Postma, C.E., et al.: Challenges of doing empathic design: experiences from industry. Int. J. Des. **6**(1) (2012)
21. Wright, P., McCarthy, J.: Empathy and experience in HCI. In: Proceedings of the SIGCHI Conference on Human Factors in Computing Systems (2008)
22. Rogers, E.M.: Diffusion of Innovations, vol. 4. The Free Press, New York (1995)
23. Stoyanov, S.R., et al.: Development and validation of the user version of the mobile application rating scale (uMARS). JMIR mHealth uHealth **4**(2), e72 (2016)
24. Patch, K., Spellman, J., Wahlbin, K.: Mobile accessibility: How WCAG 2.0 and other W3C/WAI guidelines apply to mobile, W3C (2015). Accessed 30 May 2018, https://www.w3.org/TR/mobile-accessibility-mapping/
25. Agarwal, S., et al.: Guidelines for reporting of health interventions using mobile phones: mobile health (mHealth) evidence reporting and assessment (mERA) checklist. BMJ **352**, i1174 (2016)
26. Maheu, M.M., et al.: The interactive mobile app review toolkit (IMART): a clinical practice-oriented system. J. Technol. Behav. Sci. **1**(1–4), 3–15 (2017)
27. Eysenbach, G., Consort-EHEALTH Group: CONSORT-EHEALTH: improving and standardizing evaluation reports of web-based and mobile health interventions. J. Med. Internet Res. **13**(4), e126 (2011)

Mobile Social Media Interface Design for Elderly in Indonesia

Restyandito[(⊠)], Febryandi, Kristian Adi Nugraha,
and Danny Sebastian

Fak. Teknologi Informasi, Universitas Kristen Duta Wacana,
Yogyakarta, Indonesia
{dito, febriyandi}@ti.ukdw.ac.id,
{adinugraha, danny.sebastian}@staff.ukdw.ac.id

Abstract. The most common problem faced by elderly is loneliness, especially when they live far away from familiy members. Furthermore, decreasing physical ability and mobility that comes with aging can also limit elderly's ability to socialize with others. Fortunately, modern technology offers a solution to this problem of disconnectedness. Nowadays, people are communicating through social media despite the geographical distance between them. However, due to a technological leap, the elderly in Indonesia are often left behind in adapting and using technology. In this study, a social media application interface was designed based on the results of direct interviews with the elderly. The interface is more user-friedly, with features that can be properly used by the elderly. The effectiveness of this interface and its features is supported by the test result of each feature. The contact feature (task 1) scores 80%, the call log history feature (task 2) scores 100%, the video calling feature (task 3) scores 100%, the community feature (task 4) scores 90%, the entertainment feature (task 5) scores 90%, the voice calling feature (task 6) scores 100% and the notes feature (task 7) scores 77%. The results of this study can be used as a reference for software developers in designing application interfaces for the elderly, especially those who experience technological leap.

Keywords: Gerontechnology · Social media · Interface design · Mobile

1 Introduction

In general, the most common problem faced by the elderly is loneliness. Loneliness is a personal matter that is handled differently by each individual. For some people loneliness is a normal part of life, but for some others loneliness can caused a deep sadness [1]. One of the factors causing loneliness in elderly is the lack of attention given by family members or closest relatives as a result of increased mobility among the younger generation. For example, many people migrate to other cities for work, leaving their parents at their home town. This increased mobility causes communication and interaction between elderlies and their families or relatives to decrease and become difficult to do. The possible impact of feeling lonely and lacking interaction experienced by the elderly is the feeling of isolation and depression. This causes the elderly to prefer to be

© Springer Nature Switzerland AG 2020
C. Stephanidis et al. (Eds.): HCII 2020, CCIS 1294, pp. 79–85, 2020.
https://doi.org/10.1007/978-3-030-60703-6_10

alone, which is comonly called social isolation [2]. The occurrence of depression will result in changes in the form of thought, somatic sensation, activities, health, and less productive development of mind, speech, and socialization [3]. Therefore, the impact of loneliness needs to be recognized and given more attention by the family and relatives.

Good communication is the solution to loneliness among the elderly. By taking advantage of social media, it is expected that interaction between elderly and their families, relatives and the outside world will be more affordable so that they are not limited by distance, time and place. However, the existing social media has too many features and complex functions that make it difficult for the elderly to use it. Therefore, it is necessary to design a social media that is suitable for the circumstances and needs of the elderly.

Based on Indonesian Telecomunication Statistics released by Statistics Indonesia Bureau in 2018, the percentage of population aged 50 years and older who access Internet was only 6.61% [4]. It is comparatively small to the 50.79% people of the same group who have smartphones [5]. It indicates that even though smartphones are becoming more affordable, they are not being used effectively by the elderly, who only use them to make calls and send texts. Study by Restyandito & Kurniawan [6], found that many elderlies in Indonesia do not have self efficacy in using technologies. This condition widened the techological gap between elderly and younger generation, and prevent them from utilizing technology to improve their quality of life.

There are several factors that influence product usability problem for elderly; cognition, perception, and movement control [7], consequently, to design usable interface these factors should be taken into consideration. Szeles and Kubota [8] pointed out that there are differences between regular application design and application design for elderly people in smartphone applications. For example, it must have simple features so that it is easy to use and has a suitable interface so that it does not confuse the elderly [9]. Grid menu layout is found to be easier to use compared to scrolled menu [10]. Taking into consideration user-friendly interface design for the elderly is expected to encourage them to adopt technology; hence, improve their quality of life.

2   Previous Study

Social Media has become popular as means of communication. Prior studies have shown how people spend more time socializing through digital communication services [11]. Technology enables elders to contact and share information with family and friends through text, images, voice and videos [12, 13]. Nonetheless, many social media application such as Facebook were originally designed for frequent Internet users [14] which may not be the case of elderly in Indonesia. Elderly in Indonesia are experiencing technologycal leap resulting in them not having the experience to help them understand the technology that exists today.

Coto et al. [15] pointed out it is important to take into consideration design strategies based on approaches such as human-computer interaction and participatory design that will allow designers to propose social media tools more convenient for elderly, by considering their life situations, habits and attitudes, and physical and mental conditions.

3 Method

3.1 Participants

Thirty elderly participate in this research (8 males, 22 females), age 60–83 years old (AVG = 73.2, STD = 6.66). Based on Indonesian constitution[1], a person who is sixty years of age is categorized as elderly. All participants have cellphones (60% Android smartphone, 40% feature phone).

3.2 Requirement Gathering

Indept interviews were used to understand the phenomena experienced by eldery (such as behavior, perception, motivation, action, etc.) holistically. Questions asked include the condition of the elderly, their daily activities and their experience in using cellphones.

3.3 Apparatus

Low fidelity prototype was made using Corel Draw x7 and Just in Mind 5.8.0. High fidelity prototype was developed using Android studio. The prototype was tested on Xiaomi Red Note 5 (Qualcomm Snapdrageon 636 octa core, GPU Adreno 509, RAM 6 GB).

3.4 Design

Based on the results of the interviews, it is found that most participants communicate using voice call (36.7%) followed by video call (25.31%). Only 16.46% use their cellphones to send text messages, further analysis showed most participants found fonts on their cellphones are too small; which makes it difficult for them to read. Although respondents prefer to use voice call and video call, many of them do not know how to make calls, therefore they are dependent on their families and relatives to call them (passive users). When asked about social media application used by participants, 55.88% mentioned that they used WhatsApp, only 8.82% use Facebook. The rest of the participants (35.30%) do not use social media. Data that is gathered from the in depth interviews with the edlerly is used to design the prototype of the social media interface as seen on Fig. 1.

Since many respondents who participated in this research are familiar with WhatsApp (either actively or passively) the prototype has a design similar to What-sApp, such as color scheme and icon use. By doing so, it helps users to learn using the application more quickly because they can transfer their experience in using other

---

[1] UU No. 13 Tahun 1998 tentang Kesejahteraan Lanjut Usia, Pasal 1 ayat (2),(3),(4).

Fig. 1. Example of the interface of social media application for elderly

applications [16]. Yet, only 55.88% participants use WhatsApp, consequently the icons need to be tested. Prior to developing the application, a low fidelity prototype was made to measure the comprehensive level of icons used by participants.

The application only had limited features, such as making voice call, video call, sending text, joining community, entertainment (linked to selected YouTube content based on user's preference) and making notes. These features were chosen based on the activity of the participants related to their social life (both online and offline). Since there are only a handful features needed by elderly, it will minimize physical and cognitive stress due to too many menus and symbols [17]. The application also applies grid menu and one page layout design (except for call logs which still require scrolling) as pointed out by Restyandito et al. [10]. Last but not least, the design provides many ways to perform most frequently used feature. For example, there is short cut to make voice call in any section of the application, hence reducing the need to memorize specific order to use it.

3.5   Usability Testing

The proposed design underwent usability testing using performance metrics. Participants were given 7 tasks to be completed, ranging from making video calls to find information regarding community activities. Parameter used in this test was success rate and completion time. The test result is also compared to a control group consisting of 5 university students. After completing the usability test participants were also given a self reported metric by completing a User Experience Questionnaire.

4   Results and Discussion

The performance test conducted yielded an average of 90.95% success rate. Results of the performance test can be seen in Fig. 2 and Fig. 3 respectively. Not all tasks can be completed by participants. Task 1 where participants were asked to input phone numbers in the address book, only resulted in a success rate of 80%. Task 4 where participants were asked to find announcement regarding community activities, only yield success rate of 90%. Task 5 where participants were asked to find video content, yield success rate of 90%. And Taks 7 where participants were asked to make a voice memo only yield 77%.

Further analisys showed that participants who failed in task 1 and task 7 were those who have only been using feature phones. These tasks require several steps where participants need to understand menus and icons used. Lack of familiarity [16] may contribute to the failure of participants completing the task. Many users who are not technologically savvy rely on rote learning when operating their devices, hence they may face difficulties when they need to interact with new applications or technology [18]. Participants who failed task 4 and task 5 were mostly those who are older than 75 years of age. Task 4 and Task 5 are related to finding information, participants who failed to complete these tasks perhaps due to their declining cognitive ability. In this case, they might forget the instruction resulting in providing the wrong answer [19].

Participants' completion time on average is 65.12% longer compared to the control group. From Fig. 3 we can see that the biggest difference occurs on Task 1 (138% longer) and Task 7 (73% longer). As DeFord et al. [20] pointed out, whilst young adults may rely on spatial attention in performing a task, eldery might rely on memory and executive function abilities. Since most of the participants who faced difficulties completing the task were participants who've only been using feature phone, they lack experience which they can memorized in interacting with smartphones.

Lastly, self reported metric analysis using User Experience Questionnaire (UEQ) was found satisfactory where attractiveness, perspicuity, efficiency, dependability, stimulation and novelty received an excellent score.

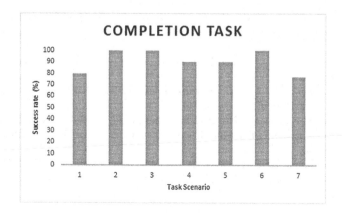

Fig. 2. Participants' success rate

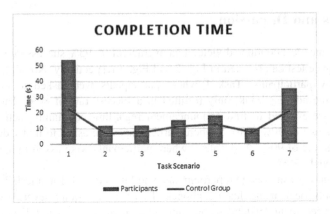

Fig. 3. Participant's completion time vs control group's completion time

5 Conclusions

The results of this case-study on designing social media interfaces for edlerly in Indonesia emphasize the need to give attention to users' experiences and cognitive abilities. Elderly in Indonesia experience two challenges in using technology: a decrease in physical and cognitive abilities, and a technological leap. Theses challenges cause them to become non-technologically savvy users. To overcome these challenges, designers should take into consideration users' prior experience in using technology. Bigger fonts and interface improves readability. Familiar interface helps users learn faster. Simple interface helps reduce users' cognitive load. Lastly, alternative ways to use features eliminate the need to memorize specific steps.

References

1. Amalia, A.D.: Kesepian dan isolasi sosial yang dialami lanjut usia: tinjauan dari perspektif sosiologis. Sosio Informa **18**(3), 203–210 (2013)
2. Kusumowardani, A., Puspitosari, A.: Hubungan antara tingkat depresi lansia dengan interaksi sosial lansia di desa sobokerto kecamatan ngemplak boyolali. Jurnal Ilmu Kesehatan 3(2), 184–188 (2014)
3. Kaplan, H.I., Sadock, B.J.: Pocket Handbook of Emergency Psychiatric Medicine. Williams & Wilkins, Baltimore (1993)
4. Utoyo, S., Sujono, T., Sari, E.: Statistik Telekomunikasi Indonesia 2018. Biro Pusat Statistik, pp. 272–274 (2018)
5. Kominfo Survei Penggunaan TIK 2017 Serta Implikasinya terhadap Aspek Sosial Budaya Masyarakat, pp. 19 (2017). https://balitbangsdm.kominfo.go.id/publikasi-indikator-tik-9.htm. Accessed 28 May 2020
6. Restyandito, Kurniawan, E.: Pemanfaatan Teknologi oleh Orang Lanjut Usia di Yogyakarta. Prosiding Seminar Nasional ke-12 Rekayasa Teknologi Industri dan Informasi (RTII 2017), pp. 49–53 (2017)

7. Siran, Z., Abidin, S.Z., Anwar, R.: Elderly usability interaction design model for home appliances: theoretical framework. In: Anwar, R., Mahamood, M., Md. Zain, D.H., Abd Aziz, M.K., Hassan, O.H., Abidin, S.Z. (eds.) Proceedings of the Art and Design International Conference (AnDIC 2016), pp. 365–374. Springer, Singapore (2018). https://doi.org/10.1007/978-981-13-0487-3_40

8. Szeles, J., Kubota, N.: Location monitoring support application in smart phones for elderly people, using suitable interface design. In: Kubota, N., Kiguchi, K., Liu, H., Obo, T. (eds.) ICIRA 2016. LNCS (LNAI), vol. 9835, pp. 3–14. Springer, Cham (2016). https://doi.org/10.1007/978-3-319-43518-3_1

9. Yusof, MFM., Romli, N., Yusof, MFM.: Design for elderly friendly: mobile phone application and design that suitable for elderly. Int. J. Comput. Appl. **95**(3) (2014)

10. Restyandito, Kurniawan, E., Widagdo, T.M.: Mobile application menu design for elderly in indonesia with cognitive consideration. J. Phys. Conf. Ser. **1196**(1), 012058. IOP Publishing (2019)

11. Cornejo, R., Tentori, M., Favela, J.: Enriching in-person encounters through social media: a study on family connectedness for the elderly. Int. J. Hum. Comput. Stud. **71**(9), 889–899 (2013)

12. Yang, Y., Yuan, Y., Archer, N., Ryan, E.: Adoption of social media and the quality of life of older adults. In: 2016 49th Hawaii International Conference on System Sciences (HICSS), pp. 3133–3142. IEEE (2016)

13. Li, Q.: Characteristics and social impact of the use of social media by Chinese Dama. Telematics Inform. **34**(3), 797–810 (2017)

14. Chou, W.H., Lai, Y.T., Liu, K.H.: User requirements of social media for the elderly: a case study in Taiwan. Behav. Inform. Technol. **32**(9), 920–937 (2013)

15. Coto, M., Lizano, F., Mora, S., Fuentes, J.: Social media and elderly people: research trends. In: Meiselwitz, G. (ed.) SCSM 2017. LNCS, vol. 10283, pp. 65–81. Springer, Cham (2017). https://doi.org/10.1007/978-3-319-58562-8_6

16. Sharp, H., Preece, J., Rogers, Y.: Interaction Design-Beyond Human-Computer Interaction, vol. 5. Wiley, New Jersey (2019). ISBN 978-1-119-54725-9

17. Sharma, S., Wong, J.: Three-button gateway smart home interface (TrueSmartface) for elderly: design, development and deployment. Measurement **149**, 106923 (2020)

18. Krisnawati, L.D., Restyandito, : Localized user interface for improving cell phone users' device competency. Int. J. Inform. Technol. Web Eng. (IJITWE) **3**(1), 38–52 (2008)

19. Liew, T.M., Yap, P., Ng, T.P., Mahendran, R., Kua, E.H., Feng, L.: Symptom clusters of subjective cognitive decline amongst cognitively normal older persons and their utilities in predicting objective cognitive performance: structural equation modelling. Eur. J. Neurol. **26**(9), 1153–1160 (2019)

20. DeFord, N.E., DeJesus, S.Y., Holden, H.M., Graves, L.V., Lopez, F.V., Gilbert, P.E.: Young and older adults may utilize different cognitive abilities when performing a spatial recognition memory test with varying levels of similarity. Int. J. Aging Hum. Devel. **90**(1), 65–83 (2020)

An Open Source Refreshable Braille Display

Victor Rocha[1(✉)] ⓘ, Diogo Silva[2], Álvaro Maia Bisneto[2] ⓘ,
Anna Carvalho[1] ⓘ, Thiago Bastos[2] ⓘ, and Fernando Souza[3] ⓘ

[1] CESAR School, Recife, Pernambuco, Brazil
{vhr, agmc}@cesar.school
[2] CESAR, Recife, Pernambuco, Brazil
{dfsls, abvmb, tab}@cesar.org.br
[3] Federal University of Perbambuco, Recife, Pernambuco, Brazil
fdfd@cin.ufpe.br

Abstract. With the exponential growth in the technological era, the need arose to bring the users a way to use Braille as a communication interface with computers and smartphones. In order to achieve this, electro-mechanical devices were created, called Braille displays, allowing users to make use of Braille on their own devices. However, access to this kind of devices is difficult, because the embedded technology makes it expensive. In this context, this work aims to create an integrated solution of hardware and software, based on the concept of one Braille cell using only open source components. The proposed system was evaluated by blind volunteers with different Braille knowledge and computer experience.

Keywords: Accessibility · Accessibility tools · Refreshable Braille display · Visual impairment

1 Introduction

According to World Health Organization (WHO), there is an estimated 285 million people worldwide who suffer from severe visual impairment. Of these, about 39 million persons are blind and, by definition, cannot walk about unaided. They are usually in need of vocational and/or social support. Many people who suffer from severe visual impairment face a lifetime of inequality, as they often have poorer health and face barriers to education and employment. These figures highlight the need to give greater attention to create solutions that enable their integration into society [1].

In order for an individual to enjoy intellectual freedom, personal security, independence and have equal opportunities to study and work, one must be literate. There is no substitute for the ability to read, therefore no digital alternative can completely replace Braille. At the same time, this can also provide visually impaired people with a unique opportunity to integrate into society and to develop their skills to their full potential. The reader of Braille is not only able to read written texts, but also to read

C. Stephanidis et al. (Eds.): HCII 2020, CCIS 1294, pp. 86–91, 2020.
https://doi.org/10.1007/978-3-030-60703-6_11

information in Braille while using different services (e.g., lifts, maps, signs) and to read information on products (food, medicines) [2].

The Braille system, also known as the white writing, was created 150 years ago and has become the reading and writing alphabet most used by blind people worldwide. The Braille system is based on a grid of six tactile dots presented in two parallel columns of three dots each. The combination of these six tactile dots signifies a specific letter. The points are in high relief, allowing, through touch, to read what is represented. The points are arranged in a rectangle, known as Braille cell [3].

There are three factors that currently work against the use of Braille as the primary reading modality for blind readers [4]: 1) The cost of refreshable Braille displays, which range from approximately $2,000 for a 18-character display to $50,000 for a half page of Braille, 2) the decline in support for teaching Braille to blind children and newly blind adults, which has resulted in a corresponding drop in levels of Braille literacy, and 3) the increasing cost of producing hard copy Braille books which has reduced the availability of recently published books in Braille format, which in turn impacts the interest in and practice of Braille reading, particularly for young readers. For all of these reasons, the pressure to develop a novel approach to the design of refreshable Braille displays is mounting [4, 5].

Refreshable Braille displays render Braille characters dynamically refreshed over time, standing to the Braille language as a computer screen or an e-reader stands to written information for sighted people. They offer the useful and unique advantage of a dynamic fruition of written information that needs to be available fast, i.e. during navigation and search of web contents, without the need of being stored on a physical sheet of paper [6]. Usually those kinds of display consist of 40 cells where the information is presented in Braille, and which is then updated on the subsequent (or previous) lines.

The fact that Braille display technology has not changed significantly for 35 years is astonishing when considered alongside the continually shifting interaction paradigms of personal computing in general. In the years since the introduction of the first piezoelectric Braille cell in 1979, we have witnessed the demise of the command line, the evolution of the Windows-Icons-Menus-Pointer (WIMP) interface and finally the birth of co-located input and output in the form of the touchscreen [4].

In particular, Braille displays most of the time uses piezoelectric or electrome-chanical array that moves pins arranged vertically to represent multiple Braille cells [6, 7]. This tends to be an expensive approach, especially because it increases the number of cells to represent all information on computer screen [4]. This paper proposes a creation of a portable and refreshable one cell Braille display, using only open source technologies.

2 Related Work

Several studies in the literature describe the importance of technological solutions for Braille reading. Most of these solutions use piezoelectric principles, which are expensive, and also there is a trend to increase the number of cells [8]. The search is on, therefore, for a low-cost refreshable display that would go beyond current technologies and deliver graphical content as well as text. Many solutions have been proposed, some of which reduce costs by restricting the number of characters that can be displayed, even down to a single Braille cell [4].

The difference between eye reading, which captures whole words and many other information almost instantly, blind people read essentially one character at a time. Based on that, some researchers have proposed a system based on a single 'bigger' Braille cell and a specific software interface and driver communication. The display was constructed using six servo motors controlled by an Arduino Uno and a computer. To read the words, the person who suffer from severe visual impairment leaves his finger on the cell while points are triggered depending on the letter that is been displayed. To display words and phrases the characters are displayed sequentially. The problem with this approach is that the size and weight of the display, although having only one cell for reading, is almost the size of a Braille display of 10 to 20 cells. Another problem is that it is not possible for this to be used with tablets or smartphones since the display must be connected to a computer to receive the information that needs to be displayed.

Drishti is another solution that propose a different approach. The idea behind this solution is use a dot matrix to represent Braille dots using Solenoids. Although the design was quite good, it faced some problems such as high power consumption and noise, caused by the use of solenoids [9].

3 Proposed Solution

This work presents a refreshable Braille display of a single cell, to be used with computers, smartphones and tablets. The Braille display proposed is inspired on the operation of a tally counter. Tally counters are digital counters built using mechanical components. They typically consist of a series of disks mounted on an axle, with the digits from 0 to 9 marked on their edge, the counter moves incrementally from right to left depending upon the number of clicks made, the logic behind the increment, follows the natural numerical order.

Braille decodes each symbol in a cell composed of up to six dots. Dots of each cell are arranged in a matrix of two columns by three rows with fixed dimensions (see Fig. 1). Each Braille character is represented by a cell with different number and positions of the raised dots [6]. Instead of using movable pins to reproduce the relief of the points of a Braille cell, the idea is to replace these pins with a plastic disc (in the format of an extruded octagon) with eight sides and in each one on each side there is the relief of each of the eight possible configurations of 3 points.

Combining two of these discs is possible to reproduce all 64 symbols of the traditional Braille system. For each of the blocks were mapped all possible combinations of the 3 points (both in relief and without), which gave a total of 8 possibilities for each block (see Fig. 1). So, each face of the extruded octagon contains one of the eight possible combinations (see Fig. 1). The mechanism is based on the principle that there isn't any difference between the combination of the dots 1, 2, 3 and the 4, 5, 6 as shown on. The pieces were printed using the 3D printer Ultimaker 2.

Fig. 1. Possible combinations for each column of Braille cell and extruded octagon [10]

Cell dimensions have to be optimal in order to allow the finger pad to cover the whole area of the cell and, at the same time, discriminate the different dots. During the years, Blind Unions and Authorities of different countries converged to a standardization of the Braille cell and dot dimensions [6]. According to the above recommendations, specifications of the Braille cells that are considered in the presented paper are summarized in Table 1.

Table 1. Braille dimensions considered in the presented work according to the European Blind Union recommendations [6]

Feature	Dimensions [mm]
Dot height	0.5
Dot diameter	1.5
Intra-cell horizontal distance	2.5
Intra-cell vertical distance	2.5
Inter-cell horizontal distance	6

Once printed, each octagon was attached to a stepper motor (model 28BYJ-48), as can be seen in Fig. 2. Each of the motors has been connected to a ULN2003 driver, that is controlled by an Arduino Nano board, with an ATmega328 microcontroller. The communication with the user device (smartphone, tablet or PC) is via bluetooth, for that a HC-06 bluetooth module was connected to the Arduino (the complete circuit diagram could be seen on Fig. 3). So, the "letters" that must be displayed on the display are sent by the device using the bluetooth protocol. Finally, the step motors were attached to a stand and placed inside a box to prevent direct contact between users and the electronics (see Fig. 2).

Fig. 2. Step motor with extruded octagon [10]

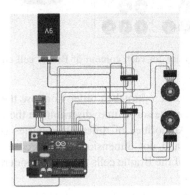

Fig. 3. Circuit diagram

4 Proof of Concept

The tests were done by five volunteers from the Instituto de Cegos Antônio Pessoa de Queiroz, from Recife, Brazil. All volunteers work in the institute and are familiar with reading in Braille. To evaluate the prototype an android application was created, where you choose a letter to be displayed on the Braille display. This letter is sent via bluetooth to the device.

The volunteers received an explanation about the Braille Display, its function and its relationship with smartphones, tablets and computers, as well as the goal of the all system. After the introduction the prototype was given to the user, the researcher chooses a character and sends it to be displayed on the display. The volunteer tries to recognize the characters represented at Braille cell, speaking aloud what character believes it is.

During the tests the volunteers were encouraged to give feedback on the use of the prototype and talk about the readability of the display. Regarding the prototype, users commented that they found it interesting and were excited about the cost of the solution, since commercial Braille displays cost more than 2000 dollars.

Some divergences between one cell solution and traditional Braille reading were detected. For example, cell points distances should be adjusted to reduce the distance between the two columns, because they were getting the impression that each column was a separate letter from the other.

On the other hand, some of the advantages of one cell Braille solution are: static reading reduces fatigue, also the price of one cell equipment is lower, simplicity, lack of line-breaking problems because the hand remained static over the device and simpler maintenance.

5 Conclusions

This work aims to contribute to the digital access of Braille by developing an integrated hardware and software solution. To this end, a single Braille cell was designed formed by two step motors controlled by an Arduino Nano. This study aimed to access the amount of effort required for reading Braille on a display formed by a single cell. It was designed to meet the demand of domestic and institutions appliances at low cost.

Experiments were focused in user's behavior, recording their evolution using the system. The use of a single cell showed promising results relating to cost and effort. The proposed solution represents an alternative way for communication of blind users, especially, young people, constantly discouraged by the traditional method of learning Braille. As a future work a mobile application is being developed to be used in conjunction with the display to teach Braille to the disabled without the need for an instructor.

References

1. WHO: Visual impairment and blindness. In: Fact Sheet (2019). http://www.who.int/mediacentre/factsheets/fs282/en/index.html. Accessed 10 June 2020
2. Marcet, A., Jiménez, M., Perea, M.: Why Braille reading is important and how to study it. Cult. Educ. **28**, 811–825 (2016)
3. Schmidt, M.B., Gustavo, L., Ramirez, A.R.G.: Single Braille cell. In: ISSNIP Biosignals and Biorobotics Conference, BRC, pp. 1–5. IEEE (2014)
4. Russomanno, A., O'Modhrain, S., Gillespie, R.B., Rodger, M.W.M.: Refreshing refreshable Braille displays. IEEE Trans. Haptics **8**, 287–297 (2015)
5. Runyan, N.H., Blazie, D.B.: The continuing quest for the "Holy Braille" of tactile displays. In: Esteve, J., Terentjev, E.M., Campo, E.M. (eds.), p. 81070G (2011)
6. Leonardis, D., Claudio, L., Frisoli, A.: A survey on innovative refreshable Braille display technologies. In: Di Bucchianico, G., Kercher, P.F. (eds.) AHFE 2017. AISC, vol. 587, pp. 488–498. Springer, Cham (2018). https://doi.org/10.1007/978-3-319-60597-5_46
7. Bisht, S., Goluguri, S.R., Maheshwari, R., et al.: Refreshable Braille display using raspberry pi and arduino. Int. J. Curr. Eng. Technol. **6**, 965–968 (2016)
8. Cook, A.M., Polgar, J.M.: Assistive Technologies, 4th edn. Mosby, St. Louis (2015)
9. Kartha, V., Nair, D.S., Sreekant, S., et al.: DRISHTI - a gesture controlled text to Braille converter. In: 2012 Annual IEEE India Conference (INDICON), pp. 335–339. IEEE (2012)
10. Hazin da Rocha, V., Silva, D., Bisneto, A.B.V.M., et al.: Ensinando a Identificação de Caracteres Braille utilizando Dispositivos Móveis e um Display Braille. RENOTE **17**, 82–91 (2019)

Frailty Assessment in Daily Living (FRAIL) - Assessment of ADL Performance of Frail Elderly with IMUs

Stephanie Schmidle[1(✉)], Philipp Gulde[2], Bart Jansen[3],
Sophie Herdegen[1], and Joachim Hermsdörfer[1]

[1] Human Movement Science, Department of Sport and Health Sciences,
Technical University of Munich, Munich, Germany
stephanie.schmidle@tum.de
[2] Center for Clinical Neuroplasticity Medical Park Loipl,
Bischofswiesen, Germany
p.gulde@medicalpark.de
[3] ETRO-VUB, Department of Electronics and Informatics, Vrije Universiteit
Brussel, Brussels, Belgium

Abstract. Frailty is accompanied by limitations in activities of daily living (ADL). These are associated with reduced quality of life, institutionalization and higher health care costs. Long-term monitoring ADL could allow creating effective interventions and thus reduce the occurrence of adverse health outcomes. The main objective of this study was to evaluate if ADL task performance can be assessed by activity measurements based on IMUs, and whether these measures can differentiate individual's frailty. ADL data was obtained from seventeen elderly who performed two ADL tasks - tea making task (TEA) and gardening task (GARDEN). Acceleration data of the dominant hand was collected using an activity sensor. Participants were split up in two groups, FRAIL (n = 6; Fried score $\geq$ 2) and CONTROL (n = 11; Fried score $\leq$ 1) retrospectively. Collected data were used to determine trial duration (TD), relative activity (RA), peak standard deviation (STD), peaks per second (PPS), peaks ratio (RATIO), weighted sum of acceleration per second (SUM), signal to noise ratio (S2N) and mean peak acceleration (MPA). STD, RATIO, SUM and MPA showed good reliability over both tasks. Four of the calculated parameters (RA, PPS, RATIO, SUM) revealed significant results differentiating between FRAIL and CONTROL (effect sizes 1.30–1.77). Multiple linear regression showed that only STD correlated with the Fried score. In summary, the results demonstrate that ADL task performance can be assessed by IMU-based activity measures and further allows drawing conclusions on the frailty status of elderly, although the predictability of the exact Fried score was limited.

Keywords: Activities of daily living · Frailty · Kinematic analysis · Wearables

C. Stephanidis et al. (Eds.): HCII 2020, CCIS 1294, pp. 92–101, 2020.
https://doi.org/10.1007/978-3-030-60703-6_12

1   Introduction

In Western societies, the prevalence of frailty and its adverse health outcomes including falls, delirium, institutionalization, hospitalization and mortality increases [1, 2]. Frailty is understood as a complex concept consisting of various cognitive, psychological, nutritional and social factors [3], representing a high burden for affected individuals, care professionals as well as health care systems [4]. According to the well-known standardized phenotype of frailty by Fried et al. [2], the following five criteria are assessed to determine frailty status: unintentional weight loss, exhaustion, slow walking speed, low grip strength and low physical activity. To be classified as *frail*, at least three criteria have to be present. In contrast, the presence of one or two indicators is categorized as *pre-frail*, whereas the absence of any indicator is termed *robust*.

Elderly people categorized as frail, show an elevated risk of disability [5, 6]. Moreover, compared to non-frail elderly frail individuals demonstrate higher rates of disability in activities of daily living (ADL), often termed as basic ADLs, which are relatively more preserved in light of declined cognitive function. In general, those activities are defined as 'activities essential for an independent life or necessary for survival, representing everyday tasks required for self-care' [7] (e.g., bathing, dressing, eating, toileting and transferring) [4]. Those activities can be separated form instrumental ADLs (IADLs), which include more complex tasks and are more sensitive to early cognitive decline [8]. Changes in ADL performance and especially altered daily activity levels are associated with poor quality of life, increased health care costs, higher mortality and institutionalization [8]. Furthermore, they can provide important information regarding functional and cognitive abilities, loss of autonomy and deterioration in health status [9].

In recent years, the interest in automated methods of real-time, unobtrusive monitoring of ambulation, activity and wellness with technologies typically basing on inertial measurement units (IMUs) has steadily increased [10]. Thus, the analysis of such data has been subject to a plethora of intense research projects including the development of feasible algorithms that are required to translate such measurements into clinically relevant markers [10]. Research focuses on automated monitoring of mobility, ADL and physiological (vital) signs of elderly adults living independently in their homes [10]. Until now, the analysis of ADL performance was limited to subjective scoring and timed actions. Regardless of their validity, these approaches are time-consuming, they often lack objectivity and they are typically bound to a standardized lab setting [11]. Decreased costs of activity tracking systems and devices that are small, mobile and reliable, offer the possibility of a stronger embedding in the clinical routine [12]. Thus, the aim of this cohort study was to assess if ADL task performance can be assessed through a commercially available activity tracking sensor, and whether these measures can differentiate individual's frailty.

2 Methods

2.1 Subjects

Seventeen older adults (≥ 60 years) participated (for detailed information, see Table 1). Subjects were recruited form care institutions and communities. Inclusion criteria for participation were defined as a minimum age of 60 years and a score of at least 24 points in the Mini Mental State Examination (MMSE) [13]. Elderly people with cognitive impairments (<24 MMSE) or severe neurological conditions were excluded. Ethical approval was given by the ethics committee of the Medical Faculty of Technical University of Munich. All participants gave written informed consent.

2.2 Tasks and Procedure

The measurements were conducted in the participants' homes or in the respective institutions. Each subject received verbal explanation of the procedure in advance. After completion of the demographics form, MMSE and frailty screening were assessed. To ensure a constant setting, the ADL performance was measured in standing position (if possible) behind a table with all equipment placed similarly in front of every participant (see Fig. 1).

Frailty Status. Adopted Fried criteria were applied according to Kunadian et al. [15].

ADL. Participants were instructed to perform two different ADLs. The ADL tasks were to either prepare a cup of tea (tea making - TEA) or to replant a plant (gardening - GARDEN).

In TEA, the following items were given: water container with approximately 250 ml of room-temperatured water, a kettle, a paper box filled with tea bags, a bowl of sugar, a plate to remove the used tea bag, a cup and a teaspoon. Standardized instruction was given to each participant as follows: '*Can you prepare a cup of tea with one spoon of sugar, standing behind the table? Please execute the task in a natural way, as you would do it at home and in a speed, which is appropriate for you*'.

In GARDEN, the following items were given: a box of soil, a watering can filled with approximately 0.5 l of water, a plant, a pot, a planter, gloves and a hand shovel.

Standardized instruction was given to each participant as follows: '*Can you replant this plant into the pot and water it, standing behind the table? Please execute the task in a natural way, as you would do it at home in a speed and a way which is appropriate for you*'.

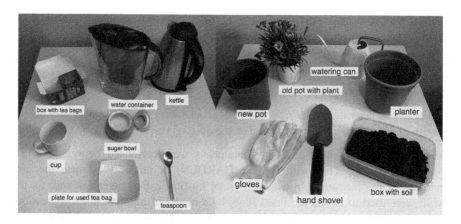

Fig. 1. Experimental set-up for the ADL TEA (left) and GARDEN (right).

During the ADL performance, the hand movements of the dominant hand were captured using a Huawei 2 (4G) smartwatch. The 3-dimensional accelerations were recorded with a sampling frequency of 100 Hz. The absolute acceleration vector was calculated, and the signal was smoothed using a 420 ms local regression algorithm [14]. An additional video recording was made to identify the individual action step of boiling time in TEA.

Kinematic Parameters. The analysis was based on previous experience with kinematic analyses of position and velocity data in different populations such as in stroke and dementia patients [16–18]. Instead of velocity, information contained in the acceleration signal was exploited. In this case of mixed, complex ADLs, commonly implemented parameters for movement smoothness, like SPARCL, could not be used [12]. All data processing was performed using MatLab R2020a (Mathworks, Natick, MA, USA). One participant (FRAIL) had to be excluded due to missing watch data. However, information about trial duration was available.

Trial Duration (TD). Time to execute the task in seconds. Time for boiling the water (if passive during this interval) in TEA was removed.

Relative Activity (RA). Period of time in which the absolute acceleration signal exceeded 0.2 m/s^2 related to TD. It ranges from 0.0 to 1.0, with 1.0 indicating the absence of any pauses.

Peak Standard Deviation (STD). Standard deviation of all acceleration peaks (maxima) in m/s^2. This parameter intends to reflect agility and the capability to adapt one's behavior to varying task demands. Low values represent a rather peculiar monotone behavior.

Peaks Per Second (PPS). Number of acceleration peaks per second.

Peak Ratio (RATIO). Ratio between the number of acceleration peaks with a minimum prominence of 0.2 m/s^2 and the total number of acceleration peaks. A measure of movement smoothness reflecting the amount of distinct movements relative to all movements including noise.

Weighted Sum of Acceleration per Second (SUM). Temporal mean of squared acceleration. A parameter to estimate energy expenditure.

Signal to Noise Ratio (S2N). Ratio of the sum of the frequency spectrum by a fast Fourier transformation from 0.01 to 3 Hz and from 0.01 to 50 Hz. A measure of movement smoothness [19].

Mean Peak Acceleration (MPA). Mean of acceleration peaks, a measure of the intensity of actions adapted from a similar measure of velocities [17].

Statistical Approach. In a first step, parameters were correlated between the two ADLs (e.g., RA for TEA with RA for GARDEN) in order to estimate the task specificity of the measures. In a second step, kinematic parameters as well as the MMSE were used to model the Fried score by a model of multiple linear regression. Third, ANOVAs (with post-hoc tests) were run in order to compare the above mentioned kinematic parameters for both tasks between groups. Due to the low sample size, we decided to differentiate between subjects with a Fried score below or equal to 1 (CONTROL) and subjects with scores above 1 (FRAIL) (resulting in a sample size of 11 and 6). Effect-sizes are given in Cohen's d, the critical variance inflation was 5.0, and α was set to 0.05. All tests were run in SPSS version 26 software (IMB, NY, United States).

3   Results

The cohort consisted of 8 males and 9 females. There was a significant difference in BMI and MMSE between the groups, whereby the frail participants represented the group with the highest BMI and the lowest MMSE values (see Table 1). From the eleven participants of the CONTROL group, 6 scored '0' on the Fried score and 5 scored '1'. From the six participants of the FRAIL group, 3 scored '2', 1 scored '3' and 2 scored '4' on the Fried score.

Not all parameters were significantly correlated between the tasks, but STD, RATIO, SUM and MPA showed significant coefficients of correlation between 0.52 and 0.67 (Table 2). Except STD, which only revealed a trend, all those measures were

Table 1. Demographics of CONTROL (Fried score $\leq$ 1) and FRAIL (Fried score $\geq$ 2).

Parameter	Age [years]	BMI [kg/m^2]	MMSE
CONTROL (n = 11)	77.9	25.9	28.5
	(5.4)	(4.6)	(2.0)
FRAIL (n = 6)	82.3	32.3	26.2
	(9.2)	(5.8)	(1.9)
Total (n = 17)	79.5	28.2	27.6
	(7.1)	(5.8)	(2.2)
p-value	0.23	**0.03**[*]	**0.04**[*]

Mean values, standard deviations and p-values (*p < .05).
BMI, Body mass index; MMSE, Mini Mental State Examination.

able to significantly differentiate between subjects with a Fried score below or equal to 1 (CONTROL) and subjects with higher Fried scores (FRAIL), when averaging over both tasks. The calculated effect-sizes were very strong, ranging from 1.30 to 1.77 (Table 4). Modelling by multiple linear regressions revealed a significant model with an $R^2_{adjusted}$ of 0.21 ($p < 0.05$), with only one factor (STD, ß-weight = -0.51) (Table 3).

Table 2. Inter-task correlations of the kinematic parameters.

Parameter	TD	RA	STD	PPS	RATIO	SUM	S2N	MPA
r	-0.22	0.49	0.61	-0.04	0.52	0.63	-0.30	0.67
p	0.42	0.06	0.01	0.89	0.04	<0.01	0.26	<0.01

Pearson's *r*, p-values.

Table 3. Model of multiple linear regression for the Fried score.

Parameter	R^2		p-value	ß-weight
Model	(adjusted) 0.21		0.04	
STD			0.04	-0.51

STD, peak standard deviation.

Table 4. Kinematic assessment of TEA and GARDEN in C (CONTROL: Fried score $\leq$ 1) and F (FRAIL: Fried score $\geq$ 2).

Parameter		TD	RA	STD	PPS	RATIO	SUM	S2N	MPA
TEA	**C**	76	0.61	0.66	2.4	0.55	36.2	0.85	0.60
		(14)	(0.10)	(0.16)	(0.5)	(0.09)	(14.1)	(0.06)	(0.15)
	F	88	0.50	0.51	3.4	0.45	26.7	0.75	0.45
		(30)	(0.06)	(0.13)	(1.2)	(0.07)	(8.0)	(0.19)	(0.12)
	p-value	0.25	0.05	0.10	0.03	0.05	0.19	0.10	0.08
	d			1.34					
GARDEN	**C**	102	0.74	0.84	3.3	0.74	85.8	0.70	0.89
		(43)	(0.02)	(0.18)	(1.6)	(0.05)	(32.7)	(0.21)	(0.16)
	F	75	0.63	0.69	2.7	0.59	42.1	0.82	0.64
		(25)	(0.14)	(0.25)	(0.8)	(0.15)	(31.3)	(0.12)	(0.20)
	p-value	0.23	0.02	0.21	0.42	<0.01	0.03	0.25	0.02
	d		1.38			1.72	1.35		1.46
Mean of TEA & GARDEN	**C**	89	0.67	0.76	2.9	0.65	61.0	0.77	0.74
		(22)	(0.05)	(0.15)	(0.9)	(0.06)	(20.6)	(0.09)	(0.14)
	F	80	0.57	0.60	3.0	0.52	34.4	0.78	0.54
		(21)	(0.10)	(0.18)	(0.8)	(0.09)	(18.2)	(0.11)	(0.15)
	p-value	0.44	0.01	0.11	0.68	<0.01	0.03	0.91	0.02
	d		1.56			1.77	1.30		1.44

Mean values, standard deviations, p-values and Cohen's *d*. N = 16 except for TD: N = 17.

TD, trail duration [s]; RA, relative activity [-]; STD, peak standard deviation [m/s^2]; PPS, peaks per second [1/s]; RATIO, peak ratio [-]; SUM, weighted sum of acceleration per seconds [m^2/s^5]; S2N, signal to noise ratio [-]; MPA, mean peak acceleration [m/s^2].

4 Discussion

The aim of this cohort study was to investigate the feasibility of assessing ADL performance in elderly by accelerometry using an IMU (smartwatch) positioned at the wrist of the dominant upper limb. We adopted and developed a series of parameters, of which four (STD, RATIO, SUM and MPA) showed good reliability over two different tasks (coefficient of correlation > 0.51 between two complex ADLs). Frailty of subjects was defined by the adopted Fried score [15], which was only correlated with the standard deviation of acceleration peaks (STD). When differentiating between subjects with lower and higher Fried scores, four of the used kinematic parameters revealed significant results with effect-sizes between 1.30 and 1.77 (Cohen's d). Interestingly, trial duration (TD) in both ADL were a) not correlated and b) not different between subjects with higher and lower Fried scores. In TEA, the FRAIL group needed on average 155 s to complete the task, whereby the CONTROL group needed 146 s. For GARDEN, the average duration time for FRAIL was 88 s and for CONTROL 75 s. Considering our experience with the increase of TD related to aging [17, 18] and neurological diseases [16] in similar tasks, we hypothesized that these prolongations are due to cognitive aspects of the tasks. However, this is the first time that TD is not a good estimate of general task performance, which should be inferior in persons with higher Fried scores, as actually illustrated by the other kinematic parameters. Since subjects of the FRAIL group did not show this prolongation in the current study, it seems that cognitive factors did not limit performance in these patients. This seems to contradict the reduced MMSE score in the FRAIL group (p = 0.04, d = 1.17). However, the MMSE score is a screening tool for dementia symptoms and probably inadequate to predict impairments of motor function. When averaging kinematic outcomes over both ADLs, subjects with higher Fried scores tended to show less continuous activity throughout the execution of the tasks (RA), less smooth or smaller movements (RATIO), less energy expenditure (SUM), and less intense changes of action (MPA). Subjects with higher Fried scores, thus, revealed a kinematic performance that appeared to be driven by energy saving strategies, which do not necessarily have to lead to different TD. Although the investigated study population and tasks differ, our study is in line with recent research showing that differences in upper limb kinematics in acquired brain injury patients can be detected via IMU sensors and, therefore, offers the opportunity for valuable addition to standardized clinical measures [20].

In summary, subjects' higher Fried scores were associated with slower, more monotonous movements and an overall reduction activity when performing the two ADLs. A smartwatch, attached to the dominant upper limb, was able to detect such kinematic differences and further, parameters showed acceptable inter-task reliability. Such approaches could, in future, help to detect changes of frailty in elderly, not only in nursing homes, but also in hospitals and clinics or in private settings. It remains unclear, if the adopted Fried score in its current form is optimal for categorizing frailty in the elderly. For instance, in our sample, subjects with higher Fried scores were rather obese (BMI: 32.9 ± 5.8, lower Fried scores BMI: 25.9 ± 4.6, p = 0.03, d = 1.20), indicating that sarcopenia and loss of appetite does not prevent strong gains in body fat mass and reflecting the huge variability of the measure. In addition, the amount of predicted variability of the exact adopted Fried score ($R^2 = 0.21$, thus 21%) by the assessment was quite limited. Given the relatively low number of participants in the present study, this analysis should however not be considered conclusive.

Despite many positive findings, this study includes several limitations that need to be addressed. First, data was collected unilateral (dominant upper limb) in two highly complex bimanual ADL tasks. Consequently, detailed evaluation of the upper limb performance including bilateral interaction was not possible. This would be of particular interest, as older adults seem to generate strategies to compensate for their decreased motor capacity probably resulting, among others, in less motor asymmetry and a more equal performance of both hands [e.g., 21], raising the question of how frailty might influence those bimanual interactions. Second, taking the verbal feedback of the participants into account, especially the GARDEN task might have been influenced by motivational factors and highly dependent on the thoroughness of each individual. Further work should consider more standardization strategies for the task set-up and instructions in domestic environment. Lastly, the study successfully proved the value of using acceleration information from an IMU in a commercially available smartwatch for assessing ADLs, while the parameters derived from more classical motion capture systems are calculated from position information and would still be considered the gold standard. Further research should implement a proof of concept by comparing the measurement accuracy and reliability of the used devices.

Even though more data on a larger number of participants is warranted, the results show, that ADL task performance can be assessed by IMU-based activity measures and further allows drawing conclusions on the frailty status of elderly people, although the predictability of the exact Fried score was limited.

Acknowledgement. The project Frailty Assessment in Daily Living (FRAIL – ID 19295) was funded by EIT Health, which is supported by the EIT, a body of the European Union. The authors acknowledge the contribution of the master students Malgorzata Lozinska, Itla das Neves Prazeres and Ioanna Rokai.

References

1. Razjouyan, J., Naik, A.D., Horstman, M.J., Kunik, M.E., Amirmazaheri, M., Zhou, H., et al.: Wearable sensors and the assessment of frailty among vulnerable older adults: an observational cohort study. Sensors (Basel) **18**, 1336 (2018). https://doi.org/10.3390/s18051336

2. Fried, L.P., Tangen, C.M., Walston, J., Newman, A.B., Hirsch, C., Gottdiener, J., et al.: Frailty in older adults: evidence for a phenotype. J. Gerontol. A Biol. Sci. Med. Sci. **56**, M146–M156 (2001). https://doi.org/10.1093/gerona/56.3.m146

3. Levers, M.J., Estabrooks, C.A., Ross Kerr, J.C.: Factors contributing to frailty: literature review. J. Adv. Nurs. **56**, 282–291 (2006). https://doi.org/10.1111/j.1365-2648.2006.04021.x

4. Vermeulen, J., Neyens, J.C.L., van Rossum, E., Spreeuwenberg, M.D., de Witte, L.P.: Predicting ADL disability in community-dwelling elderly people using physical frailty indicators: a systematic review. BMC Geriatr. **11**, 33 (2011). https://doi.org/10.1186/1471-2318-11-33

5. Boyd, C.M., Xue, Q.L., Simpson, C.F., Guralnik, J.M., Fried, L.P.: Frailty, hospitalization, and progression of disability in a cohort of disabled older women. Am. J. Med. **118**, 1225–1231 (2005). https://doi.org/10.1016/j.amjmed.2005.01.062

6. Ensrud, K.E., Ewing, S.K., Cawthon, P.M., Fink, H.A., Taylor, B.C., Cauley, J., et al.: A comparison of frailty indexes for the prediction of falls, disability, fractures, and mortality in older men. J. Am. Geriatr. Soc. **57**, 492–498 (2009). https://doi.org/10.1111/j.1532-5415. 2009.02137.x

7. van der Vorst, A., Zijlstra, G.A., Witte, N., Duppen, D., Stuck, A.E., Kempen, G.I., et al.: Limitations in activities of daily living in community-dwelling people aged 75 and over: a systematic literature review of risk and protective factors. PLoS ONE **11**, e0165127 (2016). https://doi.org/10.1371/journal.pone.0165127

8. Mlinac, M.E., Feng, M.C.: Assessment of activities of daily living, self-care, and independence. Arch. Clin. Neuropsychol. **31**, 506–516 (2016). https://doi.org/10.1093/ arclin/acw049

9. Gokalp, H., Clarke, M.: Monitoring activities of daily living of the elderly and the potential for its use in telecare and telehealth: a review. Telemed. e-Health **19**, 910–923 (2013). https://doi.org/10.1089/tmj.2013.0109

10. Khusainov, R., Azzi, D., Achumba, I.E., Bersch, S.D.: Real-time human ambulation, activity, and physiological monitoring: taxonomy of issues, techniques, applications, challenges and limitations. Sensors (Basel) **13**, 12852–12902 (2013). https://doi.org/10. 3390/s131012852

11. Gulde, P., Hermsdörfer, J.: Smoothness metrics in complex movement tasks. Front. Neurol. **9**, 615 (2018). https://doi.org/10.3389/fneur.2018.00615

12. Nguyen, H., Mirza, F., Naeem, M., Baig, M.: Falls management framework for supporting an independent lifestyle for older adults: a systematic review. Aging Clin. Exp. Res. **30**, 1275–1286 (2018). https://doi.org/10.1007/s40520-018-1026-6

13. Folstein, M.F., Folstein, S.E., McHugh, P.R.: Mini-mental state. A practical method for grading the cognitive state of patients for the clinician. J. Psychiatr. Res. **12**, 189–198 (1975). https://doi.org/10.1016/0022-3956(75)90026-6

14. Gulde, P., Hermsdörfer, J.: A comparison of smoothing and filtering approaches using simulated kinematic data of human movements. In: Lames, M., Saupe, D., Wiemeyer, J. (eds.) IACSS 2017. AISC, vol. 663, pp. 97–102. Springer, Cham (2018). https://doi.org/ 10.1007/978-3-319-67846-7_10

15. Kunadian, V., Neely, R.D., Sinclair, H., Batty, J.A., Veerasamy, M., Ford, G.A.: Study to Improve Cardiovascular Outcomes in high-risk older patieNts (ICON1) with acute coronary syndrome: study design and protocol of a prospective observational study. BMJ Open **6**, e012091 (2016). https://doi.org/10.1136/bmjopen-2016-012091

16. Gulde, P., Hughes, C.M.L., Hermsdörfer, J.: Effects of stroke on ipsilesional end-effector kinematics in a multi-step activity of daily living. Front. Hum. Neurosci. **11**, 42 (2017). https://doi.org/10.3389/fnhum.2017.00042

17. Gulde, P., Hermsdörfer, J.: Both hands at work: the effect of aging on upper-limb kinematics in a multi-step activity of daily living. Exp. Brain Res. **235**, 1337–1348 (2017). https://doi. org/10.1007/s00221-017-4897-4

18. Gulde, P., Schmidle, S., Aumüller, A., Hermsdörfer, J.: The effects of speed of execution on upper-limb kinematics in activities of daily living with respect to age. Exp. Brain Res. **237**, 1383–1395 (2019). https://doi.org/10.1007/s00221-019-05507-0

19. Gulde, P., Rieckmann, P.: A smartphone based gait assessment. In: Neurologie & Rehabilitation. 26. Jahrestagung der Deutschen Gesellschaft für Neuro-rehabilitation e. V., Leipzig, pp. 39–40 (2020)

20. Hughes, C.M., Baye, M., Gordon-Murer, C., Louie, A., Sun, S., Belay, G.J.: Quantitative assessment of upper limb motor function in ethiopian acquired brain injured patients using a low-cost wearable sensor. Front. Neurol. **10**, 1323 (2019). https://doi.org/10.3389/fneur. 2019.01323
21. Kalisch, T., Wilimzig, C., Kleibel, N., Tegenthoff, M., Dinse, H.R.: Age-related attenuation of dominant hand superiority. PLoS ONE **1**, e90 (2006). https://doi.org/10.1371/journal. pone.0000090

Auditory-Reliant Intracortical Brain Computer Interfaces for Effector Control by a Person with Tetraplegia

Daniel J. Thengone[1,2,3,4(✉)], Tommy Hosman[1,2,3],
John D. Simeral[1,2,3,4], and Leigh R. Hochberg[1,2,3,4,5]

[1] School of Engineering, Brown University, Providence, RI, USA
daniel_thengone@brown.edu
[2] Carney Institute for Brain Sciences, Brown University, Providence, RI, USA
[3] VA Medical Center, VA RR&D Center for Neurorestoration
and Neurotechnology, Providence, RI, USA
[4] Neurology, Massachusetts General Hospital, Boston, MA, USA
[5] Neurology, Harvard Medical School, Boston, MA, USA

Abstract. Brain computer interfaces (BCI) have been successful in enabling control of external effectors, such as a computer cursor or robotic arm by people with severe motor impairment. While current usage relies heavily on the users' ability to reliably utilize visual feedback from the interface, a visual-based BCI can be difficult or even unfeasible to use by people whose paralysis is accompanied by limitations of eye movements or vision. Here we present a novel auditory paradigm, and present pilot data from a person with tetraplegia performing a BCI task with auditory cues.

Inspired by previous studies, we utilize spatial auditory signals - specifically, head-response transfer functions (HRTF) - to provide task-relevant auditory feedback in real-time via headphones to the BCI user. To test the feasibility and reliability of HRTF-based feedback signals, we performed a sound source localization task in lab members and in one BCI participant with tetraplegia using intracortical recordings. Subjects were first tested on multiple azimuths of sound source, instructed to rely on the auditory cues to identify the cued spatial auditory direction, and then to navigate to the cued targets. Initial psychophysics testing suggests cursor navigation is possible in an auditory-reliant manner using the HRTF filters updated in real-time.

The results of this study demonstrate the development and implementation of a novel auditory-reliant intracortical BCI that provides real-time auditory feedback for effector control that has high potential for BCI usage in individuals with severe motor paralysis and sustained visual impairments.

Keywords: Brain computer interface · Intracortical · Auditory feedback

© Springer Nature Switzerland AG 2020
C. Stephanidis et al. (Eds.): HCII 2020, CCIS 1294, pp. 102–109, 2020.
https://doi.org/10.1007/978-3-030-60703-6_13

1   Introduction

Intracortical brain-computer interfaces (iBCIs) have been successful in providing external effector control for people with severe motor impairments [1, 2]. However, most iBCIs rely heavily on the user's visual acuity and intact oculomotor control to provide feedback regarding the effector state, such the position of computer cursor, icon, or alphabet on the screen. However in people with sustained visual impairments as a result of traumatic brain injuries, some forms of stroke, or late-stage amyotrophic lateral sclerosis (ALS), an auditory modality holds potential as a feedback method since it provides an alternate communication channel that is often intact. Previous auditory BCI studies using EEG used learned tones that vary in pitch and frequency in BCI implementations [3–5]. Recent progress has been made in developing a more intuitive way by employing spatial auditory cues for BCI control [6–8]. Motivated by this ongoing research in auditory spatial navigation [8] and, iBCI calibration for external device control [9, 10], we have developed a novel auditory-cued iBCI task and demonstrate control of a neural cursor for acquiring targets on a screen by a person with tetraplegia.

In this pilot study, we use head-response transfer functions (HRTFs) to generate a virtual environment in which spatially arranged targets on a screen have a corresponding auditory, spatially localizable tone. HRTFs provide a unique advantage enabling the ability to present virtual auditory stimuli from any direction, including the rear, without the use of loudspeakers [8].

2   Methods

2.1   Participants – Healthy Subjects and iBCI User with Tetraplegia

Participants included two lab members without paralysis and an iBCI user with tetraplegia, previously enrolled in the BrainGate pilot clinical trial (ClinicalTrials.gov ID: NCT00912041). To test the usability of spatial auditory signals, psychophysics experiments were performed in lab members (n = 2; one subject is an author, DJT). BrainGate participant T11 is a 35 year old man with C4 AIS-A spinal cord injury; as part of the ongoing trial, two 96-channel Blackrock microelectrode arrays were placed in the precentral gyrus approximately five months prior to these research sessions. The data presented here from T11 was collected on the 160th day since the neural implant.

2.2   Experimental Paradigm

Virtual sound sources via head-response transfer function were delivered as auditory stimuli through earphones. We spatialized the sound stimuli using a public domain CIPIC HRTF database [11], which contains multiple sets of HRTF measurements of human subjects measured at a range of azimuths (φ) and elevations (θ). In the first part of the study, each sound was set spatially on a horizontal plane at azimuth (φ) locations of $-90°$, $-60°$, $-30°$, $0°$, $30°$, $60°$, and $90°$ to correspond to the radially oriented directions.

2.2.1 Localization Test

We sought to determine how accurately users localized the sound sources. An auditory stimulus was presented in a random sequence from one of the azimuths, while keeping the elevation constant, and the subject reported from which direction s/he perceived the auditory stimulus. This was repeated 20 times in each direction. In total, 160 responses were obtained. Audio was presented via earphones placed in the external auditory canal (SENNHEISER IE60, Germany).

In the iBCI user, a similar localization test was performed to identify his accuracy of sound localization using the CIPIC HRTF database. The participant was seated upright in his wheelchair, facing the monitor which had an image of a head surrounded by equidistant points numbered from 1 to 35, that denoted the position of a sound source. The localization task was performed at a constant elevation ($\theta = 0$), while the azimuths were varied ($\varphi = -90, -60, -30, 0, 30, 60, 90$). Each trial started by playing an HRTF-modulated sound through the earphone, and then the participant was asked to provide a best estimate of the location of the virtual sound source, by saying a number from the image on the screen. There were 5 times more options to choose from, than the presented tones to avoid any biases the participant would acquire over multiple presentations of the same set of tones.

iBCI Center-out Radial Target Acquisition Task: During the iBCI session, the participant was seated comfortably in his wheelchair, slightly reclined from vertical and facing a 17 in flat panel monitor (34 × 27 cm, 1280 × 1024 pixels). The task that was implemented for auditory iBCI control was a Radial-8 task [1], in which the center target and 8 peripheral targets were arranged in an oval layout on the screen (Fig. 1). Specifically, with regard to the auditory signals, the targets were arranged in a virtual 3D format such that the viewer would have the illusion of being in the center of a virtual room, with each of the 8 targets uniformly distributed around the center in the front-back plane ($\theta = 0$) (Fig. 1). A trial began when a sound corresponding to the cued target location on the screen was played over earphones, with no visual cue. The participant then attempted to move the neural cursor (see neural decoding description below) to the target that corresponded to the virtual sound source and acquire the target by moving the cursor to the target and holding it there. If successful, the cued sound was heard again and the target color intensified to green briefly before turning back to blue. Trial goals alternated between one of the eight pseudo-randomly selected peripheral targets and the center target such that the task proceeded in a continuous center-out-back sequence.

2.3 Human Intracortical Recording

Motor cortical activity was recorded from the microelectrode array (4.2 mm × 4.2 mm), which had been placed in the precentral gyrus as described in [1]. Signals from this 10 × 10 array of 100 platinum-tipped silicon electrodes (400 μm spacing, 1.5 mm long, ~4 μm tip diameter) were analog filtered (Butterworth band pass filter with 1st and 3rd order corners at 0.3 Hz and 7.5 kHz, respectively) and digitized by the 96-channel NeuroPort Neural Signal Processor (NSP) at 30 k-samples s-1. Signals were

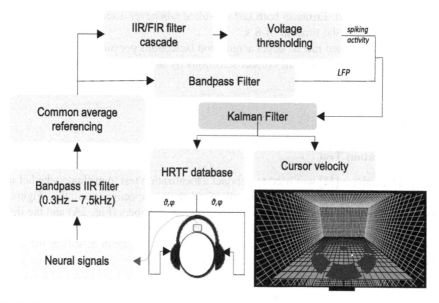

Fig. 1. Neural control paradigm: broadband neural signals recorded from the implanted microelectrode array are pre-processed to extract the multi-unit spike counts, which are then decoded to estimate intended cursor velocity. This information is used to estimate θ, φ for the auditory interface as well as the cursor position visualized by the experiment.

then filtered with a digital high-pass Butterworth filter (250 Hz 4-pole low frequency corner) prior to neural spike processing (Fig. 1).

2.4 Neural Decoding

iBCI decoder calibration was done on an open-loop version of the game as the user attempted to perform the cursor movements to the cued targets. The steady state Kalman decoder used in this task is similar to the one used by the participants in the BrainGate trial [9, 12]. Briefly, under the assumptions of a cosine tuning model, this decoder fitted the state space matrix, H (with ridge regression) in the form

$$v_t = g[Av_{t-1} + K[x_t - HAv_{t-1}]]$$

where v_t is the decoded velocity, x_t is the neural feature vector, A is the identity matrix times a smoothing factor, and g is the post-process gain, and K is the gain matrix.

2.5 Quantifying iBCI Performance

Success Rate was calculated as the proportion of successfully selected targets to the total number of targets offered during each 5–10 min task. Successful trials required that the cursor be moved to the target and a selection be executed while the cursor was placed over the target. Errors in both tasks resulted whenever a selection did not occur on the target before the timeout of 8 s.

The mean sustained rate of target acquisition (selections per minute) was calculated by dividing the total number of correct selections by the total task time including the timeout trials (8 s each).

3   Results

3.1   Localization Test

The HRTF database [11] was used to conduct a localization test to evaluate whether the presented sounds can be correctly localized to their respective azimuths. Figure 2 shows the results of the localization test in healthy lab members (Fig. 2A) and the iBCI user (Fig. 2B). All participants reported the virtual sound directions with high accuracy. The mean localization accuracy was 96.3% ± 14.4% (mean ± std) in the 2 lab members and 92.4% ± 12.1% for the iBCI participant.

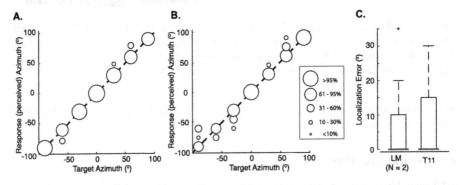

Fig. 2. Spatial sound localization test of lab members (A) and the iBCI user (B) across each direction. The horizontal axis represents the direction of the presented auditory stimulus, and the vertical axis denotes the direction the subjects' perceived direction which was reported back for each trial. The size of the circle corresponds to the proportion of responses for each test target azimuth. C shows the distribution of localization error across all HRTFs in both the lab members testing and T11. No statistical difference was present.

The localization accuracy measurements (Fig. 2C) across subjects for each presented sound direction show that median errors for all tested directions were zero, with errors of 15°–30° in the azimuths = ±30, ±60. Specifically, the incorrectly reported directions were located in adjacent locations. In lab members, the HRTF stimuli were also tested with changes in the frequencies of the tone, and slight improvements in accuracy were reported. This could be attributed to the ability of the subjects to learn the association of tones to direction. On the earlier trials, front-back confusion was evident as well. This is the known phenomenon in which sound sources that are equidistant from the left ear and the right ear (on the cone of confusion) provide identical interaural time and level differences for the listener, resulting in confusion [13]. Despite differences in perception of the absolute location of the sound sources in the subjects, overall similarities were observed in the localization accuracy and localization errors at specific azimuths (Fig. 2C).

3.2   iBCI Task Performance with the Neural Cursor

Using the spatial auditory signals, the iBCI user was able to identify the cued targets and achieve continuous neural control of the trajectory of a computer cursor to perform the center-out-and-back Radial task, selecting the correct location based only on auditory cues (Fig. 3A). Once each task started, the participant had unrestricted and continuous control of the cursor direction. Target-acquisition was executed by dwelling the cursor on any target for 1.0 s. Figure 3A shows the average cursor trajectory across multiple blocks for the 8 separate directional targets (cued using HRTF-modulated tones) over the mean trial duration. As per task instructions, the iBCI user was able to successfully utilize the spatial auditory cues to identify the targets and to navigate the cursor using motor imagery to the intended direction, and to acquire the target by executing a dwell-based selection within the allotted time. Selection times for correct trials across the blocks were 4.3407 s ± 1.4968 s, and the user attained a maximum of 6 correct targets per minute (Fig. 3B). At the initial attempt, the rate of successful target acquisition was 35%. This increased to 62% by the last block of the radial task (chance performance = 12.5%) (Fig. 3C). Errors resulted whenever the participant selected the incorrect target, or did not make a selection (i.e. dwell) within the allotted time. Similar to the performance of lab members in the localization task, many of the incorrectly reported target locations were located in neighboring locations.

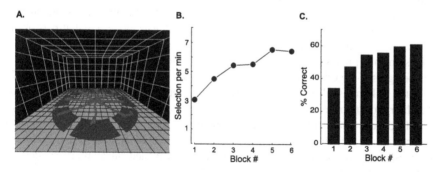

Fig. 3. A. iBCI neural cursor kinematics (mean cursor trajectory for each target during the mean trial length shown in red) during the radial center-out-and-back task that were cued with spatial auditory (HRTF) signals. **B.** The average number of targets selected per minute from shown in black. This includes trials that exceeded the allotted timeout interval of 8 s. **C.** Per-block performance on the radial task with auditory cues was evaluated as the proportion of correct target selections relative to the total number of targets. (Gray horizontal line indicates chance performance). (Color figure online)

4 Discussion and Future Work

The goal of this study was to prove the feasibility of the proposed auditory intracortical BCI as a control signal for effector usage, and to demonstrate initial use-case in a pilot study. Specifically, this study showed the use of spatial auditory signals as reliable feedback to perform a cursor movement task with an intracortical BCI by an individual with tetraplegia. The iBCI participant demonstrated clear ability to accurately identify the cued targets using auditory feedback alone, and further navigated the cursor to the targets within the first few trials. Performance from a naïve stage to reliable use was achieved within a few minutes (success rate increased from 35% to 62%, well above chance performance at 12.5%) (Fig. 3C).

Our results extend previous attempts to use HRTFs in EEG studies of spatial auditory interfaces [6–8]. EEG studies have typically tested BCI usage of event-related potentials (ERPs) and have proven to be moderately successful but mentally demanding to the user due to the need for extended periods to learn mappings between arbitrary mental imagery and the desired cursor motion. The observed increase in target acquisitions from the 1st to the last block (spanning approx. 20 min) could be attributed to the intuitive nature of the auditory signals that utilizes inherent spatial localization. The improvement in performance could be also attributed to the iBCI user's ability to quickly discern the cued target from the spatial auditory signal, and distinguish it from the previously heard tones to make the correct selections. A notable strategy used by the iBCI user on a few trials was to first move to the neighboring target before quickly adjusting to move left or right to get to the correct target. As is typical of our previous BrainGate participants [1], the iBCI participant in this study achieved cursor control using decoder coefficients computed using only a few minutes of neural signals recorded during attempted movements. Despite the marked improvements in performance over time in this task, it should be noted that the participant was already able to control the cursor using motor imagery using visual signals alone, i.e. that part of the task was familiar prior to introduction of the auditory feedback.

In sum, our pilot study demonstrates evidence for the feasibility of intracortical BCIs being used to perform a target acquisition task cued by auditory signals alone. In this initial task, a visual representation was used to ensure that the user could 'report' the auditory locations using the same iBCI strategy as he had previously learned under visual feedback. These findings greatly motivate the future investigation into spatial auditory signals for iBCI control, and the development of applications including a display of computer icons presented in auditory space, and an auditory speller for intracortical BCI usage.

References

1. Hochberg, L.R., et al.: Neuronal ensemble control of prosthetic devices by a human with tetraplegia. Nature **442**(7099), 164–171 (2006). https://doi.org/10.1038/nature04970
2. Ajiboye, A.B., et al.: Restoration of reaching and grasping movements through brain-controlled muscle stimulation in a person with tetraplegia: a proof-of-concept demonstration. Lancet **389**(10081), 1821–1830 (2017). https://doi.org/10.1016/S0140-6736(17)30601-3

3. Furdea, A., et al.: An auditory oddball (P300) spelling system for brain-computer interfaces. Psychophysiology **46**(3), 617–625 (2009). https://doi.org/10.1111/j.1469-8986.2008.00783.x

4. Kübler, A., Furdea, A., Halder, S., Hammer, E.M., Nijboer, F., Kotchoubey, B.: A brain-computer interface controlled auditory event-related potential (P300) spelling system for locked-in patients. Ann. N. Y. Acad. Sci. **1157**(1), 90–100 (2009). https://doi.org/10.1111/j.1749-6632.2008.04122.x

5. Halder, S., et al.: An auditory oddball brain–computer interface for binary choices. Clin. Neurophysiol. **121**(4), 516–523 (2010). https://doi.org/10.1016/j.clinph.2009.11.087

6. Nambu, I., Ebisawa, M., Kogure, M., Yano, S., Hokari, H., Wada, Y.: Estimating the intended sound direction of the user: toward an auditory brain-computer interface using out-of-head sound localization. PLoS ONE **8**(2), e57174 (2013). https://doi.org/10.1371/journal.pone.0057174

7. Schreuder, M., Blankertz, B., Tangermann, M.: A new auditory multi-class brain-computer interface paradigm: spatial hearing as an informative cue. PLoS ONE **5**(4), e9813 (2010). https://doi.org/10.1371/journal.pone.0009813

8. Nakaizumi, C., Makino, S., Rutkowski, T.M.: Head-related impulse response cues for spatial auditory brain-computer interface. In: 2015 37th Annual International Conference of the IEEE Engineering in Medicine and Biology Society (EMBC), Milan, August 2015, pp. 1071–1074. https://doi.org/10.1109/embc.2015.7318550

9. Hosman, T., et al.: BCI decoder performance comparison of an LSTM recurrent neural network and a Kalman filter in retrospective simulation. In: 2019 9th International IEEE/EMBS Conference on Neural Engineering (NER), San Francisco, CA, USA, March 2019, pp. 1066–1071. https://doi.org/10.1109/ner.2019.8717140

10. Brandman, D.M., et al.: Rapid calibration of an intracortical brain–computer interface for people with tetraplegia. J. Neural Eng. **15**(2), 026007 (2018). https://doi.org/10.1088/1741-2552/aa9ee7

11. Algazi, V.R., Duda, R.O., Thompson, D.M., Avendano, C.: The CIPIC HRTF database. In: Proceedings of the IEEE Workshop on Applications of Signal Processing to Audio and Acoustics, New Platz, NY, USA, pp. 99–102, October 2001

12. Simeral, J.D., Kim, S.-P., Black, M.J., Donoghue, J.P., Hochberg, L.R.: Neural control of cursor trajectory and click by a human with tetraplegia 1000 days after implant of an intracortical microelectrode array. J. Neural Eng. **8**(2), 025027 (2011). https://doi.org/10.1088/1741-2560/8/2/025027

13. Steadman, M.A., Kim, C., Lestang, J.-H., Goodman, D.F.M., Picinali, L.: Short-term effects of sound localization training in virtual reality. Sci. Rep. **9**(1), 18284 (2019). https://doi.org/10.1038/s41598-019-54811-w

Impairments in Early Auditory Detection Coincide with Substandard Visual-Spatial Task Performance in Older Age: An ERP Study

Melanie Turabian$^{(\boxtimes)}$ ⓘ, Kathleen Van Benthem ⓘ,
and Chris M. Herdman ⓘ

Carleton University, Ottawa, ON K1S 5B6, Canada
melanieturabian@cmail.carleton.ca, {kathyvanbenthem,
chrisherdman}@carleton.ca

Abstract. Investigating how the brain integrates multimodal information is critical for quantifying the effects of age on performance for tasks that rely on visual and auditory stimuli (e.g., driving or flying an aircraft). We report on how concurrent performance on a visuospatial task and a passive paired-stimulus auditory electroencephalography (EEG) paradigm were impacted by age. Outcome measures included response times and accuracy for a match-to-sample visuospatial task and event-related potentials (ERPs) derived from a 128-channel dense array EEG system. Older participants were less accurate and responded slower to the visuospatial task than younger participants, particularly in a high-workload condition. ERPs associated with cortical language processing areas showed that older participants displayed less sensory gating than the younger group for P50 and N100 ERP components. In contrast, pronounced sensory gating was found in the older participant group in the frontal cortex, which was driven by disproportionately larger N100 responses for the first stimulus. The present findings further the understanding of age-related neural changes and support the notion that a neural evaluation will one day reliably classify risk states for complex cognitive functions in older adults.

Keywords: Electroencephalography · Human-computer interaction · Neuroscience · Cognition · Aging · General aviation

1 Introduction and Background

Successful performance on tasks that integrate visual and auditory stimuli, such as driving a car or flying an aircraft, is a result of the brain's ability to integrate multimodal information. Managing risk for older adults engaged in these complex tasks is an important safety strategy, as older age is associated with an overall deterioration in performance. For example, compared with young adults, individuals aged 65–69 are 1.3–2.3 times more at risk of a critical incident while driving, a statistic that rises to 3.7–10.6 times for those 85 years and above [1]. In general aviation, pilots over the age of 60 have an increased likelihood of both critical and fatal flight incidents [2]. As of

© Springer Nature Switzerland AG 2020
C. Stephanidis et al. (Eds.): HCII 2020, CCIS 1294, pp. 110–118, 2020.
https://doi.org/10.1007/978-3-030-60703-6_14

2017, the average age of general aviation pilots was at 60.3 years and is on the rise based on earlier reports [3]. Considering the average age of pilots, and that in 2018, 97% of all aviation fatalities were within general aviation [4], there is an urgent need to develop measures that can classify risk states in older pilots. Accordingly, the implementation of objective measures of cognitive workload within the aviation domain is necessary to reliably assess pilot risk. Indices of efficient mental resource allocation may be relevant insofar as identifying aviators who experience cognitive deficits that can impact safety during flight.

1.1 Sensory Gating

Sensory gating is one index of attention resource allocation that can be measured objectively and easily using EEG. Deficiencies in gating, particularly when associated with auditory processes, may signal aviators who are at risk due to inefficient cognitive processes. To this end, the present research examined age-related changes in sensory gating linked to auditory processing.

Sensory gating refers to the neurobiological ability to filter out unimportant, or redundant information [5, 6]. In this study, sensory gating was examined using an auditory paired stimulus paradigm, a commonly used method in neural evaluations of sensory gating [7]. The paired stimulus paradigm involves the presentation of an auditory stimulus (S1), followed by an identical stimulus (S2) presented shortly thereafter [8]. Sensory gating is visible in event-related potentials (ERPs) as the attenuated response to repetitive stimuli at key latencies, such that S1 evokes a larger amplitude than S2 [9]. Latencies of interest include the P50, N100, and P200 (50 ms, 100 ms, and 200 ms after the stimulus onset).

Several studies implementing an auditory paired-stimulus paradigm have reported age-related differences in sensory gating, such that older individuals present poorer gating of repetitive stimuli at the N100 component [10–12]. There is also evidence that sensory gating at P50 and N100 components is comparable across younger and older populations [13]. The conflict regarding age-related effects of sensory gating justifies further analysis.

1.2 Current Study

The present research explored the theory that poor adaptivity in sensory gating may contribute to age-related reductions in cognitive performance. It was hypothesized that the older group would display lower accuracy and slower response times on the visuospatial task compared to the younger group. Furthermore, we hypothesized that the younger group would display more efficient sensory gating than the older group, particularly in the language [11] and frontal regions of the brain given the evidence that frontal executive function decreases with age [14].

2 Methods

2.1 Participants

A younger group of participants was recruited from a university population (n = 10, aged 18–32), and an older group from a "learning in retirement" program (n = 7, aged 57–78). Participants were compensated with either course credit or free refreshments.

Match-to-Sample Task. The task involved the presentation of two grids sequentially, and participants determined if they were the same or different, using the response pad (seen in Fig. 1.) to answer. The presentation of the visual stimuli was undertaken with a custom Python 2.7 script. The task consisted of two workload levels based on the total number of blocks in the grid and the number of filled blocks. The low workload condition had 25 blocks, of which 2 were filled. The high workload condition had 47 blocks in the grid, of which 7 were filled. In both workload conditions, only one block would move in the "different" condition.

EEG Recording and Preprocessing. EEGs were recorded at 1000 Hz using a 128-channel dense array system and a GES 250 amplifier. Net Station 4.3.1 (Electrical Geodesics, Inc.) software was used to record and reduce the data to 250 Hz. EEGLAB v.14 [15] was used to process the data, remove artifacts, and create ERPs. Data were filtered offline with a 1 to 30 bandpass. Further cleaning of the non-brain artifacts employed independent component analysis to identify and remove muscle, electrode noise, and eye-blinks. At the time of recording, triggers were inserted by the stimulus presentation software at the onset of the stimulus to mark the S1 or S2. Epochs had a baseline of 100 ms and extended for 500 ms post-stimulus. The Study function in EEGLAB computed grand averages of the epochs at each electrode for older and younger groups.

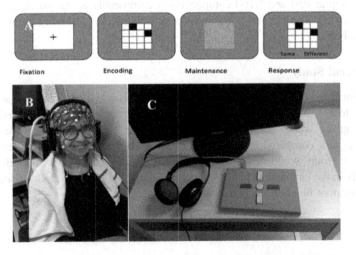

Fig. 1. Study materials/equipment: A. Visuospatial match-to-sample task (low workload condition), B. Geodesic sensor net with headphones, C. Response pad, monitor, and headphones

2.2   Procedure

Each participant completed a match-to-sample visuospatial task while wearing the EEG headset (Fig. 1). Once set up with the EEG headset, participants were presented with the match-to-sample task on an LCD monitor. After completing a baseline task consisting of watching a 5-min video of nature scenes, participants began the match-to-sample task. The starting task workload condition (low or high) was counterbalanced between participants and alternated within subjects for a total of four task blocks (two low and two high workloads).

3   Results

Data from the match-to-sample task were analyzed as 2 (Workload: low vs. high) × 2 (Age: younger vs. older) factorial ANOVAs. The ERP analysis also used a 2 (Stimulus position: first or second stimulus) by 2 (Age: younger vs. older) factorial ANOVA design with a p-value of 0.1.

3.1   Visuospatial Task

Accuracy. As shown in Fig. 2 (left panel), there was a main effect of workload where participants were less accurate in the high (72.23%) than the low (95.79%) workload match-to-sample condition, $F(1, 108) = 323.45, p < 0.001, \eta_p^2 = 0.75$. A main effect of age showed that accuracy was overall lower for the older (80.79%) than the younger group (86.08%), $F(1, 108) = 15.26, p < 0.001, \eta_p^2 = 0.13$. The interaction between workload and age was also significant, $F(1, 108) = 7.29, p < 0.05, \eta_p^2 = 0.06$. As shown in Fig. 2, older participants responded less accurately than the younger participants only in the high workload visuospatial condition.

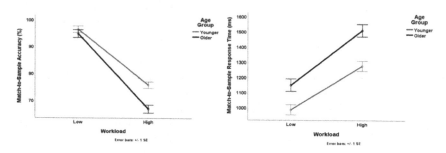

Fig. 2. Accuracy and reaction times: left panel. Mean accuracy percent by workload by age, right panel. Mean reaction time (ms) by workload by age

Response Times. As shown in Fig. 2 (right panel), there was a main effect of workload where participants took longer to respond in the high workload condition (1367.56 ms) compared to the low (1050.14 ms) workload condition, $F(1, 108) = 75.54$, $p < 0.001$, $\eta_p^2 = 0.42$. A main effect of age showed that response times were in general longer for the older group (1329.06 ms) than the younger group (1131.06 ms), $F(1, 108) = 28.03$, $p < 0.001$, $\eta_p^2 = 0.21$. There was no significant interaction between workload and age, $F(1, 108) = 0.91$, $p = 0.34$, $\eta_p^2 = 0.01$.

3.2   ERP Analyses

Postcentral Gyrus. As shown in Fig. 3, the younger group displayed expected sensory gating where S2 resulted in a significantly diminished amplitude at the P50 component ($p < 0.1$). The older group displayed less sensory gating than the younger group near the P200 component.

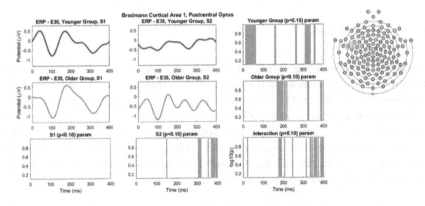

Fig. 3. Brodmann area 1, postcentral gyrus, ERP at S1 and S2 across age groups. The grey bars indicate latencies with significant effects of either age group (third row) or sensory gating (third column) at a threshold of $p < 0.1$. The top right inset shows electrode layout [16].

Frontal Eye Fields. As shown in Fig. 4, in contrast to expectations, in comparison to the younger group, the older group displayed significantly greater sensory gating at the S2 at the P50 ($p < 0.1$) component. As expected, the younger group displayed significant sensory gating at the P200 component. The older group also displayed significant sensory gating near the P50 and P200 components.

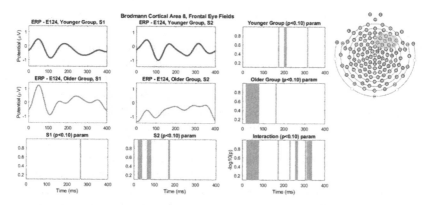

Fig. 4. Brodmann area 8, frontal eye fields, ERP at S1 and S2 across age groups. The grey bars indicate latencies with significant effects of either age group (third row) or sensory gating (third column) at a threshold of $p < 0.1$ [16].

Inferior Temporal Gyrus. As shown in Fig. 5, the younger group displays significant S2 sensory gating at P50 and N100 ($p < 0.1$) components. Additionally, the older group displays significant sensory gating at the P50 latency.

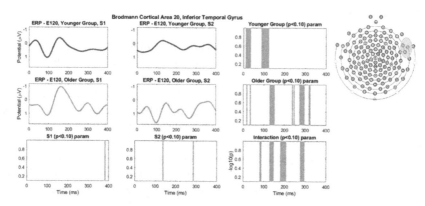

Fig. 5. Brodmann Area 20, Inferior Temporal Gyrus, ERP at S1 and S2 across age groups. In this figure, the y-axes are reversed such that the P50, N100, and P200 component polarities match the literature, as well as the other figures. The grey bars indicate latencies with significant effects of either age group (third row) or sensory gating (third column) at a threshold of $p < 0.1$ [16].

4 Discussion

The results from the match-to-sample task provided evidence in support of our hypotheses, such that the older group displayed significantly poorer accuracy and response times than the younger group. Furthermore, results revealed that the older group exhibited significantly poorer sensory gating in the postcentral gyrus and the inferior temporal gyrus.

One unexpected result appeared in activity derived from the frontal eye fields, such that sensory gating in this region was greater for older participants. There are two reasons why this may be the case. First, the older group might be expending more attention than necessary on S1, resulting in a significant difference between S1 and S2 which manifests as apparent sensory gating. As reported in Roland's [17] analysis of cerebral blood flow, prefrontal regions present greater activity during attentional tasks. Furthermore, Knight [18] determined that damage to the prefrontal cortices may result in poorer cognitive control, particularly in regard to attention and orienting systems. The second possibility is that the frontal eye field region is directly involved with processes pertinent to the match-to-sample task such as working memory, saccadic eye movements, and visuospatial attention [19]. Efficient neural processing should inhibit the unrelated stimuli to allow for more attention to the task at hand, which is apparent in the younger group given the lack of deflections, however it is not seen in the older group, given the difference between S1 and S2. Therefore, the inhibition deficits in the older group and the efficient inhibition in the younger group results in ostensible sensory gating in the older group. In sum, the ERP results suggest an inefficiency in the older participants, where they directed more attention than necessary on the auditory stimuli, perhaps leaving less attention for tasks with higher priority.

5   Conclusion

ERP analyses from language processing areas revealed differences in sensory gating, such that the older participants displayed significantly less gating than the younger group for both P50 and N100 components. In contrast, pronounced sensory gating was found in the older participant group in the frontal cortex, which appeared to be driven by disproportionately larger N100 responses for S1, when compared to the younger participant ERPs. In sum, the present results show that the older participants had impaired filtering of repetitive auditory stimuli, concurrent with lower accuracy and response times for a visuospatial task. These findings further the understanding of neural changes that transpire with age and support the notion that a neural evaluation can be used to reliably classify risk states for complex cognitive functions in older adults.

Acknowledgments. We would like to thank The NRC flight cognition laboratory for equipment assistance.

References

1. Preusser, D.F., Williams, A.F., Ferguson, S.A., Ulmer, R.G., Weinstein, H.B.: Fatal crash risk for older drivers at intersections. Accid. Anal. Prev. **30**(2), 151–159 (1998). https://doi.org/10.1016/s0001-4575(97)00090-0

2. Bazargan, M., Guzhva, V.S.: Impact of gender, age and experience of pilots on general aviation accidents. Accid. Anal. Prev. **43**(3), 962–970 (2011). https://doi.org/10.1016/j.aap. 2010.11.023

3. COPA National Homepage. https://copanational.org/en/2017/02/22/2017-membership-survey-results/. Accessed 13 June 2020

4. National Transport Safety Board: Aviation Data and Stats Page. https://www.ntsb.gov/investigations/data/Pages/AviationDataStats2017.aspx. Accessed 13 June 2020

5. Jones, L.A., Hills, P.J., Dick, K.M., Jones, S.P., Bright, P.: Cognitive mechanisms associated with auditory sensory gating. Brain Cogn. **102**, 33–45 (2016). https://doi.org/10.1016/j. bandc.2015.12.005

6. Freedman, R., et al.: Neurobiological studies of sensory gating in schizophrenia. Schizophr. Bull. **13**(4), 669–678 (1987). https://doi.org/10.1093/schbul/13.4.669

7. Gjini, K., Burroughs, S., Boutros, N.N.: Relevance of attention in auditory sensory gating paradigms in schizophrenia. J. Psychophysiol. (2011). https://doi.org/10.1027/0269-8803/a000042

8. Major, S., Carpenter, K., Beyer, L., Kwak, H., Dawson, G., Murias, M.: The influence of background auditory noise on P50 and N100 suppression elicited by the paired-click paradigm. J. Psychophysiol. (2019). https://doi.org/10.1027/0269-8803/a000245

9. Lijffijt, M., et al.: P50, N100, and P200 sensory gating: relationships with behavioral inhibition, attention, and working memory. Psychophysiology **46**(5), 1059–1068 (2009). https://doi.org/10.1111/j.1469-8986.2009.00845.x

10. Amenedo, E., Díaz, F.: Automatic and effortful processes in auditory memory reflected by event-related potentials. Age-related findings. Electroencephalogr. Clin. Neurophysiol. Evoked Potentials Sect. **108**(4), 361–369 (1998). https://doi.org/10.1016/s0168-5597(98)00007-0

11. Cheng, C.H., Baillet, S., Lin, Y.Y.: Region-specific reduction of auditory sensory gating in older adults. Brain Cogn. **101**, 64–72 (2015). https://doi.org/10.1016/j.biopsycho.2011.11. 003

12. Kisley, M.A., Davalos, D.B., Engleman, L.L., Guinther, P.M., Davis, H.P.: Age-related change in neural processing of time-dependent stimulus features. Cogn. Brain. Res. **25**(3), 913–925 (2005). https://doi.org/10.1016/j.cogbrainres.2005.09.014

13. Gmehlin, D., Kreisel, S.H., Bachmann, S., Weisbrod, M., Thomas, C.: Age effects on preattentive and early attentive auditory processing of redundant stimuli: is sensory gating affected by physiological aging? J. Gerontol. Series A Biomed. Sci. Med. Sci. **66**(10), 1043–1053 (2011). https://doi.org/10.1093/gerona/glr067

14. Rodríguez-Aranda, C., Sundet, K.: The frontal hypothesis of cognitive aging: factor structure and age effects on four frontal tests among healthy individuals. J. Genet. Psychol. **167**, 269–287 (2006). https://doi.org/10.3200/GNTP.167.3.269-287

15. Delorme, A., Makeig, S.: EEGLAB: an open source toolbox for analysis of single-trial EEG dynamics including independent component analysis. J. Neurosci. Methods **134**(1), 9–21 (2004). https://doi.org/10.1016/j.jneumeth.2003.10.009

16. HydroCel Geodesic Sensor Net. https://www.egi.com/images/stories/manuals/Printed% 20IFUs%20with%20New%20Notified%20Body/HC_GSN_channel_map_128_8403486-54_20181207.pdf

17. Roland, P.E.: Cortical regulation of selective attention in man. A regional cerebral blood flow study. J. Neurophysiol. **48**(5), 1059–1078 (1982). https://doi.org/10.1152/jn.1982.48.5. 1059

18. Knight, R.T.: Decreased response to novel stimuli after prefrontal lesions in man. Electroencephalogr. Clin. Neurophysiol. Evoked Potentials Sect. **59**(1), 9–20 (1984). https://doi.org/10.1016/0168-5597(84)90016-9
19. TCT Research Manuals Page. https://www.trans-cranial.com/docs/cortical_functions_ref_v1_0_pdf.pdf. Accessed 13 June 2020

Modeling a Low Vision Observer: Application in Comparison of Image Enhancement Methods

Cédric Walbrecq$^{(\boxtimes)}$, Dominique Lafon-Pham, and Isabelle Marc

EuroMov Digital Health in Motion, University of Montpellier,
IMT Mines Ales, Ales, France
cedric.walbrecq@mines-ales.fr

Abstract. Numerous image processing methods have been proposed to help low vision people, often relied on contrast enhancement algorithms. Their assessment is usually performed by tests on low vision subjects, which are expensive and time consuming. This paper presents a low vision observer model, fully customizable to fit various impaired visual performances, which may be used for early algorithm assessment, and avoiding unnecessary human tests. This model is fitted to visual performances of a subject with degenerative retinal disease, and applied to images processed by two edge enhancement algorithms, allowing to explain their performances in terms of blur reduction and color saturation improvement.

Keywords: Computational model · Low vision · Contrast sensitivity function · Contrast enhancement

1 Introduction

Over the past decade, numerous studies have been devoted to the development of assistive products for visually impaired people. Common principles of these aids are the use of one or more cameras to capture the real world environment, image processing aiming to enhance visibility, and display on virtual reality or augmented reality devices. Numerous image processing methods have been proposed, often aiming to contrast enhancement and some of them significantly improve performances for tasks as reading, facial expressions recognition or visual search [1]. These methods are often evaluated through tests on low vision subjects, with as far as possible standardized viewing conditions, assessment procedures and data analysis methods. When experimental conditions are correctly designed, and subject cohort well chosen, all these tests may give access to the "truth" about utility and efficiency of these enhancement methods. But tests on human subjects are expensive and time consuming. Moreover, due to the limited size of the test cohorts and to restrictive experimental protocols, their results may not be easily extrapolated to various degrees of visual deficiencies or different viewing conditions. Looking for faster alternatives, image researchers may turn to resort to so called "objective methods", with metrics based on mathematical parameters. This paper presents a low vision observer computational model, fully

© Springer Nature Switzerland AG 2020
C. Stephanidis et al. (Eds.): HCII 2020, CCIS 1294, pp. 119–126, 2020.
https://doi.org/10.1007/978-3-030-60703-6_15

customizable to fit various impaired visual performances and different technical characteristics of displays and lighting conditions. It is intended to be used in objective comparison of image enhancement algorithms or in assessment of any new digital interface for visually impaired people. This paper is structured as follows: brief presentation of recent works on Human Visual System (HVS) simulation and modeling is found in Sect. 2. The proposed model is described in Sect. 3. Application of this model to comparison to two contrast enhancement algorithms is discussed in Sect. 4. Criteria for this comparison are based on blur measurement and on color saturation assessment.

2 Related Work

Taking into account the performances and limitations of the HVS is known to improve processing in various image and video domains such as acquisition, compression, watermarking, communication, enhancement, classification, reproduction, etc. Vision is known to involve both bottom-up cues, such as luminance patterns, and top-down factors such as scene understanding. In the following, we only consider the bottom up aspect, and computational models dealing with some of the mechanisms that have significant influence on visual perception, such as light absorption, diffusion and diffraction due to the eye's optics, luminance adaptation, color representation, contrast sensitivity, frequency and orientation selective perceptual channels or visual masking. Visual saliency modeling is out of the scope of this paper. Simulation of impaired vision is achieved by modifications of appropriate parameters at these different visual information processing stages in the standard vision model. As it is known that the HVS response depends much less on the absolute luminance than on its relative local variations to the surrounding background, the Contrast Sensitivity Function (CSF) that represents the relationship between perceptible contrasts and spatial frequencies of visual stimuli is central to these models. Cottaris et al. [2] proposed to convert RGB images to cone excitation images, taking into account the wavelength-dependent point spread functions due to the eye optics, absorption in lens and macular pigment, and cone mosaic, with all the parameters extracted from physiological measurements. The CS derived from this method are in close agreement with the one measured in the standard experiment. Pattern sensitivity is simulated by a Support Vector Machine (SVM) classifier. Although the introduction of low vision parameters is straightforward in this model, it cannot be directly used for our purpose, as it is restricted to simple pattern stimuli, and hardly adapted to more complex stimuli. Peli [3] set out to define contrast in natural images by taking into account the existence of frequency selective perceptual channels in SVH, and developed a method for simulating perception by a visually impaired subject, based on SVH nonlinearities and experimental CSF measurements. Thomson et al. [4] contributed to extend this work, first by establishing a method for parametrization of standard analytical CSF model with classical clinical acuity and contrast sensitivity measurements. They have also proposed to handle color images, by translating them from RGB to CIE xyY color spaces, and then, by using CSF as a linear band pass filter for the two chromatic x and y channels. Al Atabany et al. [5] implemented a degenerative retina model with central scotoma, based on mathematical expressions of connectivity between the different neural layers within the retina. This approach allowed them to simulate foveal center-surround processing and color opponency mechanisms. Consequences of ageing on visual performances are another area where simulation approach is developed [6, 7]. Age dependent parameters such as reduced pupil size, increased scattering in ocular media and diminution of retinal cell density are introduced in standard CSF expressions.

3 The Computational Low Vision Model

Our model is intended to simulate foveal vision in photopic conditions, for viewing natural scene images on electronic displays, and therefore is concerned by color perception, light adaptation and masking effects. It must be applicable whatever the display technical characteristics, lighting conditions and distance to the screen.

3.1 Standard Vision Modeling

Among the numerous models of CSF that have been employed for instance in image quality assessment, we have chosen to build our work on Barten's model [8], as it explicitly decomposes the CSF into successive components corresponding to optical, retinal and neural processing. As it was based on luminance sine wave gratings with limited spatial frequency contents, it has to be completed to take in account wide band color stimuli.

Our model consists in four steps. The first step corresponds to pre retinal processing. RGB image is converted in device-independent and position-independent image in the CIE xyY color space. This image is then filtered by a lowpass Gaussian function modeling the Optical Transfer Function (OTF).

$$OTF(u) = e^{\left(-2.\left(\pi.\sqrt{(\sigma_0^2 + (C_{ab}.d).^2)}.u\right)^2\right)} \tag{1}$$

where u is the spatial frequency (expressed in cpd) and d the pupil size, depending on luminance adaptation level. This level is calculated by averaging Y values on the whole image, if the assumption is made that image is seen in a dark room. Otherwise, it can be set to the ambient luminance level. The σ_0 value depends on diffusion in lens and ocular media and on photoreceptor density.

The second step corresponds to retinal processing. Assuming separability between color and pattern sensitivity, separate CSF may be implemented for luminance and chromatic channels. Cone excitation image is obtained by a conversion in LMS color space, based on Smith and Pokorny approximation, and then recoded as a contrast image: for each L, M ou S component, each pixel value is divided by the mean value of its neighborhood, whose size is similar to the one used in lateral inhibition process. Neural processing that occurs in the following layers in the retina is simulated by conversion into the Krauskopf color opponent space [9]. For the achromatic components, we use the highpass function developed by Barten. He considers that lateral inhibition (modeling center surround effect because of connectivity between cones, horizontal cells and bipolar cells) is applied to visual stimuli summed with photon noise (fluctuation in the number of photons actually initiating cone excitation) and neural noise (intrinsic fluctuations in neural signals):

$$M(u) = \cfrac{1}{k.\sqrt{\left(\left(\frac{2}{T}.\left(\frac{1}{X_0^2} + \frac{1}{X_{max}^2} + \frac{u}{N_{max}^2}\right)\left(\frac{1}{\eta.p.E}.\left(\frac{\Phi_0}{\left(1-e^{\left(-(u/u_0)^2\right)}\right)}\right)\right)\right)\right)}} \tag{2}$$

where k is the Signal to Noise Ratio (SNR) allowing detection, T is the integration time of the eye, X_0 is the integration area angular size, N_{max} is the number of cycles over which the eye can integrate, η is the quantum efficiency, p is the photon conversion factor, E is the retinal illuminance, Φ_0 is the spectral density of neural noise, u_0 is the spatial frequency above which lateral inhibition disappears. For the chromatic red-green and blue –yellow components, we use the lowpass sensitivity functions described in [9].

The third step is a rough representation of the first V1 area in the visual cortex, where visual information is known to be processed by separate frequency and orientation selective cells. It is based on the Cortex transform [10]. Contrast image is decomposed into a set of subband images. In each of these image, masking effect is implemented according to [11]: contrast perception is a nonlinear process, with threshold dependent both on the contrast value and on the entropy of its neighborhood.

The last step is the reconstruction of perceived image: in each frequency subband achromatic image, each pixel value is compared to the corresponding threshold, given by CSF. Values below threshold are replaced by the local mean luminance, while values above are not modified. Thresholded achromatic and chromatic subband images are then summed, and the resulting image translated back to RGB space. The sum is restricted to the subbands that can actually be displayed by the screen, depending on its resolution.

3.2   Low Vision Modeling

As a first example, we choose to simulate low vision observer suffering from Retinitis pigmentosa (RP), an inherited retinal degenerative disease leading to the loss of photoreceptors. The first symptoms of RP are night blindness and light sensitivity, before progressive constriction of peripheral field of view [12]. Patients also report that colors appear to them as dull and washed out. Some of the model parameters have to be modified to match the pathological retina characteristics. The loss of photoreceptors is simulated by applying a factor C_{loss} lower than unity to the LMS cone response values. According to [13], foveal acuity may remained unchanged with as much as a cone loss of about 40%, and 20/50 vision is expected with only 10% of foveal cones. It is likely to assume that, among all the parameters included in the CSF model, the quantum efficiency (η), the standard deviation (σ_0) which relies on cone density and the SNR (k) have to be modified to correspond to a RP observer. Their values were varied to fit CSF from RP patients. Figure 1 shows simulation of perceived images by normal and low vision observers. The standard observer model is based on parameter values defined in [8], and the impaired ones on values chosen to fit real individual CSF, found in [14].

(a)   (b)   (c)

Fig. 1. Simulation of images perceived by normal and visually impaired individuals. (a): standard observer (k = 3, η = 0.03, σ_0 = 0.5 arcmin); (b) visual acuity 0.4 (k = 45, η = 0.01, σ_0 = 4arcmin, C_{loss} = 0.75); (c): visual acuity 0.2 (k = 75, η = 0.01, σ_0 = 6 arcmin, C_{loss} = 0.5)

4   Contrast Enhancement Algorithm Comparison

The model relevance is demonstrated by its application on images processed by three contrast enhancement algorithms. The simulated perceived images appear to be different, and suggest modifications to improve their efficiency. An attempt to quantify these differences is made, relying on blur measurement and color saturation.

4.1   Contrast Enhancement Algorithm

The first algorithm is the classical unsharp masking, with a 5 × 5 pixels Laplacian filtered image added to the initial image [15]. This algorithm is applied in RGB space. The second one is a cartoonization algorithm, as described in [5], with original RGB image Gaussian blurring, conversion to YCbCr color space, anisotropic difference filtering applied on the luminance channel, and color quantization in sixteen levels. The third algorithm is a customization of the second one, with addition of supplementary steps of luminance channel unsharpening and increase of color saturation: chrominance values are multiplied by a constant (equal to 4 in the following examples).

4.2   Blur Improvement Index

The measurement of image blurriness appears to be relevant as these algorithms are intended to improve the perception of images blurred by low acuity. The edge sharpness is strongly correlated with the amount of the existing blur in any image. A blur improvement index is computed according to the method described in [16]: for every pixel in both the reference image and the blurred image, the difference is computed between the center pixel and its height neighbor pixels, and the maximum value is calculated. Then, the average Z1 and Z2 of this maximum is calculated on the two whole images. The blur improvement index BI is calculated by the difference between Z1 and Z2. The most blurred is the processed image relative to the original, the most BI tends to 0.

4.3 Color Saturation Assessment

The cone losses in degenerative retina involve modifications in color vision. At the middle stage of the disease, environment is perceived as fade and dull. So the color saturation in processed images is a good indicator of visual perceptibility improvement. Saturation amplitude is calculated as the square rooted sum of the two squared chrominance components. Saturation index is calculated as the ratio between the saturation maximum of processed image to the maximum saturation of original image.

5 Results

The previously described algorithms were applied to 16 images extracted from the Kodak database (http://www.cs.albany.edu/~xypan/research/snr/Kodak.html), which are then processed by the low vision observer with visual acuity: 0.4. (Fig. 2).

Blur improvement index and color saturation index calculated for each image compared to the initial image are resumed in Table 1.

Table 1. Comparison

	Blur improvement index	Saturation index
Perceived original image	0.23	0.20
Perceived processed image (unsharp masking)	0.37	0.22
Perceived processed image (cartoon)	0.21	0.3
Perceived processed image (customized cartoon)	0.25	0.40

The perceived original image is significantly degraded, in terms of blur and color attenuation. Unsharp masking appears as the most efficient in blur reduction, but has minor effect on color saturation. This may explain why it was rejected by subjects in [15]. Cartoonization algorithm does not significantly improve both criteria. Increase of color saturation is only performed by the supplementary step added to the customized cartoon algorithm. It appears that using the low vision observer model might be helpful when investigating for enhancement algorithms with better efficiency for the visually impaired.

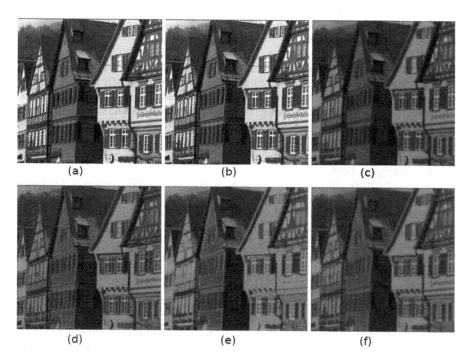

Fig. 2. Simulation of perceived images by a standard observer and a low vision observer (visual acuity: 0.4). (a): original image, (b): original image for standard observer, (c) original image for low vision observer, (d) processed image for low vision observer (unsharp filter), (e) processed image for low vision observer (cartoon filter), (f): processed image for low vision observer (customized cartoon filter)

6 Conclusion

This paper presents the first results related to a computational model of low vision observer. Its application gives cues for implementation of more efficient enhancement algorithms. Future works include further investigations on objective criteria for the measure of perceptibility increase, and experimental validation by comparison with human ranking on processed images.

References

1. Moshtael, H., Aslam, T., Underwood, I., Dhillon, B.: High tech aids low vision: a review of image processing for the visually impaired. Transl. Vis. Sci. Technol. **4**(4), 6 (2015)
2. Cottaris, N.P., Jiang, H., Ding, X., Wandell, B.A., Brainard, D.H.: A computational-observer model of spatial contrast sensitivity: effects of wave-front-based optics, cone-mosaic structure, and inference engine. J. Vis. **19**(4), 8 (2019)
3. Peli, E.: Simulating normal and low vision. In: Peli, E. (ed.) Vision Models for Target Detection and Recognition. World Scientific (1995)

4. Thompson, W.B., Legge, G.E., Kersten, D.J., Shakespeare, R.A., Lei, Q.: Simulating visibility under reduced acuity and contrast sensitivity. JOSA A **34**(4), 583–593 (2017)
5. Al-Atabany, W.I., Memon, M.A., Downes, S.M., Degenaar, P.A.: Designing and testing scene enhancement algorithms for patients with retina degenerative disorders. Biomed. Eng. Online **9**(1), 27 (2010)
6. Joulan, K., Brémond, R., Hautière, N.: Towards an analytical age-dependent model of contrast sensitivity functions for an ageing society. Sci. World J. (2015)
7. Mantiuk, R.K., Ramponi, G.: Age-dependent prediction of visible differences in displayed images. J. Soc. Inf. Display **26**(1), 4–13 (2018)
8. Barten, P.G.: Contrast sensitivity of the human eye and its effects on image quality. SPIE press, Bellingham (1999)
9. Le Callet, P., Barba, D.: Robust approach for color image quality assessment. In: Visual Communications and Image Processing 2003, vol. 5150, pp. 1573–1581. International Society for Optics and Photonics (2003)
10. Watson, A.: The cortex transform- rapid computation of simulated neural images. Comput. Vis. Graph. Image Process. **39**(3), 311–327 (1987)
11. Ninassi, A., Le Meur, O., Le Callet, P., Barba, D.: On the performance of human visual system based image quality assessment metric using wavelet domain. In: Proceedings of SPIE Human Vision and Electronic Imaging XIII, vol. 6806 (2008)
12. Hartong, D.T., Berson, E.L., Dryja, T.P.: Retinitis pigmentosa. Lancet **368**(9549), 1795–1809 (2006)
13. Bensinger, E., Rinella, N., Saud, A., Loumou, P., Ratnam, K., Griffin, S., Duncan, J.L.: Loss of foveal cone structure precedes loss of visual acuity in patients with rod-cone degeneration. Invest. Ophthalmol. Vis. Sci. **60**(8), 3187–3196 (2019)
14. Hyvärinen, L., Rovamo, J., La urinen, P., Peltomaa, A.: Contrast sensitivity function in evaluation of visual impairment due to retinitis pigmentosa. Acta Ophthalmologica **59**(5), 763–773(1981)
15. Leat, S.J., Omoruyi, G., Kennedy, A., Jernigan, E.: Generic and customized digital image enhancement filters for the visually impaired. Vis. Res. **45**(15), 1991–2007 (2005)
16. Elsayed, M., Sammani, F., Hamdi, A., Albaser, A., Babalghoom, H.: A new method for full reference image blur measure. Int. J. Simul. Syst. Sci. Technol. **19**, 4 (2018)

Usability Study of Electronic Product with Healthy Older Adults Based on Product Semantic

Yulan Zhong[1(✉)], Etsuko T. Harada[2], Shinnosuke Tanaka[2],
and Eriko Ankyu[2]

[1] School of Integrative and Global Majors, University of Tsukuba, Tsukuba,
Japan
s2030544@s.tsukuba.ac.jp
[2] Faculty of Human Sciences, University of Tsukuba, Tsukuba, Japan
etharada@human.tsukuba.ac.jp,
shin.tanaka.1127@gmail.com, ankyu@tsukaiyasusa.jp

Abstract. As a typical example of the electronic products with multi- and high-functions, integrated- function microwave oven is said to bring a much more convenient and brand-new lifestyle; however, in the meanwhile, it also compels their users to face many problems in using due to its multifunction. In this study, we conducted a usability test with healthy older adults to determine how well the elderly users can use the microwave oven, and what kinds of processes they are taking as their problem-solving. Based on the results of the usability test, we summarized several types of difficulties-in-use and tried to provide the design solutions based on product semantics, especially focusing on the process of transition between *exploration* and *reliance*.

Keywords: Usability testing · Electronic product · Healthy older adults · Product semantics

1 Introduction

With the infusion of information technology into society, the incorporation of technology into everyday life has contributed to a high and still increasing number of electronic products, especially those with multi- and high- functions. However, those products are often accompanied by complex and difficult operations, which often cause unpleasant users' experiences and mental frustrations to consumers (Moggridge 2007). Hence, proficiency in the interactions between different users and products is becoming a critical factor in successful design and development for usability-oriented products or services (You and Chen 2003).

Usability testing can help designers see what people actually do—what works for them and what does not (Barnum 2011). Specifically, usability testing involves direct observation of the users' behaviors and minds to obtain the hidden information such as "why they did it", "how they were feeling", or even "what they originally wanted to do".

C. Stephanidis et al. (Eds.): HCII 2020, CCIS 1294, pp. 127–133, 2020.
https://doi.org/10.1007/978-3-030-60703-6_16

This study chose healthy older adults as participants. It is because older adults are generally more sensitive to usability problems than younger adults (Harada 2009). That is, in situations with a design where healthy older adults are in "big troubles", also younger adults mostly have simple errors or microslips.

As a theoretical framework, we adopt the perspective of product semantics (Fig. 1), in which such "big troubles" or microslips are generally seen as disruptions between *exploration* and *reliance*. While designers are devoted to achieving meaningful interfaces by making the better transition between *recognition* (correctly identifying what something is), *exploration* (knowing how something works), and *reliance* (handling something naturally), such disruptions, however small, force users to go from *reliance* to *exploration* and back, upsetting the rhythm of the interface (Krippendorff 2006).

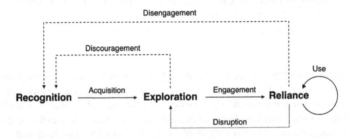

Fig. 1. Transitions between three modes of attention (Krippendorff 2006)

Therefore, the purpose of this study was to: (1) find out disruptions while older adults using the target product; (2) try to explain why they showed such disruptions; (3) come up with solutions to deal with the existing problems.

2 Usability Testing

A usability testing for an integrated-style microwave oven was conducted. Compared with the previous version of the device, the new one changed the design of the control panel, as shown in Fig. 2.

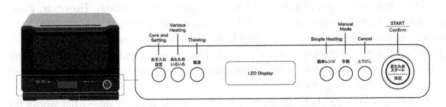

Fig. 2. The control panel of target microwave oven

2.1   Participants

A total of six older adults (3 males and 3 females, mean age 74.33, range 69–85) and, as a control participant, a younger adult (male, age 24) with an engineering background were recruited for our study. Specifically, all of them had minimum experiences with using a microwave oven, i.e., just for using to heat up some foods.

2.2   Methodology

Think-aloud protocol is one of the most common ways of usability testing. The participants are instructed to verbalize their ongoing thoughts while performing a task. It is allowed observers to know well which parts of the product do participants pay attention to and how they interpreted them. However, having a participant perform tasks and speak out at the same time is somehow "strange", especially for the beginners. Therefore, we gave participants suave explanation and demonstration, and time to practice in advance so that they can get used to it. We also use a retrospective interview, a method which is waiting until the session is complete and then asking questions about the participants' thoughts and actions (usability.gov. 2013). This method is used in case the participants were not able to think-aloud well, or their utterances are ambiguous in the context. Of course, those data had been treated carefully because their answer may be inaccurate due to the lag behind tasks.

2.3   Apparatus

Interaction between a participant and the microwave oven was recorded with three video cameras, including a wearable one; one fixed camera is focusing on the surface of the target interface for recording, especially of LED display, the other one was used to record whole process of usability testing including participant's gestures, while the wearable camera recorded the visual scope of the participant.

2.4   Tasks

The tasks range from simple heating up a retort pouch of food to cooking a dish of grilled chicken with herbs, and each task was designed to check whether the users perform well, as shown in Table 1.

Table 1. Tasks and presupposed correct usage mode

No.	Tasks	
1	Heat up a retort pouch of stew	Manual mode
2	Warm up a cup of milk	Auto mode
3	Defreeze the frozen chicken	Auto mode
4	Warm up the frozen rice	Auto mode
5	Cook an herb chicken	Auto mode/Usage of accessory
6	Add water into water tank	Usage of accessory

2.5   Procedures

Pre-Questionnaire and Think-Aloud Demonstration and Practice. After a brief introduction and informed consent, the participants were asked to fill out a pre-questionnaire, which is designed to know their initial impression of the microwave. Then the tester explained and demonstrated how to conduct a think-aloud method and asked participants to practice.

Task Execution. Participants were asked to complete a series of tasks, one by one, in the laboratory setting by him/herself, while doing think-aloud. They were handed a task card, and told to start the task with reading aloud the task at first. The tester intervened only in two situations: (1) if participants did anything dangerous; (2) if participants come to a long-time standstill. When the participant's think-aloud ceased, the tester prompted quietly by asking him/her the perceived situation (Kaiho and Harada 1993).

Post-Questionnaire and Retrospective Interview. The participants were asked to fill out a post-questionnaire once they finished tasks. The contents of the post-questionnaire were almost same as the pre-questionnaire so that we could evaluate how their feeling had changed by using the target microwave oven. Then a retrospective interview was conducted to: (1) understand what they thought about the product; (2) clarify the reason for some performances and/or utterances during the tasks.

3   Results and Discussion

To consider whether designs provide enough support to users, Krippendorff (2006) provided a checklist, including Affordance, Metonymy, Constraints, and Informative. After transcribing the verbal and behavioral protocol data and analyzing them, we extracted errors and troubles to use, i.e., *disruptions*, and summarized to mainly three types of problems in the light of product parts.

3.1   Disruptions with START Button

Direct Perception of Usability (Affordance). It is anticipatory of what can be done at present such as "pushability", "graspability", "movability" and so on (Krippendorff 2006). Here, users can control the START button by simply pressing or turning. However, more than half of the participants (01, 02, 03, 06) showed their confusion on the START button. To be specific, they did not realize that the button is also can be turned. It may be because that the button only provides the perception of press through the only cylinder. Therefore, the button should be designed into a shape that could also afford turnability.

Affordings (Informative). Affording is one of Informatives that offer guidance about the variables of an artifact and their consequences (Krippendorff 2006). Since most of the tasks required to heat something, some participants (02, 04, 06, 07) tended to depend on the microwave oven totally and directly pressed the START button as their first step. It might be because of: (1) participants' over-trusting; (2) ambiguous meaning of the START button, as shown in Table 2. Actually, there are only two words on the button: "START HEATING" and "CONFIRM". Hence, some clues which could represent the future results of different operations should be added to reduce the unnecessary mental load for memorizing.

Table 2. The meanings of START button

	Action	Meaning
	Press it directly	Heat up dishes
	Press it after choosing	Confirm what you chose
	Rotate it directly	Select Auto menu (001-179)
	Rotate it after choosing	Scroll menu

3.2 Disruptions with LED Display

Signals (Informative). Signals must succeed in competing for sensory attention with the other features of an artifact (Krippendorff 2006). In task 3, the display once showed a signal to ask users to add water into the water tank, as shown in Fig. 3. However, there were only two participants (01, 05) noticed and done it well. Even the younger adult did not realize it. Two situations can be considered: (1) they missed the signal in the display; (2) they ignored it because they did not know what did it mean. For the first situation, making it striking by changing its size, font, or position may works. For the second situation, expression with words should be changed. Furthermore, both illustration and words should be considered well to avoid users' misunderstanding it as a monitoring indicator, not as a signal, since rectangle here is also like showing the recent state of water tank.

Fig. 3. "Add water into water tank"

State Indicators (Informative). State indicators show users what their artifact is presently doing (Krippendorff 2006). Actually, the designers used it in a statement called "Measuring", which is a procedure that could estimate heating time by detecting the weight and the temperature of the food, as shown in Fig. 4. This statement has shown in task 2, 3, 4. However, it still confused the users because there is no indication of how long they have to wait and what the artifact is doing. Therefore, designs should provide more information about how much has been achieved at present.

Fig. 4. "Measuring"

3.3   Disruptions with Accessories

The function-integrated types microwave ovens generally have many accessories. With the target oven of this study, there were three accessories which were set up usually as a default (table plate, water tank, and drip pan), and two more accessories which were occasionally to be set up when it is necessarily (black plate and metal grate), as shown in Fig. 5.

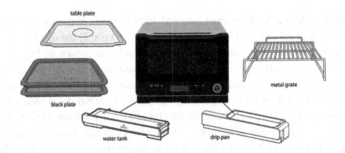

Fig. 5. The accessories of the microwave oven

Signals (Informative). Task 5 involved cooking a dish known as "Herb Chicken". Participants were given a sheet with the recipe and directions on it. Even though both the display and the instruction sheet told table plate should be used, only one participant (05) used the correct one and finished the task without any help. It may because: (1) users did not know exact differences between table plate and black plate since the task only required using table plate; (2) the information for those accessories was not enough. Therefore, the microwave should have been able to sense this error and inform the users by means of the display, because using the microwave oven function with the black plate is dangerous.

Metonymy. The last task was adding water into the water tank that is used for steaming food. This task is for those who missed the operation, which should be done in task 3. Since the lack of its signal in the display has been discussed before, we discuss another important component here, that is, metonymy. A metonymy informs users about the features of an artifact not in view, about the possible contexts of its use (Krippendorff 2006). Though designers use a text "add water" and a teardrop icon to tell users "they need to add water", it is still hard to understand where should be added water. Hence, showing where to add water may be much more efficient.

4 Conclusion

Our purposes were to investigate what and why the disruptions appeared while the user operates the target microwave oven by usability testing and consider solutions to deal with the existing problems. We recorded participants' protocols and behaviors as original materials for analysis, and finally summarized six disruptions from different parts of products. However, this study mainly focused on the analysis in the aspect of Informative. In future research, we will thoroughly consider other aspects of the *exploration* mode in the product semantics and of other modes (*recognition* and *reliance*), while verifying the validity of the solutions mentioned above.

References

Moggridge, B.: Designing Interactions. The MIT Press, Cambridge (2007)

You, H.C., Chen, K.: A comparison of affordance concepts and product semantics. In: 6th Asian Design International Conference (2003)

Barnum, C.M.: Usability Testing Essentials: ready, set … test. Elsevier, Burlington (2011)

Harada, E.T.: What do cognitive aging studies tell us? implications of memory and cognitive engineering research. Jpa. Phycol. Rev. **52**(3), 383–395 (2009). (in Japanese)

Krippendorff, K.: The Semantic Turn: A New Foundation for Design. CRC Press, New York (2006)

usability.gov. https://www.usability.gov/get-involved/blog/2013/04/moderating-usability-tests.html. Accessed 13 June 2020

Kaiho, H., Harada, E.T.: Introduction to Verbal Protocol Analysis. Shinyosya, Tokyo (1993). (in Japanese)

Virtual, Augmented and Mixed Reality

'Bring Your Own Device' in VR: Intuitive Second-Screen Experiences in VR Isolation

Konstantinos C. Apostolakis[1(✉)], George Margetis[1(✉)],
and Constantine Stephanidis[1,2(✉)]

[1] Foundation for Research and Technology – Hellas (FORTH),
Institute of Computer Science, Heraklion, Crete, Greece
{kapostol,gmarget,cs}@ics.forth.gr
[2] Department of Computer Science,
University of Crete, Heraklion, Crete, Greece

Abstract. Intuitive second screen experiences involving smartphone or tablet use are currently not possible with existing VR systems. Whenever users are immersed in a virtual reality world, interactive features and content are usually presented as pop-up windows and floating-text notifications, immediately breaking user immersion, serving as a reminder they are navigating a computer-generated environment. In this paper we discuss how to introduce second screen experiences in VR by orchestrating interplay between using handheld devices while using a VR headset. This entails allowing the users to interface with the touchscreen display despite the opaque, view-obstructing visor. We propose achieving this through a "mobile second-screen interreality system" (MSIS), referring a virtual 3D smart device representation inside the VR world, which is tightly coupled with its real-world counterpart, allowing users to manipulate, interface with, and look at the actual device screen, as if the head-mounted display were not present. This can be achieved via advanced screen-sharing technology, and pixel-perfect mapping between the real device and its virtual "double", ensuring basic functions (such as typing on an on-screen keyboard and/or tapping on application icons) can be carried out effortlessly. Advanced hand and finger-tracking can be used to represent the user's virtual hands' and fingers' movements on the screen, further enhancing virtual presence, and cementing the links established between the human brain and virtual reality space.

Keywords: Virtual reality · Smartphones · 3D pose estimation · Object localization · Screencast · Touch screen

1 Introduction

Mobile smart devices drive today's hyper-connectivity. Over the past 10 years, smartphones (and to a lesser extent, tablets) have evolved into digital extensions of ourselves, and have been revolutionizing the society ever since. Through these devices, people can instantly access a world of information, news and social contacts, all contained within the palm of their hands. Several years of experimentation and technological progress have further perfected the devices' design, making them lighter,

© Springer Nature Switzerland AG 2020
C. Stephanidis et al. (Eds.): HCII 2020, CCIS 1294, pp. 137–144, 2020.
https://doi.org/10.1007/978-3-030-60703-6_17

larger, more affordable and with significant processing capacity. In light of their proliferation, several corporations have started permitting employees to carry their own personal devices to the workplace (BYOD – "Bring Your Own Device"), which has been shown to boost productivity, efficiency and employee satisfaction [7]. On the other hand, Virtual Reality (VR) technology has started to overcome traditional barriers to its adoption, and VR headsets are quickly becoming household appliances. Furthermore, market growth in the VR head-mounted display (HMD) market is accelerated by them penetrating various business sectors, such as healthcare, advertising and defense. The way traditional VR headsets are designed however, severely restricts BYOD policies for VR applications (e.g. in business meetings), because looking at a smartphone screen would require the users to take off the headset and thus effectively exit the application, disrupting any connection they had to the VR world. Optical see-through HMDs used in Augmented Reality applications (such as e.g. Microsoft HoloLens) are currently incompatible with VR, while promising recent attempts at a hybrid solution [18] are still at an early, prototype stage, and (if VR headset adoption rates over the past 6 years are to serve as an indication) cannot be expected to overtake the VR headset market any time soon.

In this paper, we propose a pipeline for enabling smartphone and tablet use in VR using commodity headset gear, by introducing a digital double of the device into the synthetic digital world. Effectively, we propose the device to exist in two realities (real and virtual) simultaneously, maintaining a highly correlated extent of functionality. Such a system would allow users to "physically look at" the device in their hands, while they are immersed in the VR environment, and "virtually see" their hand holding that device in 3D in the VR world. To achieve the effect, both the smart device as well as the touch-based input applied in the real world will need to be efficiently tracked, and in accord to the headset, so as to carry over functionality of the device inside the virtual world. Such a system would open new avenues for transmedia/cross-device experiences, afford touchscreen interfaces to replace, or get integrated into future VR motion controller systems, and ultimately create new interaction paradigms for a variety of future VR use cases. The paper discusses, our ongoing work on implementing the concept of such a mobile, second screen interreality system (MSIS). The rest of this paper is organized as follows: Sect. 2 describes the main components toward building the proposed system. Section 3 discusses projected means of usage and the disruptive potential of MSIS across several segments of the VR market. Finally, Sect. 4 concludes with a short summary discussing the potential of the technology.

2 Proposed System Design

"Interreality systems" is a term used primarily in physics to describe virtual reality systems that are coupled to their real-world counterparts [8]. In this paper, the term is borrowed to similarly refer to a system representing the user's handheld smart device (e.g. a smartphone) in both the real and virtual realms, that are highly correlated (e.g. in terms of both device physical manipulation and functionality), so as to transfer the actual interactions of the users' hands with the device occurring in the real world into synthetic motions and visual outputs in the virtual world.

The proposed approach for achieving this combines device pose estimation and 3D tracking with user hand tracking and device sensor information. This can be achieved by mounting additional sensors on top of the users' headsets (e.g., Leap Motion, Google Soli), towards the capture of the users' natural interaction with their devices in order to be realistically transferred in the VR environment (see Fig. 1). Once the device has been properly positioned inside the virtual world, screen casting of the users' mobile devices can be based on open-source Virtual Network Computing (VNC) software.

- IR camera
- Hand tracking device (e.g., Leap Motion, Google Soli)

- Mobile front camera
- Mobile sensors (i.e., gyroscope, accelerometer)

Fig. 1. Proposed technical approach for the MSIS.

2.1 Device Localization and Tracking

In order to provide a realistic representation of user handheld devices in VR environments, efficient and accurate 3D pose estimation is required. Until recently, pose estimation employed statistical techniques to register point clouds acquired from sensory data with previously observed object models. Iterative Closest Point (ICP), is the most employed algorithm for this purpose, and many variants of ICP exist for different applications [14]. Unfortunately, ICP fails to converge due to local optimization minima if the initial pose is very different from the target pose, resulting in poor pose estimates [20]. Generative model approaches (a.k.a. model-based or top-down) employ a known model. The pose recovery process comprises two distinct parts: modelling and estimation [15]. In the first stage, a likelihood function is constructed by considering all the aspects of the problem such as the image descriptors, the structure of the human body model, the camera model and the constraints being introduced. For the estimation part, the most likely hidden poses are predicted based on image observations and the likelihood function.

More recent approaches contemplate pose estimation as an important step in the recognition process itself. Intuitively, it makes sense for pose estimation and object recognition to be performed together, since an object can look drastically different when viewed in different orientations. Only recent research has been able to merge these two steps, catalyzed by the emerging field of machine learning and, in specific, neural networks. Convolutional neural networks (CNNs), are a specialized type of deep neural network specifically designed for working with data that has spatial or temporal correlation, such as visual object recognition. [17] used a CNN for training, in order to learn feature descriptors, from RGB and RGBD data, and showed that the learned descriptors are more discriminative than HOG [5] or LINEMOD [11], succeeding high accuracy rates. This technique has the additional benefit of performing well on images lacking depth information. [4] trained a CNN to predict the 2D projections of interest points on objects, which can then be utilized to estimate the pose of the objects. This system exhibits robustness to occlusions, because if at least one interest point is visible, the algorithm can still detect the object. In [13], an improved CNN approach is proposed, which is able to obtain an initial estimate of the 3D pose, including objects with a rotational symmetry, and refine this pose estimate from the 2D representation of objects.

For the MSIS described in this paper, a novel approach for pose estimation and tracking of a mobile device is proposed, based on the fusion of three different cues: (a) images from an IR camera, mounted on the VR headset, (b) images from the front camera of the mobile, and (c) inertial data from the gyroscope and accelerometer sensors of the mobile device. In specific, a model-based mechanism is proposed, aiming the detection and tracking of the headset. This will be achieved using images from the front camera of the mobile device. In parallel, a CNN will recognize and track the mobile device from the images of the IR camera. The results of these approaches will be fused following the Extended Kalman Filter approach [6], taking also into consideration the data of the mobile device sensors. The proposed approach for estimating the location and position of users' companion devices, can overcome any occlusion problems that might occur regarding the device (e.g., while users are typing or swipe on the screen), since these situations can be compensated by the remainder of data sources (e.g., mobile front camera or sensors). In this way, the 3D coordinates of the mobile device in the user's real environment can be transferred to the VR environment.

2.2   Viewing Device Screen Content in VR

Screencasting can trace its roots to use cases such as thin-client computing [1] and remote desktops [19], where audiovisual screen content is generated by a server and is sent to a simplified client. More recently, screencasting technology has been proposed for performance-intensive and quality-driven applications, such as interactive learning [3, 16], or more commonly, for sending content from a mobile device (e.g. YouTube or Netflix videos) to a "smart" TV. Commercial standards for this latter use case include Google Chromecast and Apple Airplay, however the scientific literature has proposed several hardware- and software-based approaches [10]. VNC is a commonly used tool for screen sharing between devices, and has been adapted for mobile use to accommodate for performance considerations [9].

VR applications typically fully occupy the audio/visual sensory systems and achieve immersion by isolating the user from his/her real, physical environment. This isolation represents a huge barrier for delivering traditional second-screen experiences in VR. Screencasting software has already been used to help bring desktop PC screens (and subsequently, PC capabilities) into the VR space, allowing for social outlets (e.g. watching television content together) and collaborative efforts (desktop screen sharing). Incorporating a similar experience, but one targeting handheld smart devices instead, will not only broaden the functionality spectrum for existing VR applications, but is expected to unveil new forms for people to interact with VR content, and with each other.

3 Indicative Use Cases and Disruptive Potential

3.1 Communication and Social Interaction

For years, businesses have invested billions in customized business applications to support their employees in their jobs, performing everyday tasks. Toward this end, companies often opt for personalized solutions, developed specifically to meet their custom requirements. With the explosive growth of mobile devices and BYOD policies, companies have already started to invest in mobile development and remote desktop applications. Enterprise has also born witness to the steady penetration of VR technology, opening new and exciting avenues for online conference calls and business meetings. Mass consumers have also shown high interest in VR social interactions, opting to meet, and interact with one another and their surroundings in a variety of use cases, such as e.g. to watch a film, or a live sports match together.

It is evident that heightened interpersonal communication aspects and second-screen friendly technology can break new ground, and afford new opportunities for remote business meetings, as well as casual social interactions. MSIS could help expand current toolkits through a BYOD-friendly VR solution, one that can support numerous existing apps and embedded features (e.g. file and data sharing over smart devices) without requiring new applications to be developed specifically for the VR platform.

3.2 Games and Entertainment

Video games are the primary driver of VR consumer adoption. To meet with user demands for smoother, more immersive and interactive productions, development across both hardware and software is rapidly paced. This eventually benefits research, known to adopt game devices to the benefit of other application areas (such as e.g. healthcare). Furthermore, the experimental nature of VR allows small game development companies and individuals to experiment with the medium and deliver products that often surpass traditional gaming expectations. Other relevant business areas for VR application include game-based training, VR escape games and traditional games in virtual spaces, such as Online Casino and VR cafés.

Leveraging BYOD in VR, MSIS would enable players to enter the social-minded VR worlds together with their personally owned devices, making "game night gatherings" possible in VR spaces. Furthermore, the possibilities for "companion" mobile applications as attachments to VR games are limitless and could revolutionize the market for transmedia/cross-device play. This includes the use of smartphones as a touchscreen controller; PDA; and intuitive 2nd (e.g. player inventory or menu) screen. Other potential applications include VR Alternate Reality Games (ARGs), embedding interactive networked narratives that use the real world as a platform along with transmedia storytelling VR, rendering every imaginable context and outcome possible.

3.3   Immersive Media Experiences

VR/AR technologies are increasingly being introduced to real-time entertainment, as showcased by lifelike 360° video experiences of sports matches, theatrical plays, cinema and music concerts, which geographically distributed users can attend together through an app or web-player. Live streaming services for VR already deliver huge impact for HD broadcasting services and producers of live content, and projected means of usage span a variety of entertainment outlets. However, in order for VR to compete with traditional (social) television, sufficient work needs to be to meet requirements related to both quality, as well as audience engagement.

Through MSIS, live entertainment VR can significantly broaden the social aspects of the current technology, enabling users to remain connected throughout the experience. Second screen experiences have been used to entice audiences, enhance the viewing experience and deliver interactive, and social-minded content. With a system like MSIS new, massively online social-minded VR experiences can be orchestrated, enabling viewers to tap into live stats and companion-like capabilities for VR media consumption experiences.

3.4   Content Creation, Art and Design

VR has emerged as a medium where designers and artists can approach their craft in new and meaningful ways, offering a new dimension from which artists can work and expand their toolkits. Tools exist today that allow artists to collaborate in creating 3D art in a variety of ways: volume sculpting, virtual paints, brush strokes, etc. Through VR, artists can setup virtual workspaces, where they can construct, carve and paint their visions using a brand-new perspective, while manipulating their work in a life-size environment.

The flexibility offered by MSIS can lead to entirely new avenues for artists' creativity. Significant breakthroughs are to be expected by incorporating touchscreen interactive interfaces for 3D space exploration and in particular, object rotation for inspections. Given the diverse sensing and input capabilities of modern smart devices, MSIS will enable their use as input devices for facilitating 3D interaction in VR, in a manner that is more intuitive, comfortable and more satisfying to the users. Smart devices have revolutionized the way art is created and enjoyed, meaning artists will not have to spend significant effort and time to adjust to VR as a platform to create, also meaning adapting to the use of VR motion controllers as extensions of their virtual hands.

3.5 Commerce

VR leaves a lasting impression and is therefore a perfect solution for companies to engage their customers in new and innovative ways. VR can significantly impact e-commerce activity, through experiences that are interactive, game-like and thus, more enjoyable than browsing through online or printed catalogues. According to a recent report on VR potential, companies introducing VR elements into their advertising may experience up to 400% increase in the time customers spend on their sites, up to 27% increase in consumer activity, 100% viewer interaction, up to 400% increase in returning views and a staggering 700% increase in sharing [2].

Given the proliferation of smartphones in shopping, and the role they play in driving shoppers to the store (through micro-moments ranging from 'I-want-to-know' to 'I-want-to-buy'), MSIS can bring together elements of both VR innovation and smartphone use for brands and shoppers alike. The latter can be immediately involved in their shopping habits, e.g. by conducting local searches at home for shops during a VR experience, or using the smartphone as a source for product reviews, as well as to act as a key enabler of new paradigm shifts regarding commerce [12]. The smartphone revolution is driving change in the way shoppers behave both in and out of the store. Through MSIS, mobile is bound to have a similar –if not greater impact for an emerging VR market for e-commerce.

4   Conclusion

In this paper, we presented the ambition of kick-starting the mobile revolution in VR with a huge potential for business and leisure areas of application, where BYOD policies have gained significant traction. Incorporating a handheld reality-correlated virtual second-screen into the VR experience could revolutionize not only the way common everyday people interact with one another in private settings, but also allow corporations to understand how to incorporate a new, previously unexplored VR channel into their business strategies. Implications for business, across various verticals trying to incorporate VR into their processes could be significant.

References

1. Baratto, R.A., Kim, L.N., Nieh, J.: THINC: a virtual display architecture for thin-client computing. In: ACM SIGOPS Operating Systems Review, vol. 39, no. 5, pp. 277–290. ACM (2005)
2. Bezegová, E., Ledgard, M. A., Molemaker, R-J., Oberč, B. P., Vigkos, A.: Virtual Reality and its potential for Europe. Ecorys report (2017)

3. Chandra, S., Boreczky, J., Rowe, L.A.: High performance many-to-many intranet screen sharing with DisplayCast. ACM Trans. Multimedia Comput. Commun. Appl. (TOMM) **10**(2), 19 (2014)
4. Crivellaro, A., Rad, M., Verdie, Y., Moo Yi, K., Fua, P., Lepetit, V.: A novel representation of parts for accurate 3D object detection and tracking in monocular images. In: Proceedings of the IEEE International Conference on Computer Vision, pp. 4391–4399 (2015)
5. Dalal, N., Triggs, B.: Histograms of oriented gradients for human detection. In: IEEE Computer Society Conference on Computer Vision and Pattern Recognition, vol. 1, pp. 886–893. IEEE (2005)
6. Einicke, G.A., White, L.B.: Robust extended Kalman filtering. IEEE Trans. Signal Process. **47**(9), 2596–2599 (1999)
7. French, A.M., Guo, C., Shim, J.P.: Current status, issues, and future of bring your own device (BYOD). Commun. Assoc. Inf. Syst. **35**(1), 10 (2014)
8. Gintautas, V., Hübler, A.W.: Experimental evidence for mixed reality states in an interreality system. Phys. Rev. E **75**(5), 057201 (2007)
9. Ko, H.Y., Lee, J.H., Kim, J.O.: Implementation and evaluation of fast mobile VNC systems. IEEE Trans. Consum. Electron. **58**(4), 1211–1218 (2012)
10. Li, X., An, D.: An in-depth performance analysis and optimization for android screencast. In: Proceedings of the 2nd International Conference on Computer Science and Application Engineering, p. 69. ACM (2018)
11. Low, K.L.: Linear least-squares optimization for point-to-plane ICP surface registration. Chapel Hill Univ. N. C. **4**(10), 1–3 (2004)
12. Margetis, G., Ntoa, S., Stephanidis, C.: Smart omni-channel consumer engagement in malls. In: Stephanidis, C. (ed.) HCII 2019. CCIS, vol. 1034, pp. 89–96. Springer, Cham (2019). https://doi.org/10.1007/978-3-030-23525-3_12
13. Rad, M., Lepetit, V.: BB8: a scalable, accurate, robust to partial occlusion method for predicting the 3D poses of challenging objects without using depth. In: International Conference on Computer Vision, vol. 1, no. 4, p. 5 (2017)
14. Rusinkiewicz, S., Levoy, M.: Efficient variants of the ICP algorithm. In: Proceedings of the 3rd International Conference on 3-D Digital Imaging and Modeling, pp. 145–152. IEEE (2001)
15. Sminchisescu, C.: Three-Dimensional Human Modeling and Motion. Reconstruction in Monocular Video Sequences. Doctoral dissertation, Ph. D. Dissertation (2002)
16. Tabuenca, B., Kalz, M., Löhr, A.: MoocCast: evaluating mobile-screencast for online courses. Univ. Access Inf. Soc. **17**(4), 745–753 (2017). https://doi.org/10.1007/s10209-017-0528-x
17. Wohlhart, P., Lepetit, V.: Learning descriptors for object recognition and 3D pose estimation. In: Proceedings of the IEEE Conference on Computer Vision and Pattern Recognition, pp. 3109–3118. IEEE (2015)
18. Yamada, W., Manabe, H., Ikeda, D., Rekimoto, J.: VARiable HMD: optical see-through HMD for AR and VR. In: The Adjunct Publication of the 32nd Annual ACM Symposium on User Interface Software and Technology, pp. 131–133. ACM (2019)
19. Yang, S.J., Nieh, J., Selsky, M., Tiwari, N.: The performance of remote display mechanisms for thin-client computing. In: USENIX Annual Technical Conference, General Track, pp. 131–146 (2002)
20. Zabulis, X., Lourakis, M.I.A., Koutlemanis, P.: Correspondence-free pose estimation for 3D objects from noisy depth data. Vis. Comput. **34**(2), 193–211 (2016). https://doi.org/10.1007/s00371-016-1326-9

Automated Test of VR Applications

Adriano Gil[(✉)], Thiago Figueira, Elton Ribeiro, Afonso Costa,
and Pablo Quiroga

Sidia Instituto de Ciência e Tecnologia, Manaus, Brazil
{adriano.gil,thiago.figueira,elton.couto,afonso.costa,
pablo.quiroga}@sidia.com

Abstract. Virtual Reality (VR) is a technology that allows the creation
of immersive virtual environments. Testing VR applications is challenging due to the almost unlimited possibilites of spacial exploration. This
work presents Youkai, a framework for unit testing of Android-based
VR applications. Our preliminary results show that our method can find
objects on the screen, change camera position and it supports 6 DoF
scenarios.

Keywords: Virtual Reality · Android · Unit tests

1 Introduction

Virtual Reality (VR) technology enables a deep immersion in simulated environments in which users can explore and interact using three or six degrees
of freedom (DoF) input systems. As the number of applications increases, the
industry needs new tools to ensure the software quality.

Performing tests in VR is challenging. Repetitive tasks such as test case execution should be automated as it would allow the report and bug verification
instantaneously. When programmatically testing user interaction, it proves difficult to write automated tests when the VR platforms run standalone [2], as it
is the case of Samsung Gear VR platform.

There are several studies about how developers test general-purpose software
applications [8]. Automation of software testing has been an area of intense
interest in this field. Test cases play a vital role in achieving an effective testing
target, but generating effective test cases is an equally challenging task [12].

This work proposes Yokai, a framework for unit testing of Unity applications
targeting Android-based VR platforms. Our method allows the users to create,
execute and check the output of tasks that are being written in Python.

This work is organized as follows: Sect. 2 presents a brief overview of current
literature of VR testing; in Sect. 3 we explain how our solution works; Sect. 4 lists
some results and analysis the experience of using Youkai for testing a simple VR
application; in Sect. 5 we write our conclusions and present future works.

C. Stephanidis et al. (Eds.): HCII 2020, CCIS 1294, pp. 145–149, 2020.
https://doi.org/10.1007/978-3-030-60703-6_18

2   Related Works

Scripted testing of applications [5] is a commonplace for mobile testing where a wide range of solutions are available. [2] claims that at 2003 there were no common pattern for automated testing of VR application. Since then, some solutions came up targeting Unity-based projects as Unity has built-in support for VR development [14]. Such solutions intercept game development as game engines are also widely used for VR app development [1]. Virtual reality can be considered a challenging area regarding the inherently space interaction complexity: conventional games require a 2D environment while the nature of VR requires that a completely interactive and immersive environment to be available [13].

[7] generates functional test cases from requirements using semantic analysis and parsing the scene graph of virtual reality scene. [6] records test oracle information from haptic interfaces and employs them to evaluate the correctness of the system under test (SUT). The work [11] records test data from Android using MonkeyRunner.

Some works present test solutions for Unity applications: [11] developed a reprojection of recorded inputs of Android events into unity screen coordinate system; In [10] a solution is presented to verify image quality of 360 video player implementation, but it doesn't assess the code quality neither interact with the VR platform.

3   Automated Tests on VR

We describe an approach for writing unit testing in Python for Android-based VR platforms using a custom-made plugin. Youkai is our solution for effortlessly introspecting Unity instances from Python terminals.

In Fig. 1 we present our proposed architecture: a Python-based framework for unit testing. *YoukaiEngine* is the class to which user interacts. It makes use of a communication channel abstraction to interact with an running instance of an Unity application or even the Unity Editor.

By means of an abstraction of the communication channel, as depicted in Fig. 2, our solution connects an Unity3D application running on Android to a Python desktop application. Thus, we can automate tests of VR features by accessing the properties of the application instance, e.g, the position of virtual elements, interaction with user interfaces, among other possibilities.

4   Experiments and Results

As a testbed we implemented a simple virtual gallery to watch 360-degree videos. It is comprised by an initial menu and a separate scene for the video player. Our sample application targets GearVR since it is the most used smartphone-based platform [9].

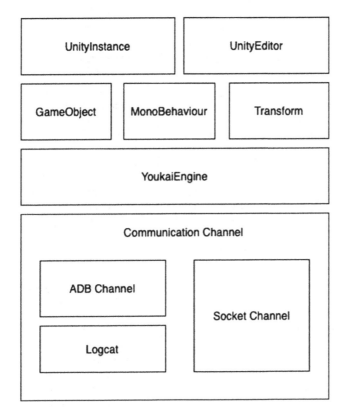

Fig. 1. Proposed architecture for our testing framework

For a small group of automation test developers, we send the task of creating unit testing using Youkai and AltUnitTester [4] and after completion we also sent a qualitative survey for comparing the experience of using both solutions. After analyzing the answers, we summarize below the elicited points:

1. AltUnitTester has a simpler setup as user only downloads its plugin from Unity Asset store and separate python module. Youkai needs the source code to be manually copied to the correct folders in Unity project.
2. AltUnitTester has a simpler interface. *YoukaiEngine* demonstrates to be complex at first.
3. The Python interface of AltUnitTester has less methods. It's not possible to inquiry about an attached component from a given GameObject. While Youkai not only allows to search for a GameObject given a name but it also has methods for handling GameObject's components.

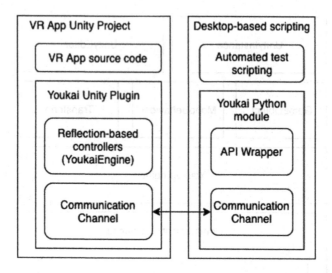

Fig. 2. A diagram of how our Desktop solution communicates with Unity instances

5   Conclusions

We propose an automated test framework for VR applications using Python-based scripts. As a test bed we presented a simple gallery application for Virtual Reality developed in Unity. In future works, we plan to improve our approach by using machine learning to generating test cases and scenarios.

Our preliminary results show that our method can find objects on the screen, change camera position, and it supports 6 DoF scenarios. We compared our solution with AltUnitTester [3], a well known testing solution available at Unity Asset Store [4], our framework have clear advantages as it is easily extensible and it has several methods to interact with Unity code what translates into improved unit tests.

References

1. Anthes, C., García-Hernández, R.J., Wiedemann, M., Kranzlmüller, D.: State of the art of virtual reality technology. In: 2016 IEEE Aerospace Conference, pp. 1–19, March 2016. https://doi.org/10.1109/AERO.2016.7500674
2. Bierbaum, A., Hartling, P., Cruz-Neira, C.: Automated testing of virtual reality application interfaces. Proc. Workshop Virtual Environ. **2003**, 107–114 (2003)
3. Cindrea, R.: AltUnity Tester-Documentation. https://altom.gitlab.io/altunity/altunitytester/index.html. Accessed 22 June 2020
4. Cindrea, R.: AltUnity Tester-UI Test Automation-Unity Asset Store. https://assetstore.unity.com/packages/tools/utilities/altunity-tester-ui-test-automation-112101. Accessed 22 June 2020
5. Coppola, R., Morisio, M., Torchiano, M., et al.: Scripted GUI testing of android open-source apps: evolution of test code and fragility causes. Empirical Softw. Eng. **24**, 3205–3248 (2019). https://doi.org/10.1007/s10664-019-09722-9

6. Corrêa, C.G., Delamaro, M.E., Chaim, M.L., Nunes, F.L.S.: Software testing automation of VR-based systems with haptic interfaces. Comput. J. (2020). https://doi.org/10.1093/comjnl/bxaa054. https://academic.oup.com/comjnl/advance-article-pdf/doi/10.1093/comjnl/bxaa054/33387955/bxaa054.pdf
7. Corrêa Souza, A.C., Nunes, F.L., Delamaro, M.E.: An automated functional testing approach for virtual reality applications. Softw. Test. Verification Reliab. **28**(8), e1690 (2018)
8. Cruz, L., Abreu, R., Lo, D.: To the attention of mobile software developers: guess what, test your app. Empirical Softw. Eng. **24**(4), 2438–2468 (2019)
9. Fuchs, P.: Virtual Reality Headsets-A Theoretical and Pragmatic Approach. CRC Press, Boca Raton (2017)
10. Gil, A., Khurshid, A., Postal, J., Figueira, T.: Visual assessment of equirectangular images for virtual reality applications in unity. In: Anais Estendidos da XXXII Conference on Graphics, Patterns and Images. SBC, pp. 237–242 (2019)
11. Hu, H., Lu, L.: Automatic functional testing of unity 3D game on android platform. In: 2016 3rd International Conference on Materials Engineering, Manufacturing Technology and Control. Atlantis Press (2016)
12. Jain, N., Porwal, R.: Automated test data generation applying heuristic approaches–a survey. In: Software Engineering, pp. 699–708. Springer (2019). https://doi.org/10.1007/978-981-10-8848-3_68
13. Jerald, J.: The VR Book: Human-Centered Design for Virtual Reality. Morgan & Claypool, San Rafael (2015)
14. Linowes, J.: Unity Virtual Reality Projects. Packt Publishing Ltd., Birmingham (2015)

Augmented Reality Signage in Mixed-Use Shopping Mall Focusing on Visual Types of Directional Signage

Yoojin Han and Hyunsoo Lee[✉]

Yonsei University, Seoul, Republic of Korea
{yoojin79,hyunsl}@yonsei.ac.kr

Abstract. This study aims to explore the effective types of signage in augmented reality (AR) environments. Although AR, a state-of-the-art technology, has been utilized in diverse contexts, its application in real-world situations is limited. This study examines the effectiveness of AR signage in mixed-use shopping malls in terms of wayfinding, which is a continuous problem. First, the time it took to make a decision was measured for three categories of signage: existing signage, AR-textual signage, and AR-graphic signage. Thirty directional sign images from the three categories of signage were used in the experiment. The sign images of the current sign system at the mixed-use mall were used as the control condition. Second, subjects were asked in a questionnaire to evaluate each AR-enhanced sign type in 5 aspects: uniformity, continuity, legibility, clarity, and aesthetics. The result found that AR-graphic signage is the most effective type in terms of decision-making time and aesthetics. However, it was found that for legibility and clarity of signage, textual elements should be adjusted in AR signage environments. Thus, this research suggests the use of mixed graphic and textual signage in AR environments.

Keywords: Augmented Reality (AR) · Signage · Wayfinding · Mixed-use shopping mall

1 Introduction

As the experiential aspect of shopping has emerged, traditional shopping malls have changed to perform mixed functions, e.g., shopping, dining, working, and entertaining [11, 12]. However, significant research has determined that, in mixed-use shopping malls, wayfinding can be difficult [1, 2, 6, 10]. In these circumstances, augmenting the physical environment with virtual images (i.e., AR) can be a solution. In retail environments, augmented reality (AR) has been applied in diverse contexts to transform traditional experiences [3, 4]. This research suggests that applying AR in sign systems for mixed-use shopping malls will not only enhance experiential engagement but also improve wayfinding. As both textual and graphic elements in the sign system are important to support wayfinding in traditional systems [2], this paper also examines the effective types of AR signage, particularly in terms of direction decision-making and improved cognitive experience.

© Springer Nature Switzerland AG 2020
C. Stephanidis et al. (Eds.): HCII 2020, CCIS 1294, pp. 150–155, 2020.
https://doi.org/10.1007/978-3-030-60703-6_19

2   Methodology and Methods

This study explores the viability of AR-enhanced signage in mixed-use shopping malls and analyzes the most effective type for wayfinding. To this end, among the four types of signs defined by Gibson [10], the directional sign, which plays an important role in enclosed environments, was set as the primary target for the research. An experiment and survey were established with the following aims: 1) to compare decision-making time in the mixed-use space when assisted by each type of AR signage, and 2) to investigate the subjective experiences of the subjects by type of AR-enhanced signage.

Three main research hypotheses were examined.

- **H1**: People can find directions faster when they use an AR-enhanced sign system than the existing sign system, regardless of its visual type.
- **H2**: People can find directions faster when they use graphic signage than textual signage in an AR environment.
- **H3**: In terms of sign design, graphic signage is the most effective in an AR environment.

2.1   Experiment

The experiment primarily focused on investigating the viability of AR signage to improve wayfinding. Thus, the decision-making time to find a direction was measured for each type of signage. As wayfinding is a dynamic process affected by various environmental cues [5, 8, 9], the experiment was based on the image to eliminate the environmental influence. The decision-making time was defined as the reaction time taken by the subject to press the direction cue for the guided destination after being presented with the sign images. The participants were encouraged to press the arrow button right after they determine the direction for the destination. The decision-making time is recorded in milliseconds to press the right direction for the given destination. The experiment was programmed with Python using keyboard arrow buttons and images.

Experimental Conditions. As illustrated in Fig. 1, the experimental conditions were divided into three categories of signage: existing signage, AR-textual signage, and AR-graphic signage. The AR-graphic signage contained pictograms or logos. As a control condition, the existing sign systems in a shopping mall were also presented to compare the effectiveness of AR. The AR-enhanced signage was developed with the existing signage as a guideline. The design features of the AR signage, including pictogram, font, and color, were controlled to be the same as the existing sign system. The position of the AR-enhanced signage is placed at eye-level. The size and number of the text and graphics were controlled to be consistent.

Participants. There were 51 participants who took part in this study voluntarily (23 males and 28 females). Consumers aged between 20 to 40, who were relatively familiar with AR technology, were selected. Moreover, the participants who are not familiar with the presented shopping mall and have normal vision were selected. The experiment was conducted in the same condition for all participants.

(a) Existing Signage   (b) AR-Textual Signage   (c) AR-Graphic Signage

Fig. 1. Three categories of signage

Procedure. The experiment was conducted in a seminar room at a university. The steps of this experiment are the following. First, the researcher explained the purpose and method of the experiment to the subjects. Subsequently, a practice session was offered to the participants to help them familiarize themselves with the experiment environment. The destination was given to them. They were then asked to press the arrow button on the keyboard based on the sign images. They were encouraged to find their direction intuitively. If they chose the wrong direction, they did not advance to the next step and were asked to choose again. Thirty directional sign images were presented in total. The main experiment took a total of five minutes on average.

2.2 Survey

After the experiment, a survey about features of the AR-enhanced signage was conducted. The five features of sign design (uniformity, continuity, legibility, clarity, and aesthetics) were rated by dividing them into three types: text, pictogram, and logo. The participants were asked to rate their subjective perception on a seven-point scale ranging from 1 = Not at all to 7 = Extremely.

3   Findings and Discussion

3.1 Decision-Making Time

As shown in Table 1, 1530 decision-making time data were obtained through the experiments. The results show that, regardless of the visual type, participants determined the direction faster when using AR-enhanced signage than existing signage. On average, the participants spent 1.644 s (SD = 0.899 s) when viewing the AR-enhanced signage, whereas they spent 2.529 s (SD = 1.282 s) in the existing system. In addition, participants found their way slightly faster with graphic signage (mean = 1.567 s; SD = 0.922 s) than textual signage (mean = 1.721 s; SD = 0.869 s) in AR settings. When people saw the AR-graphic signage, they found their direction on average 0.154 s faster than the AR-textual signage. It can be due to the fact that the cognitive load to understand graphics is relatively low [7]. Therefore, this result supports hypothesis 1 and hypothesis 2.

Table 1. Decision-making time (in Sec)

Categories	Time				
	n	Min	Max	Mean	SD
Existing signage	510	0.886	11.982	2.529	1.282
AR-textual signage	510	0.769	8.036	1.721	0.869
AR-graphic signage	510	0.541	10.611	1.567	0.922
Total	1530	0.541	11.982	1.939	1.122

3.2   Sign Design Evaluation

Table 2 demonstrates the result of the survey that assessed participants' perceptions of different visual types of signage. All mean ratings on the five features were above the midpoint (3.5) of the seven-point scale. Firstly, the participants responded that pictogram is the most uniform in AR environments (5.569). In addition, they rated pictogram at a high level in continuity (5.549). As the ratings in uniformity and continuity were similar, there is expected to be a connection between the two factors in the AR environment. On the other hand, participants responded that AR-textual signage was legible with a rating of 6.039. In terms of clarity, pictogram (5.902) and text (5.882) were evaluated as the most effective types at a similar level, whereas the rating for the logo was only 4.294. Finally, the type assessed to be the most aesthetic was pictogram with a rating of 5.255. While the pictogram signage was rated as the most aesthetic, the textual signage was considered the most readable in AR settings. The logo was assessed differently from others with the lowest rating in all factors except aesthetics.

Table 2. Sign design evaluation (n = 51)

Types	Ratings (Mean)				
	Uniformity	Continuity	Legibility	Clarity	Aesthetics
Text	5.275	5.314	6.039	5.882	4.118
Pictogram	5.569	5.549	5.843	5.902	5.255
Logo	4.078	4.608	4.549	4.294	4.588

3.3   Summary

Table 3 illustrates the outcomes from the hypothesis testing. In summary, people could find directions quickly when viewing AR-enhanced signage. Especially, AR-graphic signage was the most efficient type to find way faster in a complex indoor environment. Although graphic signage was the most effective in terms of time spending, textual signage was expected to be highly readable in AR environments. Moreover, in contrast to the case of the pictogram, the logo received a low evaluation. Therefore, it would be better to apply both graphics and text, avoiding the logo to improve wayfinding experience.

Table 3. Results of hypotheses testing

	Hypotheses	Result
H1	People can find directions faster when they use AR-enhanced sign system than the existing sign system, regardless of its type	Supported
H2	People can find directions faster when they use graphic signage than textual signage in AR environments	Supported
H3	In terms of sign design, graphic signage is the most effective in an AR environment	Not supported

4   Conclusion

Consumer experience in commercial spaces has a significant role in terms of purchasing intensions. However, the wayfinding difficulty in mixed-use shopping malls has been creating a negative customer experience. In these circumstances, improving wayfinding experience to eliminate negative experiences is critical for sustainable growth. Thus, the current study focused on investigating the viability of AR-enhanced signage to enhance wayfinding in mixed-use shopping malls. In terms of decision-making time, people found their directions faster with AR-enhanced directional signage. Besides, graphic elements not only improved wayfinding ability but also received high praise for the aesthetics of sign design. On the other hand, when it comes to legibility and clarity, the textual type was the most effective. Therefore, this study suggests the active use of both graphic and textual elements for AR-enhanced signage. Although this research was limited to the directional signage in shopping malls, the present paper shows the many possibilities for AR in a wayfinding context. Finally, this research proposes the wider application of AR to solve diverse problems in real-world situations.

Acknowledgements.   This work was supported by the BK21 Plus funded by the Ministry of Education of Korea.

References

1. Chebat, J.C., Gélinas-Chebat, C., Therrien, K.: Lost in a mall, the effects of gender, familiarity with the shopping mall and the shopping values on shoppers' wayfinding processes. J. Bus. Res. **58**(11), 1590–1598 (2005)
2. O'Neill, M.J.: Effects of signage and floor plan configuration on wayfinding accuracy. Environ. Behav. **23**(5), 553–574 (1991)
3. Poushneh, A., Vasquez-Parraga, A.Z.: Discernible impact of augmented reality on retail customer's experience, satisfaction and willingness to buy. J. Retail. Consum. Serv. **34**, 229–234 (2017)
4. Scholz, J., Smith, A.N.: Augmented reality: designing immersive experiences that maximize consumer engagement. Bus. Horiz. **59**(2), 149–161 (2016)
5. Weisman, J.: Evaluating architectural legibility: way-finding in the built environment. Environ. Behav. **13**(2), 189–204 (1981)

6. Bolen, W.H.: Contemporary Retailing. Prentice Hall, Upper Saddle River (1982)
7. Paas, F., Renkl, A., Sweller, J.: Cognitive load theory and instructional design: recent developments. Educ. Psychol. **38**(1), 1–4 (2003)
8. Passini, R.: Wayfinding in architecture (1984)
9. Arthur, P., Passini, R.: Wayfinding: people, signs, and architecture (1992)
10. Gibson, D.: The Wayfinding Handbook: Information Design for Public Places. Princeton Architectural Press, Princeton (2009)
11. Gensler Research Institute: Shaping the future of cities. Design Forecast, Gensler (2019)
12. Gensler Research Institute: Transforming the urban experience through design: Reinventing the mall, Dialogue 35, Gensler (2019)

Preliminary Study on the Influence of Visual Cues, Transitional Environments and Tactile Augmentation on the Perception of Scale in VR

Tobias Delcour Jensen, Filip Kasprzak, Hunor-Gyula Szekely, Ivan Nikolov[✉],
Jens Stokholm Høngaard, and Claus Madsen

Aalborg University, Rendsburggade 14, Aalborg 9000, Denmark
{tdje16,fkaspr16,hszeke16}@student.aau.dk, {iani,jsth,cbm}@create.aau.dk

Abstract. Virtual reality (VR) is being used more and more as a way to easily visualize and share ideas, as well as a step in product designing. The initial study presented in this paper is part of a project for getting the general public involved in the design of new busses for Northern Jutland in Denmark, by using VR visualization. An important part of VR visualizations is the correct understanding of scale. Studies show that the perception of scale in VR undergoes compression compared to the real world. In this paper we test how additional visual cues, transitional environments and tactile augmentation in a VR environment can help with the perception of scale. We show that familiar visual cues can help with the perception of scale, but do not remove the compression of perception. We can further mitigate the problem by introducing transitional environments and tactile augmentation, but transitional environments provide a better perception of scale than tactile augmentation.

Keywords: Virtual reality (VR) · Scale perception · Visual cues ·
Tactile augmentation · Transitional environments

1 Introduction

Virtual reality (VR) has become an important part in involving users during the design and testing process of manufacturing, before the final product is made. VR as a medium, allows for early and inexpensive public testing of products, resulting in a more rapid design process. This paper is part of a project to involve the populace in the design of new buses, before the final product is finalized. To make the process less time consuming and costly a VR visualization is selected. One of the main requirements for the project is to design the environment with a correct sense of scale and judgement of distances. This can become a problem because egocentric and exocentric distance perception in virtual reality gets affected by the compression of scale. In general, the estimated dimensions of virtual environments are about 74% of the actual modeled dimensions [1,2]. It

© Springer Nature Switzerland AG 2020
C. Stephanidis et al. (Eds.): HCII 2020, CCIS 1294, pp. 156–164, 2020.
https://doi.org/10.1007/978-3-030-60703-6_20

has been suggested that the cause of the compression is related to higher-level cognitive issues in the interpretation of the presented visual stimulus [3].

As humans perceive size and distances in many different ways, there are a variety of techniques used to estimate how big and how far away an object is in a scene. In this paper we present two experiment studies into how the user's perception of scale is influenced by three common factors:

1. Familiar objects as visual cues (VC) - the familiar size of an object influences the perceived size in agreement with the size-distance invariance [4];
2. Transitional environment (TE) - the change between real and virtual world can help with immersion and the perception of the virtual environment [13];
3. Tactile augmentation (TA) - the introduction of additional modalities and the insertion of the human body in VR helps with scale understanding and immersion [5–7].

The results confirmed that the availability of objects with a familiar scale increases the accuracy of scale perception. Having both a transitional environment and tactile augmentation greatly reduces the compression of scale, with the transitional environment proven to have a greater influence than tactile augmentation.

2 State of the Art

One way of decreasing the compression is through visual cues, such as binocular disparity, motion parallax and relative size. Loyala [9] found out that having multiple visual cues available helps explaining inaccuracies in dimension estimation in VR, especially for egocentric dimensions. Furthermore the findings indicates a trend that the accuracy of estimations rises with the level of cues available.

Another proven method is the introduction of a transitional environment. A replica of the real world can be made in VR and users can first start in that environment, making their transition into VR smoother and their sense of presence higher. Furthermore, gradually transitioning users from the virtual replica to a different scene, increases their presence in the real world [10,13].

Finally, tactile augmentation can be created when a virtual environment mixes real-life physical objects with their artificial representations, resulting in the user being able to touch real physical objects while being inside a virtual environment [11,12,14]. Allowing the users to interact physically with the objects through both visual and tactile cues, is found to increase presence and immersion [5,6].

In this paper we build upon these findings, by testing how combining these three elements can influence the perception of scale in VR.

3   Experimental Setup

As a basis for the experiments the virtual environment used is a 1:1 replica of the laboratory[1] (Fig. 2c) where the tests are carried out. It was created by measuring the laboratory and modeling all of its interior and positioning it in the correct places. The VR system used is the HTC Vive, as it provides the possibility for easy movement tracking, as well as both controller and tracker support. For creating the testing application, Unity was used together with StreamVR, while the interior was modeled using Maya. An overview of each of the experimental environments is given below.

3.1   Familiar Objects as Visual Cues

The laboratory environment was used as the testing environment. The first experiment introduced six real-world objects - bottle of water, mug, coca-cola can, milk carton, pendrive and a tennis ball. Virtual objects are created by modeling real world equivalents in Maya and scaling them to absolute real world scale, except the tennis ball, which is the one that users would need to scale. They are then placed corresponding with their real-life position (Fig. 1). The objects were deemed recognizable to the general public, as they represented items normally found in an office or home environment. All interactions are carried on with the use of the Vive controllers.

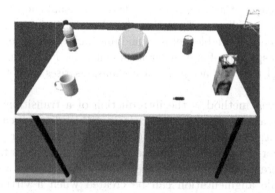

Fig. 1. The six modeled objects on a table in VR. The object are used for the first test-scaling the tennis ball correctly by using visual cues from the other objects.

3.2   Transitional Environment and Tactile Augmentation

The laboratory environment is used as the transitional environment. The second experiment introduces a real world bus chair and pole Fig. 2a, which are remade

---

[1] Model freely available from `graphics.create.aau.dk`.

in VR Fig. 2b, together with a bus model Fig. 2d, for test participants to walk around and interact with. The models are created in Maya, using real life images and sketches. The interaction with the environment are carried out using both the HTC Vive controller and a tracker for users hand. The modeled objects are also tracked using additional trackers.

Real-world chair, with attached tracker at the end of the pole

Render of the replica model of the chair

The laboratory environment

The bus environment

Fig. 2. The solution used a bus seat as a tactile augmented object and had two different environments

Because of the size of the bus, teleport points are used to move the user around, and from the transitional environment to the bus environment. Users can also move freely if needed. The outside environment was created with a 360 sphere textured with a simple real world location wrapped on the inside of the sphere. The outside environment was created with the intention of preserving the users focus on the inside environment of the bus, while still preserving the immersion of being inside a bus.

4   Experiments and Results

To evaluate people's perception of scale inside a virtual environment we designed two experiments. In the first one, the effects of familiar objects on the scale perception were assessed. In the second test, we tested the effects of Transitional Environment and Tactile Augmentation on the users' perception of scale.

4.1   Familiar Objects as Visual Cues Setup

The first experiment focused on testing whether the different visual cues added to the scene improve user's perception of scale. A total of 15 students participated in the experiment, all of them naive users of VR, with normal or corrected-to-normal vision.

At the beginning of the test, the participants saw a physical ball and were put in the replica of the testing lab in VR. They were tasked with scaling a VR ball to its real world size, using the controller to make adjustments. After confirming, the facilitators noted down the size. Then the participants took of the HMD and were presented with the ball and table with 5 additional objects in the real world. The same items were displayed on the table in the VE in the corresponding locations. Participants were then instructed again to scale the ball and after confirming the test was concluded. Each time the ball started from a different size.

4.2   Results

The data was found to be approximately normally distributed through Shapiro-Wilk's test. A paired T-test between the two case - with and without visual cues, was conducted and results were found to be significant ($p = 0.0256$, $p < 0.05$). A vast majority of the participants reported using the added objects as a point of reference when re-scaling the ball in the second part of the test.

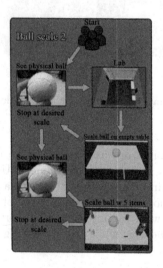
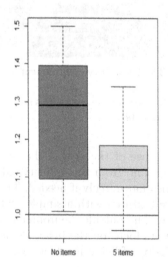

Fig. 3. Setup of the experiment 3a and the scale results in percentage from the first experiment, with and without items 3b. Red line shows correct scale. (Color figure online)

The participants on average over-scaled the ball by 25% in the condition without the visual-cues and 14% with the visual-cues (Fig. 3b). The difference in means suggests that adding visual cues to the virtual environment improves people's perception of scale, yet they still tend to over-scale the object. This general tendency to over-scale the object could mean that the participants try to compensate for the scale compression. This is further explored in the second experiment.

4.3   Transitional Environment and Tactile Augmentation Setup

The second experiment investigates how a transitional environment (TE) and tactile augmentation (TA) can further affect the users' perception of scale. A total of 40 participants have taken part in the experiment, 10 participants per condition in a between subject experiment. The participants are a combination of naive and experienced users and all have normal or corrected to normal vision.

The participants are tasked with scaling a bus they are in. The difference between the real scale of the bus and the participants' chosen scale is measured as accuracy. The test incorporates the model of the real laboratory as the TE, where users start the test, before being teleported to the bus model. The TA part of the experiments is in the form of a real bus chair and pole.

The test is split into four conditions in order to evaluate separate and combined effects of TE and TA on scale perception, these will be referred to as A, B, C and D respectively going forth.

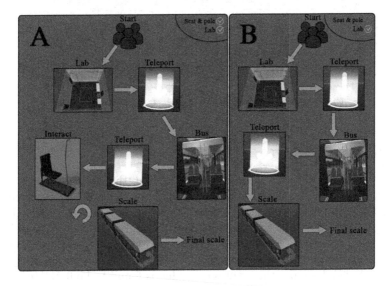

Fig. 4. Experimental Procedure for A and B conditions

The most complex setup is A (Fig. 4a) where the participants are first put in the replica of the lab as their TE. They are instructed to teleport out of the room to the bus when they felt ready. In the bus they can move around using three fixed teleport points located in the back, middle, and front of the bus and move freely in short distances. They can freely interact with the TA objects which are located in a fixed position in the bus. Afterwards they are instructed to adjust the scale of the bus, until they feel it is right. The scaling is performed on the whole model of the bus, including the TA objects. After confirming the scale the test is concluded.

Condition B (Fig. 4b) has the same procedure, excluding the interaction with the TA object. The model of the chair is still included in the bus environment, however the physical chair is not there for the participants to interact with. In the condition C (Fig. 5c) the participants started the test already in the bus, without the use of TE, but are allowed to interact with the TA objects. The last condition D (Fig. 5d) neither the TA or the TE are present, but the procedure stays the same.

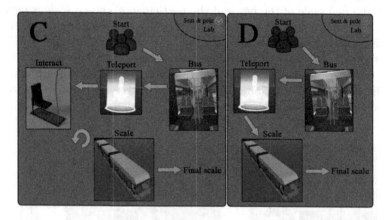

Fig. 5. Experimental Procedure for C and D conditions

4.4   Results

The Shapiro-Wilk test for normality showed that the data is approximately normally distributed for three out of the four groups. The p-values for Conditions A, B and C are 0.087(A), 0.437(B), 0.056(C) but for condition D it was 0.034(D), meaning that the data was not normally distributed. Furthermore, Levene's tests is performed, comparing condition A to B, C and D respectively, and confirmed that homogeneity requirements are met. The Kruskai-Wallis test is performed on the gathered data and the resulting p-value is found to be 0.211 ($p > 0.05$), meaning that no significant difference can be found. However, by looking at graphical representation of the data we can see that there is a difference between the means, as seen in Figs. 6a and 6b.

The results suggest that the use of TE before entering a VR simulation improves scale perception among participants. Those exposed to the replica of the lab before entering the bus (A, B), were able to scale its size more accurately

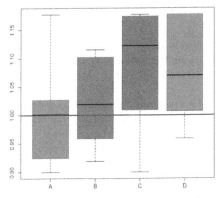
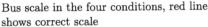

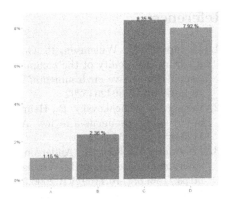

Bus scale in the four conditions, red line shows correct scale

Mean difference from 1:1 scale in % for all four conditions

Fig. 6. Results from the second experiment. Even if the results are shown to have no statistical difference, the calculated means demonstrate positive effect of TA and TE. (Color figure online)

to its real-life size, while participants in the conditions without TE (C, D) tended to overscale the bus around them, further suggesting that they were compensating for the compression of scale. This tendency resulted in the non-normal distribution in Condition D where 4 out of 10 participants set the scale to its maximum, and some even expressed that they would scale it up more if allowed to. The results also show that TE affects perception of scale more significantly than the use of TA element.

5   Conclusion

In this paper we presented a user study conducted on various ways to improve the perception of scale in VR, in a context of visualizing bus models. We tested three common factors - adding visual cues, transitional environment and tactile augmentation.

We demonstrate that every day objects, as visual cues alleviate the problems with perceiving scale, but the scale compression is still a problem. A second experiment is conducted introducing a transitional environment and tactile augmentation, in the form of a 3D modeled laboratory and a bus chair and pole. We show that scale compression is mostly reverted using both and a transitional environment gives better results on its own. With this we shown that the topic is worth further investigation. As future work we would like to verify the results using more participants, as well as test with different representations of the three factors.

References

1. Thompson, W., Willemsen, P., Gooch, A., Creem-Regehr, S., Loomis, J., Beall, A.: Does the quality of the computer graphics matter when judging distances in visually immersive environments? Presence **13**, 560–571 (2004). https://doi.org/10.1162/1054746042545292
2. Renner, R., Velichkovsky, B., Helmert, J.: The perception of egocentric distances in virtual environments-a review. ACM Surv. **46**, 1–40 (2013). https://doi.org/10.1145/2543581.2543590
3. Interrante, V., Ries, B., Anderson, L.: Distance perception in immersive virtual environments, revisited. In: Virtual Reality Conference, vol. 3–10. IEEE (2006). https://doi.org/10.1109/VR.2006.52
4. Predebon, J.: Perceived size of familiar objects and the theory of off-sized perceptions. Percept. Psychophys. **56**(2), 238–247 (1994)
5. Ahmed, FW., Cohen, J., Binder, K., Fennema, C.: Influence of tactile feedback and presence on egocentric distance perception in virtual environments. In: Proceedings-IEEE Virtual Reality, vol. 195–202 (2010). https://doi.org/10.1109/VR.2010.5444791
6. Zhao, Y., Forte, M., Kopper, R.: VR touch museum. In: 2018 IEEE Conference on Virtual Reality and 3D User Interfaces (VR), Reutlingen, pp. 741–742 (2018)
7. Chessa, M., Caroggio, L., Huang, H., Solari, F.: Insert Your Own Body in the Oculus Rift to Improve Proprioception, pp. 755–762 (2016). https://doi.org/10.5220/0005851807550762
8. Cutting, J.E., Vishton, P.M.: Perceiving layout and knowing distances : the integration, relative potency, and contextual use of different information about depth. Percept. SP Motion **22**(5), 69–117 (1995). https://doi.org/10.1037/0096-1523.22.5.1299
9. Loyola, M.: The influence of the availability of visual cues on the accurate perception of spatial dimensions in architectural virtual environments. Virtual Reality **22**(3), 235–243 (2018). https://doi.org/10.1007/s10055-017-0331-2
10. Steinicke, F., Bruder, G., Hinrichs, K., Lappe, M., Ries, B., Interrante, V.: Transitional environments enhance distance perception in immersive virtual reality systems. In: Proceedings of the 6th Symposium on Applied Perception in Graphics and Visualization (APGV'2009). Association for Computing Machinery, New York, NY, USA, pp. 19–26 (2009). https://doi.org/10.1145/1620993.1620998
11. Hoffman, H.G., et al.: Tactile Augmentation: Enhancing presence in virtual reality with tactile feedback from real objects (1996)
12. Hoffman, H.G.: Physically touching virtual objects using tactile augmentation enhances the realism of virtual environments. In: Proceedings-Virtual Reality Annual International Symposium, vol. 59–63 (1998). https://doi.org/10.1109/vrais.1998.658423
13. Sisto, M., Wenk, N., Ouerhani, N., Gobron, S.: A study of transitional virtual environments. In: De Paolis, L.T., Bourdot, P., Mongelli, A. (eds.) AVR 2017. LNCS, vol. 10324, pp. 35–49. Springer, Cham (2017). https://doi.org/10.1007/978-3-319-60922-5_3
14. Di Franco, P.D.G., Camporesi, C., Galeazzi, F., Kallmann, M.: 3D Printing and Immersive Visualization for Improved Perception of Ancient Artifacts, pp. 243–264. MIT Press, Cambridge (2015)

Comparative Analysis of Cricket Games in VR and Other Traditional Display Environments

Md. Zarif Kaisar[1,2]([⊠]), Md. Sirajuddin Borno[1,2], Fahim Estiyak[1,2], Md. Shayanul Haq[1,2], Farhana Sayed Juthi[1,2], and Khandaker Tabin Hasan[1,2]

[1] Department of Computer Science, American International University Bangladesh, Dhaka, Bangladesh
zarif.kaisar@gmail.com
[2] American International University Bangladesh, Dhaka, Bangladesh
info@aiub.edu
https://fst.aiub.edu/

Abstract. This research is study involves around a VR based cricket game. It uses the technology of VR to simulate the environment of a player playing cricket in the stadium. The research tries to state that how this type of game creates a more immersive and interactive experience compared to regular 2D/3D video games played in traditional display environments.

Keywords: Virtual reality · Video game controllers · Immersive experience · Human centered computing · Cricket video games

1 Introduction

Virtual Reality (VR) is a simulated experience that can be similar to or completely different from the real world. It is used for computer technology to create a simulated environment. Unlike traditional user interfaces, VR places the user inside an experience. Instead of viewing a screen in front of them, users are able to have immersive experience and able to interact with artificially generated3D worlds. By simulating as many senses as possible, such as vision, hearing, touch, even smell, the computer is transformed into a gatekeeper to this artificial world. The only limits to near-real VR experiences are the availability of content and cheap computing power. It could range from creating a video game to having a virtual stroll around the universe, from walking through our own dream house to experiencing of playing cricket on virtual ground. This creates and immersive and interactive experience [14].

Cricket is an international game that is pretty popular these days. The games that are played in traditional display environments such as laptops, monitors,smartphone screens etc. are developed in 3D or 2D, which makes it harder for the user/player to have the immersive and interactive experience that VR gives.

© Springer Nature Switzerland AG 2020
C. Stephanidis et al. (Eds.): HCII 2020, CCIS 1294, pp. 165–172, 2020.
https://doi.org/10.1007/978-3-030-60703-6_21

In this research we try to analyze the whole paradigm of cricket games in these platforms and compare them head to head to identify how our VR based simulation cricket game creates a more immersive and interactive experience compared to 2D, 3D games played with traditional controllers such as joysticks, Dualshock, keyboards and other forms of controllers.

2   Literature Review

The **Cricket VR** game we had developed is a virtual reality game which is similar to the normal cricket game like *Cricket 2007,King of Spin* etc. but it is a realistic cricket simulator compared to the previously mentioned games which are played with either mouse and keyboard or game controllers in traditional display environments such as monitors, tv's, phone displays etc. (Fig. 1).

Fig. 1. VR vs. 3D [2,3]

The VR games of cricket from *steam* and other platforms differ from the 3D games drastically as they are played from very different perspectives. Cricket 3D games such as *Cricket 2007* [10], *Cricket 19* [11], *Ashes Cricket* [13], *Don Bradman Cricket 14* [13] etc. can provide such a nice gaming experience but they are not immersive, interactive and nonetheless way less realistic. The existing cricket games developed in VR such as *Cricket Club* [5], *Balls! Virtual Reality Cricket* [6], *JUST BAT (VR CRICKET)* [7], *CricVX - VR Cricket* [8], *VR Cricket* [7], *King of Spin VR* [2] etc. are very realistic and that is why have more enjoyable experience due to their immersive and interactive nature.

3   Methodology

Although there are tons of VR based cricket games out there we wanted to create one of ourselves for this research so that we can structure the game with our own rules and optimize it as well as have a better control over the game mechanics.

It is a cricket simulator game we have developed called **Cricket VR** was developed in Unity [4]. It contains One big cricket stadium, ball, bat, stump and a score board are used in the game. We designed the game to mimic the real life feel of the cricket game. The player sits at the batting position for now. The bowling or fielding simulation has not been implemented yet.

Some important information about the game:

- Different colliders such as *mesh collider* were implemented in unity.
- Different types of Algorithms were developed to spawn new ball for changing the direction of the ball after drop.
- In the game balls keep coming and you hit the ball with the bat.
- The number of balls, wickets and run is shown in the bill board inside the stadium.

3.1 Gameplay Demonstration

Fig. 2. Gameplay demonstration

This gameplay demonstrates from the first person perspective of the player. Hitting the balls coming towards the players (Fig. 2).

3.2 Survey Questionnaire Preparation Procedure

We designed a survey questionnaire consisting 9 questions with *Survey Monkey* [1]. We used Likert scale in the questionnaire. The surveys were conducted by hand using the offline app of *Survey Monkey* after letting the participants play the game for a few minutes. We asked questions about the learning curve, intuitiveness, interactivity, performance and the overall gameplay experience with VR. The target audience consisted of three age groups. 13–18 were teenage and school, high school years. 19–24 were college or university years and finally 25–35 consisted of people from the industry. The three most likely age groups who will most definitely play the game. In total there were 16 respondents. All of them participated in the survey voluntarily.

4 Results and Analysis

4.1 Results

The results of the aforementioned survey are given below:

Q1. How realistic is the game environment?

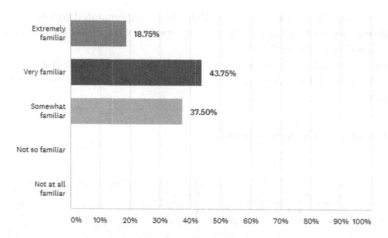

Q2. What is your age group?
Unfortunately we couldn't conduct survey on the first and last groups. We only conducted survey on age groups of 19–24.

Q3. Is the game-play and controller setup interactive and responsive?
Everyone responded yes that they found the controller to responsive and interactive.

Q4. Was it intuitive and easy to learn?
Everyone responded yes that they found the controller to responsive and interactive.

Q5. Is the haptic feedback properly working?

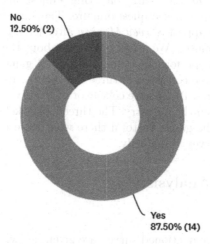

Q6. Which is more intuitive and enjoyable for this type of game?

All of the participants enjoyed the cricket game in VR more than the 3D flat display experience they get while playing in monitors.

Q7. How was your overall experience while playing in VR?

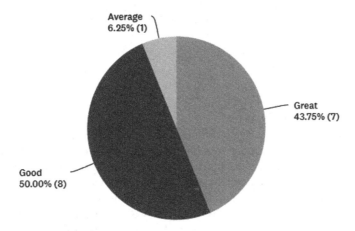

Q8. Is the game worth playing in VR?

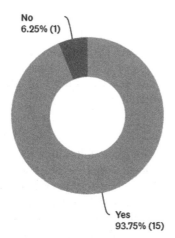

Q9. What were the major problems you have faced in the game?

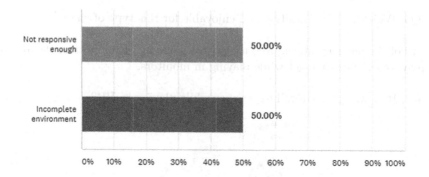

4.2 Analysis

Statistical Data Analysis
The data shows that if the environment was complete the responses the participants would have felt more familiar with the game environment. But that depends on his/her experience playing cricket as well. Other than that, data clearly shows that the game with the controllers was way more immersive than any keyboard based games. They found it easy to learn and very intuitive. All of them responded that they think that the VR game was more intuitive and enjoyable than their 2D/3D counterparts. Also, hap tic feedback and responsiveness needs to be improved a bit. While most of them enjoyed the game in VR some of them would have preferred a better overall experience. Most of them think the game was worth playing in VR which was more than 90%. But still I think we need to up our sample size. We identified the two core problems of this research that is our incomplete environment and occasionally unresponsive gameplay. Statistics show that both of the problems go head to head because half of the participants selected one and the other half selected the other problem. We need to put emphasis on fixing both.

Comparative Analysis
In compared to other games our game falls short because of short development time. Those games have significantly more features and are much better in many ways. But compared to the 3D games it was quite a bit more enjoyable experience according to the results. And comparing to the other 2D, 3D cricket games we didn't include to let the participants play back to back in 2D/3D and VR, but we will incorporate them in the next research plan.

5 Limitations

There are certain limitations of this project. They are:

- Occasionally unresponsive Gameplay.
- Incomplete Environment.
- Lack of Bowling, Fielding mode.

- Bat hit throws the ball in random directions sometimes.
- Insufficient number of features.
- Insufficient Sample Size.

6   Future Work

- Making it properly responsive.
- Incorporating the Bowling and Fielding mechanics of the game.
- More Features.
- A more in depth comparative analysis between experience of 2D/3D games and VR cricket games by letting the players play each type of game back to back.
- Bigger Sample Size.
- Better and more improved questionnaire.

7   Conclusion

VR technology is comparatively new to the general public. Although people are catching up to it and the technology is getting better everyday, it would take a while for everyone to take it as a norm of life. But in the world of gaming experiences VR is way more realistic and gives a much more immersive experience. And with the controllers improving it, is becoming seamless day by day. VR would certainly be more popular than non VR games.

Acknowledgments. During the development of the project *Cricket VR* assistance provided by another student named Eraj from our university (AIUB) department of CSSE was greatly appreciated.

References

1. Survey Monkey HomePage. https://www.surveymonkey.com/. Accessed 25 Aug 2019
2. King of Spin VR Image. https://www.indiedb.com/games/king-of-spin-vr/images/image-3. Accessed 25 Aug 2019
3. Cricket 2007 Image. https://ea-sports-cricket.en.softonic.com/. Accessed 25 Aug 2019
4. Unity Homepage. https://unity.com/. Accessed 25 Nov 2019
5. Cricket Club. https://store.steampowered.com/app/772180/Cricket_Club//. Accessed 25 Nov 2019
6. Balls! Virtual Reality Cricket. https://store.steampowered.com/app/517220/Balls_Virtual_Reality_Cricket/. Accessed 25 Nov 2019
7. JUST BAT (VR CRICKET). https://store.steampowered.com/app/525950/JUST_BAT_VR_CRICKET/. Accessed Nov 2019
8. CricVRX - VR Cricket. https://store.steampowered.com/app/1109550/CricVRX_VR_Cricket/. Accessed 25 Nov 2019

9. VR Cricket. https://store.steampowered.com/app/951110/VR_Cricket/. Accessed 25 Nov 2019
10. Cricket 2007. https://www.ea.com/games/cricket/cricket-2007. Accessed 25 Nov 2019
11. Cricket 19. https://store.steampowered.com/app/1028630/Cricket_19/. Accessed 25 Nov 2019
12. Ashes Cricket. https://store.steampowered.com/app/649640/Ashes_Cricket/. Accessed 25 Nov 2019
13. Don Bradman Cricket 14. https://store.steampowered.com/app/216260/Don_Bradman_Cricket_14/. Accessed 25 Nov 2019
14. What is Virtual Reality? [Definition and Examples]. https://www.marxentlabs.com/what-is-virtual-reality/. Accessed 25 Nov 2019

Molecular Augmented Reality for Design and Engineering (MADE): Effectiveness of AR Models on Discovery, Learning, and Education

Hyejin Hannah Kum-Biocca[(⊠)] [ID], Edgardo T. Farinas [ID],
Nisha Mistry, and Yutong Wan

New Jersey Institute of Technology, Newark, NJ 07102, USA
hannahbiocca@gmail.com

Abstract. The design and manipulation of chemical systems involves understanding the form or morphology of chemical structures. An understand of the form of chemical structure includes an understanding of the components of chemical structure, the functions of the forms and sub-components, and changes in the structure of chemical systems during interaction, maturation, or chemical processes. Viewed from a computer graphic viewpoint these chemical processes can be described and modelled as three-dimensional structures, changing shape, and interacting with other 3D structures. Furthermore, our intuition was that the visualization should be as embodied as possible and open for collaboration.

In this project we seek to create a tool for collaborative, embodied visualization of biomolecules. To achieve this interaction with targeted for hand on visualizations allowing for biomolecular exploration and scientific visualization within immersive augmented reality platforms. We anticipate a tool where components can assist both in (1) biomolecule discovery and design and a subset applicable for (2) education in biomolecules. We conducted some formative research to analyze user value and requirement.

For the prototype we focused on the visualization of DNA binding protein, called Zip Proteins. These proteins are transcription factors. This system is implemented across two devices that support AR capabilities: head mount display (HMD) and the mobile phone. Key development is the porting of these molecules to immersive augmented reality environment for direct interaction.

Describing the advantage of the platform for this application at the broadest level, we can say that augmented reality platforms allow for full embodied interaction with the structures at any scale and contextualized by the physical background. We also discuss future plans for this platform.

Keywords: Augmented reality · Chemistry · Education · Scientific visualization

1 Introduction

Efficient design, optimization, engineering, and investigation of biological and chemical systems are necessary for a variety of industrial and biotechnological goals. Design of biological systems includes, but is not limited to, drug design, improving enzymes

© Springer Nature Switzerland AG 2020
C. Stephanidis et al. (Eds.): HCII 2020, CCIS 1294, pp. 173–180, 2020.
https://doi.org/10.1007/978-3-030-60703-6_22

for green chemical synthesis and bioremediation, and creating new materials. If the molecular mechanisms can be uncovered, then the ultimate goal of molecules designed to order can be fulfilled.

1.1 Manipulating Form and Structure: The Bridge Between Biochemistry and 3D Visualization

The design and manipulation of chemical systems involves understanding the form or morphology of chemical structures. An understanding of the form of chemical structure includes an understanding of the components of the chemical structure, the functions of the forms and sub-components, and changes in the structure of chemical systems during interaction, maturation, or chemical processes.

So often, both chemistry discovery and education deal with understanding 3D structures of molecules, the components of these structures, and their functions. Both use this understanding to iterate new forms or to manipulate the forms. Discovery in the chemical and biological sciences have been advanced by tools for capturing and visualizing molecular forms at small scales. For example, scientists analyze microscopic entities at increasingly powerful scales to gain a greater visual understanding of chemical compounds at an atomic level.

Viewed from a computer graphic viewpoint these chemical processes can be described and modelled as three-dimensional structures, changing shape, and interacting with other 3D structures. Understanding and becoming intuitively familiar with these 3D forms is applicable in the design of new biomolecules and education involve the ability to discover and visualize chemical compounds and chemical reactions.

Interactive visualizations provide the ability to discover and visualize chemical compounds and chemical reactions on a molecular level to create an interactive exploration of simulation of a chemical compound. Additionally, a visualization tool for biomolecules can aid in the fulfillment of educational needs and investigate basic science questions.

Molecules and biomolecules are best understood when visualized in 3-dimensions in simulations that approximate the physical structures in nature. The intuitive grasp of the physical structures can be lost in the traditional course format that relies solely on lectures, textbooks, and PowerPoint presentations. Improving the visualization in 3-dimensions of chemical processes can help "bridge the gap" between theoretical concepts and practical application.

1.2 Development Background and Goals

In this project we seek to create a tool for collaborative, embodied visualization of biomolecules. We anticipate a tool where components can assist both in (1) biomolecule discovery and design and a subset applicable for (2) education in biomolecules.

Beginning stages of development of the augmented reality (AR) visualization system focused on formative research, prototyping and design, and development.

Research consisted of understanding the current industrial and biotechnological tools and processes used to investigate complex chemical compounds. These included visualization tools. The details are reported elsewhere.

Furthermore, our intuition was that the visualization should be as embodied as possible and open for collaboration. To achieve this interaction with targeted for hand on visualizations allowing for biomolecular exploration and scientific visualization within immersive augmented reality platforms. Technological functionalities, developmental limitations, and usability goals were the primary focus when prototyping and designing the augmented reality visualization system.

2 Formative Research

2.1 User Discovery and Requirements

Through the NSF-I Corps customer discovery process we were able to discover and understand our target user and requirements. By iterating through multiple business model canvases, we were able to establish two distinct user and customer segments with corresponding requirements and value propositions [1]. The two distinct groups of customers included life science professionals and those interested in education, such as educators, students, parents, and museum educators, and school systems (Fig. 1).

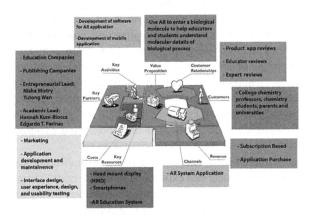

Fig. 1. Business model canvas (20 interviews (7 Educators, 12 Chemistry Students, and 1 Life Science Professional))

For life science professionals, our value proposition was to use AR to enter a biological molecule, which would help identify targets faster and cheaper. Life science professionals would efficiently design, optimize, engineer and investigate biological and chemical systems for a variety of industrial and biotechnological goals. They can use drug design, improvement of enzymes for green chemical synthesis and bioremediation, which assists in the creation of new materials.

For those interested in education, our value proposition was to help them understand molecular details of the biological process. It would aid in the fulfillment of educational needs and investigate basic science questions. Furthermore, it would provide life science professionals and those interested in education the ability to discover and visualize chemical compounds and chemical reactions on a molecular level to create an interactive exploration experience. Lastly, they would be able to analyze microscopic entities and gain a greater visual understanding of chemical compounds at an atomic level.

2.2 User Discovery Interviews

After identifying our target markets, we conducted interview individuals from those groups to understand requirements of the interface and how it would be of use for them. Before interviewing our selected customer segments, we developed interview questions. The questions included general questions such as what their day to day looked like, what struggles they faced, etc. However, certain questions were specific pertaining to each customer segment.

Through the 20 interviews, we found that educators believe that experiential learning is an effective teaching method. Therefore, through AR we will be able to accelerate student's educational benefits. Since we were focusing on educators and students, we interviewed chemistry professors and chemistry students at New Jersey Institute of Technology (NJIT). Most students preferred when professors utilized videos when lecturing as it was a more engaging way to understand the material. They felt that textbooks and PowerPoints were the least effective methods when teaching chemistry concepts, as it difficult to conceptualize and visualize the material. Additionally, most students felt that using an AR system to learn complex chemistry concepts, as it would provide a new avenue that current learning methods do not provide.

Introducing new technology to the field required extensive involvement in the customer discovery process accomplished through The National Science Foundation's Innovation Corps (NSF-I Corps) Program. Through the process, we were able to identify customer segments, their needs, and limitations, and establish values propositions for key customer divisions.

Our goal was to implement an augmented reality visualization system to allow a wide range of users to manipulate and explore complex chemical compounds. Through our AR system, users would be able to scale the visualization for embodied interaction with the models. As a result, engagement and interactivity through augmented reality will help users to understand complicated structures more easily.

3 Design Approach and Prototype

3.1 Prototype Target: Molecular Model

An understanding of research-valid chemical composition and molecular structures play a critical role when creating 3-dimensional models. It was important to continuously work and validate our 3D molecular models to create a scientifically informed and authentic experience. The ability to accurately design, as well as effectively integrate the 3-dimensional models into the physical world, require multiple design iterations.

3.2 Design Iterations

For the prototype we focused on the visualization of DNA binding protein, called Zip Proteins. These proteins are transcription factors. They have clinical importance. For example, overexpression can lead to cancer. As a result, they are anticancer targets.

The models in Fig. 2 are of Eukaryotic DNA binding protein. The protein is composed of 2-alpha helices. It resembles a two-pronged fork. The stem forms a coiled-coil. The top view is a coiled-coil from above. In this visualization we can label each residue as we go down the helix a-g, the it repeats again. The top part of the Zip protein binds to DNA. Structure of just coiled coil ball and stick. DNA contacts the protein at the fork by basic residues. DNA binding occurs in the major groove.

The visualization includes a color spectrum to make the structures more distinguishable at different angles of examination (from Chimera X).

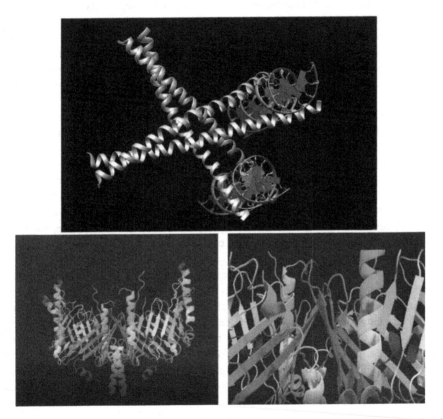

Fig. 2. Visualization of DNA binding protein, called Zip Proteins, complex structures rendered more meaningful under rotation and examination.

Models were acquired and exported from UCSF Chimera to Unity for visualization and interaction with the models. Chimera is broad featured program for interactive visualization and analysis of molecular structures. It includes data, density maps, supramolecular assemblies, sequence alignments, docking results, trajectories, and conformational ensembles.

3.3   Use of Augmented Reality Technology for Biochemistry

This system is implemented across two devices that support AR capabilities: head mount display (HMD) and the mobile phone. The head mount display includes the HoloLens 2. The platform allows for a more immersive experience, while the mobile phone is able to reach a larger number of users, as it is more widely accessible. Both devices allow users to manipulate molecules in a live setting.

While biomolecules can be visualized in different platforms, there are a number of reasons to interact with these complex structures in augmented reality versus the most common virtual platforms mobile phones and PCs.

Describing the advantage of the platform for this application at the broadest level, we can say that augmented reality platforms allow for full embodied interaction with the structures at any scale and contextualized by the physical background. We can unpack this statement in different features that are valuable for examining and manipulating complex models in this domain.

However, an advantage of utilizing an HMD device, such as HoloLens 2, is that it allows for a hands-free experience. Unlike the mobile device, where the user is required to occupy one hand holding the phone, the HMD device allows users to utilize both hands when interacting and exploring chemical compounds.

In the augmented reality system users directly use their hands to scale and rotate objects while interacting. Users move their bodies around the structures to understand the forms while they can scale the structures around their body to any size. Through these AR devices and implementation of molecular visualization software, users can "shrink" to the size of the atoms or they can scale up the molecule to gain a closer insight on molecular morphology.

This embodied exploration can be done in groups of users each positioned around the models, gesturing, and interacting with the simulations and visualization (Fig. 3).

Augmented reality (AR) can be integrated into design, optimization, engineering, and investigation of biological and chemical systems. It may be critical to gain a deep understanding of chemical processes that take place on a molecular scale and then transform these processes into an AR platform. A molecular visualization system thus created allows the scientists, molecular engineers, and biological architects to manipulate and explore complex chemical compounds.

Fig. 3. 3D molecular visualization models implemented Mobile Phone (left), HMD (Right)

3.4 The Applications of the AR Visualization System

The AR visualization platform can be used by pharmaceutical and chemical industries, specifically to visualize physiological processes of complex chemical compounds. Engagement and interactivity through augmented reality help easily relay complicated structures. AR allows the integration of computer-generated models into the physical world, creating a familiar, but authenticate experience, possibly mitigating restrictions experienced in a traditional lab setting. The ability to virtually touch and manipulate 3-dimensional models enables a detailed experience.

The utilization of augmented reality to visualize and manipulate 3D molecular models for an education application cultivates a highly captivating learning environment. It provides a new dimension to supplement the curriculum, allowing engagement and interactivity amongst students. Educators can modernize and enhance study material and accompany the traditional teaching approach, by letting students connect with the educational material through AR. Using AR to engage with chemical compounds and reactions in a safer environment, which is still a "hands-on" approach for students. Furthermore, mobile AR is a convenient tool that students can access on the palm of their hands. Experiential learning is gaining popularity in the education system and through AR we can accelerate student's educational benefits.

4   Use and Prospective Development

4.1 Continued Development of the MADE AR Visualization System

We continuously work and validate our 3D molecular models to create an authentic experience. The ability to accurately design, as well as, effectively integrate the 3-dimensional models into the physical world also require multiple design iterations.

Future development for the AR visualization system across both devices HMD and mobile device requires user study.

We anticipate a user study to provide key developmental insight on functionalities and features that may be implemented. The study will determine the effectiveness of our visualization software in comparison to the traditional learning method. Participants will be divided into three groups, one group will utilize the traditional learning methods, one group will use head mount display with AR visualization software, and one group will use the AR visualization software with mobile phone. Traditional learning methods include lectures, textbooks, and PowerPoint presentations taught in a standard classroom setting. We will measure the differences between the groups including learning abilities, information retention, quality of visualization, and the efficacy of the education system. Through research and usability testing we will be able to revise and tailor the application for user's needs.

Furthermore, it will be integral to gain user feedback through user testing, preferably in a laboratory or classroom setting, to gage an understanding of the effectiveness of the application in comparison to the traditional teaching method of lectures, PowerPoints, and textbooks.

Reference

1. Steve Blank Business Model versus Business Plan. https://steveblank.com/category/business-model-versus-business-plan/. Accessed 04 Mar 2020

Towards Motor Learning in Augmented Reality: Imitating an Avatar

Eva Lampen[1,2]([✉]) [iD], Maximilian Liersch[1,2], and Jannes Lehwald[1] [iD]

[1] EvoBus GmbH, Neu-Ulm, Germany
{eva.lampen,jannes.lehwald}@daimler.com
[2] CITEC, Bielefeld University, Bielefeld, Germany

Abstract. Divers methods to train motions exist in multiple domains such as sports, rehabilitation or in industrial use cases. With regard to findings considering imitation learning in real world scenarios and social interaction guidelines in extended realities (XR), in this paper the transferability of these real world effects to AR is investigated within an assembly scenario. On that basis, a comparative user study ($N = 12$) was conducted analysing implicit imitation learning as well as the impact on the performance. Therefore, besides the measurement of the completion time, motion data are captured and a first analysis of the data is conducted. Whereas in terms of the cumulative completion time, no significant differences between trained and untrained subjects can be measured, the avatar's motion was imitated differently between the groups. More precise, for the similarity of motion pattern between the avatar's motion and the motion of the subjects it was shown that the untrained imitated the motions significantly more often than the trained, but both groups imitated in general. The results provide a first insight of the possibilities and limits of imitation learning in AR. With respect to the specific assembly use case, an avatar assistance method could enhance the learning, considering performance parameters and could lead to an implicit imitation of ergonomic motion patterns while having free cognitive capacity for conducting the specific processes.

Keywords: Augmented reality · Motion similarity · Human computer interaction · Assistance

1 Introduction

Learning of manual tasks (i.e. motor learning) has a wide-ranging relevance in various domains, such as sports, rehabilitation or in industrial use cases like the assembly. The development of divers assistance methods with the goal of motor learning gain importance, especially utilizing augmented reality (AR) methods [12]. However, only a few putting emphasis on the development of applications on the basis of observation of an avatar [1,2,11] or parts of an avatar [6] and thus utilizing the effects of imitation learning. Particularly, within the assembly use case, procedural skills of knowing how to suitable conduct a specific task are

© Springer Nature Switzerland AG 2020
C. Stephanidis et al. (Eds.): HCII 2020, CCIS 1294, pp. 181–188, 2020.
https://doi.org/10.1007/978-3-030-60703-6_23

important [21]. Therefore, a process-oriented assistance for an accurate motion execution without the consequence of performance loss or an unergonomic task execution is essential. With regard to findings considering imitation learning in real world scenarios and social interaction guidelines in XR, in this paper the possibility of implicit imitation learning in AR is investigated within a manual assembly use case.

2   Related Work

In the following an overview concerning the related work of imitation learning of motions and social interaction guidelines in XR is given.

2.1   Motor Learning by Imitation

Imitation of motion performed by self and others is an important learning concept requiring complex mechanisms [17]. Among other things, by implicating the so-called mirror system, which responds during action observation and action execution [16], perceived actions can be mapped onto the own body [17]. Besides the learning of unknown motion pattern, already known ones are consolidated or even adjusted by the comparison of an observed motion to the existing representation. Due to the adaption of the observed motion and therefore the possibility of learning an inaccurate motion, there is a need of expert-based motion presentation within imitation learning. Whereas the concept of expert-based learning is widely adopted, a shortage of such experts for real world motor learning exists [12]. Furthermore, real world imitation learning relies on the expert knowledge. Although experts perform accurate motion, they could be unaware of the importance of specific parts of the motion and their explicit demonstration [15]. To overcome the mentioned limitations of real world imitation learning, digital sensor-based learning by imitation gain importance and has the opportunity of process simplification [12]. With the goal of free attention capacities for the task performance, especially AR methods are beneficial in terms of cognitive savings [10]. Due to the fact that if the information is presented true to scale and with spatial correctness, the cognitive effort is minimized to the transfer from external space to an egocentric perspective, likewise in real world imitation learning. Whereas in the literature, evaluations on explicit learning of correct motions by imitation in extended reality (XR) exists [1,2,6], implicit imitation learning in XR is rarely investigated.

2.2   Social Interaction Guidelines in XR

Research on social interaction effects in XR gain importance, due to the potential of such methods [7]. To realize imitation learning in AR and thus presenting an augmented human to the user, the consideration of general social interaction guidelines in XR is crucial. With respect to the visualization of an augmented human, the findings of [8] indicate the importance of body presence of a digital assistant and furthermore an increasing acceptance of the digital avatar if motions are realized. Besides the parameter of acceptance and with consideration of performance parameter, [13] proved evidence of the occurrence of social facilitation and inhibition effects in AR, in addition to discomfort being inside the avatar. To overcome a performance decrease due to the feeling of a presence of another person, a personalized avatar could alter that feeling into embodiment. With respect to the gender [5] and furthermore the appearance [20], a personalization of an avatar results into an increased persuasive power and body ownership and therefore, could minimize the feeling of a presence of another person. Considering the presented motion, a natural presentation is important. Additionally to the goal of learning accurate motions and therefore the need of proper motion presentations, the acceptance of the avatar is increased with a natural occlusion [9].

3   Evaluated Process-Oriented Assistance

With respect to the stated related work of social interaction guidelines in XR and the assumption of lacking knowledge considering implicit imitation learning in AR, a process-oriented assistance visualizing a human avatar is utilized for the evaluation.

To minimize possible effects due to the avatar's appearance, the anthropometry of the avatar is in accordance to the 50th percentile German male [14]. Moreover, to enable the imitation of realistic motions, the visualized poses are based on motion data captured with the XSens system [18]. Therefore, an employee with manual assembly experience as well as similar anthropometry to the body data of the avatar, served as a basis for the target motion data. For neglection of a random conduction of similar movement pattern, multiple solution strategies with regard to the upper body (see Fig. 1(a)) and likewise the lower body parts (see Fig. 1(b)) are captured and visualized. In general, the entire body of the avatar is presented. However, if body parts obscuring relevant parts or objects, only the arms and hands are visible henceforth. Furthermore, only the end effectors are visible at the end of the visualized motion. Therefore, the user is still aware of the hand's end pose without feeling uncomfortably by stepping inside the avatar.

4   Evaluation

A user study utilizing the process-oriented assistance was conducted, were we investigated the implicit imitation of motion pattern in a binary way and furthermore, the effects to the completion time.

4.1   Experimental Design

A laboratory hardware setup with respect to a stationary real world working environment was designed. The car door assembly setup consists of a start/end

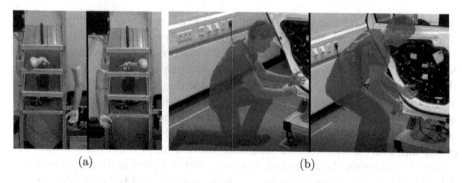

(a)   (b)

Fig. 1. Exemplary visualization of the process-oriented assistance with different motion pattern concerning (a) the upper body and (b) the lower body. For example, once the grasping is performed with the right hand and within another take with the left hand. Motion pattern considering the lower body parts, are for instance doing a lunge or a forward bend.

zone, picking zone, pre-assembly zone and assembly zone. The participants wore a AR-HMD, i.e. HoloLens, for the visualization of the presented process-oriented assistance and besides that, a Xsens MVN motion capture suit [18]. Each participant had to assemble the car door two times and each run consists of nine visualized sequences. For taking limited capacity of the working memory into account [4], a sequence includes only interactions with a specific object at one zone. For example, being in the start zone, the following assistance sequence comprises the walking to the picking zone and furthermore, the grasping of the relevant objects. To differ between the car door assembly qualification levels, i.e. trained and untrained, a training period was conducted for 50% of the participants. For the grouping, to neglect differences due to prior AR knowledge, this was used as blocking factor in a randomized block design. Furthermore, during the learning period a goal-oriented pictorial paper-based assistance method, without presenting human poses, was utilized. Thus, learning effects considering the usage of the assistance method can be neglected. And beyond that, trained participants need to develop their own solution strategies. The learning period lasted at least five runs and was finished when no improvements higher 10% could be recognized (M = 6.50 runs and SD = 1.23 runs), considering the power law of practice [19]. Afterwards, a simple test task was conducted for each of the participants with the objective of familarization with the presented process-oriented assistance method. During the subsequent experimental period the visualized motion pattern of the process-oriented assistance changed in a randomized way, however with the specification that every participants experiences every motion pattern once. For the evaluation of implicit imitation learning, the participants were only informed that the overall goal is to assemble the door correctly and at a moderate speed, without being aware of the motion similarity evaluation criteria.

4.2   Results

Overall twelve participants, students and research engineers took part in the multi factorial study. The participants were aged between 21 and 28 years (untrained: 25.00 ± 3.03, trained: 23.83 ± 1.17). To neglect possible effects due to dissimilarity with the visualized avatar and possible effects due to the handedness, all of the participants were male and right-handed. Furthermore, as a specification the difference in human height (untrained: $1.78\,\text{m} \pm 0.06\,\text{m}$, trained: $1.81\,\text{m} \pm 0.07\,\text{m}$) was less than 10% compared to the avatar's height of $1.75\,\text{m}$. Prior AR knowledge, reported by a 5 point Likert scale rating, was comparable among the groups (untrained: 1.83 ± 1.17, trained: 1.83 ± 0.98). The results, considering the binary evaluation of motion similarity were statistically analysed using a mixed ANOVA. For the cumulative completion time an unpaired two sample t-test was utilized.

Motion Similarity. To analyse motion similarity, the captured Xsens video data are visually compared to the related avatar's motion in terms of performed motion pattern. Therefore, six tasks are analysed per participant, which are demonstrated by the avatar in two different ways, i.e. twelve recordings. The analysed tasks are categorized in accordance to the adjusted general assembly task model [3]. Precisely, the *Locate Part* category comprises the tasks the upper body is positioned with the goal to grasp a part. *Locate Pos* is defined as category with tasks in which the carried part is aligned with the target position. Besides the analysis of motion patterns concerning upper body parts, motion patterns with regard to lower body parts are examined. The binary analysis is depicted in Fig. 2(a). The average of similar motion pattern over all task categories is for the trained participants 63.33% (SD = 18.21%) and for the untrained participants 88.33% (SD = 18.21%). With regard to the different task categories the trained group shows the highest accordance of conducted motion pattern within the *Locate Part* category with M = 75.00% and SD = 20.92% (*Locate Pos + Upper Body*: 60.00% $\pm$ 22.36%, *Locate Pos + Lower Body*: 60.00% $\pm$ 14.91%). The untrained participants imitated the tasks the most within the category of *Locate Pos + Upper Body* with M = 100.00% and SD = 0.00% (*Locate Part*: 95.00% $\pm$ 11.18%, *Locate Pos + Lower Body*: 70.00% $\pm$ 13.94%). The results of the mixed ANOVA reveals a significant difference for the qualification level with $p < 0.01$, however none for the task categories ($p > 0.05$) and none for interaction effects ($p > 0.05$).

Cumulative Completion Time. With regard to the cumulative completion time, the assembly was completed when the car door was correctly assembled twice. Due to the sequential demonstration of the single tasks, the cumulative completion time is summed. In Fig. 2(b) the results for the cumulative completion time are visualized. The trained group needed less time with an average of 242.27 s (SD = 28.79 s) compared to the untrained group (M = 271.04 s, SD = 31.17 s). However, the results are not significantly different with $p > 0.05$.

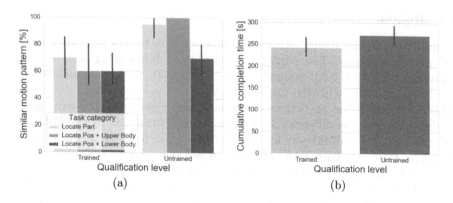

Fig. 2. Results of (a) motion similarity and (b) cumulative completion time.

4.3   Discussion

As from real world imitation learning expected, an implicit imitation of the demonstrated avatar's motion is occurred, both for the untrained and the trained. Although the untrained imitated the motion pattern significantly more often. Due to the fact that the different tasks are conducted twice and for every trial a different motion pattern is demonstrated, an random conduction of similar movement pattern could only explain 50% of similar motions. However, thus the percentage of motion similarity for trained and untrained is higher than 50% a general imitation can be assumed. Interestingly, the trained group imitated the avatar although basic task solution strategies should be developed during the training process. Perhaps, due to the fact that the trained group's task-dependent cognitive load was less, the free attention capacities are dedicated to the demonstrated instructions and with respect to the related work, an adjustment of the existing representation occurred for situations rated as appropriate. Bringing this together with the results indicating no significant difference of the cumulative completion time between the trained and untrained, the imitation of motion pattern during learning scenarios or even during working scenarios could enhance a consolidation and implicit imitation of ergonomic motion patterns without minimizing the time performance significantly. Because of the subject's unawareness of the motion similarity criteria, an implicit imitation can be assumed instead of an explicit imitation.

Regarding the imitation of different task categories, no significant differences are stated. However, for the category taking the lower body into account the smallest percentage of similar motions are recorded. Eventually, due to the possibility the upper body was rated as more important because of the interaction with assembly parts, a dedication of attention capacities mainly to the avatar's upper body appeared. Furthermore, the limited field of vied (FOV) of the AR device could have lead to missing information, although on the basis of the procedure the FOV should have superimposed the relevant motions entirely.

5   Conclusion and Future Work

Within this paper we evaluated a process-oriented assistance method in terms of motor learning by imitation. The presented results reveal the existence of implicit motion imitation in AR, comparable to real world effects. With respect to the manual assembly use case, the results further assume the opportunity of learning ergonomic motions without a substantial performance loss considering the time component. Moreover, for experienced employees with physical limitations a process-oriented assistance method could enable an adjustment of existing motion pattern representations and therefore lead to an ergonomically appropriated task conduction. However, due to the small sample size and the late breaking work character the topic of imitation learning in AR is ongoing research and the results reveal only a first insight.

The authors intend further work on the basis of the captured data, considering the analysis of motion imitation in terms of similarity of joint angle trajectories. Hence, compared to the utilized visual analysis, the analysed task categories can be extended to more complex tasks such as assembly tasks, and the results can be analysed related to their task complexity.

Acknowledgement. The authors acknowledge the financial support by the Federal Ministry of Education and Research of Germany (MOSIM project, grant no. 01IS18060A-H).

References

1. Anderson, F., Grossman, T., Matejka, J., Fitzmaurice, G.: YouMove: enhancing movement training with an augmented reality mirror. In: Proceedings of the 26th Annual ACM Symposium on User Interface Software and Technology - UIST 2013, pp. 311–320. ACM Press (2013). https://doi.org/10.1145/2501988.2502045
2. Chen, X., et al.: ImmerTai: immersive motion learning in VR environments **58**, 416–427. https://doi.org/10.1016/j.jvcir.2018.11.039
3. Funk, M., Kosch, T., Greenwald, S.W., Schmidt, A.: A benchmark for interactive augmented reality instructions for assembly tasks. In: Proceedings of the 14th International Conference on Mobile and Ubiquitous Multimedia - MUM 2015, pp. 253–257. ACM Press. https://doi.org/10.1145/2836041.2836067
4. Ganier, F.: Factors affecting the processing of procedural instructions: implications for document design **47**(1), 15–26. https://doi.org/10.1109/TPC.2004.824289
5. Guadagno, R.E., Blascovich, J., Bailenson, J.N., Mccall, C.: Virtual humans and persuasion: The effects of agency and behavioral realism, p. 22 (2007)
6. Han, P.H., Chen, K.W., Hsieh, C.H., Huang, Y.J., Hung, Y.P.: AR-arm: augmented visualization for guiding arm movement in the first-person perspective. In: Proceedings of the 7th Augmented Human International Conference 2016 on AH 2016, pp. 1–4. ACM Press (2016). https://doi.org/10.1145/2875194.2875237
7. Kim, K., Billinghurst, M., Bruder, G., Duh, H.B.L., Welch, G.F.: Revisiting trends in augmented reality research: a review of the 2nd decade of ISMAR (2008–2017) **24**(11), 2947–2962. https://doi.org/10.1109/TVCG.2018.2868591

8. Kim, K., Boelling, L., Haesler, S., Bailenson, J., Bruder, G., Welch, G.F.: Does a digital assistant need a body? The influence of visual embodiment and social behavior on the perception of intelligent virtual agents in AR. In: 2018 IEEE International Symposium on Mixed and Augmented Reality (ISMAR), pp. 105–114. IEEE (2018). https://doi.org/10.1109/ISMAR.2018.00039

9. Kim, K., Maloney, D., Bruder, G., Bailenson, J.N., Welch, G.F.: The effects of virtual human's spatial and behavioral coherence with physical objects on social presence in AR: Virtual human's spatial and behavioral coherence in AR **28**(3), e1771. https://doi.org/10.1002/cav.1771

10. Kosch, T., Funk, M., Schmidt, A., Chuang, L.L.: Identifying cognitive assistance with mobile electroencephalography: a case study with in-situ projections for manual assembly **2**, 1–20. https://doi.org/10.1145/3229093

11. Lampen, E., Teuber, J., Gaisbauer, F., Bär, T., Pfeiffer, T., Wachsmuth, S.: Combining simulation and augmented reality methods for enhanced worker assistance in manual assembly **81**, 588–593. https://doi.org/10.1016/j.procir.2019.03.160

12. Limbu, B.H., Jarodzka, H., Klemke, R., Specht, M.: Using sensors and augmented reality to train apprentices using recorded expert performance: a systematic literature review **25**, 1–22. https://doi.org/10.1016/j.edurev.2018.07.001

13. Miller, M.R., Jun, H., Herrera, F., Yu Villa, J., Welch, G., Bailenson, J.N.: Social interaction in augmented reality **14**(5), e0216290. https://doi.org/10.1371/journal.pone.0216290

14. Deutsches Institut für Normung, e.V.: DIN CEN ISO/TR 7250–2: Wesentliche Maße des menschlichen Körpers für die technische Gestaltung Teil 2. Anthropometrische Datenbanken einzelner nationaler Bevölkerungen. https://doi.org/10.31030/1935074

15. Patterson, R.E., Pierce, B.J., Bell, H.H., Klein, G.: Implicit learning, tacit knowledge, expertise development, and naturalistic decision making **4**(4), 289–303. https://doi.org/10.1177/155534341000400403

16. Rizzolatti, G., Fogassi, L., Gallese, V.: Neurophysiological mechanisms underlying the understanding and imitation of action **2**(9), 661–670. https://doi.org/10.1038/35090060

17. Schaal, S., Ijspeert, A., Billard, A.: Computational approaches to motor learning by imitation **358**(1431), 537–547. https://doi.org/10.1098/rstb.2002.1258

18. Schepers, M., Giuberti, M., Bellusci, G.: Xsens MVN: Consistent tracking of human motion using inertial sensing. https://doi.org/10.13140/rg.2.2.22099.07205

19. Snoddy, G.S.: Learning and stability: a psychophysiological analysis of a case of motor learning with clinical applications **10**(1), 1–36. https://doi.org/10.1037/h0075814

20. Waltemate, T., Gall, D., Roth, D., Botsch, M., Latoschik, M.E.: The impact of avatar personalization and immersion on virtual body ownership, presence, and emotional response **24**(4), 1643–1652. https://doi.org/10.1109/TVCG.2018.2794629

21. Webel, S., Bockholt, U., Engelke, T., Gavish, N., Tecchia, F.: Design recommendations for augmented reality based training of maintenance skills. In: Alem, L., Huang, W. (eds.) Recent Trends of Mobile Collaborative Augmented Reality Systems, pp. 69–82. Springer, New York (2011). https://doi.org/10.1007/978-1-4419-9845-3_5

Innovation of Interactive Design from the Perspective of Safety Psychology— Based on VR Technology

Feng Liu[1], Yu Dong[1], Xianheng Yi[2], and Haiming Zhu[3(✉)]

[1] School of Journalism and Communication, Shanghai University, Shanghai, People's Republic of China
[2] College of Foreign Languages, Shanghai Jianqiao University, Shanghai, People's Republic of China
[3] Shanghai Municipal Engineering Design and Research Institute (Group) Co., Ltd., Shanghai, People's Republic of China
zhuhaiming@ecust.edu.cn

Abstract. With the rapid development of science and technology, the era of "Internet of everything" is imminent, and "interaction" has emerged a new connotation. Interactive design should be reconsidered and defined in view of many new application scenarios. From the perspective of safety psychology, how to innovate interactive design methods and improve the effect of safety education become a problem that designers should take in to account. This greatly broaden the application scope of interactive design, and create more conditions for updating the application concept of interactive design and grasping the new connotation of interactive design based on the new technical environment. The traditional methods of safety education are hard to stimulate the participation of audiences, which fails to produce active and effective interactions, and then, conceptual update and innovation of interactive design is very difficult to take effect. The development of VR created the condition for the application of more novel visualization and interaction patterns, and interactive design can be innovated with the application of VR in Safety Education. Based on the characteristics of VR and its impact on interaction behaviors of human beings, this paper combining with the relevant viewpoints and requirements of safety psychology makes an exploratory analysis on the innovation methods of VR-based interactive design.

Keywords: Safety psychology · Interactive design · VR

1 Introduction

With the rapid development of science and technology, the era of "Internet of everything" is imminent, and "interaction" has emerged a new connotation. Interactive design should be reconsidered and defined in view of many new application scenarios. Safety education plays a significantly important role in human production and life. Scientifically designed contents and methods of safety education can effectively improve the safety awareness and behavioral ability of the audience and meanwhile

C. Stephanidis et al. (Eds.): HCII 2020, CCIS 1294, pp. 189–196, 2020.
https://doi.org/10.1007/978-3-030-60703-6_24

reduce the incidence of injury events. From the perspective of safety psychology, how to innovate interactive design methods and improve the effect of safety education become a problem that designers should take into account. The development of technical conditions provides new conditions for us to realize the innovation of interactive design methods. Based on the characteristics of VR and its impact on interaction behaviors of human beings, this paper combining with the relevant view-points and requirements of safety psychology makes an exploratory analysis on the innovation methods of VR-based interactive design.

2   Interactive Design Concept from the Perspective of Safety Psychology

Safety psychology was initially developed on the basis of other disciplines such as industrial psychology, psychologists engaged in the design of machines, tools, equipment and working environment, working procedure that is suitable for psycho-logically and physiologically actual need of from the perspective of safety, in order to alleviate fatigue and prevent accidents. From such a specific perspective, a safety psychology has been gradually formed [1]. Safety Psychology is also known as Occupational Health Psychology [2], which refers to guide people to prevent from injuries and accidents by regulating their mental state. Safety psychology also has comprehensive and cross discipline attribute. Infact, "stress-response theory" [3] "self-regulation model" [4] were put forward by the psychologist so as to promote the application of safety psychology. Furthermore, Robert Heath developed the "Safety psychological intervention mode" [5] based on previous studies, which plays a sig-nificantly essential role in the industries of safety education.

The applied research of safety psychology in different industries has created good conditions for the purpose of improving the scientific level of safety education and safety psychology intervention. For example, UNOH used the driving simulator as the test platform to set up the stress scene of suddenly driving out of the vehicle at the intersection. It aims to have a study on the stress hedging behaviors of drivers at different ages, and further provide specific stress response training programs for dif-ferent age groups [6]. In addition, Crundall et al. designed a Faros GB3 simulator to study the training methods of verbal warning of potential risks for 9 different stress risk scenarios [7].

The development of safety psychology lays a foundation for the extension of the application scope of interactive design, and also suggestively puts forward new requirements. Safety psychology pays closer attention to timely identify severe safety in the process of application of psychological reaction of the individual. At the same time, it puts forward targeted intervention respectively according to its main reason based on both mental state and psychological problems. Besides, it concentrates on individual coping mechanisms, and is beneficial to improve the individual ability to cope with actual situations, in order to achieve a relative balance of physiological and mental state. It finally assists to adapt to the production process as well as obtains the optimum state of body and mind in its own conditions. After all, it is difficult for traditional design methods to meet these requirements. On the one hand, designers should deeply grasp the constructive needs of safety psychology in specific scenes. On the other hand, they need to creatively use interactive design methods to meet the above requirements. In general, both factors greatly broaden the application scope of interactive design, and create more conditions for updating the application concept of interactive design and grasping the new connotation of interactive design based on the new technical conditions.

3   The Application Dilemma of Interactive Design Concept in the Traditional Scene of Safety Psychological Education

Different from general product designs, on the one hand, the content of safety education requires not only integrating and arranging interactive designs and safety materials, but also thinking about how to present safety education materials to the audience more effectively. On the other hand, from the perspective of products, if interactive functions were realized, many safety education scenarios tend to require larger scale venues, higher-cost machines and equipment and other hardware bases, which are greatly limited in flexibility, portability and application range. Therefore, the concept of interactive design has obvious application difficulties in the scene of traditional safety psychological education. The realization of "interactivity" in terms of traditional safety psychological education is restricted by many factors. For example, simple words, pictures and other safety education information contents are difficult to arouse interests and attentions of training personnel and audiences. As a matter of fact, the environment and way of traditional safety education are hard to stimulate the participation of audiences, which fails to produce active and effective interactions. Under such a scenario, conceptual update and innovation of interactive design is very difficult to take effect.

As the scenario of safety psychological education is mainly applied in the industrial, engineering and specific life scenes, the application of interactive design in this area in addition to following the general design requirements for product interaction, should take these factors into overall consideration the relationship and interaction between various factors, such as human beings between, human and facilities, facilities between, human and material contents. it should take efforts to fully mobilize various elements. Therefore, the interactive design in this scenario goes beyond the design of product interactive "interface" in the traditional sense, and meanwhile the interactive design concept should be further integrated into every link of safety education design. The realization of this interactive design effect requires not only the conceptual update of the designers, but also the support of advanced technology. If there was no innovative technology that broke the physical and functional boundaries between different elements, the innovation of interactive design concept and method should not be realized. This is an original application dilemma in the traditional scene of safety psychology education. On the one hand, conceptual interactive design needs to be updated. On the other hand, there is a lack of innovative technical support.

4 Opportunities for Innovation in Interactive Design Under the Background of VR Technology Development

The development of VR technology created the condition for the application of more novel visualization and interaction patterns [8]. In fact, VR can not only make use of advanced digital technology to simulate the three dimensional space and provide users with a sensible, visible virtual scene, but also accomplish real-time interaction between people or between people and things with the help of intelligent terminal in the virtual scene. On the basis of these technical features, VR become an effective hardware support for interactive design work. According to a study of Majid Mastli et al. it suggests that applying VR technology to construction safety education and training and simulating real scenes can significantly improve the effect of construction safety training [9]. In addition, VR technology applied in safety education can provide various possibilities for innovative interactive design.

In the first place, VR-based innovative interactive design can reduce the cost of education. Although the design of VR safety education and training system has a large one-time investment, in fact, it can be used repeatedly for a long time. In despite of a continuous and large-scale safety training, VR-based safety training is more cost-saving than traditional training.

In the second place, VR-based innovative interactive design can break a variety of restrictions. VR-based safety education and training tend to break the limitation of time and space. Through scientific design, trainees can carry out centralized exercises in different time and place. At the same time, they are able to quickly obtain the results of the exercise for evaluation and improvement. In terms of remote training, VR technology can also be used in the exercise synchronously. In addition, trainees can repeat the exercise according to their own time, which greatly increases the exercise time.

Thirdly, VR-based innovative interactive design can stimulate trainees' initiatives. Through effective interactive design, VR safe education training can achieve a "scenario-typed" + "experiential-typed" effect. Not only is it built on the basis of objective practice environment, but its practice is closer to production and living in line with the actual situation. A rehearsal scene with high-fidelity model makes trainees hard to tell true and false, and meanwhile interactivity of VR technology can make the training more interesting and funnier, motivate employees to participate in training the enthusiasm and passion, especially welcoming young employees.

Fourthly, VR-based innovative interactive design can expand the application scenarios of safety education. Safety education in many industries involves dangerous factors such as falling high, electric shock, limited space, poisonous and harmful gas, etc. Actual operation is often accompanied by huge risks. If new employees are rushed to carry out on-the-spot practical training with any careless mind, it may cause heavy loss of life and property. Hence, training with VR technology can effectively avoid above risks. Trainees can remove the burden of potential accidents and carry out drills as much as possible, so as to quickly improve their skills and safety awareness.

In a word, VR-based technology is conducive to promoting the application and development of interactive design concept in intelligent, intensive and convenient safety training mode. By applying VR technology, designers are able to propose for a comprehensive integrated simulation scene, set scientific interactive content and mode of science, simulate such risk scenarios as electric shock damage, falling, drowning, limited space, toxic or harmful gases. In fact, unlike previous propaganda and education models in a didactic or indoctrinatory way, experiencers are immersive in such a real-like accident. Such as physical simulation can not only make experiencers further understand safety accidents and effectively improve the efficiency and effect of safety training, but also provide opportunities for the conceptual and strategic innovation of interactive design from the perspective of safety psychology.

5   Research on Innovative Ways of Interactive Designs Based on VR Technology

Based on VR technology, the development of interactive design should be considered more from the perspective of safety psychology. It shows that interactive design is not only an update of design methods, but also a breakthrough of design philosophy. The breakthrough of interactive design concept is not only reflected in the design of products or interactive interface, but also in the process of product conception, design, production, use and even feedback optimization. Based on these advantages of VR technology in immersion and interaction, this paper discusses how to realize the innovation of interactive design from the following four aspects such as the production of interactive basic content, environmental research and development of VR-based interactive design, specific design of interaction mode as well as feedback and optimization.

First of all, it is the production of interactive basic content. VR-based interactive design should not only systematically cope with a lot of information and comprehensively take each element in VR virtual scene into consideration, but also pay attention to how these elements should be scientific arrangement in order to achieve the optimal foundation interaction effect. In general, Interactive design work based on VR technology gives a priority to produce basic content used for interaction comprehensively and scientifically. For example, before designing VR-based safety education system, basic training courseware should be completed over, which differs in the content of classroom teaching. It should take into full consideration the characteristics of interaction between people and devices in VR virtual environment, and conform to the basic principles of safety psychology.

During the production of basic contents, it is necessary to design and develop a set of propagable safety training content characterized with comprehensive contents and various forms for needs of different sectors, combined with the characteristics of the work scene as well as relevant hazards prevention and control of training exercises, all kinds of emergency plans. Training contents include teaching materials, courseware and videos, all of which are exampled for a typical accident case analysis, the process, information, scientific principle, theoretical knowledge and practical experience of major dangerous crafts, etc.

Secondly, it is research and development of VR interactive environment. This is an environment where interactive design can be realized. 3D models of work scenes can be created through digital technology. In this way, all the equipment, facilities and various instrument tables in the specific work can be input to simulate a real scene for trainers and audiences for teaching and training. The research and development of interactive environment can give full play to the advantages of VR technology. For example, the virtual prototype system can simulate dangerous scenes such as electric shock, falling high and limited space, so that the audience can feel the same feeling and constantly improve safety awareness and skills in avoid of dangers in work and life.

The virtual prototype system of safety production training based on VR-based interactive environment can be used as a critical technology of safety education, training and assessment system. Its design is divided into two modules such as teaching and assessment. On the one hand, in terms of teaching, audiences can directly feel the objective work scenes, main equipment and facilities and functions through VR technology, which opens a variety of work operation exercises, and practices safety awareness and related skills in a variety of simulated dangerous events and environments. In terms of assessment module, audiences are tested with related processing and reaction check through the simulation of VR dangerous environment, where they are able to complete various interactive behaviors under a harmless virtual environment. As a result, they can judge the behavior of the print operators according to all functions and processes based on such teaching mode. In addition, combined with the analysis of examination score data, it is able to make an objective evaluation on individual safety skill level quickly and accurately, thus and finally find problems existing in their interaction.

Thirdly, it is specific design of interaction mode. Technical factors play a vital role in VR-based interactive design. Therefore, specific design of interaction mode should be based on a comprehensively thorough understanding of technical factors. If there were greater technical conditions, it is better to develop a set of simulation environment integration center equipment based on interactive VR technology. For example, a combined device for VR interactive scene operation should be developed and manufactured, which consists of front experience area and backstage control area. Front experience area is an interface of direct contacts or an occasion of direct immersion activities, which contains educational training, simulation and assessment test of experiencer. In fact, experiencers are able to enjoy all kinds of risk factors and events in such a virtual reality scene, such as electric shock, fire, falls, etc. Furthermore, they can also use virtual devices in the dangerous scenes, and carry out the simulation operation instructions based on VR systems in the virtual environment. In the design process, it is necessary to pay attention to how to set the VR trap to capture the movement information of experiencers in the space in real time, guide the experiencer to operate the VR terminal to control the items in the virtual environment, and add gestures and other operations to realize such functions as environment switching and menu selecting.

Background control area is the operation control area in the whole VR interactive system, which provides various resources such as sound source, light source and power source to support for front experience area and meanwhile ensures a smooth operation of the system. This control system includes a series of supporting services such as video monitoring, sound, photoelectric and VR system, so that the staff in the background control area can effectively guide the experientials in the front experience area to carry out various activities, and are able to take necessary corrective measures in case of abnormalities. At the same time, background control area can monitor the running state of the facilities and equipment in the whole center, which provides the basis for maintenance. Certainly, background control area is not a simple underlying technical hardware in the traditional sense, but a crucial part of interactive design. Many functions of front experience area should take effect with the real-time cooperation of the background control area.

Fourthly, it is the design of feedback and optimization methods. Interactive design based on VR technology should give full play to the advantages of digital technology. Currently behaviors of interactive design accurately produce large amounts of data which can be stored in real-time through database technology. Besides, these behaviors can be digged out a lot of potential problems existing in the interaction based on data analysis, which provides a scientific reference to interactive behavior of the optimization and interactive design. In the process of interactive design, the consciousness of feedback and optimization should be reflected in each link. At the same time, the data of experiencers should be collected according to system settings. In addition, based on theoretical methods and tools from the perspective of safety psychology, a better optimization scheme and a further improvement of safety awareness of experiencers should be explored and discussed by means of combining investigation, statistics and data analysis. Therefore, VR-based interactive design can play a greater role in safety education.

To sum up, it shows that from the perspective of safety psychology, on the one hand, VR-based interactive design not only is beneficial for interactive designs to open wider application scenarios, but also provides a new technical conditions and practical strategy for safety psychological education. In addition, it is able to prevent audience from being hurt or injured by the objective risk scenario, and runs well in a virtual simulation scenario with enjoying safety experience and education as well as learning safety skills. On the other hand, the application of the theories and methods of safety psychology also provides reference for the application and innovation of interactive designs in related fields. The combination with theories of other disciplines and interactive designs can promote the innovation of interactive design concepts and design methods. In terms of designers, in addition to constantly improving their design level and accumulating design skills, they also need to broaden their horizons and pay more attention to the application requirements of different fields. Before the specific design work, a large number of systematic preliminary work should be done well. According to the needs of different customers, through investigation and research, safety risks and dangers in their industries and fields should be taken into consideration. Furthermore, designers should participate in the production of safety training content for these specific risks. Only when the above preparations are made can it be clear that which links can be set up with interaction and how to do so when building VR scenes.

Acknowledgements. This paper is supported by "Research on key technology and prototype system of integrated security simulation integration center" (Shanghai urban drainage Co., Ltd.), China social science foundation project "Research on the space production of newsroom under the background of media content convergence" (19FXWB025) and Shanghai social science foundation project "Research on the reproduction of newsroom space under the background of 5G" (2019BXW004).

References

1. Munsterberg, H.: Psychology and Industrial Efficiency (1912)
2. Chen, S.: Safety Psychology. Tianjin University Press, Tianjin (1999)
3. Jin, Y.: An Overview of Modern Stress Theory. Science Press, Beijing (2008)
4. Lin, Z.: A review of self-regulated learning theory. Psychol. Sci. **26**(5), 870–873 (2003)
5. Heath, R.: Crisis Management. CITIC Press, Beijing (2003). Wang Cheng, Song Binghui, Jin Ying, Translated
6. Uno, H.: Aged drivers' avoidance capabilities in an emergent traffic situation. Trans. Soc. Autom. Eng. Jpn. **32**, 113–118 (2001)
7. Crundall, D., Andrews, B., Van Loon, E., et al.: Commentary training improves responsiveness to hazards in a driving simulator. Accid. Anal. Prev. **42**(6), 2117–2124 (2010)
8. Wolfartsberger, J.: Analyzing the potential of Virtual Reality for engineering design review. Autom. Constr. **104**, 27–37 (2019)
9. Mastli, M., Zhang, J.: Interactive highway construction simulation using game engine and virtual reality for education and training purpose. In: Computing in Civil Engineering, pp. 399–406 (2017)

Virtual Reality in Model Based Systems Engineering: A Review Paper

Mostafa Lutfi[(✉)] and Ricardo Valerdi

Department of Systems and Industrial Engineering, The University of Arizona,
Tucson, AZ 85721, USA
mostafalutfi@email.arizona.edu

Abstract. Model Based Systems Engineering (MBSE) thrived in the recent
decades in order to overcome the increasing complexity within systems. MBSE
envisioned replacing document centric systems engineering by model centric
systems engineering. MBSE can handle systems complexity efficiently by representing each entity in the model only once and generating different viewpoints.
Most commonly used MBSE language is the "Systems Modeling Language
(SysML)". Virtual Reality can play a bigger role on creating truly model centric
systems engineering approaches. The core application of MBSE approach
implies utilization of a single system model, which will act as "source of truth"
to all embedded system analyzing tools. Thus, the system model can communicate back and forth with Virtual Reality Environment to analyze the system
performance. Systems engineer can conduct interactive immersive simulation of
a scenario described in the system model and return the results obtained from the
Virtual Reality Environment to the system model. Requirements analysis can be
performed more efficiently by ensuring participation of the customers early in
the product lifecycle utilizing the VR environment. A customer can walk into
VR environment and see how the system design would look like and interact
with it. Based on the interaction results, the systems engineer can modify the
product/service specifications and design. This paper reviewed the works been
done to incorporate virtual reality environment with SysML. The paper also
proposed a framework on how VR environment can be implemented with
SysML to perform true MBSE practice.

Keywords: MBSE · Virtual reality · SysML · VR · Systems engineering

1 Introduction

1.1 Virtual Reality

Virtual Reality (VR) is one of the most emerging technologies of the last four decades.
Coates in 1992 defined VR as electronic simulation of environments with head-
mounted eye goggle and wired clothing, which allows the end user in realistic three-
dimensional situations to interact [1]. A simple VR system comprises of virtual
environment design software, head mounted display, tracking sensors, input devices,
tactile feedback devices and users [2, 3]. Immersion, Presence, and Interactivity are the
three defining pillars of VR [4]. Immersion in VR is a sensation of being present in a

© Springer Nature Switzerland AG 2020
C. Stephanidis et al. (Eds.): HCII 2020, CCIS 1294, pp. 197–205, 2020.
https://doi.org/10.1007/978-3-030-60703-6_25

non-physical environment. Presence is the level of engagement felt by the user in the VR environment. Immersion is a "technological component" of VR, whereas, presence depends on psychological, perceptual and cognitive behavior of the user being immersed [5].

1.2 Model Based Systems Engineering

Model Based Systems Engineering (MBSE) focuses on formalized application of modeling to support systems engineering artifacts development from the conceptual design phase throughout the end of the system of interest (SOI) lifecycle [6]. Dr. Wayne Wymore at the University of Arizona in his book Model Based Systems Engineering first introduced the term MBSE in 1993 [7]. Systems engineers are in an era in which modern systems are increasingly complex [8]. Model Based Systems Engineering is the proposed solution for managing the systems complexity by various researchers [9, 10]. Different methodologies have been developed to implement the MBSE approach namely INCOSE Object-Oriented Systems Engineering Method (OOSEM), IBM Telelogic Harmony-SE, IBM Rational Unified Process for Systems, Engineering (RUP SE) For Model Driven Systems Development (MDSD), Vitech Model-Based System Engineering (MBSE) Methodology, JPL State Analysis (SA), Object-Process Methodology (OPM) and Arcadia [11, 12].

In recent years, Systems Modeling Language (SysML) has been the most common method for implementing MBSE approaches [13, 14]. SysML has its root from the Unified Language Modeling (UML) [15]. SysML follows the Object-Oriented Systems Engineering Methodology (OOSEM) developed by INCOSE [16]. SysML consists of nine diagram types distributed over four pillars, namely Structure, Behavior, Parametrics and Requirements [16]. Figure 1 below shows the SysML diagram taxonomy.

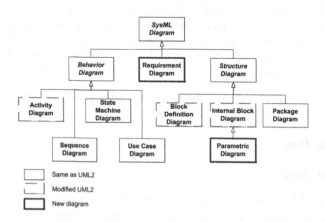

Fig. 1. SysML diagram taxonomy [17]

1.3   Objective

VR has the potential to improve the MBSE practices in various system development and analysis. VR application in the field of Model Based Systems Engineering is increasing day by day. This paper reviews the work conducted to incorporate VR into MBSE by different researchers in recent years. As SysML is the most widely used MBSE language, the paper limited its focus to SysML driven MBSE approaches. The paper also outlines a VR-MBSE Framework to facilitate the integration between VR and SysML more convenient, which is currently under development.

2   Methodology

The authors searched two widely used electronic databases-Google Scholar and Scopus for the research papers reviewed in this paper [18, 19]. The search terms used to select the papers were- "VR and MBSE", "Virtual Reality and MBSE", "VR and SysML" "Virtual Reality and SysML" and "Application of VR in MBSE". The authors only considered publications after 2010. This inclusion criterion was set considering research availability, novelty and advancement. The minimum citations to consider a research paper for inclusion in this review paper was set to four. In addition, the language of the included research papers was English. The authors evaluated the identified research papers on their feasibility of data extraction, first by abstract and, ultimately, by reading the full text. From the included research papers, authors extracted information on (i) research objective (ii) methodology (iii) year of publication and (iv) software used.

3   Application of VR in MBSE Practice

Akshay Kande in 2011 was one of the first to conduct a thesis on the integration of MBSE and VR tools for system design [20]. The author used an open source software, namely Virtual Engineering (VE) suite, which consist of three core engines- VE Conductor, VE Computational Engine and VE Explorer. User can create interface through the VE conductor API and built in libraries. Computational Engine manages the integration between the COTS tools and Virtual Engineering framework. Explorer works as the graphical engine responsible for developing the virtual environment. The main objectives of the virtual systems modeling approach developed in the thesis paper are executable SysML Modeling in a MBSE tool, providing a graphical interface to demonstrate the system of interest and operations, enabling a decision making environment for the stakeholders, performing sensitivity analysis of the design parameters and maintaining a consistent information flow by providing an integrated environment. The major steps of the methodology followed in this thesis are structural model development in SysML, analytical model development in SysML, creation of VE-suite model and connecting the two analytical model and VE-suite model using relationship constructs.

A. Madni in his research paper published in 2014 demonstrated a novel approach that mapped systems engineering (SE) artifacts modeled in SysML to virtual worlds within which various storylines can contextualize [21]. The methodology developed in this paper acts as a bridge between Model Based Engineering (MBE) and Story Based Engineering (StBE). The core steps involved in the mapping process are experiencing system CONOPS and system design in virtual environment, incorporation of SysML model with the virtual environment and story authoring. The author demonstrated the whole process with an illustrative example of Campus Security System (CSS). The author used Unity 3D software to create the virtual environment and Magicdraw software for the SysML model build up. Moreover, the paper also proposed a Dynamic Interaction Matrix (DIM) to capture the possible and actual interactions among technical story elements namely system elements, actors, environments, other system entities etc.

In another journal paper published in the same year (2014), A. Madni et al. proposed MBSE+ i.e. bolstering MBSE with the integration of storytelling techniques [22]. The authors also suggested an Experiential Design Language (EDL), which is the combination of SysML and experiential perspective developed in the virtual world. In this research paper, the authors presented a framework showing the relationship between system models, experiential perspective and storytelling in the virtual world. The authors also demonstrated the transformation steps between the system design and storytelling spaces. The steps are as follows- (a) developing system models in SysML in BDD, activity and use case diagrams, (b) mapping systems models with storytelling space defined by VR world entities, (c) rendering VR world entities and their behaviors in order to tell the stories and (d) story extraction and data collection in the VR world. The authors also presented an illustrative example of a "diverted aircraft scenario" to execute the steps described in the methodology.

Abidi et al. in their 2016's paper utilized interactive VR simulation and SysML model to facilitate real time simulation of production flows in a lean environment [23]. The paper utilized the MASCARET framework, which provides a logical connection between system engineering artifacts and VR environment [24]. The methodology comprised of the following basic steps: (1) Conversion of the simulation model of the proposed system to a SysML model, (2) Exporting as XMI description, (3) Preparation of the MASCARET framework in order to analyze the XMI description, (4) Mapping the XMI description with VR environment and (5) Connecting the simulation tool (ARENA) with the VR environment through the RTI infrastructure. Interactive VR environment was created through Unity 3D. "OpenSlice" (an open source RTI supported library) enabled the data exchange between different tools of the proposed system. Moreover, the author created a custom interface namely "UnityInterface.dll" using C# to facilitate the connection between VR environment and RTI. The authors also mentioned some difficulties they encountered while developing the methodology namely building a custom data exchange module between ARENA and VR system, forced partial virtual design of the total simulation and transformation of ARENA models to SysML.

Mahboob et al. in their paper titled, "Model based systems engineering (MBSE) approach for configurable product use-case scenarios in virtual environments" introduced a concept of defining behavior description of a use case inside SysML model to create VR environment [25]. This approach will facilitate the development of product's life cycle specific VR models for early production evaluation, which in turn will help the stakeholders (product designer, production manager, customer, investors etc.) to achieve better knowledge of the product behavior in the later phases. The core methodology of the research papers are as follows: (1) VR scene is composed of the product, the environment and human actor(s), (2) Product, Environment and actor(s) have structural and behavioral components, which are modeled in SysML, (3) combination/modification of product, environment and actor(s) used to construct specific VR scenarios. This combination/recombination/modification of the VR components are performed with the use of SysML behavior diagrams. The use of proposed method eliminates the rigorous task of scripting the whole VR scenario for individual use cases throughout the product's lifecycle. Finally, the authors used vacuum cleaner as an illustrative example to implement the methodology (Table 1).

Table 1. Review summary

Title	Year of Pub.	Objective	Methodology	Software used
Integration of model-based systems engineering and virtual engineering tools for detailed design,	2011	Executable SysML Modeling in a MBSE tool	(1) Structural and analytical model development in SysML, (2) Creation of VE-suite model and (3) Connecting the two analytical model and VE-suite model	VE Suite
Expanding stakeholder participation in upfront system engineering through storytelling in virtual worlds	2014	Mapping systems engineering (SE) artifacts modeled in SysML to virtual worlds	(1) Experiencing system CONOPS and system design in virtual environment, (2) Incorporation of SysML model with the virtual environment and (3) Story authoring	Unity 3D, MagicDraw
Toward an experiential design language: augmenting MBSE with technical storytelling in VW	2014	MBSE+: bolstering MBSE with the integration of storytelling techniques	(1) Developing system models in SysML (2) Mapping systems models with storytelling space In VR (3) Rendering VR world entities (4) Story extraction/VR data collection	Unity 3D, MagicDraw

(*continued*)

Table 1. (*continued*)

Title	Year of Pub.	Objective	Methodology	Software used
Contribution of virtual reality for lines production's simulation in a lean manufacturing environment	2016	Interactive VR simulation and SysML model to facilitate real time simulation of production flows in a lean environment	(1) Conversion of the simulation model of the proposed system to a SysML model, (2) Exporting as XMI description, (3) Preparation of the MASCARET framework in order to analyze the XMI description, (4) Mapping the XMI description with VR environment and (5) Connecting the simulation tool (ARENA) with the VR environment through the RTI infrastructure	Unity 3D, OpenSlice, ARENA, MASC-ARET
Model based systems engineering (MBSE) approach for configurable product use-case scenarios in virtual environments	2017	Defining behavior description of a use case inside SysML model to create VR environment	(1) VR scene is composed of the product, the environment and human actor(s), (2) Product, environment and actor(s) have structural and behavioral components, (3) Combination/modification of product, environ-ment and actor(s) used to construct specific VR scenarios.	Cameo systems modeler, CAVE Systems

4 Proposed VR-MBSE Framework

All the reviewed papers incorporated VR into SysML though some custom made plugins and conversion techniques (XMI conversion, MASCARET etc.). These may hinder the mass use of VR-enabled SysML due to time and effort needed to set up those systems. Hence, we propose a VR-MBSE framework (see Fig. 2) which utilizes most widely used tools namely Cameo Systems Modeler (CSM), Unity 3D and Unreal Engine in an efficient way [26–28]. The proposed methodology for the framework is as follows:

(1) Systems behavior and structural Modeling in SysML through CSM, (2) Simulation set up in Cameo Simulation Toolkit of CSM and (3) Communication with VR Engine through CSM's scripting API (C# for Unity/Python for Unreal Engine). This framework will make the SysML model executable by incorporating VR in order to support design, analysis and verification activities early phases of the system lifecycle through enabling co-simulation.

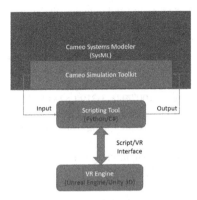

Fig. 2. VR-MBSE framework

5 Discussion

VR can incorporate real time simulation, virtual storytelling, requirements verification and product/service performance evaluation early in the lifecycle of a product or service through the integration with MBSE approach. SysML is the most widely used MBSE tool. Hence, various efforts are taking place to develop VR enabled SysML. The reviewed papers are the most notable efforts happened in recent years to accomplish this goal. MBSE thrives under the principle that the whole systems engineering artifacts will be based on a "system model as the source of truth". By utilizing the VR enabled SysML model, later phases of system lifecycle can be simulated/analyzed early in the early phases of the System of Interest (SOI). Moreover, SysML model can be used as an ontological repository for the creation of different VR scenarios (instead of creating each scenario separately).

6 Conclusion and Future Work

The paper reviewed major research efforts to apply VR in MBSE practice through SysML. The review results are summarized in a table.Then, the authors proposed a VR-MBSE framework that can make the VR-enabled SysML approach more accessible to everyone. Finally, the authors discussed major implications of the VR enabled SysML in a systems engineering lifecycle. To further the research, the authors intend to build the proposed VR-MBSE framework and test it using a use case.

References

1. Steuer, J.: Defining virtual reality: dimensions determining telepresence. J. Commun. **42**(4), 73–93 (1992). https://doi.org/10.1111/j.1460-2466.1992.tb00812.x
2. Biocca, F.: Virtual reality technology: a tutorial. J. Commun. **42**(4), 23–72 (1992). https://doi.org/10.1111/j.1460-2466.1992.tb00811.x

3. Bamodu, O., Ye, X.M.: Virtual reality and virtual reality system components (2013). https:// doi.org/10.4028/www.scientific.net/AMR.765-767.1169
4. Mütterlein, J.: The three pillars of virtual reality? Investigating the roles of immersion, presence, and interactivity, January 2018. https://doi.org/10.24251/hicss.2018.174
5. Berkman, M.I., Akan, E.: Presence and Immersion in Virtual Reality. In: Lee, N. (ed.) Encyclopedia of Computer Graphics and Games, pp. 1–10. Springer International Publishing, Cham (2019). https://doi.org/10.1007/978-3-319-08234-9_162-1
6. Hart, L.: Introduction To Model-Based System Engineering (MBSE) and SysML, p. 43
7. Wymore, A.W.: Model-Based Systems Engineering, 1st edn. CRC Press Inc., Boca Raton (1993)
8. Calvano, C.N., John, P.: Systems engineering in an age of complexity. Syst. Eng. 7(1), 25–34 (2004). https://doi.org/10.1002/sys.10054
9. French, M.O.: Extending model based systems engineering for complex systems. In: Presented at the 53rd AIAA Aerospace Sciences Meeting, Kissimmee, Florida, January 2015. https://doi.org/10.2514/6.2015-1639
10. Asan, E., Albrecht, O., Bilgen, S.: Handling complexity in system of systems projects–lessons learned from MBSE efforts in border security projects. In: Complex Systems Design and Management, pp. 281–299 (2014). https://doi.org/10.1007/978-3-319-02812-5_21
11. Estefan, J.A.: Survey of Model-Based Systems Engineering (MBSE) Methodologies, p. 70 (2008)
12. Yaroker, Y., Perelman, V., Dori, D.: An OPM conceptual model-based executable simulation environment: implementation and evaluation. Syst. Eng. 16(4), 381–390 (2013). https://doi.org/10.1002/sys.21235
13. Peak, R.S., Burkhart, R., Friedenthal, S., Wilson, M.W., Bajaj, M., Kim, I.: Simulation-based design using SysML part 1: a parametrics primer (2007). https://doi.org/10.1002/j.2334-5837.2007.tb02964.x
14. Sage, A.P., Lynch, C.L.: Systems integration and architecting: an overview of principles, practices, and perspectives. Syst. Eng. 1(3), 176–227 (1998). https://doi.org/10.1002/(SICI)1520-6858(1998)1:3%3c176:AID-SYS3%3e3.0.CO;2-L
15. Hampson, K.: Technical evaluation of the systems modeling language (SysML). Procedia Comput. Sci. 44, 403–412 (2015). https://doi.org/10.1016/j.procs.2015.03.054
16. A Practical Guide to SysML - 3rd edn. https://www.elsevier.com/books/a-practical-guide-to-sysml/friedenthal/978-0-12-800202-5. Accessed 7 Aug 2019
17. What is SysML? | OMG SysML. http://www.omgsysml.org/what-is-sysml.htm. Accessed 7 Aug 2019
18. Google Scholar. https://scholar.google.com/. Accessed 18 June 2020
19. Scopus - Document search. https://www.scopus.com/search/form.uri?display=basic. Accessed 18 June 2020
20. Kande, A.: Integration of model-based systems engineering and virtual engineering tools for detailed design, p. 79
21. Madni, A.M.: Expanding stakeholder participation in upfront system engineering through storytelling in virtual worlds. Syst. Eng. 18(1), 16–27 (2015). https://doi.org/10.1002/sys.21284
22. Madni, A.M., Nance, M., Richey, M., Hubbard, W., Hanneman, L.: Toward an experiential design language: augmenting model-based systems engineering with technical storytelling in virtual worlds. Procedia Comput. Sci. 28, 848–856 (2014). https://doi.org/10.1016/j.procs.2014.03.101
23. Abidi, M.-A., Lyonnet, B., Chevaillier, P., Toscano, R.: Contribution of virtual reality for lines production's simulation in a lean manufacturing environment. IJCTE 8(3), 182–189 (2016). https://doi.org/10.7763/IJCTE.2016.V8.1041

24. Chevaillier, P., et al.: Semantic modeling of virtual environments using MASCARET. In: 2012 5th Workshop on Software Engineering and Architectures for Realtime Interactive Systems (SEARIS), March 2012, pp. 1–8 (2012). https://doi.org/10.1109/searis.2012.6231174

25. Mahboob, A., Weber, C., Husung, S., Liebal, A., Krömker, H.: Model based systems engineering (MBSE) approach for configurable product use-case scenarios in virtual environments. In: DS 87-3 Proceedings of the 21st International Conference on Engineering Design (ICED 17), Product, Services and Systems Design, 21–25 August 2017, Vancouver, Canada, vol. 3 (2017). https://www.designsociety.org/publication/39633/Model+based+systems+engineering+%28MBSE%29+approach+for+configurable+product+use-case+scenarios+in+virtual+environments. Accessed 19 June 2020

26. Cameo Systems Modeler. https://www.nomagic.com/products/cameo-systems-modeler. Accessed 22 Dec 2019

27. Technologies, U.: Unity Real-Time Development Platform | 3D, 2D VR and AR Visualizations. https://unity.com/. Accessed 19 June 2020

28. The most powerful real-time 3D creation platform - Unreal Engine. https://www.unrealengine.com/en-US/. Accessed 19 June 2020

Designing of a Seamless Training Experience Delivered Through VR Simulator for Winder-Operator

Chandni Murmu[✉]

Indian Institute of Technology, Hyderabad 502285, Telangana, India
chandni2104@gmail.com

Abstract. Winder-operators are responsible for the lives that they move down deep into the mines and bring them back safely to the surface. So, in order to have the same sense of responsibility in the training simulator, the user experience needs to be seamless and natural, including all the risks and surprises that a winder-operator faces in his real-world scenarios. To bring this objective to life, field studies, customer experience audits (interviews) and recordings were done to gather qualitative and physical data. Contents were inventoried, audited and analysed for body-storming and drawing up of the mental model of winder-operators. User persona was defined to maintain focus, even when expert reviews were taken. A contextual design process was followed to develop the simulator which included rigorous and multiple usability testing by the developer, designer and the winder-operators (end users).

Keywords: UX · User experience · Experience · Design · Design process

1 Introduction

A hoist operator is a certified worker of sound physically and mentally health. He is also known as winder operator. The employer examines the operator on his knowledge on the regulations and procedures associated with the safe execution of the duties and decides on his competence (Safety Standard for Hoist Operations 2010). A man-hoist operator's responsibility is to lower and raise conveyances within the mine shaft occupied with mining workers.

A typical hoist operator works for a 12-h shift per day, with very few time offs. In such a fragile environment, having trainee hoist operators in the same cabin as the authorized winder operator, though it may just be for observation, will not only be counter-productive, but may also lead to a catastrophic incident, due to distraction. Hence, to provide an effective on-hands training, a VR simulator, simulating the essential features and experiences of a winder, was developed. The simulation was developed with close attention to design methodologies and was process oriented.

A meaningful and better product can be built, by understanding and empathizing with users. Insights on methods and strategies to inculcate user emphasis were drawn from Martin and Hanington 2012. A collaborative research model for product development (Isaksson 2016; Shelly et al. 2005) ensured frontloading of the real-life

© Springer Nature Switzerland AG 2020
C. Stephanidis et al. (Eds.): HCII 2020, CCIS 1294, pp. 206–213, 2020.
https://doi.org/10.1007/978-3-030-60703-6_26

challenging scenarios in the research practices and warranted a common understanding of key challenges across the teams. The work of Savage (2000) was used as a precautionary guide for user observations and the field research. Further, the works of Eyal and Hoover 2014, Rosenfeld et al. (2015) and Nodder (2013) were key instructors for strategy development and user motivation directed towards using and learning from the simulator

2 The Design Process

The steps in the design process were developed taking inspiration from the contextual design method, a user-centered process that makes the ways in which designers work concrete, explicit and sharable, anchored in user data (Holtzblatt et al. 1998).

2.1 User Research

As the designed simulator had to be very user centric, it was very essential to do a detailed study of the user. Therefore, an extensive user research was done in order to understand user's intellectual and behavioral aspects.

Field Studies, Interviews and Recordings. Through multiple visits to a state owned mine, every single aspect of the operation of mine and its interaction on hoist operator were studied. Interesting observations were made such as only winder drums (see Fig. 1), on which the conveyance rope winds and unwinds, are visible to the operator from his cabin and the buzzer systems, indicator for hoist request origin was custom designed for that particular mine.

Evolutionary development was ensured with structurally planned and formulized field visits. For instance, the first visit was observational, to observe the placement of the equipment and monitor the schedule of the day. Further visits' objectives were broken down into smaller objectives based on the first visit, so that the visits could sync with pre-structured research sessions with worksheets utilization (where observations were entered), checklists (to keep track of covered pre-thought scenarios) and recording any form of behaviors and events (Martin and Hanington 2012).

Authorized interactions were set-up. To obtain maximum possible answers, a thoughtful questionnaire was drawn, on the basis of the operator's profile. The answers were tallied by cross-checking with another operator. In case of any discrepancy, a third user-interview was conducted, to capture most of the plausible scenarios. These questionnaires captured information on the users' thoughts, characteristics, feelings, perceptions, behaviors or attitude (Martin and Hanington 2012). Background studies, done on mine shaft and its operators, provided design inquiry structure and control which was helpful in analysis later. Information collected in these interviews were primary in verifying and humanizing the data obtained from other sources.

All the interviews were recorded, for transcription and analysis purposes. A week-long videos and audios, of operators operating the machine, were made with cameras placed inside the operator's cabin and just outside the cabin. These were helpful in empathizing with them and understand their physical experience. They were used for

Fig. 1. A typical Winder operator's cabin (Left) and Winder drums (Right).

bodystorming, generate user situations and contextually configure the simulator. A lot of understanding on decision making cognition, interactive experiences and emotional responses came from these recordings (Burns et al. 1994).

2.2   Content Inventory

To get an affinity of what the content is, what structure can be deduced and quick access to relevant information, it is important to have all the content inventoried. Carefully organized and easy to access spreadsheets were aggregated as the outcome of the quantitative exercise.

Transcription and Record Labeling. For text based qualitative and quantitative verbal-behavioral analysis, the recordings were converted to transcripts. Interview transcripts were very handy for decision justifications. They were constructive in affinity diagrams (Holtzblatt et al. 1998), cognitive mapping (Kelly 1995) and persona definition. For inventory purposes, audio record summary, after listening the audio, was used as record label in spreadsheets. The video recordings were labeled on the basis of either the operator's name or by the major task being done in the recording or any latent occurrences, if any. These were real time savers in quick access, collaborative or delegatory activities, assuring consistency in interpretation of the content.

2.3   User Persona

User personas consolidate archetypal descriptions of user behaviour patterns into representative profiles, so as to humanize design focus, test scenarios, and aid design communication (Cooper 2004). Defining a persona was essential for the project and the product team's focus.

Transcript Analysis, Pattern Identification. Above mentioned qualitative data, converted into quantitative transcripts, were analyzed for various physical and emotional touch points of the user. To get a 360-° view of hoist operator, these touch points where seen in different perspective, with the help of lenses mentioned by Jesse Schell (Schell 2015). Pattern were identified and segregated categorically with key behavioral aspects.

Fig. 2. (Left) An illustration of spreadsheet used for qualitative transcript analysis and (Right) spreadsheet for pattern identification from transcript analysis.

To avoid discrepancies in pattern, due to diversity in opinions; very difficult to govern, the number of analysts working on this task was limited to 1 to 3, only.

Persona Definition. Core motivational drives and pain points were identified using octalysis framework (Chou 2015). The most influential drive for respective patterns were quantitatively decided by a designed system. The persona for the simulator was structured by this system and octalysis. Multiple decision-making, for the product features, as well as, justification of the value-added delivery to the other stakeholders, were dependent on the persona definition.

2.4 Functionality Design

All the features and functionalities of a mine winder were listed down, to construct the simulator and design the seamless experience. However, the features were imparted to the user in stages, and not all at once, as it would diminish the experience and would nullify the objective.

Feature Identification, Segregation and Prioritization. Various hoist manuals helped in listing features and functionalities. User research revealed that features from the manual's content were not enough, as, many mines' hoist gets customized due to geographical and situational limitations, that cannot be eliminated. Such variants were identified and listed, as a separate category. Frequent revisiting of persona definition was important, to ensure that the simulator was engaging, user friendly and core oriented. The features were segregated into categories that reflected the major motivations and pain points and were contextual. After segregation, the features were prioritized, to ensure continued engagement, quality learning and training of the user, without creating any kind of frustration or learning fatigue (Osterwalder et al. 2014) (Fig. 3).

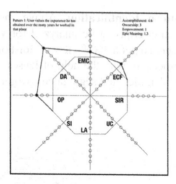

Fig. 3. Example of octalysis framework applied to one of the patterns (Chou 2015).

Module Creation and Visual Aids. Appropriately ascending skill level and user-centric modules, distributed in a consumable and engaging fashion, were created with the help of storyboarding and user task flow. These modules, called levels, spreading from level 0 to level 25, left room for flexibility required if any alteration was needed upon user testing and also for accessing any level, on the basis of skill status of the user (Schell 2015). There were supporting features identified during the user research and persona definition, apart from the core functionalities. These were incorporated as visual aids, that indicated the learning progress to the winder operator. A timer, for example, informed the user on time taken to complete a task, instruction text bar (instructions for the task to be completed), a red bar (provide on top of the two drums for visual aid to judge the drum levels alignment), visual light indicators (on shaft scale), a console (with prominent physical quantity indicators), were provided.

2.5 Usability Testing

Winder operators, the tasks and responsibilities, they were required to meet, were the focus of the usability testing, and empirical evidences were sought on, to improve the usability and purpose of the simulator (Gould et al. 1985).

Developers' Contribution. The developers performed feature tests, for every feature to behave in the intended manner, to make sure that the functionality and the outcome the tasks are due to actions taken by the user. In order to have a structured qualitative testing, the lists of features were referred and functionality was tested, level after level. Agile process was followed after each round of testing, to rectify any failures.

Designers' Contribution. Ideally, after the developers give the confidence to go ahead, designer do the testing. However, for this project, to shorten the turn-around time, testing from designer's side happened parallelly. Spreadsheets, which included visual components positioning, simulator's interactivity and functionality, experiences felt while using the VR simulator, instructional content consistency, visual queue, and other design aspects, were maintained by designer, too, for quality checks. The spreadsheets were shared with the developer, after each round, to make amends in VR environment in the best possible way, to make the experience better.

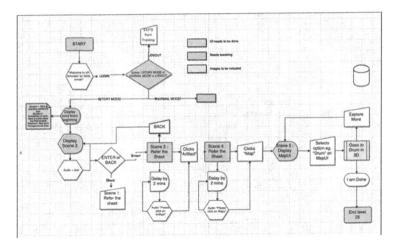

Fig. 4. User task flow sample.

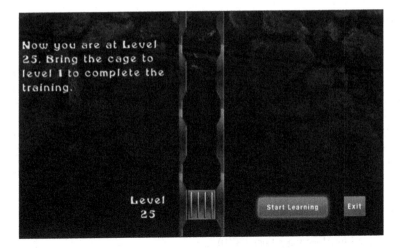

Fig. 5. One of the initial contextual design for learning module levels.

End User Testing. The simulator was taken to the mine at the end of each developer and designer testing cycle, where it was setup in a room similar to the intended size that would get allocated for the training purposes. They were allowed to play with VR head set and haptic devices for a duration after a basic explanation on how to use them, to make them comfortable with the device. Once comfortable, the simulator was introduced to the user. As the instructions on the task needed to be performed were inbuilt, the user took on from there. Heatmap generator was integrated with the build, for tracking purposes, which was recorded for later analysis. Video recordings of the screen and user were done, for later analysis. Shortcomings were identified from these analyses and were taken for the subsequent improvement process cycles.

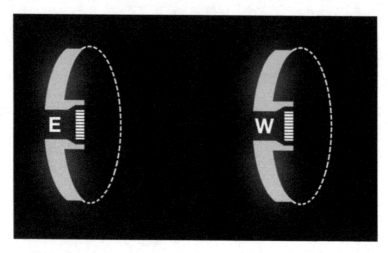

Fig. 6. Indicative interactive component for east and west drum clutch being in safe mode.

3 Future Work and Conclusion

Functionally perfect simulator, providing intended seamless experience, does not mark the end of the journey. To enhance the learning and training experience, many more possibilities and inclusions are there that can be integrated to the VR simulator. Data science, for example, can be augmented to the system for collecting quantitative data, for analysis of the user behavior with the simulator and allowing flexibility for customizing the simulator, to ensure that at the end of the training program a quality winder operator emerges and, thus, with the support of quantitative data, satisfying all the stakeholders.

References

Safety Standard for Hoist Operations (2010)

Martin, B., Hanington, B.: Universal Methods of Design: 100 Ways to Research Complex Problems, Develop Innovative Ideas, and Design Effective Solutions. Rockport Publishers, Beverly (2012)

Isaksson, O.: Design research model–an aerospace manufacturer's view. In: Chakrabarti, A., Lindemann, U. (eds.) Impact of Design Research on Industrial Practice. Springer International Publishing Switzerland (2016). https://doi.org/10.1007/978-3-319-19449-3_24

Shelly, A.W., Lutz, W., Smyth, N.J., Charles, S.: Integrating Research and Practice: A Collaborative Model for Addressing Trauma and Addiction. Taylor and Francis Inc. (2005). https://doi.org/10.1080/15434610590956930

Savage, J.: Participative observation: standing in the shoes of others?. Qual. Health Res. **10**(3), 324–339 (2000). Sage Publications

Eyal, N., Hoover, R.: Hooked: How to Build Habit-Forming Products. Penguin, London (2014)

Rosenfeld, L., Morville, P., Arango, J.: Information Architecture for the World Wide Web: Designing for the web and beyond, 4th edn. O'Reilly Media Inc., Sebastopol (2015)

Nodder, C.: Evil by Design: Interaction Design to Lead Us into Temptation. Wiley, Indianapolis (2013)

Holtzblatt, K., Beyer, H.: Contextual Design: A Customer-centered Approach to Systems Design. Morgan Kaufmann, Burlington (1998)

Kelly, G.: The Psychology of Personal Constructs (Volumes 1 and 2). Norton, New York (1955)

Cooper, A.: The Inmates Are Running the Asylum: why High-Tech Products drive Us Crazy and How to Restore the Sanity. Sams - Pearson Education, Indianapolis (2004)

Schell, J.: The Art of Game Design: A Book of Lenses. 2nd edn. CRC Press, Taylor and Francis Group, 6000 Broken Sound Parkway NW, Suite 300 (2015)

Chou, Y.-K.: Actionable Gamification: Beyond Points. Packt Publishing Ltd., Badges and Leaderboards (2015)

Osterwalder, A., Pigneur, Y., Bernarda, G., Smith, A.: Value Proposition Design: How to Create Products and Services Customers Want. Wiley, Hoboken (2014)

Burns, C., Dishman, E., Verplank, W., Lassiter, B.: Actors, hairdos and videotape informance design: using performance techniques in multidisciplinary, observation-based design. In: CHI 94 Conference Companion, pp. 119–120 (1994)

Gould, J.D., Clayton, L.: Designing for usability: key principles and what designers think. Commun. ACM **28**(3), 300–311 (1985)

Design and Cognitive Considerations for Industrial Mixed Reality Systems

Prithvi Raj Ramakrishnaraja[✉]⬤, Abhilasha⬤,
and Srinjoy Ghosh⬤

Siemens Corporate Technology, CT RDA UXD-IN, Bengaluru, India
{prithvi.ramakrishnaraja,abhilasha,
ghosh.srinjoy}@siemens.com

Abstract. In this paper we expound our theoretical hypothesis covering Design and Cognitive factors to be considered while designing an effective Augmented/Mixed Reality system solution for industrial use cases. For demonstration purposes, the targeted scenario chosen is an offshore oil-rig maintenance scenario: this scenario involves critical tasks in the areas of equipment maintenance, quick error recognition, safety, and effectiveness. With the goal towards enhanced effective Situational Awareness of the Oil Rig industrial system, the scenario involves oil-rig stakeholder collaboration/ participation and remote assistance.

An additional aim of the paper is introducing new perspectives for effective operations in an industrial maintenance scenario using mixed reality systems: the perspectives extends towards the following principles of study - Experience Design, Usability, Cognitive Science and Situational Awareness. Using Cognitive Science principles and Design Thinking approach, we try to bridge the existing white gap in the research space and intend to spearhead research towards surfacing the points to be considered in effectively designing Mixed Reality systems in such Industrial scenarios. The use of multimodal sensory augmentations such as sound and haptics to aid a better experience in performing a particular task, is also given attention. Elucidation of a functional prototype built using Microsoft Hololens1 is shared and next steps and targets are showcased as well.

Keywords: Mixed Reality · Experience Design · Cognitive factors · Situational Awareness

1 Introduction

New forms of 'realities' have emerged. 'Reality' technologies such as Mixed Reality, Augmented Reality, Virtual Reality and Augmented Virtuality are increasingly becoming indispensable to industry. Ranging from traditional application domains of architecture, design, and learning; these novel realities are the cornerstones for the this digitalization prone and smart-centric century: in a nutshell, these realities replace or merge with the normal physical world and subsequently be molded to enhance specific design comprehension, collaborating activities [7], and visualization activities [10]. These realities though promising on many fronts (industry wise) and having the ability

C. Stephanidis et al. (Eds.): HCII 2020, CCIS 1294, pp. 214–220, 2020.
https://doi.org/10.1007/978-3-030-60703-6_27

to integrate seamlessly with the IoT revolution pose new challenges to the inherent aspects of decision making, integration of newer social-cultural and cognition capabilities (here recalibration) and influences. Clark and Chambers [2] in their groundbreaking article 'The Extended Mind', showcase the human cognition has the behavioral ability to realize familiar mental states and physical skills in structures and processes located beyond the scope of their immediate sense modalities; and the complete realization of a situation requires various forms and tendencies of external scaffolding and support (stimulus) oriented mechanisms. Involving user centric mixed reality in this context is a calculated extension, and as Doswell and Skinner [4] opine that 'scientifically-grounded methods for identifying appropriate information presentation, user input, and feedback modalities in order to optimize performance and mitigate cognitive overload' is a challenge for Human-computer interaction ecosystems, and similar is the case with AR and other forms of MR which base their ecosystem on delivering maximum user interaction.

There are three important features for any MR system:

(1) combining the real-world object and the virtual object;
(2) interacting in real-time; and
(3) mapping between the virtual object and the real object to create interactions between them [6].

The main goal of MR is the creation of a big space by merging real and virtual environments wherein real and virtual objects coexist and interact in real-time for user scenarios [1]. This focus of user immersion for the output of productive decision making in ICT trends today requires appropriate visualization strategies that take into account the 'extended' capabilities of a human user and this informs -the design of the application cognitively.

For the purposes of this paper, we showcase the initial steps of integrating adaptive cognition elements (user centric) and expound our theoretical hypothesis covering Design and Cognitive factors to be considered while designing an effective Augmented/Mixed Reality system solution for an offshore oil rig maintenance scenario. This use case involves critical tasks in the areas of equipment maintenance, quick error recognition, safety, effectiveness etc. This involves multiple stakeholders. With the goal towards enhanced effective Situational Awareness of the Oil Rig industrial system, the experimental setup and prototypes designed would be elaborated. The paper extends towards identifying the key basic Cognitive and Design principles that designers need to consider while designing an industrial experience such as this.

2 Situational Awareness and Its Requisites for Sense Making

Situation Awareness (SA) of the user is of prime importance for an integrated and productive industrial workflow. With the scenario showcasing an OIM maintaining an offshore oil rig (from the mainland on an extended scenario), a stabilized depiction of tailored situational inputs becomes the key. Highlighting this journey of SA and incorporating Endsley's initial theoretical framework of SA [5] and involving the Lundberg's holistic visuo-spatial centric enhancement [9], we have incorporated AR/MR integration for enhancement of an OIM's task in the sense of making it more streamlined, direct and most importantly the possibility of him being productive on the go. Endsley's framework consists of three interconnected parameters:

a. Perception of elements in the current situation within a volume of time and space
b. Comprehension of their meaning
c. Projection of future status

Importantly, the three conducive parameters are affected by visual display support and automation aids.

Lundberg [8] enhances on this by incorporating specific visual artifacts that act as stimulus input for the user and is of the opinion that the visuo-spatial input is 'anchored in the present' but performs as the 'locus of decision-making' to incorporate the past scenarios and proceed towards a future action in the present midst of an 'ongoing, dynamic, uncertain process'. This locus that he points out rests in the sensemaking and the data driven frame that the user (in our case) is exposed to: this centrality of framing data is resting on the correct symbiosis (again this has to be generated by the OIM) being deduced and affected upon. Critically, sense making opens up the gaps of requisite imagination [11] and requisite interpretation during the comprehension of the present situation [8]: both of which are inherent problematic concerns for a high-stress positionality of an OIM's work output. Taking this crucial factor of mitigating the sense-making gap, our approach is detailed out in the next section of the paper which highlights an oil-rig maintenance use case.

3 Application Use-Case and Generation of Cognitive Prototype Design

The application use case is Oil-Rig motor maintenance and the persona defined is an Offshore Installation manager (OIM). The key tasks of an OIM are monitoring, updating and allocating resources, delegating tasks to maintenance engineers (ME), collaboration and communication, implementing the plan and assessment of the situation given the information. In an oil rig, while the OIM can benefit from digital information, there is also an increased need for the OIM to remain in contact with physical reality when using several sophisticated tools. Nevertheless, the OIM is also responsible for recognizing the signs of stress, ensuring that all staff are regularly updated on situation along with demonstrate flexibility and adaptability as plan of action and goals change.

Moreover, there is not just one but too many factors (visual elements) within the person's environment that constantly compete for visual awareness and control of action. In such an overwhelming situation information overload is bound to happen. To tackle with this problem of information overload, our attention system actively and rapidly prioritizes and selects information according to its relevance for processing and achieving the goal. But one cannot deny the fact that detection of the relevant information while ignoring the irrelevant one might get affected by the increased cognitive load on the system. Therefore, in oil rig having knowledge of objects, situations, or locations in the environment is not only useful but even life-critical for workers as they may require assistance with (1) dangers, obstacles, or situations requiring attention; (2) visual search; (3) task sequencing; and (4) spatial navigation.

Some situations would involve instances where responses are novel, dangerous and technically difficult while a few would involve planning and informed decision making, need for troubleshooting and error correction. Others may require a need to overcome some strong habitual response. But in most of the cases the most important thing that is common for all the activities is rapid generation of behavior in response to a new situation.

Hence, the design of the AR/MR system had to be as such to enable the detection of inconsistencies for OIM in the easiest manner possible for effective and efficient decision making.

The goal was to streamline the process of performing tasks where consideration is given to the related integration of cognitive functions while sparing OIM from the functional cues that are of no immediate need. Hence, the primary goal was addressing the human needs and how to augment human capabilities to overcome cognitive limitations in a decision-making process. The secondary goal was to make the system smarter as a result of the primary goal.

The prototype design defines a specific OIM workflow where the steps in the process of motor maintenance are listed as follows –

1. OIM is currently working on a task using Hololens. He is focused on his current task of analyzing a Large Drive as a part of his daily routine.
2. OIM attention is directed to an emergency. A visual cue is provided in his periphery indicating an emergency.

AR suffers a major setback that hinders the complete realization of its potential – The field-of-view (FoV) of the AR hardware is severely lacking as compared to the human eye, or even VR. With this context, the design was particularly perceptive to the aspects of the applications that focused on subtle, yet fairly accurate cues which fulfilled their purpose of guiding the user's attention to certain elements in the application environment.

3. OIM uses voice command to attend to the emergency.

Spatial tracking allows OIM to interact through pointing and natural voice commands.

4. The system opens OIM main dashboard with the error card details. Error information and rectification to enable the detection of inconsistencies for OIM in the easiest manner possible for effective and efficient decision making (Fig. 1).
5. OIM chooses to deep dive into the task.

The system by allowing selection gives OIM a perceived sense of control.

6. A confirmation message is popped up checking if the OIM would want to leave the current task and take up the new one.

System confirming the action to be taken.

Fig. 1. Showcases steps 1–4.

7. a) The OIM confirms to take up the task and is asked to place the 3D model in a location wherever convenient. - System allowing comfortable navigating and move around easily.

b) The model is placed and the error details is showcased. The physical error location on the Oil Rig is also highlighted.

c) Spatial tracking to allow OIM to interact and have the perception of 'Where I am'.

d) OIM clicks on the object to deep dive to next and consecutive level. Presentation of relevant information while ignoring the irrelevant ones.

e) OIM is at the final stage with details of error information.

System is in a ready state for the OIM to delegate tasks to the Maintenance engineer. The maintenance engineer then gets instructions in their HoloLens to work on an existing maintenance task at hand (Fig. 2).

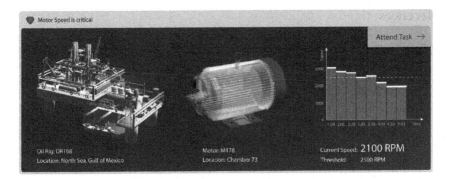

Fig. 2. Steps 5 to 7 have been highlighted.

4   Conclusion

The system has been designed in such a manner that it addresses the OIMs needs and augments capabilities to overcome cognitive limitations in his/her decision-making process. It also considers the following three aspects that has not yet been well-developed from an industrial experience point of view: First, not everything in the physical world is interactable or tagged. Second, the users still do not have well developed mental models of AR applications that might exist. Third, the visual language that these AR applications need to follow has still not reached its potential.

Incorporating of the above mentioned cognitive centric aspects help to give designers a perspective on how to evolve the visual language and develop an application that attempts to deliver the best in class visual immersive experience. The observed cues are along 3 dimensions – the goal to be accomplished (task), the extent to which the cue blends in with the environment (markedness), and the context in which the cue is triggered into the user's visibility (trigger) within the context. The challenge lies in keeping these cues minimalistic yet informative enough, so that the OIM remain immersive enough and the information is easy to understand and distinguishable from the environment. The result of this activity would be a smarter system that effectively incorporates expectations of the physical environment into the AR application and parallelly develops a well-defined visual language for the AR systems in an industrial setup.

However, our immediate next step which is already in process is the scientific validation of the prototype with actual users. Verification and validation with data from eye tracker and user-specific tasks activity will focus on the following:

1. Validating with the actual users
2. Quantitative validation - latency and accuracy
3. Scalability of the framework to additional industrial use cases and domains.

Additionally, we shall also focus on developing a more robust and texture specialized Visuo-Haptic Mixed Reality layer [3], as a continuation of the work mentioned in this paper.

References

1. Chen, L., Day, T.W., Tang, W., John, N.W.: Recent developments and future challenges in medical mixed reality. In: Proceedings of 16th IEEE International Symposium on Mixed and Augmented Reality (ISMAR) (2017)
2. Clark, A., Chalmers, D.J.: The extended mind. Analysis **58**, 7–19 (1998)
3. Cosco, F., et al.: Visuo-haptic mixed reality with unobstructed tool-hand integration. IEEE Trans. Vis. Comput. Graph. **19**(1), 159–172 (2013)
4. Doswell, J.T., Skinner, A.: Augmenting human cognition with adaptive augmented reality. In: Schmorrow, D.D., Fidopiastis, C.M. (eds.) AC 2014. LNCS (LNAI), vol. 8534, pp. 104–113. Springer, Cham (2014). https://doi.org/10.1007/978-3-319-07527-3_10
5. Endsley, M.R.: Toward a theory of situation awareness in dynamic systems. Hum. Factors J. **37**(1), 32–64 (1995)
6. Hoenig, W., Milanes, C., Scaria, L., Phan, T., Bolas, M., Ayanian, N.: Mixed reality for robotics. In: Proceedings of the IEEE/RSJ International Conference on Intelligent Robots and Systems (IROS), Hamburg, Germany, 28 September–2 October 2015. IEEE, Piscataway (2015)
7. Lukosch, S., Billinghurst, M., Alem, L., Kiyokawa, K.: Collaboration in augmented reality. Comput. Supported Coop. Work (CSCW) **24**(6), 515–525 (2015). https://doi.org/10.1007/s10606-015-9239-0
8. Lundberg, J., Johansson, J.: Resilience, stability, and requisite interpretation in accident investigations. In: Proceedings of 2nd Resilience Engineering Symposium, pp. 191–198 (2006)
9. Lundberg, J.: Situation awareness systems, states and processes: a holistic framework. Theor. Issues Ergon. Sci. **16**(5), 447–473 (2015)
10. Schnabel, M.A., et al.: From virtuality to reality and back. In: Poggenpohl, S. (ed.) International Association of Societies of Design Research 2007 (IASDR 2007), School of Design, The Hong Kong Polytechnic University 2007 Core A, The Hong Kong Polytechnic University Hung Hom, Kowloon, Hong Kong, 12–15 November 2007, Digital Proceedings, Day 4, Session D: Interaction/Interface (2007). ISBN 988-99101-4-4
11. Westrum, R.: A typology of resilience situations. In: Hollnagel, E., Woods, D.D., Leveson, N. (eds.) Resilience Engineering Concepts and Precepts. Safety Culture and Resilience Engineering: Theory and Application in Improving Gold Mining Safety. Ashgate Publishing, Aldershot (2006)

Augmented Reality Space Informatics System

Olivia Thomas[(✉)] [ID], Daniel Lambert [ID], and Beatrice Dayrit

Boise State University, Boise, ID 83725, USA
{oliviathomas,daniellambert,
tricedayrit}@u.boisestate.edu

Abstract. The Augmented Reality Space Informatics System (ARSIS) is a Microsoft HoloLens application developed for the NASA SUITS (Spacesuit User Interfaces for Students) challenge that provides an augmented reality (AR) interface for information display and communication to be used by astronauts during extravehicular activity (EVA) procedures. Astronauts are required to deal with complex and changing circumstances on EVA. The current status quo requires heavy reliance on voice communication with Mission Control Centers (MCCs) for everything from biometric data to assistance with procedures. ARSIS is designed with the dual purpose of increasing astronaut autonomy and making communication with MCCs more effective. Features of ARSIS include voice and gaze user interface (UI) navigation, anchored menus, planetary navigation aids, biometric information display, procedure instructions, and a suite of tools for enhanced communication with Mission Control including spatial telestration. User experience (UX) testing results for ARSIS have been generally positive overall, with the biggest takeaway being that users would prefer alternative modes of UI navigation to voice control. Eye tracking for UI navigation is a promising area of exploration in the future.

Keywords: Augmented reality · Mixed reality · Virtual reality · Aerospace · Computer supported collaborative work · Telestration · Telepresence

1 Introduction

The Augmented Reality Space Informatics System (ARSIS) was designed for the NASA SUITS (Spacesuit User Interfaces for Students) challenge as a prototype for a heads-up display (HUD) interface to be integrated into astronauts' helmets. During EVA missions, it is important to be able to communicate complex data and instructions to crew members. By showing this information in the astronauts' physical space instead of on a traditional monitor, information can be communicated in a more direct, natural manner. ARSIS has a dual purpose of increasing astronaut autonomy and efficiency of communication with Mission Control.

AR overlays additional information onto physical reality (PR). Mixed reality (MR) integrates these digital elements into PR. Virtual reality (VR) is an immersive experience which obscures PR. ARSIS uses a combination of all three, with AR/MR used by the astronaut and VR used by MCCs.

One of the guiding design principles of ARSIS is the concept of embodied interaction. Embodied interaction reflects on a person's familiarity with the real world to

© Springer Nature Switzerland AG 2020
C. Stephanidis et al. (Eds.): HCII 2020, CCIS 1294, pp. 221–228, 2020.
https://doi.org/10.1007/978-3-030-60703-6_28

direct an experience in the digital world. Embodied interaction is the "creation, manipulation, and sharing of meaning through engaged interaction with these embodied phenomena" [1]. Research suggests that this concept may be useful when MR integrates into physical space. When a user interface is integrated into the physical space, the line between real and digital is blurred, allowing for more intuitive interaction.

A major application of embodied interaction in ARSIS is spatial telestration between astronauts and Mission Control. This is used as a method of computer-supported cooperative work (CSCW). The goal of CSCW is to "allow people to cooperate by overcoming barriers of space and time" [2]. In a setting where effective communication is critical, telestration can make communication more natural, providing operatives the ability to show the astronaut what they mean through visual cues rather than relying solely on audio explanations. This also provides the ability for asynchronous communication between the astronauts and Mission Control, which is useful in space exploration past our moon where significant communication lag may be encountered.

2 Background

ARSIS was designed for NASA in response to the NASA SUITS challenge. The intended user is an astronaut on EVA. ARSIS also contains communication features to be utilized by Mission Control operatives.

NASA provided specific requirements for ARSIS which were the primary consideration in the design. The next sections describe the users of ARSIS and the design requirements in more detail.

2.1 User Profiles

Astronauts. Astronauts are required to deal with complex and changing circumstances on EVA. Nominal procedures are read to NASA astronauts over voice by an intravehicle (IV) crew member [7]. Astronauts also use a paper cuff checklist secured to their wrist containing emergency procedures and their own notes [3, 7]. Former astronaut Steve Swanson spoke to his experience on EVA at the International Space Station (ISS), saying, "We have to rely on Mission Control to help us out. They monitor our suit data, so we don't really get that insight into a lot of things that we are doing" [7]. A major goal of ARSIS is displaying more information to the astronaut to increase autonomy. Another important consideration is that EVAs can last up to 8 h [4]. Fatigue may set in, making the minimization of cognitive load crucial. Studies have shown that use of MR UIs through a HUD does not increase cognitive load [5]. According to a review of 87 studies by Santos et al. as cited by Leonard and Fitzgerald [6] MR can even reduce cognitive load. Finally, while current EVAs take place primarily on the ISS, ARSIS is also designed to be used for planetary exploration on the moon and Mars. Astronauts will face new challenges on planetary EVAs including navigating terrain, documenting and sampling geology features, and more [8].

Mission Control Operatives. Mission Control operatives provide support to the astronaut on EVA. Swanson spoke to the experience of Mission Control operatives, noting that constant voice communication with astronauts slows them down. "Right now there is so much communication from the crew that they are always listening and trying to figure out what is going on, and then the little bits of time that they have that people aren't talking they get a lot of work done. It would be more efficient if we could communicate without all of the voice" [7].

2.2   Design Requirements

Following are the design requirements for the SUITS 2020 challenge [8]:

1. EVA task instructions shall be displayed
2. The astronaut must be able to access the status of the spacesuit at any time
3. The astronaut shall be able to communicate with ground control at any time
4. A caution and warning system must be implemented to inform the astronaut about a spacesuit anomaly
5. In case of an interruption, the astronaut must be able to continue the task on hand seamlessly
6. The user interface shall not permanently impede the astronaut's ability to perform
7. All hand gestures must be operable with EVA gloved hands (like heavy ski gloves)
8. The user interface shall take field notes for lunar sampling

3   UI Navigation

One of the most important design challenges tackled by ARSIS is UI navigation. Many HoloLens applications use hand gestures as a primary form of user input. However, this is not practical for the intended user of ARSIS. Astronauts currently wear thick gloves on EVA [3] and need to use their hands for their work. Voice control is an alternative available in HoloLens 1 and which is already being developed for control of robots in space by The German Aerospace Center in partnership with Mozilla [9].

Thus, ARSIS uses two interchangeable modes of UI navigation: voice commands and gaze + voice. These modes are detailed in Sects. 3.1–3.2. A third possibility for navigation is eye tracking, which studies have shown has promise as a mode of UI navigation [10, 11].

Menus are anchored in space and appear directly in front of the user when opened. Users can close a menu by using a voice command while looking at it. Multiple different menus can be opened at a time, although not multiple copies of the same menu. If a user attempts to do this, the currently open menu will be moved to where the user is looking.

Some information, such as sensitive biometric data, warnings, and an indicator of microphone input, is configured to appear at the corner of the user's view instead of staying anchored in space. This information is non-interactable.

3.1 Voice Commands

All ARSIS functions are accessible by a unique voice command. Voice commands must be prefaced by the "Adele" keyword to aid in accurate recognition.

Many voice commands, such as the commands to open menus, can be called at any time. On the other hand, commands which act on an open menu are only recognized when that menu is open. Menus include buttons with the names of possible voice commands to aid in navigation of the voice interface and memory of commands. A help menu contains a list of commands. During testing, users are also given an arm sleeve which holds a printed list of common voice commands.

A microphone icon at the top left of the ARSIS display modulates in size based on the volume of audio input. When a command is recognized, the icon turns red and the name of the command appears briefly next to the microphone icon. This was designed to mitigate user confusion over whether their command was understood correctly.

In case of voice command failure, a manual override can be called by Mission Control. This is detailed in Sect. 4.5.

3.2 Gaze + Voice

When a user looks directly at a button on a menu (determined using headset rotation), the button will light up. The user can then use the "Adele choose" voice command to select that button. This is a useful alternative for buttons with titles that would be long or ambiguous to pronounce (e.g. selecting a field note by date to view more details). This is also useful if a user finds that a voice command is not recognized reliably.

4 Features

ARSIS is a fully functional HoloLens 1 application which allows users to do the following, detailed in Sects. 4.1–4.5:

- Record and view spatial translation information
- View procedures via menus anchored in physical space
- Monitor biometric data
- Enter field notes through an interactive questionnaire
- Communicate with Mission Control through spatial telestration
- Receive additional help from Mission Control including remote UI navigation and real-time procedure and diagram updates

Translation
ARSIS includes several systems that can be used to help the astronaut navigate to the work location. One system provides collaborative communication through telestration. This system is described in Sect. 4.4. Additionally, another system provides an autonomously controlled "breadcrumb" trail. When activated, the system renders a trail in the space showing the user's location over time. These paths can then be saved and used to navigate back to the starting point, or for navigation to the same location in the future.

ARSIS also includes a toggleable top-down map which shows users the spatial mapping data gathered from the HoloLens infrared sensors, as well as the user's current position on the map denoted by a red dot. This map is pictured in Fig. 1.

Fig. 1. Top-down map (Color figure online)

4.1   Procedure Instruction

Upon reaching the work location, the user can activate the procedure instruction interface, shown in Fig. 2. This interface allows astronauts to view task instructions anchored in space. The user can open the appropriate procedure and navigate through it using commands such as "next" and "previous." Commands are also available for displaying diagrams.

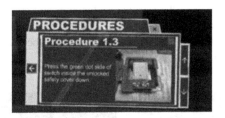

Fig. 2. Example procedure instruction

4.2   Biometrics

ARSIS displays biometric information including suit pressure, oxygen, and other relevant values. Currently this information is simulated over a web server.

All measured information is shown in the biometrics menu, with colors indicating whether each value is in the expected range. However, it is important for astronauts to monitor the most sensitive information without having to open a menu. For this reason, a time left value (the smaller of oxygen time and battery time) is always shown persistently in the bottom left of the display. If biometric values are outside of the expected range or if another anomaly is encountered, a warning will be shown on the display.

4.3 Field Notes

The field notes interface presents users with an interactive questionnaire used to document information about geology features. At the end of the questionnaire, users are asked to take a picture of the geology feature. Both the image and the questionnaire answers are stored on the device for future reference.

4.4 Telestration

When astronauts encounter unexpected scenarios or difficulties with procedures, voice communication with Mission Control is the current standard for resolving these issues. Spatial telestration adds a visual layer to the interaction. Spatial telestration has already been successfully implemented in surgical procedures [12]. It also allows for a form of asynchronous communication that may be beneficial in situations with communication delay. According to Swanson, back and forth communication is difficult with a com delay. He remarked, "If you can do it visually... that's going to give the person much more information more quickly and in a way where they are not going to have a conversation back and forth" [7].

ARSIS includes two Ground Station applications through which telestration can take place, one in VR and one which can be used on a desktop computer. This feature builds upon work such as that by Kato and Billinghurst [13]. In ARSIS, spatial mapping data from the HoloLens is sent over a network to the Ground Station applications. This data is then rendered in VR or on the desktop. Mission Control operatives can see a marker of the astronaut's location and can move around the space to see it from different angles. They can draw annotations in a manner similar to that described by Arora et al. [14]. The annotations will then be sent back and rendered in real space on the HoloLens display, as shown in Fig. 3.

Fig. 3. Spatial telestration – Mission Control drawing (right) and HoloLens view (left)

Operatives can also choose from a selection of preset icons (arrows, circles, etc.) to place in the space instead of or in addition to drawn annotations.

4.5 Additional Mission Control Features

If the astronaut is unable to use voice commands due to noise, a failure in the system, etc., Mission Control operatives can use a web portal to call commands remotely. The web portal also includes functionality to upload new procedures and diagrams to be displayed on the HoloLens. In the future, this web portal could be combined with the desktop telestration application for a more cohesive experience.

5   Testing Results

ARSIS underwent testing at Johnson Space Center (Houston, Texas, USA). During these tests, astronauts and industry experts successfully used the system to complete simulated EVA tasks.

In a separate UX test conducted at Boise State with 15 participants, 100% of users (high school students, parents, and university staff) reported that they would prefer ARSIS to complete a task over instructions delivered via paper or a tablet. 75% of users reported that the interface (which at the time used only voice navigation with no gaze option) was either somewhat or extremely easy to use. However, ease of using voice commands was a common complaint and 67% reported difficulty using the voice interface in a loud environment. The problem of noise would be less prevalent in outer space. However, these results prompted the addition of gaze-based navigation and the consideration of eye tracking as a future possibility. According to Swanson, a navigation solution which does not require voice would be beneficial as it would avoid taking up voice loop time with Mission Control [7].

The spread of COVID-19 in the United States in Spring 2020 prevented UX testing of the features developed during that time, including extensive testing of telestration features. Additional testing is planned in the future.

6   Conclusion

Further work on ARSIS will explore additional methods of interaction between the Ground Station applications and HoloLens system, approaching telepresence. Other areas of possible expansion include object recognition, eye tracking for UI navigation, and solutions for high and low light scenarios.

While applied specifically to the field of aerospace, the information display and communication methods demonstrated in ARSIS have applicability in a wide variety of instructional and operational scenarios where displaying information in space and/or collaborating with a remote expert are of value. As more and more information and communication become available digitally, the importance of displaying this information in a meaningful, context-driven manner, as accomplished by spatial systems like ARSIS, will only increase.

Acknowledgements. Special thanks to our faculty advisors, Dr. Karen Doty and Dr. Steve Swanson, as well as our community advisor Charles Burnell.

References

1. Dourish, P.: Where the Action Is. MIT Press, Cambridge (2001)
2. Wexelblat, A.: Virtual Reality: Applications and Explorations. Academic Press, Cambridge (1993)
3. NASA EMU Hardware Data Book. https://www.nasa.gov/sites/default/files/atoms/files/esoc-13_rev._v_emu_hardware_data_book_jsc-e-daa-tn55224.pdf. Accessed 14 June 2020
4. NASA General EVA Guidelines. https://msis.jsc.nasa.gov/sections/section14.htm#_14.1_GENERAL_EVA. Accessed 14 June 2020
5. Cometti, C., Païzis, C., Casteleira, A., Pons, G., Babault, N.: Effects of mixed reality head-mounted glasses during 90 minutes of mental and manual tasks on cognitive and physiological functions. PeerJ **6**, e5847 (2018)
6. Leonard, S., Fitzgerald, R.: Holographic learning: a mixed reality trial of Microsoft HoloLens in an Australian secondary school. Res. Learn. Technol. **2160**(26), 1–12 (2018)
7. Former Astronaut Steve Swanson, personal interview
8. NASA SUITS Challenge Descriptions. https://microgravityuniversity.jsc.nasa.gov/docs/suits/SUITS%202020%20Mission%20Description.8.22.19.pdf. Accessed 14 June 2020
9. Astronauts adopt Mozilla speech tech to control Moon robots. https://www.zdnet.com/article/astronauts-adopt-mozilla-speech-tech-to-control-moon-robots/. Accessed 14 June 2020
10. Boudoin, P., Otmane, S., Mallem, M.: Design of a 3D navigation technique supporting VR interaction. In: AIP Conference Proceedings, vol. 1019, no. 1, pp. 149–153 (2008)
11. Zhu, D., Gedeon, T., Taylor, K.: "Moving to the centre": a gaze-driven remote camera control teleperation. Interact. Comput. **23**(1), 85–95 (2011)
12. Jarc, A.M., et al.: Beyond 2D telestration: an evaluation of novel proctoring tools for robot-assisted minimally invasive surgery. J. Robotic Surg. **10**(2), 103–109 (2016). https://doi.org/10.1007/s11701-016-0564-1
13. Kato, H., Billinghurst, M.: Marker tracking and HMD calibration for a video-based augmented reality conferencing system. In: Proceedings 2nd IEEE and ACM International Workshop on Augmented Reality (IWAR), San Francisco, CA, USA, pp. 85–94 (1999)
14. Arora, R., Kazi, R.H., Anderson, F., Grossman, T., Sign, K., Fitzmaurice, G.: Experimental evaluation of sketching on surfaces in VR. In: Proceedings of the CHI, Denver, CO, USA (2017)

Mercury's Boots: Extending Visual Information and Enabling to Move Around a Remote Place for VR Avatar

Koki Toda[✉] and Sayuki Hayashi

Revetronique, Tokyo, Japan
koki.t.kmd@gmail.com, revetronique@gmail.com

Abstract. In this research, we develop a mobile telepresence robot displaying a light field image of the VR avatar synchronizing its posture to that of the VR performer and VR controlling application rendering a point cloud of the scene before the robot to the VR system with an RGB-D camera. Both our robot and application communicate with each other via WebRTC. Our remote communication system compresses depth data approximately 100 kB, sends every about 200 ms and decodes it for 20 ms in average as the result of our performance test. In our online survey, 105 subjects generally expected our expecting effects, but some of them worried or suspected the limitation concerned to VR technology, network, or emotional expression of avatars.

Keywords: VR avatar · Telepresence · Remote communication

1 Introduction

Under today's widespread of communication devices and networking infrastructure in the world, enormous remote communication services or applications have been launched [1]. Some of them use a CG model called "avatar" to communicate with others [2]. Eventually, social VR services or "VTubers", who are live streamers performing as a digital character have appeared in recent years [3]. Though using an avatar for remote communication become popular today, there are significant limitations for bidirectional communication or interaction such as running around live stages, eye contact, hug, or shake hands.

By the way, telepresence robot is used for various purposes from business to personal use [4]. These robots can take people having physical, economic, or health problems to distant places, work in dangerous areas or situations, and move in or interact to the real world unlike video contents or software. However, it can hardly produce complex gestures and facial expressions, or its reliability, robustness, and maintainability will be decreased even if required components are installed.

In this study, we develop a mobile telepresence robot displaying a light field image of the VR avatar and VR application showing a point cloud of the remote area to the VR performer so that a VR performer and his or her audience can communicate with each other as if they feel they are in the same place (Fig. 1).

© Springer Nature Switzerland AG 2020
C. Stephanidis et al. (Eds.): HCII 2020, CCIS 1294, pp. 229–237, 2020.
https://doi.org/10.1007/978-3-030-60703-6_29

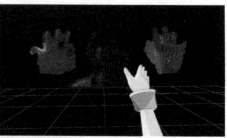

Fig. 1. VR player performing as a virtual character makes a communication with audience in remote space via our developing robot (left). VR player can watch the audience in the place where our avatar robot stands sterically through a point cloud (right).

Our research features and contributes are in the followings.

- VR: performer
  - 3D rendering of a remote place using RGB-D images and point cloud.
  - Enhancement of the sense of immersion in a remote location through VR
- Robot: audience.
  - Emphasizing the presence of avatars by showing a light field image.
  - Move an avatar in the real world.
  - Represent emotional expression such as gesture or face.

2   Related Works

2.1   Virtual Avatar

Recently, besides social VR services, platforms of virtual avatars, which is specialized in delivering live performance or live chat, were getting fulfilled [5]. Live shows of virtual avatars have been held in succession [6], and facilities for supporting live shows with virtual avatars also opened [7]. In addition, we can find some cases utilizing virtual avatars in economic or social activities [8, 9].

2.2   Avatar Robot

Until today, large number and variety of telepresence robot have been researched and developed [4]. One of the representative robots is TELESAR researched and developed by Prof. Tachi and his laboratory [10]. "Orihime" has been provided for people with disabilities, especially for ALS patients [11].

2.3   Researches for Interaction Between VR and Real

There are also some researches or applications connecting VR to the real. Chagué et al. used IR tracking cameras to capture physical objects for their VR experience [12]. Some remote communication systems using an RGB-D camera to unite distance places were launched [13]. Levitar displayed a stereoscopic image of a VR avatar which moved corresponding to the VR player's head [14].

3 System

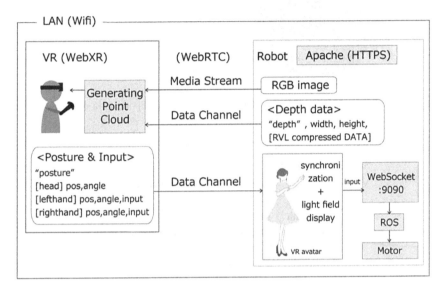

Fig. 2. System configuration.

We depict the configuration of our system in Fig. 2. Our VR system and robot are connected to the same wireless LAN via wifi. It utilizes WebRTC API for communication processes, WebGL for drawing 3DCG models, and WebXR for VR.

The VR side is simply composed of a VR-ready computer and VR devices (HMD, tracking cameras, and VR controllers). On the other hand, robot side is built with a microcontroller unit (MCU), RGB-D camera, light field display, and two-wheel differential driving unit. The MCU manages communication process, 3DCG drawing process, and controlling its driving unit. The RGB-D camera scans the 3D geometry of audiences and their place, and the driving unit moves the VR avatar as the VR player's operation. We also adopt a light field display of the video output device for enhancing the presence of the avatar.

4   Implementation

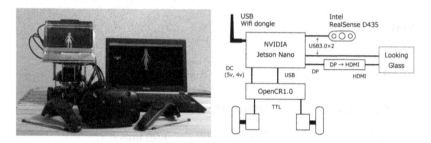

Fig. 3. All devices in our system (left). Connection of all components in our robot (right).

Table 1. Hardware components.

Side	Component	Device
VR	Computer	VR-Ready PC (with NVIDA GTX 1070)
	VR HMD	HTC Vive
Robot	Drive unit	TurtleBot3 Burger
	MCU	NVIDIA Jetson Nano (Ubuntu 18.04)
	Camera	Intel RealSense D435
	Display	8.9″ Looking Glass

All devices used in our system are in Fig. 3 (light), and every component is listed in Table 1. We also develop Web applications for VR and robot side with html5, css3, and javascript. Our applications are stored in a web server built with Apache 2, and our VR system and robot execute each corresponding application by accessing it.

4.1   VR Side

Our VR system draws a VR avatar with using WebGL and WebXR. Every frame the posture of the VR HMD and controllers is applied to the avatar.

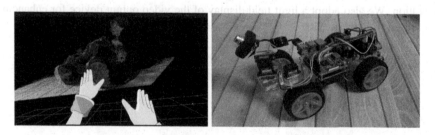

Fig. 4. Point cloud shown in the VR (left). The object captured with an RGB-D camera (right).

The VR performer can see a 3D image (point cloud) of the remote place captured from the RGB-D camera attached to the robot (Fig. 4). It renders a point cloud of the remote place from an RGB and depth image received via WebRTC.

The rendering processes are the followings.

1. Decoding the compressed depth image data with RVL (see Sect. 4.2).
2. Converting the raw depth image from unsigned short to float.
3. Generating a texture from a transformed array.
4. Drawing a point cloud based on the generated depth texture and RGB image.

4.2 Robot Side

Figure 3 (right) illustrates the connection of all components in our robot. This robot shows an image of the VR avatar sterically with the light field display, and also obtains the 3D geometry of the scene before the robot by using the RGB-D camera. Captured image has a resolution of W424 × H240 pixels and is transferred to the VR application after compressing the depth image with RVL compression algorithm [15]. This robot can be moved by the VR performer and the avatar image shown in its display synchronizes to his or her posture.

4.3 Media and Data Communication

Our VR system and robot share the posture and input of the VR performer and the three-dimensional geometry of the scene in front of the robot via WebRTC.

Table 2. Directions and contents of our communication system with WebRTC.

API	From	To	Content
Media stream	Robot	VR	RGB image from RGB-D camera
Data channel	Robot	VR	Tag: "depth" Width and height of depth image Array data of compressed depth image
	VR	Robot	Tag: "posture" Posture and input of VR performer

The details of the whole data the system exchanges are listed in Table 2. All data exchanged via Data Channel are converted to JSON format. Owing to sending a large-size data depth image, the system disables ordered transfer and limit re-transmission time within 500 ms when opening a data channel. We aim to compress the data size by setting the depth over a certain threshold to zero so as to increase the number of chunks of zero-pixels.

5 Experiment

5.1 Performance Test

We evaluated our system to display a point cloud of the remote place by measuring the interval of receiving a depth data, the receiving and decoding time, and compressing size and rate of it. Support that compressed depth data is contained in a 32-bit unsigned integer array and raw depth image in a 16-bit unsigned integer array, compressing rate is calculated with the following equation:

$$(\text{Compressing rate}) = (L_{cd} * 4)/(w * h * 2) \tag{1}$$

where L_{cd} is the data size, w is the width, and h is the height of the depth image (Table 3).

Table 3. Measurement results among thresholds of distance.

Threshold	Transfer interval (ms)	Receiving time (ms)	Decoding time (ms)	Data size (kB)	Compressing rate
1000 mm	218.37 ± 32.45	21.08 ± 3.95	3.23 ± 0.98	89.80 ± 13.76	0.44
2000 mm	241.01 ± 26.27	18.36 ± 2.34	3.10 ± 0.98	127.99 ± 10.05	0.63

First, we compared its performance by changing the depth threshold to (a) 1000 mm and (b) 2000 mm (the size of depth image is W424 × H240) (Table 4).

Table 4. Measurement results among sizes of depth image.

Image size	Transfer interval (ms)	Receiving time (ms)	Decoding time (ms)	Data size (kB)	Compressing rate
424 × 240	241.01 ± 26.27	18.36 ± 2.34	3.10 ± 0.98	127.99 ± 10.05	0.63
480 × 270	269.24 ± 34.31	18.71 ± 1.93	2.97 ± 1.82	117.18 ± 21.93	0.45
640 × 480	279.60 ± 24.98	17.73 ± 1.48	2.33 ± 0.33	100.12 ± 1.19	0.16

Second, we also compared its performance by changing the size of depth image to (a) W424 × H240 (same as the case (a) in the previous test), (b) W480 × H270, and (c) W640 × H480 (the depth threshold is 2000 mm).

On the whole, even the system spent nearly 20 ms to decode, it took over 200 ms in average and the framerate of redrawing a point cloud goes down to less than 5 fps. We will improve it by optimizing arrangement of depth data in an array because the size of compressed data itself is relatively large (over 100 kB).

5.2   Preliminary Survey

In order to expect potential and utility of our proposal system, we conducted a web survey in Japan. We have finally collected answers from 105 people from 20s to 50s who had VR experiences (of which 50 males, 53 females and 2 non-respondents). We mainly asked their impressions of CG avatars utilized for economic or social activity and expectation to our proposal system.

The subjects rated 6 types (P1: easy to talk, P2: familiarity, P3: presence, P4: credibility, P5: psychological distance, and P6: discomfort) of impression to them on a 5-point scale (1: not at all - 5: definitely agree), and wrote their impressions of the experience, problems, and desired interactions. Then, they also rated and wrote about their impression and expecting features of our developing system after seeing its operating images. The whole questions in five-point scale evaluation are Q1) More realistic than display, Q2) More powerful than display, Q3) Psychological distance closer, Q4) Familiar than mechanical robots about our robot, and Q1) More realistic than display, Q2) Feel as if you talk with remote people in the same place, Q3) Psychological distance closer, Q4) More immersive in remote areas, Q5) Make the environment and situation of distant places comprehensive about our VR system.

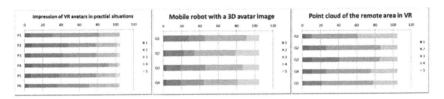

Fig. 5. Results of the 5-point scale evaluation for the impression of VR avatars (left), mobile robot with a 3D avatar image (middle), and point cloud of the remote area in VR (right).

The results of the evaluation are shown in Fig. 5. None of the items were extremely positive or negative towards the real world use of avatar, while our remote communication system was generally rated 4 or more favorably. Especially for the VR system, the question 1 and 5 were rated 4 or higher by more than 80% of subjects.

We also summarize some remarkable impressions and opinions in below:

- Utilizing an avatar for economic or social activity
  - More realistic than they expected.
  - Something different from a real person because of the gap between their appearance and voice, psychological distance, and incomplete expressions.
  - Technical limitations or problems, especially in VR sickness or time lag.
  - Presenting the five senses, physical actions from the avatar, participation in events in remote areas, and solving social isolation were desirable.
- Mobile robot that displays a light field image of an avatar
  - Useful for visiting remote areas, guide, signage, and live performances.
  - The two main problems are the drive unit is large and display area is small.

– Point cloud of the remote place rendered in VR
  • Enhancing the presence and reality of the remote place.
  • Useful for visiting remote areas, working at dangerous sites, and collaborative work with people in a remote place
  • Subjects requested sharpening image, presenting thermal or tactile sense.

6 Conclusion

For the purpose of extending remote communication, we develop a new mobile telepresence robot and VR application with using a VR avatar. Our robot enables a VR avatar to move around a distant place by displaying a light field image of the avatar and driving its wheels as the VR performer's control. In our VR system, the VR performer can see a point cloud of the remote place through the HMD.

We conducted a performance test and online survey of our system. In the performance test, we inspected our transfer system for compressed depth data. The decoding time was about 20 ms, while the average transfer interval was almost always over 200 ms because the data size exceeded 100 kB. We also conducted a preliminary survey for 105 people with VR experience. Our system was generally rated highly. Some subjects told that our system could be used for remote visit, signage or facility guidance, and collaborative work in remote areas.

In future, we will improve the compression algorithm, enable a VR performer to represent emotional expressions as his or her will, and examine how our proposal system effects remote communication through user studies.

References

1. Odlyzko, A.: The history of communications and its implications for the internet. SSRN Electron. J. (2000). https://doi.org/10.2139/ssrn.235284
2. Ventrella, J.J.: Virtual Body Language: The History and Future of Avatars: How Nonverbal Expression is Evolving on the Internet. ETC Press, Pittsburgh (2011)
3. Bredikhina, L.: Designing identity in VTuber era. In: Proceedings of Laval Virtual VRIC ConVRgence 2020, pp. 182–184. https://doi.org/10.20870/IJVR.2020...3316
4. Kristoffersson, A., Coradeschi, S., Loutfi, A.: A review of mobile robotic telepresence. Adv. Hum. Comp. Int. **2013** (2013). Article 3, 1 page. https://doi.org/10.1155/2013/902316
5. Wright Flyer Live Entertainment Inc.: Reality (2018). https://reality.wrightflyer.net/
6. Ichikara Inc.: Virtual to Live in Ryogoku Kokugikan (2019). https://event.nijisanji.app/vtlryougoku2019/
7. Pony Canyon, Inc.: Harevutai (2020). https://harevutai.com/#
8. ADVAC Corp.: Vataraku (2018). https://saisyun-kaiba.com/vataraku/
9. Heroes Inc.: AVASTAND (2019). https://www.heroes-tokyo.com/
10. Fernando, C.L., et al.: Design of TELESAR V for transferring bodily consciousness in telexistence. In: 2012 IEEE/RSJ International Conference on Intelligent Robots and Systems, Vilamoura, pp. 5112–5118 (2012). https://doi.org/10.1109/iros.2012.6385814
11. Ory Laboratory: OriHime (2012). https://orihime.orylab.com/

12. Chagué, S., Charbonnier, C.: Real virtuality: a multi-user immersive platform connecting real and virtual worlds. In: Proceedings of the 2016 Virtual Reality International Conference (VRIC 2016), article 4, pp. 1–3. Association for Computing Machinery, New York (2016). https://doi.org/10.1145/2927929.2927945
13. Stocking, H., Gunkel, S.N.B., De Koninck, T., van Eersel, M., Kok, B.: AR/VR for conferencing and remote assistance. In: Proceedings of Laval Virtual VRIC ConVRgence 2020, pp. 175–177 (2020). https://doi.org/10.20870/IJVR.2020...3316
14. Tsuchiya, K., Koizumi, N.: Levitar: real space interaction through mid-air CG avatar. In: SIGGRAPH Asia 2019 Emerging Technologies (SA 2019), pp. 25–26. Association for Computing Machinery, New York (2019). https://doi.org/10.1145/3355049.3360539
15. Wilson, A.D.: Fast lossless depth image compression. In: Proceedings of the 2017 ACM International Conference on Interactive Surfaces and Spaces (ISS 2017), pp. 100–105. Association for Computing Machinery, New York (2017). https://doi.org/10.1145/3132272.3134144

Comparison of Different Information Display Modes for Smart Glasses Assisted Machine Operations

Chao-Hung Wang[1], Chih-Yu Hsiao[1], An-Ting Tai[1],
and Mao-Jiun J. Wang[2(✉)]

[1] Department of Industrial Engineering and Engineering Management,
National Tsing Hua University, No. 101, Sec. 2, Guangfu Road, Hsinchu 30013,
Taiwan R.O.C.
[2] Department of Industrial Engineering and Enterprise Information, Tunghai
University, No. 1727, Sec. 4, Taiwan Boulevard, Xitun District, Taichung 40704,
Taiwan R.O.C.
mjwang@ie.nthu.edu.tw

Abstract. A pair of commercially available smart glasses, Epson BT-200, was evaluated with different information display modes for assisting machine operators. Two information display modes were selected, displaying animated images only, and displaying animated images with text illustrations. Direction prompts were added in the system. Whether the prompts are helpful or not was also discussed in this study. Task completion time and error rate were collected during the experiment. System Usability Scale (SUS) and NASA-Task Load Index (NASA-TLX) were used to collect subjective information after each experiment. Twenty participants (10 males and 10 females) were recruited. The results showed that the display mode of having smart glasses displaying animated images versus displaying animated images with text illustrations showed no significant difference in task completion time and error rate. But the significant difference was found in the result of SUS scores. Participants preferred the display mode of animate images with text illustrations according to the SUS scores. Moreover, the results indicated that the use of direction prompts had significant influences upon all the measures. Participants completed the tasks faster and had lower error rate by using the smart glasses with direction prompts. And the results of subjective ratings also showed higher SUS score and lower NASA-TLX score were associated with using smart glasses with direction prompts. Thus, the implementation of using smart glasses to guide machine operations should be considered the design of adding direction prompts to increase efficiency and effectiveness of the operations.

Keywords: Augmented reality · Information display · Smart glasses

© Springer Nature Switzerland AG 2020
C. Stephanidis et al. (Eds.): HCII 2020, CCIS 1294, pp. 238–243, 2020.
https://doi.org/10.1007/978-3-030-60703-6_30

1   Introduction

With the trend of promoting Industry 4.0, the awareness of developing smart factory is becoming more universal around the world. Smart glasses are considered to be advantageous for assisting machine operators in smart factory environment. Smart glasses can simultaneously assist operators to work with their hands free, and provide required information through the lens [1]. The transparent displays of smart glasses allow operators to read instructions virtually, and the functionality of augmented reality (AR) have been identified helpful for the operators in shop-floor [2]. Paelke (2014) [3] proposed virtual instructions for assembly tasks in a pair of optical see-through glasses, and indicated that participants without prior experience in assembly tasks were also able to complete the tasks. Zheng et al. (2015) [4] designed a wearable solution for industrial maintenance tasks by using Google Glasses, which contained virtual work-flow guidance via pictures, videos, and voice annotations. Smart glasses or head-mounted displays (HMDs) were widely used in the industry universally, various evaluations of smart glasses/HMDs used in factory floors were exhibited in recent years. Such as, comparing video see-through glasses with optical see-through glasses for displaying virtual annotations [5], comparing Google Glasses with tablet PC for assembly tasks [6], or comparing different types of augmented reality smart glasses on the market [2]. However, research focusing on the information display of smart glasses for the machine operations was few.

Augmented reality technology has been widely applied in various fields. By superimposing virtual objects and animations onto the scenes in real environment, AR was considered a promising technology for assisting maintenance operations, including dis/assembly, repair, inspections, and training [7]. In order to enhance the effect of AR, cues or prompts were added to help operators to understand the direction or sequence. Tonnis and Klinker (2006) [8] compared 3D arrow with bird's eye perspective demonstration for an AR head-up display tasks, and indicated the 3D arrow was preferable for the participant drivers. Henderson and Feiner (2010) [9] designed an AR head-worn display system for assisting mechanics, where virtual arrows were also included to guide mechanics' attention. Rehrl et al. (2012) [10] proposed a mobile AR system for navigating pedestrians, and they put semi-transparent circles on the overlay for cuing users the destination. Sanna et al. (2015) [11] exhibited an AR step-by-step assembly task, and they provided arrows for operators to travel among steps. Renner and Pfeiffer (2017) [12] demonstrated different virtualizations for a picking and assembly task, and they discovered the in-view image and in-situ line guiding methods were preferred.

Based on the review of previous studies, different guidance and information modes led to different results. Thus, this study aimed to evaluate the performance of machine operation under two information modes (animated images only and animated images with text) and two situations of direction prompts (with prompts or without prompts). Completion time and error counts were collected during the experiment as the objective performance measures, system usability scale (SUS) [13] and NASA task load index (NASA-TLX) [14] questionnaires were filled after each experiment for understanding the satisfaction and mental workloads.

2   Materials and Methods

2.1   Participants

Twenty participants (10 males and 10 females) were recruited, the average age was 22.8 (±1.33) years. All of them were graduate students of engineering school at National Tsing Hua University (Taiwan). They had basic knowledge of machine operations. Participants had to wear the BT-200 during the experiment. Thus corrected vision of 20/20 was required for each participant.

2.2   Apparatus and Materials

A coil straightener machine was selected as the research target in this study. The whole operation process contains 14 steps. The instruction of each step was designed and displayed in the smart glasses—BT-200. Two types of information modes (animated image only and animated image with text) were included. The appearance of animated images for both modes were consistent. The only difference was the text illustrations.

Besides, considering the real situation of operating a coil straightener, operators have to move back and forth aside the machine. Direction prompts were added to the experimental design to find out whether the prompts can affect the performance or not. The appearance of direction prompts was designed as a little yellow arrow with text of the next step. Figure 1 shows the two information modes and the direction prompt.

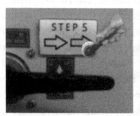

Fig. 1. The illustration of display with animated image only mode (left), animated image with text mode (middle), and the appearance of direction prompt (right).

2.3   Experimental Design

A factorial design was employed. The independent variables were information display modes (animated image only, and animated image with text) and direction prompts (with, and without). The dependent variables were completion time, error counts, SUS, and NASA-TLX scores. Each participant had to complete the 14-step procedure in each sub-experiment, and 4 sub-experiments were included (animated image with prompts, animated image without prompts, animated image with text and prompts, and animated image with text and no prompts) in the whole experiment. In order to reduce the learning effects, all the sub-experiments were randomly arranged and the machine parameters were varied every time.

2.4   Statistical Analysis

The recorded data was first processed in Microsoft Excel. Two-way analysis of variance (ANOVA) were conducted using SPSS 17.0 (IBM Inc) with $\alpha = 0.05$.

3   Results

Table 1 shows the summarized ANOVA results, both the objective and subjective measures were listed. Information mode showed significant effect in SUS score. The use of direction prompt showed significance in completion time, error counts, SUS, and NASA-TLX scores. No interaction was found between information mode and direction prompt.

Table 1. Z. Summarized ANOVA results for objective and subjective measures.

	Objective		Subjective	
	CT	ERR	SUS	TLX
Information mode			*	
Prompt	*	*	**	**
Information mode*Prompt				

Note: * p < 0.05; ** p < 0.01; *** p < 0.001
Note: CT = completion time; ERR = error counts; SUS = system usability scale; TLX = NASA-TLX scale.

3.1   Information Display Mode

As Table 1 shows, the significant effect of information display mode was only found in SUS score ($p = 0.02 < 0.05$). Animated image with text received a better score of 76.5 (± 17.52) than the animated image having the average score of 67.38 (± 17.95).

3.2   Direction Prompt

The use of direction prompts affected all objective and subjective measures. The average completion time for operations with prompts (160.48 s) was significantly lower than the average completion time for operations without prompts (179.78 s). In addition, operations with prompts had significantly lower error counts (0.43) than the error counts for operations without prompts (0.78).

As for the SUS scores, the average rating for operations with prompts was 77.63 (± 14.81), and was significantly higher than the average rating for operations without prompts 66.25 (± 19.67). And for scores of NASA-TLX, the average rating for operations with prompts was 30.08 (± 13.95), and was significantly lower than the average rating for operations without prompts 40.42 (± 17.10). Figure 2 showed the differences direction prompt effect for both the objective (left) and subjective (right) measures.

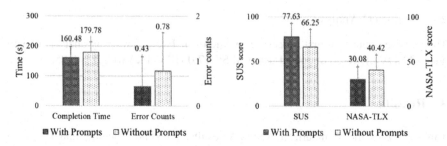

Fig. 2. The comparisons of operating with and without direction prompts on objective (left) and subjective (right) measures.

4 Discussion

The results showed the information display mode effect was significant on SUS score. The participants were more satisfied with the information display mode of animated image with text. Since the operation process contained various actions, such as pressing a button, lifting a handle, or adjusting a roller, some of the steps were hard to comprehend by viewing the animated images without any illustration. Diaz et al. (2015) [15] reported that AR application using audio and text as supplementation can lead to a better quality of learning. As for the system usability of animated image without text, the rating score was only 66.25, which was below 70 and was considered as "poor" system usability [16].

Moreover, operations with direction prompts received an overall positive outcome compared to the operations without prompts. Operating with direction prompts had less completion time and error counts, and had a lower NASA-TLX score and a higher SUS score. For AR applications of using virtual objects to guide users, Henderson and Feiner (2010) [9] used 2D and 3D arrows to direct mechanics' attention. Volmer et al. (2018) [17] compared different kinds of cues for AR procedural tasks, and reported that using "lines" to guide users had the best outcome, and the condition of using none cues had the longest response time and higher errors.

5 Conclusions

This study focused on evaluating the effect of information display for machine operation tasks using the BT-200. The results of objective performance showed no difference between the two information display modes (animated image and animated image with text), but the results in SUS score was significant. More conditions of information display modes should be included in the future. The results showed that the use of direction prompts were helpful to accomplish this task. The outcome was reasonable, due to the operation process of the coil straightener machine required participants to move back and forth. In conclusion, direction prompts should be considered in similar situations, to guide the operators and to increase operation performance.

References

1. Barfield, W.: Fundamentals of Wearable Computers and Augmented Reality. CRC Press, Boca Raton (2015)
2. Syberfeldt, A., Danielsson, O., Gustavsson, P.: Augmented reality smart glasses in the smart factory: product evaluation guidelines and review of available products. IEEE Access **5**, 9118–9130 (2017)
3. Paelke, V.: Augmented reality in the smart factory: supporting workers in an industry 4.0. environment. In: Proceedings of the 2014 IEEE Emerging Technology and Factory Automation (ETFA), pp. 1–4. IEEE, September 2014
4. Zheng, X.S., Matos da Silva, P., Foucault, C., Dasari, S., Yuan, M., Goose, S.: Wearable solution for industrial maintenance. In: Proceedings of the 33rd Annual ACM Conference Extended Abstracts on Human Factors in Computing Systems, pp. 311–314, April 2015
5. Baron, L., Braune, A.: Case study on applying augmented reality for process supervision in industrial use cases. In: 2016 IEEE 21st International Conference on Emerging Technologies and Factory Automation (ETFA), pp. 1–4. IEEE, September 2016
6. Wille, M., Scholl, P.M., Wischniewski, S., Van Laerhoven, K.: Comparing Google glass with tablet-pc as guidance system for assembling tasks. In: 2014 11th International Conference on Wearable and Implantable Body Sensor Networks Workshops, pp. 38–41. IEEE, June 2014
7. Palmarini, R., Erkoyuncu, J.A., Roy, R., Torabmostaedi, H.: A systematic review of augmented reality applications in maintenance. Robot. Comput. Integr. Manuf. **49**, 215–228 (2018)
8. Tonnis, M., Klinker, G.: Effective control of a car driver's attention for visual and acoustic guidance towards the direction of imminent dangers. In: 2006 IEEE/ACM International Symposium on Mixed and Augmented Reality, pp. 13–22. IEEE, October 2006
9. Henderson, S., Feiner, S.: Exploring the benefits of augmented reality documentation for maintenance and repair. IEEE Trans. Visual Comput. Graphics **17**(10), 1355–1368 (2010)
10. Rehrl, K., Häusler, E., Steinmann, R., Leitinger, S., Bell, D., Weber, M.: Pedestrian navigation with augmented reality, voice and digital map: results from a field study assessing performance and user experience. In: Gartner, G., Ortag, F. (eds.) Advances in Location-Based Services. LNGC, pp. 3–20. Springer, Heidelberg (2012). https://doi.org/10.1007/978-3-642-24198-7_1
11. Sanna, A., Manuri, F., Lamberti, F., Paravati, G., Pezzolla, P.: Using handheld devices to support augmented reality-based maintenance and assembly tasks. In: 2015 IEEE International Conference on Consumer Electronics (ICCE), pp. 178–179. IEEE, January 2015
12. Renner, P., Pfeiffer, T.: Evaluation of attention guiding techniques for augmented reality-based assistance in picking and assembly tasks. In: Proceedings of the 22nd International Conference on Intelligent User Interfaces Companion, pp. 89–92, March 2017
13. Brooke, J.: SUS-a quick and dirty usability scale. In: Usability Evaluation in Industry, vol. 189, no. 194, pp. 4–7 (1996)
14. Hart, S.G.: NASA-task load index (NASA-TLX); 20 years later. In: Proceedings of the Human Factors and Ergonomics Society Annual Meeting, vol. 50, no. 9, pp. 904–908. Sage Publications, Sage CA, Los Angeles, October 2006
15. Diaz, C., Hincapié, M., Moreno, G.: How the type of content in educative augmented reality application affects the learning experience. Procedia Comput. Sci. **75**, 205–212 (2015)
16. Bangor, A., Kortum, P., Miller, J.: Determining what individual SUS scores mean: adding an adjective rating scale. J. Usability Stud. **4**(3), 114–123 (2009)
17. Volmer, B., et al.: A comparison of predictive spatial augmented reality cues for procedural tasks. IEEE Trans. Visual Comput. Graphics **24**(11), 2846–2856 (2018)

Building a Firefighting Training System in MR

Kazuya Yamamoto[1]([⊠]) and Makio Ishihara[2]

[1] Graduate School of Computer Science and Engineering,
Fukuoka Institute of Technology,
3-30-1, Wajiro-Higashi, Higashi-ku, Fukuoka 811-0295, Japan
mfm19104@bene.fit.ac.jp
[2] Fukuoka Institute of Technology, 3-30-1, Wajiro-Higashi, Higashi-ku,
Fukuoka 811-0295, Japan
m-ishihara@fit.ac.jp

Abstract. This manuscript builds a firefighting training system using AR functionality designed for home use. In the system, the user can practice manipulating a fire extinguisher to put out the fire burning in the room. The speed of fire is examined to yield the sense of urgency and a pilot experiment is conducted. The result shows that the mechanism a fire's flame continues to spread if nothing is done, could give the subject a sense of urgency while there are opinions that the image quality of the camera is low, and that the brightness of the virtual object is different.

Keywords: Pilot experiment · Firefighting training · Disaster prevention · Mixed reality

1 Introduction

In recent years, with the development of virtual reality or VR technology, the use of VR in evacuation training for disasters has become reality. Unlike real evacuation training, the training in VR can be performed safely in any location and time. However, for the use of VR, it is necessary to prepare a tracked open space to avoid collisions between the user and objects during the training because the real space is invisible to the user. So, it is not so easy to train at home. Kawano et al. [1] developed an evacuation training method in augmented reality or AR using a tablet PC. AR is a technique of displaying computer-generated objects overlaid on the real space simultaneously and it provides the user with a feeling as if those objects existed in the real space. In their method, the user carries a tablet PC and does the training intuitively and safely. However, it is difficult for the user to feel the sense of urgency because the user sees the AR space just through a small screen of the tablet PC, resulting in lack of reality, immersion, and feelings of those virtual objects in existence. In addition, it is difficult to operate virtual objects. In that respect, the HTC VIVE allows a wide range of training that can be performed using the controller. Therefore, in this study, a prototype of a fire fighting training system in AR using a head mounted display or HMD is built and a pilot experiment in sense of urgency is conducted. An HMD provides a wide field of view with the user's eyes to yield high reality, high immersion,

© Springer Nature Switzerland AG 2020
C. Stephanidis et al. (Eds.): HCII 2020, CCIS 1294, pp. 244–250, 2020.
https://doi.org/10.1007/978-3-030-60703-6_31

and high fidelity of existence of virtual objects. Referring to the research of Yoshioka et al. [2], it was found that a sense of time leads to a sense of urgency. In this study, the speed of the fire's flame spreading is discussed to have the user feel the sense of urgency.

2 Firefighting Training System

In our system, a subject wears a video see-through HMD and puts out a fire with a fire extinguisher, which has occurred at a preset location in the AR space. Table 1 shows the hardware setups and their specs used for our system. To simulate a fire in the AR space, our system employs the game engine of Unity and VIVE SRWorks SDK 0.9.0.3 for adding AR functions to VIVE Pro. For example, a 3-dimensional representation, called a mesh, of the surrounding objects such as walls, desks, chairs, ceiling and other things are built and available in real time. The fire has already been burning when the system starts to run, and it spreads over time. As the user sweeps the nozzle of the fire extinguisher on the fire, it gradually gets smaller and eventually goes out. Figure 1 shows a mesh of the surrounding objects built by VIVE Pro, and Fig. 2 shows a stereo image of a simulated fire which is placed on the mesh. Spreading time of the fire is assumed to be 20 s for general households and an amount of smoke increases in proportion to the size of the fire's flame. The user sprays materials from the nozzle of the fire extinguisher by pressing a button on the VIVE controller. The controller vibrates during spraying. The position of the simulated fire is hopefully chosen on the mesh in a random manner, but it is constant now of our system.

Table 1. Hardware setups

HTC Vive pro	Resolution	2880 * 1600 pixel
	Refresh rate	90 Hz
	Viewing angle	110°
	Weight	765 g
PC	CPU	Intel core i7 7820x
	Graphics Card	GeForeceGTX1080ti
	Memory	16.00 GB
	OS	Windows10pro 64bit

Fig. 1. The obtained mesh

Fig. 2. Computer-generated fire in Unity

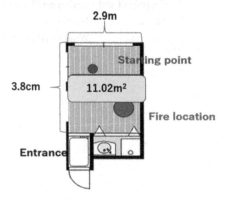

Fig. 3. A floor plan and dimensions of the room where the experiment is conducted

Fig. 4. A subject who is performing the firefighting in our training system

3   Experiment

The purpose of this experiment is to make a prototype of a firefighting training system and conducts a pilot experiment in sense of urgency. To evaluate the sense of urgency, the questionnaire with a five-point scale of 1 being no and 5 being yes shown in Table 2 is employed, referring to Yoshioka et al. [2] and Iimura et al. [3]. Figure 3 shows a sketch of the room used for the experiment. The subject's starting point is shown in blue, and the fire-starting point is shown in red. Figure 4 shows a scene of the experiment, and Figs. 5 and 6 show the progress of firefighting.

There are 7 subjects (7 males) with the ages between 20 and 24. The flow of the experiment is shown below.

Step 1. Ask the subject to wear an HMD and use our system until they get used to manipulating the VIVE controller and handling how to use the fire extinguisher.
Step 2. Instructs the subject to put out the fire.
Step 3. The training lasts until the size of the fire's flame reaches the ceiling or disappears completely.
Step 4. Remove the HMD and ask the subject fill out the questionnaire and note down an overall impression of the system.

Table 2. Questionnaire

Q1	Did you feel as if you were in a fire?
Q2	Did you feel you had to put out the fire soon?
Q3	Did you feel the flame approaching?
Q4	Did you feel sick during the experiment?
In addition, note down an overall impression of the system	

Fig. 5. A stereo image from the HMD view at the beginning of the experiment

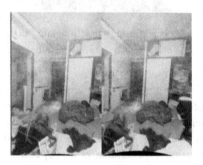

Fig. 6. An HMD view where the room is filled out with a large amount of smoke

4 Result

Figure 7 shows the questionnaire result. For the questions Q1 till Q3, the average of evaluation points is considerably larger than the neutral evaluation point of 3. For the question Q4, all the subjects answered 1. The Wilcoxon signed-rank test shows that the average is significantly different from the neutral evaluation point of 3 at all the questions [$T(7) = 0$ at $p < .05$, $T(7) = 0$ at $p < .05$, $T(7) = 0$ at $p < .05$, $T(7) = 0$ at $p < .05$]. Table 3 shows the list of overall impression of the system obtained from the subjects.

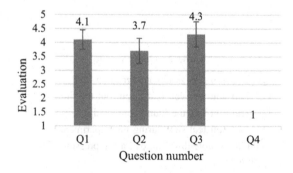

Fig. 7. Questionnaire result

From the results, our system seems to provide the sense of urgency with the subjects while some points in improvement were found.

Table 3. Subject's impression

Comment 1	I was surprised when the flame spread and approached
Comment 2	Feeling that the brightness of the real-world image and the virtual reality object are different
Comment 3	Feel like low resolution
Comment 4	Feel a little lag

Figure 8 shows the change of frame rate for one of the subjects during the experiment. The horizontal axis shows the sequence number of frames and the vertical one does the number of frames per second or FPS. From the figure, the FPS increased to 90 at some points while it was stabilized at approximately 40. Considering if it is practical, the FPS of 60 is necessary and some improvements in terms of both the software and hardware aspects are required.

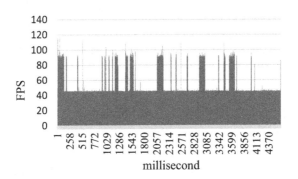

Fig. 8. FPS during the experiment

5 Conclusion

This manuscript built a firefighting training system using AR for home use and conducted a pilot experiment in performance and evaluated if our system would yield the sense of urgency by questionnaire. The results showed that the mechanism a fire's flame continues to spread if nothing is done, could give the subject a sense of urgency but there is still room to take a consideration into speed of spreading.

In the future, we would like to prepare several speed patterns and conduct comparative experiments.

References

1. Kawano, T.: Development of disaster evacuation training method applying simulated experience using AR. Ergonomics **52**(Suppl.), S358–S359 (2006)
2. Yoshioka, T., Takebe, K., Suzuki, K.: The effects of fire evacuation on stress and crisis avoidance behavior. Architectural Inst. Japan **615**, 69–74 (2007)
3. Iimura, K., Nakamura, H., Okura, N., Komatsu, T.: Experiment of quantification and evaluation of realism and reality. In: Japan Ergonomics Society 53rd Conference (2012)

Learning

Technology for Training: Acquisition Recommender Support Tool

Julian Abich IV$^{(\boxtimes)}$ and Eric Sikorski

Quantum Improvements Consulting, Orlando, FL 32817, USA
{jabich, esikorski}@quantumimprovements.net

Abstract. Immersive technologies, such as augmented and virtual reality (AR/VR), are increasingly being utilized for training in various domains, especially the military. Although immersive technology's potential for meeting specific training needs should be analyzed prior to implementation, an in-depth analysis is not always feasible. Therefore, military acquisition personnel often take an approach focused on logistical constraints when making decisions about acquiring new technology for training though no solution exists to guide these acquisition personnel through that selection process. The goal for this effort is to develop a software tool that will equip acquisition personnel with the ability to make evidence-based decisions about technologies for training prior to their acquisition. This support tool will help users make informed acquisition decision by inquiring about parameters (e.g. group size) and practical constraint (e.g. outdoor environment) considerations through various data extraction techniques. The ultimate goal is more efficient training as a result of guidance during the training technology acquisition process.

Keywords: Training · Immersive technology · Defense acquisition · Support tool

1 Introduction

The Department of Defense (DOD) acquisition workforce is defined as "uniformed and civilian government personnel, who are responsible for identifying, developing, buying, and managing goods and services to support the military [1]." The DOD is continuously attempting to reform the defense acquisition process with the goal to reduce wasteful spending and mismanagement of programs [2, 3]. While efforts have been made to improve acquisition efficiency and effectiveness by enhancing workforce capabilities, task loads and contract complexities continue to hinder progress. Further, the Defense Acquisition University (DAU) educates and trains the acquisition workforce across a variety of career fields (e.g. engineering, auditing, logistics, etc.), yet there does not appear to be any focus on learning science, instructional design, or training methodology as standalone or integrated within related courses (e.g. Science and Technology Management). There currently is no solution available to provide acquisition personnel with training focused guidance when determining the most effective technological training solutions. Therefore, when acquisition personnel are faced with the task of acquiring new technology to support learning and training within

© Springer Nature Switzerland AG 2020
C. Stephanidis et al. (Eds.): HCII 2020, CCIS 1294, pp. 253–258, 2020.
https://doi.org/10.1007/978-3-030-60703-6_32

the military, they may not have a solid foundation to make critical decisions when choosing optimal technology to facilitate training. The goal for this project is to develop a software support tool that guides acquisition personnel through a learning and training perspective, granting them the ability to make evidence-based informed decisions when acquiring technology for training.

As the proliferation of new immersive technologies flood the market, the desire to utilize them for training applications increases. Acquisition personnel must not succumb to temptation by the face validity (e.g. replicates the real-world or operational environment) of these technologies to support training outcomes. Instead, decisions to leverage new technologies, regardless of the type, should be based on specific criteria related to learning objectives and desired training outcomes [4]. Further, they must provide the trainee with the opportunity to learn the specific components of the tasks and eventually support practice of those tasks as they would occur in the operational environment. The benefits of replicating the operational environment, along with other types of fidelity [5], are only realized when fidelity is aligned with the appropriate phases of training [4, 6, 7]. Since acquisition personnel are not specifically educated on training methodology, they are challenged when faced with the decision to acquire technology that will be the most effective to facilitate successful training outcomes while reducing cost of diminishing returns.

1.1 Our Approach

The research team is developing an acquisition support tool prototype. The tool features a series of questions for the user in areas such as learning objectives, fidelity, and environmental factors. The questions are being developed based on the assumption that its users (i.e. acquisition personnel) do not typically have advanced knowledge of training methodologies or instructional design principles. The types of questions and wording in the tool guides the user rather than relies on knowledge of training. The output will be a set of technology recommendation based on user responses as well as research-based recommendations of immersive technology applications for training. To develop a prototype, the sample of technology options available for recommendation are scoped down to include only augmented and virtual reality (AR/VR) devices that were available in 2019.

1.2 Aim for This Paper

This paper will focus on the design approach to extract user knowledge of the acquisition process, describe how the information will be translated into design documents for communication with the development team, and explain how the tool will be used. To inform tool development, a literature review was conducted on the acquisition process for non-major (i.e. below a few million dollars) technology acquisition. Front-end analysis, such as structured interviews with subject matter experts, are underway to understand gaps that exist between the current and desired acquisition process. These results will drive the design of the conceptual framework, requirements specification, content architecture, user flows, wireframes, and mockups.

A user-centered design methodology taking an iterative development approach is being applied. Ideally, there is a linear sequence of activities during this process though variability in executing them is typical, due to external events (e.g. inability to access SMEs). The process described here will discuss some of the steps that have been executed along with the challenges faced thus far and implemented resolutions. The intent is to present the lessons learned to inform future design processes.

2 Methodology

2.1 Front-End Analysis

A front-end analysis was conducted to build a knowledge foundation of the defense acquisition process. The Defense Acquisition System (DAS) established acquisition categories (ACAT) to manage the decision-making, execution, and compliance for each category type. The main categories range from ACAT I through IV. The general differences in the categories lie in the total funds procured, where in the acquisition process a program resides, and who has decision authority. The customer indicated this tool will support ACAT IV which is specific only to the U.S. Navy and Marine Corps.

Challenge. ACAT IV is defined as "ACAT programs not otherwise designated as ACAT III [8]." The same definition exists for ACAT III, meaning the criteria for categorization is that it does not fall into any preceding category. The challenge becomes apparent by the nature of that definition. Very little documentation about the process exists, making this step strongly dependent on stakeholder, SME, and user input and feedback. Another challenge is trying to gain access to SMEs or users that have ACAT IV acquisition experience.

Resolution. To resolve this challenge, the intent of the support tool was re-evaluated. Instead of trying to integrate the current acquisition process into the tool, the tool was reconceptualized to educate acquisition personnel about the importance of basing technology acquisition decisions on specific task objectives. By reviewing the course curriculum and descriptions provided by the DAU, it was realized that none provided education on training methods or instructional design. This realization was confirmed with the customer and allowed us to go forth with the reconceptualized design.

2.2 Conceptual Framework and Concept of Operations (CONOPS)

A conceptual framework for the support tool was created leveraging the information gathered in the front-end analysis combined with the literature found on training device design and implementation. This provided a basis for the components that guide the technology acquisition recommendation process. Once established, the CONOPS was generated that provided the characteristics of the support tool and described the process a user would go through when using the tool.

Challenge. The initial framework was complex and strongly emphasized the concepts of designing a training device, rather than capturing an approach for the acquisition process. The CONOPS reflected this in terms of components of the support tool and the steps a user would take to achieve the technology recommendation.

Resolution. Through repeated discussion and brainstorming sessions with the internal design team, external development team, and stakeholder feedback, both documents were revised to reflect only the essential training related components that the acquisition personnel would need to generate the technology recommendation. Sample content was generated to better understand the information that would be presented to the user and how to format it.

2.3   User Flow

The user flow provides a visual diagram of a prototypical user's path through the decision support tool. After refining the conceptual framework and CONOPS, a basic user flow was designed for the support tool. Beyond the basic login and profile creation, the flow illustrated each step the user would go through to reach the technology recommendation.

Challenge. The process must guide users in determining if technology is appropriate and, if so, then which one. The acquisition tool may not recommend a technology, if technology is not the most appropriate solution, which helps to mitigate the issue of wasteful spending. Combining this concept into the process poses a challenge as the knowledge needed to make this decision is usually outside the user's training and that user, as an acquisition professional, may be biased toward acquiring technology.

Resolution. After further evaluation of the of the user flow and components, an evaluation of the process was conducted using a sample use case derived from the literature. Utilizing the use case, the original flow was evaluated at each decision point. Each decision point is an opportunity to extract pertinent information from the end user to refine the final technology recommendation. An in depth understanding of the goals to be achieved at each step were mapped out and described to show how output in one step would support the input of the next. Through this evaluation, extraneous components were identified and either removed or integrated into subsequent steps as a way to preserve the contribution of these components but to present them in an appropriate format for the acquisition users.

2.4   Mockups

The mockups provide the visual details of the user interface, such as typography styles, colors, and scale of content, to provide a realistic representation of the final support tool user interface. These mockups reflect the functionality of the system in a visual format to convey critical design information to the development team.

Challenge. This support tool is being integrated into a previously designed tool intended to provide decision support for training researchers. When designing the user interface for a completely new system, there is more opportunity for creative freedom. For this support tool, the challenge was designing the interface for a different user than for whom it was originally conceived while maintaining the look and feel of the original solution.

Resolution. Through the iterative design process, a mix of wireframes and mockups were generated and tested internally with the design team. Once an agreed upon design was set, input from the development team was gathered and integrated. This process resulted in a final mockup set that was presented to the stakeholders to ensure the support tool was aligned with their vision and expectations.

3   Future Steps

Validation is the next major project milestone. First approach requires validation of the design documents. At this stage, the mockups will need to be reviewed by potential users or at least someone with experience and knowledge of the ACAT IV acquisition process. The best candidates will be the Navy researchers that have both the expertise in training and experience with the acquisition process. They will understand the process from both perspectives and will be able to provide valuable insight into the practicality of the support tool.

Another recommended validation activity is to test the support tool against a full stakeholder provided use case. By implementing a stakeholder use case, the support tool can be tested on its ability to provide recommendations to a situation most familiar to them. A second and third validation approach is to leverage a use case that is a current challenge the users face or a retro-analysis from a past technology acquisition, respectively. A current use case will allow the system to be evaluated for a new training technology acquisition decision. A use case alone will not determine how effective the recommended technology so a training effectiveness evaluation should also be conducted. Alternatively, a retro-analysis would provide insight into whether the technology recommendation aligns with what was acquired. The limitation of the retro-analysis is that although a particular technology was acquired, it may not have been the most effective solution. Therefore, the best solution is to execute all three approaches to provide a robust validation of the support tool as each may uncover different opportunities for improvement.

4   Conclusion

The goal for this project is to develop a support tool for Navy and Marine Corps acquisition personnel when executing ACAT IV acquisitions. Specifically, this tool is designed to help provide informed decision making for personnel with no instructional design or training development background. The support tool presented here is still a work in progress but was presented to highlight the accomplishments and challenges overcome throughout the design process. These provide lessons learned for future design work.

This support tool can help avoid DOD wasteful spending associated with acquiring technology not aligned with training outcomes. Further, with proper implementation, this tool will lead to more effective training, which in turn could result in additional cost savings while better preparing trainees for operational tasks.

Acknowledgements. This research was accomplished under Contract No N68335-19-C-0089. The views and conclusions contained in this document are those of the authors and should not be interpreted as representing the official policies, either expressed or implied, of NAWCTSD or the US Government. The US Government is authorized to reproduce and distribute reprints for Government purposes notwithstanding any copyright notation hereon. NAWCTSD Public Release 20-ORL043 Distribution Statement A – Approved for public release; distribution is unlimited.

References

1. Gates, S.M., Keating, E.G., Jewell, A.D., et al.: The Defense Acquisition Workforce, An Analysis of Personnel Trends Relevant to Policy, 1993-2006. RAND Corporation, Santa Monica (2008)
2. Schwartz, F., Francis, K.A., O'Connor, C.V.: The Department of Defense Acquisition Workforce: Background, Analysis, and Questions for Congress. Congressional Research Service (CRS Report R44578), pp. 1–14 (2016)
3. U.S. Government Accountability Office (GAO). Homeland Security Acquisitions: Identifying all non-major acquisitions would advance ongoing efforts to improve management (Report GAO-17-396), Washington, D.C. (2017)
4. Kinkade, R.G., Wheaton, G.R.: Training device design. In: Van Cott, H.P., Kinkade, R.G. (eds.) Human Engineering Guide to Equipment Design, pp. 667–699. Library of Congress, Washington, D.C. (1972)
5. Liu, D., Macchiarella, N.D., Vincenzi, D.A.: Simulation fidelity. In: Vincenzi, D.A., Wise, J. A., Mouloua, M., Hancock, P.A. (eds.) Human Factors in Simulation and Training, pp. 61–74. CRC Press, Boca Raton (2009)
6. Andrews, D.H., Carroll, L.A., Bell, H.H.: The future of selective fidelity in training devices (Report AL/HR-TR-1995-0195). Air Force Material Command, Brooks Air Force Base, TX (1996)
7. Padron, C., Mishler, A., Fidopiastis, C., Stanney, K., Fragomeni, G.: Maximising return on training investment in mixed reality systems. In: Proceeding of the Interservice/Industry Training, Simulation, and Education Conference (I/ITSEC) (2018)
8. Defense Acquisition University. Acquisition Category (ACAT). https://www.dau.edu/acquipedia/pages/articledetails.aspx#!313. Accessed 10 Mar 2020

Meta-Analysis of Children's Learning Outcomes in Block-Based Programming Courses

Jen-I Chiu[✉] and Mengping Tsuei

Graduate School of Curriculum and Instructional Communication Technology,
National Taipei University of Education, Taipei, Taiwan
chiujeni@gmail.com, mptsuei@mail.ntue.edu.tw

Abstract. In the last two decades, the importance of research on block-based programming education has grown. The use of block-based programming tools is receiving attention not only in computer science courses, but also in robotics education. The effects of such programming on children's learning outcomes have been examined, but the results have been inconclusive. The purpose of this meta-analysis was to examine the mean effect of block-based programming compared with traditional instruction (i.e., text-based programming) on children's learning outcomes, including problem-solving skills, programming skills, computational thinking and motivation. The effect size and effects of moderators (publication year, sample size, publication sources and study region) were also examined. The database search yielded 19 publications with 31 effect sizes (n = 1369). Block-based programming had a significantly larger effect size than did traditional instruction for overall learning outcomes. More specifically, we found a large effect size for problem-solving skills, small effect sizes for programming skills and computational thinking, and a trivial effect size for motivation. No moderating effect was detected. Effect sizes for outcomes were large in research conducted in the Americas and Asia, medium in studies conducted in Europe and trivial in studies conducted in the Middle East. No evidence of publication bias in the studies was detected. These study findings support the benefits of block-based programming education for children's learning outcomes, especially their problem-solving skills. Future research should examine additional dependent variables.

Keywords: Block-based programming · Meta-analysis · Visualized programming language

1 Introduction

In the last two decades, the importance of research on programming education has grown. Programming education has been shown to benefit students' reading, writing and problem solving (Felleisen et al. 2004). Students show stress and low motivation when using traditional text-based programming tools because the procedures they describe are difficult to remember, leading to susceptibility to syntax error. Bau et al. (2017) noted that block-based programming is easy to learn, reduces cognitive loading

---

The original version of this chapter was revised: The typesetting error in the Table 1 has been corrected. The correction to this chapter is available at https://doi.org/10.1007/978-3-030-60703-6_83

and syntax error and increases motivation. Findings from several other studies suggest that block-based programming improves learning outcomes (Brown et al. 2008; Wang et al. 2009; Hermans and Aivaloglou 2017).

Although most scholars agree that the use of block-based programming leads to positive learning outcomes, some argue against this conclusion. Costa and Miranda (2019) found no significant difference in logical thinking skills among students with low socio-economic status exposed to traditional and block-based programming. Similarly, Nam et al. (2010) found no difference in problem-solving skills among students exposed to traditional and block-based programming. The purposes of this meta-analysis were to compare the mean effects of block-based programming and traditional instruction on children's learning outcomes, and to identify factors moderating these effects.

2 Block-Based Programming

Recently, many researchers have suggested that block-based programming facilitates children's acquisition of programming, computational thinking and problem-solving skills. Block-based programming tools have user-friendly interfaces that enable students to 'drag and drop' blocks for composite programming. Commonly used tools for children include Alice (Costa and Miranda 2019), Scratch (Oh et al. 2012) and APP Inventor (Papadakis et al. 2016). Numerous studies have shown that children who use these tools have significantly better programming skills than do those receiving traditional instruction (Wang et al. 2009; Hermans and Aivaloglou 2017). Primary-school and sixth-grade students who use Scratch have been shown to have significantly better problem-solving and mathematical skills, respectively, than students receiving traditional instruction (Lai and Yang 2011; Calao et al. 2015). Durak (2018) also noted significantly enhanced self-efficacy among fifth-grade children who had taken block-based programming courses.

Other researchers, however, have reported negative effects or no specific effect of block-based programming courses. Cooper et al. (2003) noted that the use of block-based programming might make children miss the opportunity to do 'real' coding. Kormaz (2016) found no significant difference in the programming skills of children receiving block-based and traditional programming instruction.

Many recent studies have examined the efficacy of block-based programming, but the results have been inconclusive. Our findings will be useful for teachers and researchers when instructional design.

3 Method

This meta-analysis included 19 publications dating to 2008–2019. We followed meta-analytic procedures, including the gathering of studies and coding of features to calculate the effect size and moderating effects (Cheng et al. 2019). As existing research focused on 'children' refers to primary- and secondary-school students.

3.1   Inclusion and Exclusion Criteria

The titles, keywords and abstracts of identified publications were read to determine their applicability to this study. Eligible publications described studies comparing block-based programming (treatment) with traditional programming (control) instruction. The exclusion criteria were: 1) no use of a (quasi) experimental approach, 2) provision of insufficient data for effect size calculation, 3) use of an undergraduate or older sample and 4) inaccessibility of full text.

3.2   Publication Selecting and Coding

The EBSCOhost platform, ACM Digital Library and IEEE Xplore Digital Library were searched to identify relevant studies published between 2008 and October 2019. Data on the author, year of publication, title, publication source (e.g. journal, conference proceeding), sample size, participant nationality, block-based tool (i.e. Scratch, Alice, APP Inventor), learning outcomes and quantitative results (e.g. means, standard deviations, t and p values) were extracted.

After the removal of duplicates, the sample comprised 19 publications (11 journal articles and 8 conference proceeding papers) and 31 effect sizes ($n = 1369$), including eleven journal articles and eight conference proceedings. The independent variables were the block-based programming tools (Scratch, Alice and APP Inventor). The dependent variables were programming skills, computational thinking skills, problem-solving skills and motivation. The included studies were conducted in the Americas, Asia, Europe and the Middle East.

3.3   Effect Size Calculation

The Comprehensive Meta-Analysis (version 2.0) software was used to calculate effect sizes and assess publication bias, using the standardised measures of Cohen's d and Hedges' g (Cheng et al. 2019). The formula for Cohen's d is as following. Where $\bar{X}_1$ and $\bar{X}_2$ represent the mean scores, n_1 and n_2 represent the sample sizes, and S_1^2 and S_2^2 represent the variances of two groups.

$$\text{Cohen's } d = \frac{\bar{X}_1 - \bar{X}_2}{\sqrt{\frac{(n_1-1)S_1^2 + (n_2-1)S_2^2}{(n_1 + n_2 - 2)}}}$$

Hedges' g has the best properties for small sample size, the formula of Hedges' g is:

$$J = 1 - \frac{3}{4(N-2)-1}; \text{Hedge'g} = J \times \text{Cohen's } d$$

The effect sizes > 0.2 were considered to be small, those of 0.5 were considered to be medium, and those of 0.8 were considered to be large (Cohen 1992, 1998). As the region and year of publication varied widely among publications, a random-effects model was used (Borenstein et al. 2007). Publication bias was evaluated using the fail-safe N procedure.

4 Results

4.1 Overall Effect of Block-Based Programming

The total sample comprised 1369 children who received block-based ($n = 779$) and traditional ($n = 590$) programming instruction. The overall effect size was medium ($g = 0.71$, 95% confidence interval –2.32 to 5.88; $Z = 2.68$, $p = .01$). For learning outcomes overall, the effect size for block-based programming was significantly larger than that for traditional instruction.

4.2 Publication Bias

We used the classic fail-safe N test to examine publication bias; the formulas are:

$$\text{Fail - safe number}_{(.05)} = 19s - n; \text{Tolerance level} = 5K + 10$$

where $s - n$ represents the difference in the number of studies yielding significant and nonsignificant differences and K represents the total number of studies. When the fail-safe number, which is the number of missing studies needed to render the overall mean effect size trivial, exceeds the tolerance level, the absence of publication bias is suggested (Rosenthal 1991). The fail-safe N (422) exceeded the tolerance level (105), indicating the absence of evidence of publication bias.

4.3 Effects on Learning Outcomes

Table 1 shows effect sizes for the learning outcomes examined. The effect sizes were large for problem-solving skills ($n = 5$; $g = 1.11$, $p = .07$), small for programming skills ($n = 11$; $g = 0.64$, $p = .07$) and computational thinking ($n = 4$; $g = 0.57$, $p = .29$), and trivial for motivation ($n = 11$; $g = 0.13$, $p = .38$).

Table 1. Effect sizes on four moderator variables

	Effect size and 95% confidence interval							Heterogeneity		
	K	g	SE	Lower limit	Upper limit	Z	p	Q	df	p
Problem-solving	5	1.11	.62	−.11	2.32	1.79	.07			
Programming	11	.64	.35	−.05	1.33	1.83	.07			
Computational thinking	4	.57	.54	−.48	1.62	1.06	.29			
Motivation	11	.13	.15	−.16	.42	0.88	.38			
Total between								4.14	3	.25

Effect According to Publication Sources. The results provide the effect sizes on four moderator variables: publication source, study region, publication year and sample size.

In terms of publication source, the effect sizes were large for conference proceedings papers ($n = 8$; $g = 0.96$, $p = .02$) and medium for journal articles ($n = 11$; $g = 0.53$, $p = .16$). The effects on learning outcomes were not moderated by the publication source ($Q = 0.61$, $p = .44$) (Table 2).

Effects According to Study Region. The effect sizes of study region indicated that effect sizes were large for research conducted in the Americas ($n = 3$; $g = 1.18$, $p = .03$) and Asia ($n = 6$; $g = 0.95$, $p = .03$), medium for studies conducted in Europe ($n = 6$; $g = 0.66$, $p = .43$) and trivial for studies conducted in the Middle East ($n = 4$; $g = 0.05$, $p = .80$). The effects on learning outcomes were not moderated by the study region ($Q = 7.04$, $p = .07$) (Table 2).

Effects According to Publication Year. Effect sizes were large for studies published in 2016–2019 ($n = 9$; $g = 1.05$, $p = .09$) and small for those published in 2012–2015 ($n = 7$; $g = 0.47$, $p = .08$) and 2008–2011 ($n = 3$; $g = 0.31$, $p = .18$). The effects on learning outcomes were not moderated by the publication year ($Q = 2.22$, $p = .33$) (Table 2).

Effects According to Sample Size. Effect sizes were large for samples ≥ 30 ($n = 13$; $g = 0.94$, $p = .00$) and small for samples < 30 ($n = 6$; $g = 0.69$, $p = .70$). The effects on learning outcomes were not moderated by the publication year ($Q = 1.66$, $p = .20$) (Table 2).

Table 2. Effect sizes on four moderator variables

	Effect size and 95% confidence interval							Heterogeneity		
	K	g	SE	Lower limit	Upper limit	Z	p	Q	df	p
Publication source										
Journal articles	11	.53	.38	−.21	1.27	1.41	.16			
Conference- proceedings	8	.96	.41	.17	1.75	2.37	.02			
Total between								.61	1	.44
Study Region										
Middle East	4	.05	.18	−.30	.39	0.25	.80			
Asia	6	.95	.45	.08	1.83	2.14	.03			
The Americas	3	1.18	.53	.13	2.22	2.20	.03			
Europe	6	.66	.83	−.98	2.29	0.79	.43			
Total between								7.04	3	.07
Publication year										
2008–2011	3	.21	.15	−.09	.51	1.36	.18			
2012–2015	7	.47	.26	−.05	.99	1.77	.08			
2016–2019	9	1.05	.62	−.17	2.26	1.69	.09			
Total between								2.22	2	.33
Sample size										
Less than 30	6	.19	.49	−.77	1.15	.39	.70			
Above 30	13	.94	.32	.31	1.58	2.91	.00			
Total between								1.66	1	.20

5 Discussion and Conclusions

This meta-analysis of 19 publications showed that block-based programming courses contribute to the improvement of children's programming, problem-solving and computational thinking skills, but have a trivial effect on their motivation. Effect sizes for overall learning outcomes were large for research conducted in the Americas and Asia, medium for studies conducted in Europe, and trivial for studies conducted in the Middle East. They were large for conference proceedings papers and studies published in 2016–2019, medium for journal articles and small for studies published in 2008–2015. They were large for samples more than 30 and small for samples less than 30. No moderating effect was detected.

One possible reason for the trivial effect on children's motivation is that most children included in the studies were novice programmers. Programming learning may still challenge tasks for children. The children might have struggled to learn in the block-based environment. We recommend that teachers should consider children's programming skills during courses and using teaching strategies to familiarise them with block-based programming.

The trivial effect size observed for studies conducted in the Middle East is likely due to the small sample ($K = 4$). More empirical research on the effects of block-based programming in the Middle East is needed.

Overall, the results of this study suggest that the development of programming, problem-solving and computational thinking skills using block-based programming tools improves the performance of primary- and secondary-school students. We suggest that block-based programming not only could be used in computer science courses, but also could be integrated into courses in other disciplines (i.e. mathematics, language and art).

This preliminary research on block-based programming education limited by its focus on studies involving children. The findings, however, provide a basis for future research of meta-analyses on other dependent variables.

References

References Marked with an Asterisk Indicate Studies that are Included in the Meta-Analysis

Bau, D., Gray, J., Kelleher, C., Sheldon, J., Turbak, F.: Learnable programming: blocks and beyond. Commun. ACM, 72–80 (2017). https://doi.org/10.1145/3015455

Borenstein, M., Hedges, L., Rothstein, H.: Meta-analysis: fixed effect vs. random effects (2007). www.meta-analysis.com/downloads

*Brown, Q., Mongan, W., Kusic, D., Garbarine, E., Fromm, E., Fontecchio, A.: Computer aided instruction as a vehicle for problem solving: scratch boards in the middle years classroom. In: Proceedings of 2008 Annual Conference & Exposition, Pittsburgh, Pennsylvania (2008)

*Calao, L.A., Moreno-León, J., Correa, H.E., Robles, G.: Developing mathematical thinking with scratch. In: Conole, G., Klobucar, T., Rensing, C., Konert, J., Lavoue, E. (eds.), Design for teaching and learning in a networked world, Toledo, Spain (2015). https://doi.org/10. 1007/978-3-319-24258-3_2

Cheng, L., Ritzhaupt, A.D., Antonenko, P.: Effects of the flipped classroom instructional strategy on students' learning outcomes: a meta-analysis. Educ. Technol. Res. Dev. 67(4), 793–824 (2019). https://doi.org/10.1007/s11423-018-9633-7

Cohen, J.: Statistical Power Analysis for the Behavioral Sciences, 2nd edn. Erlbaum, Hillsdal (1988)

Cohen, J.: A power primer. Psychol. Bull. 112(1), 155–159 (1992). https://doi.org/10.1037/0033-2909.112.1.155

Cooper, S., Dann, W., Pausch, R., Pausch, R.: Teaching objects-first in introductory computer science. ACM SIGCSE Bull. 35(1), 191–195 (2003). https://doi.org/10.1145/792548.611966

*Costa, J.M., Miranda, G.L.: Using alice software with 4C-ID model: effects in programming knowledge and logical reasoning. Inf. Educ. 18(1), 1–15 (2019). https://doi.org/10.15388/infedu.2019.01

*Durak, Y.H.: Digital story design activities used for teaching programming effect on learning of programming concepts, programming self-efficacy, and participation and analysis of student experiences. J. Comput. Assist. Learn. 34(6), 740–752 (2018). https://doi.org/10.1111/jcal.12281

Felleisen, M., Findler, R.B., Flatt, M., Krishnamurthi, S.: The teach scheme! project: computing and programming for every student. Comput. Sci. Educ. 14(1), 55–77 (2004). https://doi.org/10.1076/csed.14.1.55.23499

*Hermans, F., Aivaloglou, E.: Teaching software engineering principles to k-12 students: a MOOC on scratch. In: Proceedings of 2017 IEEE/ACM 39th International Conference on Software Engineering: Software Engineering Education and Training Track, Buenos Aires, Argentina (2017). https://doi.org/10.1109/icse-seet.2017.13

*Ideris, N., Baharudin, S.M., Hamzah, N.: The Effectiveness of scratch in collaborative learning on higher-order thinking skills in programming subject among year-six students. In: Paper presented in 4th ASEAN Conference on Psychology, Counselling, and Humanities, Universiti Sains, Malaysia (2019). https://doi.org/10.2991/acpch-18.2019.99

Korkmaz, Ö.: The effect of Scratch-based game activities on students' attitudes, self-efficacy and academic achievement. Int. J. Mod. Educ. Comput. Sci. 8(1), 16–23 (2016). https://doi.org/10.5815/ijmecs.2016.01.03

*Lai, A.F., Yang, S.M.: The learning effect of visualized programming learning on 6th graders' problem solving and logical reasoning abilities. In: Proceedings of 2011 International Conference on Electrical and Control Engineering, Yichang, China (2011). https://doi.org/10.1109/iceceng.2011.6056908

*Master, A., Cheryan, S., Moscatelli, A., Meltzoff, A.N.: Programming experience promotes higher STEM motivation among first-grade girls. J. Exp. Child Psychol. 160, 92–106 (2017). https://doi.org/10.1016/j.jecp.2017.03.013

*Moreno-León, J., Robles, G., Román-González, M.: Code to learn: where does it belong in the K-12 curriculum. J. Inf. Technol. Educ. Res. 15, 283–303 (2016). https://doi.org/10.28945/3521

*Nam, D., Kim, Y., Lee, T.: The effects of scaffolding-based courseware for the Scratch programming learning on student problem solving skill. In: Wong, S.L., (eds.) 18th International Conference on Computers in Education, Putrajaya, Malaysia (2010)

*Oh, J.C., Lee, J.H., Kim, J.A., Kim, J.H.: Development and application of STEAM based education program using scratch: focus on 6th graders, science in elementary school. J. Korean Assoc. Comput. Educ. **15**(3), 11–23 (2012). https://doi.org/10.1007/978-94-007-6738-6_60

*Oluk, A., Saltan, F.: Effects of using the scratch program in 6th grade information technologies courses on algorithm development and problem solving skills. Participatory Educ. Res., 10–20 (2015). https://doi.org/10.17275/per.15.spi.2.2

*Papadakis, S., Kalogiannakis, M., Zaranis, N., Orfanakis, V.: Using scratch and app inventor for teaching introductory programming in secondary education: a case study. Int. J. Technol. Enhanced Learn. **8**(3–4), 217–233 (2016). https://doi.org/10.1504/ijtel.2016.10001505

*Rodríguez-Martínez, J.A., González-Calero, J.A., Sáez-López, J.M.: Computational thinking and mathematics using Scratch: an experiment with sixth-grade students. Interact. Learn. Environ., 1–12 (2019). https://doi.org/10.1080/10494820.2019.1612448

Rosenthal, R.: Applied Social Research Methods: Meta-Analytic Procedures for Social Research. SAGE, Thousand Oaks (1991). https://doi.org/10.4135/9781412984997

*Sáez-López, J.M., Román-González, M., Vázquez-Cano, E.: Visual programming languages integrated across the curriculum in elementary school: a two year case study using "Scratch" in five schools. Comput. Educ. **97**, 129–141 (2016). https://doi.org/10.1016/j.compedu.2016.03.003

*Su, A.Y., Yang, S.J., Hwang, W.Y., Huang, C.S., Tern, M.Y.: Investigating the role of computer-supported annotation in problem-solving-based teaching: an empirical study of a Scratch programming pedagogy. Brit. J. Educ. Technol. **45**(4), 647–665 (2014). https://doi.org/10.1111/bjet.12058

*Tekerek, M., Altan, T.: The effect of scratch environment on student's achievement in teaching algorithm. World J. Educ. Technol. **6**(2), 132–138 (2014)

*Wang, T.C., Mei, W.H., Lin, S.L., Chiu, S.K., Lin, J.M.C.: Teaching programming concepts to high school students with alice. In: Proceedings of 2009 39th IEEE Frontiers in Education Conference, San Antonio, TX, USA (2009). https://doi.org/10.1109/fie.2009.5350486

*Yünkül, E., Durak, G., Çankaya, S., Abidin, Z.: The effects of scratch software on students' computational thinking skills. Electron. J. Sci. Math. Educ. **11**(2), 502–517 (2017)

A Framework for the Design of Plant Science Education System for China's Botanical Gardens with Artificial Intelligence

Lijuan Guo[(✉)] and Jiping Wang

School of Art Design and Media,
East China University of Science and Technology, Shanghai, China
kerryglj@163.com, wangjpl08@163.com

Abstract. The framework of the traditional plant science education has lagged, which is hard to meet the needs of various visitors in China. In the following paper, we propose a unified interaction framework to help the design of the plant science education system. That is suitable for various visitors from China. They are from young to old with different levels of education, and some of them have dialect or accents. Inspired by the background, we try to design a new framework that takes advantage of the variety of the visitors' output, aiming to make the plant science education system very smart to understand what the visitors want to learn. Firstly, all the plants are numbered with the non-linear digital numbering method, which can be seen as the label of the training process for deep learning networks. Afterward, the interaction continuously collects the visitors' plant-related voice data as the input of the deep learning networks during the operation of the system to improve the performance and the stability of the plant science education system. Through continuous training, the overall accuracy of the system could be improved, and the system can gradually understand the regular pattern and central issue of people cares for the plant. The framework provides a new idea for the science education of the botanical garden and further improves the level of science education in China. This framework helps achieve sustainable development and environmental protection.

Keywords: Plant science education · Botanical gardens · Artificial intelligence

1 Introduction

As world populations become more urbanized, botanical gardens are increasingly recognized as among the important cultural resources of industrialized nations [1]. China is one of the largest countries that owns a large variety of plants. For multiple purposes, such as scientific research, species conservation, and science education, Although the major contemporary objective of botanical gardens is to maintain extensive collections of plants, this paper aims to address the problem of mainly discuss plant science education.

This paper focuses on the effect of the design for plant science education. Considering that plant science education relates to the issue of environmental protection and public literacy.

© Springer Nature Switzerland AG 2020
C. Stephanidis et al. (Eds.): HCII 2020, CCIS 1294, pp. 267–271, 2020.
https://doi.org/10.1007/978-3-030-60703-6_34

In modern times, these botanical gardens not only contain a large number of plants, but also utilizes many modern techniques to effectively protect the plants, show rare plants, and satisfy the public's needs of science knowledge. Compared with other places, the botanical garden is more suitable to carry out environmental education on plant science. Their key advantage is the wide variety of plants could attract the public's interest and motivate them to look inside the deeper information of the plants in practice.

However, although the botanical garden upgrades their equipment well, the interaction is not well design, thus could hardly achieve satisfactory effects. A good design framework of Artificial Intelligence(AI) could provide visitors of all ages with the opportunity to connect with nature and promote environmental literacy.

2 Botanical Garden Science Education

Education in Botanical gardens relates closely to many scientific disciplines [2]. China has built more than one hundred botanical gardens, which are "open-air science museums" where numerous plants lead visitors to discover science [3]. From the 1950s to the 1980s, the plant science education in China's botanical gardens began. In this early period, with the construction progress in the botanical gardens, traditional plant science education was gradually carried out [4].

Nowadays, people have a new understanding of environmental protection and plant science education. Traditional botanical science education cannot meet the increasing demands of people [5]. The Chinese botanical gardens play a significant role in the plant science education of the residents. However, for a long time, the plant science education work of the Chinese Botanical Garden still relies on old methods such as nameplates, bulletin boards, and manuals. These methods have poor effect at the aspects of interaction with visitors.

Initiatives to support plant science education innovation should be taken to adapt to changes in the pace of technology. In this paper, plants are numbered according to existing species in the botanical garden with a non-linear digital method. The voice was interactive with the science education program focused on deep learning that supports the Chinese botanical garden 's artificial smart and digital transformation. So that people can enjoy the benefits of education by the advancement in science and technology.

3 Voice Interaction

Voice interaction establishes communication between humans and machines through voice, and usually have the feature of speech recognition, semantic understanding, speech synthesis, and dialogue management [6]. Artificial intelligence allows more connectivity between people and systems, thus making the system more friendly. Voice recognition has gained prominence and is widely used in various applications since the improvement of computing power. It could be seen as one of the most suitable and feasible ways to communicate with visitors and plants. The friendly interaction way frees hands and could be used under various weather conditions for visitors of all ages because it also requires very little for them. A typical scenario is that the visitors receive education in the way of talking to the plants., making the uncommon knowledge get closer to visitors. We believe that it is the trend of plant science education, which is conducive to the humanized construction of the system of the botanical garden.

The effect of voice interaction relies on how smart the plant education science system is. The combination of artificial intelligence and voice interaction system makes the science education of botanical garden smarter. Benefit from the convenient operation of voice interaction., the education system could obtain large amounts of users' voice data if the visitors agree to upload their dialogue data with the system to improve the effect. Once the system collects more data, it will dig deeper into the needs behind the collected voice data. The team of the botanical garden can discover the interest of visitors from the collected data, and then display customized content of plant sciences. The system has a very positive impact on the continuous improvement of botanical garden services. From the perspective of the obtain of automatic feedback, the intelligent voice interaction system promotes the development of plant science education and improves the satisfaction of visitors.

4 Deep Learning

Generally, training deep neural networks need voice data as the basic input and the label as the output. However, if the interaction mode is not well designed, the scale of the voice data will be small and the quality of the data will be poor. Besides, the label can also be hard to obtain. Specifically, the challenges of voice interaction technology remain three aspects. Firstly, a large proportion of the names of the plants in Chinese characters seems uncommon and the names of some plants share similar pronunciations, which tremendously increase the recognition difficulty of the voice interaction system. Furthermore, China is a big country with diverse culture and nature, people from different regions has different dialects Finally, in the open-air environment of the botanical gardens, noise must be taken into consideration when using the voice recognition technology.

To address these problems, we design a novel framework. In this framework, visitors only need to say a combination, i.e., code+name. The coding of the plant name is generated with an expansive nonlinear coding method. This coding strategy converts the non-linear digital number obtained from the visitors into the index, which corresponds to the plant science knowledge stored in the system. The use of non-linear digital numbering enhances the recognition rate of the plant science education system and minimizes environmental interference. In such cases, even if visitors do not know the name of the plants, they can obtain the expected knowledge quickly. The voice interaction system of nonlinear numbered plant science education is more friendly to children and the elderly. This framework increases efficiency and improves user experience.

The framework based on deep learning seems like the computer "understands" the words and in turn "communicate" with the people. This process involves speech recognition and natural language processing. The framework takes the number said by visitors as the label of the deep learning neural network during the training process. Then, the system analyzes it, extracts features as the voice features vectors, and performs supervised training. Through the iterative process, the system establishes a set of corresponding patterns and the optimal network can be used. Compare these voice parameters with the data in the pattern set, the framework recognizes the voice, and finally, output the corresponding speech for feedback, as shown in Fig. 1. The voice interaction system recognizes and uses human language that stimulates the human brain's process of language processing and communication. It converts the voice information input by visitors into fluent spoken output analyzed by the system.

Fig. 1. Voice interaction process based on deep learning

The artificial intelligence system of plant science collects a large amount of plant-related voice data generated from visitors during the tour as input to the deep learning networks. The stability of plant science education is continuously improved through training. As more and more users interact with voice recognition technology, the voice recognition system will have more data and information to feedback into the neural networks, thus improving the capabilities and accuracy of the plant science education system. By analyzing massive amounts of input data, the system gradually evaluates the plant-related issues that are a public concern. Based on the above process, recognition and analysis of visitors' voice input can be realized, responding to visitors' needs, and providing visitors with high-quality intelligent science education services.

5   Conclusion

We have demonstrated that artificial intelligence technology can be used in the plant science education of botanical gardens. By using the non-linear numbered voice interaction system based on deep neural networks, the difficulties, such as the uncommon and similar names, the diverse dialects, and the environmental noise, are addressed and continuous improvements have been achieved. Benefited from well-designed interaction mode and the continuous optimization of the neural networks, this framework enhances the effect of plant science education of China. This framework is a reference for the interaction design of the Chinese botanical gardens.

References

1. Abotanic garden. https://www.britannica.com/science/botanical-garden-study-and-exhibition-garden. Accessed 18 June 2020

2. Yourun, L., Zhenhua, X.: Discussion on the issue of "Botanical Gardening". Plant Res. **24**(3), 379–384 (2004)
3. Fengjun, G.: The development and innovation of plant science education. Trop. Agric. Eng. **43**(02), 210–214 (2019)
4. Ling, X., Jin, C., Daguang, L., et al.: Exploring the development of science popularization in Chinese botanical gardens through three botanical gardens. Sci. Popularization Res. **4**(22), 80–83 (2009)
5. Nan, W.: The current situation and development of landscape science education. Heilongjiang Agric. Sci. **6**, 130–132 (2017)
6. Zhikang, P.: Research on voice interactive product design based on user experience. Public Lit. **19**, 139–140 (2019)

Research on Human-Computer Interaction of Online Course System for "New Media Management" Course of the Major of Journalism and Communication

Xiuyuan Guo[✉] and Yuxuan Xiao

Hunan University, Changsha, China
guoxiuyuan@hnu.edu.cn, 22155075@qq.com

Abstract. During this special period, many classes have become an online curriculum, including dissemination of Journalism and Communication major. This paper starts from the problem of human-computer interaction of the online course system for "New Media Management" course of the Journalism and Communication Major, method based on an online survey from 13 teachers and 157 students, we studied the influence and role of online teaching methods on teachers and students of dissemination of news major. Based on the research purposes, the human-computer interaction behavior, demand, and usability of teachers and students in 13 online class hours are studied on field research. Research shows that the real-time interaction, integration of multi-channel interaction, situation awareness, and practical mode of dissemination of news majors are the key problem of the online teaching system of dissemination of news majors, then we improved the online course system and completed the design of the online course system.

Keywords: New media management · Online course system · Human-computer interaction

1 Introduction

Online courses because of the small space limitations, time relatively free, low marginal cost advantage, has become a trend. In the form of human-computer interaction, however, the effect of knowledge dissemination and evaluation has obvious difference polarization. From the perspective of curriculum setting, some courses are naturally suitable for human-computer interaction, and their technical means can assist teaching presentation, students' perception and practice. But for other courses, the teaching method of human-computer interaction may become obstacle to the communication effect for some extent. From the perspective of audience perception, the difference of individual knowledge system will also bring great differences in communication effect. This study is based on the online teaching practice of the series of "New Media Management" courses in the field of Journalism and Communication. The audience is all college students majoring in Journalism and Communication, and they have relatively consistent background of knowledge and learning ability. Therefore, the impact

C. Stephanidis et al. (Eds.): HCII 2020, CCIS 1294, pp. 272–280, 2020.
https://doi.org/10.1007/978-3-030-60703-6_35

of audience differences on this study is relatively small, which is more conducive to in-depth discussion from the perspective of curriculum setting.

In the field of online education, the teaching of journalism and communication is always a special research object. How to develop news production and dissemination on the latest Media always brings New challenges to "New Media Management" series of courses. On the other hand, the change from offline teaching to online teaching is not achieved through good teaching research and long-term validation, but is by necessity to a large extend. In this case, this study has a practical significance.

The research shows that:

(a) In terms of teaching methods and design, the teaching syllabus does not present significant changes for online teaching.
(b) In terms of the selection of teaching platforms, teachers generally use professional online education platforms in the commercial market.
(c) The use of online teaching function, playback is favored by the students.
(d) The interaction between teachers and students based on online teaching is significantly higher than that on offline.
(e) In terms of human-computer interaction situation, the duration of teacher's image appears are random distribution. And so on.

2 Related Work

Currently, relevant researches are mainly carried out at the following levels:

First, the design and development of the human-computer interaction platform for online teaching are introduced, which is mainly carried out in the basic computer field. For example, Ovaska et al. [1] introduced the operation mechanism and teaching content of some large-scale online open courses (MOOC) in User Experience and Learning Experience in Online HCI Courses.

Second, the research on the evaluation and achievement system of online teaching from the perspective of human-computer interaction are introduced. Tang et al. [2] put forward a bottom-up evaluation index system in Construction of "Bottom-up" Evaluation Index System of Open Online Course Based on the Delphi Method.

Third is an empirical study of online teaching in a curriculum field is introduced. Leventhal and Barnes et al. [3] outlined a project-oriented human-computer interaction course in Two for One: Squeezing Human-Computer Interaction and Software Engineering into a Core Computer Science Course.

Fourth the research and reflection on the advantages and disadvantages of human-computer interaction teaching mode are introduced. Henk [4] starting from the concept of "the right to education", discuss Open courseware (OCW) to provide a wider range of potential opportunities provided by the higher education opportunity.

Fifth, the utility of human-computer interaction teaching mode is studied. Cheng et al. [5] designed and implemented a real-time Attention Recognition and Feedback System to measure The change of learners' Attention state.

3 Method

This paper mainly uses the methods of questionnaire survey and interview the participating students and teachers of new Media Operation course researching on human-computer interaction behavior, demand and usability. The research in-volves real-time interaction, situational awareness and other issues in the teaching process of journalism major, and puts forward suggestions on the design of network course system.

4 Experiment

4.1 Student Needs and Platform Availability

The common results of students' questionnaires and teachers' interviews show that:

- Platform Usage Survey
  Statistic of "What is the teaching platform used for this course?" shows (Fig. 1):

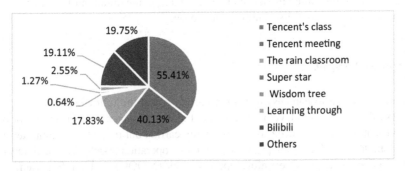

Fig. 1. Distribution map of online course teaching platform (Self-designed Form)

Statistical results show that the maximum data is from Tencent's class, was 55.41%, and the teachers' interview also reflects its main advantage is that the system has relatively high stability, simple operation, functional switching is also in a easy way, which is suitable for theoretical class. Most teachers have tried more than one teaching platform and finally confirmed one as the main teaching platform.
- Teaching Styles
  For "What is the teacher's online teaching method?", 90.45% of real-time online teaching, 3.82% of Video broadcast. Meanwhile, Besides attending classes, most teachers used other auxiliary teaching methods to assist the job, 76.92% of teachers released electronic Courseware, 84.62% issued a syllabus and teaching plan, etc., 53.85% of teachers allowed to use Courseware Playback, 100% of teachers participated in group discussion between teachers and students (WeChat group, etc.), and 84.62% of teachers set communication with students one to one. Teachers have a relatively high level of engagement in devoting to the online teaching on the whole, and they are generally concerned about the students' attention.

- Course Playback

  On the subject, there is a bigger difference between teachers and students answer. How many times do you think students need to watch the replay of the class after the first live broadcast of the class (or play the class video) is over? For this point, teachers believe that if the students want to master the corresponding classroom knowledge, 53.84% of the course need to watch the replay, and 7.69% of them even need to replay 5–10 times. But only 38.52% of the students had watch playback, and watch the replay of students, a large proportion is from other than "classroom knowledge not mastered" why choose to watch a replay, as shown in the Table 1.

Table 1. The reason of students playback (Self-designed Form).

The reason of students playback	Rate (%)
The course is very difficult	26.11
The course progress is fast	31.21
The course requires students to follow and carry out practical operation in real time	28.66
High interest in the course content	29.94
Poor reception in the first class due to network reasons	9.11
The course feedback channel is not unobstructed, so it is inconvenient to ask questions immediately	15.29
Others	10.83

The statistical results show that teachers and students have great deviation in judging the difficulty of the course. Teachers believe that in the case of online teaching, it is impossible for students to master the practical knowledge and complete homework through a course because they cannot gradually guide students to complete the operation face to face. And there is obviously a part of students think they can. However, as far as the concerned shows in interview of teachers, it does not see that there is an obvious increase of error rate and other negative situation in students' homework.

4.2 Multi-channel and Real-Time Interaction

According to the common results of student questionnaire survey and teacher interview, teachers and students generally believe that during the online teaching process, the frequency of teacher-student interaction has been greatly improved and the overall interaction is in good condition. In the online class, only 1.27% of students never participate in the interaction. Actively engaging with teachers in the course accounted for 54.78% of the students. 40.76% of the students can follow the teacher to answer questions. This level of interaction is much higher than that of offline teaching.

- Student Participation Ways in the Interaction
  According to student questionnaires, there are two channels for students to participate in online interaction: "using the built-in function of the teaching platform" and "using channels other than the teaching platform". However, different interactive channels have no significant impact on "whether to participate in interaction" (Table 2).

Table 2. The channels of online class interaction (Self-designed Form).

The channels of online class interaction	Rate (%)
On the platform, use voice interaction	32.9
On the platform, use text to interact	89.68
On the teaching platform, use pictures (including emoticons, gifs, etc.) to interact	18.06
On the platform, use video interaction	8.39
Outside the teaching platform, use social groups (such as qq group, WeChat group, etc.) to interact	45.81
Others	0.65

Many teachers and students interact on two or more platforms. Some teachers said that this practice was out of concern for the special circumstances such as "the poor quality of sound". In addition, online classroom interaction has obvious fragmentation characteristics. Due to the limitation of platform condition, most teachers reduce the interactive design of students' group discussion and oral presentation in class, and set more simplified topics that can easy reply in words and symbols, which may be part of the reason for the students' cognition of the course as low challenge.

- Interactive intention and content
  There are 74.52% of students take the initiative to communicate with teachers, this proportion is much higher than offline data (Table 3).

Table 3. Students' active intention statistics (Self-designed Form).

Students' active intention statistics	Rate (%)
No intention of active communication	25.48
Wants to communicate with the teacher about the extension of the curriculum	63.06
Wants to communicate with the teacher in writing papers (research papers, graduation papers, etc.)	22.93
I want to communicate about academic planning	14.01
Interested in the teacher's research direction, consider participating in the teacher's research project or team	14.65
Wants to communicate about life, entertainment and other non-curriculum contents	15.92
Others	1.27

Studies show that online classes actually bring teachers and students closer together. Even in 31.85% of the online classes, the teacher's image never appears in the visual area of students, but because students are individually alone in the real situation of attending class, there is the psychological feeling of "the teacher seems looking forward to me", to some extent, the long-term isolation from the group atmosphere also improves the desire for their individual expression.

4.3 Human-Computer Interaction Situation

Teachers and students generally have a high evaluation on the human-computer interaction condition in this course, but they have underestimate on appealing for the human-computer interaction design of this course. However, this does not prevent the communication effect of the course from showing a good tendency.

- Course satisfaction in human-computer interaction

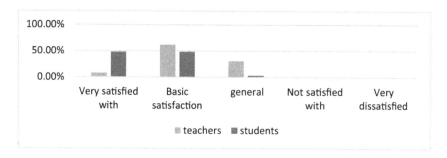

Fig. 2. Online course satisfaction profile (Self-designed Form)

With the exception of very few individuals, most of the teachers and students are satisfied with the online class. Especially among the students, 47.77% very satisfied with it and 48.41% of them with basic satisfaction. Among the teachers, 61.54% have basic satisfaction. None of teachers rated "Not satisfied with" and "Very dissatisfied" (Fig. 2).
- Human-Computer Interaction Situations Effects on Concentration

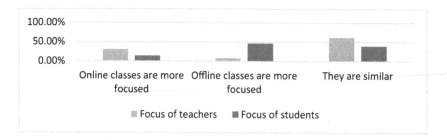

Fig. 3. Online course concentration comparison chart (Self-designed Form)

Research shows that only 14.01% of students think online classes are more focused, to some extent, we can realize that the students listening to lectures online are under the condition of relatively low concentration, still finished tasks properly, which made us consider other reason for this change. Teachers are significantly more focused on online teaching, with 30.77% believing that online classes are more focused and 7.69% believing that Offline classes are more focused. Objectively, more teachers invest more attention in online teaching and spend more time and energy to think about the way to improve (Fig. 3).

- The Influence of Human-Computer Interaction Condition on the Teaching Effect
  In terms of the presentation and perception of the effect, teachers and students majoring in journalism and Communication show relatively different judgments (Fig. 4).

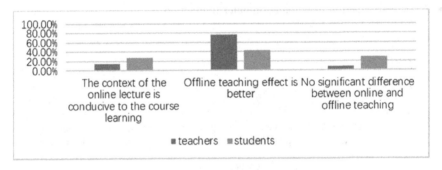

Fig. 4. The comparison chart of online class interpersonal interaction situation evaluation (Self-designed Form)

General speaking, most of teachers and students think offline teaching would has better effect, only 15.38% of the teachers and 28.03% of the students think the context of the online lecture is conducive to the course learning. but it is interesting to note that these judgments are inconsistent with the actual data from the performance of the communication effect. It is evident in the dramatic increase in the frequency of student interaction and in the fact that student's mastery of knowledge has improved than teachers' expectation.

5   Conclusion

Based on the above data analysis, the research says that: first, in terms of student demand and platform availability level, the online teaching platform used by the current courses has its advantages and disadvantages, which can generally meet the students' online learning needs of information transmission. However, as for the details of human-computer interaction settings, which needs to be used in different courses, such as the inability to import operational procedures for teacher-student alternations and inspections in practice classes, there is still a room to grow. Secondly, on the real-time interaction and multi-channel interaction level, the current course platforms have obviously deficiencies on the user service function. However, in this study, students' enthusiasm for interaction is motivated by the particularity of interpersonal interaction, and teachers' non-confidence in network communication objectively stimulate the number of interactions. In fact, that improving the degree of interaction between teachers and students is conducive to enhancing the communication effect of online courses. Moreover, it unconsciously constitutes the basic situation of positive interaction, which can even compensate for the lack of hardware in some points of view. Thirdly, in the context of human-computer interaction, the course produces a good situation which is not easily perceived by teachers and students, but this does not obstruct the improvement of the communication effect. The efficiency of students' knowledge acquisition has been improved, and students have generally completed learning at much lower playback rate than that estimated by teachers. This conclusion can be supported by homework completion and accuracy rate. The interaction between teachers and students is significantly enhanced. Due to the psychological implication of one-to-one teaching and the absence of personal image in class, students feel reduce the risk of wrong answer, improve the willingness of communication, and form a good virtuous circle and communication expectation.

Based on these, the following aspects should be improved in setting the online teaching system of New Media Operation in the future. First, a special online teaching platform should be built according to the teaching requirements of different disciplines, designed access ports for various practical operating software. Second is to reduce the systematic and deliberative topics setting of class interaction, increase the schedule of extracurricular teacher-student interaction that is not limited to the course content, and the establishment of close relationship between teachers and students. Third, enhance the perception ability of teachers and students majoring in news communication for human-computer interaction situation, avoid the effect perception barriers caused by different professional fields, miss the human-computer interaction situation data that really contributes to the communication effect, and tend to take their own feelings and experience as evaluation criteria.

In addition, because the course has not yet completed the final evaluation, the assessment of students' knowledge understanding is mainly based on several current assignments, therefore, systematic data presentation has not been achieved in the evaluation of online communication effect of this course. There is flaws here, that is expected to be in a follow-up study to continue carrying out the analysis.

References

1. Ovaska, S.: User experience and learning experience in online HCI courses. In: Kotzé, P., Marsden, G., Lindgaard, G., Wesson, J., Winckler, M. (eds.) INTERACT 2013. LNCS, vol. 8120, pp. 447–454. Springer, Heidelberg (2013). https://doi.org/10.1007/978-3-642-40498-6_34
2. Tang, X.J., Lu, Y., Liu, N., Wang, H.W., Gongyuan, Q.: Construction of "bottom-up" evaluation index system of open online course based on the delphi method. In: 2016 International Conference on Power Engineering & Energy, Environment (PEEE 2016), pp. 1–9 (2016)

3. Leventhal, L., Barnes, J.: Two for one: squeezing human-computer interaction and software engineering into a core computer science course. Comput. Sci. Educ. **13**(3), 177–190 (2003)
4. Henk, H, Tas, B, David, B.: OpenCourseWare, global access and the right to education: Real access or marketing ploy. In: International Review of Research in Open and Distance Learning, 2008, vol. 9, no. 1, p. 13 (2008)
5. Cheng, P.Y., Chien, Y.C., Huang, Y.M.: The design and implementation of a real-time attention recognition/feedback system in online learning course. In: 2017 International Conference of Educational Innovation through Technology (EITT). IEEE (2017)

Modeling Learners' Programming Skills and Question Levels Through Machine Learning

WooJeong Kim[1], Soyoung Rhim[1], John Y. J. Choi[2], and Kyungsik Han[1(✉)] (iD)

[1] Ajou University, Suwon, Republic of Korea
{gks3284,ter194,kyungsikhan}@ajou.ac.kr
[2] Coding Robot Lab, Inc., Seoul, Republic of Korea
john.choi@codingrobotlab.com

Abstract. Many universities have started to adopt online programming tools to support students' programming practice, yet the services currently offered by the existing tools are somewhat passive with respect to considering a student's programming skill level and providing appropriate code questions. To enhance students' learning experience and improve their programming skills, it would be helpful to examine students' programming abilities and provide them with the most suitable code questions and guidelines. Machine learning can play a role in modeling the level of students' programming skills as well as the difficulty of questions by taking the students' programming experience and code submissions into account. This paper presents a study on the development of machine learning models to classify the levels of students' programming skills and those of programming questions, based on the data of students' code submissions. We extracted a total of 197 features of code quality, code readability and system time. We used those features to build classification models. The model for the student level (four classes) and the question level (five classes) yielded 0.60 and 0.82 F1-scores, respectively, showing reasonable classification performance. We discuss our study highlights and their implications, such as group and question matching based on code submissions and user experience improvement.

Keywords: Programming · Machine learning · Learning matching

1 Introduction

The popularity of programming continues to rise. The importance of programming education to help with mathematical and logical thinking has been emphasized around the world, and there have been many educational efforts to cultivate talented programmers at the national level. For example, the United States has adopted programming as a subject of formal education in many public schools, including those in Florida, Arkansas and California[1]. In Finland, programming

---

[1] https://advocacy.code.org/.

© Springer Nature Switzerland AG 2020
C. Stephanidis et al. (Eds.): HCII 2020, CCIS 1294, pp. 281–288, 2020.
https://doi.org/10.1007/978-3-030-60703-6_36

education has been mandatory for elementary school students since 2016 [3]. India has designated software education as an elementary, middle and high school requirement since 2010. The demand for skilled programmers is high. Not only IT companies but also companies in various fields such as finance, biotechnology, health care, manufacturing and distribution are actively recruiting talented software engineers. The demand for fostering students into good programmers at the university level is similarly high as well.

Despite high popularity, expectations and demands, many students majored or minoring in computer science or engineering, as well as those from other departments (e.g., humanities) who want to learn programming, are struggling in programming classes. According to Bennedsen and Caspersen's research [2], the average failure rate of students taking CS1 ("Introduction to computer programming") in 2017 was 28%. Similarly, Watson and Li's article about failure statistics reported the average failure rate of CS1 at 33.3% [8]. These results indicate that almost one third of students fail the introductory course. This problem is also reflected in the high dropout rate of students majoring in computer science. The Higher Education Statistics Agency (HESA) indicated that the percentage of dropouts from the computer science major was 9.8% during the 2016–17 academic year, which is greater than that of other majors such as business and administration (7.4%) or engineering and technology (7.2%)[2].

To mitigate such challenges, universities have been making many efforts such as expanding and strengthening programming practice and providing online or video-recorded lectures, etc. In particular, many universities have adopted an online programming support tool that may be used in classrooms, or available to students individually to assist them with their programming practice. To name a few of the anticipated benefits, it is expected that students can use the programming tool to access many step-by-step, thematic programming questions and improve their programming skills by evaluating their submitted code (e.g., LeetCode[3], Baekjoon[4], Exercism[5]).

Despite many advances and the expanding roles of programming support tools, our review on the current tools indicates that the services presently being offered are somewhat passive for learners; code questions are provided in a simple list by theme, and learners (randomly) select the desired questions from each topic to solve the problem. Many of the tools are designed to support students who want to participate in coding competitions (e.g., ICPC by ACM) and prepare for job interviews, which may not (yet) be the objective of students who are new to programming (e.g., freshmen, students from non-computer science departments) and who need more programming guidelines. This means that the service of providing learner-customized questions through the analysis of the learner's code submissions does not seem well supported or explicitly highlighted in the current tools. We believe that artificial intelligence (machine/deep

---

[2] https://bit.ly/37izVmz.
[3] https://leetcode.com/.
[4] https://www.acmicpc.net/.
[5] https://exercism.io/.

learning) technology can play a role in modeling a learner's programming skill level and providing a better learning environment; however, based on our review, research on the possibility and specific applications of machine/deep learning in the context of programming learning has not been extensively conducted to date.

The purpose of our research is to increase the effectiveness of learning by providing learners with the most suitable questions based on large-scale data of code submissions. In this paper, we present a study on the development of machine learning models to classify levels of programming skills and those of question levels, based on the code data submitted by college students using a cloud web, IDE-based programming learning tool[6]. For two semesters (around 8 months in total), we collected data (2574 code submissions) from 644 students (302 freshmen, 219 sophomores, 86 juniors and 37 seniors) in the seven "Introduction to Computer Programming" and three "Data Structures" classes. We extracted a total of 197 features based on *code quality* and *code readability*, which are essential aspects of the code, and system time-related features. We used the features to build the classification models. As a result, the classification models yielded 0.60 and 0.84 f1-scores for the user-level and the question-level classification, respectively. The performance seems reasonable and also suggests room for improvement and opportunities (e.g., peer and question matching) in the future.

Our study highlights the possibility of classifying the level of learners and questions through code analysis. This is meaningful in that learners can be assigned to learning groups whose members have similar programming skills, and be provided with the most necessary questions using a recommendation approach. Depending the learner's performance, he/she can move up or down to another level and access the most suitable questions. Thus, it is expected that learners will experience a better environment for conducting programming exercises and improving their programming skills. Unlike existing measurement studies [7,9], our measurement framework brings new opportunities for data analysis to the fields of educational data mining and learning analytics [5].

2   Feature Extraction

2.1   Code Quality Features

To capture code quality (185 features in total), we used two measurements: OCLint[7] and C-Quality Metrics[8]. First, OCLint is a static code analysis tool for C, C++, and Objective-C codes that looks for the following potential problems: possible bugs, unused code, complicated code, redundant code, etc. It relies on the abstract syntax tree of the source code for better accuracy and efficiency. Second, C-Quality Metrics [6] reads the code from its standard input and prints on its standard output a single line with features including size, complexity, used

---

[6] http://calmsw.com/.

[7] http://oclint.org/.

[8] https://github.com/dspinellis/cqmetrics.

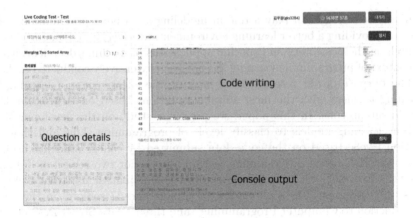

Fig. 1. Software used for data collection

keywords, comments and documentation, use of the C preprocessor and observed formatting style (e.g., number of lines, empty lines, functions, specific keywords, declarations and many occurrence cases) (Fig. 1).

2.2   Code Readability Features

We used an Automatic Readability Checker[9] that takes a code sample and calculates the number of sentences, words, syllables and characters. The checker plugs these numbers into the following nine popular readability formulas: Flesch Reading Ease formula, Flesch-Kincaid Grade Level, Fog Scale, SMOG Index, Coleman-Liau Index, Dale Chall, Spache, Automated Readability Index and Linsear Write Formula.

2.3   System Time Features

Our programming tool provides the following three types of information that we used as the system features: minimum/maximum/average execution times.

2.4   Target Variable

We considered two target variables – *user level* and *question level* – in this study. The user level was determined based on student grade (from freshman to senior), meaning that students in a higher grade are more likely to have more programming experience and skill, which will be reflected in their codes. Our correlation analysis between student grade and score in our sample showed positive results ($r = 0.10$, $p < 0.05$), thus our assumption is valid. The number of samples in each class was as follows: freshmen (302), sophomores (219), juniors

---

[9] More information about each formula is explained at https://bit.ly/2viSaen.

(86) and seniors (37). The question level was determined based on the average score of the question, meaning that students are likely to have lower scores if the question is difficult. Given that the range of the score is from 0 to 100, we divided the score into five sections (by 20) and used these sections as the target variables. The number of samples in each class was as follows: scores between 0–20 (485), 20–40 (879), 40–60 (577), 60–80 (369), and 80–100 (264).

3   Model Development and Performance

3.1   Code Cleaning

When students use the system, each question is presented with a pre-defined code template; it asks the students to type the essential code to run the program and see the score for their submission. Students do not have to use the template. They can clean the template and start programming from scratch.

We found that most students actually kept the template and added their code. The problem here is that even if a student submits only a template code, the features of that code will be calculated and can be used for modeling. Therefore, in order to more accurately apply code quality and readability to model development, we removed the submission samples that only had the template code based on cosine-similarity between the sample and the template. Based on our qualitative analysis, scores above 0.95 indicate that the submission and the template are almost identical. We thus removed the corresponding submissions and had 2574 submissions for the analysis.

3.2   Model Development Procedure

We developed two models that classify (1) the level of a student's programming and (2) the difficulty of a programming question. We normalized all of the features through a min-max normalization.

We used LightGBM (Gradient Boosting Model) as a model algorithm [4]. LightGBM is a gradient boosting framework that uses tree based learning algorithms, designed to be distributed and efficient with several advantages, such as faster training speed and higher efficiency, lower memory usage, better accuracy, and the capacity to handle large-scale data. We prepared 60% of the data as the training data, 20% as the validation data, and 20% as the test data. We applied 10-fold cross-validation. Note that our intention in conducting this research was to assess the feasibility of classifying user levels and question levels based on the quality and readability of the code, not to achieve the best performance of the model through a rigorous model comparison analysis. We consider the latter objective to be the subject of future studies.

3.3   Model Performance

Table 1 shows the overall performance of the model. In addition to accuracy as a metric, because the sample sizes of each class were unbalanced, we used

Table 1. Model performance results

	User level (4 classes)	Question level (5 classes)
F1-score	0.60	0.82
Accuracy	0.64	0.83

F1-score. The model yielded 0.60 and 0.82 F1-score (0.64 and 0.83 accuracy) for classifying user level and question level, respectively. These findings indicate the feasibility of using code quality and readability to assess a learner's skill level in programming and the difficulty of the question.

It appears that identifying user level is a bit challenging. As we looked more deeply into our sample data, we found some cases in which some freshmen had high test scores while some juniors and seniors had relatively lower test scores, which can be easily explained in many real scenarios. On the other hand, classifying question level yielded reasonably good results. This further means that the level of a learner's submitted codes can be measured and assigned to a proper group of code questions. Then the learner can be provided with questions that are more relevant to his/her learning and any related programming materials (e.g., related data structure algorithms, sample codes) can be provided, increasing user experience in learning.

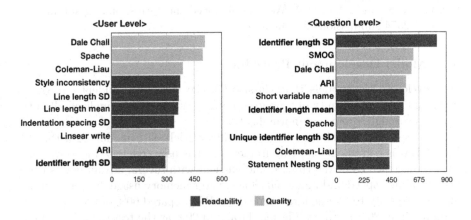

Fig. 2. Feature importance for the user level and the question level

3.4   Feature Importance

We measured the importance of the features to see how much influence the three main feature groups – code quality, code readability and system time – had in model performance. Figure 2 illustrates the top ten features for the user and the question levels. The results indicate that the quality and readability groups influenced the model performance quite evenly. The system time features were not included in the list. Readability features, some of them are length-related (e.g., line length, identifier length), tended to highly influence the user level, while those related to identifiers highly influenced the question level. Quality features for the user and question levels were quite overlapped; these included Dale Chall, Spache, Coleman-Liau and ARI. We paid close attention to the fact that many readability features are length-related. This indicates that the basic programming rules (e.g., not having long lines of code) do not seem to be well followed by many students; such programming practices could be addressed by providing learners with proper feedback.

4 Discussion and Conclusion

Our study demonstrates the possibility of classifying the level of learners and questions through code analysis with machine learning. The model could be improved by collecting more samples (e.g., programming submissions, diverse classes from multiple departments), building more complex models (e.g., multimodal models, sequence-based deep learning), applying additional features (e.g., code2vec [1]), having additional important target variables, etc.

Our study insights are meaningful in that through the use of the classification model, learners can be assigned to learner groups based on programming skills and be provided with the most suitable programming questions through a recommendation technique. Depending on their programming performance, learners can move up or down to another level and be provided with questions appropriate to each level. Through this process, it is expected that learners can experience a better environment for engaging in programming exercise, improve their programming skills and possibly contribute their experience to helping other learners and peers.

References

1. Alon, U., Zilberstein, M., Levy, O., Yahav, E.: code2vec: learning distributed representations of code. In: Proceedings of the ACM on Programming Languages 3(POPL), pp. 1–29 (2019)
2. Bennedsen, J., Caspersen, M.E.: Failure rates in introductory programming: 12 years later. ACM Inroads 10(2), 30–36 (2019)
3. Hiltunen, T.: Learning and teaching programming skills in finnish primary schools-the potential of games. University of Oulu (2016). Accessed 16 Dec 2016
4. Ke, G., et al.: LightGBM: a highly efficient gradient boosting decision tree. In: Advances in Neural Information Processing Systems, pp. 3146–3154 (2017)
5. Romero, C., Ventura, S.: Educational data mining: a review of the state of the art. IEEE Trans. Syst. Man Cybern. Part C (Appl. Rev.) 40(6), 601–618 (2010)
6. Spinellis, D., Louridas, P., Kechagia, M.: The evolution of c programming practices: a study of the unix operating system 1973–2015. In: 2016 IEEE/ACM 38th International Conference on Software Engineering (ICSE), pp. 748–759. IEEE (2016)

7. Wang, Z., Bergin, C., Bergin, D.A.: Measuring engagement in fourth to twelfth grade classrooms: the classroom engagement inventory. School Psychol. Q. **29**(4), 517 (2014)
8. Watson, C., Li, F.W.: Failure rates in introductory programming revisited. In: Proceedings of the 2014 Conference on Innovation & Technology in Computer Science Education, pp. 39–44 (2014)
9. Zhou, M., Ma, M., Zhang, Y., Sui, A,K., Pei, D., Moscibroda, T.: EDUM: classroom education measurements via large-scale WIFI networks. In: Proceedings of the 2016 ACM International Joint Conference on Pervasive and Ubiquitous Computing, pp. 316–327 (2016)

Reviewing Mobile Apps for Learning Quran

Omar Mubin, Bayan M. Alsharbi[✉], and Mauricio Novoa

Western Sydney University, Victoria Rd., Rydalmere, NSW 2116, Australia
18516887@student.westernsydney.edu.au

Abstract. The Quran is the holy book for millions of Muslims around the world and is read and learnt in Arabic. We are witnessing a spawning of many mobile apps claiming to provide a digitised experience of Learning Quran. In our research we present a thorough review of 37 such apps from the Google Play Store and 85 apps from iOS Apple Store. Our results shows that while most apps provide tailored interaction, in general the main target group remains adult Arabic speaking users. Moreover, real time feedback remains a sought after feature, due to limitations in speech recognition. Accreditation and authentication of the sanctity of these apps remains a key worry for most users. In conclusion, we present design implications emerging from our results that could be applied to mobile apps for Quranic teaching.

Keywords: Mobile apps · Arabic · Quran · Islamic education

1 Introduction

Religious sculptures and writings have been passed on from generations and are such integral to the sanctity of the religion. The use of digital technology can provide us with a mechanism to not only maintain the consistency of the teachings but also establish a real time learning experience for users. Islam is one of the largest religions in the world with almost 1/5th of the world's population being of Muslim faith (Hackett et al. (2015)). Since the birth of the religion took place in Saudia Arabia of today, most rituals, teachings and practice related to Islam is done in the Arabic language. Although, the holy book of Islam: The Quran is translated in many languages it is also read in Arabic as a matter of principle and custom. A common myth regarding Muslims is that they all can speak Arabic - current estimates indicate that only 20% of Muslims speak Arabic as their first language (Mohammed (2005)). Hence many Muslims in non-Arabic environments either rely on rote learning of Arabic verses within Islam without a focus on proper pronunciation, especially in younger children. This is particularly a dilemma if Arabic instructors are not available, as correct recitation of the Quran is imperative as a matter of principle (Kamarudin and Salam (2012)). Traditionally all forms of Islamic teaching in the Muslim world, particularly learning and reading of the Quran and praying begins from young ages (as little as 7 years

© Springer Nature Switzerland AG 2020
C. Stephanidis et al. (Eds.): HCII 2020, CCIS 1294, pp. 289–296, 2020.
https://doi.org/10.1007/978-3-030-60703-6_37

old). Additionally reading and understanding Quran forms an integral part of muslims and many continue the learning process well into adulthood (Ahmad et al. (2016)). Currently, most Islamic education takes places in dedicated religious schools (Madrassahs), mosques, Islamic specialized private schools, or at home by either parents or religious scholars (Anzar (2003)). Further, most Quranic teaching is established on the basis of "memorization", which we already know on the basis of pedagogical literature (Orlin (2013)) is a challenge, particularly in order to retain the attention of the student. State of the art research indicates that there is recent intersection of Islam and technology. Advancements in Arabic speech recognition have allowed checks and verification of Tajweed Khir et al. (2016); i.e. pronunciation of verses from the Quran (Muhammad et al. (2012); Elhadj (2010)). We can observe the proliferation of mobile apps in the developing world and the uptake of the same to teach languages (Godwin-Jones (2011)) such as Arabic (Gharawi and Bidin (2016)). A seminal overview (Campbell et al. (2014)) of such apps showed that search terms related to Islam and Christianity resulted in more than 3000 hits on iTunes. Therefore, therein lies great potential in further utilising mobile computing technology to promote Quranic education (Kamarudin and Salam (2012)) particularly to the non native speakers of Arabic.

The aim of this work was to set out to perform a review of existing Islamic religion based commercial applications in the market to understand the gaps, trends, learning styles and user preferences. To the best of our knowledge such an overview does not exist, one exception being (Machfud and Mahmud (2016)), however the stated overview did not focus on pedagogical or Quranic recitation methodologies associated with learning the Quran. Another exception is (Rippin (2013)), however it only focuses on web solutions meant to teach Quran. We contribute towards Educational technology literature by providing design implications extracted from our review, which are firstly, relevant to apps aimed to teach Quran but some findings can be generalised and applied to other religious apps.

2   Method

Our meta analysis of mobile apps is a commonly followed methodology or paradigm in health informatics or educational technology literature (Mateo et al. (2015); Crompton et al. (2017)). For our overview we focused on apps available on the Android platform as well as the Apple Store. We performed a thorough search on both App stores to shortlist relevant apps. Keywords that we utilised were "Learning Quran", "Memorising Quran", "Reading Quran", "Understanding Quran" and their Arabic translations. Since more than half of the research team was bilingual (spoke both Arabic and English), we included any app that used English, Arabic or both in combination as the mode of interaction. Apps that we could not browse or download were excluded from our analysis. We only focused on apps which were meant for teaching Quran as there are a number of apps which provided general Islamic education.

2.1 Coding Scheme

The coding scheme comprised of a number of extracted variables. The codes are summarized here under:

1. Medium of instruction, which was either Arabic or English
2. The second code attempted to classify the main target group of the app into children, adults or the elderly
3. The third code was the type of learning focus or main pedagogical technique employed by the apps which we coded into the following possibilities:
   (a) Tajweed: Tajweed refers to the correct elocution, pronunciation of Quranic verses with a suitable speed of articulation (Ibrahim et al. (2015)). Any app which focused on this learning style was placed into this category.
   (b) Tafseer: Tafseer is referred to as the science of the mode of articulating the expressions of the Quran, its linguistic indications and singular and composite rules, its meanings interpreted as composite constructions and related matters al (Andalusi (1970)). Apps dealing with the semantics were hence placed into this category.
   (c) Hifiz: An app that employed Hifiz as its mode of teaching concentrated on memorisation of Quranic verses by heart through repeated recitations (Nawaz and Jahangir (2015)).
   (d) Noorani Qaida: The Noordani Qaida is a teaching method for the Quran that explains the basic pronunciations of various phonemes. It is typically intended for children or for those who are beginning to learn the Quran.
   (e) General: An app was placed into this category if it used two or more of the aforementioned pedagogical techniques in combination.
4. The modality of learning interaction made it as the fourth code, where we checked if the app utilised audio, video or an interactive combination thereof (listen and repeat, listen and record).
5. As a fifth code we also noted the Human Computer Interaction elements comprised within the apps, pertaining to their specific features, functionalities and interaction styles.
6. The last three codes were quantitative in nature and were sourced from the App stores. They were:
   (a) Number of downloads as a range
   (b) total number of reviews
   (c) average app rating

All codes had a possibility to mark a category as not applicable or not available. Two coders independently coded 25% of the apps to resolve any ambiguities or disagreements in the coding scheme.

3 Results

In this section, we present our results and findings in two subsections where the first sub-section provides our findings from the Google Play store and the second sub-section summarizes our findings from the Apple store.

3.1 Google Play Store

Initially our search gave us 256 apps upon which we applied exclusion criteria mentioned earlier giving us a total of 37 Learning Quran apps which were short-listed for further analysis. Most of the apps were targeted specifically towards Arabic speakers (16). There only 7 apps meant primarily for non native Arabic speakers. Similarly there were only 6 apps designed for younger users such as children. With regards to the learning focus of our selection of apps the popular type was Hifiz or memorisation with almost 1/3rd in number. Tajweed and Tasfeer in comparison were adopted in fewer apps (around the 25% and 10% mark respectively). More than 2/3rd of the apps employed a listening to audio approach with about half of them also providing an opportunity to the user to repeat the verses. Only 6 apps facilitated the recording of user audio. We noticed that the apps incorporated a wide variety of features and Human Computer Interaction aspects. Most apps allowed users to create profiles and consequently design tailored and guided lesson plans. A number of interaction strategies were designed to motivate the learners, for example through recording, sharing and comparing performance in online quizzes with others. In addition, most apps also provided offline interaction, allowing users to use the app without a data connection. Customisation was a key feature; most apps allowing users to choose particular verses to learn through a number of recitation or memorisation settings. Real time detection of phonological errors and searching for words through voice was a novel feature, present in only 2 apps (such as in Quran Tutor. In order to replicate student scholar interaction as is in conventional learning of the Quran, some apps used video snippets of scholars reciting verses or phonemes which users could use to practice (such as in Learn Quran - Qaaida Noorania).

We also recorded the range of total downloads and associated user reviews made on each app to gauge their popularity. Around 50% of the apps were downloaded between 100,000 and 1,000,000 times. On average, each app received a total of 12,065 reviews and a rating of 4.56. The most popular apps were Al Quran and Ayat Al Quran with more than 5,000,000 downloads, 100,000 user reviews and ratings of 4.5 and 4.7 respectively. We explored these two apps with some detail to analyse their features and design aspects. Al-Quran had a number of key attributes which stood out, such as it allowed for easy navigation between the various chapters and sections of the Quran. Users were also able to go back to their active session conveniently. In addition, Al-Quran provided a two way mechanism to explore the Quran (scrolling or paging). Ayat Al Quran supported different techniques to learn the Quran (Tafseer, Tajweed and memorisation). It also allowed users to drill down and select specific verses for recitation.

3.2 Tunes Store

Our search in the iTunes store gave us approximately 250 apps upon which we applied exclusion criteria mentioned earlier giving us a total of 85 Learning Quran apps. 20 apps (23.5%) were meant for Arabic speakers only, unlike Google Play, many apps were found to be targeting non-native speakers. iOS apps that were meant to teach Quran by translation to another language were 54 in number. Interestingly, 24 apps were designed for young users and children. Similar to the Android platform, the learning focus of iOS apps was on Hifiz (more than 1/3rd of our sample), followed by Tajweed. The proportion of apps that utilised Tafseer as the main aspect were more in comparison to the Android platform (27% vs 10%). There were only 6 apps that did not employ a listening to audio approach, while 18 apps intended to use an interactive approach for teaching.

Similar to our findings in Android apps, most apps on the iOS platform incorporated a wide variety of features and Human Computer Interaction aspects. A majority of the apps were visual in nature relying on graphics and animations during the interaction. Hovering upon particular words and then highlighting them while being pronounced by the app was also an interesting technique. Profiling, customisation and tailoring the lesson plan to one's own preferences was widely seen. Users could choose what to learn, in which order and how many repetitions. Most apps also allowed users to choose particular verses to learn through a number of recitation or memorisation settings. In order to replicate student scholar interaction as is in conventional learning of the Quran, some apps used audio snippets of scholars reciting verses or phonemes which users could use to practice (such as Al Qaida Al Nooraniya). Another key user interaction featured employed by iOS apps was the usage of motivation such as in Quran Star. In this app, numerous reward mechanisms were seen. For example, earning 3 gold stars on every surah read or sharing accomplishments and performance with friends on social media. Quran Star was seen to comprise of a recording feature built into the app that allowed the user to test their memorization of each surah and send recordings to friends and family. Finally, in the app the unique HuroofMeter counted the number of letters read through each ayah.

4   Discussion

Results from our review of mobile apps intended to teach Quran on the Android and iOS platform have revealed that although a number of relevant apps are present there are still some open gaps in the field. Our findings show that the primary target group for such apps is adult native Arabic speakers. In comparison there were fewer apps for children and Muslims whose first language was not Arabic. It is commonly acknowledged that most digital solutions used to learn and read the Quran are tailored to Arabic speakers (Elsayess and Hamada (2013)). In addition, is it also known that there is a dearth of Islamic apps specifically tailored for children (Machfud and Mahmud (2016)). Our findings also show that real time feedback on correctness of pronunciation of Quranic verses is a rarely present feature, possibly due to challenges of voice recognition. Prior work shows that Arabic speech recognition is still a work in progress venture with fluctuating recognition accuracy rates. Challenges of processing the Arabic language are also known (Farghaly and Shaalan (2009)).

Our overview also shows that most app developers realise the importance of providing a customised user experience when using mobile apps to learn the

Quran. A wide user base who wish to learn the Quran requires mobile solutions to adapt to different learning styles, skill levels and convenience (Ibrahim et al. (2015); Ragab (2009)). Self-Customisation and user-profiling of learning patterns and styles would be an essential design feature of any app which promotes educational aspects of a religion, such that users can learn, read and practice at their own pace. Providing discrete and private learning opportunities is well understood in educational literature (Cheong et al. (2012)), primarily with the focus of being "inclusive" and allowing students with different personality traits an equal opportunity to learn.

Our analysis also shows that about 1/3rd of our short listed apps provided the possibility of reading and learning the Quran through Tajweed. This is not as large a number as we would expect given the importance of (Tajweed Elhassan et al. (2015)). Tajweed relies on audio and visual feedback hence apps which intend to incorporate Tajweed may be susceptible to technical limitations. The review of the apps also illustrated that there was no evident mechanism to establish or verify the veracity and authenticity of the sacred content presented in the mobile apps. For example information about accreditation or certification can be stated in the about us section or through an appropriate logo on the home page. We were unable to establish if this was the case in the apps that we considered, at least such information was not immediately visible.

5   Conclusion and Future Work

In this paper, we have presented an overview of mobile apps dedicated to teach Quran as a result of which we present certain implications for Quranic app design which could also be considered for apps from other religions. We believe that the category of Quranic apps is still in embryonic stage as the combination of Islam and technology is a sensitive issue (Khan and Alginahi (2013)), particularly if unintentionally errors occur during interaction. Furthermore, uptake of mobile apps to read Quran is still met with resistance by some users, as face to face learning or reading the physical copy of the Quran ("Mushaf") may be a preference (Muhammad Nasrullah (2015); Kamarudin and Salam (2012)). In addition, we may still be a fair way away from the mass usage of such Quranic apps in local Islamic teaching setups, primarily due to issues related to stereotypical perception of technology, lack of support from the educational boards and simply the diversity in pedagogical methods followed in Islamic education. Our review has also indicated that there is a shortage of apps focusing on non native Arabic speakers. Our long term research endeavor is to utilize mobile technology to promote the uptake and learning of Arabic, Islamic teachings and Quran in non-Arabic speaking users. As a first step in our user centered design process we aim to involve Sheikhs (religions scholars) from our community and internationally as a means to ground and validate our findings and design ideas. We also aim to complete our overview by considering apps from the iTunes store.

References

Ahmad, N.A., Zainal, A., Kahar, S., Hassan, M.A.A., Setik, R.: Exploring the needs of older adult users for spiritual mobile applications. J. Theoret. Appl. Inf. Technol. **88**(1), 154 (2016)

al Andalusi, A.H.: Tafsir Al bahr Al muhit al Mujallad 2 (1970). https://books.google.com.au/books?id=aNOONQEACAAJ

Anzar, U.: Islamic education: A brief history of madrassas with comments on curricula and current pedagogical practices. Paper for the University of Vermont, Environmental Programme (2003)

Campbell, H.A., Altenhofen, B., Bellar, W., Cho, K.J.: There'sa religious app for that! a framework for studying religious mobile applications. Mobile Med. Commun. **2**(2), 154–172 (2014)

Cheong, C., Bruno, V., Cheong, F.: Designing a mobile-app-based collaborative learning system. J. Inf. Technol. Educ. Innov. Pract. **11**, 97–119 (2012)

Crompton, H., Burke, D., Gregory, K.H.: The use of mobile learning in PK-12 education: a systematic review. Comput. Educ. **110**, 51–63 (2017)

Elhadj, Y.O.M.: E-halagat: an e-learning system for teaching the holy Quran. TOJET Turkish Online J. Educ. Technol. **9**(1), 54–61 (2010)

Elhassan, E.M., et al.: Investigating the Role of Mastering the Rules of Holy Quran Recitation in English Pronunciation. Ph.D. thesis, Sudan University of Science and Technology (2015)

Elsayess, M., Hamada, S.E.: Using mobile application in teaching correct recitation of the holy Quran. In: 2013 Taibah University International Conference on Advances in Information Technology for the Holy Quran and its Sciences, pp. 535–551. IEEE (2013)

Farghaly, A., Shaalan, K.: Arabic natural language processing: challenges and solutions. ACM Trans. Asian Lang. Inf. Process. (TALIP) **8**(4), 14 (2009)

Gharawi, M.A., Bidin, A.: Computer assisted language learning for learning Arabic as a second language in Malaysia: teacher perceptions. Int. J. Inf. Educ. Technol. **6**(8), 633 (2016)

Godwin-Jones, R.: Emerging technologies: mobile apps for language learning. Lang. Learn. Technol. **15**(2), 2–11 (2011)

Hackett, C., Connor, P., Stonawski, M., Skirbekk, V., Potancoková, M., Abel, G.: The future of world religions: Population growth projections, 2010–2050. DC, Pew Research Center, Washington (2015)

Ibrahim, N.J., Idris, M.Y.I., Yusoff, M.Z.M., Anuar, A.: The problems, issues and future challenges of automatic speech recognition for quranic verse recitation: a review. Al-Bayan J. Qur'an Hadith Stud. **13**(2), 168–196 (2015)

Kamarudin, N., Salam, S.: Tajweed understanding among malaysian muslim (a preliminary findings). In: 2012 Proceedings of 1st International Conference on Mobile Learning, Applications and Services (Mobilecase2012), Kuala Lumpur, pp. 1–4 (2012)

Khan, M.K., Alginahi, Y.M.: The holy Quran digitization: challenges and concerns. Life Sci. J. **10**(2), 156–164 (2013)

Khir, M., et al.: ITAJweed to enhance the interactive learning modules for the users. Int. J. Comput. Sci. Inf. Technol. Res. **4**(2), 281–291 (2016)

Machfud, F.M., Mahmud, M.: A survey on Islamic mobile applications for children. In: Critical Socio-Technical Issues Surrounding Mobile Computing, pp. 1–29. IGI Global (2016)

Mateo, G.F., Granado-Font, E., Ferré-Grau, C., Montaña-Carreras, X.: Mobile phone apps to promote weight loss and increase physical activity: a systematic review and meta-analysis. J. Med. Internet Res. **17**(11) e253 (2015)

Mohammed, K.: Assessing English translations of the Qur'an. Middle East Q. **12**, 59–72 (2005)

Muhammad, A., Ul Qayyum, Z., Tanveer, S., Martinez-Enriquez, A., Syed, A.Z.: E-hafiz: Intelligent system to help Muslims in recitation and memorization of Quran. Life Sci. J. **9**(1), 534–541 (2012)

Muhammad Nasrullah, R.: My tajwid mobile application (2015)

Nawaz, N., Jahangir, S.F.: Effects of memorizing Quran by heart (Hifz) on later academic achievement. J. Islamic Stud. Cult. **3**(1), 58–64 (2015)

Orlin, B.: When memorization gets in the way of learning. The Atlantic (2013)

Ragab, A.H.: Using the adaptive e-learning styles in learning and teaching the holy Quran (2009)

Rippin, A.: The Qur'ān on the internet: implications and future possibilities. In: Hoffmann, T., Larsson, G. (eds.) Muslims and the New Information and Communication Technologies. MGSS, vol. 7, pp. 113–126. Springer, Dordrecht (2013). https://doi.org/10.1007/978-94-007-7247-2_7

Designing Discussion Forum in SWAYAM for Effective Interactions Among Learners and Supervisors

Neha$^{(\boxtimes)}$ and Eunyoung Kim$^{(\boxtimes)}$

School of Knowledge Science, Japan Advanced Institute of Science
and Technology, 1-1 Asahidai, Nomi-shi, Ishikawa 923-1292, Japan
neha.balhara92@gmail.com, kim@jaist.ac.jp

Abstract. Discussion forum boards play a crucial role in the interactions among learners and supervisors on e-learning. SWAYAM (Study webs of Active Learning for Young Aspiring Minds) is the first Indian MOOC (Massive open online course) adopted in all higher education institutes, high schools, and vocational schools as a database of their learning materials and discussions. However, being in its initial stage, SWAYAM lacks a well-designed structure in its discussion forums which is necessary for encouraging student engagement in learning.

In this study, we aim to redesign the discussion forum systematically by classifying queries to enhance the learner-supervisor interactions in SWAYAM. In a previous study, FENG [1] developed a model with a convolutional neural network on Rossi's data set to classify posts in the discussion forum of Coursera which helped to improve the course quality in MOOCs and students' learning effect. Our study initially adopted a manual classification while in the future we will implement a hybrid approach of machine learning along with the Rule-Based expert system to predict a type of query in the discussion forum of SWAYAM. This proposed system will segregate the comments of the discussion forum using specified indicators and identify repetitive comments. The learners can acquire knowledge frequently from the discussions instead of navigating all the comments separately or retrieving the visual learning materials. On the other hand, subject matter experts (SME) can answer the relevant queries at once after indicator-based segregation of queries and need not to reply to every query distinctly.

Keywords: MOOCs · Discussion forum design · Classification · Learner supervisor interaction

1 Introduction

With the rapid development of information technology, E-learning became an essential approach to enhance our way of learning new knowledge and developing skills. Increasing demands for learning centers such as universities and colleges cannot be fulfilled by the conventional way of teaching. In this regard, MOOCs platform has been developed to provide knowledge or information in the form of course content for

© Springer Nature Switzerland AG 2020
C. Stephanidis et al. (Eds.): HCII 2020, CCIS 1294, pp. 297–302, 2020.
https://doi.org/10.1007/978-3-030-60703-6_38

various types of learners. There are numerous MOOCs platforms like Coursera, edX, FutureLearn, etc.

Swayam is an Indian-based platform that all the courses are provided free of charge except for the certification. It delivers all the courses that are taught from class 9 to postgraduate in India. It is developed by the Ministry of Human Resource and Development, National Program on Technology Enhanced Learning and Indian Institute of Technology Madras with the help of Google Inc. and Persistent Systems Ltd along with nine national coordinators. Currently, around 12,541,992 students are enrolled in this platform but only 654,664 students passed the course certification [2].

According to the Learning pyramid developed by the National Training Laboratory Institute, 50% of the learning process depends upon discussion and this discussion phase relies on student's interaction with studying materials and instructors [3]. If we compare with traditional classroom learning and many intelligent tutoring systems, MOOC learners face difficulty in the interaction with instructors. A well-structured discussion forum benefit learners, instructors, and developers of MOOC.

This paper aims to re-design the discussion forum systematically through the following three steps: (1) Identification of queries in the discussion forum; (2) Manual classification of queries based on the specified indicators; (3) Recommendation of tasks for instructors and learners. The ultimate goal of this study is to provide a system that can automatically classify queries/comments with a new platform of discussion form, not only for the learner but also for the instructor. Moreover, classification based on different indicators will be explored.

2   Related Work

Several research efforts have been devoted to supporting the discussion forum in MOOCs for its importance. Feng et al. regarded the discussion forum as the only way for students and instructors to communicate in MOOCs [1]. They expressed 18 features based on user interaction behaviour and performed on a limited data set. Thomas et al., reported that an online discussion forum actively encourages cognitive engagement and critical thinking. Despite this fact, the virtual learning of it did not support coherent and interactive dialogue which is important for conversational learning [4]. Feedback is information about the content and understanding of the construction that students have derived from the learning experience [5].

Diyi Yang et al. studied confusing states from MOOC's forum which are mainly caused by neither receiving a response nor support from the instructor timely. The large number of learners registered in MOOC which often enable face to face interaction with the instructors or other well-performing learners. Classification of discussion threads in MOOC forums is essential and should be reasonable for the better utilization of MOOC forums [6].

The quality of questions and chances of getting answers can be increased by understanding the factors that contribute to questions being answered as well as questions remain ignored which can further help the discussion forum users [7]. The manual effort can break the continuation of the evaluation and efficiency of instructors as it requires a considerable amount of time. Data and text mining can be a solution to decline the problems faced by instructors, but it requires a highly specified domain [8]. The implementation of machine learning and expert system achieves a precision that is comparable to top-ranked methods and there is no need to train with human experts [9]. Thus, this study will adopt a hybrid approach of machine learning and expert system.

3   Research Procedure

3.1   Data Collection

In the Discussion forum of SWAYAM, there are unstructured comments. Comments may cover questions, phrases, sentences, paragraphs, replicated ones, etc. Usually, a course in SWAYAM is for 12 weeks and a learner can put comments in an online discussion forum of a particularly registered course. These comments may be related to the content, quiz, assignment, enquires. In this study, we selected two computer courses as shown in Table 1 representing their information.

Table 1. Information about the two computer courses

Course title	Computer architecture	Computer networks
Category	Programming in Teaching	Computer Science & Eng.
Duration	16 weeks	12 weeks
Start Date	3 September 2019	16 January 2020
End Date	31 December 2019	18 April 2020
No. of registered students	7,318	11,939
Total no. of posts	95 (as of 4 March 2020)	16 (as of 4 March 2020)

3.2   Data Coding

We manually classified queries of the discussion forum in these two computer courses, but their classification is challenging due to their high volume and unstructured nature [10]. The system will follow the statistical procedure as it will take the input data from the short description box which is already present while asking questions in SWAYAM. Then it will map these input data with five indicators to classify comment and these indicators are Content related (CR), Assignment related (AR), Quiz related (QR), Time related (TR) and Others(O) depending on the query. In the initial stage, a data set of manual classification or human coded data is required to secure the accuracy of indicator-based segregation. After that, a classifier will be trained to predict the query. The construction of the classifier can be done by checking the repository data or log file where we can find the previously asked queries. In case some comments/queries do not contain any of the categorized tags then in this situation, the system will categorize it as "others". This will help in segregating relevant and irrelevant parts. Further, we need an expert system that will use simple rules based on the logic expression for fine-tuning. Some keywords from the short description box may overlap with others. For instance, it will categorize the query based on the number of terms that satisfy the logical expression. Each input is then tested for acceptance, rejection or for the option to categorize as "others".

3.3 Data Analysis

One of the roles of feedback is to determine the quality and standard of teaching and learning. In classroom teaching, there is an advantage that a learner can ask questions at any point, but some learners feel shy while asking questions at the same time. In E-learning, it takes a lot of time by the supervisor to answer every post and it becomes more difficult when the comments are unstructured. Sometime there may be a repetition of comments also occurs. We can solve such problems by focusing on discussions in online learning.

Segregation of comments in the discussion forum can make the task easier for the subject matter expert (SME) in SWAYAM to answer the queries effectively. It can save the time of the learner and the SME simultaneously because, in this situation, SME does not need to answer every post and the learner can get the knowledge frequently from discussions. For instance, queries related to the content part can be answered separately. Analysis of coded data can be done by calculating the students taking part in the discussion forum of a course over students enrolled in that course. Analyzing the type and number of queries can help in determining the most occurring problem. After solving queries related to an indicator, we can evaluate by observing the learner participation experience. For instance, there is a quiz system in SWAYAM so maybe solving queries related to the quiz can enhance the numbers of quiz takers and the same can be done in case of assignment, content, etc.

4 Results

4.1 Analysis of Various Posts in the Discussion Forum of Two Computer Courses

In Fig. 1, there is an analysis of various posts of SWAYAM discussion forum in computer networks (Course A) and computer architecture course (Course B) and these posts are Content related (CR), query related (QR), assignment related (AR), time-related (TR) and others which are not related to these specified indicators. We can observe the highest number of queries are asked by learners is of content related in both the courses. In Course A, the content related queries are 38% while in Course B its 49%.

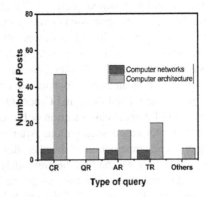

Fig. 1. Frequency of various posts

4.2 Interactions Among Learners and the Supervisor

It is rare to find the thread of similar queries in the discussion forum. For example, in the case of a computer architecture course, there are 95 posts in the discussion forum in which there are 4 queries which were posted in a single thread but all the queries have a reply from the instructor (see Fig. 2) and a single reply was from a learner. Overall, only 9 queries out of 95 which got a reply from the instructor. On the other hand, the computer networks course has only 16 posts so far, as of the 7th week of the total 12th week's course, and 10 posts from them were answered by the instructor and a single post by the learner. However, gradually when the number of posts increases, it results in a mingling of comments.

It becomes very difficult for an instructor to answer individually to all the posts. It was found that there is still no reply from the instructor regarding several queries related to the course content. However, CR queries are most important part of an online discussion forum in E-leaning platform and should be higher. As Table 2 suggest, interactions regarding CR queries for Course A and Course B is 50% and 19% respectively, while interactions about AR (Course A 83% and Course B 25%) and TR (Course A 60% and Course B 25%) queries are comparatively high. Also, the total percentage of interaction between learners and supervisors in course A is 69% and in course B is 19% which is very low compared to registered students.

Table 2. Interactions among learners and supervisor

Query type	Course A		Course B	
	No. of posts	Posts with interactions	No. of posts	Posts with interactions
CR	06	03 (50%)	47	09 (19%)
QR	00	00 (-)	06	00 (-)
AR	06	05 (83%)	16	04 (25%)
TR	05	03 (60%)	20	05 (25%)
Others	00	00 (-)	06	00 (-)
Total	16	11 (69%)	95	18 (19%)

Fig. 2. Screenshot of a Discussion forum with a single query; and similar queries

5 Conclusion

The findings of our study can be summarized as follows:

- Similar queries clustered at the same place are more expected to answer by the instructor.
- After the segregation of comments or queries, learners can acquire frequent knowledge from discussion instead of navigating all the comments.
- Classification helps the instructor to work on the specified area after finding the number of queries relating to specified indicators.

However, our study has limitations that we manually classified repetitive comments and we couldn't identify the factors that are responsible for less interactions among learners and supervisors. In our future study, we will implement a hybrid approach of machine learning and rule-based systems to classify queries and try to find the responsible factors to design a discussion forum platform.

References

1. Feng, L., et al.: Classification of discussion threads in MOOC forums based on deep learning. In: 2nd International Conference on Wireless Communication and Network Engineering, (WCNE 2017). https://doi.org/10.12783/dtcse/wcne2017/19907
2. SWAYAM. https://swayam.gov.in/about. Accessed 04 Mar 2020
3. Bloom, B.S.: Taxonomy of Educational Objectives, vol. 1. Cognitive Domain. McKay, New York (1956)
4. Thomas, M.J.: Learning within incoherent structures: the space of online discussion forums. J. Comput. Assist. Learn. **18**, 351–366 (2002). https://doi.org/10.1046/j.0266-4909.2002.03800.x
5. Hattie, J., Timperley, H.: The power of feedback. Rev. Educ. Res. **77**(1), 81–112 (2007). https://doi.org/10.3102/003465430298487
6. Yang, D., et al.: Exploring the effect of confusion in discussion forums of massive open online courses. In: ACM Conference on Learning (2015). https://doi.org/10.1145/2724660.2724677
7. Fong, S., Zhuang, Y., Liu, K., Zhou, S.: Classifying forum questions using PCA and machine learning for improving online CQA. In: Berry, M.W., Mohamed, A.H., Wah, Y.B. (eds.) SCDS 2015. CCIS, vol. 545, pp. 13–22. Springer, Singapore (2015). https://doi.org/10.1007/978-981-287-936-3_2
8. Laurie, P., Ellis, D.T.: Using data mining as a strategy for assessing asynchronous discussion forums. J. Comput. Educ. Arch. **45**(1), 141–160 (2005). https://doi.org/10.1016/j.compedu.2004.05.003
9. Villena, J.: Hybrid approach combining machine learning and a rule-based expert system for text categorization. In: Artificial Intelligence Research Society Conference (2011). https://aaai.org/ocs/index.php/FLAIRS/FLAIRS11/paper/view/2532
10. Rantanen, A.: Classifying online corporate reputation with machine learning: a study in the banking domain, emerald insight (2019). https://doi.org/10.1108/intr-07-2018-0318

Educational Convergence with Digital Technology: Integrating a Global Society

Margel Parra[1]([✉]), Cecilia Marambio[2], Javier Ramírez[3],
Diana Suárez[4], and Henry Herrera[4]

[1] Corporación Universitaria Reformada,
38 Street #74 -179, Barranquilla, Colombia
Margel.alejandra@gmail.com
[2] Universidad Andrés Bello, Republica 239, Santiago de Chile, Chile
[3] Corporación Universitaria Latinoamericana,
58 Street #55-24a, Barranquilla, Colombia
[4] Universidad de la Costa, 58 Street #55-66, Barranquilla, Colombia

Abstract. The current society of change places the human being in a situation of new learning in emerging moments, therefore, it is necessary to place the teacher and the student in this new social paradigm. The objective of the present study was directed towards understanding the role of the educational technological society as an integrated component for the promotion of citizenship within virtual spaces. The methodology used in this study had a quantitative approach, this being a research with a descriptive level and a non-experimental and field design; where it was selected a sample of forty (40) faculty from three (3) universities in the city of Barranquilla for data collection, which was supported by a 120 question questionnaire related to the use of information technologies in education and the promotion of values within these environments. The results allowed to recognize that within the educational institutions that made part of the sample there is an optimal level in the use of information technologies, as well as in the promotion of the values in these institutions by teachers. The article concludes with a reflection of how the web spaces of today are the door for new generations to be more interconnected and informed, nourishing themselves in their growth process as individuals and citizens.

Keywords: ICT · Digital citizenship · Virtual education

1 Introduction

In today's globalized world, interconnection figures as the catalyst factor for information and access. In this way, it is recognized that new technologies are a fundamental element for the unification of a global integrated system where people can be part of it [1].

Considering the role of information technologies within the processes of globalized society, it is essential that individuals can adapt and become part of the process. Various studies recognize that international efforts to provide digital spaces for citizens are growing and much more transparent, therefore new platforms are generated in the private sector making the link to digital spaces more attractive.

© Springer Nature Switzerland AG 2020
C. Stephanidis et al. (Eds.): HCII 2020, CCIS 1294, pp. 303–310, 2020.
https://doi.org/10.1007/978-3-030-60703-6_39

However, it is noted that beyond the efforts made to link the population, the need to generate the promotion of digital citizenship is developed involving generic competences constituting human development [2].

In addition, there is a human being who appropriates technology to serve society in building a digital system that contributes to the development of information in the expansion of knowledge. In the need to generate knowledge management not only within administrative processes in schools, today it becomes urgent to educate young people towards the development of knowledge management within an experiential learning process for the development of wisdom which results in a knowledge of practice that leads us to improve the deficiencies of culture. Which should make sense in the different implications of socio-educational processes to form towards continuous and autonomous training.

The cultural deficit is reflected in the lack of the development of wisdom, so there is a stagnation in alluding to a socially and democratically shared and built knowledge. Wisdom is from an ontological dimension with a qualifying assessment. The components that will be able to support a school's open vision to change are the possibilities of developing: action research, semantic thinking, knowledge management and solidary education [3].

These postulates lead to reflection on how to develop the information society in such a way, that all students can agree to develop meaningful learning, in a cooperative learning action, making use of information technologies and connecting to a virtual world that is now global [4].

In this way, the importance of providing virtual spaces to students is visualized; in the same way as the training needed to operate within these spaces in a civic way and with a critical perspective [4]. With this point, it is stated that the objective of this study was aimed at understanding the role of educational technology society as an integrated component for the promotion of a citizenship within virtual spaces.

1.1 The State of ICT in the Classroom Nowadays

In a very broad sense, technologies have managed to transform the most intimate core of education, that is, the teaching and learning processes [5], technology is essential, influences and improves what students are taught.

In this regard, there is a significant divergence between the potential of computer technology to contribute to a meaningful learning, in the generation of positive attitudes and the facilitation of active learning modes, and the observed use of these resources in the establishments.

Different investigations show that there is little pedagogical use of computing resources, even though their potential is recognized as a tool capable of transforming learning environments [3].

Technological media offer great possibilities for education. These resources are valuable because they can bring about significant changes in pedagogical practices, in teaching methodologies and in the way students' access and interact with the diverse knowledge.

It should be noted that the most important thing that investigations have pointed out, regarding the integration of technological resources into learning and teaching, it is not to make use of technology, it is how to do it. In this sense, it is vital to examine the purpose of the lesson and how technology fits within that purpose.

On the other hand, in addressing the, educational model for the development of meaningful learning: information processing from Schmeck [6]; it is noted that curricular management makes it necessary to adopt a model of learning strategies that will profile an institutional pedagogical policy, that manages to structure educational quality in the training processes of students, resulting in an effective school, with high performance and able to develop meaningful learnings in students [7], to this end, the proposal by the American psychologist Ronald Schmeck is presented, whose study corresponds to an analysis of research into the structure of memory and the functions of how and what students learn.

For Schmeck, a style of learning, is simply the cognitive style that an individual manifests when faced with a learning task, and reflects the student's preferred, common and natural strategies for learning, hence it can be located somewhere between personality and learning strategies, for not being as specific as the latter, nor as general as the first [6]. Which allows for the evolution of cognitive structures in the student related to the design of strategies that allow the development of higher cognitive skills [7].

For Professor Schmeck, learning and memory are a byproduct of thought and strategies are those that have the greatest impact on thought [6]. Schmeck defines learning strategies as the activity plan a person uses in information processing when they need to perform a learning task and sets differences with learning styles, pointing out that these are understood as predisposition towards certain strategies, so a style is a set of strategies that are used consistently [2].

This will distinguish itself for each learning style, a set of tactics, which are defined as more specific observable activities performed by the individual when executing a certain strategy. The acquisition of strategies is part of the process of personal development of students, until, according to their use, they will create a style of learning. Changing the strategy means influencing the style that is part of the student's personal characteristics, so strategies and learning style reflect the way students will develop thinking. Getting academics to master information technologies to promote their research and interact with their students, moves the process towards a placed learning, where students meditate with their teacher on research bodies and develop research skills using digital tools, provoking a social reach of generating advanced human capital, for this it is important to incorporate the ICT as explained below:

The technological tools needed to support this approach should contribute and favor information search, analysis and contrast activities, reflection on the phases and time of organization and management, as well as the communication and interaction of students [3].

To systematize student's progress towards critical thinking as raised by Álvarez & Nadal and Marambio, authors who point to Professor Schmeck's theoretical model [2, 3], which identifies three dimensions of learning and information processing styles, these are: deep, elaborate and superficial, each is characterized by using a particular learning strategy and different learning levels, ranging from simple to complex:

- Superficial Processing: students using a memorization-focused strategy; the student only remembers the reviewed content while studying, achieving a strategy for facilitating low-level learning. It involves assimilating information as perceived and not, rethinking it, attending to more phonological and structural aspects, repeating and memorizing information in its original form.

- Elaborate Processing: students who use the personalized strategy, the content of their study must be directly related to themself, to their experiences, to what have happened or what they think will happen, achieving a strategy of facilitating mid-level learning. It involves how to process information in such a way that it is enriched, made more concrete and personally relevant.
- Deep Processing: students who use the conceptualization strategy, which means that when they study, they abstract, analyze, relate, organize abstractions achieving a high-level learning facilitating strategy.

2 Method

This study was developed with a quantitative approach, this being a descriptive level research, thus studying the use of information technologies within higher education institutions. On the other hand, the design used was of a non-experimental, field, and transactional cut; where data was obtained from its original source, in a single measurement and without manipulating the variables.

The study population was constituted by forty (40) teachers from three universities in Barranquilla (Colombia) with a full-time dedication and faculty members of economic sciences and psychology. It is provided that within the context there is a finite number of subjects, determined and accessible for their handling; therefore, the sample was equal to that population, this being an intentional sample.

The data collection tool used, was a questionnaire developed for this study, which allowed to know the use and level of information technologies within the university context. To determine the reliability of the instrument, the Alfa Cronbach method was applied, resulting in rtt: 0.80, for the instrument, which determines that they were highly reliable. The instrument applied consisted of 120 questions in fifteen (15) sections which were distributed in five (5) dimensions: Institutional portal, Virtual Education Platform, Institutional Mail, Computer Rooms and Digital Citizenship.

3 Results

Below, the exposition of the results from the data collection instrument applied to the sample under study (Table 1):

When analyzing the use of the technological platforms utilized by teachers within academic processes in the field of higher education, in the first instance the indicator called institutional portal represents that institutions use it as an educational resource, counting with telematic networks for the implementation of the various learning activities.

Table 1. Use of technology platforms

Indicator	Section	Always		Almost Always		Sometimes		Almost Never		Never		Sections	Indic	Total
		FA	%	FA	%	FA	%	FA	%	FA	%			
Institutional portal	1	11	27%	29	73%	0	0%	0	0%	0	0%	4	4,2	4,10
	2	0	0%	40	100%	0	0%	0	0%	0	0%	4		
	3	11	27%	28	70%	0	0%	1	3%	0	0%	4		
Virtual Education Platform	4	2	5%	28	70%	9	23%	0	0%	1	3%	4	3,6	
	5	1	3%	20	50%	19	48%	0	0%	0	0%	4		
	6	0	0%	11	27%	29	73%	0	0%	0	0%	3		
Institutional mail	7	20	50%	11	28%	9	23%	0	0%	0	0%	4	4,2	
	8	13	33%	18	45%	9	23%	0	0%	0	0%	4		
	9	11	27%	29	73%	0	0%	0	0%	0	0%	4		
Computer rooms	10	30	75%	10	25%	0	0%	0	0%	0	0%	5	4,3	
	11	0	0%	30	75%	10	25%	0	0%	0	0%	4		
	12	11	27%	28	70%	1	3%	0	0%	0	0%	4		
Digital citizenship	13	0	0%	40	100%	0	0%	0	0%	0	0%	4	4,2	
	14	0	0%	30	75%	10	25%	0	0%	0	0%	4		
	15	30	75%	9	23%	1	3%	0	0%	0	0%	4		

This was found by reviewing that the at 73%, 100% and 70% (respectively for Sect. 1, 2 and 3) of the sample choose the response almost always, with an average of 4.2, which allows to set its frequency according to the scale. Its tendency being the high identification with the existence of the institutional portal.

Then, on the indicator virtual education platform, results are inclined towards the use in a continuous way, which is based on the institutions having virtual education platforms, as well as educational resources in electronic versions, in addition the platforms provides information to the university community.

Considering the respondents' responses, it is observed that, for section four (4) the percentage towards almost always was 70%, while section five (5) almost always received 50% and sometimes 48%. Then in section six (6) the option almost always got 27% and sometimes 73%, resulting in a total dimension average of 3.5, these achievements demonstrate the existence of the virtual education platform.

On the other hand, with regard to institutional mail, for section seven (7) there was a 50% representation in the always option about the involvement of mail in university processes, where it was also achieved a 27% in almost always, and 23% for the option sometimes. Also, on section eight (8) addressed to know if mail is used as a dissemination way in teaching work, it was known that 45% answered almost always, 33% always, while 23% sometimes.

Then, in section nine (9), with the intention to know if it is conceived as a necessary service for the educational process, 73% leaned towards the option almost always, while 27% did so with always. In this way, it is emphasized that the average within this institutional mail dimension was 4.2 establishing the frequency of its use.

On the other hand, with regard to the size of the computer room, the responses associated with the section indicate the existence of it as part of the technological platform in the higher education institutions in Barranquilla, since 75% of the population considered the option always, while 25% almost always within section ten (10).

In relation to section eleven (11), 75% of the population considered the option almost always, while 25% sometimes, establishing that institutions under study, have computer rooms that allow the development of academic and research activities. As for section twelve (12) which involves whether if the computer rooms promote the relation between work, and communication, 70% assumed the option almost always, while 27% always. Its average was 4.3, giving a high trend towards an adequate process of using computer rooms as a process of dynamization of learning.

With the last dimension, it was analyzed the so-called digital citizenship, where teachers were asked about the various processes, they develop to promote the appropriate and critical use of digital media provided by the institutions. Having 75% of the sample taking the option always and 23% almost always and just 3% choosing sometimes. In this regard, it is noted that the average in this dimension was 4.2, which allows to recognize the processes developed by teachers to promote values within the use of ICT.

4 Discussion and Conclusions

To begin results' discussion, it is provided that for Moreira the technologic platform represents the whole of the components that are part of the material part of a computer. It refers to the logical components required to enable the completion of a specific task, i.e. it is a set of instructions for them to be executed by a processor [8].

Backed by the opinion of Sánchez who states that technology platforms are container systems of courses, but, in addition, they incorporate tools of communication and monitoring of students. Others refer to the space in which learning takes place [9]. For others, the nuance of the content or the sequence of learning activities is what is significant.

In this regard, Moreira states that educational portals of an informative nature are those to access for obtaining a specific information or data, they are of a formative nature, in addition they have been created to generate a particular process of learning and teaching [8].

It should be noted that in Colombian higher education institutions the educational portal provides information to the university community, as well as tools to develop internet research, providing educational resources of all kinds, free and usable directly from the internet (online teaching materials) or from computers.

The process of teaching and learning through ICT enables the possibility of adapting information to the needs and characteristics of users, both for the levels of training they may have, and for their preferences regarding the channel by which they want to interact, or simply by the formative interests planned by the teacher [7].

Ferro, Martínez & Otero consider that this network society is the current society whose structure is built around information networks from microelectronic information technology structured on the internet, this is an environment that covers the organizational form of society equivalent to what was the factory in the industrial age or the large corporation in the industrial age [1]. The internet is the heart of a new technical partner paradigm that is the technological basis of our lives and our forms of relation, between work and communication.

In conclusion, it is considered that easy adaptation to change will be a necessity to live in this global scenario, which will generate an open mind to new knowledge. These skills must be borne in mind in the new educational approaches, because from there, a new concept of education will have to be generated that prepares children and young people to face 21st century society. In schools, nowadays, the work is focused on training the citizen of this global world.

If it has to be introduce a new concept in education, the following premise should not be overlooked: the people who will be part of society are formed and this society expects from them the attitude of a dynamic, productive being with the possibility of contributing to social and cultural progress, therefore the curriculum approach, that allows 21st century schools to respond to the learning needs of new generations should focus on managing cognitive skills, accompanied by the development of emotional intelligence and the mastery of information technologies.

It is an open door to curriculum innovation to take on technological and scientific changes inside the classroom. The relevant part is that young people leave school prepared to face this technological social world, and able to handle all kinds of knowledge required by the information society. Above all, try to break from schools the digital division that produces so much inequality today the development of cultural capital. Certainly, the linkage of ICT within educational processes allows not only the training of individuals capable of developing in electronic media as professionals, but in doing so demonstrate civic behaviors within these new virtual contexts.

References

1. Ferro, C., Martínez, A., Otero, M.: Ventajas del uso de las TICs en el proceso de enseñanza-aprendizaje desde la óptica de los docentes universitarios españoles. Edutec. Revista Electrónica de Tecnología Educativa **29**(1), 1–12 (2016)
2. Marambio, C.: Estrategias para estimular competencias cognitivas superiores en estudiantes universitarios. Revista Contextos Estudios de Humanidades y Ciencias Sociales **38**(1), 107–123 (2017)
3. Álvarez, G., Nadal, J.: Escenarios de aprendizaje diseñados en conjunto por estudiantes y docentes en la universidad: el caso de la asignatura Tecnología Educativa. Virtualidad, Educación y Ciencia **10**(19), 57–74 (2019)
4. Castell, M.: Globalización, sociedad y política en la era de la información. Bitácora Urbano Territorial **1**(4), 42–53 (2000)
5. Brunner, J.: Nuevos Escenarios Educativos. PREAL, Santiago de Chile (2000)
6. Schmeck, R.: Learning Strategies and Learning Styles. Springer Science & Business Media, New York (2013)
7. Godoy, M., Calero, K.: Pensamiento crítico y tecnología en la educación universitaria. Una aproximación teórica. Revista espacios **39**(25), 36–42 (2018)
8. Moreira, M.: Aprendizaje significativo crítico. Instituto de Física da UFRGS, Porto Alegre (2005)
9. Sánchez, C., Cesar, A.: Creación de Conocimiento en las Organizaciones y las Tecnologías de Información como Herramienta para alcanzarlo (2005)

A Similarity-Calculation Method of Geometric Problems for Adaptive e-Learning

Shunichi Tada[✉] and Susumu Shirayama

University of Tokyo, Bunkyo-ku, Tokyo, Japan
tada-shunichi513@g.ecc.u-tokyo.ac.jp

Abstract. In the recent years, increasing attention has been drawn toward adaptive e-learning, which is a learning method that uses educational big data to flexibly change the learning content according to the proficiency of a learner. In this study, we proposed an overview of an adaptive e-learning system that focuses on the solution procedure, which comprises the knowledges and operations used by a learner to solve a problem. Using the example of elementary geometric problems, we develop a prototype of our proposal in which the situations of learning are formalized on the basis of an adaptive e-learning context model, which is represented using a meta-network. This prototype comprises three subsystems. One is an expert system that automatically generates various solution procedures for a given problem. The other two are an inference system that identifies the procedures that a learner is using by calculating their similarity with the procedures generated by an expert system and a classification system of given problems by calculating the similarity of the procedures of each problem; the similarity is calculated using both the Levenshtein distance and Needleman–Wunsch algorithm, respectively. Compared with conventional methods, the proposed system might provide more detailed support for learners.

Keywords: Adaptive e-learning · Meta-network · Expert system · String-similarity metric

1 Introduction

Currently, the education reform by EdTech is being promoted as a part of "Society 5.0" advocated by the government of Japan [1]. In the promotion of the education reform by EdTech, adaptive e-learning is mentioned as a task that should be immediately started. Adaptive e-learning is defined as the learning method that delivers the right content to the right person, at the proper time, in the most appropriate way [2]. The existing adaptive e-learning services suffer from various issues regarding the manner of providing content. For example, Truong, after reviewing adaptive e-learning research from the year 2004 to 2014,

© Springer Nature Switzerland AG 2020
C. Stephanidis et al. (Eds.): HCII 2020, CCIS 1294, pp. 311–318, 2020.
https://doi.org/10.1007/978-3-030-60703-6_40

suggested that learning styles were important in adaptive e-learning [3]. According to Truong, many adaptive e-learning studies use the Felder and Silverman model [4], which determines the learning style by calculating the tendency of each of the following four-axis: active–reflective, sensing–intuitive, visual–verbal, and sequential–global. However, the aforementioned model merely categorizes an individual's learning behaviors that are not even associated with the domain of learning. Therefore, the adaptive e-learning service based on this model cannot consider the parameters of the learning behavior that is specific to the learning domain; the examples of such learning behavior include the manner of solving each problem. In addition, Barr et al. suggested that the behavior of a learner could be analyzed to provide real-time support upon combining learning record store (LRS) and learning management system [5]. However, the research that utilizes LRS for adaptive e-learning services is still in its infancy.

Based on these backgrounds, the purpose of this study is to develop a new adaptive e-learning system that can provide real-time learning analysis and support. To that end, we consider the solution procedure as a parameter that is specific to the domain of study, as well as the learning style of a learner. In addition, we attempt to automatically classify problems on the basis of the solution procedure.

2   Implementation

To identify a learning context that includes the situation of learners and their progress, we defined a context model of adaptive e-learning. Generally, adaptive e-learning is a system in which a learner studies alone using a computer or tablet terminal; therefore, there are no instructors in the system. This style of learning is called self-studying. We extend the meta-network model by [6], which represents socio–cultural systems by defining several types of nodes, to an educational form, and we then define another meta-network model for self-studying. In Table 1, we present the contextual elements that comprise self-studying, and in Table 2, we list the interrelationships between the elements.

Table 1. Elements in self-studying

Type of elements	Description
Agents	The individual learner
Knowledges	Knowledges or operations required for answering
Resources	Learning histories regarding the manner in which the learner solves a problem
Tasks	Listed problems

Table 2. Relations between the elements in self-studying

Types	Knowledges	Resources	Tasks
Agents	Proficiency	Access to resources	Problems assignment
Knowledges	Dependencies among knowledges and operations	Knowledges and operations used in learning history	Knowledges and operations required for problems
Resources		Time series of learning histories	Problems solved in each learning history
Tasks			Priorities of problems

In Table 3, we present the changes expected from the conventional self-studying in the meta-network model when our proposed system is applied. In the conventional self-studying, we assumed that the learners do their homework, which is assigned at the elementary school, at their home. In Table 4, we summarize the functional requirements for the adaptive e-learning system to realize the changes expected.

Table 3. Changes in self-studying

Changes	Elements or relations	Conventional self-studying	Adaptive e-learning
Change 1	Resources Tasks	Paper media such as notebooks and textbooks	Electronic terminals such as tablets
Change 2	Agents - Knowledges Agents - Resources	The learner investigates his/her own proficiency and progress by looking back at his/her answers	Automatically visualize the proficiency and progress of the learner by using learning histories
Change 3	Agents - Tasks Tasks - Tasks	The order of the problems is specified, and no support is available while answering	The order of problems dynamically changes according to the proficiency of the learner, and support is provided as needed while answering

Table 4. Functions of the AL system

Changes	Functions
Changes 1	Hold problems and learning histories in an expression format that can be used on a computer
Changes 2	Quantify the proficiency of knowledges and operations required for answering
Changes 3	Varying the order of problems on the basis of both the knowledges and operations required for answering and the proficiency of the learner

2.1   Problem Model

We developed a model to describe elementary geometric problems. The model is used to automatically generate possible solution procedures in the expert system. The model describes the following three aspects of a problem, and these aspects are implemented using Prolog [7]. Using this knowledge, the system infers both the necessary knowledge and order of operations to solve the problems.

1. **Figure structure**
   The data describe the structural features of the figures given in the problems. The following three components comprise a geometric figure: points, segments, and polygons. In addition, various geometric relationships exist between the components. We defined Prolog predicates to describe the components as facts. In Table 5, we present the predicates of each component, and in Table 6, we list the relationships between the components.

Table 5. Components of the geometric shapes

Component	Predicate	Description
Point	point(P, X, Y)	P: name of the point
		X: x coordinate of the point
		Y: y coordinate of the point
Segment	segment(L, P1, P2)	L: name of the segment
		P1, P2: name of the endpoint
Polygon	polygon(Poly, Ps)	Poly: name of the polygon
		Ps: vertexes of the polygon
Regular polygon	regular_polygon(Poly, Ps)	Poly: name of the regular polygon
		Ps: vertexes of the regular polygon

2. **Problem condition**
   This data describe the physical quantities such as the length and angle set for each problem and the object asked in the problem, and these are also represented as Prolog facts.
3. **Mathematical knowledges and operations**
   This data represent the knowledges and operations required to solve problems, and these are also represented in Prolog facts and rules. In this study, we regarded axioms and formulas as knowledges, and we considered editing geometric shapes such as drawing auxiliary lines as operations.

Table 6. Relations between the components

Components	Predicate	Description
Point - point	reflect(P1, P2, P0)	Point P1 is the symmetry point of point P2 with respect to point P0
Point - segment	on_line(P, L)	Point P is on segment L
Point - polygon	vertex(P, Poly)	Point P is a vertex of polygon Poly
Segment - segment	straight(L1, L2)	Segment L1 and segment L2 are on the same line
	parallel(L1, L2)	Segment L1 and segment L2 are parallel
Segment - polygon	edge(L, Poly)	Segment L is a side of polygon Poly

2.2   Similarity-Calculation Method

To support learners by setting an appropriate order of problems or providing a hint while they are answering, we must calculate the similarity of the solution procedures. The first reason is that to set an order of problems, the system must classify all the problems according to the correct solution procedure of each problem. The second reason is that to provide learners a hint while they are answering, the system must compare the correct solution procedure of the problem they are answering with the actual procedure they performed thus far, and then judge the content that they are overlooking. The solution procedure for a graphic problem is represented as a finite number of overlapping permutations that comprise axioms, formulas, and operations. To calculate the similarity between sequences such as character strings, both the Levenshtein distance [8] and Needleman–Wunsch (NW) algorithm [9] are often used.

The Levenshtein distance is the number of editing operations required to convert from one character string to another. We considered the following three operations as editing operations: insertion, deletion, and character replacement. If two character strings are similar to each other, the number of editing operations required to convert the character strings is small. Conversely, if the strings to be compared are significantly different from each other, the number of operations required for the conversion should increase. That is, the magnitude of the Levenshtein distance between character strings indicates the similarity between them.

The NW algorithm is used to calculate the similarity between character strings in the same manner as the Levenshtein distance does. The NW algorithm was developed to extract the common parts between amino-acid sequences and

DNA molecular sequences, and it has become a common technique in the domain of bioinformatics.

3   Results

3.1   Generation of Solution Procedures

In this study, we prepared 31 problems of plane figures and attempted to generate their correct solution procedures by using an expert system. Notably, the expert system could generate the correct solution procedures of eight problems asking an angle. However, it failed to generate the correct solution procedures of the other 23 problems. Particularly, all the problems that involved area calculations could not be solved. There are various reasons, but one of the major reasons is regarding the order in which Prolog inferences are performed. In the inference process, references are made in an order starting from the top of the source code; therefore, the facts and rules written at the bottom may not be referenced, thereby resulting in incorrect procedures.

In Fig. 1, we depict one of the solvable problems, and in Fig. 2, we show one of the unsolvable ones.

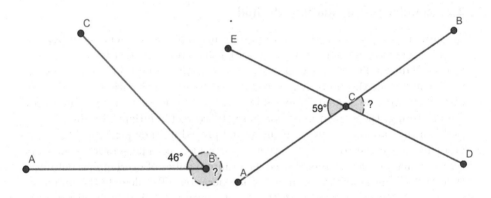

Fig. 1. Solvable problem   **Fig. 2.** Unsolvable problem

3.2   Calculation of Similarities

We attempted to calculate the similarity using both the Levenshtein distance and the NW algorithm, respectively, for the solution of the problem group depicted in Fig. 3, 4, 5 and 6. Problems 1 and 2 required operations that were related to parallel lines such as complex angles. However, Problems 3 and 4 required operations that employed regular polygons and isosceles triangles. Therefore, we expected high similarity between Problems 1 and 2, and that between Problems 3 and 4.

Table 7. Calculation using the Levenshtein Distance

	Problem 1	Problem 2	Problem 3	Problem 4
Problem 1		0.75	1.0	0.95
Problem 2			0.83	0.95
Problem 3				0.75
Problem 4				

Table 8. Calculation using the NW algorithm

	Problem 1	Problem 2	Problem 3	Problem 4
Problem 1		0.25	0	0.05
Problem 2			0.17	0.05
Problem 3				0.25
Problem 4				

The calculation results obtained using the Levenshtein distance are presented in Table 7, and those obtained using the NW algorithm are listed in Table 8. Expectedly, the similarity between Problems 1 and 2, and that between Problems 3 and 4 were higher than those between other problem pairs, in both the calculation methods.

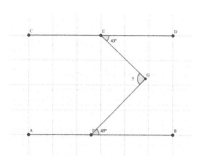

Fig. 3. Problem 1

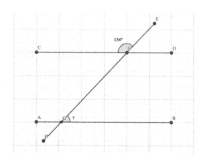

Fig. 4. Problem 2

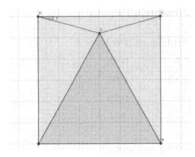

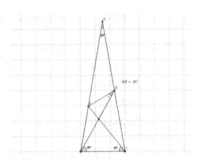

Fig. 5. Problem 3   **Fig. 6.** Problem 4

4 Conclusion

In this study, we proposed a new adaptive e-learning system that considered the solution procedure while aiming the real-time learning analysis and support, and we built the problem model to automatically generate the solution procedure. In addition, we applied both the Levenshtein distance and NW algorithm to calculate the similarity between the solution procedures. Further studies must be performed to solve more types of problems, and now we are considering to introduce the similarity of each knowledge and operation in order to develop a similarity-calculation method that is based on the NW algorithm.

References

1. Ministry of Education, Culture, Sports, Science and Technology homepage. http://www.mext.go.jp/. Accessed 17 Nov 2019
2. Shute, V., Brendon, T.: Adaptive e-learning. Educ. Psychol. **38**(2), 105–114 (2003)
3. Truong, H.M.: Integrating learning styles and adaptive e-learning system: current developments, problems and opportunities. Comput. Hum. Behav. **55**, 1185–1193 (2016)
4. Felder, R.M., Silverman, L.K.: Learning and teaching styles in engineering education. Eng. Educ. **78**(7), 674–681 (1988)
5. Barr, A., Robson, R.: Missing pieces: infrastructure requirements for adaptive instructional systems. In: Sottilare, R.A., Schwarz, J. (eds.) HCII 2019. LNCS, vol. 11597, pp. 169–178. Springer, Cham (2019). https://doi.org/10.1007/978-3-030-22341-0_14
6. Carley, K. M., Pfeffer, J.: Dynamic network analysis (DNA) and ORA. Advances in Design for Cross-Cultural Activities Part I, 265–274 (2012)
7. Kowalski, R.: Logic for problem solving. Department of Computational Logic, Edinburgh University (2014)
8. Levenshtein, V.I.: Binary codes capable of correcting deletions, insertions, and reversals. Soviet Phys. Doklady **10**(8), 707–710 (1966)
9. Needleman, S.B., Wunsch, C.D.: A general method applicable to the search for similarities in the amino acid sequence of two proteins. J. Mol. Biol. **48**(3), 443–453 (1970)

Effects of Virtual Reality Mudslide Games with Different Usability Designs on Fifth-Grade Children's Learning Motivation and Presence Experience

Mengping Tsuei[✉] and Jen-I Chiu

Graduate School of Curriculum and Instructional Communications Technology, National Taipei University of Education, Taipei, Taiwan
mptsuei@mail.ntue.edu.tw

Abstract. Mudslide disaster prevention education is important for children who face related life-threatening situations in their daily lives. The purpose of this study was to compare the effects of two virtual reality (VR) mudslide games with different usability designs on children's presence experience and learning motivation. The games provided users with three options (riverside, bridge and hillside) for escape from a mudslide disaster. Sixty-six fifth-grade students in Taiwan participated; 18 students played Game 1 and 48 students played Game 2 individually for 10–15 min. A 24-item questionnaire assessing the students' learning motivation and presence experience was administered after game play. Questionnaire responses indicated that the students had positive attitudes toward learning via the two games. Learning motivation, presence and total questionnaire scores were higher among students who played Game 2 than among those who played Game 1, but these differences were not significant. All three scores were higher among boys than among girls who played Game 2, as indicated by nonparametric analysis. The results indicate that the low-polygon VR mudslide game designed for usability facilitated children's, and especially boys', learning about mudslide disaster prevention.

Keywords: Virtual reality · Mudslide education · Disaster prevention · Children

1 Introduction

Mudslides are usually caused by earthquakes, volcanic eruptions, melting snow or downpours of rain. In recent years, typhoons and downpours of rain have consistently caused serious mudslide-related disasters in mountainous areas of Taiwan [1]. Mudslide disaster prevention education is thus an important educational focus in Taiwan.

Lave and Wenger [2] indicated that situated learning may improve prevention and risk reducing. Virtual reality (VR) immersion scenarios can be used to simulate problem-solving experiences for real-world disasters, and students can improve their disaster prevention knowledge by interacting with the virtual learning environment. The use of VR in disaster prevention training has had successful outcomes, helping

© Springer Nature Switzerland AG 2020
C. Stephanidis et al. (Eds.): HCII 2020, CCIS 1294, pp. 319–323, 2020.
https://doi.org/10.1007/978-3-030-60703-6_41

participants to develop skills related to fire safety [3], street crossing [4], flood risk [5] and earthquake risk [6]. Thus, VR application for mudslide prevention education has important potential.

In our previous work, we developed a VR mudslide game for children, played with the HTC Focus Plus headset. In a preliminary study, children were satisfied with the usability of the game [7]. This study extends our work; we compared the effects of two VR mudslide games with different usability designs on fifth-graders' presence experience and learning motivation.

2 Related Works

VR can be used for disaster simulation, prevention drills and training. Ren, Chen, Shi and Zou [8] developed a VR system in which users navigate a virtual building with an active fire, and perform emergency evacuation drills. The system's properties can be configured to simulate various types of flame and smoke. The researchers did not explore the user's tests.

Cakiroğlu and Gökoğlu [3] developed a VR system for fire safety training for children. In the system's multi-user virtual environment, children interact with avatars, including mentors and teachers. The researchers found that children developed fire safety skills in VR and face-to-face training sessions, and could transfer the skills acquired with the VR system to real-life conditions.

Yamashita, Taki and Soga [6] developed an augmented reality (AR) system with animation of furniture falling during an earthquake. They found that system users developed significantly better abilities to estimate safety and danger zones and to prepare for earthquake disasters than did a control group by training in face to face.

3 Method

3.1 VR Mudslide Games

The effects of two VR mudslide games were compared in this study. The first game was designed by the Shadowork studio in Taiwan. Our research team collaborated with the Shadowork studio to develop the second game. In both games, the user is presented with three options (riverside, bridge and hillside) for escape from a mudslide disaster. Game one was designed with real-time rainfall calculation and simulation of a mudslide scene (Fig. 1); the user wears an HTC Vive headset and uses eye-gaze points to play. The other VR game (Game 2) has the same content, but features a low-polygon mudslide scene; the user wears an HTC Focus Plus headset and uses a controller to play.

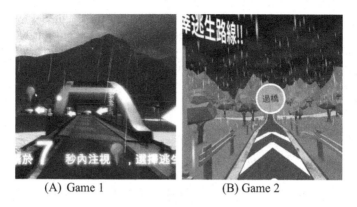

(A) Game 1   (B) Game 2

Fig. 1. Mudslide scenes in the two virtual reality games.

3.2 Participants

Sixty-six fifth-grade students (36 boys and 30 girls) in an elementary school in New Taipei City, Taiwan, participated in the study. Most participants had no prior experience with VR games.

3.3 Assessment of Users' Learning Motivation and Presence Experience

A questionnaire was administered after the VR game-playing sessions to assess the students' learning motivation and presence experience. Learning motivation was assessed using eight items adapted from the Motivated Strategies for Learning Questionnaire (MSLQ) [9]. Sixteen items were used to address presence, based on a previous study [10]. The alpha coefficient for the questionnaire was 0.94, indicating adequate internal consistency.

4 Results

The questionnaire scores reflected students' overall strongly positive attitudes toward both VR mudslide games (Table 1). Learning motivation, presence experience and total questionnaire scores tended to be higher among students who played Game 2 than among those who played Game 1, but these differences were not significant.

Table 1. Mean questionnaire scores and differences between games

Score	Game 1	Game 2	t
	Mean (SD)	Mean (SD)	
Overall	4.51 (0.65)	4.65 (0.41)	−0.98
Learning motivation	4.57 (0.76)	4.75 (0.41)	−1.26
Presence experience	4.46 (0.58)	4.54 (0.47)	−0.58

We used nonparametric analysis to compare boys' and girls' attitudes toward use of the two games. Among students who played the second game, boys had significantly higher learning motivation ($Z = 2.72$, $p < 0.01$), presence experience ($Z = 2.08$, $p < 0.05$) and total ($Z = 2.44$, $p < 0.05$) scores than did girls (Table 2).

Table 2. Mean questionnaire scores among boys and girls

Score	Game 1		Z	Game 2		Z
	Boys ($n = 7$)	Girls ($n = 11$)		Boys ($n = 29$)	Girls ($n = 19$)	
Overall	9.64	9.41	−0.09	28.47	18.45	−2.44*
Learning motivation	8.86	9.91	−0.44	28.66	18.16	−2.70**
Presence experience	10.36	8.95	−0.54	27.88	19.34	−2.08*

*$p < 0.05$, ** $p < 0.01$.

5 Discussion and Conclusions

The present study revealed significant benefits of the use of VR mudslide games. Improvements in children's learning motivation and presence experience were observed, especially after the use of Game 2. Among students who played Game 2, boys had significantly greater learning motivation and presence experience than did girls. These results are in agreement with those of previous studies [3–6] examining the use of virtual environments in disaster prevention education.

Our results indicate that the low-polygon design was more suitable for disaster prevention education than was the realistic scene design. Thus, designers should focus on the usability design. They also indicate that VR game play using the HTC Focus Plus controller was more intuitive than was interaction via eye-gaze. Moreover, they revealed that icons with which users interact in VR games designed for children need to be large and consistent, permitting easy recognition and manipulation. This study adds to existing knowledge about the efficacy of VR learning environment used in disaster prevention education.

Acknowledgments. This work was supported by funding from the Ministry of Science and Technology of Taiwan (MOST-107-2622-H-152-002-CC3).

References

1. Taiwan Ministry of the Interior, Mudslide information. https://246.swcb.gov.tw/
2. Lave, J., Wenger, E.: Situated Learning. Legitimate Peripheral Participation. Cambridge University Press, New. York (1991)
3. Cakiroğlu, Ü., Gökoğlu, S.: Development of fire safety behavioral skills via virtual reality. Comput. Educ. **133**, 56–68 (2019)

4. Morrongiello, B.A., Corbett, M., Milanovic, M., Beer, J.: Using a virtual environment to examine how children cross streets: advancing our understanding of how injury risk arises. J. Pediatr. Psychol. **41**, 265–275 (2016). https://doi.org/10.1093/jpepsy/jsv078
5. Zaalberg, R., Midden, C.J.H.: Living behind dikes: mimicking flooding experiences. Risk Anal. **33**, 866–876 (2012)
6. Yamashita, N., Taki, H., Soga, M.A.: Learning support environment for earthquake disaster with a simulation of furniture falling by mobile AR. In: 2012 International Conference on Information Technology Based Higher Education and Training (ITHET), pp. 1–5. IEEE Press (2012). https://doi.org/10.1109/ithet.2012.6246053
7. Tsuei, M., Chiu, J.-I., Peng, T.-W., Chang, Y.-C.: Preliminary evaluation of the usability of a virtual reality game for mudslide education for children. In: Trescak, T., Simoff, S., Richards, D. (eds.). Proceeding of 25th ACM Symposium on Virtual Reality Software and Technology (VRST 2019), Article No.: 85, pp. 1–2. Association for Computing Machinery, New York (2019). https://doi.org/10.1145/3359996.3364710
8. Ren, A., Chen, C., Shi, J., Zou, L.: Application of virtual reality technology to evacuation simulation in fire disaster. In: Proceeding of CGVA Conference, pp. 15–21 (2006)
9. Pintrich, P.R., Smith, D.A.F., Garcia, T.W., McKeachie, J.: Reliability and predictive validity of the motivated strategies for learning questionnaire. Educ. Psychol. Measur. **53**, 801–813 (1993)
10. Witmer, B.G., Jereme, C.J., Singer, M.J.: The factor structure of the presence questionnaire. Presence **14**, 3-198-312 (2005)

Rethinking Continuous University Education for Professionals – A Podcast-Based Course on Service Design and AI

Pontus Wärnestål[1][(✉)] and Jeanette Sjöberg[2]

[1] School of Information Technology, Halmstad University, Halmstad, Sweden
pontus.warnestal@hh.se
[2] School of Education, Humanities and Social Sciences, Halmstad University, Halmstad, Sweden
jeanette.sjoberg@hh.se

Abstract. The knowledge demand in the intersection between human-centered design and Artificial Intelligence (AI) has increased rapidly in both the private and public sectors. However, higher education is struggling to provide relevant content to already established senior professionals in a flexible and timely way. Mobile learning (m-learning) provides a promising way, but more research and practice is needed to design and launch efficient m-learning initiatives. In this paper, we share our experiences in designing and launching a flexible and self-paced podcast-based, free university course for established professionals on the topic of human-centered design and AI. We present our design process and highlight the findings from our on-going student survey evaluation. The questions addressed in this paper are: (1) How can educators design podcast-based courses for professionals in Higher Education? (2) What impact does a podcast-based format have on a student's engagement in higher education? Preliminary results indicate that the podcast-based format is an appreciated form of flexible learning, and that the content of human-centered design and AI is of high interest for a multidisciplinary community of professional practitioners.

Keywords: M-learning · AI · Higher education · Podcast · Course design

1 Introduction

The knowledge demand in the intersection between User Experience (UX) Design, Service Design and Artificial Intelligence (AI) has increased rapidly in both the private and public sectors [1]. At the same time, 46% of EU workers feel their skills will become outdated in the next five years [2]. The EU Commission is increasing its annual investments in AI by 70% and will reach EUR 1.5 billion for the period 2018–2020. One of the central aims is to increase trust and utility of human-centric AI [3]. University education caters mostly to young people getting a full-time campus-based education before entering the professional workforce. Changes in the curriculum therefore takes several years before their effects reach the profession.

Flexible education usually includes digital technology in teaching, stimulating the development of distant learning [4]. However, contemporary HEIs are often criticized

© Springer Nature Switzerland AG 2020
C. Stephanidis et al. (Eds.): HCII 2020, CCIS 1294, pp. 324–332, 2020.
https://doi.org/10.1007/978-3-030-60703-6_42

for their slow pace when it comes to adopting new pedagogical approaches in relation to emerging digital technology [e.g. 5]. Simultaneously, learners have become accustomed to using digital technology for learning [6]. "'Going to the classroom' will be less identified with spending time in a well-defined and constrained physical location. The classroom has become virtual and may exist everywhere and at all times of the day" [7]. In 2015, 49% of students had taken an online course and this number is increasing as more online learning opportunities become available [8]. This, in turn, generates new issues about changing conditions for learning and teaching in higher education and the implementation of digitally based pedagogical approaches [9, 10]. Hence, emerging digital technologies in everyday life need to be related to the pedagogical methods being used [11].

Podcast-based education is an example of mobile learning, or m-learning, which is a subset of e-learning in higher education [e.g. 12, 13]. The focus in m-learning is on student mobility through interaction with portable technologies, and research shows that key factors for students' usage of m-learning are perceived usefulness, ease of use [13] and accessibility [14]. Podcasting as a form of m-learning consists of educational audio episodes that are listened to on a mobile device. Podcast episodes automatically pushed to a subscribing device of a "show" (i.e. a collection of episodes), so that the most updated content is available, and possibly also synchronized across different devices. This "push" functionality reduces the effort to search for, and manually load, relevant content [15], and allows learners to choose when and where they study [12]. When it comes to podcasting in education, one of the most important questions within research has to do with how podcasts optimally can be designed in order to improve student learning [e.g. 16].

Several practitioners within the field of higher education claim that podcasting has a major pedagogical potential when it comes to enhancing teaching and learning [15, 17, 18]. According to previous research, however, much indicates that the most common use of podcasts in higher education is either teacher-distributed lectures or student-generated podcasts [17, 19], which raises concerns that podcasts are used in a regressive way, focusing on recording lecture materials and study questions [e.g. 20], rather than adapting the medium for unique learning opportunities and thus utilizing its full potential.

Our work has a twofold purpose: First, to develop new course content at the intersection between AI and human-centered UX and Service Design in order to increase the professional skill and ability for AI and design professionals in private and public sector organizations. The question guiding this part of the work is: what skills do professionals in this cross-disciplinary field need in order to build human-centered AI-driven services that provide value to individuals, organizations, and society at large?

Second, the project explores a new course format for flexible and short courses at an advanced level for practitioners. The target group for this type of course is experienced and operates in advanced knowledge-intensive environments. Furthermore, the target group works in a time-pressured context where knowledge and skills need to be continuously developed, but where traditional full- time campus- education often is unrealistic. The course format needs to be flexible, modularized, remote, and self-paced.

The questions addressed in this paper are:

1. How can educators design podcast-based courses for professionals in Higher Education?
2. What impact does a podcast-based format have on a student's engagement in higher education?

2   Design of the Podcast-Based Course

In order to systematically design a podcast-based course in the intersection of human-centered design and AI that is relevant for professionals, a working group consisting of industry representatives, pedagogical experts, as well as researchers in the fields of HCI, digital service innovation, and AI and Data Science was formed. All participants in the group are active podcast listeners and use podcasts as a way to learn and develop their own skill set. The group met weekly for four months (January through April 2019) in order to answer three key questions:

1. What are the critical characteristics of the target learner group?
2. What content do professionals in this cross-disciplinary field need in order to build human-centered AI-powered services that provide value to individuals, organizations, and society at large?
3. What format should be used to design a good learning environment based on podcast-based m-learning, given the target group and the content?

2.1   Learner Target Groups

The aim of the course is to concretize and make knowledge available about AI and human-centered user experience (UX) design and service design for professionals and contribute to flexible and self-paced learning. The target group for this course thus has specific characteristics that need to be taken into account when designing both content and format. Based on workshops with the project's working group, as well as five complementing interviews with people from industry outside of the working group, a list of characteristics for two different target groups was compiled. It was expected from the outset – and confirmed in the workshops and interviews – that the target group of professionals for this course are either (a) professional designers who want to learn more about how AI and Data Science will influence and benefit their design work, or (b) engineers and developers who are already knowledgeable in the technology and algorithmic aspects but want to learn how to apply this knowledge in human-centered services, beyond the mere technical aspects. Learners in both target groups typically exhibit the following general characteristics:

- Deep practical knowledge in their field. Learners have deep experience in a concrete application domain (such as automotive, MedTech, or telecom), or in the case of design professionals, a strong ability to apply human-centered design principles in any domain.

- Learners have varying academic backgrounds. Even in senior positions, academic backgrounds range from self-taught to PhD degrees.
- Focused on practical, day-to-day matters in order to deliver value in several simultaneous projects.
- Time-pressured with limited possibilities to take external courses. Flexibility in learning is critical.
- Senior and strategic mindset. Even though some of them have not started any practical AI implementations yet, they are in the process of shaping offers and positioning in the area of AI-powered service development.
- International work environment. English is often the official workplace language for designers and AI developers, who work in multinational companies, and most articles and literature in the field is only available in English.

2.2   Content and Scope

Since the topic of human-centered design for AI-driven services is open-ended and a vast topic, some effort had to be put into a relevant and suitable scoping of the content. The knowledge demand in the area of AI and human-centered design has increased rapidly recently within both industry and public sector. Putting AI to use in real-life implementation is a prioritized goal for companies as well as national and international policymaking [cf. 3, 21]. And even though there is considerable literature and research available for each of these two fields, there is still theory and methodology lacking in terms of combining the two. Therefore, one of the goals of the course is to find examples of the interdisciplinary overlap between the fields. Furthermore, as there are considerable and complex ethical implications when implementing AI-powered services in society, an underlying theme in the course is ethical considerations for designing and implementing data-driven and AI-powered services.

In order to serve both target groups and to be relevant to professionals' practical work on AI in human-centered services, it was decided that the course should first establish a common ground and consistent technical vocabulary, and then move into application areas and examples. It was also decided that the course "Human-Centered Machine Learning" should be short – roughly equivalent to 3 ECTS (European Credit Transfer System) in scope. However, there are three reasons for offering the course as a MOOC (Massive Open Online Course) without ECTS. First, due to the varying background of the target learner group, prerequisites to enter the course would have to be individually assessed which would be very resource consuming. Second, an official ECTS course comes with an administrative overhead which would limit the reach to a large audience. Third, by giving the course freely available without examination and grading, the course development work can focus on podcast design and production, and without examination dates, learners can be completely self-paced. Fourth, in previous internal surveys among students in other short courses aimed at senior professionals there is a clear attitude that credits are of little – if any – importance when deciding to take the course.

The working group iterated the content and episode design and decided on a total of twelve episodes. The first six episodes focus on technical aspects of AI and are followed by six design-oriented and applied episodes. Ethical considerations are part of all episodes, but the final episode is dedicated to ethical considerations. The participants in the episodes are experts in their fields, and include both researchers and practitioners from academia, research institutes, and companies. Table 1 summarizes the episodes and content of the course.

Table 1. Human-centered machine learning podcast overview. Download count is generated by the Spreaker platform from October 1, 2019 to February 29, 2020.

Episode	Topic	Episode participants	Downloads
1	Introduction	Researchers in AI (2), HCI (1), and Pedagogy (1)	552
2	What is Artificial Intelligence?	2 AI researchers, 1 senior AI expert from a research institute	490
3	Machine Learning: Theory	2 AI researchers, 1 senior AI expert from a research institute	310
4	Practical Machine Learning	2 AI researchers, 1 senior AI expert from a research institute	218
5	Deep Learning	2 AI researchers, 1 senior AI expert from a research institute	187
6	Generative Adversarial Networks (GAN)	2 AI researchers, 1 senior AI expert from a research institute	186
7	Designing AI Services	1 HCI researcher, 1 CEO of a company with end-user AI service development experience	182
8	Agentive Technology	1 HCI researcher, 1 design expert and author of a seminal AI design textbook	125
9	AI for Learning and EdTech	1 Pedagogy researcher, 1 AI researcher and EdTech expert	122
10	AI in Healthcare	1 HCI researcher, 1 CEO of a company in data-driven healthcare	132
11	AI and Mobility	1 HCI researcher, 1 AI researcher, 1 mobility researcher from a research institute	125
12	Ethical Challenges	1 HCI researcher, 1 AI researcher, 1 Design Ethnography researcher	354
Total downloads			3,042

2.3 Format and Production

During the workshops several participants in the working group highlighted that the podcast format presents a unique opportunity to "listen in" on experts in dialogue with each other, or in dialogue with a skilled interviewer. Expert guests were recruited and booked, and the episodes were recorded during August-September. Based on the insights on the international target group, and the mother tongue of some of the guests, it was decided that all content should be given in English.

The podcast episodes were recorded in the university's recording studio and edited using the GarageBand™ software. Recordings were made with state-of-the-art multi-channel studio equipment and directed microphones. The only exception to this was Episode 8, which was recorded backstage on an international design conference where one of the speakers was interviewed. The equipment used for that particular episode was a Zoom H5 portable digital recorder with two directional microphones.

After two weeks of post-production, the entire collection of episodes was published in October 2019. All episodes were published as a podcast show with the course name "Human-Centered Machine Learning" on the Spreaker[1] platform that generates an RSS feed, allowing for publication on all major podcast platforms, such as Apple Podcasts, Google Podcasts, and Spotify. All episodes were also embedded on the course's own website[2]. The website holds additional learning resources connected to each episode.

3   Evaluation

For the purpose of evaluating the podcast-based approach to course development, we continuously monitor an online anonymous survey directed at people from the learner target group (professionals working with either human-centered design or AI technology and software development). This paper reports on the first seven complete responses.

3.1   Participants

The anonymous participants in the evaluation group all finished the twelve episodes within three weeks. Their age span is between 25 and 54 years. Six participants identify as male, and one as female. Three participants have a professional background in HCI (including titles such as UX Designer, Service Designer, and Interaction Designer), two participants have a technical profession (Software Engineer and Programmer), and two participants have a business or management background (Project Manager and CEO). Five of the participants have more than 11 years of relevant professional experience, one has 6–10 years, and one is in the 3–5-year span.

3.2   Flexibility

The results of the survey indicate that students value the flexibility offered by m-learning in the form of podcasts. They appreciate that they can listen in contexts where they usually cannot access traditional e-learning resources. Participants listened to the course while commuting, exercising, doing household chores, walking, and driving. Only one person said s/he listened to one of the episodes sitting at his/her desk at work.

---

[1] http://www.spreaker.com.

[2] http://dap.hh.se.

3.3 Content and Learning

The topic of human-centered AI sparks interest and is perceived as being highly relevant by all participants. Two participants commented on the interdisciplinary aspect of the course, and highlight self-reflection of their own skills and knowledge in relation to the course content:

"It was a good mix of different researchers and different themes. I will probably go back and listen to the first episodes, they would probably be more beneficial to me as I'm not that proficient in these areas."

"Nice overview of the field. [...] Enjoyed the more techie episodes the most, but that's probably because I know least about this."

Learning resources beyond audio, such as articles and links to other resources, are only available via the course's website. Regular podcast channels only support audio, and learners accessing the course via regular podcast outlets therefore need to actively go to the course's website. Four of the seven participants said that they used the external resources available on the website. All seven participants indicate that they would like to take more podcast-based courses in the future.

3.4 Format and Listener Experience

The interview genre was appreciated, which is consistent with previous research findings, claiming that higher education professionals "can provide content-rich educational content related to an authentic context, by producing and implementing podcasts linked to their field of study or interest" [22, p. 428]. One participant contrasts the interview genre with the traditional lecture genre:

"Very interesting and diverse. Unique position between tech and human-centered design. I like the 'interview' format, instead of just "lectures" as in most e-learning courses I have taken before."

The user experience of a podcast is naturally very sound-dependent. Therefore, it is critical to invest in technology and know-how to ensure high sound quality. For example, making sure that speakers are positioned correctly in relation to microphones and setting recording levels correctly is required to ensure that listeners have good experience even in noisy environments, such as when walking in a city environment or listening on the subway.

Another aspect of a good auditory experience is in relation to language. About half of the speakers in the episodes are native Swedish speakers and speak English as a secondary language. One of the reviewers commented on this:

"Listening to Swedes speaking non-perfect English is a bit annoying, but these are minor details."

However, by using English the course serves listeners all over the world. According to the listener statistics, 62% listened in Sweden, and the remaining 38% accessed the podcast from other countries (predominantly with listeners from the USA, the UK and Germany).

4 Conclusion and Future Directions

The overall research aim of this work is to explore how podcast-based courses can be designed, and what features facilitate and challenge the learning experience for professionals. A second aim, and of particular interest to the HCI and design community, is to provide content in the intersection of AI and human-centered design. We have provided an account of the experiences in designing and launching a podcast-based course from a course development perspective, and provided initial insights on the impact of a podcast-based format from the learners' perspective.

Seven responding participants in the evaluation is a too small number for extracting statistical significance. However, the responses give indications of podcasts as a promising way to provide accessible and relevant content for time-sensitive knowledge professionals. The format of interviews and listening in on dialogues between experts was listed as helping build a positive learning experience by several of the respondents. One drawback based on the responses include the lack of visual learning, such as using figures and diagrams for example. A second drawback highlighted by the developers of the course (but not present in the learners' evaluation so far) is the lack of interactive aspects and student-generated discussions. The combination of existing pushed podcast technology and interactive m-learning is an interesting area of future research for education and HCI researchers. One idea that comes to mind is to provide question-and-answer episodes injected between the regular episodes, where students can pose questions to be discussed by experts in the studio. Live broadcasts with students having the ability to write or call in, could also be a possible way to add interaction. These ideas, however, could limit the desired flexibility and self-paced experience for some learners.

Acknowledgements. This research was supported by VINNOVA. We thank the members of the working group, Halmstad University's technical staff for help in the studio, and the invited external experts who provided insights and expertise in the podcast episodes.

References

1. Noessel, C.: Designing Agentive Technology: AI That Works for People. Rosenfeld (2017)
2. Skills Panorama: Skills Obsolescence EU Commission Report. European Centre for the Development of Vocational Training (2019). https://skillspanorama.cedefop.europa.eu/en/indicators/skills-obsolescence. Accessed 20 Feb 2020
3. EU Commission: Artificial Intelligence Policy (2019). https://ec.europa.eu/digital-single-market/en/artificial-intelligence. Accessed 20 Feb 2020
4. Ferri, F., D'Andrea, A., Grifoni, P., Guzzo, T.: Distant learning: open challenges and evolution. Int. J. Learn. Teach. Educ. Res. **17**(8), 78–88 (2018)
5. Buzzard, C., Crittenden, V.L., Crittenden, W.F., McCarty, P.: The use of digital technologies in the classroom: a teaching and learning perspective. J. Market. Educ. **33**(2), 131–139 (2011)
6. Moos, D.C., Honkomp, B.: Adventure learning: motivating students in a minnesota middle school. J. Res. Technol. Educ. **43**(3), 231–252 (2011)

7. De Meyer, A.: Impact of technology on learning and scholarship and the new learning paradigm. In: Weber, L.E., Duderstadt, J.J. (eds.) University Priorities and Constraints, Gilon Colloquium Series, no. 9, Economica, London, Paris, Geneva (2016)
8. Statista: Global student online course usage rate, 7 December 2015. https://www.statista.com/statistics/548112/online-course-student-access-worldwide/. Accessed 20 Feb 2020
9. Liu, C.: Social media as a student response system: new evidence on learning impact. Res. Learn. Technol. **26** (2018)
10. Jain, A., Dutta, D.: Millennials and gamification: guerilla tactics for making learning fun. South Asian J. Hum. Resour. Manag. **6**(1), 1–16 (2018)
11. Hansson, E., Sjöberg, J.: Making use of students' digital habits in higher education: what they already know and what they learn. J. Learn. Dev. High. Educ. (14) (2019). ISSN: 1759-667X
12. Evans, C.: The effectiveness of m-learning in the form of podcast revision lectures in higher education. Comput. Educ. **50**(2), 491–498 (2008)
13. Sabah, N.M.: Exploring students' awareness and perceptions: influencing factors and individual differences driving m-learning adoption. Comput. Hum. Behav. **65**, 522–533 (2016)
14. Crescente, M.L., Lee, D.: Critical issues of m-learning: design models, adoption processes, and future trends. J. Chin. Inst. Ind. Eng. **28**(2), 111–123 (2011)
15. Campbell, G.: There's something in the air: podcasting in education. EDUCAUSE Rev. **40**(6), 32–47 (2005)
16. Drew, C.: Edutaining audio: an exploration of education podcast design possibilities. Educ. Media Int. **54**(1), 48–62 (2017)
17. Dale, C.: Strategies for using podcasting to support student learning. J. Hospitality Leisure Sport Tourism Educ. **6**(1), 49–57 (2007)
18. Abdous, M., Facer, B.R., Yen, C.-J.: Academic effectiveness of podcasting: a comparative study of integrated versus supplemental use of podcasting in second language classes. Comput. Educ. **58**, 43–52 (2012)
19. Hew, K.: Use of audio podcast in K-12 and higher education: a review of research topics and methodologies. Educ. Tech. Res. Dev. **57**, 333–357 (2009)
20. Hew, K., Cheung, W.: Use of web 2.0 technologies in K-12 and higher education: the search for evidence-based practice. Educ. Res. Rev. **9**, 47–64 (2013)
21. Future of Life Institute: National and International AI Strategies (2020). https://futureoflife.org/national-international-ai-strategies/. Accessed 8 Mar 2020
22. Norkjaer Nielsen, S., Holm Andersen, R., Dau, S.: Podcast as a learning media in higher education. In: Ntalianis, K., Andreats, A., Sgouropoulou, C. (eds.) Proceedings of the 17th European Conference on e-Learning (2018)

COVID-19 Pandemic: A Usability Study on Platforms to Support eLearning

Cui Zou[⊠], Wangchuchu Zhao, and Keng Siau

Missouri University of Science and Technology, Rolla, USA
{tracyzou, wzkt2, siauk}@mst.edu

Abstract. With the COVID-19 pandemic, the higher education communities throughout almost the entire world have moved from traditional face-to-face teaching to remote learning by using video conferencing software and online learning applications and platforms. With social distancing requirements, it is expected that eLearning will be part of the delivery modalities at least until an effective vaccine is widely available. Even after the pandemic is over, it is expected that remote learning and online education will be part of the "new or next normal." Such online and remote learning modalities are not simply restricted to academic institutions. Businesses are using online and remote learning to re-train, re-tool, and re-educate their employees. The students, in general, are not enthusiastic about the virtual classroom. Niche.com surveyed 14,000 undergraduate and graduate students in April 2020 and found that more than 2/3 of them thought online classes are not as effective as in-person and teacher-centered classes. This unplanned change in teaching modes caused by COVID-19 and the negative feedback from students creates some serious concerns for educators and universities. How to enhance the eLearning experience for students? How to choose from many eLearning platforms on the market? Which eLearning platform is the most user friendly and the best suited for online classes? Which eLearning platforms enable the best class participation and student involvement? In this research, we apply the eLearning usability heuristics to evaluate the major video conferencing platforms (e.g., Cisco Webex, Microsoft Teams, and Zoom).

Keywords: COVID-19 · Pandemic · eLearning · Online teaching · Video conferencing software · Higher education · Usability heuristics · Virtual classroom

1 Introduction

eLearning is learning conducted via electronic media, typically using the Internet. Synchronous and asynchronous eLearning are methods to substitute the traditional face-to-face learning method to improve learning performance and meet the social distancing requirement amid the COVID-19 outbreak. Educators and instructors have numerous options when choosing from different eLearning platforms based on features and purposes [1, 2]. The purpose of this study is to present a comparison of three popular eLearning platforms by functions and rank the platforms by the evaluation results. Usability is the key factor in eLearning [3]. To date, some research projects

© Springer Nature Switzerland AG 2020
C. Stephanidis et al. (Eds.): HCII 2020, CCIS 1294, pp. 333–340, 2020.
https://doi.org/10.1007/978-3-030-60703-6_43

have sought to understand the various technologies and tools (e.g., video conferencing, learning management systems, multimedia, virtual reality, gamification) used in eLearning, the usability of different eLearning tools, the usability of mobile technologies, and the impact of usability on student performance [4–6, 8–17]. Previous research has also investigated mixed usability heuristics, from the "Nielsen's 10 general heuristics" to some recent domain-specific heuristics targeting web sites, mobile applications, virtual reality, video games, and eLearning environments [17–20]. Evaluation heuristics to study the eLearning platforms in higher education during a pandemic is new because the situation is unprecedented. With COVID-19, we are relying almost completely on online and remote learning with hardly any face-to-face interactions [21]. Further, many instructors and students are forced into the situation and they have not self-selected to participate in eLearning. Although many articles online have discussed the pros and cons of popular eLearning platforms, again, these studies are focusing mainly on the needs of business users and not higher education.

Our research seeks to fill this gap by using a set of evaluation heuristics tailored for eLearning and using the evaluation heuristics to review the usability of major eLearning platforms. The results can be used to guide educators in boosting learners' participation and involvement in an eLearning by selecting the most appropriate platforms. The results can also help the developers of eLearning platforms to improve and tailor their products to better support pedagogical requirements.

2 Literature Review

2.1 Heuristic Evaluation

One of the popular evaluation heuristics is the one proposed by Nielsen and Molich [17]. This evaluation method usually involves a group of usability experts to examine an interactive software system based on a set of guidelines (so-called "Nielsen's Heuristics" [18]) to capture and categorize problems in the system. Compared to full-scale usability study involving actual users, heuristics evaluation is cost-effective and efficient. However, Nielsen's heuristics were considered too general to evaluate domain-specific user interfaces. Therefore, a considerable number of new sets of usability heuristics have been developed to target the needs of different domains by modifying Nielsen's heuristics and/or adding new heuristics. For example, some researchers designed heuristics tailored to domains such as virtual worlds [3], social networks, mobile interfaces [5], and u-Learning applications [6]. However, according to a systematic review of 70 studies of domain-specific heuristics, many heuristics propositions lack validation and less than 10% of all the studies report acceptable robustness and rigorousness. Further, more than 80% of the studies adopted similar heuristics as Nielsen's [20].

The use of eLearning as the domain of our study arises from the COVID-19 pandemic and the sudden need to transfer from face-to-face teaching to remote learning and virtual classroom [21]. Nielsen's heuristics are not sufficiently specific for eLearning, especially when using video conferencing platforms. As a result, we decided to use the Virtual Learning Environments (VLEs) heuristics developed by

Figueroa *et al.* (see Table 1) [20]. It is a new and validated set of usability heuristics that is not only applicable to this specific domain but it also provides the evaluation of the virtual learning environment for educational purposes. It also takes user acceptance during the learning and teaching processes into consideration.

Table 1. VLEs heuristics developed by Figueroa *et al.* [20].

Id	Name of VLEs Heuristics
H1	Visibility of system status
H2	Match between system and the real world
H3	User control and freedom
H4	Consistency and standards
H5	Error prevention
H6	Recognition rather than recall
H7	Flexibility and efficiency of use
H8	Aesthetic and minimalist design
H9	Help users recognize and diagnose from errors and recover from errors
H10	Help and documentation
H11	System elements consistency
H12	Web standards and symbols
H13	Teaching-Learning process indicator
H14	Flexible configuration of resources and learning objects
H15	Storage capability
H16	Interactive communication
H17	Multiple devices adaptation
H18	Measuring learning

2.2   eLearning and Blended Learning

eLearning and blended learning provide learners with flexibility in terms of time, place, and learning pace in higher education. They reduce person-to-person interaction to ensure social distancing during the pandemic. However, traditional learning approaches provide learners with an enhanced sense of participation and involvement. Online and traditional learnings have their advantages and applicable scopes [22]. Blended learning is a mixture of online and traditional learnings and provides learners and trainees with a wide range of basic online resources that are suitable for students with different backgrounds and needs. Some researchers [7, 8] suggest that blended learning stimulates learners' interests in participating in an interactive classroom and results in significantly higher academic performances and better learning outcomes.

2.3   eLearning Platforms

Zoom is a cloud-based and web-based conference tool that people can use to virtually communicate and interact. Zoom offers several unique features that increase its popularity among small-, medium-, and large-sized groups of people. Zoom offers multiple free functions such as online meeting either by video or audio or both for 100 people maximum with a 40-min time limit, and other free functions such as live chat, screen sharing, and recording. Zoom provides functions and performances across multiple operating systems including Windows, Mac, Linux, iOS, Android, and Blackberry [23]. Over half of Fortune 500 companies reportedly used Zoom in 2019 [24], and Zoom has gained even more users worldwide since the outbreak of COVID-19 because of its versatility and compatibility. With the number of users soaring, Zoom and its products are placed under the spotlight. Some cybersecurity researchers pointed out the vulnerabilities, security flaws, and data leaking risks when using Zoom. As a result, the Pentagon [25], German government [26], Taiwan government [27], and Singapore teachers [28] were warned about or restricting Zoom use. Even though the founder of Zoom, Eric Yuan, admitted the "missteps" and committed to focusing on privacy and security [29], security concerns remain.

Cisco Webex is another popular online conference platform on the market. Webex has similar functionalities as Zoom and has comparable pricing plans as Zoom. The key difference between the two is that Webex's free plan allows users to host meetings of any length of time whereas Zoom's free plan limits a meeting to 40 min. As the typical length of a class is longer than 40 min, Webex is more suitable for a longer class session and Zoom is suitable for a short group meeting. Compared to Zoom, Webex's pricing for the next two tiers designed for small teams and mid-sized teams are cheaper at $13.50/mo per host and $17.95/mo per host respectively. With Zoom, it costs $14.99/mo per host for small teams and $19.99/mo per host for mid-size teams [30]. Thus, Webex is commonly used for mid-sized classrooms or large group meetings whereas Zoom is popular with small classrooms or small group meetings.

Microsoft Teams is a digital hub that brings conversations, meetings, files, and applications into a single learning management system. Microsoft Teams allows individual teams to self-organize and collaborate across different business scenarios. In Microsoft Teams, teams are a collection of people, content, and tools surrounding different projects and outcomes within an organization. Channels are dedicated sections within a team to keep conversations organized by specific topics, projects, and disciplines. It is estimated that by the end of 2020, 41 percent of organizations will be using Microsoft Teams globally [31]. Similar to the Zoom and Webex, Teams allows audio, video, and desktop sharing.

Technology has played and continues to play an important role in the development and expansion of eLearning [32–34]. This paper investigates the functionalities that various platforms can offer educators in higher education institutions.

3   Research Procedures

The usability of some popular online and remote learning platforms was evaluated using the new and validated set of VLE usability heuristics in this research. Some of the popular eLearning technologies that have been used in eLearning are Cisco Webex, Microsoft Teams, and Zoom. Different eLearning platforms have their unique strengths and each platform emphasizes different functionalities. In this research, Cisco Webex,

Microsoft Teams, and Zoom were evaluated based on the 18 VLE usability heuristics by two evaluators. The results summarize the pros and cons of each focusing on their usage in higher education institutions.

4 Results and Discussions

The usability of Microsoft Teams, Webex, and Zoom are generally very good and that is probably the reason for their popularity in the market place. The three also have very similar features and functions. The market is hyper-competitive and a useful feature in one is quickly adopted by the others. Further, the lock-in features of these platforms are weak. In other words, customers can switch easily from one platform to another. Usability, functionalities, and costs are keys for competition in such circumstances.

In the following, we provide some suggestions to further enhance their usability for eLearning environments. Some of the suggestions provided below may not be relevant to corporate customers. Again, it should be emphasized that the evaluation was done with higher education environment in mind.

After evaluating Microsoft Teams, Webex, and Zoom using the VLEs heuristics, we found several areas of improvement related to heuristics 2, 6, 7, 16, and 18 for eLearning.

Sharing screen is common in eLearning and online teaching environments. For these three platforms, screen sharing is not as intuitive and simple as it should be for a novice user. The interaction needs to be made more natural and obvious. Also, for pedagogy, the instructors may need to view the screen of the students. For example, the instructors may be giving a test and need to ensure that the students are not searching for answers online. In the face-to-face environment, the instructors would be walking around to proctor the test. Although formal exams may need the professional proctoring service, proctoring of simple quizzes in eLearning can be accomplished easily when the instructors can view the screen of the students. This feature needs not be activated all the time – just when needed (e.g., during quizzes) and with the consent of the students. This is related to heuristic 2 – match between system and the real world. Proctoring of tests and exams is related to heuristic 18 – measuring learning.

One effective way to evaluate eLearning involvement is to check on class attendance. While Teams gives a one-click tool to download the attendance list from the side menu, Webex and Zoom make the operation a little more complicated – the instructors have to go through a few steps before they can download the attendance lists. One suggestion is to make commonly used/needed features to be accomplished in one-click. This is related to heuristics 7 and 18 – flexibility and efficiency of use, and measuring learning.

Although Teams provide a neat user interface during video conferencing, the meeting icon used to open a video meeting can be made more visually distinct and easily recognizable. The icons used should be easily identifiable and conforming to the norm (i.e., what is commonly used at this time) [35]. This is related to heuristics 6 and 7 – recognition rather than recall, and flexibility and efficiency of use.

Another suggestion is related to heuristic16, interactive communication. Compared to face-to-face classroom, eLearning calls for a more engaging interactive communication to keep students involved and instructors informed of students' statuses [36]. This is important for some eLearning sessions where the instructors are lecturing and would like to know the students' statuses. Teams, Webex, and Zoom have features that address this need – embedded non-verbal feedback using icons such as raise hand, clap, and go slow. These icons enable the students to provide feedback and allow students to express their understanding of the course content. However, these icons are not visible unless a chat screen is open. One suggestion is that these icons can be made more visible and a few more such icons can be included (e.g., an icon for "Please Elaborate/Explain") for eLearning environment. This is also related to heuristic 2 – match between system and the real world.

5 Conclusions

COVID-19 propels the importance of eLearning platforms to a new height. In this research, we investigated three eLearning platforms – Cisco Webex, Microsoft Teams, and Zoom. The Virtual Learning Environments heuristics was selected as the evaluation criteria. The evaluation results show that the three platforms score well in usability and have similar basic functions including online meetings using video and/or audio, live chat, screen sharing, and recording. The evaluation also reveals some areas where the three platforms can be enhanced for eLearning. Features that can be enriched include ease of sharing screens, employ intuitive icons, and tailor the platforms to pedagogical needs such as collecting class attendance and viewing of students' screens during tests.

Cisco Webex, Microsoft Teams, and Zoom are not designed specifically with eLearning in mind. With COVID-19, millions of students in many countries are suddenly forced to use these platforms to continue their education. Their experience and exposure to different eLearning platforms will change the pedagogical landscape post-pandemic. It will not be education as usual after COVID-19 is managed and controlled. Issues to resolve to further enhance the acceptance of eLearning include security, privacy, and trust [37–40]. Nevertheless, a massively huge market is there to be grabbed for the platforms that are best designed for eLearning! Usability is a critical success factor in this competition! [41]

References

1. Chen, X., Siau, K.: Technology-mediated synchronous virtual education: an empirical study. J. Database Manag. **27**(4), 39–63 (2016)
2. Eschenbrenner, B., Nah, F., Siau, K.: 3-D virtual worlds in education: applications, benefits, issues, and opportunities. J. Database Manag. **19**(4), 91–110 (2008)
3. Rusu, C., Muñoz, R., Roncagliolo, S., Rudloff, S., Rusu, V., Figueroa, A.: Usability heuristics for virtual worlds. In: Proceedings of the Third International Conference on Advances in Future Internet, IARIA, pp. 16–19 (2011)
4. Chen, X., Siau, K., Nah, F.: Empirical comparison of 3-D virtual world and face-to-face classroom for higher education. J. Database Manag. **23**(3), 30–49 (2012)

5. Yáñez Gómez, R., Caballero, D., Sevillano, J.: Heuristic evaluation on mobile interfaces: a new checklist. Sci. World J. (2014)
6. Sanz, F., et al.: A set of usability heuristics and design recommendations for e-learning applications. Information Technology: New Generations. AISC, vol. 448, pp. 983–993. Springer, Cham (2016). https://doi.org/10.1007/978-3-319-32467-8_85
7. Gilboy, M., Heinerichs, S., Pazzaglia, G.: Enhancing student engagement using the flipped classroom. J. Nutr. Educ. Behav. **47**(1), 109–114 (2015)
8. Thai, N., De Wever, B., Valcke, M.: The impact of a flipped classroom design on learning performance in higher education: Looking for the best "blend" of lectures and guiding questions with feedback. Comput. Educ. **107**, 113–126 (2017)
9. Nah, F., Schiller, S., Mennecke, B., Siau, K., Eschenbrenner, B., Sattayanuwat, P.: Collaboration in virtual worlds: impact of task complexity on team trust and satisfaction. J. Database Manag. **28**(4), 60–78 (2017)
10. Siau, K., Ling, M.: Mobile collaboration support for virtual teams: the case of virtual information systems development teams. J. Database Manag. **28**(4), 48–69 (2017)
11. Siau, K., Nah, F., Ling, M.: National culture and its effects on knowledge communication in online virtual communities. Int. J. Electron. Bus. **5**(5), 518–532 (2008)
12. Gao, S., Krogstie, J., Siau, K.: Adoption of mobile information services: an empirical study. Mob. Inf. Syst. **10**(2), 147–171 (2014)
13. Gao, S., Krogstie, J., Siau, K.: Development of an instrument to measure the adoption of mobile services. Mob. Inf. Syst. **7**(1), 45–67 (2011)
14. Sheng, H., Siau, K., Nah, F.: Understanding the values of mobile technology in education: a value-focused thinking approach. ACM SIGMIS Database **41**(2), 25–44 (2010)
15. Sheng, H., Nah, F., Siau, K.: strategic implications of mobile technology: a case study using value-focused thinking. J. Strateg. Inf. Syst. **14**(3), 269–290 (2005)
16. Katerattanakul, P., Siau, K.: Creating a virtual store image. Commun. ACM **46**(12), 226–232 (2003)
17. Nielsen, J., Molich, R.: Heuristic evaluation of user interfaces. In: Proceedings of ACM CHI 1990 Conference, pp. 249–256 (1990)
18. Nielsen Norman Group. https://www.nngroup.com/articles/ten-usability-heuristics/. Accessed 8 July 2020
19. Hermawati, S., Lawson, G.: Establishing usability heuristics for heuristics evaluation in a specific domain: is there a consensus? Appl. Ergon. **56**, 34–51 (2016)
20. Figueroa, I., Jiménez, C., Allende-Cid, H., Leger, P.: Developing usability heuristics with PROMETHEUS: a case study in virtual learning environments. Comput. Stand. Interfaces **65**, 132–142 (2019)
21. Zou, C., Zhao, W., Siau, K.: COVID-19 calls for remote reskilling and retraining. Cutter Bus. Technol. J. **33**(7), 21–25 (2020)
22. Suda, K., Sterling, J., Guirguis, A., Mathur, S.: Student perception and academic performance after implementation of a blended learning approach to a drug information and literature evaluation course. Currents Pharm. Teach. Learn. **6**(3), 367–372 (2014)
23. Coronavirus (COVID-19): 'Zoom' application boon or bane. https://ssrn.com/abstract=3606716. http://dx.doi.org/10.2139/ssrn.3606716. Accessed 8 July 2020
24. What is Zoom and how does it work? Plus tips and tricks. https://www.pocket-lint.com/apps/news/151426-what-is-zoom-and-how-does-it-work-plus-tips-and-tricks. Accessed 8 July 2020
25. Pentagon Issues New Guidance on Zoom Use. https://www.voanews.com/silicon-valley-technology/pentagon-issues-new-guidance-zoom-use?utm_medium=social&utm_campaign=dlvr.it. Accessed 8 July 2020

26. US Senate, German government tell staff not to use Zoom. https://www.zdnet.com/article/us-senate-german-government-tell-staff-not-to-use-zoom/. Accessed 8 July 2020

27. Taiwan instructs government agencies not to use Zoom. https://www.zdnet.com/article/taiwan-instructs-government-agencies-not-to-use-zoom/. Accessed 8 July 2020

28. MOE suspends use of Zoom in home-based learning following breaches involving obscene images. https://www.channelnewsasia.com/news/singapore/moe-suspends-zoom-home-based-learning-obscene-images-12626534. Accessed 8 July 2020

29. Zoom CEO responds to security and privacy concerns: 'We had some missteps'. https://www.theverge.com/2020/4/5/21208636/zoom-ceo-yuan-security-privacy-concerns. Accessed 8 July 2020

30. What users are saying about Webex Meeting vs Zoom. https://www.trustradius.com/compare-products/cisco-webex-meetings-vs-zoom#:~:text=Webex%20Meetings%20and%20Zoom%20have,to%2040%20minutes%20per%20meeting. Accessed 8 July 2020

31. Microsoft: Welcome to Microsoft Teams (2018). https://docs.microsoft.com/en-us/microsoftteams/teams-overview. Accessed 8 July 2020

32. Erickson, J., Siau, K.: Education. Commun. ACM **46**(9), 134–140 (2003)

33. Siau, K.: Education in the age of artificial intelligence: how will technology shape learning? Glob. Anal. **7**(3), 22–24 (2018)

34. Siau, K., Messersmith, J.: Analyzing ERP implementation at a public university using the innovation strategy model. Int. J. Hum. Comput. Interact. **16**(1), 57–80 (2003)

35. Siau, K.: Human-computer interaction-the effect of application domain knowledge on icon interpretation. J. Comput. Inf. Syst. **45**(3), 53–62 (2005)

36. Siau, K., Sheng, H., Nah, F.: Use of a classroom response system to enhance classroom interactivity. IEEE Trans. Educ. **49**(3), 398–403 (2006)

37. Siau, K., Wang, W.: Building trust in artificial intelligence, machine learning, and robotics. Cutter Bus. Technol. J. **31**(2), 47–53 (2018)

38. Siau, K., Shen, Z.: Building customer trust in mobile commerce. Commun. ACM **46**(4), 91–94 (2003)

39. Wang, W., Siau, K.: Artificial intelligence, machine learning, automation, robotics, future of work, and future of humanity – a review and research agenda. J. Database Manag. **30**(1), 61–79 (2019)

40. Siau, K., Wang, W.: Artificial intelligence (AI) ethics – ethics of AI and ethical AI. J. Database Manag. **31**(2), 74–87 (2020)

41. Stephanidis, C., et al.: Seven HCI grand challenges. Int. J. Hum. Comput. Interact. **35**(14), 1229–1269 (2019)

HCI, Culture and Art

Visualizing Ancient Culture Through the Design of Intermodal Extended Reality Experiences

Joseph Chambers[1,2(✉)]

[1] The Ohio State University, Columbus, OH 43210, USA
chambers.459@osu.edu
[2] Department of Design,
100 Hayes Hall, 108 North Oval Mall, Columbus, OH 43210, USA

Abstract. The purpose of this paper is to propose findings on a process for developing and designing a hybrid Virtual Reality/Augmented Reality (VR/AR) system that facilitates artifact discovery and meaning-making at the Guard dig site near the Little Miami River. Both researchers and visitors use this active archeological dig site. The content for this system uses a combination of computer-generated and photogrammetry type models to show the world of the Ft. Ancient people. The virtual presentation of these artifacts uses both a VR and AR system or Extended Reality (XR) system, to share critical cultural stories about this ancient culture. Approaching the design of this project demanded the use of designerly thinking, design research and co-design principles with archeologists, the local community, and potential visitors. This process, based on agile methodologies, ensures the needs of researchers, stakeholders, and visitors are met. The research highlights the challenges facing, exhibit, museum and historical landmark designers as they strive to create a more vibrant and dynamic experience while at the same time creating a historically accurate recreation. The main issues facing an immersive designer consist of the blending of relevance, expectations, engaging interpretation, and finally creating a cultural hub.

Keywords: Design · Extended reality · Virtual cultural heritage · Archeology · Virtual reality · Augmented reality · Museum · Ft. ancient culture

1 Introduction

In his book, Space and Place, Yi-Fu Tuan has remarked, "As social beings and scientists we offer each other truncated images of people and their world. Experiences are slighted or ignored because of the means to articulate them or point them out are lacking. The lack is not due to any inherent deficiency in language. If something is of sufficient importance to us, we usually find the means to give it visibility" [1]. This passage is rather poignant to the design research conducted in this project as several emerging technologies were designed to tell stories; that engage and immerse the visitor in more informative ways.

© Springer Nature Switzerland AG 2020
C. Stephanidis et al. (Eds.): HCII 2020, CCIS 1294, pp. 343–351, 2020.
https://doi.org/10.1007/978-3-030-60703-6_44

The idea of placing a visitor in a time and place that connects them to an ancient people and transports them through time is a way to immerse a user or visitor in a particular culture. This type of transportation has been a goal of artists and philosophers since ancient times. Aristotle proclaimed in his classic Poetics, "…Tragedy is an imitation, not of men, but of an action and of life, and life consists in action, and its end is a mode of action, not a quality" [2]. Immersive technology like Augmented Reality (AR) and Virtual Reality (VR) allows us to insert action into lessons and shared experiences, thus recreating a "life" that was once limited to passive experiences. A fully immersive VR project allows us to build, play, and manipulate artifacts within a virtual world. The technology of AR inserts computer-generated models into a user's place and space and then allows them to not only see those objects but also interact with them. The blending of the technology can provide an engaging extended reality experience for a historical, cultural heritage site.

2   Expert Domain

2.1   Subject Matter Experts and Stakeholders

While approaching the beginning stages of the design, it is helpful to identify who the stakeholders and domain experts are for the project. The VR and AR expertise is provided by the project designer, but the domain experts were those fluent in Ft. Ancient culture. The subject matter experts consisted of faculty from The Ohio State University Department of Anthropology, the University of Wisconsin-Milwaukee, the Archeological Research Institute, and others from The Ohio State University Department of Anthropology. The stakeholders, as described in this paper, are also the community at large and visitors to the site.

2.2   Ft. Ancient Culture

The origins of the Ft. Ancient Culture date back to roughly 1000 AD [3]. At this time, the culture was a weak and stagnant group. Most of the houses were pit-house style, and they farmed mostly corn, bean, and sunflower. Ft. Ancient society was a melting pot of cultural influences. They borrowed from many different peoples and civilizations. This melding helped the culture become fuller, more productive, and it grew more substantial as a result. This is also when European made goods found their way into the villages through trade. The foreign objects would include brass, glass, steel, and other products. Along with the increase in trade and material came the introduction of infectious diseases. Around 1300 AD many Ft. Ancient sites were abandoned in Southwest Ohio and Southeastern Indiana due to social and ecological changes that they encountered [3].

3   Designing for a Specific Domain

3.1   Adopting Design Principles

Design thinking is a powerful tool that is useful when looking to build alternative learning environments [4]. In researching what process would be necessary to design current immersive learning experiences, the process of design thinking emerged as a critical candidate. Brown states there are "three spaces of innovation: *inspiration*, the problem or opportunity that motivates the search for solutions; *ideation*, the process of generating, developing, and testing ideas; and *implementation*, the path that leads from the project room to the market" [4]. In proceeding with the first part of this project, inspiration was realized from the Archeologist group. The ideation phase of this project consisted of a collaboration with stakeholders using a framework of co-design principles used throughout the ideation process. An agile methodology heavily influences the implementation path.

3.2   Identifying the Strengths of Each Medium

To identify what medium, when comparing AR to VR, would be most useful, a rating system was put in place to quantify the ability of AR and VR to accurately portray the affordances each area supports (see Fig. 1 and 2). It was readily apparent some design elements would lend themselves to AR, while others VR. For instance, if you want to control every aspect of an environment, like weather, VR would be a better option visually as we could control the elements no matter what season it is. In contrast, viewing AR snow in the middle of July wouldn't have the same effect. Particular areas of interest received a rating to help identify which medium would work best.

Fig. 1. Rating AR vs VR

Fig. 2. AR vs VR data

3.3   General Issues in Designing for XR

Virtual Reality Design Considerations. It is helpful to briefly describe some of the most active elements of VR and AR so that they can be used to communicate effectively. As VR scholar Jason Jerald points out, "A fully immersive VR experience is more than merely presenting content. The more a user physically interacts with a virtual world using their own body in intuitive ways, the more than a user feels engaged and present in the virtual world" [5]. This enhanced engagement can make the experience more relatable to others. It can create a new world around us, which allows us to build, play, and manipulate objects within that world. This play and learning are at the heart of the project, so being able to have a system that can utilize these important traits is essential. VR will transport a guest to a new place, a new time, and give them a new perspective.

Augmented Reality Design Considerations. Augmented Reality is a technology that changes the visual views of its user. According to Papagiannis, "(In AR) you are more deeply immersed and engaged with your surroundings via newfound contextual understanding assisted by technology" [6]. The technology of AR inserts computer-generated objects into a user's place and space and then allows them to not only see those objects but also interact with them. This ability to "augment" a scene allows for visual overlays, object interactions, and instructions to engage a user seamlessly. Paired with the ability to set up physical trigger markers and GPS beacons, the immersive designer can place those digitally designed artifacts at specific locations and create a method of discovery learning.

3.4   XR Design Considerations for Historical and Cultural Heritage

The current exhibit, museum and historical landmark designer has several issues they need to address in order to create a vibrant and dynamic immersive experience for cultural heritage purposes. The main problems facing a designer consists of some blend of relevance, expectations, and engaging interpretation [7]. For this project, it was helpful to consider the following elements throughout the process.

Fig. 3. Website for domain experts   **Fig. 4.** Guard dig site in Indiana

Engagement. Active user participation enhances the cognitive processes in the areas of problem-solving, decision-making and evaluation. Active user participation encourages the visitor to engage with the subject matter. Engagement theory can involve collaboration, discovery and visionary types of motivation [8].

Flow. Additionally, there are design elements like FLOW and user engagement that need to be considered [9]. When the visitor comes to the location of the site, they should feel like they are visiting the past. This feeling of both arousal and control should never leave the visitor throughout the entirety of the experience. We offer a guide to assist the user throughout the teaching moments.

Gamification and Interaction Design. The interactivity of the project was considered, designed, and tested for. When approaching the design of non-gaming systems, 'gamified' elements can be used to increase a visitor's interest and motivation. Providing motivational powers to goals through mastery seeking, reputation, and identity signaling of valued accomplishments are just a few of the techniques that can be explored through these design elements [10].

Interface Design. The virtual interface was considered very carefully. If the interface does not amplify the power and control a visitor has over content, the interface can become a wall. The visitor should be provided with information that isn't obvious by just looking around the field or perusing the artifacts in the museum. The way the information is delivered to the visitor is considered [11].

Inclusivity. Research was done by going to museums and noting what all age groups do and say. This helped influence the conceptual designs for each group. Identifying topics to be addressed included how small interactions and environmental spaces can provide a meaningful outcome. It also meant having a place for the stakeholders to view the project in various states. To address this, a website was developed to share models created by individuals like OSU graduate student Jiaxing Gao with archeologists and subject matter experts (see Fig. 3).

Appropriate Visual Representation. It is challenging for a scientific researcher to share their discoveries with others outside their field. This is simply due to the very complex and dynamic elements that inhabit a historical space. While the archeologist knows the intimate experience through their hours of research and examination, much of the cultural relevance that is attached to the fragment is lost on the public without more extensive explanation. A solution to this might be to virtually incorporate emerging theories about a culture. It is important to know how a digital artifact's value is being considered by the user [1].

4 Extracting Methodology and Design Principles

4.1 Co-design and a Designerly Approach

As design researcher Sanders points out, "Approaches to design research have come from a research-led perspective and from a design-led perspective" [12]. Work by Sanders also bounds design research using both an expert mindset and a participatory mindset, referring to an approach that acknowledges the community around a project and the creators of the project. It was using this mindset that sparked discussions that informed this design. Much of the archaeologist's work is written, hand-drawn, or is research in progress, so it became critical that to connect with the archeology lab at subject matter experts. The Ft. Ancient culture is particularly hard to visualize. While this group has unearthed many artifacts, there is no modern culture to investigate and no physical structures to visit (see Fig. 4). Because of the Ft. Ancient's quick departure and their tendency to burn dwellings that were old, or inhospitable, there is little material culture left. Discussions led to an agreement about digitally visualizing three significant areas: the spiritual journey through a central village pole, a family domicile that relates to daily activities, and finally, the wilderness outside the village stockade.

4.2   Combining Co-design with Agile Methodology

By using a co-design methodology that treats the domain experts and the visitors as first-class members, we can combine design techniques used in Human-Computer Interaction, software development, and mutual learning. This project uses an interpretation of the agile co-design methodology as presented by designers at the University of Southampton [13]. This system creates scope and shared understanding upfront, then uses an iterative development process to move the project forward. The first stage is defining the problem and understanding the requirements of the stakeholders. Continuing the understanding between the stakeholders and designers from phase one, we move on to creating personas, scenarios, and activity diagrams. The next step is to develop, test and refine elements from stakeholders and possible users.

4.3   User Profiles and Journey Maps

User profiles and journey maps, also known as user personas, can help to discover the complex elements and help to aid in approaches to human-centered design. The persona and journey maps created can provide a broad picture of a participant's thoughts and the benefits associated with some of the more complex issues a design is trying to address. As Newton and Riggs point out, the personas can help to "identify broader trends, including common issues or inquiries made by particular client types" [14]. In the case of this project, the client types are the archeologists, the visitors and the local residents (see Fig. 5 and 6).

Fig. 5.   User persona

Fig. 6.   User journey map

4.4   Experience Roadmap

In addition to personas and user maps, there is a need to create a roadmap, or storyboard of the experience so that the designers and creators can identify what elements are essential to create a working prototype. Experience diagrams and storyboards are the tools of choice. These diagrams (see Fig. 7 and 8) were chosen because as Walsh states, "visual presentation of ideas helps respondents to identify themselves with the use situation and enhance imagination [15].

Fig. 7. Experience map

Fig. 8. Ancient culture

4.5   Importance of a Prototype

Continuing with an agile co-design methodology, there is a need to build and showcase a working prototype. Wensveen states in discussions about design research, "the practice of prototyping, as a means of inquiry often receives the least attention as a research contribution, it is often the case that a prototyping process has been vital for the exploration and further development of research directions, or has provided a conceptual background for the later stages of research" [16]. The effect on creating a prototype for the stakeholders provided them with the ability to see what this technology is capable of and what type of stories they can afford to the public.

AR Prototype. The AR prototype places artifacts in the desired location at the Guard site and connects the visitor to the history contained there. The artifacts include information about discovery and purpose. The user's ability to move around and see the artifact in its native surroundings was tested. The project supports physical movement through a location-based AR experience (see Fig. 9 and 10).

Fig. 9. AR prototype iPad

Fig. 10. AR prototype of pole

VR Prototype. The VR prototype places the visitor in a remote location like a museum but virtually transports them to the site (see Fig. 11 and 12). Annotation and information is contained in each artifact and presented to the visitor. By acknowledging individuals who learn best when encouraged to explore physical space, the project was leveraged by introducing historical artifacts with immersive technologies. Embodiment and movement are achieved using VR.

Fig. 11. Village in VR - night   **Fig. 12.** Village in VR - day

4.6   Considerations

- Appealing to a wide range of ages and backgrounds
- Networking will allow functionality and learning with a mass mindset
- Given the time and resources available, there could be limitations in visualizing all the areas the domain experts would like to have.
- Weather
- Technology changes

5   Conclusion

Immersive designers should take note of designerly thinking and the ability to use the design tools to enhance their design. Using personas, scenarios and prototypes are vital tools throughout the design process. Moreover, weaving the subject matter experts and stakeholders into the development process, even if they have limited experience with extended reality systems, is needed to ensure the project is accurately representing a cultural heritage site. A primary goal of this project is to raise awareness of this culture. There is a need to allow the design of these immersive experiences the ability to build more than just a walkthrough, but a place that can offer an enhanced culturally immersed experience. This can only happen through collaboration and the sharing of design choices.

References

1. Tuan, Y.-F.: Space and Place: The Perspective of Experience. U of Minnesota Press (1977)
2. Fergusson, F.: Aristotle's Poetics. Macmillan (1961)
3. Cook, R.A.: Continuity and Change in the Native American Village: Multicultural Origins and Descendants of the Fort Ancient Culture. Cambridge University Press (2017)
4. Brown, Tim, Katz, Barry: Change by design. J. Prod. Innov. Manag. **28**(3), 381–383 (2011)
5. Jerald, J.: The VR Book: Human-Centered Design for Virtual Reality. Morgan & Claypool (2015)
6. Papagiannis, H.: Augmented Human: How Technology is Shaping the New Reality. O'Reilly Media, Inc. (2017)
7. VernerJohnson Homepage. http://www.vernerjohnson.com/. Accessed 14 Feb 2020
8. Kearsley, G., Shneiderman, B.: Engagement theory: a framework for technology-based teaching and learning. Educ. Technol. **38**(5), 20–23 (1998)
9. Csikszentmihalyi, M.: Flow: the psychology of optimal experience (Nachdr.) (2009)
10. Deterding, S.: Gamification: designing for motivation. Interactions **19**(4), 14–17 (2012)
11. Schell, J.: The Art of Game Design: A Book of Lenses. CRC Press (2008)
12. Sanders, L.: An evolving map of design practice and design research. Interactions **15**(6), 13–17 (2008)
13. Millard, D., Howard, Y., Gilbert, L., Wills, G.: Co-design and co-deployment methodologies for innovative m-learning systems. In: Multiplatform E-Learning Systems and Technologies: Mobile Devices for Ubiquitous ICT-Based Education, pp. 147–163. IGI Global (2010)
14. Newton, K., Riggs, M.J.: Everybody's talking but who's listening? Hearing the user's voice above the noise, with content strategy and design thinking (2016)
15. Walsh, T., Nurkka, P., Koponen, T., Varsaluoma, J., Kujala, S., Belt, S.: Collecting cross-cultural user data with internationalized storyboard survey. In: Proceedings of the 23rd Australian Computer-Human Interaction Conference, pp. 301–310 (2011)
16. Wensveen, S., Matthews, B.: Prototypes and prototyping in design research. In: The Routledge Companion to Design Research. Taylor & Francis (2015)

Information Design of an On-Site Interpretative Game

Chun-Wen Chen(✉) ⬤ and Wei-Chieh Lee

Taipei National University of the Arts, No. 1 Hsueh-Yuan Road, Peitou District,
Taipei 11201, Taiwan
junbun@ahe.tnua.edu.tw

Abstract. This research proposes to develop a design and application model for interpretative media for ecomuseums and other exhibit facilities. With perspective of information design, we consider the form of an on-site interpretative game to combine the benefits of field interpretation and game tasks. This research takes Beitou area in northern Taiwan as the sample site of ecomuseum, to develop the contents of the interpretative game. With different styles of information design, including the order of task and interpretative text, and the use of realistic or schematic image, a card-based on-site interpretative game is designed and made. We conduct on-site user tests to understand the difference and features of usability and satisfaction among combinations of different styles of information design. Quantitative and qualitative data is collected to be analyzed. The guidelines for information design of on-site interpretative game are concluded and proposed.

Keywords: Information design · Interpretation design · Game-based learning

1 Introduction

Ecomuseum is a kind of museum in concept. The concept is to utilize real sites or objects of culture, history or nature as subjects for visiting, but not to collect them in museum. Because the subjects are not located in controllable venues, how to process an appropriate exhibit interpretation becomes an important issue. This research proposes to develop a design and application model for interpretative media for ecomuseums and other exhibit facilities.

With perspective of information design, we consider the form of an on-site interpretative game to combine the benefits of field interpretation and game tasks. It could be guided by an interpreter or operated by users themselves, to improve the visiting experience. The interpretative tool should be compact to carry and can demonstrate the functions of interpretative media well. It should have a concise form to provide basic and important site information, as well as to match the needs and styles of tasks and the context.

This research takes Beitou area in Taiwan as the sample site of ecomuseum, to develop the contents of the interpretative game. This paper is the pilot study that tested the paper prototypes on the real site with fewer participants. Guidelines are concluded to make the final test model of the on-site interpretative game.

C. Stephanidis et al. (Eds.): HCII 2020, CCIS 1294, pp. 352–358, 2020.
https://doi.org/10.1007/978-3-030-60703-6_45

2   Literature Review

2.1   Interpretation

Interpretation is a kind of educational activity. It is multiple methods and media of demonstration and explanation for visitors to understand the themes and contents of exhibits. Tilden [11] provided a definition of *interpretation* for dictionary purpose as follows:

> *An educational activity which aims to reveal meanings and relationships through the use of original objects, by firsthand experience, and by illustrative media, rather than simply to communicate factual information* (p. 33).

Beck and Cable [2] took interpretation as a procedure of transmitting information and inspiration for us, to promote the understanding, appreciation, and protection to cultural and natural heritage. We can see that interpretation is a method of education, with direct experience and explanative information, to inspire the understanding and insights of visitors to the themes and contents of exhibits, and to actively promote the protection of the cultural and natural environment. It is also the purpose of this research.

The effect of direct experience on learning has been richly discussed in literature, mainly due to the benefits of multiple sensory stimulation and connection. Experiential learning (or experience-based learning) is a way of learning through experience, especially learning by reflection in operation.

Kolb [6] proposed the experiential learning theory that defines experience learning as the process of knowledge generation through the conversion of experience. Kolb's experiential learning model (ELM) is divided into four stages, from individual concrete experience, reflective observation, abstract conceptualization, and finally to verification of the concept (active experimentation). Knowledge is obtained by summing up experience from actual situations, and promoted from verification and application. This is originally a natural way to obtain usable knowledge from experience, but it is more efficient for us to directly utilize the experience gathered by our predecessors, with means such as reading. Now we lose the ability to learn directly from experience, and also lose the learning effect of multiple senses. Kolb is to retrieve this original learning method.

Tilden [11] believes the two concepts that the interpreter must think about. One is that the statement must go beyond the facts to inspire more important meanings behind the facts. The other is that the explanation should make full use of human curiosity to enrich and enhance human intelligence and mind. This means that interpretation can use people's instinct of curiosity for novelty, to provide multiple experiential environments, just like puzzles to be solved, to trigger learning motivation, and to open up potentially important meanings.

The interpretative media is the medium that conveys the content of the message. Broadly speaking, it also covers the means and methods of using the media to elicit the reaction of the recipient, including the methods, facilities and tools of communication. Sharpe [10] divides the interpretative media into two categories: staff interpretation and non-staff interpretation. 1. Personal or attended service: the use of personnel to explain directly to tourists. 2. Non-personal or attended service: using a variety of facilities to explain the subject matter, without personnel explanation. This research conducted test with a means of non-personal service.

2.2 Information Design

The name *information design* is derived from the field of graphic design, and is also traditionally called information graphics. It is a method of explaining facts and numerical concepts by combining graphics and text. In the development of human civilization, it is natural to use graphics and text to convey ideas at the same time. After the development of many pioneers in modern times, it has gradually become an integrated design professional field. Information design is defined by the International Institute for Information Design (IIID) [5]: is "the defining, planning, and shaping of the contents of a message and the environments in which it is presented, with the intention to satisfy the information needs of the intended recipients."

Information architecture refers to a set of methods for describing the structure of an information system, including how information is organized, how information is navigated, and vocabulary and term selection [1]. Morville and Rosenfeld [7] believe that the information structure can be divided into four parts: organization system, labeling system, navigation system, and search system.

Information graphics is a comprehensive graphic and text to explain the facts and numerical concepts. There are many different views on the scope and classification of information graphics. Wildbur and Burke [13] divide information graphics into three categories according to their usage: 1. Organized presentation of facts or data; 2. Methods to understand the situation or process; 3. Design of control systems.

2.3 Game-Based Learning

Game-based learning (GBL) is a learning method that uses games to achieve specific learning purposes. It includes games through various media, such as computers, video games, paper cards, board games, etc. The game-based learning using digital media is called digital game-based learning (DGBL). In recent years, there are researches on the effectiveness of digital game-based learning. Although many results have proved to be beneficial to learning, the disputes continue [3, 8, 12].

The most questioned question about the strategy of attracting visitors in museum exhibition with entertainment is: Regardless of whether the visitors pay attention to and understands the theme information, the entertainment effect can still be achieved. It is difficult to determine whether the visitors have learned something. Screven [9] proposed two modes of participation: *passive participation* and *interactive participation*. Passive participation usually only plays the role of the initiator. The visitors can see the dynamic demonstration, but has no power of choice. This kind of participation is one-way only, and the system has the same response to all feedback. While interactive participation does not only provide visitors a chance to make a decision. The focus is to encourage visitors to find the answer from the exhibit to achieve the best cognitive learning effect before visitors make a decision. Interactive participation is closer to the ideal way of participation in education and entertainment.

About digital games on real site, Hwang, Tsai and Yang [4] discussed the location-based mobile learning environment on the topic of context-aware ubiquitous learning environment. They suggested the learning environment should be environment-aware, that is, the state of the learner or environment can be detected before the system can perform learning activities. And the learning environment should provide personalized support or prompts at appropriate paths, locations, and times that based on the learner's personal, environmental factors and learning process.

3   Method

This research takes Beitou area in northern Taiwan as the sample site of eco-museum, to develop the contents of the interpretative game. In Beitou, many cultural and historic spots are very worth visiting. We select some important spots to form an appropriate visiting path. With different styles of information design, including the order of task and interpretative text, and the use of realistic or schematic image, a card-based on-site interpretative game is designed and made. Every card matches a specific spot with its task description, interpretative text and image (see Fig. 1).

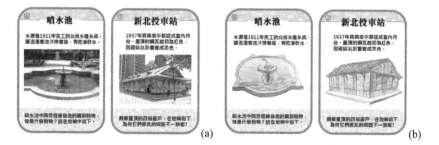

Fig. 1. Game cards: (a) with realistic photos; (b) with hand drawing.

In this pilot study, paper prototypes were tested in three stages by eight participants. Paper prototypes were made with three design factors: (1) order of task and text, (2) realistic or schematic image, and (3) with or without background color under lower texts. A hand-drawing map and puzzle booklet like elementary school homework were also designed as parts of the game (see Fig. 2). Each group of two participants took one prototype with a combination of the factors and started to arrange a suitable route for all spots on the cards. They had to follow the task directions on the cards to complete the tasks on the spots and also try to solve the number puzzle on the booklet. After a group of participants finished their tasks and solved the puzzle, a group interview was conducted to understand the problems and satisfaction that participants met. After each test stage, the prototype was modified to make new version.

We will conduct on-site user tests to understand the difference and features of usability and satisfaction among combinations of different styles of information design. Quantitative and qualitative data is collected to be analyzed.

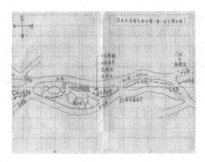

Fig. 2. Game map

4 Results and Discussion

This pilot study collects qualitative data in three group interviews. The results show three categories of reflections and insights about the game design: (1) process and puzzle design: the game integration and puzzle solving, (2) information and visual design: the order of objects and visual styles, and (3) task design: how the experience can be gather.

Stage 1. Two participants. (1) Process and puzzle design: Users can understand how the game progresses from documents and cards. The puzzle solving is processed on the booklet, so it should provide obvious hints and directions.

(2) Information and visual design: "Title, introduction, image, task" is the most acceptable visual order of information presented. Users think that tasks are more important than introduction. You need to know what the mission is before you start to explore. The task texts should be emphasized. The yellow background can highlight the task texts. The images that utilize hand-drawing style got better satisfaction. User can explorer the spots with hints in the drawing images. The routes on the map can provide the function of positioning to locate personal position.

(3) Task design: The task on the card can make users want to go inside the train station to find the answer. It is good to get experience of problem solving. The tasks should have clear instructions and have obvious correspondence with the spots (Fig. 3).

Fig. 3. On-site test in Thermal Valley, Beitou.

Stage 2. One participant. (1) Process and puzzle design: Relevance and priority of tasks and puzzle solving is important. If there is no relevance, it is easy to guide users focus on the puzzle solving and ignore the experiential tasks. The time without limitation is good for users to get more experience in the site. The free exploration is encouraged. Users also like the manner that users can freely arrange their routes to go through the spots shown on the cards. But they like a clear method to finish the tasks, such as blank squares to fill the answers.

(2) Information and visual design: The mapping between cards and the map is well for wayfinding. The landmarks on the map should be showed on the correct related positions so that they can be referred easily.

(3) Task design: The task should be designed with answer searching or rich field experience to prevent users to skip the tasks. Users could start drawing after deep observation: such as the task that starts observation on Thermal Valley and try to draw witch image from the scene. Finally, the clear and important knowledge can be understood, such as the story that Beitou waterway system was completed in 1911.

Stage 3. Four participants. (1) Process and puzzle design: Users will also observe things that are not card tasks. The path they have taken is that we have not traveled before. There are two groups that will compete and have more fun. A group is suitable for 2–3 people to cooperate through barriers.

(2) Information and visual design: The arrangement of tasks above and introduction below will be misunderstood that the instruction below is the answer. Observation skills can be trained, and card clues can assist in correspondence. The map does not need to be drawn with too much details, and this map is just good. And real photos used in the cards are less fun. It makes the card designed more like a sightseeing manual.

(3) Task design: They also pay attention to the information along the road to see if they can find the answer for the tasks. They like the interactive way on site, such taking pictures in the Little Bath and finding a green-building book in the library.

The tested cards can be used as a self-guided interpretation tool. It can fulfill the most principles by Tilden [11]. It can provide experiential connection between users and knowledge. The interpretation function works better than mere information by tasks that can stimulate people's imagination.

5 Conclusion

The guidelines for information design of on-site interpretative game are concluded and proposed.

(1) The simple on-site game can provide similar functions of a person's interpretation. The tasks are good to get experience of problem solving. The tasks should have clear instructions and have obvious correspondence with the spots.

(2) In the game context, "Title, introduction, image, task" is the most acceptable visual order of information presented. Users think that tasks are more important than introduction. The task texts should be emphasized.

(3) The images that utilize hand-drawing style got better satisfaction. User can explorer the spots with hints in the drawing images. Real photos used in the cards are more formal and less fun.
(4) Relevance and priority of tasks and puzzle solving is important. If there is no relevance, it is easy to guide users focus on the puzzle solving and ignore the experiential tasks.
(5) The free exploration is encouraged. The time without limitation is good for users to get more experience in the site.
(6) The mapping between cards and the map is important for wayfinding. The landmarks on the map should be showed on the correct related positions so that they can be referred easily.

This pilot study shows that without a real person's interpretation, this game can play a similar role to interact with visitors and bring rich experience on the real site.

Acknowledgments. This research was partly sponsored by grants, MOST 108-2410-H-119-003, from the Ministry of Science and Technology, Taiwan.

References

1. Barker, I.: What is information architecture? https://www.steptwo.com.au/papers/kmc_whatisinfoarch/. Accessed 2019
2. Beck, L., Cable, T.: Interpretation for the 21st Century: Fifteen Guiding Principles for Interpreting Nature and Culture, 2nd edn. Sagamore, Urbana (2002)
3. Bedwell, W.L., Pavlas, D., Heyne, K., Lazzara, E.H., Salas, E.: Toward a taxonomy linking game attributes to learning: an empirical study. Simul. Gaming **43**(6), 729–760 (2012)
4. Hwang, G.-J., Tsai, C.-C., Yang, S.J.: Criteria, strategies and research issues of context-aware ubiquitous learning. J. Educ. Technol. Soc. **11**(2), 81–91 (2008)
5. International Institute for Information Design Definitions. https://www.iiid.net/home/definitions/. Accessed 2018
6. Kolb, D.: Experiential Learning as the Science of Learning and Development. Prentice Hall, Englewood Cliffs (1984)
7. Morville, P., Rosenfeld, L.: Information Architecture for the World Wide Web. O'Reilly Media, Sebastopol (2006)
8. Prensky, M.: Digital game-based learning. Comput. Entertainment **1**(1), 21 (2003)
9. Screven, C.G.: Information design in informal setting: museum and other public spaces. In: Jacobson, R. (ed.) Information design, pp. 131–192. MIT Press, Cambridge, MA (1999)
10. Sharpe, G.W.: Interpreting the Environment, 2nd edn. Wiley, New York (1982)
11. Tilden, F.: Interpreting our Heritage, 3rd edn. University of North Carolina Press, Chapel Hill (1997)
12. Van Eck, R.: Digital game-based learning: it's not just the digital natives who are restless. Educause Rev. **41**(2), 16–30 (2006)
13. Wildbur, P., Burke, M.: Information Graphics. Thames and Hudson, London (1998)

Augmented Reality as an Educational Resource Applied to the Teaching of Pre-Columbian Cultures Settled in the Pumapungo Archaeological Park

Edgar Marcelo Espinoza Méndez[(✉)] [ORCID]

Universidad de Cuenca, Cuenca 010112, Ecuador
marcelo.espinoza@ucuenca.edu.ec

Abstract. The objective of the project focuses on the use of Augmented Reality and free software applied to a playful, puzzle-like game that serves as didactic support in the teaching and diffusion of archaeological patrimony in museums.

For the study case, we choose The Pumapungo Museum and The Archaeological Park located in the city of Cuenca, Ecuador, which have an important archaeological and patrimony reserve and are also located on one of the most important Inkas settlements in the country. According to its statistics, around 164,000 thousand tourists visit it annually, and 14.64% of them are children; therefore, based on these data, the defined audience of users for the study were primary school children between 6 and 8 years of age.

As a pedagogical methodology, the learning theories in education were used, by Seymour Papert (Constructivism) and John Dewey (Learning by doing), tools that have improved the learning process through exploration and experience. Likewise, we worked with formal and non-formal learning schemes that allow improving the interaction of children with the museum environments, reinforcing the knowledge from the guided visits.

The results show that the use of Augmented Reality in the learning process arouses the interest and curiosity of children in a given topic because it allows them to get involved in real time in historical contexts and therefore learn about the material and intangible heritage or patrimony of their country.

The research and development of the project was carried out in 2015, so the technological and bibliographic references correspond to that date.

Keywords: Augmented Reality · Free software · Pedagogy · Constructionism · Learning by doing · Game · Museum

1 Introduction

Augmented Reality as technology has allowed the development of multiple applications in cultural, scientific or educational fields, showing the versatility that it offers not only on computers but also on mobile devices; In the time of the study, examples such as from the School of Computing and Information Systems, University of Tasmania, where several work is carried out to reduce the problems of students for the study of

© Springer Nature Switzerland AG 2020
C. Stephanidis et al. (Eds.): HCII 2020, CCIS 1294, pp. 359–366, 2020.
https://doi.org/10.1007/978-3-030-60703-6_46

Anatomy with the use of haptic Augmented Reality, with results expressed by their authors as "promising" (Yeom 2011); An investigation was carried out In Bogotá, Colombia about the use of Augmented Reality to enhance the main points of tourist interest through a website (Cuervo et al. 2011); According to (Fabregat 2012) the Adaptive Hypermedia Systems and The Augmented Reality can be coupled for the benefit of students when teaching, through the use of e-learning platforms, as a tool in adaptive environments; In more specific cases and related to this project, studies have also been carried out where "... the possibilities that Augmented Reality offers in museum environments have been observed, taking into account its pedagogical nature, since the simplicity of the applications makes them adapt to a wide spectrum of public..." (Ruiz Torres 2011, p. 223).

Based on the mentioned cases, we can say that Augmented Reality has proven to be an optimal resource to be applied as a didactic and pedagogical tool, which is in accordance with the public policies of the Network of National Museums of the Ministry of Culture of Ecuador, that promotes the valuation, preservation of Ecuadorian cultural patrimony so that museums could be "a powerful tool for content transmission and non-formal pedagogical complementarity" (Celi et al. 2010, p. 3), besides contributing to the main objective of this project, which is to demonstrate that the didactic experience of visitors to the Pumapungo Archaeological Park can be reinforced and improved, through the use of a game based on Augmented Reality and free software; technologies that allow the creation of highly useful applications, at a lower cost and with the scope of being able to mix multimedia elements such as video, sound and 3D.

2   Materials and Methods

2.1   Theoretical Framework

To conceive the application design in Reality, we relied on the following concepts:

Teaching in Museums. It proposes formal and non-formal learning that contributes to teaching methodologies within these spaces of historical collectivity. If we rely on the concepts of formal education, museums would fulfil a similar objective of a library "... from the perspective of formal education, we should go to the museum and do what is not possible to perform in school or look for answers to previously raised questions" (Santacana 1998). It is then when processes must be organized to follow before, during and after the visit to a museum, where dialogue and coordination with educational entities is a fundamental part of it.

As a consequence of formality, we can talk, then, of non-formal learning, where the museum's visitor himself is the person who must interact directly with the object or space intentionally prepared for the visit, culturally stimulating their knowledge and potential questions or answers, generating a self-interest of knowledge as a user. Although its name is called "non-formal" (Papert 1981) this does not mean that this type of learning is completely removed from the processes; in other words, the experimentation on the object is potentiated and the subject becomes part of the previously designed process.

Seymourt Papert - Constructivism. His theoretical approach is based on the fact that computers would be a useful tool to improve the development of children's creativity and learning, as well as the possibility that, in the future, these machines would be a personal object of each student.

As a result of his theory about computers in education, he developed a programming language called "LOGO" (Turtle Language), a tool with which children, in this case, and machines, can communicate in an easy and attractive language, becoming the developers of their own learning universe, but also working together with the educator; that is, children understanding that the educator is also a student and that everyone, including the teacher, learns from their mistakes, "Sharing the problem and the experience of solving it allows the child to learn from the adult, not "doing what the teacher says "but" doing what the teacher does"" (Papert 1981, p. 137).

John Dewey - Learning by Doing. His theory is based on the fact that children develop precise skills to solve problems established by themselves, through exploration and investigation within a space; that is, learning from their experience, seeking to generate inquiry and interest in them, stimulating a more creative response for future situations that occur in their learning.

In "Experience and Education" Dewey conceives a theory of experience, this way configuring a "corpus of certainties" and prescriptions that the school should promote:

– The student as the center of educational action.
– Learning by doing.
– The school as the place

Didactic or Playful Games, What Benefits Do They Have for Pedagogy in Children. In children the word "game" is directly related to fun, and in pedagogy with learning and how it can stimulate in them. If it is not their main activity, games are presented as a stimulant to children so that they develop different cognitive, concentration or social interaction skills. Playing can be seen as a distracting action, but also as an effective guide applied to make a child understand reality. Through this, people, especially the little ones, experience learning as a way to make them grow in the educational environment. Regardless of their age, playing becomes part of the recreational activities that will accompany their knowledge.

> Children grow up playing therefore, a very important part of their development has to do with games, since it stimulates the growth of their intelligence and creativity; didactic games help children to think more, to be able to reason better and to have a greater capacity for analysis and synthesis. (Educational toys: Invite to learn)

Augmented Reality and Free Software. Augmented Reality is basically the mixture of virtual information of any kind: images, text, 3D figures or video, with physical information, on the same scene and in real time, it aims to expand the reality that we perceive with our senses, enrich a real physical object, with any type of digital information, using technological devices and of course a computer system (Fig. 1).

In the development of work in Augmented Reality, the use of specialized software and libraries is very important, on the internet you can find some applications that were based on the concepts of free software and open source code and are available to users,

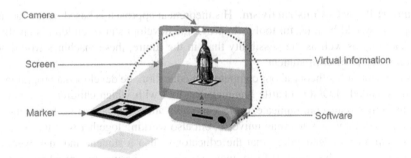

Fig. 1. Scheme of the necessary components for an Augmented Reality system

since this allows the exchange of knowledge, updates, improvements and contributions to increase the benefits that each of them can offer.

Richard M. Stallman, founder of the Free Software Foundation, a non-profit organization dedicated to promoting the use and development of free software, defined the four freedoms or principles of free software as:

1. The freedom to run the program for whatever purpose.
2. The freedom to modify the program to adjust it to your needs. (For effective freedom in practice, you must have access to the source code, because without it the task of incorporating changes into a program is extremely difficult.)
3. The freedom to redistribute copies, either for free, or in exchange for paying a price.
4. La libertad de distribuir versiones modificadas del programa, de tal forma que la comunidad pueda aprovechar las mejoras introducidas. (Stallman 2004, pág. 19)

The project was developed with tools such as: Blender for 3D modeling, ARToolKit Marker Generator Online for creating markers, OpenCollada plugin for handling 3D files and Adobe Flash Builder (software with license) with free source code for game programming.

2.2   Methodology

Taking into account the aforementioned concepts, the design process of the Augmented Reality application was developed under the following work scheme:

- Evaluation of the different spaces and elements of the park to determine what the main archaeological attractions are that will form part of the prototype of the game.
- Research on the Inca settlement in Pumapungo, current city of Basin.
- Research on the types of free software with which you can program the game.
- Creation of a storyboard for the narrative of the game.
- Design of the different elements of the game.
- Prototyping and testing.

3 Game Design

The game in Augmented Reality is called "Pumapungo World", and its objective is to hypothetically teach how the Inca site could have been in Pumapungo, using graphical elements of this culture taking as a reference the illustrations of the indigenous chronicler Felipe Guamán Poma de Ayala.

The Pumapungo World is made up of the main architectural spaces (scenarios) that the Incas built on the site (The Kancha, The Barracks o Kallankas, The Aqlla Wasi, The QuriKancha, Canal-Bathrooms-Lagoon and Outer Palace) and the context that revolves around it so that children can idealize What this wonderful settlement could have looked like (Table 1).

Table 1. Scheme of relationship between architectural spaces and other elements of the Puzzle.

Ground	Living area	Character	Environment	Video
Represents the space where the settlement Inca was	It represents the main constructions or vestiges found on the site	It shows who used the houses or buildings	It exemplifies a context of the agricultural work of the Inca people	It is narrative type and complements the 3D information presented
Stage stand	The Kancha	Inca people	Open space, place of gathering of the people	Video related to the topic
Stage stand	The Barracks o Kallankas	Soldiers	Rooms for the armies of the empire	Video related to the topic
Stage stand	Aqlla Wasi	Aqllas and Mamaconas	Species of convent inhabited by women consecrated to the sun	Video related to the topic
Stage stand	The Qurikancha	Priests	Greater temple and astronomical observatory, symbolizes religious power	Video related to the topic
Stage stand	Canal - Bathrooms - Lagoon	Inca Emperor	Space dedicated to the God Tiksi Wiraqucha	Video related to the topic
Stage stand	Outer Palace	Inca Royalty	Architectural construction	Video related to the topic

The game starts from the conception of a thematic puzzle made up of four chips and a support base, each one incorporates a marker (element that activates Augmented

Reality) with topics related to archaeological spaces of the Pumapungo Park (Fig. 2 and Table 2).

Table 2. Chart of 3D graphics and markers using the Aqlla Wasi scenario as an example.

Marker	Element	3D Graphic / Video
	Logo introduction to the Pumapungo World	
	Terrain / Stage Support	
	Character	
	Aqlla Wasi	
	Environment	
	Video	

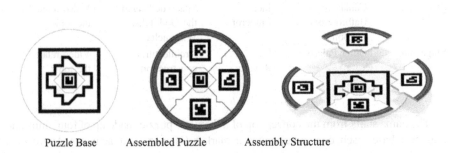

Puzzle Base   Assembled Puzzle   Assembly Structure

Fig. 2. Puzzle tabs with their own Augmented Reality markers

For the development of the application, programming tests were carried out, first with Flash Builder version 4.6, plus libraries and free use codes based on multimarkers and video loading for Augmented Reality which were created with the ARToolKit Marker Generator Online tool. The modeling and animation of 3D elements were made with 3D Studio Max software. A second test was performed with AR Media software; its plugin was used to 3D Studio Max and marker generation with AR Media marker Generator, this software allows the assembly of the elements of the application in the same 3D program while creating an executable file for its operation (Fig. 3).

Fig. 3. Evaluation tests of the app

4   Results

The evaluation of the prototype was done with 20 children from a rural school in the city because they have less contact with computers and new technologies for their scarce economic resources; by observing usage and behavior, the strengths and weaknesses of the proposed model were determined.

The puzzle was perhaps the most involved element. The majority of opinion from the children is that more tiles should be included in order to see more 3D animations, in some cases the apparent complexity of the puzzle due to the shape of the puzzle did not allow them to assemble it easily; This led to unintended individual activity becoming a group activity because of other children's interest in helping to solve the puzzle. The level of interaction of the children with the game was high since the size of the tiles allowed them to correctly manipulate and observe each of the elements.

The use of Augmented Reality in the field of education allows children to become more involved in learning about a specific subject. By showing a different perspective of an intangible reality, we managed to awaken curiosity in children, first, about the operation of the application and, second, about the theme presented. It must be emphasized that the motor and cognitive development is different in each child, so in some cases the instructions on how the puzzle works should be personalized.

This technology can provide the user with new experiences in non-immersive environments, since its easy use makes it totally attractive, especially for children who, in general, are more and more accustomed to the technological advances that stimulate their minds.

The proposed application can be adapted and modified, according to the needs of the Park and in its first stage was limited to an emblematic area previously analyzed by the park managers. The use of technologies based on free software allows the realization of applications of great utility and at a lower cost. The application that gave the best result when doing the tests prior to the final evaluation was 3D Studio Max plus the AR Media plugin.

References

Yeom, S.-J.: Augmented reality for learning anatomy. In: Ascilite, pp. 1377–1383 (2011)

Cuervo, M.C., Salamanca, J.Q., Aldana, A.A.: Ambiente interactivo para visualizar sitios turísticos, mediante Realidad Aumentada implementando Layar. Ciencia e Ingeniería Neogranadina **21**(2), 91–105 (2011)

Fabregat, R.: Combinando la realidad aumentada con las plataformas de e-elearning adaptativas. Enl@ce: Revista Venezolana de Información, Tecnología y Conocimiento **9**, 69–78 (2012)

Ruiz Torres, D.: Realidad Aumentada, educación y museos. Revista Icono **14**(2), 212–226 (2011)

Celi, I., Bedoya, M., Cevallos, P.: Propuesta del Sistema Ecuatoriano de Museos y Política Nacional de Museos. Ministerio de Cultura del Ecuador, Ecuador (2010)

Santacana, J.: Museos, ¿al servicio de quién? Iber (15), 39–50 (1998)

Papert, S.: Desafío a la Mente. Computadoras y Educación. Galápago, Buenos Aires (1981)

Juguetes didácticos: Invitan a aprender. (s.f.). Recuperado el Julio de 2014, de Proquest. http://search.proquest.com/docview/307174190/EF49A4CA43FF4B1CPQ/5?accountid=36552

Stallman, R.: Software libre para una sociedad libre, vol. 1. Traficantes de Sueños, Madrid (2004)

Research on the Design of Regional Cultural and Creative Products Based on Consumer Cognition

Da-wei Fan[1,2(✉)]

[1] Jincheng College of Nanjing University of Aeronautics and Astronautics,
Nanjing 211156, China
david121121@163.com
[2] College of Economics and Management, Nanjing University of Aeronautics
and Astronautics, Nanjing 211106, China

Abstract. Products are of commemorative significance when associated with regional culture, whose differences in design themes and cultural attributes cause consumers to have different perceptions of regional culture. In view of this, this paper took the regional culture of Nanjing as an example to study the consumer cognition of two types of products in five attributes including cultural and historic natures, cultural story-based natures, local characteristics, cultural connotations, and cultural art, with cultural and creative products designed for architecture and IP roles as the research objects. The research findings show 1. Consumers had different cognitions towards design attributes of regional cultural and creative products of Nanjing, which have different design themes. 2. Consumers had different cognitions towards design attributes of regional cultural and creative products of Nanjing on different design levels. 3. Cognition of design attributes of regional cultural and creative products of Nanjing was influenced by design themes and design levels. The research can provide a reference for the design of regional cultural and creative products, help designers master consumer demands better and prevent design deviations.

Keywords: Consumer cognition · Regional culture · Cultural and creative products

1 Introduction

Culture and design influence each other. Through abstractive and refined application of cultural information of different themes (such as architecture, clothing and language) in cultural and creative products, the regional culture has been continued and propagandized, which can help consumers understand natures and connotations of regional culture. According to classification of three levels of cultural products by Wu, Tyan-Yu et al. [1], we can classify regional cultural and creative products into symbolic design with direct transplantation of cultural elements, functional design highlighting product practicality and metaphor design highlighting cultural connotations. As for the same regional culture, due to different design themes and skills of designers, consumers will have different cognitions towards cultural and creative products with different design

© Springer Nature Switzerland AG 2020
C. Stephanidis et al. (Eds.): HCII 2020, CCIS 1294, pp. 367–374, 2020.
https://doi.org/10.1007/978-3-030-60703-6_47

themes. Therefore, whether a design is successful depends on whether the product can effectively convey natures and connotations of regional culture to consumers. Hence, it is quite necessary to design cultural products which have local characteristics and satisfy consumer cognitions. Therefore, the paper aims to, from the perspective of consumer cognition, explores design strategies of regional cultural and creative products and help designers effectively grant products with unique cultural features during design of cultural and creative products, so as to establish associations with local culture in consumers' cognition.

2   Relevant Studies

2.1   Design and Development of Regional Cultural and Creative Products

Regional culture refers to a unique type of culture given regional marks, which is formed through the integration of culture with surroundings in a certain regional environment. Based on regional traditional culture, it absorbs essences of external culture and features inheritance, growth and inclusiveness [2]. As believed by the UNESCO, cultural products carry economic and cultural natures and become a carrier of cultural features, values and significances through use and preservation of cultural heritage [3]. As proposed by Lin Rongtai (2007), cultural and creative products can be designed through scene application and storytelling. The design comprises four steps, namely investigation (set a scenario), interaction (tell a story), development (write a script) and implementation (design a product). In addition, designers shall assess features, significances and adaptability of products and perfect the design according to assessment results [4]. Yi Jun et al. (2018) aiming at design and development of cultural and creative products proposed construction of a service platform including sub-platform for integration of design resource of regional culture, design assistant sub-platform, and rapid prototyping manufacture sub-platform. This platform involves all processes of product design and development, wherein each module is mutually independent and realizes mutual cooperation and influences, acquisition paths of cultural resources are simplified, and design efficiency is increased [5].

2.2   Consumer Cognition

As believed by Zhi Jinyi (2007), consumers' cognition responses towards products to a certain extent involve the selection of visual perception and are directly associated with consumers' former visual experience, memory and image arising [6]. Consumers' cognition of products is influenced by product factors and consumer factors. The information generated from product design, including functions, forms, textures, colors and styles will bring consumers with aesthetic experience. Social and cultural environment, educational level, age, job, gender, customs and other factors of consumers will influence their cognition and experience of products. During the design of cultural and creative products, designers will according to the cognition of the regional cultural object use the design knowledge mastered to conduct the design. If the designed product has proper content and information on regional culture, correct cognition responses of consumers will arise, so accurate cognition matching can be acquired [7].

Therefore, in the research, cultural targets of architecture and IP roles are used as the design themes. In addition, cultural and creative products designed based on these two themes were selected for the research from three design levels such as symbolization, functionality and metaphor. In this way, consumers' cognition and preferences for cultural and creative products are judged, and design references can be provided for designers in the design of regional cultural and creative products.

3 Experimental Design

The research is divided into two stages. Firstly, preliminary survey: Literature research was conducted in the first stage. 30 testing samples were extracted from Jiangsu Travel Commodity Website and Qinhuai Gift Taobao Official Flagship Store. Their design levels and themes were researched and classified. Through collection of comments of five experts in the design field, six representative products were screened as experimental samples. In the second stage, questionnaire survey was conducted on cognition preferences of 131 tests. Survey results were analyzed by SPSS statistical software. ANOVA analysis of design themes (IP roles, architecture) × design levels (symbolization, functionality, and metaphor) was conducted, so consumers' cognitions and preferences towards regional cultural and creative products of Nanjing were explored.

Hypothesis 1: Consumers have the same cognition towards design attributes of regional cultural and creative products of Nanjing with different design themes.

Hypothesis 2: Consumers have the same cognition towards design attributes of regional cultural and creative products of Nanjing with different design levels.

Hypothesis 3: Design themes and design levels cannot influence the design attributes of regional cultural and creative products of Nanjing at the same time.

3.1 Tests

Main consumers of regional cultural and creative products are basically young people [8–10]. Thus, in the research, young people of 18–40 years old (34.09% for males, and 65.91% for females) were taken as the research objects. In total, 131 valid questionnaires were collected for statistical analysis.

3.2 Samples of Cultural and Creative Products

As one of the Chinese cities with deepest cultural deposits, its culture integrates elements in North and South, features inclusiveness and embodies uniqueness. There are abundant cultural and creative products with Nanjing culture as the research target. In the paper, samples of cultural and creative products were extracted from Jiangsu Travel Commodity Website and Qinhuai Gift Taobao Official Flagship Store. According to the sales ranking, 30 testing samples were selected and classified according to design levels and design themes. Then, five experts in the design field of cultural and creative products were invited to choose 6 representative products as experimental samples.

3.3   Items of Attributes of Cultural and Creative Products

Survey questionnaires were sorted through a literature review. In total, five dimensions of cognition towards cultural and creative products were obtained, which include Cultural historical nature, Cultural story-based nature, Local characteristic, Cultural connotation, Cultural artistic nature.

3.4   Implementation of Experiment

Based on the reference review and preliminary survey, 6 products and 5 dimensions were collected from samples. For purposes of the research, scores of 1–5 points were marked for preferences of 6 cultural and creative products and cognition of 21 design attributes in the questionnaire. 5 points refer to the highest intensity of attribute recognition, and 1 point refers to the lowest intensity of attribute recognition. Then, scores were graded for preferences of product samples, wherein 1 refers to "dislike the most" and 5 refers to "like the most".

4   Results and Discussion

4.1   Cultural Historical Nature and Cultural Artistic Nature

1. Design levels of cultural and creative products had significant influences on consumers from the perspective of cultural historical natures ($F_{(2, 260)} = 125.09$, $p < .001$). It is shown through Scheffe method: consumers' cognition towards the levels of symbolization and functionality was significantly stronger than that of the metaphor level, while there was no significant difference between cognitions on the levels of functionality and symbolization. In other words, as for consumers' cognition of cultural historical natures in cultural and creative products, the design level of metaphor is the least perceivable one for consumers in comparison with design levels such as functionality and symbolization (see Table 1).
2. Design themes and design levels had significant interactions in consumers' cognition of cultural historical natures, wherein $F_{(2, 260)} = 3.539$, $p = 0.03$. Further simple main effects were checked. Results are as follows: as for levels such as symbolization, functionality and metaphor, design themes had significantly simple main effects ($F_{(1, 390)} = 8.38$, $p = 0.004$; $F_{(1,390)} = 5.94$, $p = 0.015$; $F_{(1,390)} = 33.50$, $p < 0.001$). Consumers' cognition of architecture-themed cultural and creative products on three levels ($M = 4.03$, $SD = 0.64$; $M = 4.01$, $SD = 0.65$; $M = 3.43$, $SD = 0.84$) was stronger than that of IP role cultural and creative products on the same level ($M = 3.84$, $SD = 0.69$; $M = 3.85$, $SD = 0.72$; $M = 3.05$, $SD = 0.87$).

In addition, as for cultural artistic natures, consumers' cognition of attributes of cultural and creative products was similar with that of cultural historical natures; the design level has significant effects on consumers' cognition of cultural artistic natures ($F_{(2, 260)} = 15.667$, $p < .001$), while the metaphor level of design is the least perceivable aspect for consumers (see Table 1). However, as for cultural artistic natures, there was no significant interaction between design themes and design levels.

4.2   Cultural Story-Based Natures and Cultural Connotation

According to research results, consumers had similar cognitions towards cultural story-based natures and cultural connotations of cultural and creative products, which are mainly manifested in the following aspects:

1. Design levels of cultural and creative products had significant effects on consumers' cognitions towards attributes of cultural story-based natures and cultural connotations (F (2, 260) = 70.113, p < .001; F (2, 260) = 48.841, p < .001). As shown through Scheffe method, as for consumers' cognitions towards cultural story-based natures and cultural connotations in cultural and creative products, the functionality was most easily perceived by consumers, with design on the symbolization level ranking the second place; in comparison with design levels of functionality and symbolization, the metaphor design level was least perceivable by consumers.
2. Design themes and design levels of cultural and creative products had significant interactions as for consumers' cognition on cultural story-based natures and cultural connotations (F (2, 260) = 30.407, p < 0.001; F (2, 260) = 11.222, p < 0.001). Further simple main effect testing was conducted, as follows:
   (1) As for the symbolization level, design themes has significant simple main effects (F (1, 390) = 5.43, p = 0.020; F (1, 390) = 58.98, p < 0.001); but differently, consumers' cognition towards cultural story-based natures of cultural and creative products of architecture (M = 3.12, SD = 0.95) was weaker than that of IP roles (M = 3.26, SD = 0.82); the results was opposite for cognition of cultural connotations, namely the cognition for architecture (M = 4.02, SD = 0.62) was stronger than IP roles (M = 3.58, SD = 0.80). As for the functionality level, design themes also had significant simple main effects (F (1,390) = 61.22, p < 0.001; F (1,390) = 4.39, p = 0.037). Consumers' cognition towards attributes of cultural and creative products of IP roles (M = 3.31, SD = 0.76; M = 3.97, SD = 0.66) was weaker than that of architecture (M = 3.78, SD = 0.71; M = 4.09, SD = 0.66). As for the metaphor level, design themes had no significant simple main effects from the level of cultural story-based natures (F (1,390) = 2.24, p = 0.135). However, as for cultural connotations, design themes had significant simple main effects on the metaphor level. Cognition of architecture (M = 3.64, SD = 0.79) was stronger than that of IP roles (M = 3.51, SD = 0.74)).
   (2) As for cultural and creative products of IP roles, the design level had significant simple main effects (F (2, 520) = 21.90, p < 0.001; F (2, 520) = 33.26, p < 0.001). As for cognition of cultural story-based natures, the symbolization level was weaker (M = 3.26, SD = 0.82) than that of the functionality level (M = 3.31, SD = 0.76). However, as for cognition of cultural connotations, the symbolization level (M = 3.58, SD = 0.80) was stronger than the functionality level (M = 3.97, SD = 0.66). As for architecture products, the design levels had significant simple main effects (F(2,520) = 87.61, p < 0.001; F(2,520) = 31.74, p < 0.001), while the functionality (M = 3.78, SD = 0.71; M = 4.09, SD = 0.66) was stronger than symbolization (M = 3.12, SD = 0.95; M = 4.02, SD = 0.62).

4.3   Local Characteristics

1. Design levels had significant effects on consumers' cognition of local characteristics ($F_{(2, 260)}$ = 66.764, p < .001). As shown in Scheffe method, consumers' cognitions towards the functionality level (M = 3.82, SD = .74) and the symbolization level (M = 3.65, SD = .73) were significantly stronger than that of the metaphor level (M = 3.28, SD = .89) (p < 0.001). Meanwhile, symbolization was significantly stronger than functionality. In other words, as for consumers' cognition of local characteristics in cultural and creative products, functionality was most easily cognized by consumers, with the symbolization-level design ranking the second place; in comparison with design levels of functionality and symbolization, the metaphor design level was the least perceivable for consumers.
2. Design themes and design levels had significant interactions as for consumers' cognition of local characteristics ($F_{(2, 260)}$ = 15.115, p < 0.001). As found in further simple main effect testing that: as for levels of symbolization, functionality and metaphor, design themes had significant simple main effects ($F_{(1, 390)}$ = 3.94, p = 0.020; $F_{(1,390)}$ = 67.97, p < 0.001; $F_{(1,390)}$ = 16.99, p < 0.001); cognition of architecture (M = 3.71, SD = 0.66; M = 4.09, SD = 0.62; M = 3.41, SD = 0.82) was stronger than that of IP roles (M = 3.58, SD = 0.80; M = 3.55, SD = 0.76; M = 3.14, SD = 0.94).

As for IP roles, design levels had significant simple main effects ($F_{(2, 520)}$ = 31.79, p < 0.001); cognition of the symbolization level (M = 3.58, SD = 0.80) was stronger than that of the functionality level (M = 3.55, SD = 0.76). As for architecture products, the design levels also had significant simple main effects ($F_{(2,520)}$ = 61.10, p < 0.001); cognition of functionality (M = 4.09, SD = 0.62) was stronger than that of symbolization (M = 3.71, SD = 0.66).

Table 1. Scheffe's post hoc test and Interaction Analysis of Design Attribute Cognition

Items	Scheffe's post hoc test	Interaction
Cultural historical nature	Symbolization (M = 3.94, SD = .67) > metaphor (M = 3.24, SD = .87) (p < 0.001)); Functionality (M = 3.93, SD = .69) > metaphor (p < 0.001)	p = 0.03
Local artistic nature	Functionality (M = 3.98, SD = .69) > metaphor (M = 3.77, SD = .74) (p < 0.01)); Symbolization (M = 3.95, SD = .69) > metaphor (p < 0.01)	p = .239
Cultural story-based nature	Functionality (M = 3.55, SD = .77) > symbolization (M = 3.19, SD = .89) > metaphor (M = 2.98, SD = .88)	p < 0.001
Cultural connotation	Functionality (M = 4.03, SD = .66) > symbolization (M = 3.80, SD = .75) > metaphor (M = 3.58, SD = .77)	p < 0.001
Local characteristic	Symbolization (M = 3.65, SD = .73) > functionality (M = 3.82, SD = .74) > metaphor (M = 3.28, SD = .89)	p < 0.001

5 Conclusion

With the regional culture of Nanjing as the example, the paper studies cultural and creative products based on design themes of architecture and IP mages so as to explore consumers' cognition towards five attributes including cultural historical nature, cultural story-based nature, local characteristics, cultural connotation and cultural artistic nature of two products. Results show:

1. Consumers' cognitions were different towards design attributes of regional cultural and creative products with different design themes. As for historical nature/artistic nature/connotation and local characteristics of cultural and creative products, consumers' cognition towards cultural and creative products of architecture was stronger than that of IP roles; however, as for cultural story-based natures, consumers' cognition towards cultural and creative products of architecture was weaker than that of IP roles. The cause may be that cultural and creative products of architecture mainly have concrete forms which can relatively directly convey attributes of design themes. As for cultural story-based natures, shaping and manifestation of IP roles can more easily cause consumers' emotional resonance, so as to help them understand story contents conveyed by cultural and creative products.

2. Consumers' cognitions are different towards design attributes of regional cultural and creative products of Nanjing based on different design levels. Research findings show that as for cognition of five attributes of two types of products, consumers' cognitions of design attributes on levels of functionality and symbolization were stronger than those of the metaphor level. In other words, attributes of cultural and creative products implied on the metaphor level were least perceivable by consumers.

3. Design themes and levels could influence the cognition of design attributes of regional cultural and creative products of Nanjing at the same time. Except for cultural artistic natures, as for historic nature/connotation/story-based nature and local characteristics of cultural and creative products, design themes and levels of cultural and creative products had interactions. Thus, through the rational combination of design themes and design levels, consumers can better cognize regional attributes of cultural and creative products.

The research can provide a reference for the design of regional cultural and creative products, help designers better know about consumers' cognition and prevent the occurrence of design deviations.

Acknowledgements. The research is sponsored by Qing Lan Project of Jiangsu Colleges and Universities and the 2018 Philosophy and Social Science Research Fund of Jiangsu Colleges and Universities (2018SJA2093).

References

1. Wu, T.-Y., Hsu, C.-H., Lin, R.: The study of Taiwan aboriginal culture on product design. In: Proceedings of Design Research Society International Conference Paper, vol. 238, pp. 377–394 (2004)
2. Liu, X., Xu, Q., Feng, X.: Creative cultural product and strategy of increment of value based upon cultural research. Hundred Sch. Arts **32**, 54–57 (2016)
3. UNESCO: Convention on the Protection and Promotion of the Diversity of Cultural Expressions (2005)
4. Lin, R.-T.: Transforming Taiwan aboriginal cultural features into modern product design: a case study of a cross-cultural product design model. Int. J. Des. **1**, 2 (2007). Chinese Institute of Design
5. Yi, J., Zhang, Z.: Construction of service platform for regional cultural creative product design. Packag. Eng. **39**, 108–114 (2018)
6. Zhi, J.: Analysis of product visual references influencing consumer cognition. Packag. Eng. **28**, 124–126 (2007)
7. Shang-shang, Z.H.U.: Study of regional cultural image in modern product design. Packag. Eng. **5**, 1 (2009)
8. Zhang, X.B.: Suggestions on the market positioning and marketing strategy of the palace museum. Forbid. City **1**, 168–181 (2016)
9. Niu, L.Q.: Museum "cultural and creative blue ocean". New Econ. Guide **3**, 25–29 (2015)
10. Zhu, Y.: 600-year-old Forbidden City is also "selling Moe" cultural and creative industry chain has not yet opened. Bus. Sch. **Z1**, 27–30 (2017)

The Soundomat

Astrid K. Graungaard, August E. Enghoff, Johanne L. Fogsgaard[✉],
Laura K. Schmidt, and Marc D. Hansen

Aalborg University, Rendsburggade 14, 9000 Aalborg, Denmark
Jfogsg18@student.aau.dk

Abstract. This paper will examine the interactive sound sculpture The Soundomat, constructed with the aim of making an engaging experience while challenging our perception of music.

The concept of music will be discussed through people's reaction, to an installation which is based on musique concrète. Furthermore, it will analyze and investigate where the project originated from, through methods of idea development, designing, coding and conceptualization. It will illustrate and describe what inspired the work, and the reasoning behind the choices that were made. The installation is playful in its design, and It has the intention to stir imagination, curiosity and provoke playfulness, while looking intriguing with its vibrant color scheme and 'turntable' element. Additionally, we will discuss and analyze the interaction between The Soundomat and the participants, through interviews, observations and the feedback received. It observes that people had two different ways of interaction. Either they picked the soundblocks based on the materials and the sounds they expected from them, or they worked in a more systematic manor and only added one soundblock at a time. There was no clear indicator, why some used one method over the other. Even though some of the participants were not aware of the concept musique concrète, they described the soundscape from The Soundomat in a way that corresponds with the definition of musique concrète. Lastly it will be analyzed, whether the project fulfills its intent, as well as its future work and improvements.

Keywords: Sound · Machine · Musique concréte · Design · Interaction · Creativity · Curiosity

1 Introduction

"Sound installations, for better or for worse, get us listening to the world" (Rogill 1989). Sound installations often use sounds from our everyday life, these sounds are usually not noticed, either they are ignored, or our brain filters it out as noise. Many of the sounds seem recognizable but are easily discarded as the noise of the world. What if we listened? This question has led us to the problem formulation:

> "How does people react and interact, either alone or together, with an installation that encourages and inspires the users, to experiment with different materials to create a soundscape from their own creativity and curiosity, and thereby challenges the users perception of music?"

© Springer Nature Switzerland AG 2020
C. Stephanidis et al. (Eds.): HCII 2020, CCIS 1294, pp. 375–381, 2020.
https://doi.org/10.1007/978-3-030-60703-6_48

We wanted to facilitate this investigation and exploration in an intriguing way that stirred the user's imagination, curiosity and provoked playfulness. To this purpose, we developed The Soundomat.

The Soundomat is an engaging sound installation that aims to explore the relation between sound, noise and music, based on the theory and concept of musique concrète introduced by Pierre Schaeffer in 1948. As he describes in an interview: "Musique concrète is music made of raw sounds: thunderstorms, steam-engines, waterfalls, steel foundries... The sounds are not produced by traditional acoustic musical instruments. They are captured on tape (originally, before tape, on disk) and manipulated to form sound-structures" (Hodgkinson 1987).

The Soundomat aims to experiment and investigate raw sounds, it allows the participants to investigate the properties, textures and sounds through 'soundblocks'. Soundblocks consists of raw materials, which are placed on Velcro strips around the artefact, they can then be placed on the turntable. Contact microphones pick up and enhance the sound of the different materials. Users are encouraged to create their own composition and soundscape, and through this process listen to the world anew.

During the exhibition at Aalborg University we gathered data, through interviews and observations, about the user's experience, their creative approach, and their perception of sound and Music. This will be analysed and discussed.

2 Method and Design

In this section we will account for the design process and discuss our choices in term of the design we chose to make an artefact as clear to understand and as user-friendly as possible. The process started with the idea of having a pickup bar with contact microphones, which would allow the participants to experiment with sound and music.

To expand on this idea and to find a systematic order to the ideas and the process we chose to work with mind mapping and concept mapping. Through both mapping-concepts it helped to expand our creative design thinking further and get even more ideas written down for discussion. Nick Pride puts it this way: "Drawing out everything that's in your mind gets rid of the ideas that you've used before that clutter your brain.

Get these down, know that they're out of your mind, then you can turn the page and get on to the new." (Pride, as cited in Ingeldew 2016). The team took the advice into consideration and worked with a-no-fear-process towards each other– it was crucial for the idea – and design process that all team members never left an idea unsaid and that everybody came over their fear of embarrassment: "Get over this fear of humiliation and always voice your wildest ideas" (Ingeldew 2016) - and so, we did.

We used an iterative design process, developing ideas before starting over with new concepts. While this design method was not planned, it did allow us to improve the important elements of the design through the multiple iterations. One aspect of the design which changed over time and in the end was dropped was the space around the pickup bar. We started of wanting to create a room and closing off the space by having it be a dome with the pickup bar built into it. Trough iterations this chanced to a half dome and a roof overhanging the turntable to still create a room and encompass the participant. In the end the roof was removed from the design altogether. This way the artifact could include more people both working together but also making it possible for them to observe and share the experience. By making the artifact including for the participants around it we discovered when the participants worked individually everybody else became spectators. The artifact became a stage for everybody to become an artist.

A key aspect of the artifact was to have it be intuitive and be user-friendly. To achieve this, we wanted to guide the user's eyes by using bright colors, to indicate where and how to interact with the artefact. The use of velcro helped make it clear to participants that the soundsblock were movable and where they should be moved to.

To draw the participant eyes to the rotating plate it was made in a different material than the rest of the artifact. We placed LED lights beneath the plate which would change colors slowly, this combined with the rotating plate made it the only moving part of the artifact. We also made the walls of the exterior structure narrow towards the top to again help guide the user's eyes up.

It was important for the artefact to be as inviting and eye-catching as possible. The bright colors, that were used to make the artefact intuitive, were not only useful for usability but is was also an excellent choice to make the artefact very eye-catching and intriguing.

Through an iterative design process and especially design thinking as a method we were able to create an artifact which challenged the participants perception sounds and music by facilitating an engaging and user-friendly experience. At the exhibition the team discovered that the participants of all ages and different musical backgrounds found it intuitive and entertaining.

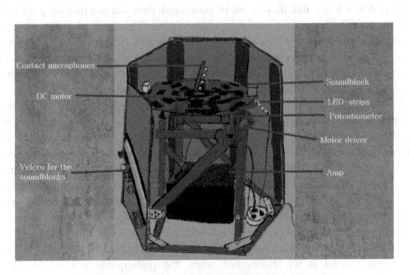

3   Analysis of Interaction

To collect data from the participants of The Soundomat we used the general interview guide approach; This gave us the possibility to interact with the participants in a relaxed though formal manner. As part of our data collection we talked with dozens of people at an exhibition and further interviewed 12 people. Additionally, we coupled this with observations of the participants interaction with the artifact.

We observed two main approaches to creating a soundscape. The first approach depended on the participants worked in a systematic fashion and here by placing the soundblocks on the artifact one at the time to gain knowledge about the individual sound of every soundblock or rotating it to find the most satisfying sound. One participant using this method stated as followed: "I am curious about which different sounds the materials could make but when you put all the soundblocks together, you have no idea, how it will sound"

The team discovered when the participants chose a soundblock, they got an expectation of which sound they also wanted to add to the soundscape. Somehow the participants who worked in a systematic manor also planned how the soundscape should sound through expectations to the soundblocks. When they chose a soundblock that lived up to their expectations, they then sought to discover a new sound which then led the way to a new plan and new expectations to the soundscape.

The other approach relied on people's expectations of the materials on the soundblocks. We observed multiple participants touching or tapping the soundblocks before placing them. Before testing whether this method would match with the sound produced. They would place several soundblocks before hearing the sound it makes, with a clear expectation of how it would sound. This despite none of them having experience with contact microphones. One user who mistook a soundblock with plastic for glass described their expectation as follows:

"Glass appealed to me, because I assumed it would have a high-pitched sound. I also listed to the leather which reminded me of a bass. So, I tried to choose sounds, based on where they might fit in the timbre."

The participants who used this method would often be surprised by the finished soundscape as it would not match their expectations. This forced them to experiment further, often still using their expectation to the material but now in tandem with their new knowledge of how the materials sounds through contact microphones. However, they would still change several soundblocks at a time making it difficult to distinguish the different sounds, this did not seem to hinder the participants from creating a soundscape they were satisfied with.

We see that participants using either method worked using their expectations but in very different ways. Perhaps this shows how people cannot help but use expectations as a tool for learning even when faced with an artifact which works in such a way, they have no prior experience with. There was no clear distinction between participants with high or low level of musical experience and which method they used when interacting with The Soundomat. It would be interesting to see if participants with experience making musique concrète would interact differently, but we were unable to arrange this.

"When ask whether or not they would classify the soundscapes as music the participants never gave a clear answer. They would start pondering the definition of music, arguing with themselves back and forth before concluding that it was music. Some gave the reasoning that because there was a rhythm it must be music. While another argued that the fact it was intentionally created made it music. A lot of participant stated while they did not necessarily enjoy it, they would classify it as music. It was clear that experimenting with The Soundomat made them question and reevaluate what they would normaly define as music."

Musique concrète has a clear process of creation. It helps define which music that is concrete and which music that is defined as regular music (According to Pierre Schaeffer). The participants that worked with The Soundomat worked in a way that corresponds with the process of creation dictated by Pierre Schaffer.

The participants who contributed to the interview were asked if they had heard of the concept 'musique concrète', of which they all answered 'no'. Further in the conversation the participants mentioned musical genres as 'stomp' and 'beatboxing' – these modern musical genres are good examples of what musique concrète is, even though the participants who mentioned it knew of musique concrète. Additionally, the participants compared The Soundomat to 'stomp' and 'beatboxing'. The interesting part in this assertion is that the participants did not know of musique concrète, but they managed to mention genres that is known as subgenres to musique concrète right after they interacted with The Soundomat. It that case we can derive a comparison of the participants between musique concrète and the The Soundomat, despite not knowing the concept.

At the exhibition we were able to observe participants interaction both working in groups and alone. Some felt frustrated working in groups, they felt it kept them from freely experimenting. While others felt working together made the experience better, these people would often stay longer to observe other people's soundscapes even after the people they had collaborated with had left. It was not possible based on our observations and interviews to come up with any hypothesis to why people felt differently.

4 Conclusion

We conclude that we succeeded in creating an installation that made its users think about their understanding of music by allowing them to make their own soundscape by experimenting with different materials and their creativity. They did this either by reflecting on their expectations to the sounds of different materials or by experimenting with limited expectations and working only by pure curiosity. Many of the participants were surprised by the sounds coming from the soundblocks, but this only contributed with more curiosity and experimentation.

Some of the participants chose to work by systematically placing a single or few soundblocks at the time and then adjusting each of them to get the exact rhythm they wanted. Others chose the soundblocks more randomly without putting a lot of thought into the process.

Most of the participants would describe their soundscapes as music, though often only after some contemplation and afterthoughts. They wondered about the definition of music and were often thinking about different definitions before they would conclude that they would describe their soundscapes as music.

The Soundomat both challenges and facilitates the creation of musique concrète. The installation has inspired and encouraged the participants to use creativity to discover sonic properties of different materials and experiment with these to challenge and question their perception of what they would define as music.

References

Hodgkinson, T.: An interview with Pierre Schaeffer – Pioneer of Musique Concréte. ReR Q. Mag. **2**(1) (1987)

Ingledew, J.: How to Have Great Ideas: A Guide to Creative Thinking. Laurence King Publishing, London, UK (2016)

Rogill, R.: Sound Sculpture: Turning into the world (1989). https://search.proquest.com/docview/398074795/abstract/745E18D5881D4959PQ/1?accountid=8144

Design of Form and Meaning of Traditional Culture in Virtual Space

Jingjing He[✉]

Shanghai University, Shanghai, China
yasminehjj@sina.com

Abstract. On the background of innovative concepts for the creation of cultural virtual spaces, the article discusses the fiction of form and meaning of traditional culture within virtual worlds. It argues that current digital forms in virtual worlds obscure and separate their cultural context. Moreover, commercially motivated design masks the separation of form and meaning, and the growing realism of virtual reality facilitated by technology is imperceptibly contributing to the intensification of this separation. This has a negative impact on the communication of traditional cultural values within virtual worlds. That is one of the problems between traditional culture, human, machine and virtual environment in modern society. Therefore, by speculating about the relationship and characteristics of the virtual form and the real meaning of digital culture, by means of the design of virtual narrative environments, citing the traditional cultural form and meaning as props, analyzing the relationship between designers and audiences, grounding our observations on design experiments and measurements of data, we can explore the new design ideas of virtual form and meaning of traditional cultural in the virtual environment.

Keywords: Digital traditional culture · Form · Meaning · Virtual reality · Virtual narrative environments

1 Introduction

Benjamin has already regarded the new technology as the principle and form of generating new meanings in the book "The Little History of Photography". "We can also get hints from the descriptions of the excitement that surrounded the introduction of stereoscopic mirrors in the 19th century" [1]. For the first time, the world was faithfully reproduced in another medium, and the image in the other medium was also controlled by the person who created them. Redesigning, disguising, tampering, and purposeful editing of meaning has become convenient and simple. These artistic meaning makers no longer have to depict the world of divine greatness with reverence, just like operating new inventions. Like the machine, the digital art is used to manipulate the form, and the artistic image is used to charm the eyes of the human being.

Project Source: "Speculation and Evidence: Theory and Teaching Mode of Intelligent Design for Product Combined with Augmented Reality" (No.: C19100, Shanghai University). Education Research Project, Shanghai Municipal Education Commission, 2019.

C. Stephanidis et al. (Eds.): HCII 2020, CCIS 1294, pp. 382–389, 2020.
https://doi.org/10.1007/978-3-030-60703-6_49

2 The Form and Meaning of Digital Culture

The reason why digital culture has a great impact on human life is that the human brain has the most complicated way of thinking. The digital culture only constantly satisfies and reflects the human thinking through more and more realistic avatars. And the most direct chemical effect on thinking is the visual form. Therefore, rather than saying that digital culture is affecting human life, it is better to say that it is constantly satisfying human thinking by using virtual visualizations. Is caffeine-free coffee a coffee? The coffee without caffeine masks the absence of caffeine (the real meaning) in the virtual form of coffee, and the caffeine separated by the technique obtains a false existence by means of the virtual form. It is not difficult to find that the marketing has realized this kind of discipline, that is the separation of form and meaning, and given satisfaction, and look forward to meeting the spiritual needs of customers.

3 Speculative Design of the Form and Meaning of Traditional Culture Fiction

As far as the virtual designer of traditional culture is concerned, speculate the problem of the digital expression of traditional cultural form and meaning is that it is fictitious and depends on the imagination of the designer. The aforementioned advertisement is a typical representative of the relationship between virtual form and meaning. The author uses the analogy analysis method to speculate on the fictional design of traditional culture. One of the methods is to pay attention to the props [2] of the virtual form in the advertisement (visual elements). According to the intimation of the props, the audience can understand and imagine the virtual world to which the fictional object belongs in accordance with their own ideas. Props must definitely support advertising appeals, with the characteristics of recognizability, readability, experience and synesthesia, but it destroys the possibility of the audience to create surprises and challenges from advertising, and the passive audience can only rely on the designer's imagination to get the meaning (this meaning is not necessarily true). In fact, rather than the audience wants to be the person in the advertisement or get the product in the advertisement, it is more concerned with whether the product can really achieve the expected effect of the advertisement. It is difficult for designers to achieve this. Advertising can only provide the concept of virtual form, but the audience wants more to get the result of real meaning. Traditional culture has a specific form and meaning, which is different from general business and consumer culture and has clear social attributes. Therefore, "I don't want to create, but I want to quote… More importantly, learn as much as possible about contemporary imagery that has long been ingrained in human consciousness" [3]. This is the main difference between the advertising props and the fiction of the traditional cultural virtual design.

4   The Design of Virtual Narrative Environments

In the virtual world of traditional culture, the designer's role is to create a virtual environment (environmental narrative story designer). The so-called environmental narrative is to design a story purposefully, or to make a certain story possible, just like a literary story intended to spread ideas and information, and the story is not like everyday life [4–7]. By citing the elements of traditional cultural forms and images, the designer designs story props that can trigger the audience's imaginative feedback. With the explicit (the form that interacts directly with the audience: images, words, objects, and face-to-face conversations, etc.) and implicit (comprehension of meaning in the virtual environment narrative experience: shape, scale, color, light, sound, material and human behavior, etc.) communication of the narrative environment, so that the audience can generate their own ideas and build a world shaped by their own ideals, values and beliefs, and form the cultural memory. "After the end of the creation, the designer loses control of the meaning in the virtual form" [8], and the person who enters the virtual environment enjoys the satisfaction of the virtual form for his fictional needs. Meanwhile also experience the meaning in the subconscious. When designers start to adopt the reference strategy, it may make the audience's understanding of the virtual object more difficult. It is necessary to encourage the audience to participate more actively in the design and change the state of passively accepting information. Spatial narrative can promote learning and interactive communication, support business, form community and cultural memory, develop and establish specific values in power relations and knowledge order [9–12]. Therefore, this virtual narrative environment of citing traditional culture is an effective place for new discourse practice and cultural innovation.

5   People in Virtual Reality Environment

In the virtual world, the accurate expression of traditional cultural form and meaning depends on the communication and feedback of people (including designers and audiences) in the virtual environment, and the audience needs to be involved in the design process, through "participate in design" [13], "active design" [14] and "Flexible System Design" [15, 16] to achieve the meaning communication and education process (social embodiment). "The designer is both a producer and a maintainer, and also a professional participant. It needs to remain open, willing to be weak, exposed to the public, accepting itself as a participant, not a leader in the design process" [17]. The audience should act as a producer and feedback participant. The traditional culture cited by the designer exists as a virtual prop, which also makes the experience more vivid, energetic and intense. As described by Professor Ezo Mancini, "the resilience system characterized by diversity, redundancy, feedback and continuous experimentation makes the vitality of the public space more visible and tangible" [18].

6   Empirical Analysis

The author's work "Shan Hai Jing: Shen You" (2017.12, Fig. 1) exhibited at the Liu Haisu Art Museum in Shanghai, "China Creation World Myth - Internet Art Exhibition", cites some of the stories of the traditional Chinese culture "Shan Hai Jing" and the image of the fish, using AR technology, the fictional design is presented in a surreal way, allowing the audience to follow the fish in the exhibition hall with electronic mobile device, to be able to participate in the greatest extent and to give feedback. The project does not contain any position or assertion of the designer, but only shows the audience some possibility. Because of the individual, each person will see or feel different virtual worlds, and the audience decides whether to agree.

Fig. 1. Shan Hai Jing: Shen You

The project design team conducted on-site audience sampling data survey and measurement analysis on the effect of the work, and effectively investigated the number of visitors is 921. First, to study whether individual characteristics will affect the audience preferences, including gender, age, occupation, education, the level of understanding of AR technology, etc. through descriptive statistical analysis (Table 1). The ratio of male to female is quite similar. The sample selection is more suitable to ensure the objectivity of the research results. According to data analysis of the audience in Shanghai, the audience is mainly concentrated in the 18 to 40 age group, followed by the 41 to 65 years old audience. Academic qualifications are mainly concentrated in junior college, undergraduate and below, accounting for more than 90%. Students, state agencies, enterprises, research and education units are the main groups, followed by manufacturing and transportation industries, and art workers account for the least. The proportion of people with a low level of understanding of AR technology is only a quarter. As far as China's current situation is concerned, people generally have a high degree of interest in the digital display form of traditional culture. The influence of age, education, occupation and other factors is low, but the familiarity with AR technology is not high, indicating that the rate of the education of related knowledge is low. Thus, the introduction of appropriate education and training related technologies in the above industry applications, will improve the efficiency of the work. At the same time, the public is also looking forward to the virtual form of traditional culture, and it is expected to increase their social experience and cultural quality.

Table 1. Statistics of individual characteristics of the audience.

Audience basic information		Proportion	Audience basic information		Proportion
Gender	Male	453	Occupation	Student	31.16%
	Female	468		State Agencies, Enterprises, Research and Education Units	24.1%
Age	Under 18	17.15%		Private Enterprise	8.36%
	18–40	38.98%		Digital Information Related Professional Technical and Service	12.7%
	41–65	27.58%		Manufacturing and Transportation	16.07%
	Above 65	16.29%		Artistic or Designer	3.69%
Education	High school or Below	40.07%		Others	3.91%
	College and Undergraduate	53.2%	Familiarity with AR	Know well	25.2%
	Master Degree or Above	6.73%		Do not know much	63.95%
				Hardly Know	10.86%

Second, the individual psychological factors are the motivation for the formation of viewers' preferences. The author measures the three dimensions of emotion, cognition and intention of the work, and confirms these factors through reliability analysis and factor analysis. Among them, emotional factors include satisfaction, positive and negative effects of the work, and feedback on the use of equipment (Table 2). The survey results show that the audience is more satisfied with the work, the proportion of positive affecting factors is balanced (M2—M6), the M3 and M4 indexes are higher, and M2 and M5 are second. This shows that this work has a positive impact on the audience with the design of virtual narrative environment story, guiding the audience to participate in interactive communication, feedback and so on.

Cognitive factors include popularity, evaluation, and image cognition. For cognitive factors analysis, the author selected the more popular virtual design works on the

Table 2. Descriptive analysis of the individual emotional factors of the audience.

Measurement dimension	Measurement item	Audience basic information	Proportion	Serial no.
Emotion factor	Satisfaction	35.32% very satisfied; 43.48% satisfied; 16.69% general; 2.68% not satisfied; 1.83% extremely dissatisfied		M1
	Positive Effect	The content design is novel and interesting, helping to understand traditional culture and stimulate the fun of learning new knowledge	39.97%	M2
		Can generate more interaction with others (friends, strangers, family, etc.)	50.43%	M3
		Open up the horizon and be attracted by the application of new technologies	52.5%	M4
		More interesting than traditional forms of presentation	41.78%	M5
		Protect exhibits better and avoid damage	30.09%	M6
	Negative Effect	Lack of aesthetics of the exhibit itself	38.61%	M7
		Just a new technology show, content design is not attractive enough	40.68%	M8
		There are too many people in the pavilion, the order of the visit is chaotic, affecting the experience	37.15%	M9
	Equipment Use	The exhibition equipment is easy to operate and convenient	22.78%	M10
		Dissatisfied with the way that user needs to carry electronic mobile devices	49.7%	M11
		Long-term use will be slightly dizzy	38.37%	M12

market, such as IKEA "Home Guide", Tokyo "Sunshine Aquarium App", AR real scene selection color "Yocli", Pokemon "Pokemon Go", Dinosaur APP "AR Dino-pank", AR scale tool "Aug Measure", the audience satisfied with IKEA "home guide" satisfaction accounted for 47.38%, this work accounted for 43.73%, ranked second. In terms of image recognition, we have listed virtual works of digital traditional culture on the market. The results of various age groups show that a small number of understandable indexes are high, and most of them are understandable. Among them, more than 63% of the audience under the age of 18 and over 65 believe that only a small number of people understand the meaning of the work.

88.31% of the audience expressed their willingness to participate in the experience, participate in content design, provide design related materials, feedback and other intent. They most interested in the AR application of the virtual restoration of the real face of the exhibit, the resurrection of the exhibit and interaction with it, and the AR navigation in the hall. Most of the audience expressed satisfaction and expectation for this kind of cultural education display and communication form of AR exhibition hall or AR classroom. Especially the group over 65 years old think that digital classroom is very helpful to understand traditional culture or learning knowledge.

Finally, the author interviewed dozens of experts and scholars in the art design profession. It is understood that most traditional culture and art workers believe that the current artistic aspects of most virtual works are quite different from the original works. Most of them are only the display of new technologies, lack the design of connotation and depth of cultural communication, and even the misunderstanding of the audience, which remains to be seen. Therefore, the development of traditional culture needs to be strengthened in the virtual narrative, highlighting the attraction of culture.

7 Conclusion

The currently existing cultural virtual design works on the market are mainly concentrated in specific places such as museums, exhibition halls, tourist attractions, etc. The design content is still set at the designer's unilateral information transfer level, and the audience's design engagement and feedback rate are low. The author seems that the cultivation of innovative thinking about narrative virtual environment and the citing imagination of traditional cultural fictional design is the primary problem at present, and it is necessary to pay attention to the social nature of fictional culture. "Although design speculation has always existed (such as auto show, future vision, high fashion show, etc.)" [19]. In the face of domestic cultural inheritance and development issues, designers should not only create a virtual environment. At the same time of commercial design, they should face more social goals and exert more social imagination to satisfy the public and not only consumers' demands. You can try to solve both problems at the same time [20].

References

1. Gang, L., Wei, G.: Visual Culture Reader, pp. 203, 206. Guangxi Normal University Press, Guilin (2003)
2. Dunne, A., Fiona, Li, Z.: Speculative: Design, Fiction and Social Dreams. (Dunne, A., Raby, F.: Speculative Everything – Design, Fiction, and Social Dreaming. The MIT Press (2013)), p. 70. Jiangsu Phoenix Fine Arts Publishing House (2017)
3. Stuart Candy. The Child Who Praises Humanity, The Sceptical Futuryst Blog, 12 April 2008. http://futuryst.blogspot.com/2008/04/in-praise-of-children-of-men.html

4. Aristotle, translated by H.S. Butcher. Poetics. Hill and Wang, New York (1989)
5. Bal, M.: Narratology, Introduction to the Theory of Narrative. University of Toronto Press, Toronto (1997)
6. Kermode, F.: The Art of Telling, Essays on Fiction. Harvard University Press, Cambridge (1978)
7. Porter Abbott, H.: The Cambridge Introduction to Narrative. Cambridge University Press, Cambridge (2008)
8. He, J.: Digital art space in the digital age. Art Des. (Theory) (286), 86–88 (2014)
9. Austin, T.: Enhancing Social Cohesion through the Design of Narrative Environments in the Pubic Realm. Open Your Space: Design Intervention for Urban Resilience, p. 183. Tongji University Press, September 2017
10. Foucault, M.: The Order of Things. Tavistock Publication, London (1970)
11. Hooper Greenhill, E.: Museums and the Shaping of Knowledge. Routledge, London (1992)
12. Lefebvre, H.: The Production of Space. Blackwell Publishers, Oxford (1991)
13. Ni, Y., Zhu, M.: Open Your Space: Design Intervention for Urban Resilience. Tongji University Press, September 2017
14. Fang, X.: On Active Design, Decoration, no. 267. Tsinghua University Press, July 2015
15. Gunderson, L.H., Holling, C.S. (eds.): Panarchy: Understanding Transformations in Systems of Humans and Nature. Island Press, Washington DC (2002)
16. Scheffer, M., Carpenter, S., Foley, J.A., Folke, C., Walker, B.: Catastrophic shifts in ecosystems. Nature **413**, 591–596 (2001)
17. Williams, D., Cuoco, R.: Co-creating a city spectacle: fashion as facilitator of social ties and forms. CoR website (2016)
18. Manzini, E., Till, J. (eds.): Cultures of Resilience: Ideas. Hato Press, London (2015)
19. Dunne, A., Raby, F.: Speculative Everything – Design, Fiction, and Social Dreaming. The MIT Press, Cambridge (2013)
20. Clark, S.R.L.: The Future of Philosophy, p. 17. Peter Lang, Frank furt am Main (2011)

The Chladni Wall

Anca-Simona Horvath[1]([☒])[iD] and Viola Rühse[2][iD]

[1] Research Laboratory for Art and Technology, Aalborg University,
Rendsburggade 14, 6223 9000 Aalborg, Denmark
ancah@hum.aau.dk
[2] Department for Images Science, Danube University Krems,
Dr.-Karl-Dorrek-Straße 30, 3500 Krems, Austria
viola.ruehse@donau-uni.ac.at,
https://vbn.aau.dk/da/persons/143403
https://www.donau-uni.ac.at/de/universitaet/organisation/
mitarbeiterinnen/person/4295238221

Abstract. This article describes a practice based artistic investigation which produced a participatory installation consisting of sculptural objects informed by sound vibration patterns. The installation, called the "Chladni Wall", brings together Chladni bricks. These are based on analogue 2D Chladni patterns made with granular material scattered on a plate and activated by sound vibrations. One or more Chladni patterns are transformed into 3D sculptures. Four areas where Chladni pattern informed 3D objects could be applied further are identified. Namely, for (1) educational curricula which integrate teaching acoustics, 3D modelling and digital fabrication, (2) for designing objects with special acoustic properties, (3) as help in voice training and with speech impediments and finally (4) for providing sonic experiences to the hearing impaired.

Keywords: Computational design · Digital fabrication · Visualization of sound · Form-finding · Chladni patterns

1 Introduction

1.1 Context: Visualisation of Sound Waves Through History

One significant characteristic of sound is its transitoriness, hence there have been several visualization attempts in the past. These visualizations are connected to the research of sound waves that has a longer history. The first beginnings can be dated back to the Renaissance. Leonardo mentioned in his notebooks that "when a table is struck in different places the dust that is upon it is reduced to various shapes of mounds and tiny hillocks." [1] Afterwards Galileo Galilei described marks related to sound vibrations in "Dialogues Concerning Two New Sciences" (1632):

Aalborg University.

"As I was scraping a brass plate with a sharp iron chisel in order to remove some spots from it and was running the chisel rather rapidly over it, I once or twice, during many strokes, heard the plate emit a rather strong and clear whistling sound: on looking at the plate more carefully, I noticed a long row of fine streaks parallel and equidistant from one another." [2]

The English scientist Robert Hooke (1635–1703) observed nodal patterns in association with the vibrations of a glass plate with flour caused by a violin bow on July 8, 1680 [3]. In Germany, Ernst Chladni (1756–1827) repeated and developed Hooke's experiment further. He scattered sand over a thin metal plate and by striking a violin bow against the plate noticed the sand grain accumulating in certain areas. He perfected his method and was able to create different patterns published in "Entdeckungen über die Theorie des Klanges [Discoveries in the theory of sound] (1827) [4] for the first time and later in his famous book "Die Akustik [Acoustics]" (1802) [5]. He tried to develop mathematical formulas and his public demonstrations of the experiment became very popular. The patterns were admired by contemporaries such as Johann Wolfgang von Goethe [6].

Physicists such as Michael Faraday and Lord Rayleigh developed Chladni's results further in the 19th and early 20th centuries [7]. In addition, singers such as Margaret Watts-Hughes and vocal therapists such as Holbrook Curtis began to experiment with them [8,9]. Hans Jenny published a widely received book on his experiments inspired by Chladni patterns [10] and introduced the term 'Cymatics' to describe the study of visible sound vibration.

Most artistic explorations of Chladni patterns and cymatics today are conducted, unsurprisingly, by sound artists and musicians, and come in the form of projections or holograms. The work of musician and sound artist Nigel Stanford 'CYMATICS: Science Vs. Music' is notable in showing sound vibration patterns in various mediums [11]. The number of other artistic applications and research experiments where sound is visualized through real objects derived from sound informed 3D models is smaller. These projects tend to take advantage of technological advances in computational design and digital fabrication and they fit within a strand of art and technology which explores (or simply exposes) scientific phenomena.

German researchers Skrodzki et al. describe a method for the digital production of 3D models based on the mathematical equations of Chladni patterns and present several rendered images [12]. Architects V. Yücel and İ. Yıldan describe a software application which visualizes Chladni patterns based on mathematical functions. The application allows users to create their patterns by playing with parameters such as frequency and amplitude and to export images. Derived from one image, a fabrication method using CNC milling is presented. The authors suggest that this strain of research can have possible applications in sectors such as architecture, product design, or interior design [13]. In 'Spatial Cymatics', L. M. Tseng and J. H. Hou further investigate the physical production of Chladni pattern informed 3D objects. The authors describe a setup they design to create Chladni patterns using sounds controlled through a script. These patterns are then digitised and four algorithms are compared to process the images. Finally, they present a 3D printed piece based on processing images of Chladni patterns [14]. Dutch designer Ricky van Broekhoven used Chladni patterns to informs the shape of the "Soundshape Speaker" which was exhibited during the Dutch Design Week 2013 [15].

There are aspects that are still under-explored in the current state of the art of Chladni pattern informed production of physical artefacts. Effective 3D modelling methods that are fabrication-ready need more investigation. Only a few workflows for going to patterns to 3D models have been reported. Experiences of artists and designers working across design spaces (sound, 3D modelling, fabrication) are yet to be analyzed [16]. Participatory works that involve audiences in developing sculptural pieces from sound vibration patterns can be investigated in more detail.

The Chladni Wall was used as a medium for art-based action research [17] on making invisible sounds tangible through an artifact. More specifically, by thinking through making, and in a participatory setup, it was asked: what possible applications can come from the process of taking a sensory-somatic experience (of creating a Chladni pattern) to a technologically mediated representation (an index, or symbol) of it. From sound to pattern to virtual 3D shape and afterward to fabricated sculpture. A preliminary analysis and reflections upon areas of possible applications are presented in this paper.

2   Method

In this section, the workflow of producing the Chladni Wall is described. 16 participants were involved and 17 bricks sculptural Chladni bricks were created. This process was framed as a two-week workshop with Art and Technology students and as part of a course meant at introducing 3D modelling and digital fabrication. During this workshop, the artistic potential of working with 2D Chladni patterns was enlarged by taking advantage of current 3D modeling and fabrication technologies.

In order to understand where sound-informed fabricated shapes can find their applications, this process of art-based action research was observed and reflected upon. Additionally, participants completed a survey after the completion of the artefact. Two main aspects were interrogated in detail:

1. knowledge about sound, the physicality of sound, and relationship to own voice
2. their feelings during the creative exploration.

2.1   Workflow of Producing the Chladni Wall

The shape of the Chladni Wall was pre-designed and divided into bricks. Each of the 16 participants was asked to create one or more bricks. The requirements were to use 2D Chladni patterns to inform the 3D design of the brick, to use laser cutting for production, to use the same wood material, and to maintain the outside shell of each brick so that the wall can be assembled and exhibited.

A simple setup made up from a vibration generator triggering a small rectangular metal plate and connected to a microphone was introduced to participants. Scattering salt or sugar on the rectangular plate and playing sounds into the microphone allowed participants to visualize sounds through Chladni patterns. Higher frequencies would create more complex patterns, while lower frequencies would result in simpler ones. The steps in the production process were:

1. to create Chladni patterns using the setup.
2. to digitize these patters
3. to place the patterns in a 3D modelling software
4. to create a 3d model informed by the patterns - here participants had full explorative freedom
5. to place this 3d model inside the 3d model of the pre-assigned brick and to merge these two
6. to slice the object for fabrication using laser cutting
7. to fabricate the layers and glue them together to form a Chladni brick
8. to assemble the Chladni bricks in a wall.

3 Results

This section presents the final result of the Chladni wall together with a preliminary analysis of how participants explored the different design spaces - namely that of producing sounds, that of creating 2D patterns through sound vibration, the 3D environment and the fabricated objects.

The layered wooden bricks were informed by 1, 2 or 3 Chladni patterns and most of the pieces had symmetry on one or more axes (see Fig. 1). In general, the visual grammars are organic and the initial patterns are vaguely recognizable.

3.1 Producing Sounds and Relationship with Own Voices

There were no binding instructions on how to use the analogue Chladni setup for the participants. Most of them preferred to create sounds using instruments such as frequency generation phone apps or sound or music pieces played from their laptops. Engaging with their own voices would have been interesting to observe, but most seemed too shy to do so. The survey questions which investigated how they feel about their own voices showed that the majority have a negative attitude to this (10 out of 16). 5 Participants declare that they "cannot stand their own voice." and 4 feel they do not control their voice in daily life. One reports having no consciousness of the voice "I am not listening to my own voice".

Only one-third of participants have a very good/positive attitude towards their own voice: one says they have the feeling that their own voice has 'magical powers' and two report they enjoy hearing their own voice.

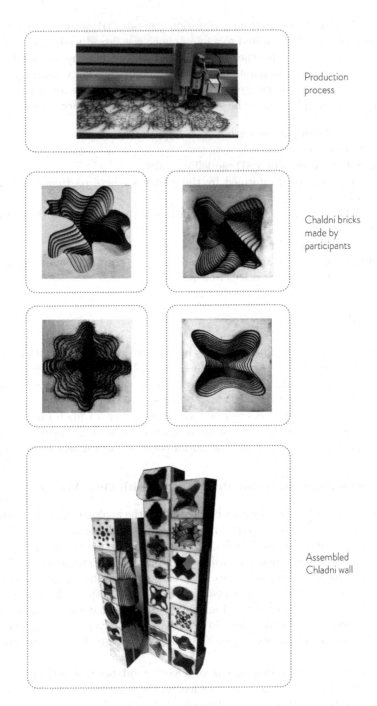

Production
process

Chaldni bricks
made by
participants

Assembled
Chladni wall

Fig. 1. The production process, a selection of Chladni bricks, and the assembled Chladni Wall

3.2 Preliminary Reflections on the Process of Producing Chladni Pattern-Inspired Objects for Digital Fabrication

When asked to talk about their experiences of making sounds, Chladni patterns, 3D models, and sculptural objects, 12 participants reported having a deep attachment to the brick and their 3D models. Interesting remarks were made about the sizes of the design spaces which were explored: 4 participants reported that the Chladni patterns were not "unique enough" or that "frequencies cannot be owned". By contrast, the 3D models and the fabricated objects were considered as "their own works". This can be because there is a limited number of significantly different Chladni patterns which can be created on a plate of a certain size, as opposed to a considerably larger array of 3D models to explore. The physical shape was seen as a visual "memory" of the ephemeral sounds. In general, the project was also seen as a good learning example for 3D modelling.

4   Discussion and Conclusion

This paper presented a participatory sculptural artifact which brought together sound experimentation, 3D modelling, and digital fabrication. By thinking through making and reflecting along the creative process [17], possible applications of Chladni pattern informed geometries are identified. In general, 3D Chladni patterns still have under-explored potential for application in various fields.

The most obvious application is to use them in educational setups which introduce 3D modelling and digital fabrication together with sound exploration. This can be done at different levels. The use of 3D Chladni visualisations as an educational tool for teaching acoustics to school children is generally accepted and apps available for free have been developed for it [20]. Merging the teaching of acoustics with that of 3D modelling and digital fabrication can be a way to enhance classroom engagement with science but also allow creative freedom. A possible next step to such explorations is the development of objects with special acoustic properties, given that Chladni patterns are used to inform the design of string musical instruments.

Given the relatively large number of participants who have negative feelings about their own voices, using Chladni patterns to encourage vocal somatic experimentation can also prove interesting. This method could then also be used as practice training for speech impediments. Cymatic visualisations have been used as a therapeutic tool that improves sensory impaired patients such as people with autism, but so far, only 2D Chladni images have been tested in this field [18,19].

3D models derived from Chladni patterns could find applications for speech development of the hearing impaired as a supplement to conventional computer-based training methods for instance after cochlear implantation. A workshop similar to the one used to produce the Chladni Wall installation would be also relevant for initiatives such as 'CymaSpace' in Portland who focus on offering cymatic experiences, especially for the deaf and hearing-impaired [21].

References

1. da Vinci, L.: Notebooks of Leonardo da Vinci, Arranged, Rendered into English and Introduced by Edward McCurdy, p. 542. Reynal and Hitchcock, New York (1939)
2. Galilei, G.: Dialogues Concerning Two New Sciences (1632), p. 101. Macmillan Co., New York (1914)
3. Hooke, R.: The Diary of Robert Hooke 1672–80. Taylor & Francis, London (1935). p. 448 (entry of July 8, 1960)
4. Chladni, E.F.F.: Entdeckungen über die Theorie des Klanges. Weidmanns Erben und Reich, Leipzig (1787)
5. Chladni, E.F.F.: Die Akustik. Breitkopf und Härtel, Leipzig (1802)
6. de la Motte-Haber, H.: Musik und Licht - Zeitfarben. In: Böhme, G., Olschanski, R. (eds.) Licht und Zeit, p. 87. Wilhelm Fink Verlag, Munich (2004)
7. Ullmann, D.: Chladni und die Entwicklung der Akustik von 1750–1860. Birkhäuser, Basel (1996). p. 11 and p. 25 f
8. Watts-Hughes, M.: Eidophone. Christian Herald, London (1904)
9. Curtis, H.: The Tonograph. Sci. Am. **76**(33), 345–346 (1897)
10. Jenny, H.: Kymatik. Wellen und Schwingungen mit ihrer Struktur und Dynamik/Cymatics. The structure and dynamics of waves and vibrations. Basilius Presse, Basel (1967)
11. Stanford, N.: CYMATICS: Science Vs. Music, music video (2014)
12. Skrodzki, M., Reitebuch, U., Polthier, K.: Chladni Figures Revisited: A Peek Into The Third Dimension. In: Proceedings on Bridges 2016: Mathematics, Music, Art, Architecture, Education, Culture, pp. 481–484. Tesselations Publishing, Phoenix (2016), p. 481
13. Yücel, V., Yildan, İ.: Form follows algorithm: differentiation of chladni patterns through mathematical functions in processing. In: Proceedings on XX Generative Art Conference, GA (2017). https://www.generativeart.com/. Accessed 20 Mar 2020
14. Tseng, L.M., Hou, J.H.: Spatial Cymatics, Conference Paper presented at ArtsIT 2019–8th EAI International Conference: ArtsIT, Interactivity and Game Creation, November 6–8. Aalborg, Denmark (2019)
15. Madlener, A.: Soundshapes by Ricky van Broekhoven, frameweb Homepage, 16 November 2013. https://www.frameweb.com/news/soundshapes-by-ricky-van-broekhoven. Accessed 15 Mar 2020
16. Horvath, A. S., Rühse, V.: Chladni Patterns gone 3D: computational design and digital fabrication methods for producing sound-informed geometries. In: AMPS2020 Canterbury: Connections: Exploring Heritage, Architecture, Cities, Art, Media (2020). https://tinyurl.com/y7u2djm3. Accessed 18 June 2020
17. Coghlan, D., Brydon-Miller, M.: The SAGE Encyclopedia of Action Research (Vols. 1–2). SAGE Publications Ltd., London (2014). https://doi.org/10.4135/9781446294406
18. CymaScope Homepage. http://www.cymascope.com. Accessed 24 May 2020
19. McGowan, J. et al.: CymaSense: a novel audio-visual therapeutic tool for people on the autism spectrum. In: ASSETS 2017: Proceedings of the 19th International ACM SIGACCESS Conference on Computers and Accessibility, pp. 62–71. Association for Computing Machinery, New York (2017)

20. "Resonant Chladni patterns" app. Technical University Munich website, Application Library of the Chair of Vibroacoustics of Vehicles and Machines. https://tinyurl.com/ybwd7vp9. Accessed 15 May 2020

21. CymaSpace, 5040 SE Milwaukie Ave, Portland OR 97202, USA. https://www.cymaspace.org/. Accessed 15 May 2020

A Study on Framework Development and Augmented Reality Technological Factors Consumers' Evaluation for Cultural and Creative Products

Yu-Ju Lin[(⊠)]

Department of Commercial Design and Management, National Taipei University of Business, Taoyuan 32462, Taiwan
naralin@ntub.edu.tw

Abstract. Following the rapid development of high-technology industries, digital applications have been applied in various technologies, bringing people a whole new daily living experience. Interactive technology has led to breakthrough innovations. Application of augmented reality (AR), in addition to people's approaches to interact with the physical world, has changed industry owners' methods in designing products. This reveals the criticality of designing products with AR technology and new forms of interactions. This study investigated the current status regarding the cultural and creative products in consumer markets and the effectiveness of incorporating AR technology into cultural and creative product design courses. Data were analyzed to clarify said effectiveness and confirm the feasibility of AR technology in cultural and creative product design. A survey was performed on the cultural and creative products in the National Palace Museum located in Taipei and those designed by university students majoring in design to explore the effect of AR technology employed in cultural and creative product design on consumers' review of and purchase intentions for the products. The following conclusion was reached: (1) The scale constructed to evaluate the cultural and creative products designed using AR technology was feasible. (2) AR technology positively affected participants' review of and purchase intentions for cultural and creative products. (3) The products created by students according to the teaching method employed exhibited business value of high interactivity. Future cultural and creative product design courses can employ AR technology in their principles and practices in training innovative talents that satisfy the market demand. The design principles developed thereof can also serve as a reference for industry owners in designing cultural and creative products.

Keywords: Cultural and creative product design · Augmented reality (AR) · Evaluation · Purchase intention

© Springer Nature Switzerland AG 2020
C. Stephanidis et al. (Eds.): HCII 2020, CCIS 1294, pp. 398–405, 2020.
https://doi.org/10.1007/978-3-030-60703-6_51

1   Introduction

With evolutions in society and technology, developments in interactive and experiential technology have enhanced teaching and learning; people are increasingly learning in a virtual rather than physical space. Experiential technology emphasizes interactivity in thee connections and communications hat users have with a product or service; such technology stimulates all our senses and makes user participation more fun and meaningful. Digital technology is capable of disseminating large quantities of information; is versatile, being capable of applications in a variety of fields; is time-sensitive and interactive; is capable of furnishing immersive visual stimuli; and is capable of being applied in different forms. Excellent interactive design is key to retaining users of this technology and providing them with an immersive experience.

2   Literature Review

2.1   Cultural and Creative Products in the Age of Interactive Experience

Interactive developments have made contact more sensory, intimate, and integrated. Therefore, the application of interactive digital technology has become an inevitable trend in design and creation. Cultural and creative product designs integrate art, culture, and science. Such designs convey various ideas and facilitate cultural contexts in products not related to their functions and in doing so, redefine lifestyles. Therefore, products must feature technological and aesthetic innovation to induce an emotional experience in customers, thus facilitating customer retention [1]. To make homogeneous cultural and creative products more competitive in the market, in addition to making them more functional and aesthetically pleasing, the delivery and construction of consumer knowledge must also be improved. Such improvement in knowledge helps users better learn about and interact with these products; users can also better appreciate the intangible meanings embedded in the products and better identify with them, similar to how a museum's visitors feel toward the exhibits.

2.2   Applying Augmented Reality (AR) and Related Models in Cultural and Creative Products

Aauma, AR affords users a deeper interaction with the real world and the opportunity to gain experiences that cannot be otherwise acquired; AR brings users closer to their everyday environment and improves their use experience [2]. Therefore, cultural and creative product designers should consider the user's physical sensations and psychological state. The integration of AR into cultural and creative product designs enables users to improve data acquisition methods, visualize data, and optimize product performance using real-time data; in doing so, users can better interact with and control the product [3–6].

2.3   Effect of AR Integration in Cultural and Creative Products on Consumer Preferences and Purchase Intention

Witmer, Jerome and Singer organized the factors influencing sense of presence into four dimensions: involvement, sensory realism, adaptation/immersion, and interface quality. Involvement refers to how natural interactions and experiences are in a virtual environment; an user who becomes involved has a firm control of their activities within the environment and is focused on their experience in the environment [7]. With the recent emergence of digital technology and consumer awareness, the development of new products must involve encouraging consumer purchases through the stimulation of the consumer's senses [8, 9].

3   Research Methods

3.1   Participant Selection and Testing

This study selected 10 samples, five of which were commercial works and the other five were student works; the student works were assignments in a cultural and creative product design course taught by the researcher. The commercial works were those on sale in the shop of the National Palace Museum. A commercial work was chosen if it satisfied all of the following conditions: (1) it is a bestselling product during the research period, (2) its design is based on a collection in the museum, and (3) it is an article for daily use. As for student works, a work was chosen if it satisfied all of the following conditions: (1) it is an exceptional works incorporating AR technology, (2) its design is based on one or more collections in the National Palace Museum, and (3) it serves an everyday function (Fig. 1).

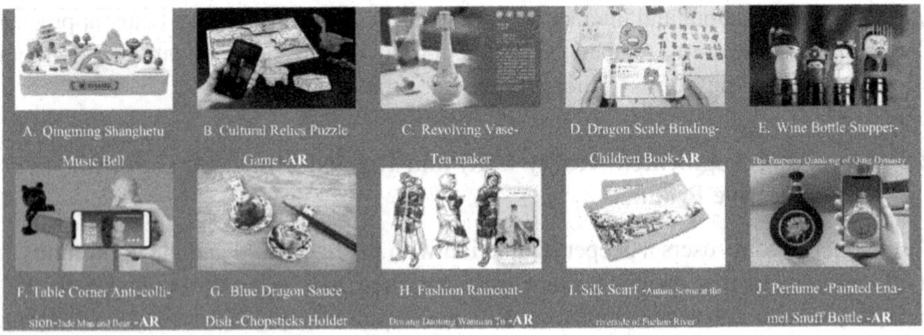

Fig. 1. Research object

3.2   Research Instruments

The dimensions and evaluation in the questionnaire's scale measured the sensory, emotional, cognitive, behavioral, and relational aspects of experiential cultural and creative product designs as well as consumer purchase intention and preference. The questionnaire comprised seven dimensions, encompassing 21 items. To verify the feasibility of the questionnaire, a confirmatory factor analysis (CFA) was performed after the survey was complete.

3.3 Experiment Design

Creative values are determined by how consumers feel toward products. Before consumers actually use or view a specific product, they cannot accurately determine the creative values the product affords them. Therefore, experiential marketing must emphasize creating various modes of experience for consumers. In the present study, a total of 127 participants, 42 of whom were male and 85 were female, were selected through purposive sampling. Most of the participants were tourists with a basic understanding of the given historical culture and relics, and tourists are the primary consumers in the cultural and creative product market. The participants were shown the sampled creative works, namely the products sold in the National Palace Museum Shop and students' works created with AR technology.

4 Research Results and Discussion

4.1 Confirmatory Factor Analysis

The standardized factor loadings (SFLs) for the sensory, emotional, cognitive, behavioral, and relational dimensions of cultural and creative products were 0.39–0.94, 0.50–0.75, 0.56–0.69, 0.82–0.90, and 0.42–0.62, respectively; the SFL for purchase intention was 0.70–0.91. The estimated SFLs of all the items were >0.6, indicating that the scale satisfied the requisite standards. Furthermore, the convergent reliability and average variance extracted (AVE) of the scale were 0.56–0.85. This indicated that the research model had acceptable internal consistency. According to the diagonal values, the square roots of the AVEs of the dimensions ranged between 0.55 and 0.86, larger than the correlation coefficient of each dimension and constituting $\geq 75\%$ of the overall comparative values. Therefore, the discriminant validity of the research model was satisfactory (Tables 1 and 2).

4.2 Structural Model Analysis and Research Hypothesis Verification

Nearly all the indices in the model attained or were close to the level of acceptance, indicating a satisfactory fit between the structural model and the theoretical framework with the empirical data (Table 3).

According to the model path analysis results, the factors related to cultural and creative product designs were critical; experiential design, consumer preferences, and consumer purchase intention mutually influenced each other. As revealed in the structural equation model, the pleasure factors under the experiential design dimension significantly influenced consumer preferences, but none of the hypotheses related to the other factors were supported. Accordingly, all the factors pertinent to emotional designs should be integrated to increase purchase intention and make consumer preferences

Table 1. Table of CFA results for the research model

	Variable	M	SD	SK	KU	SFL(t)	SMC	EV	CR	AVE
Experiential Design of Cultural and Creative Product	S. Sense	**5.69**							**0.80**	**0.48**
	S1 This product is fashionable	5.62	1.01	−0.29	−0.57	0.39 (11.37)	0.11	0.91		
	S2 This product has good style and proportions	5.84	0.89	−0.46	−0.19	0.70 (26.12)	0.21	0.62		
	S3 The colors are consistent with the overall style of the product	5.63	0.79	−0.00	−0.21	0.40 (13.50)	0.15	0.53		
	S4 This product features outstanding details in design	5.70	0.91	−0.24	−0.63	0.84 (34.61)	0.71	0.25		
	S5 This product is interactive	5.68	0.95	−0.23	−0.74	0.94 (39.74)	0.88	0.11		
	Mardia	7.29						**P**		

(P + 2) = 5 × 7 = 35F. Feel5.710.690.43F1 This product brings me a sense of happiness5.780.94−0.34−0.740.50 (15.99)0.250.65F2 This product takes me to a story context5.620.98−0.41−0.370.75 (21.26)0.560.42F3 This product is fun5.730.87−0.44 −0.170.70 (20.40)0.490.05Mardia0.06P(P + 2) = 3 × 5 = 15T. Think5.900.700.37T1 This product is practical5.930.79−0.450.050.69 (21.55)0.470.33T2 This product is novel6.030.79 −0.690.740.56 (17.64)0.310.43T3 This product is original and innovative5.940.76 −0.470.480.56 (17.51)0.310.40T4 This product has a strong association with a cultural relic5.710.97−0.24−0.810.60 (19.02)0.360.60Mardia3.23P(P + 2) = 4 × 6 = 24A. Act5.880.850.74A1 I intend to share this product5.880.91−0.38−0.550.90 (22.83)0.000.17A2 I intend to learn more about the cultural relic and its history5.880.85−0.32−0.240.82 (22.83) 0.000.23Mardia3.00P(P + 2) = 2 × 4 = 8R. Relate5.780.560.30R1 This product is unique5.770.82−0.20−0.530.62 (27.93)0.390.42R2 This product enables me to discover fun in life5.870.83−0.29−0.400.42 (20.52)0..840.11R3 This product teaches me about cultural values5.710.85−0.34−0.140.58 (19.37)0.340.48Mardia3.24P(P + 2) = 3 × 5 = 15Purchase IntensionPI. Purchase Intension5.690.830.62PI1 I intend to purchase this product5.770.90 −0.13−0.800.70 (26.12)0.490.42PI2 I intend to buy similar products that I find appealing5.610.82−0.03−0.440.91 (35.26)0.830.12PI3 I intend to buy this product ifs someone else recommends it to me5.690.79−0.08−0.070.74 (28.03)0.550.28Mardia6.596P

(P + 2) = 3 × 5 = 15Product PreferencePR1 I like this product5.780.77−0.00−0.52Note 1: *α = 0.05, indicating the level of statistical significance.

Note 2: M = mean; SD = standard deviation; SK = skewness; KU = kurtosis; SFL = standardized factor loading; SMC = square multiple correlation; EV = error variance; CR = convergent reliability; AVE = average variance extracted.

Note 3: p = the number of observed variables.

Table 2. Table of CFA results for the research model

Code	Facets	Amount	Correlation coefficient					
			S.	F.	T.	A.	R.	PI.
S.	Sense	5	**0.69**					
F.	Feel	3	0.57^{**}	**0.66**				
T.	Think	4	0.68^{**}	0.68^{**}	**0.61**			
A.	Act	2	0.41^{**}	0.64^{**}	0.60^{**}	**0.86**		
R.	Relate	3	0.52^{**}	0.58^{**}	0.60^{**}	0.50^{**}	**0.55**	
PI.	Purchase Intension	3	0.40^{**}	0.52^{**}	0.52^{**}	0.53^{**}	0.66^{**}	**0.79**

Note 1: The variable mean indicates the aggregate mean of all the items.
Note 2: The diagonal value indicates the square root of the AVE of the latent variable, which should be larger than the nondiagonal value.
Note 3: $*\alpha = 0.05$ indicates a significant correlation between the variables.

Table 3. SEM-analysis results

	SFL	C.R.	P	Hypothetical test
Purchase Intension ← Experiential Design of Cultural and Creative Product	0.33	16.75	***	Effective
Product Preference ← Experiential Design of Cultural and Creative Product	0.55	23.41	***	Effective
Purchase Intension ← Sense	−0.06	−3.37	***	Effective
Product Preference ← Sense	0.08	3.17	0.00	Invalid
Purchase Intension ← Feel	0.03	1.75	0.08	Invalid
Product Preference ← Feel	0.07	2.92	0.00	Invalid
Purchase Intension ← Think	0.08	4.99	***	Effective
Product Preference ← Think	−0.04	−1.60	0.11	Invalid
Purchase Intension ← Act	0.15	8.20	***	Effective
Product Preference ← Act	0.17	7.03	***	Effective
Purchase Intension ← Relate	0.28	13.93	***	Effective
Product Preference ← Relate	0.47	19.54	***	Effective
Purchase Intension ← Product Preference	0.57	27.54	***	Effective

Note: $*p < 0.05$, $**p < 0.01$, $***p < 0.001$

more favorable toward the product. Factors relating to manufacturing, marketing, and cost were excluded in this study. According to the afore mentioned results, due to a well-planned teaching model for design, the AR-integrated products created by the students exhibited considerable potential for commercialization; compared with the commercial works in the museum shop, the works integrated with AR made the participants' preferences and purchase intention more favorable (Table 4).

Table 4. Regression weights

	The commercial works from the shop				Student-made AR-integrated works			
	SFL	C.R.	P	Hypothetical test	SFL	C.R.	P	Hypothetical test
Purchase Intension ← Experiential Design of Cultural and Creative Product	0.16	4.91	***	Effective	0.26	9.87	***	Effective
Product Preference ← Experiential Design of Cultural and Creative Product	0.29	7.53	***	Effective	0.53	15.53	***	Effective
Purchase Intension ← Sense	−0.15	−5.36	***	Effective	0.09	3.85	***	Effective
Product Preference ← Sense	0.06	1.54	0.12	Invalid	0.09	2.66	0.01	Invalid
Purchase Intension ← Feel	−0.06	−2.08	0.04	Invalid	0.09	3.87	***	Effective
Product Preference ← Feel	0.05	1.38	0.17	Invalid	0.04	1.12	0.26	Invalid
Purchase Intension ← Think	0.11	3.80	***	Effective	−0.11	−4.57	***	Effective
Product Preference ← Think	−0.13	−3.68	***	Effective	0.07	2.08	0.04	Invalid
Purchase Intension ← Act	0.14	4.71	***	Effective	0.16	6.82	***	Effective
Product Preference ← Act	0.16	4.43	***	Effective	0.07	2.08	0.04	Invalid
Purchase Intension ← Relate	0.25	8.13	***	Effective	0.22	8.18	***	Effective
Product Preference ← Relate	0.33	9.02	***	Effective	0.50	14.60	***	Effective
Purchase Intension ← Product Preference	0.54	17.25	***	Effective	0.62	22.75	***	Effective

Note: $*p < 0.05$, $**p < 0.01$, $***p < 0.001$

5 Conclusion

The results of this study provide a reference for the implementation of AR in cultural and creative products. The results were as follows.

- Data analyses confirmed that the structural equation modeling fit of the scale was satisfactory, indicating the feasibility of the scale. The structure of the instrument was based on interactive experience; it was designed to investigate the effect of AR integration in cultural and creative products, providing a reference for product design education and value-added product design in the relevant industries.
- As revealed in the structural equation model analysis, the integration of AR technology in cultural and creative products significantly affected the participants' purchase intention; the dimensions for experiential design, customer preference, and purchase intentions mutually influenced each other. As for experiential design, act and relate factors clearly and directly influenced preferences; the other three factors were also necessary for experiential design's influence even though they directly influenced either consumers' preference or consumer purchase intention. These factors also affected preferences in a joint manner. In designing cultural and creative products, interactivity, story contexts, strong association with cultural relics, the enhancement of knowledge on the relics in question and their history, and the

delivery of cultural value should be considered. Moreover, preference was confirmed to substantially mediate the relationship between experiential design and purchase intention; applying AR technology in cultural and creative products influenced the participants' preferences for the products, thereby heightening their purchase intention.

- This study explored the differences between the commercial works from the shop of the National Palace Museum and the student-designed AR-integrated works with respect to consumer preferences and purchase intention. The results revealed that the AR-integrated works exhibited strong potential for commercialization, even exhibiting higher commercial values than did the commercial works.

This study clarifies the focal points of AR integration in cultural and creative products for future studies. Studies and educational practices have revealed that the design thinking and design methods employed in students' technological innovations have challenged the conventional production procedures employed in various industries. Institutions should first, train designers who fulfill contemporary market demands, and second, enable the capacity for high-quality and culturally rich product design in the relevant industries. In doing so, the experience economy and the visibility and competitiveness of cultural and creative industries can be enhanced.

References

1. Yan, H.Y.: A study on framework development and emotional design factors affecting consumers' preferences for cultural and creative products. J. Des. **23**(4), 21–44 (2018)
2. Azuma, R.T.: A survey of augmented reality. Presence Teleoperators Virtual Environ. **6**(4), 355–385 (1997)
3. Burdea, G.C., Coiffet, P.: Virtual Reality Technology. Wiley, Hoboken (2003)
4. Kikuo, A.H., Tomotsugu, A.: Augmented instructions-a fusion of augmented reality and printed learning materials. In: Fifth IEEE International Conference on Advanced Learning Technologies (ICALT05), pp. 213–215 (2005)
5. Kung, C.H.: The Application of Augmented Reality for Product Concept Promotion. Graduate School of Art and Design, National Taipei University of Education (2017)
6. Hsu, K.F.: Expand reality application business opportunities and industry trends. J. Autom. Intell. Robot. **27**, 24–29 (2018)
7. Witmer, B.G., Jerome, C.J., Singer, M.J.: The factor structure of the presence questionnaire. Presence Teleoperators Virtual Environ. **14**(3), 298–312 (2005)
8. Tsai, Y.C.: The Study and Design of Augmented Reality technology used in the digital interactive advertising display. Graduate School of Design, National Taiwan Normal University (2012)
9. Tsai, M.T.: Exploring the Applicability of Augmented Reality in Brand Communication: A Case Study of AR-Assisted IKEA 2013 Catalogue. Graduate School of Public Relations and Advertising, Shih Hsin University (2013)

Digital Signage for a Guided Tour
at the Science Museum

Miki Namatame[1(✉)], Meguru Ohishi[1], Masami Kitamura[1],
Chie Sonoyama[2], and Seiji Iwasaki[2]

[1] Tsukuba University of Technology, Ibaraki 3058520, Japan
miki@a.tsukuba-tech.ac.jp
[2] National Museum of Nature and Science, Tokyo 1108718, Japan

Abstract. In our previous survey (February 2018, Japan), 70 people with
hearing loss indicated the lack of necessary information at museums. The d/Deaf
or hard-of-hearing visitors at museums want sign language interpreters. Therefore, we organized guided tours with a curator explaining in sign language on
the B1 floor [Evolution of Life -Exploring the Mysteries of Dinosaur Evolution-
] at the National Museum of Nature and Science in Tokyo, Japan. The guided
tours showed that many jargons did not have corresponding signs in the sign
language, which made seeing some exhibitions difficult. We had to support with
written text to convey these jargons. We prepared a portable digital signboard.
A tablet PC attached to a portable stand displayed technical terms and jargons in
Japanese. The curator was able to navigate the exhibition floor easily while
carrying the signboard. As the digital signboard was self-supporting, the curator
could use both the hands freely. It was effortless, involved low technology
(hence, inexpensive), and very convenient to use at museums. This practice
paper will report the design method to support technical terms in written
Japanese. While displaying in writing, we recommend the following: 1. Use
easy Japanese; 2. Proper nouns must be written; 3. Add Kana for difficult Kanji;
4. Display structured information; 5. Align text to the exhibition layout. These
methods will be useful not only for the d/Deaf or hard-of-hearing but also for the
hearing. We aimed at improving information accessibility of the museum based
on "universal design" and "design for all."

Keywords: Design method · Written content · d/Deaf guide

1 Introduction

We surveyed 70 d/Deaf or hard-of-hearing people from June 30, 2017 to February 21,
2018, in Japan. The results indicated the lack of necessary information or knowledge at
museums. Therefore, we provided guided tours with a sign language interpreter at the
National Museum of Nature and Science in Tokyo, Japan, on April 29, 2019 [1]. The
experimental guided tours showed that communication at the science museum for the
d/Deaf is facilitated by sign language. However, it is difficult to convey technical terms
and jargons in sign language.

© Springer Nature Switzerland AG 2020
C. Stephanidis et al. (Eds.): HCII 2020, CCIS 1294, pp. 406–410, 2020.
https://doi.org/10.1007/978-3-030-60703-6_52

2 Research Questions

In our experimental guided tours at the museum by a d/Deaf curator who explained the exhibition using sign language, we had to provide support by showing many technical terms and jargons in writing. The research questions for this paper were:

1. Which display device is most useful on a guided tour for a d/Deaf curator?
2. How can we provide support to convey these jargons in writing?

3 Design Method

In this research, we used the methodology of inclusive design principle. The team consisted of five members: a d/Deaf trainee, two museum staff, a sign language interpreter, and a designer. Two museum tour workshops and three design workshops were conducted. At the beginning of the workshop, the trainee chose his favorite theme. He picked up "Evolution of Life -Exploring the Mysteries of Dinosaur Evolution-." The first workshop was a guided tour for the d/Deaf trainee by the museum staff to the permanent exhibition at the museum with a sign language interpreter and KAHAKU Navigator (Ka-ha-ku navi) Audio Guide on a tablet [2] (Fig. 1). The tour was planned for about 45 min. After the tour, the trainee wrote about his guided tour scenario and got it checked by the museum staff. The three design workshops focused on the following: 1. Consideration of device; 2. Design to convey meanings of jargons in writing; and 3. Modification of design to convey meanings of technical terms in writing. The final workshop was a guided tour for the museum staff by the d/Deaf trainee with the sign language interpreter.

Fig. 1. Snapshot of the guided tour for the d/Deaf trainee

4 Outcome of Inclusive Design

4.1 Which Display Device Is Most Useful?

In order to find the answer to this question, we prepared three display devices. Table 1 shows the merits and demerits of these devices. The most crucial point was that both the hands of the trainee had to be free as he had to explain the exhibitions in sign language. The first device was designed to hang on the neck and was made of paper. It was not heavy but presented only limited information. The second device was a tablet PC that was also hung on the neck, but the trainee commented on experiencing some difficulties; the sign language was hiding the displayed information and the device caused a neck strain. The third one was a tablet PC fitted on a portable stand, which freed the hands of the trainee. This display style was very comfortable for the guide who used sign language, but it had to be ensured that the set-up was not causing inconvenience to the other visitors in the crowded museum.

Table 1. Merits and demerits of the display devices

	Trial 1	Trial 2	Trial 3
Title	Hang on the neck(made of paper)	Hang on the neck (Tablet PC)	Portable stand (Tablet PC)
Display Style			
Merits	• Both hands can be used freely • Not heavy to hang on the neck	• Both hands can be used freely • Presented unlimited information	• Both hands can be used freely • Presented unlimited information • Sign language does not hide the display
De-Merits	• Presented limited information • Sign language hides the display • Cannot be used on dark floors	• Heavy to hang on the neck • Sign language hides the display • Too bright on dark floors	• Get in the way of other visitors

4.2 How to Write and Communicate Jargons?

Moreover, representation of scientific jargons in writing was considered. The communication problems on the dinosaur evolution floor were: 1. As the name of the dinosaur was not known, the sign interpreter showed it in writing, but reading manual alphabets was challenging; 2. The jargons were not familiar sounds. Even if visitors understood the content of the explanation, they could not understand the meaning. Even if jargons were indicated in written Kanji, visitors could not read it. 3. Content of the guided tour was linear, but the exhibition at the museum was not, because evolution had a process of differentiation. The guide needed to explain and clarify this evolutionary process to promote audience understanding. 4. The exhibition of dinosaurs was huge, and there was some distance between the exhibits and audience on this floor. A small scheme was, therefore, required to associate a layout on display with the real space of the museum. In order to solve these problems, the following methods in writing were adopted (Table 2).

Table 2. Representation in writing and the guide's scripts

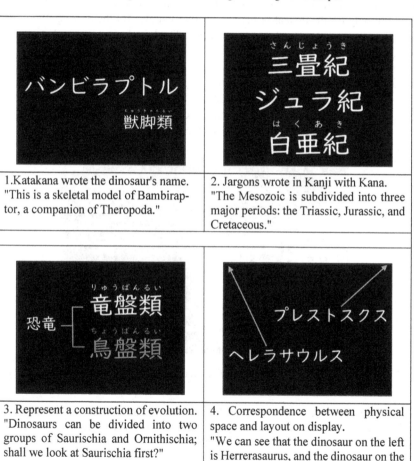

 1.Katakana wrote the dinosaur's name. "This is a skeletal model of Bambiraptor, a companion of Theropoda."	2. Jargons wrote in Kanji with Kana. "The Mesozoic is subdivided into three major periods: the Triassic, Jurassic, and Cretaceous."
3. Represent a construction of evolution. "Dinosaurs can be divided into two groups of Saurischia and Ornithischia; shall we look at Saurischia first?"	4. Correspondence between physical space and layout on display. "We can see that the dinosaur on the left is Herrerasaurus, and the dinosaur on the right is Prestosuchus."

5 Conclusions

In this practice paper, we discussed the design method to support jargons using written Japanese. We considered the most useful display device for a guided tour by a d/Deaf curator at the museum. We proposed to attach a tablet PC to a compact stand. The guide moved with it while explaining the points. Both hands of the guide were completely free, and the sign language did not hide the display of the device.

While displaying jargons in writing, we recommend the following: 1. Use easy Japanese; 2. Proper nouns must be written; 3. Add Kana for difficult Kanji; 4. Display structured information; 5. Align text to the exhibition layout. These methods will be useful not only for the d/Deaf or hard-of-hearing but also for the hearing. We aimed at improving the museum's information accessibility based on "universal design" and "design for all."

Figure 2 is a snapshot from the final guided tour workshop at the museum for the museum staff by the d/Deaf trainee with a display attached stand. The digital signage proposed by inclusive design was beneficial for both the audience and guide. This guided tour was successful. In the future, we will evaluate the digital signage displaying jargons and guided tours in the science museum.

Fig. 2. Snapshot of the curator having a guided tour using sign language and a digital signage

Acknowledgments. We thank the National Museum of Nature and Science in Tokyo and the four students of the Tsukuba University of Technology. Furthermore, we also gratefully acknowledge the grant from JSPS KAKENHI (#18H01046).

References

1. Namatame, M., Kitamura, M., Iwasaki, S.: The science communication tour with a sign language interpreter. In: Pacific Rim International Conference on Disability & Diversity. 4th coming (2020). https://pacrim2020.exordo.com/programme/presentation/509
2. KAHAKU navigator (Ka-ha-ku navi): audio guide by tablet to permanent exhibition. National Museum of Nature and Science. https://www.kahaku.go.jp/english/userguide/access/id/index.html

SmArt Spaces: Restructuring Art Galleries as Interactive Portals

Glenn A. Terpstra[✉] and Laura A. Huisinga

California State University Fresno, Fresno, CA 93702, USA
terpstra@mail.fresnostate.edu

Abstract. Continued oscillation between digital environments and physical realities has created a demand for hyper-interactive community spaces. Because the overall cost of prototyping extended reality (XR) experiences can require large initial investments of time and money, current art spaces could be used for prototyping digital environments with physical spaces. Integrating an art gallery with digital sensors, cameras, and projectors could allow for rapid prototyping of XR development, solving rudimentary problems found with spatial navigation, sensory exposure, and psychological ramifications in a more cost efficient manner.

Not only do these SmArt Spaces provide pivotal community engagement centers, they act as cultural hubs transcending divisions based on location. Connecting multiple spaces with virtual, and mixed reality experiences embrace concepts of the omni-connected environments in the near future. Integrating the primal functions of both art and an art gallery in the form of experience engages those willing to enter the space and provides an excellent opportunity for XR prototyping case studies. These spaces would naturally develop as community research centers and allow for a centralization of cultural experience and organization.

This writing aims to establish a baseline of artistic explorations relating to the interconnectivity of all humans through technology. Combining culture, location, and communication this seminal work attempts to better define underlying truths to how humans experience while providing a synthesis of physical and digital elements in order to create future SmArt Spaces

Keywords: Experience design · Mixed reality · Art and design

1 Introduction

This research explores controlled spatial designs, such as art galleries, showing how people navigate space and different interactive components in a physical environment, to better design digital Extended Reality (XR) environments. The results of this research provides a potential framework for future interactive community collectives of digitally charged art galleries world-wide. Experience is one of the foundations to human existence and should be used as a vehicle to better explain where we come from as well as represent where we are currently.

Experience design goes well beyond technology and it is pertinent to question the assets we currently have in our communities, ripe for adaptation to social equalizing

© Springer Nature Switzerland AG 2020
C. Stephanidis et al. (Eds.): HCII 2020, CCIS 1294, pp. 411–418, 2020.
https://doi.org/10.1007/978-3-030-60703-6_53

design philosophies. The primary goal of this research is to connect different environments that define cultural norms seen in artistic expressions throughout the world. These art spaces can act as technology safe havens where anyone has access to super computing power and connect with anyone in similar SmArt Spaces. Because divisions of technology there is a rising gap beyond just having the technology but, between those embracing all computing power possible versus the majority of computing being done from a phone or mobile device. These are elements beyond the scope of this research but are considered as a reason and purpose for community based technology infused engagement points.

1.1 History and Future Needs

On the most basic level a work of art shares an idea, art galleries share collections of ideas, different towns or cities have different collections of galleries, regions and beyond all establish definitive and measurable inferences of how we all see the world differently, not only because of our independence, but the environments that influence us. "The number of basic colors depends largely on who you ask: a neurophysiologist, a psychologist, a painter, a philosopher, a photographer, a painter, a stage designer and a computer graphics expert will all have different answers" [1]. If all perspectives are original then it becomes critical to allow the viewer of art influence the art they are seeing. With recent advances in XR interfaces possibilities of interconnected communication and shared experiences can reach a new level for all humanity.

1.2 Simple and Scalable

Producing a low-cost interactive space from art galleries opens communities, both urban and rural, to an unattainable operating system. Everyday art viewers, local makers, artists, researchers, and community endeavors would all benefit from a space that reacted to their presence and reminded of the global perspective. As these spaces develop beyond simple art installations, they will evolve to collect measurable data that can influence or change environments in a different part of the world.

Embracing the artistic exploration of experience design removes the limits sciences places on exploration and engages not only raw human interaction but the cultural, emotional, and openness imagination allows for. By releasing specific constructs researchers and designers are able to infer solutions that were previous not visible.

Viewers entering an art gallery space could change what they are looking at. Based on the collapsing powers of experience all art is perceived as a unique documentation of a point in space and time, while in truth, art is not real until experienced. Acting as a founding principle to experience itself, it becomes critical to analyze and dissect experience through relative terms and if possible, through the quantifiable structures of bigdata and artificial intelligence processing.

One art show experience connecting several art galleries throughout the world could be used as a metric to compare data produced by viewers in the space on an infinite level of complexity. The purpose comes back to the average community member being able to interact with a specific environment either controlled by or controlling how they interact in the space. This concept investigates physical environments, through virtual reality art galleries, to provide a constantly changing art experience. As a result this produces qualitative data charged with psychologic undertones based in spatial design.

2 Background

The Intelligent Interior Design Framework (IIDF) Developed by Professor Holly Sowles [2] defines three domains, Smart Geometry, Information Modeling and Ambient Intelligence. Smart Geometry uses parametric or algorithms to create designs. Information Modeling uses integrated software to create kinetic deployable designs. Finally, Ambient Intelligence uses sensors that are activated through interaction and interfaces to provide non-obtrusive assistance. The vision for these SmArt Spaces utilizes all three of the IIDF domains [2].

2.1 Experience Design

Experience design is the relationship we have with the world. We do not usually notice when an experience is well designed but we certainly notice when one is poorly designed. Often experience design is talked about in the realm of websites or applications, however experience design is all around us and covers many aspects of our lives. How we move through spaces or interact with our environment is often influenced by the design of that experience.

2.2 Environmental vs Digital Environments

As we engage with developing 5G technologies, the Web 3.0 or the Spatial Web, can start to come online.

> "The term "spatial" in the Spatial Web references how our future interfaces enable a web that extends beyond the screen to integrate and embed spatial content and interactions, facilitated by distributed computing, decentralized data, ubiquitous intelligence and ambient, persistent, edge computing [3]".

The Spatial Web will enable an extended reality to permeate our physical reality and allow a blending of the physical and digital environments. When this happens our physical environments, or hardware will be activated by dimensions of information seen as the software overlay. Data blends the two worlds seamlessly and the results leave us wondering where the significance of experience resides.

2.3 Navigating Space or Space Navigating You

We navigate through space on a daily basis but do not consider how we are choosing to navigate or if we are really making decisions of how we navigate. The cartesian mind would infer we can move in relative terms to previous known positions. Descartes *cogito, ergo sum*, or *I think therefore I am*, leaves us with significance placed on experience in order to determine our own realities.

Intentionally designed environments create a flow of movement through the space that guides our experience in the space. Even when making decisions about how we navigate, the way an environment is designed sets up the experience we will have in the space. Signage and wayfinding can direct us through a space but strategically placed interior elements and the use of ambient intelligence can drive an experience that seamlessly moves us through a space in an intentional way.

3 Evidence

The primary form of evidence for this research begins with an experience designed art installation in the January 2020 at the Conley Art Gallery at California State University, Fresno. The purpose of the show provides the viewer with five experience driven art installations that challenges how we look at art on a wall in an art gallery. Attention to how we see rather than what we are looking at is worth questioning as all elements and events will be recorded and reviewable in the future altering our perceptions of time. The work has artistic merit with each work independently, but the whole experience of the space and who you share the space with matters just as much if not more. This is the first art space manipulation by the SIXhalf Artist Collective in order to develop SmArt Spaces as a community engagement point. The two contributing artists Robert Hagen and Glenn Terpstra produced the environment as a way to begin the discussion of what people expect from art galleries both locally and globally.

3.1 Perspectrum: A Human Eye Versus the Word [4]

Perspectrum is an artistic installation that places the viewer in a variety of environments intended to make them think twice about how and what they perceive as art in a gallery. Breaking the stereotype of framed work on a wall, this exhibit capitalizes on sensory experience to provide a new lens to understand the world around us. How we conduct ourselves in a community space has certain connotations and expectations that can be shifted when the anticipated environment is rewired or flipped upside down. This action encourages the same reflection on our current cancel culture and post-truth society.

Though the work presented is deeply rooted in intelligent interiors research, the installations take advantage of the chaos and influence new technologies have on our current and future lives. Simultaneously each piece subtly questions what you had previously been looking at, due to a change of perspective. Micro/macro relations, moments of time, and the collapse of a superposition creates an environment worthy of slowing down, reflecting, and realizing the power held with perception.

Showing installations and paintings in changing light drives a core theme of the exhibit, to encourage a shift in perspective, in order to better understand innate perceptions. By creating works that alter how we look at, hear or experience an idea, points to the significance of uniqueness and individuality. Each of us have a history of values and culture influencing our perceptions–realizing the wide range of perspectives is critical if we are to navigate the development of Artificial Intelligence and should be thought of as a spectrum over ones and zeros.

3.2   Word Wall and a Full Range of Emotion

Being directed to the left upon entering the exhibit a viewer is faced with choice from the beginning, follow the flow or go right, ignoring signage and entering through the exit. Comprised of 19 triangle panels with screen printed words on them, this work is arranged by students at California State University, Fresno through a workshop held in the Conley gallery. Three teams of students collaborated to produce design proposals for the space and defended their experience designs to the group as a whole.

The arrangement of the first six triangles represent stability and structure while the second arrangement of six triangles indicate stability is not guaranteed. Ultimately chaos consumes attempts of order as triangles randomly scattered through the space. This arrangement looks at the constant flux between order and chaos through physical arrangement of panels, constant lighting changes, and the directed experience by following the flow of the space.

Each of these panels produce a unique collection of words, six colors have been chosen to represent six essential emotions, (Happy-Pink, Disgust-Green, Sadness-Violet, Anger-Yellow, Fear-Blue, Orange-Surprise). The words chosen to print are synonyms of these six core words. When light matching the colors used for each emotion causes them to fade away and reveals alternative emotions. The interplay of words and emotions begins to question how different lighting can alter emotion and even influence experience.

Once passing the installation, a reveal to the entirety of the galley gives the viewer a choice of navigation rather than a suggested path as experienced with the initial entrance. To the left is a sound installation intended to shift how we think of sound. This data driven work is comprised of recordings from Fresno, California sounds based on current environment conditions. the walls are white boxes with color changing circles and a five panel print installation. Centrally located is an interactive living installation with a motion responsive coffee table, and to the right is a wall of lenses looking through the wall of light from the first installation. At this point the viewer must reflect on which space to enter and react to the idea that others could have been watching their experience previously.

3.3   Small Worlds

The collection of paintings has been encased in white boxes mounted to the wall, small holes cut into the face of these boxes allows changing light to take the form of floating circles. When viewed from a distance it is hard to not compare the different worlds, though the details of these worlds can not be determined. When moving closer to any one world changes fixation from the series as a whole to an individual cluster of circles in one world. This transition forces the decision of what hole to look through that tends to lead to looking through an additional hole for comparison.

The purity of curiosity drives a constant change to what is being viewed and in is the collapse of a superposition established prior to looking through one hole. This choice creates a singularity of perspective, observing a world that is still changing due to the light within the box. It is hard to put a limit to which hole is looked through, but if this was the case, using technology could provide more information than is observable with the naked eye. Placing a smartphone camera to one of these holes could reveal the entirety of any painting with a wide-angle lens. Taking a photo of one of these tinyworlds would flatten the observable reality and represent a moment of time for that world. Sharing this world on social media is an entirely different mechanism all together and is a launching point for new interpretations and experience beyond gallery spaces.

Technology is seen as a great equalizer and seeing in these boxes can be enhanced through the use of a digital advantage. According to principles of universal design, this work would fail greatly due to limitations of access. This is intentional as a means to reflect on what is not accessible to all requires mechanisms of equalizations in how we interact with our environments. Making all things accessible helps all to access them.

The paintings within these boxes have several layers of color that shift how the world is viewed and imply the quantum nature of the world around us. Because the worlds are in constant flux the color theory of the painting results in different layers coming forward and going backward, activating an otherwise stagnant environment. The layers of paint and the chaotic nature of application reflect on the post impressionists, but through the lens of an RGB LED world of light over natural light. Lighting has the ability to adjust experience and can greatly impact how one interprets that experience. It is critical to reflect on the impact exposure to unnatural lights from our devices and screens both physically and psychologically.

3.4   Listening

Audio visual artist Robert Hagen continues with describing the next environment altering installation,

> Listening is a dynamic composition and musical space that draws upon live data streams retrieved from Fresno itself and programming methods to create an ever-changing music. Lacking motivic, melodic, or harmonic structure, Listening is driven purely by Fresno as a community, a city, and the layers of data that comprise it. The sound of Listening is always unique from day to day and moment to moment - each moment unrepeatable.

> Here you can listen to Fresno, the nearby seismic activity, the humidity, the quality of the air, the direction of the wind, the sounds of the San Joaquin River. Listening invites the listener to meditate in a space which reflects its exterior. The outside is brought in, creating an ambient intelligence that asks the listener to listen wholly and look inwards [4].

The sound field is constantly generating new waves of auditory exploration and provides a space that alters how you can use your ears for new ways of interpretation. The deep blue and violet fabric walls dampen external sounds and allow the listener to not be distracted by visuals but rather focus on the sound field produced by eight hanging speakers and two subwoofers. A rich neon violet rope light illuminates the end of the room, activating the fabrics and mimicking the rhythm of the San Joaquin River, where the installation sounds originate from. Fluctuations of the various source samples depend on actual input data from nature surrounding Fresno, California.

This experience produces new ways to interpret this data and paints an auditory picture of how these sounds come together. If the weather outside the gallery is uncomfortable the sounds in the installation reflect this discomfort. If there were to be an earthquake the seismic readings as an input to the installation would force an audio output reflecting this extreme intensity with loud rumbling.

3.5 Living

Creating an environment where a viewer can fantasize about the future technology is possible with motion sensing cameras that change the content of your physical experience. Hagen continues to explain,

> Living envisions the coffee table book of an unknown future - one that is perhaps human, or perhaps enhanced by AI, sentient computing, or other advanced robotics. In a broken modernity where devices and tech serve as walls between people, Living presents an interactive and intelligent screen which encourages people to gather together. Gesture and space are intuitive and expansive in rooms that have awareness of their designers and guests.

> Sustainable and intelligent design can improve and enhance daily life without being novel in the extreme. Smart furniture may reinvent the former centerpieces of a home such as the dining table and television but Living also questions the necessity of the coffee table book and other excesses of materialism. [4].

3.6 Levelalls

This series of 5 prints comes from an 8" × 10" painting and shows how scale, medium, and reproduction changes interpretation. The subject matter shows the last scramble for resources experienced by the Levelalls who inhabit earth in the future. Waste left behind by humans, has till this point, proved to be a valuable energy supply and is now running out. The mass chaos that occurs symbolize the over-saturation of content we experience today. Tones of magenta plague the environment and tie the space and time back to our current attention seeking culture.

Using magenta is crucial to the exhibit as a whole because of the short circuiting that happens in our brains in order to see this color. Red, Blue, and Green cones in our eyes produce a good range of hue for us to understand our environments but, on an electromagnetic level, the frequency for a magenta color struggles to exist within our visible spectrum. This is a lie our brains fabricate to suggest a circular connection of the colors we experience but has a greater impact with the creation of RGB LEDs. Breaking this painting up into five distinct prints isolates the content of the whole and allows for deconstruction of an otherwise overwhelming environment.

3.7 Results

The designed space of the Perspectrum exhibit provides several real-world case examples worthy of exploring further, such as how people view work or generating a heatmap of viewer movements. Determining universal design principals can help ensure accessibility to all experiences equally, or at a minimum help determine where some sticking points arise in spatial design or designed environments. When we think of art spaces, they tend to be made of art on a wall or podium, when in reality the spaces tend to be designed to manage movement of the viewer between these points. Considering how one engages with an element is just as significant as the element itself and why this research will continue to determine how people interact with space.

4   Connections

How we see the world and navigate daily challenges is mostly done without thinking. When a gallery space is predictable it becomes formulaic, leading to an inefficient mechanism for an artist to share their work. We are inundated with visual stimulus from the moment we wake to sleep and do not consider what this does to our actions and way of life. Moving screens closer and closer to our eyes will lead to the point of transition, where the content is within us and we no longer share what we are looking at.

4.1   Theory to Model

Beyond this dark interpretation, it is significant to research how we move through physical environments and question how people would interact with a space they can control. Ideally there is a dualism of an art exhibit where physically movable elements of various sizes act as markers within the space and can be arranged by all who visit the space. By moving these elements in the physical space, a virtual gallery of the space would change as a result. This may not seem significant, but the process begins to show threads of a double blind study. Giving people permission to move art frees the constructs of a gallery space and since it is in the name of art, more liberty and subliminal intuitions come to the surface. An art space as a data collecting interactive hub of digital program development would save time and money for XR by moving prototype development to an improved starting point based on the highly authentic data driven results.

4.2   Conclusions

The ending of this research is the beginning of a new chapter, the results are still being processed and will continue to evolve over time. The ultimate take away is that people strive for community discussion and forgotten art galleries could solve an endless array of problems for a multitude of situations. Considering the great things an artist makes on a miniscule budget, give artists access to good tech and the digital synthesis of neighborhoods will naturally follow.

References

1. Elkins, J.: How to Use Your Eyes, p. 202. Routledge, New York (2000)
2. Sowles, H.M.: Distributed knowledge in interior design: an emerging theory for the future of intelligent interior design. Doctoral dissertation, Washington State University (2016)
3. Rene, G., Mapes, D.: In the Spatial Web: How Web 3.0 Will Connect Humans, Machines, and AI to Transform the World (2019)
4. Hagen, R.J., Terpstra, G.A.: Perspectrum: A Human Eye Versus the Word, California State University Fresno, Fresno, CA (2020). www.sixhalfstudios.com/perspectrum

Health and Wellbeing Applications

Lokahi: The Wearable Body Pillow to Foster an Intimate Interaction Between Two Users Through Their Heartbeat Awareness

Beste Özcan[(⊠)] [iD] and Valerio Sperati [iD]

Institute of Cognitive Sciences and Technologies, National Research Council of Italy
ISTC-CNR, Rome, Italy
{beste.ozcan,valerio.sperati}@istc.cnr.it

Abstract. We present the design concept *Lokahi*: a soft, interactive, wearable device which aims to promote a pleasant, intimate closeness sensation between two people. Its shape is designed to encourage hugging, while the embedded electronics –through pulsating coloured lights– lets the users to visualise their own heartbeats, so that they are aware of each other's current affective state. Lights hues mix according to the synchronisation of the two heartbeats, possibly producing a single hue: such shared visual feedback can potentially be used in relaxing and meditative exercises, where two people try to synch their own heartbeats.

Keywords: Bio-feedback · Intimacy · Design · Well-being

1 Introduction

We were designed to be emphatic, to emotionally connect with each others. Sharing an affection for other individuals is a feature deeply grounded in our human nature, and makes us feel like part of a group [22]. Social interaction is consequently a very crucial feature of our species: through emotions, Man interprets and understands the circumstances and the interactions with his own kind [11]. Emotional competencies are then critical for our behavior, as they convey information about people's thoughts and intentions and coordinate social encounters [13]. From the viewpoint of a product designer, such issues can be very important when conceiving an idea. In particular, designing a product for engaging social interactions, and at the same time furnishing emotional experiences to users, is a really challenging task. Indeed, the affective information is still not much considered in the design perspective [17], while it is clear that experience-based interaction involving emotions is becoming a more and more important issue, especially in Human-Computer Interaction (HCI) field [2]. New technologies can be exploited in this regard: for example, sensors for detection of physiological parameters (e.g. Heart Rate Variability or Electrodermal Activity) started to be embedded in smart clothes, like t-shirts or wristbands, mainly for use in sport

© Springer Nature Switzerland AG 2020
C. Stephanidis et al. (Eds.): HCII 2020, CCIS 1294, pp. 421–429, 2020.
https://doi.org/10.1007/978-3-030-60703-6_54

Fig. 1. On left, the front view of *Lokahi*; on right, the device used during a hug: the two pockets host two sensors detecting the heartbeats of the partners, displayed by the blue and red pulsating lights (respectively for first and second partner). (Color figure online)

activities or health monitoring [16]. Interestingly, such devices provide data that can also be used to detect the affective states of the user [21]: communicating emotions through wearable technology can potentially introduce new approaches to social interaction, and enhance the human body's role in mediating the communication. Designers could take an advantage of such technologies and conceive new ways of physical interactions and experiences between "smart" products and their users [10].

Although the advances in technology can provide new means for enhancing social communication, we should not forget that humans are beings that relate to external world through senses. The current work mostly focuses on the sensation of intimacy and social connectedness, relying on the senses of touch and sight. About the first, we mainly look at the importance of a fundamental human gesture: an intimate hug. Through hugging, people have a close physical contact characterised by a rich haptic feedback. Touch not only functions for identifying an object but also plays a major role in social interaction [21]. From the very first stage of the human beings touch sense exists to experience and express emotions [15]. Psychological studies show that touching has an important affect in emotional development for both infants and adults too [4]. Since touch is an intimate way of communication and emotional expression, it is crucial in interpersonal relationships [20]. Therefore, it can work as a therapeutic tool making people experience positive and calm feeling which reduces anxiety [8].

In this paper we present *Lokahi*, an interactive, wearable body pillow designed to enhance the feeling of closeness between two partners (see Fig. 1). Its shape is meant to encourage an intimate hug, during which embedded coloured lights pulsate at the rhythm of users' heartbeat. We propose that such combined haptic and visual feedback can potentially create a deep emotional connection in people, facilitating relaxing and soothing sensations. We call this positive experience *co-feeling*, which means *experiencing to feel together*.

In the next 3 sections we firstly overview related works on technologies promoting social connectedness, then we describe the current *Lokahi* prototype, and finally we discuss and suggest potential scenarios for the use of the device.

2   Related Works

The research on perceived social connectedness by means of technological applications is a relatively new field of study. The proposed ideas are often based on the detection and sharing of important physiological signals. For example in [14] the authors developed *imPulse*, a device which senses the user's heartbeat and translates it into a pleasant pulsating light and a vibration; if a second user is present with his own device, the two units get wirelessly connected and the visual and haptic feedback are shared, so that the partners are aware about the internal status of each other. Authors propose the use of *imPulse* for meditative moments between people at distance. A similar idea was investigated in [19], where authors observed the effect of Heart Rate (HR) feedback on social perception: in this study couples of participants wearing an heartbeat chest belt shared the HR information of each other -through visual or aural feedback from a connected laptop- reporting pleasant feelings of connectedness, especially when there was a physical distance between them. The explicit synchronisation between users of emotionally relevant informations was observed in the social game *SinKin* [23]: here two facing players were equipped with sensors measuring brain, heart and electrodermal activities, while a cam detected their facial expressions. All this data, available to users on a display, were then combined into a single, general measure of *emotional* syncronisation between players. As reported by authors, people found very amusing and engaging the activity and -interestingly- called it as *Friendship Game*.

Although emotion-based bio-signals are clearly very important in such type of studies, feelings of togetherness can be conveyed even through simpler sensory feedback, as shown in the design concept *The Hug*, meant to keep alive the social relationships of elderly people [5]: this is an interactive pillow, the shape of which encourages the gesture of hugging. When a user embraces and pets it, the information is wirelessly transmitted to a twin device in the hands of a second, far user. The receiver pillow starts then to vibrate softly and to slowly warm up, creating a pleasant perception of emotional closeness between users across distance.

With respect to the previous concepts, *Lokahi* aims to enhance the intimate interaction between two people who are actually in physical contact, combining the haptic feedback inherent to hugging, and a visual feedback (pulsating lights) reflecting the users heartbeats and their synchronisation.

3   Design of the First Prototype

The design of *Lokahi* for user experience impacts what kind of feelings become shareable, how they can be shared and how others can respond to these shared experiences. Persuasive design of the product influences positive behaviors such as encouraging two people to hug each other. This positive touch can relieve negative effect and evoke pleasure [6]. Another design affordance of the product to promote pleasurable touch is having soft, furry material: Harlow states in his experimental studies with monkeys that soft, fluffy things provide a sense of security and comfort [9].

Fig. 2. On left: in a room with dim light, the pulse of lights on *Lokahi* are clearly visible to both users; on right, *Lokahi* can also be used as a separate object, and placed in the middle of a couple.

Lokahi is a kind of soft, interactive and wearable body pillow, which lets two users visualise their own heartbeat –through synchronised pulsating lights– and promotes an intimate hug between users (see Fig. 2, left). They can see, hear, touch and talk during a hug, so they become *human interfaces* to interact with each other. As an interdisciplinary project combining design, engineering, and psychology, it is expected to experiment positive effects of physical closeness through touch (intended as hugging) and heartbeat visualisation. Two pulsating lights, embedded in transparent silicone shapes displaced on the sides of the device, display blue and red colors, respectively for the first and second users. The pace of pulse mirrors the users heartbeats. During a hug (or similar personal circumstance, as staying on the same bed, see Fig. 2, right), if the same heartbeats rhythm is detected by the pillow, the two colors mix into a unique magenta shade[1]. Sharing this intimate experience can potentially provide calming, trusting, affection effect between two users.

3.1   Hardware Specifications

The device is based on the principle of photoplethysmography (PPG), a non-invasive technique to measure the blood volume variations in tissues using a light

---

[1] See supplementary video material at link https://vimeo.com/427703690.

source and a detector. Since the change in blood volume is synchronous to the heartbeat, this method can be used to detect the heart rate. Two PPG sensors (or pulse oximeters) are embedded within two *Lokahi* pouches, where users can put their index fingertip. Power is supplied by a rechargeable 3.7V LiPo battery. Lights are implemented with a single addressable LED strip composed by 10 LEDs (5 per each sensor); lights are diffused through a silicone shape. A custom PCB hosts an ATmega328 chip and the electronic circuit (adapted from [7]). Each PPG sensor is implemented assembling a standard red LED (as a light emitter) and a standard IR detector (as a signal detector) in a thimble-like structure, where the user's index fingertip can be hosted.

3.2 Signals Filtering

Given the hardware features, each pulse oximeter reports a raw, continuous PPG value x close to 800^2 when a heartbeat is detected, and close to 0 otherwise, producing then a cyclic square wave. We then transformed x in a binary value y through a step function:

$$y = \begin{cases} 1, & \text{if } x > 750 \\ 0, & \text{otherwise} \end{cases} \tag{1}$$

Filtering y through a Leaky integrator function with temporal parameter $\tau = 4$ [1] we obtained a signal u:

$$u_t = u_{t-1} + \frac{1}{\tau}(-u_{t-1} + y_t) \tag{2}$$

Equation 2 produces a smooth value in $[0, 1]$ which gently increases when $y = 1$ and gradually leaks a small amount when $y = 0$ (see Fig. 3). Given that *Lokahi* presents two pulse oximeters, we have two signals denoted as u^a and u^b respectively for the user a and the user b.

3.3 Synchronisation Computation

In order to compute a signal s reflecting a synchronisation between data u^a and u^b, we first computed the *mean squared error* (MSE) between two vectors containing the last $L = 100$ values of u^a and u^b. Since sensors are updated each 20 ms, the vectors contain data for two seconds[3] MSE will be close to 0 if the two heartbeats data are equal, and positive otherwise, with greater and greater value as the signals increase their difference. We normalised the obtained value in $[0, 1]$, fixing an arbitrary maximum threshold $\alpha = 0.4$ observed when the two signals are reasonably different[4]. Formally s is then computing with the following equation:

---

[2] Analog inputs on ATmega328 range in $[0, 1023]$.
[3] The current value of L was set to 100 due to memory limits of the chip.
[4] This was done generating random noise on both sensors.

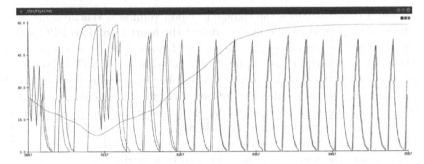

Fig. 3. Signals visualisation (screenshot from Arduino serial plotter): red and blue lines represent the heartbeats of two wearers (after filtering), i.e. u^a and u^b; green line represents the sync value. In this example, noisy signals were deliberately generated by a single user (who played the role of both partners) simply moving the fingers within the sensors; around step 9200 fingers were then correctly arranged and heartbeats were revealed. As shown, the sync signal properly computes the matching between u^a and u^b values. (Color figure online)

$$s = 1 - \left(\frac{1}{L} \sum_{n=1}^{L} (u_n^a - u_n^b)^2 \right) \cdot \frac{1}{\alpha} \tag{3}$$

Given the Eq. 3 the variable s will be close to 1 when users heartbeats will be equal (i.e synchronised), and will reach 0 when signals are reasonably different. In order to have a synchronisation value with a smooth temporal development, we computed a moving average of s in the last L steps, obtaining s_{mov}. Variables s_{mov}, u^a and u^b were then used to select the hue and intensity of the two light effectors[5], for user a and user b, namely *colour u^a* and *colour u^b*:

$$colour\ u^a = \begin{cases} red = u^a \\ green = 0 \\ blue = s_{mov} \cdot u^b \end{cases} \qquad colour\ u^b = \begin{cases} red = s_{mov} \cdot u^a \\ green = 0 \\ blue = u^b \end{cases} \tag{4}$$

Fig. 4. Red and blue lights pulse respectively with heartbeats of users a and b. The two lights turn to magenta hue when heartbeat synchronisation between users is detected, otherwise individual colors are maintained. (Color figure online)

---

[5] LEDs hue is based on three values in [0, 1] respectively for red, green and blue.

Equation 4 make the two effectors light up respectively in red and blue hue, according to the heartbeats signals. However, according to the synchronisation signal intensity, blue and red can be mixed to produce a magenta colour (see Fig. 4).

4 Conclusion and Future Work

We presented *Lokahi*, the wearable body pillow designed to provide an intimate, emotional experience of closeness between two people. Its simple shape with two pockets and soft material which is pleasant to touch encourage positive behaviors such as hugging or lying down to calming together. Through embedded electronics, *Lokahi* displays to the users their heartbeats, through pulsating coloured lights which are synchronised with their heart rates. Furthermore, the device computes the level of synchronisation between users signals and mixes the lights shades accordingly. We hypothesize that these visual feedback –along with the haptic feedback due to hugging– can potentially create a close, interactive loop between users, resulting in a shared experience characterized by intimacy and deep connection ("Lokahi" means *harmony* and *balance* in Hawaiian language). We call this positive experience as *co-feeling* which means *experiencing to feel together*. The logic behind our supposition is that such feedback are directly in touch with a (philosophically) meaningful, essential process of life itself: the beats of one's own heart. In the next research step, we plan to experiment *Lokahi* on pairs of people, with two main purposes. First, we want to test our design hypothesis and see –through an evaluation of emotional involvement of participants– if *Lokahi* helps to develop a better social interaction between people (with possible potential benefits on the treatment of neurodevelopmental conditions involving social impairments like Autism Spectrum Disorders [3]). As a second purpose, we want to see to what extent users manage to synchronise their heartbeats, during meditation exercises. This last point is particularly relevant for scientific research on biofeedback: it is well known in fact that heart rate can be voluntarily influenced if the right feedback is furnished and that such awareness can have positive effects on well-being [12,18].

Acknowledgments. This paper was funded by Regione Lazio, project +me: motivating children with autism spectrum disorders to communicate and socially interact through interactive soft wearable devices (Progetto di Gruppo di Ricerca finanziato ai sensi della L.R. Lazio 13/08).

References

1. Abbott, L.F., Dayan, P.: Theoretical Neuroscience: Computational and Mathematical Modeling of Neural Systems. MIT Press Ltd., Cambridge (2001)

2. Blythe, M.A., Overbeeke, K., Monk, A.F., Wright, P.C. (eds.): Funology: from Usability to Enjoyment, vol. 3. Springer, Dordrecht (2005). https://doi.org/10. 1007/1-4020-2967-5

3. Boucenna, S., et al.: Interactive technologies for autistic children: a review. Cognit. Comput. **6**(4), 722–740 (2014)

4. Bush, E.: The use of human touch to improve the well-being of older adults. A holistic nursing intervention. J. Holist. Nurs. **19**(3), 256–270 (2001)

5. DiSalvo, C., Gemperle, F., Forlizzi, J., Montgomery, E.: The hug: an exploration of robotic form for intimate communication. In: 2003 2003. Proceedings of the 12th IEEE International Workshop on Robot and Human Interactive Communication, ROMAN 2003, Millbrae, CA, USA, pp. 403–408. IEEE (2003)

6. Ellingsen, D.M., Leknes, S., Løseth, G., Wessberg, J., Olausson, H.: The neurobiology shaping affective touch: expectation, motivation, and meaning in the multisensory context. Front. Psychol. **6**, 1986 (2016)

7. Embedded Lab: Introducing Easy Pulse: A DIY Photoplethysmographic Sensor For Measuring Heart Rate (2012). https://bit.ly/2At0V5v

8. Gallace, A., Spence, C.: The science of interpersonal touch: an overview. Neurosci. Biobehav. Rev. **34**(2), 246–259 (2010)

9. Harlow, H.F., Zimmerman, R.R.: Affectional responses in the infant monkey. Science **130**(3373), 421–432 (1959)

10. Höök, K.: Knowing, communicating, and experiencing through body and emotion. IEEE Trans. Learn. Technol. **1**(4), 248–259 (2008)

11. Lazarus, R., Lazarus, B.: Passion and Reason: Making Sense of Our Emotions. Oxford University Press, New York (1994)

12. Lehrer, P.M., Gevirtz, R.: Heart rate variability biofeedback: How and why does it work? Front. Psychol. **5**, 756 (2014)

13. Lopes, P.N., Brackett, M.A., Nezlek, J.B., Schütz, A., Sellin, I., Salovey, P.: Emotional intelligence and social interaction. Pers. Soc. Psychol. Bull. **30**(8), 1018–1034 (2004)

14. Lotan, G., Croft, C.: imPulse. In: CHI 2007 extended abstracts on Human factors in computing systems - CHI 2007, p. 1983 (2007)

15. Montagu, A.: Touching: The Human Significance of the Skin. William Morrow Paperbacks, 3 edn. (1986)

16. Nag, A., Mukhopadhyay, S.C.: Wearable electronics sensors: current status and future opportunities. In: Mukhopadhyay, S.C. (ed.) Wearable Electronics Sensors. SSMI, vol. 15, pp. 1–35. Springer, Cham (2015). https://doi.org/10.1007/978-3-319-18191-2_1

17. Overbeeke, K., Djajadiningrat, T., Hummels, C., Wensvveen, S., Frens, J.: Let's Make Things Engaging. In: Blythe, M.A., Overbeeke, K., Monk, A.F., Wright, P.C. (eds.) Funology: from Usability to Enjoyment, chap. 1, pp. 7–17. Springer, Dordrecht (2005)

18. Schoenberg, P.L.A., David, A.S.: Biofeedback for psychiatric disorders: a systematic review. Appl. Psychophysiol. Biofeedback **39**(2), 109–135 (2014)

19. Slovak, P., Janssen, J., Fitzpatrick, G.: Understanding heart rate sharing: towards unpacking physiosocial space. In: Proceedings of the SIGCHI Conference on Human Factors in Computing Systems (CHI 2012), New York, NY, USA, pp. 859–868. ACM (2012)

20. Thayer, S.: History and strategies of research on social touch. J. Nonverbal Behav. **10**(1), 12–28 (1986)

21. Uğur, S.: Wearing Embodied Emotions: A Practice Based Design Research on Wearable Technology. Springer, Mailand (2013). https://doi.org/10.1007/978-88-470-5247-5

22. de Vignemont, F., Singer, T.: The empathic brain: how, when and why? Trends Cogn. Sci. **10**(10), 435–441 (2006)

23. Wikström, V., Makkonen, T., Saarikivi, K.: SynKin: a game for intentionally synchronizing biosignals. In: CHI EA 2017 Proceedings of the 2017 CHI Conference Extended Abstracts on Human Factors in Computing Systems, pp. 3005–3011. ACM (2017)

Strong Stimulation with Virtual Reality Treatment for Acrophobia and Its Evaluation

Su Chang[1][✉] and Makio Ishihara[2]

[1] Graduate School of Computer Science and Engineering, Fukuoka Institute of Technology, 30-3-1, Wajiro-Higashi, Higashi-Ku, Fukuoka 811-0295, Japan
mfm18201@bene.fit.ac.jp
[2] Fukuoka Institute of Technology, 30-3-1, Wajiro-Higashi, Higashi-Ku, Fukuoka 811-0295, Japan
m-ishihara@fit.ac.j

Abstract. This manuscript discusses an acrophobia treatment procedure using virtual reality of VR technology and conducts a pilot experiment on feasibility. The core of our treatment produce is a exposure therapy with a strong shock. In our treatment produce, patients wear a head-mounted display or HMD and they are left on the top of a mountain in a virtual space. They are given five minutes to find a way down the mountain and only a way down is to jump off. There are some artifacts for them to do that by themselves. A strong stimulation is given to the patients at the moment of jumping. The experiment results show that our treatment procedure demonstrates the potential for alleviating acrophobia and a stronger stimulation is acceptable for alleviating acrophobia.

Keywords: Pilot experiment · Shock treatment · Exposure therapy · Virtual reality · Acrophobia

1 Introduction

About the treatment of acrophobia, now the common treatment for acrophobia is exposure therapy, the core of which is to make patients repeatedly face the scene and things they are afraid of and stimulate them constantly so that they adapt to the stimulation. Finally, they feel numb and insensitive to the things they are afraid of. So the reality treatment requires professional guidance and facilities [1]. Our treatment is performed with virtual reality technology and lets subjects experience the feeling of falling from the height instead of just walking and watching in a virtual space. The core idea of our treatment is strong stimulation. The preliminary experiment result [2] shows that adding some powerful stimulation of fear may have a certain positive effect in treating acrophobia and the aim of this manuscript is to evaluate it. In our treatment procedure, subjects are allowed to move freely on a very high mountain with a lot of open space as watching waterfalls and lightning, listening to howling of the wind and thunder. This surrounding noise could distract the subjects from suffering from fear of height so that they could have little burden of jumping off the mountain top. It results in making them feel smug and find confidence in chance of alleviating acrophobia.

© Springer Nature Switzerland AG 2020
C. Stephanidis et al. (Eds.): HCII 2020, CCIS 1294, pp. 430–435, 2020.
https://doi.org/10.1007/978-3-030-60703-6_55

2   Related Work

If people adopt a method of virtual reality technology for acrophobia treatment, the treatment just completes in a closed room without any professional guidance and facilities but the effect of the treatment is not obvious [3]. However, most VR treatment techniques are limited to specific mobile routes and specific treatment methods such as taking sightseeing elevators, flying in the sky and so on. Their stimulation to patients is smooth without any fluctuation [4]. In addition, there are many different ways to move in a VR space for acrophobia treatment such as use of whole-body movement, use of hand controllers, or moving along the established route without any operating procedures and the survey [5] found that use of whole-body movement made patients feel more involved while it did them feel dizziness about VR, having them only operate with the controller. In our VR environment, patients will receive stimuli with strong fluctuations and the way to move is diversified. The hand controller is combined with use of the whole-body movement.

3   Experiment

3.1   Our VR System

Our system runs on a Windows10 desktop powered by UNITY 3D and an HTC-Vive system, which provides subjects with an immersive VR environment. Figure 1 shows the HMD view from the virtual world. From left to right is a panoramic view of the virtual world, the subject's view from the edge of the mountain, and the view after landing. The VR space is set in a natural environment of 10 km^2, among which the highest peak is set at about 80 m. The subject stands at the top in the beginning and he/she is asked to find the way down the mountain in 5 min. The subject finally finds that there is no way down the mountain except for jumping down the mountain in a tight time, during which the subject is greatly shocked. If subjects choose to use the controller, they will use the HTC handle to operate: the round button on the slide handle to move in the direction.

Fig. 1.   HMD view from the virtual world

3.2   Procedure

Eighteen patients with severe acrophobia are chosen as subjects through the acrophobia questionnaire introduced in [6]. They are divided into two groups of A and B. The group A performs our treatment procedure and it takes about three minutes once a week for four weeks. The group B performs a simple reality treatment procedure about three minutes once a week for four weeks as well. The subjects in the group B just simply look down from the top of an eight-story building over the window frame.

All the subjects from the two groups are asked to take the acrophobia test and the acrophobia questionnaire to assess the level of acrophobia before and after the given four-week treatment procedure. For the test, the subjects are asked to look down from a high-rise building and their biological data is obtained for assessment. When people are nervous and afraid, their heart rate will increase and their ECG rhythm will become irregular [7]. The change of heart rate (beat per minute or BPM) and the balance (LF/HF) of low frequency (LF) to high frequency (HF), which is represented by Eq. (1), are used to estimate the level of acrophobia:

$$LF/HF = \frac{\int_{0.04HZ}^{0.15HZ} f(\lambda)d\lambda}{\int_{0.15HZ}^{0.40HZ} f(\lambda)d\lambda},$$

(1)

where $f(\lambda)$ is the power spectrum at the given frequency λ for the obtained RRI.

3.3 Acrophobia Questionnaire [6]

The questionnaire is designed to determine whether the subjects have acrophobia and its level of acrophobia. At the beginning, this questionnaire will ask some simple questions, such as do you feel afraid if you stand tall in your life, do your heart rate increase, etc. These questions are used to screen the subjects for acrophobia, and the next stage of the problem is to identify their level of acrophobia. There are 13 levels and the most severe is 13. People with severe acrophobia will have a level of nine or more.

4   Result

Table 1 is the comparison results between the two groups of A and B. Figure 2 and Fig. 3 show the mean change in BPM and mean change in the balance before and after the treatment in group A and B. The results show that there is little change in BPM before and after treatment in two groups and there is no significant difference on it. As regards the balance, there is significant change for group A before and after treatment $[t(8) = 4.750$ at $p < .05]$ and the group B does not show any significance.

Table 1. Experiment results

Items	Group A	Group B
Mean of changes in BPM	−2.2	−1.9
LF/HF before treatment	2.95 ± 0.93	2.95 ± 0.97
LF/HF after treatment	2.10 ± 1.26	2.61 ± 0.65
Mean of change in LF/HF	−0.98	−0.2

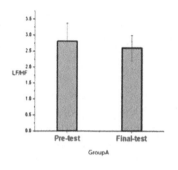 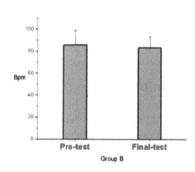

Fig. 2. Mean change in BPM

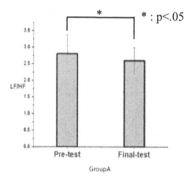 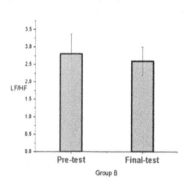

Fig. 3. Mean change in balance

According to scores from the acrophobia questionnaire, the result is shown in Fig. 4. From the figures, although there is a slight difference before and after treatment for both the groups. Both the group $A[t(8) = 3.833$ at $p < .01]$ and $B[t(8) = 2.896$ at $p < .05]$ have a significant difference.

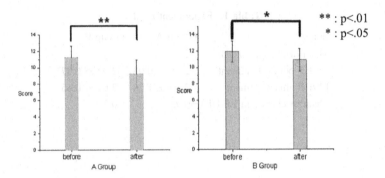

Fig. 4. Questionnaire scores from group A and B

5 Evaluation

In this experiment, subjects were greatly stimulated in the process of falling. To show that, Fig. 5 is one of the subject's BPM during the treatment. The horizontal axis is the elapsed time from top to bottom in 25 mm/s and the vertical one is voltage in 10 mm/mV. From the figure, at first the subject's heart rate was steady, as he toured the virtual world, and then as time pressed his heart rate began to increase. The second page is the heart rate of the experimenter during the descent, which varies greatly due to the involuntary avoidance and the BPM accelerated sharply in the process of falling, meaning that stimulation was properly given to subjects. In addition, some patients showed a sign of sudden instability at the moment of landing on the ground in the virtual world. This is because they were fully immersed in the sensation.

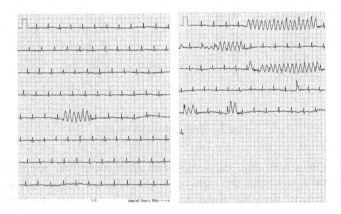

Fig. 5. An electrocardiogram taken by a subject in group a during the experiment

The acrophobia questionnaire results before and after the experiment, it was obvious that our treatment made the subjects choose a grade of two lower points on average, indicating that their acrophobia symptoms had some alleviation.

According to the results from the acrophobia test and the feedbacks from the questionnaire, this experiment can indeed have alleviation to the fear of heights but not sure it has the effect of completely cured acrophobia because of the limitation of experimental periods as well as professional technology. To make sure the definite therapeutic effect, it a further experiment is needed with some extra experimental period, for example, to join the guidance of professional doctors, etc.

6   Conclusion

This manuscript discussed the acrophobia treatment using VR technology and conducted a pilot experiment on feasibility. The results showed that our treatment demonstrated the potential for alleviating acrophobia and a stronger stimulation was acceptable for alleviating acrophobia.

References

1. Chang, S., Ishihara, M.: Preliminary experiment of virtual reality treatment for acrophobia. In: Proceedings of the 2020 IEICE General conference, March 2020
2. Pan, Q.X.: A case report of psychological counseling with acrophobia. Educ. Sci. Manage. Yunnan university, 650500, China, 263–263 (2013)
3. Yi, W.: Design of virtual reality exposure therapy for acrophobia. Drama House **09**, 272–274 (2017)
4. Coelho, C.M., Waters, A.M., Hine, T.J., Wallis, G.: The use of virtual reality in acrophobia research and treatment. J. Anxiety Disord. **23**(5), 563–574 (2009)
5. Kritikos, J.: Comparison between full body motion recognition camera interaction and hand controllers interaction used in virtual reality exposure therapy for acrophobia. Sensors (Basel). **20**(5), pii: E1244 (2020)
6. Huppert, D., Grill, E., Brandt, T.: A new questionnaire for estimating the severity of visual height intolerance and acrophobia by a metric interval scale. Front. Neurol. **8**, 211 (2017)
7. Miyada, Y.: New Physiological Psychology 1 volume Basis of Physiological Psychology. Taiyou Press (1998)

Technology-Enhanced Monitoring of Physical Activity

Albert Espinoza[1] ⓘ, Bernardo Restrepo[2] ⓘ,
and Edwar Romero-Ramirez[3](✉) ⓘ

[1] Universidad Ana G Mendez, Gurabo, PR, USA
[2] Polytechnic University of Puerto Rico, Orlando, FL, USA
[3] Florida Polytechnic University, Lakeland, FL, USA
eromeroramirez@floridapoly.edu.edu

Abstract. Traditional activity trackers use acceleration sensors to trace when individuals are walking, running, or standing still. The programming in these devices then determines the number of steps, walking or running distance, floors climbed, and calories associated with the physical activity throughout the day. Other than counting steps, there is little interaction to motivate an increase in pace or to provide feedback into how vigorous the activities are, besides heart rate sensors. The same number of steps walked represent different calories burned at different speeds. Thus, more energetic exercises provide enhanced physical activity. This work describes a wearable tracking device for enhanced monitoring of physical activity. An accelerometer was used to measure the acceleration level at the wrist location and compared against a threshold to illuminate a series of LEDs based on the number of lights turned on and color emitted. This wearable prototype provides visual feedback to let the user know how energetic the activity level is.

Keywords: Monitoring · Physical activity · Accelerometer

1 Introduction

Wearable electronics can enhance the functions of traditional activity tracking devices. Fitness wearables are one of the technologies used to monitor physical activity. Many of them use three-axis accelerometers to determine the intensity of a motion that is communicated wirelessly to smartphones for continuous monitoring. Numerous smartphone applications provide additional data analysis capabilities, from the number of steps or distance walked, to graphical representations of the level of activities performed (stairs climbed, calories). Since most of them are wrist-worn, they might be affected by gesturing, among other unintentional motions. In addition, activity trackers may overestimate the step count [1]. Most trackers count the number of steps and provide means to estimate the distance walked. However, calories are burnt at different rates based on speed and body mass [2]. Thus, providing feedback about how energetic the physical activity might help to estimate the calories burn per minute in addition to calories per distance traveled.

© Springer Nature Switzerland AG 2020
C. Stephanidis et al. (Eds.): HCII 2020, CCIS 1294, pp. 436–441, 2020.
https://doi.org/10.1007/978-3-030-60703-6_56

Wearables can also be used to measure the activity level for health care applications as well. According to a UN report [3], by 2050, near 22% of the US population will be over the age of 65. This number will climb to almost 30% in Europe while Japan will be nearly 40%. Due to the increase in longevity and decrease in bird rates [4], health care will be in higher demand. Thus, physical activity monitoring might be used as well for health monitoring and to increase higher levels of physical activity exposure.

This work proposes enhanced monitoring of the physical activity by using multiple sensors (three-axis accelerometers) at various body locations (near the joints) for a more accurate representation of the physical activity tracking. The enhanced monitoring can be either provided by visual feedback of LED changing colors (representing low, medium, and high-intensity activities) or by smartphone integration with applications for additional enhanced trackin. Upper limbs and lower limbs can be tracked separately for different levels of monitoring. Thus, we propose using experimental acceleration results from activity tracking of individuals walking at varying speeds as a threshold for activating the LED lights. This provides immediate visual feedback of the exercise intensity to the wearer.

2 Methodology

A database set is analyzed first to perform data comparison against a threshold to provide feedback. Then, the acceleration measurement is compared against this limit for the body location. A different set of colored LED lights can indicate a low, medium, or high-intensity level to provide visual clues of how energetic a motion is. For this purpose, a portable prototype was designed to activate the corresponding LED color based on the acceleration level to be worn at the wrist.

2.1 Body Acceleration

Body acceleration data for walking and running is required to have a baseline to determine patterns for these two activities. A study were ten individuals were evaluated for walking (5 women, 5 men, age 29.4 ± 5.8, weight 62.9 ± 12.8 kg, height 1.68 ± 0.1 m) and other ten when running (5 women, 5 men, age 28.7 ± 7.0, weight 63.2 ± 12.4 kg, height 1.69 ± 0.1 m) on a treadmill was used as a reference [5]. Nine body locations were selected (ankle, knee, hip, wrist, elbow, shoulder joint, chest, side of the head, and back of the head), as shown in Fig. 1(a). Acceleration was measured using multiple sensors (3-Axis ±3G ADXL335, 3-Axis ±6G MMA7260Q, and 2-Axis ±18G ADXL321 accelerometers). Treadmill walking speeds varied from 1.0–4.0 mph (0.45–1.79 m/s) and running ranged from 2.0–5.0 mph (0.89–2.24 m/s).

The results can be used to characterize walking and running activities by the step frequency, as shown in Fig. 1(b). Walking was shown to have step frequencies ranging from 1.2 to 2.2 Hz while running showed a step frequency near 2.5 Hz. Furthermore, walking speeds can be used to distinguish between younger pedestrian (walking speeds higher than 1.3 m/s) and older pedestrians (walking speeds lower than 1.3 m/s) [6]. Figure 2 shows the summary of the results of the localized acceleration results at different body locations from each acceleration axis.

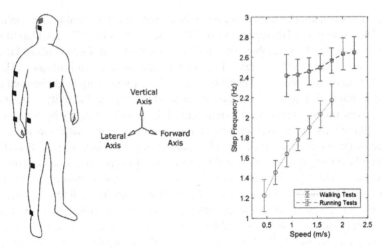

Fig. 1. Body acceleration measurement locations and the relationship between step frequency from walking and running [3]. Error bars represent one standard deviation distribution.

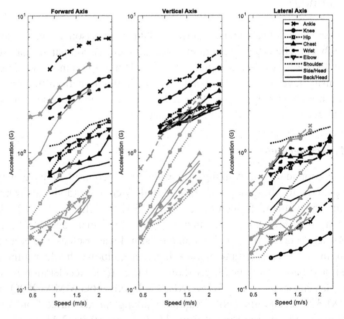

Fig. 2. Average acceleration results from walking (grey-colored lines) and running (bold-colored lines) for the 3-axes measured. (Color figure online)

2.2   Measurement Processing

A portable platform was developed using off-the-shelf components. An ATmega328P single-chip microcontroller was used with a commercial development board (Arduino

Nano) for data acquisition, analysis, and control of the LEDs. A breakout board containing the MPU-6050 was used for acceleration data acquisition. This IC contains a 3-axis gyro and 3-axis programable accelerometer (± 2 g, ± 4 g, ± 8 g, and ± 16 g). Programming for the MPU-6050 followed the datasheet for I2C communication and acceleration selection. The resultant acceleration from Fig. 3 (combining the measurements of the forward, lateral, and vertical axes) was used to determine a threshold, as shown in Table 1. For instance, establishing the resultant acceleration at the wrist location while walking at 1.3 m/s was used as a threshold for a worn wrist device. A strip of eight RGB LEDs (Adafruit NeoPixel Stick) was used to provide a visual cue of the level of the acceleration (based on light intensity and color change). Figure 3 shows the prototype developed. Arduino programming makes it possible to map the acceleration thresholds for each individual location to the maximum scale of the LED strip. Thus, the same wearable device can be used in multiple locations with little modification other than selecting the body location with full. These kinds of devices are microcontrollers that can be paired with smartphone applications for real-time monitoring and data recording using Bluetooth connectivity for simplifying this task for the final user.

The sensor measures acceleration simultaneously on 3-axes, and since the sensor should be oriented along the major plane of motion, then a normalized acceleration value should be used to account for alignment differences. The resultant of the individual acceleration component in each axis are combined into one acceleration that is representative of the body location without requiring alignment with the cartesian planes. Equation (1) shows the normalized acceleration formula used. Calibration was performed along each individual axis aligned with the vertical under rest until a 1 g (9.8 m/s^2) was obtained. Once the resultant acceleration was calculated from Eq. (1), the sensor outputs 1 g of acceleration irrespectively of its orientation of the sensor under rest. Then, additional programming was developed to map acceleration levels to light intensity and the number, and color, of the LEDs, turned on.

$$A_{normalized} = \left(A^2_{x-axis} + A^2_{y-axis} + A^2_{z-axis} \right)^{1/2} \tag{1}$$

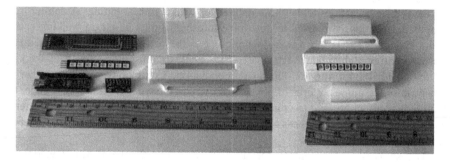

Fig. 3. The wearable prototype. Left, components and custom shield. Right, assembled unit.

Table 1. Acceleration thresholds from treadmill walking (0.4–1.8 m/s) and running (0.9–2.2 m/s).

Body Location	Walking acceleration threshold (g)	Running acceleration threshold (g)
Ankle	2–4	4–7
Knee	0.9–3	2–4
Hip	0.3–2	1–3
Chest	0.3–1	1–3
Wrist	0.2–0.6	1–2
Elbow	0.2–0.6	1–2
Shoulder	0.2–0.6	1–3
Side of head	0.3–0.9	1–2
Back of head	0.3–0.9	1–2

3 Results and Discussion

A test was performed on a treadmill machine while walking to determine the visualization of the acceleration based on the threshold data set. This preliminary investigation was carried on the wrist for the prototype shown in Fig. 3. An external battery bank was used to power the device. This makes the wearer aware of the displayed energy level during regular activities. This can entice users to implement more energetic activities. For instance, by analyzing step-frequency (walking <2.2 Hz, running >2.4 Hz), the microcontroller can be programmed to select the intensity level automatically, providing a fluid transition with no input from the user. The initial prototype was designed as a proof-of-concept. Future devices require a smaller form factor with an integrated battery and wireless connectivity to an smartphone for enhanced tracking and history of the activities to determine physical activity patterns.

4 Conclusion

This paper presents a method to provide visual cues of physical exercise intensity based on the acceleration threshold from a dataset for walking and running. A dataset from nine body locations was used to determine threshold limits based on walking speed. Color-changing LEDs were used to represent if the activity level was found to be lower, equal, or higher than the database. This can be used for fitness feedback tracking or for health monitoring for the aging population. Continuous monitoring can be practical to determine patterns of physical activity to the wearer. At the same time, the light indicator can be used to entice the wearer to develop motions with higher energy expenditure for enhanced fitness or targeted physical conditioning due to the immediate feedback.

This study provides a dataset for other researchers in this field. App development for multiple body monitoring locations can increase the functionality of fitness devices.

Future work might consist of establishing additional models for other types of exercises or body motion activities with smartphone tracking and/or control.

References

1. Hernandez, A., Ajisafe, T., Lee, B.C., Xie, J.: Commercial activity trackers overestimate step count: implications for ambulatory activity monitoring. In: Stephanidis, C. (ed.) HCII 2019. CCIS, vol. 1034, pp. 446–451. Springer, Cham (2019). https://doi.org/10.1007/978-3-030-23525-3_60
2. Hall, C., Figueroa, A., Fernhall, B., Kanaley, J.A.: Energy expenditure of walking and running: comparison with prediction equations. Med. Sci. Sports Exerc. **36**(12), 2128–2134 (2004)
3. United Nations: Department of Economic and Social Affairs, World Population Prospects 2019, Demographic Profiles, United Nations, New York, vol. 2 (2019)
4. Gavrilov, L.A., Heuveline, P.: Aging of population. In: Demeny, P., McNicoll, G. (eds.) The Encyclopedia of Population, pp. 32–37. Macmillan Reference (2003)
5. Romero, E., Warrington, R., Neuman, M.: Powering biomedical devices with body motion. In: 32nd International Conference of the IEEE EMBS, 31 August–4 September, Buenos Aires, Argentina, pp. 3747–3750 (2010)
6. Knoblauch, R.L., Pietrucha, M.T., Nitzburg, M.: Field studies of pedestrian walking speed and start-up time. Transp. Res. Rec. **1538**, 27–38 (1996)

Smart Service Design Facilitate and Develop the FCMC (Family-Centered Maternity Care)

Bo Gao[✉] and Xinyue Dai[✉]

Tongji University, 1239 Siping Road, Shanghai, People's Republic of China
gaobo@tongji.edu.cn, adele_dai@outlook.com

Abstract. The demand for women who are in pregnancy transforms form medical birth service to high-quality life gestation. The family-centered approaches to maternity care present an important direction for fitting the needs of pregnant women, the better pregnancy experience, and more emotional care. In this paper, we explore design issues in developing a smart service product system for pregnant women and her family. As a prototype, we have developed a service to provide the family-centered maternity health care link with a pregnant woman, her family, and maternity hospital. The prototype includes an application provide telemedicine support, antenatal report visualization, and maternity information sharing for the whole family. These features are designed and implemented based on the principle of family-centered maternity health care, which will highlight how to dissolve the boundary between the medical system and pregnant women's family, and how to increase the emotional link between the puerpera and her family members. The contribution of this paper is to research on maternity health service lies in a complete set of smart service design processes based on FCMC mode and discussion on the relationship on medicine, puerpera, and her family.

Keywords: Family-centered maternity care · Maternity health · Smart service design

1 Introduction

In the advent of the twentieth century, with the introduction of modern maternity professional care, the direction of maternity care transfer from family to the hospital, pregnant women have to go to the hospital to have the antenatal examination and give births. The iatrogenic form of care is dominated by physician-led antenatal care, which is largely limited to biomedical health indicators and fertility. Also, because of the unbalanced match of a large number of people and the relatively limited and uneven medical resources, the quality of maternity care in hospital is not satisfactory. There are problems such as excessive staff pressure, insufficient time for each visit, and incomplete provision of maternity care knowledge [1] While the service satisfaction of nursing staff is not very high, and patients do not receive enough reputation and attention [2], especially for pregnant women, who need more emotional and personalized care. For example, relevant medical services adapted to each pregnant woman's different gestational weeks. However, pregnant women's emotional care is not the focus of the hospital, except for a few expensive private care institutions, like some

© Springer Nature Switzerland AG 2020
C. Stephanidis et al. (Eds.): HCII 2020, CCIS 1294, pp. 442–449, 2020.
https://doi.org/10.1007/978-3-030-60703-6_57

maternity hotel. But those maternity hotel is more about providing more professional personalized nursing service, not totally focus on emotion.

Although the health of pregnant women was medically guaranteed in modern obstetric hospital, the family's status was excluded from the current nursing service system. But it is going to see the change: returning the initiative to pregnant women is becoming a trend. *"Newborn belongs to the family, not to the caregivers or the hospital. Because the family is the constant factor in the life of a new human being [3]."* Future care scenes will gradually shift to consumer-centric health/virtual homes and communities [4]. And the family scene must be the focus of the return of care services. The value of home-based nursing services has been proven to bring benefits to the physical and mental health of women, especially in China. That's because delivery is not only the birth of a new life but also the continuation of the family, which directly link the traditional "family culture" of China. From a medical point of view, the FCMC model reduces the difficulty rates, and improving obstetric quality has positive effects [5].

Based on family-centered maternity health care theory, this paper explores how a smart service design system can enhance pregnant women's experience by strengthening cooperation between hospitals and families, and improving pregnant women's sense of support from family members to get a better experience and sense of security. Promote the birth of the "medical consortium", which redefine the service diversion between family and hospital, to provide a new one-stop smart family doctor health management solution [6].

2 Family-Centered Maternity Care

There is a medical term for this type of home care that centered on pregnant women, called FCMC (Family-centered maternity care). FCMC is a new model of obstetric care since 1960. It means including the father in childbirth preparation classes and in the birth itself. Over time, even as family members were welcomed in the birthing room, technology played an increasingly significant role in the birth experience. The FCMC model creates a lot of responses. There are already some FCMC mode practices in western countries. For example, the Public Health Agency of Canada released its national guidelines for family-centered care in 2000. In response to the Institute of Medicine's publication of "Crossing the Quality Chasm", many professional organizations have published statements on "family-centered care" or "patient-centered care." Of course, the FCMC model is more suitable for about 77% of low-risk pregnant people and daily care, while the hospital's tasks are more focused on difficult diseases, which is also useful for minimizing unnecessary hospitalizations, interventions and expenses [7].

In FCMC, active family intervention in pregnancy care can provide care to pregnant women both physically and emotionally, thus ensuring the health and safety of pregnant women and fetuses. From a medical point of view, parental participation in nursing has a higher rate of spontaneous delivery and lower rates of dystocia. For the family, their participation during pregnancy can increase the sense of responsibility of each family member in raising children to enhance self-confidence. The proactive attitude of pregnant women and their families will help create a better healthy environment for children in the future [8].

3 Methodology

The research has been planned in 3 stages: a preliminary study, field research, prototyping and verification. The preliminary study consisted of the literature review on the development and application of family-centered health care mode. The field research collects user data and opinions from several maternity hospitals in Shanghai and the pregnant women and their families. We went to three first-class hospitals, two gynecology hospital, and one private hospital. Then we did the in-depth interview with eight pregnant women, two family members, and three doctors. Service design kits help us better understand every detail of the birth process, which is essential because pregnancy is a long time. The prototype is to elaborate on possible scenarios and service, try to build a new service process, and verify that the Settings of the contacts in the process are reasonable, by designing and making the touchpoint of the service, and verifying our concept in user interview and usability test.

Table 1. Items of interview guide (for pregnant women)

Items	Investigation contents
General profile	Age, family size, the number of pregnancy, Gestational age, the relationship between family members
Experience in hospital	The choice of the different hospital, the hospital facilities, Antenatal examination items and process, the understanding of examination report, the feeling in hospital
Personal behavior and feeling during pregnancy	Lifestyle change during pregnancy, the emotional needs, the daily activity of family members, the social connection between puerpera group
Information collection	The information content, where to get the healthcare information, the knowledge level during pregnancy
Used product/service	The used pregnancy product/service, the judgment of those product/services

Table 2. Items of interview guide (for pregnant women's family)

Items	Investigation contents
General profile	Age, knowledge of Puerpera's pregnancy, housework sharing,
Experience in hospital	Antenatal examination company situation
Life during pregnancy	Lifestyle change during pregnancy, the communication situation between puerpera and family members, current health care way from family members
Opinion about pregnancy	Preparation about pregnancy, anxious or pressure, opinion about puerpera, the knowledge of taking care of puerpera, the knowledge level during pregnancy
Used product/service	The used pregnancy product/service, the judgement of those product/service

Table 3. Items of interview guide (for doctor/nurse)

Items	Investigation contents
General profile	Doctor's qualifications, the working situation, the main work content, hospital shift system, the reason to be the gynecologist/obstetrician
Diagnosis process	Frequency of receiving pregnant women, contents of medical orders, the way to convey the medical orders, the communication situation between pregnant women and doctors/nurses, the common problem when doing diagnosis
Antenatal examination report	The content of the examination report, the important level of Indicator in the report, the communication situation when explaining the report

Table 4. User journey about pain points and needs during pregnancy

Stage	Activity	Pain point of puerpera	User needs
Knowing about pregnant	Do a gynecological examination to confirm the pregnancy, then understand the current pregnant situation	- Lack of full knowledge of the impending pregnancy - Unclear knowledge of medications during prepregnancy - Physical discomfort caused by early pregnancy reactions	Know about pregnant itself
First times antenatal examination	Nurse build the puerpera profile and inform the antenatal examination process, then make the appointment of the next examination	- The queue time is too long - Cannot find the right examination room - Doctors don't have enough time to explain the whole process - Poor communication between doctors and pregnant women leads to misunderstandings and conflicts - The husband is forbidden to enter, and the second transmission of the doctor's advice is not effective	- Understanding of the procedure and location of hospital pregnancy test - Planning the pregnancy examination cycle in advance
The middle period of pregnancy	Line up antenatal examination for a long time, then get the examination report and give it to doctors. Pregnant women should relay medical advice to family members. Then they usually use some pregnancy APP to search for more information	- The technical terms of the examination report are hard to understand - Pregnant women sometimes do not understand medical advice - Ordinary pregnant women cannot judge the information professionalism of non-professional channels	- Clear interpretation of inspection data - Families can better participate in the pregnancy care

(*continued*)

Table 4. (*continued*)

Stage	Activity	Pain point of puerpera	User needs
The late period of pregnancy	Do fetal heart monitoring at home and in the hospital	- Lack of awareness of the importance of fetal monitoring - No professional knowledge of fetal monitoring	- Learn about fetal status in real time - Mood changes during the third trimester and more emotional support is needed
Delivery	Prepare delivery items and be admitted to the hospital on the due date	- Health problems and anxiety and depression caused by inadequate knowledge of nursing, parenting and psychological preparation - Lack of nursing awareness in the family leads to nursing ineptness and conflict of ideas	Adequate preparation for delivery Prenatal adequate psychological construction

Insight from Research. In our research of pregnancy care services, it has been found that supply and demand mismatch between pregnant women and hospital, the user journey shows the different problems during different gestation stages. The medical institutions offer hospital-centered care, but pregnant women have a family-centered expectation. The central contradiction between them is that the existing medical resources are challenging to support the individualized needs of each pregnant woman's family.

By analyzing the research from the user interview, the most critical finding is that the pregnant woman needs to have a family member's companion, but the participants are unsatisfied. It has caused by many complex reasons, such as space and time limitation in the hospital, which prevent family members involving in the nursing process. The neglect of family members in hospital pregnancy education makes them unfamiliar with the relevant knowledge and has no perceived control. Also, the hospital services don't regard to the difficulties and anxiety that terminology can cause when interpreting a pregnant woman's condition, which affects how well pregnant women and their families know about their health, which is partly associated with prenatal anxiety [9].

4   Result: Service System and Interaction Design

It is important to design services and interactive design from "birth service" to "life gestation", starting from technology, maternal and family needs, and existing hospital care resources. The FCMC service design can build a new type of pregnancy family-centered care service with the help of smart technology to track and visualize puerperia's data, with professional support from telemedicine doctors to give health care suggestion and activate families member's participatory by pregnant care education.

At the beginning, it is intention to solve the problem of giving a sense of control. Through some research, the fear, anxiety, mental tension comes from lack of knowledge and experience in childbirth [10]. So by redesigning the communication channel between pregnant woman, the hospital, and the family, the communication barriers will be reduced, so that the mood of pregnant women could get better. Pregnant women as the core of the service, and are also the people who have the greatest demand for communication. Therefore, in this stage of research, we use an APP as a touch point. The function of this interaction design is (a) pre-learning of antenatal examination and medical order record, (b) the visualization of antenatal examination report, and (c) family information shared platform.

(a) Pre-learning of antenatal examination, hospital guidelines, and medical order record. Mainly solve the communication problem between pregnant women and the hospital. Pregnant women can click on the APP to view the time and place of birth inspection and learn the contents of the birth inspection project in advance. APP also provides the navigation route of the department in the hospital. And quickly records the doctor's order during the diagnosis.

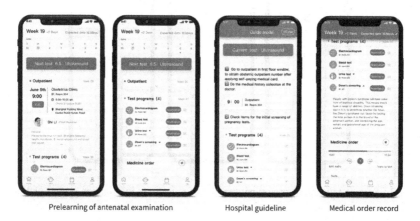

Prelearning of antenatal examination   Hospital guideline   Medical order record

Fig. 1. Service touchpoint prototype: the updating the communication channel between pregnant woman and the hospital in APP.

(b) The visualization of the antenatal examination report. To upload the original antenatal examination report, identify and interpret the text, and display the specific explanation of this indicator and the reference of the numerical range visually.

(c) Family information shared platform. The APP has family ports to use by mom or dad. The smart APP assistant automatically communicates the results of the antenatal examination and the precautions of the gestational week to the family, reminding the family to care for the pregnant woman correctly.

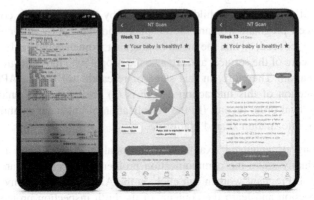

Fig. 2. Service touchpoint prototype: the visualization of prenatal examination report.

Fig. 3. Service touchpoint prototype: the family pregnancy information shared platform.

5 Conclusion and Prospect

Through feedback from the prototype, a useful tool and service can help family members participate in the maternal health care process together with the pregnant women, can bring a better experience to pregnant women indeed. In our prototype design, we tried to solve the problem of medical communication, broke the professional barriers of medical terminology, and established a family information platform for synchronizing maternal health information.

However, current research stage was just the first step. The future maternal health care system could be smarter and integrated in the service system map in Fig. 4: a fully developed personalized smart services supported by the Internet and big data, interact and connect with the hospital (doctors, nurses) medical services in real-time, and openly share data with pregnant women and their families to make them take the initiative. The obstetricians and midwives with assessment from the artificial intelligence diagnosis and treatment assistants provide localized nursing service support as professional team support.

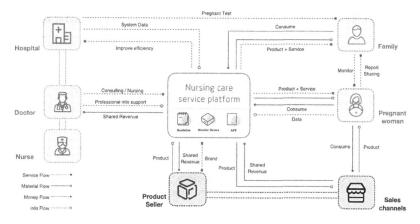

Fig. 4. The FCMC service system map.

References

1. Geng, Z., Yuan, X., Jia, H., Yan, X., Tian, L.: Investigation on the health care work during pregnancy and maternity needs in Tianjin. Tianjin J. Nurs. **27**(2), 150–153 (2019)
2. Yang, W., Cao, Q.: Research on optimization of health care service model during pregnancy. J. Math. Med. **30**(3), 421–423 (2017)
3. Zwelling, E.: Trendsetter: celeste phillips, the mother of family-centered maternity care. J. Obstet. Gynecol. Neonatal. Nurs. **29**(1), 90–94 (2000)
4. The future of health: Paper presented at deloitte insights. https://www2.deloitte.com/us/en/insights/industry/health-care/forces-of-change-health-care.html?icid=dcom_promo_featured| us;en. Accessed 13 Apr 2019
5. Hou, Q., Wang, C.: Evaluation of the clinical effect of a new model of family-centered obstetric services. China Matern. Child Health Care **24**(24), 3339–3341 (2009)
6. Idowu, I.O.: Artificial Intelligence for detecting preterm uterine activity in gynecology and obstetric care. In: 2015 IEEE International Conference on Computer and Information Technology; Ubiquitous Computing and Communications; Dependable, Autonomic and Secure Computing; Pervasive Intelligence and Computing, pp. 215–220 (2015)
7. Huang, W., Peng, Z.: The impact of family-centred prenatal education on maternal delivery and breastfeeding. Mod. Clin. Nurs. **19**(7), 26–29 (2013)
8. Li, J., Qiao, K., Zhang, P., Li, H.: Analysis of influencing factors of pregnant women's prenatal anxiety and childbirth outcomes. China Eugenics Yuyu **19**(2), 86–89 (2013)
9. Zheng, R.: The influence of doula delivery on labor process and pregnancy outcome. Int. J. Nurs. **31**(012), 2277–2278 (2012)
10. Betancourt, T.S., Abrams, E.J., McBain, R., Fawzi, M.C.S.: Family-centred approaches to the prevention of mother to child transmission of HIV. J. Int. AIDS Soc. **13**, S2 (2010)

ABLE Music: Arts-Based Exercise Enhancing LongEvity

Paula Gardner[1], Stephen Surlin[1]([✉]), Caitlin McArthur[2],
Adekunle Akinyema[1], Jessica Rauchberg[1], Rong Zheng[1],
Jenny Hao[1], and Alexandra Papaioannou[2]

[1] McMaster University, Hamilton, ON, Canada
surlins@mcmaster.ca
[2] GERAS Centre for Aging Research, McMaster University,
Hamilton, ON, Canada

Abstract. The ABLE Music platform is co-creation project in collaboration with older adults with dementia and their caregivers, to provide unique pair or group interactions and intergenerational play by transforming movement into art experiences (digital painting and musical creation) in order to enhance wellness (physical, mood, cognitive). The ABLE Music platform advances current research on dementia that tends to, a) not be interactive, b) not exploit digital tools, and c) doesn't take advantage of the opportunity to engage families and caregivers, reduce their stress, and restore identity, dignity and relationships. These advancements are built on research that demonstrates the benefits of: bright colour palettes' ability to stimulate older adults with dementia, music and painting experiences that reflect the memories and preferences of older adults, and intergenerational gaming that will allow younger children and adults to teach older adults digital gaming skills. Art combined with movement has a synergistic effect – it has the power to enhance mood, physical health and cognition. Reducing depression makes us less susceptible to cognitive & memory impairment, due to depression ageing the brain. Arts-based and Montessori-based approaches increase communication, episodic memory, and relationships between People with Dementia (PwD) and their family members and caregivers. Crip approaches to design can help researchers center PwD and caregiver perspectives in treatment plans, in addition to rethinking how power can influence the research process.

Keywords: Co-Design · Art based experience · Dementia

1 ABLE Music Platform Research Background

1.1 Co-Design with Older Adults and Care Networks

The ABLE Music platform (AMP) uses a method of co-creation with older adults with varying degrees of dementia and their caregivers. Our team will work with pairs or groups that include older adults in a series of interactions and intergenerational play in order to develop the AMP. The AMP uses interactive software and hardware technology that has the ability to transform movements, gestures and voice into art

C. Stephanidis et al. (Eds.): HCII 2020, CCIS 1294, pp. 450–454, 2020.
https://doi.org/10.1007/978-3-030-60703-6_58

experiences that include: digital painting, musical composition and gaming. The goal of these interactions is to enhance the wellness of the participating older adults, which is measured in terms of their physical, mood and cognitive well-being.

Our co-creation research method is a novel approach to collaborating on the design of interactive multimedia interfaces with older adults that contrasts with recent research that: lacks interactivity, does not engage critically with digital tools and does not engage the families and caregivers of the older adult collaborators. These choices are intended to maintain dignity, cultural identity and relationships between older adults and their care networks.

1.2   The Dementia Epidemic and Caregiver Crisis

Dementia currently affects over 500,000 Canadians, primarily those over 65, and mostly women. With 76,000 new diagnoses annually, numbers are projected to rise to 937,000 in 2 decades. Dementia creates a host of symptoms that often go untreated and thus worsen. As longevity increases in Canadians, a staggering 7% percent of the Canadian population over 65 lives with dementia, mostly women over 65, while 486,000 (or 6%) of Canadians aged 65 or above care for an individual with dementia. Seniors with dementia experience high levels of immobility, pain & discomfort, isolation, and depression. This produces boredom, confusion, agitation, wandering and sometimes, aggressive behaviour, requiring persistent care that is rarely available (Canada Public Health Service 2020).

Levels of exhaustion and stress - Half of People with Dementia (PwD) live at home, cared for primarily by unpaid family and neighbours, while the remaining reside in retirement and long-term care residence environments, 2/3 of which house this population. Family, neighbours and professional staff alike struggle to provide adequate care to treat these diverse, ongoing symptoms. Staff and particularly unpaid caregivers report debilitating rates of isolation, distress and depression (Canada Public Health Service 2020).

1.3   Housing Crisis

Disruptive adults are often removed from or denied acceptance to residential care facilities or treated via use of restraints and potentially inappropriate antipsychotics. There is no current plan to confront this escalating health care crisis, which impacts those with dementia and their caregivers. The Dementia deficit also presents a financial crisis costing Canada $8.3 billion today and estimated to increase to $16.6 in 2031. (Canadian Institute for Health Information 2020).

1.4   Older Women at Risk

As age increases, Women have been found to be more affected by dementia than men. Above the age of 80, women have a 1.3 times higher rate of dementia than men (20.8% versus 15.6%). Attention will be given to women with dementia (the majority of those with depression) and women with depression (Canadian Institute for Health Information 2020).

2   ABLE Music Platform Design Principles

Low Level Exercise for Short Durations
AMP will prioritize designing short duration exercise/movement experiences with older adults and their caregivers based on recent research that shows that light intensity exercise is associated with healthy brain aging:

- 10 min or short bursts of mild exercise is associated with enhanced memory (2017, Stubbs et al./London), enhanced brain volume, and improved physical and cognitive health in older adults (Tse et al. 2015)
- Higher amounts of activity is linked to reduced rates of cognitive decline (Suwabe et al. 2019), and increased brain volume (Spartano et al. Spartano et al. 2019; Suwabe et al. 2019)

Reduce Depression to Fend Off Dementia
Our collaborative design method and interactive software for artistic expression is intended to reduce depression that makes people less susceptible to cognitive & memory impairment, due to depression ageing the brain (Esetlis/Yale 2019; Gaysina and John/Sussex 2018; Al Hazzouri/Miami et al. 2018).

Synergistic Impact of Art and Movement
Art combined with movement has a synergistic effect – it has the power to enhance mood, physical health and cognition (Schiphorst 2007). This is an important component of the AMP. Arts-based and Montessori-based approaches increase communication, episodic memory, and relationships between PwD and their family members and caregivers (Wilks et al. 2019; Camp 2010; Ducak et al. 2018; Cheon et al. 2016; Nagahata et al. 2004).

AI and Machine Learning for Cognitive Enhancement
Artificial intelligence systems hold potential to improve cognitive enhancement for PwD to live independently without relying on pharmacological treatments (Sonntag 2015; Tyack et al. 2017; Camic et al. 2014; Spartano et al. 2019). The AMP intends to integrate machine learning to gain insights into the quality and effectiveness in the platforms ability to create enjoyable experiences.

Crip Theory and Disability Research
Crip theory approaches to design can help researchers center PwD and caregiver perspectives in treatment plans, in addition to rethinking how power can influence the research process (Hamraie and Fritsch 2019; Yeargeau 2017; Schalk 2013).

3 The ABLE Music Platform Hardware and Software Iterative Design Process

3.1 Initial Hardware Design

The ABLE Music platform will connect to a computer using an MbientLabs Meta-Motion R+ werable sensor (see **Error! Reference source not found.**). The sensor will connect via Bluetooth (BLE) to the host computer to translate the user's gestures into motion-based sound and art on the screen. The user can clip on the sensor, housed in a silicone case, to their sleeve, a glove or wear it like a watch. The user can then move their hand or extremity that the sensor is attached to in 3D space to create art and music in an application on the host computer.

Machine learning algorithms will aid in the recognition of gestures made by the user. This can aid in recognizing patterns that can help improve the enjoyability of the interaction and aid in the recalling of memories for the user and their caregivers (Figs. 1 and 2).

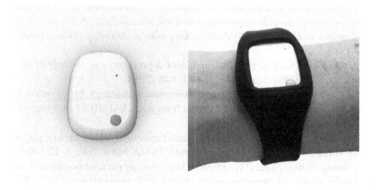

Fig. 1. (Left) MbientLabs MetaMotion R+werable sensor, (Right) MetaMotion R+werable sensor in the watch style silicone case.

Fig. 2. Movement and gesture by the user is sent to the ABE Music painting and music application to generate audio, visual and haptic feedback (through the sensors vibration motor).

References

Camic, P.M., Tischler, V., Pearman, C.H: Viewing and making art together: a multi-session art-gallery-based intervention for people with dementia and their carers. Aging Mental Health **18**(2), 161–168 (2014)

Camp, C.J.: Origin of montessori programming for dementia. Nonpharmacol. Ther. Dement. **1**(2), 163–174 (2010)

Canadian Institute for Health Information: https://www.cihi.ca/en/dementia-in-canada/how-dementia-impacts-canadians. Accessed 9 Apr 2020

Canada Public Health Service: https://www.canada.ca/en/public-health/services/publications/diseases-conditions/dementia-strategy.html. Accessed 9 Apr 2020

Cheon, C.Y., et al.: Creative therapy in an acute care setting for older patients with Delirium and Dementia. Dement. Geriatr. Cogn. Disord. **6**(2), 268–275 (2016)

Ducak, K., Denton, M., Elliot, G.: Implementing Montessori methods for Dementia in Ontario long-term care homes: recreation staff and multidisciplinary consultants' perceptions of policy and practice issues. Dementia **17**(1), 5–33 (2018)

Hamraie, A., Fritsch, K.: Crip Technoscience Manifesto. Catal. Feminism Theory Technosci. **5**(1), 1–34 (2019)

Nagahata, K., Fukushima, T., Ishibashi, N, Takahashi, Y., Moriyama, M.: A soundscape study: what kinds of sounds do elderly patients with dementia recollect? Noise Health **6**(24) (2004)

Schalk, S.: Coming to claim crip: disidenitification with/in disability studies. Disabil. Stud. Q. **33**(2) (2013)

Schuch, F.B., et al.: Physical activity and imminent depression: a meta-analysis of prospective cohort studies. Am. J. Psychiatry **175**(7), 631–648 (2018)

Sonntag, D.: Kognit: intelligent cognitive enhancement technology by cognitive models and mixed reality for dementia patients. In: Papers from the AAAI 2015 Fall Symposium, pp. 47–53 (2015)

Spartano, N.L., et al.: Association of accelerometer-measured light-intensity physical activity with brain volume: the Framingham heart study. JAMA Netw. **2**(4), 1–12 (2019)

Tse, A.C.Y., Wong, T.W.L., Lee, P.H.: Effect of low-intensity exercise on physical and cognitive health in older adults: a systematic review. Sports Med. Open **1**(1), 1–13 (2015). https://doi.org/10.1186/s40798-015-0034-8

Tyack, C., Camic, P.M., Heron, M.J., Hulbert, S.: Viewing art on a tablet computer: a well-being intervention for people with Dementia and their caregivers. J. Appl. Gerontol. **36**(7), 864–894 (2017)

Wilks, S.E., Boyd, P.A., Bates, S.M., Cain, D.S., Geiger, J.N.: Montessori-based activities among persons with late-stage dementia: evaluation of mental and behavioral health outcomes. Dementia **18**(4), 1373–1392 (2019)

Yergeau, M.: Authoring Autism: on Rhetoric and Neurological Queerness. Duke University Press, Durham (2017)

Fundamental Study for Analysis of Walking Considering Base of Support for Prevention of Stumble Accident

Masaya Hori[1]([✉]), Yusuke Kobayashi[2], Tatsuo Hisaoka[2],
Takuya Kiryu[2], Yu Kikuchi[2], Hiroaki Inoue[3], and Shunji Shimizu[3]

[1] Graduate School of Engineering and Management,
Suwa University of Science, Chino, Japan
gh19701@ed.sus.ac.jp
[2] Shimizu Laboratory, Suwa University of Science, Chino, Japan
SRL@ed.sus.ac.jp
[3] Department of Applied Information Engineering, Suwa University of Science,
Chino, Japan
{hiroaki-inoue,shun}@rs.sus.ac.jp

Abstract. Recently, in developed countries, especially in Japan, the population of elderly people are increasing. Physical function of elderly people deteriorates due to age, it causes stumble accident. A stumble accident of an elderly people leads to a bone fracture. In elderly people, it is very dangerous to become bedridden by bone fractures and injuries. Thus, it is important for elderly people to prevent stumble accident. The "Base of Support" (BoS) has been reported to be related to stumble accident. We have been executing experimental consideration regarding stumble accident and BoS. In this study, we executed measurement and analysis of walking movement for human and analyzed based on the dynamic change for BoS. This experiment, we measured and analyzed walking movement using optical and inertial sensor type motion analysis device. In addition, we measured the step length using the camera. The Subjects walked straight for approximately 10 m indoors. Moreover, they executed heel strike according to the timing when the metronome sounds. Also, we changed the rhythm of the metronome every 10 bpm from 90 bpm to 140 bpm. As for experimental results, the dynamic change of BoS increased as walking rhythm changes faster. This is considered to be increasing movement of gravity center of human body. In this study, we executed measurement and analysis of walking movement for human and analyzed the dynamic change for BoS. In the future, we aim to establish an index of the dynamic stability evaluation of human walking movement.

Keywords: Motion analysis · Walking movement · Evaluation method · Base of Support (BoS)

C. Stephanidis et al. (Eds.): HCII 2020, CCIS 1294, pp. 455–463, 2020.
https://doi.org/10.1007/978-3-030-60703-6_59

1   Introduction

Recently, the number of elderly people is increasing in developed countries especially in Japan [1]. Elderly people's physical function decline with age causes stumble accident. Therefore, it is dangerous for the elderly people to fall. Around the world, an estimated 646,000 peoples die each year from stumbling accidents, and elderly people over 65 years old are said to cause the most fatal stumbling accident [2]. There are many accidents involving the elderly people, and according to statistics from the Tokyo Fire Department, approximately 81.4% of the elderly people who have been urgently transported in the past five years have been urgently transported due to stumbling [3]. There are internal and external factors for a reason of stumble accidents of the elderly people. Internal factors include muscle weakness, vision loss, decreased understanding and judgment, depression and polypharmacy [4]. External factors include slippery floors and the carpet edge turn over. If an elderly people falls, it may cause a fracture even if it is not fatal. In particular, femoral neck fracture reduces walking ability in the elderly people. A decrease in walking ability reduces the amount of exercise and narrows the scope of daily life. In addition, elderly peoples who have fallen feel anxious and limit their activities. Therefore, the physical strength of the elderly peoples may be reduced, causing a bedridden state. It is important and pressing necessity for elderly peoples to prevent stumble accident [5, 6]. Also, we think that prevention of stumble accident is effective in living an independent life. A lot of study about stumble accident have been reported [7]. However, there are few products that prevent stumble accident. Thus, there is a need to develop equipment that prevents stumble accident. Final purpose of this study is develop equipment to prevent stumble accident. In this study we focused on "Base of Support" (BoS) that should be related to stumble accident [8]. We performed measurement and analysis of walking movement for human and consider to analyze the dynamic change for BoS (Fig. 1).

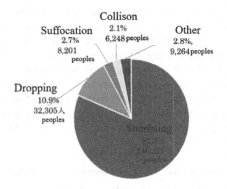

Other: Stabbed, Drown, Laceration, etc.

Fig. 1. Elderly emergency carrier for each type of accident in the past five years from 2017.

2 Experimental Method

2.1 Base of Support

BoS can be defined by a body part in contact with the ground surface as shown in Fig. 2. In addition, when a cane is used, the BoS can be defined including the contact position of the cane. The assumed line that extends vertically downward from the center of gravity of the body is called the center of gravity line [9]. In the case of a healthy people, if this center of gravity line deviates from the bottom BoS, it will either fall over or prevent it from stumbling. Body stability is basically affected by the height of the center of gravity relative to BoS and the width of the BoS and the position of the center of gravity line. In addition, it is said that if the center of gravity is located more higher, the stability will decrease. If the center of gravity is located more lower, the stability will increase (Fig. 3).

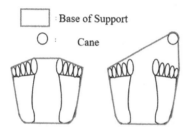

Fig. 2. Base of support image.

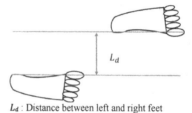

L_d : Distance between left and right feet

Fig. 3. Measurement image of distance between left and right feet.

2.2 Measurement of Footsize

The subject were eight 20s males. In order to estimate the BoS, we measured the values of the lower limbs of the subjects in preliminary experiments. Typical results are shown in Table 1 and 2. First, we performed to measure the distance between the left and right foot in a stable gait when subjects performed walking motion. Next, the width of the foot, the length from the foot point to the little finger MP joint, the maximum width of the forefoot, and the maximum width of the hindfoot were measured. The foot point mean the point at the tip farthest from the heel point. Also, The little finger MP joint mean the joint at the base of the little finger. The length between these two was measured. These values will be used later to calculate the area of BoS (Figs. 4, 5 and 6).

Table 1. Subjects information.

	Age	Height [cm]	Weight [Kg]	L_F	L_d
Subject1	22	174	75.3	27	9.5
Subject2	23	165	61.5	24	8
Subject3	21	165	46.35	23.5	8.2
Subject4	21	171.2	61.65	25.2	6.8
Subject5	22	170.7	67.55	24.8	5.6
Subject6	22	163.8	59.45	25.5	6.5
Subject7	22	175.8	52.3	24.6	12
Subject8	22	171.3	58.9	26	8.4

L_F: Foot length
L_d: Distance between left and right feet

Table 2. The width of each foot and the length from each point to the little finger MP joint.

	L_{FWR} [cm]	L_{FWL} [cm]	L_{RWR} [cm]	L_{RWL} [cm]	$L_{t\text{-}mpR}$ [cm]	$L_{t\text{-}mpL}$ [cm]
Subject1	10.5	10.5	5.5	5.5	7.0	7.0
Subject2	10.0	10.0	5.5	5.5	7.0	7.0
Subject3	10.2	10.0	6.2	6.5	8.4	8.5
Subject4	9.0	8.5	6.0	6.0	6.0	6.5
Subject5	10	9.8	6.2	6.6	7	6.6
Subject6	9.5	9.6	5.2	5.3	8.6	8.5
Subject7	9.5	9.8	5.0	5.6	8.8	9.4
Subject8	10.2	9.0	7.0	6.6	9.0	7.8

L_{Fw}: Forefoot maximum width, L_{FwR}: Right foot, L_{FwL}: Left foot
L_{Rw}: Maximum rear foot width, L_{RwR}: Right foot, L_{RwL}: Left foot
$L_{(t\text{-}mp)}$: Length from the apex to the little finger MP joint
$L_{(t\text{-}mpR)}$: Right foot, $L_{(t\text{-}mpL)}$: Left foot

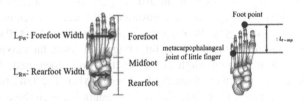

Fig. 4. Measurement of foot width and length between foot point and little finger MP joint.

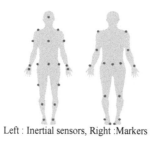

Left : Inertial sensors, Right :Markers

Fig. 5. Inertial sensor and motion capture marker

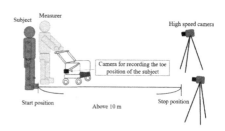

Fig. 6. Experimental landscape mounting positions.

2.3   Measurement Equipment

NOITOM's Perception Neuron was used as the inertial sensor type 3D motion analyze. And we used the motion capture which was products by Nobby Tech. Ltd.

2.4   Measurement of Walking Movement

We measured walking movement using optical and inertial sensor type motion analysis devices. At the same time, we also measured the stride required to estimate the area of the support base using an optical camera. The subject walked about 10 m indoors. The subjects walked while looking at the gazing point at a constant rhythm so that the left and right feet were grounded in time with the timing of the metronome. We repeated experiments with different rhythm of the metronome every 10 bpm from 90 bpm to 140 bpm. A camera was attached to a carriage and translated with the subject to measure subject's stride. We carried out these experiments with informed consent of the subjects following the approval of the Suwa University of Science Ethical Review Board.

2.5   Calculation Method of Dynamic Base of Support Area

To analyze the dynamic BoS, the model in Fig. 7 was simplified. In this model, the position of the outside of the foot that touches the next heel from the kicking is on the same straight line. We assumed six points coordinates on the model in Fig. 7. Assumed coordinates include values such as the maximum width of the forefoot and hindfoot measured in the experiment preparation and the step length measured by the camera from the experiment. Next, each coordinate is explained. To estimate the area, the length of the part where the heel is in contact with the ground: L_h is the same as the length from the apex to the little finger MP joint. Next, the length of each side surrounding the area of the support base was calculated using each coordinate. Then, the lengths of point B, point C, and point D were calculated from the origin O, and four triangles were assumed (Fig. 8). The assumed triangles are $\triangle OAB$, $\triangle OBC$, $\triangle OCD$, $\triangle ODE$, respectively, and their areas are S1, S2, S3, and S4. The respective areas S1,

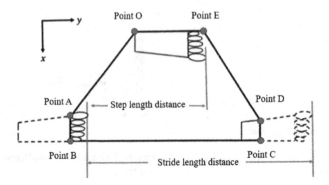

Fig. 7. Base of support model.

S2, S3, and S4 were obtained using Heron's formula (1) (Fig. 9). Then, the area S of the support base was obtained by adding the areas of the triangles .

$$S = \sqrt{s(s-a)(s-b)(s-c)}$$ (1)

$$s = a + b + c/2$$

- Point: O (0,0)
- Point: A (Ax, Ay)
  Ax: $L_{Fw} + L_d$
  Ay: $-\left(L_F + L_{t-mp}\right)$
- Point: B (Bx, By)
  Bx: $L_{Fw} + L_d + L_{Fw}$
  By: $-\left(SL - L_F + L_{t-mp}\right)$
- Point: C (Cx, Cy)
  Cx: $L_{Fw} + L_d + L_{Fw}$
  Cy: $WC - L_F + L_{t-mp} + L_h$
- Point: D (Dx, Dy)
  Dx: $L_{Fw} + L_d + L_{Fw} - L_{Rw}$
  Dy: $WC - L_F + L_{t-mp} + L_h$
- Point: E (Ex, Ey)

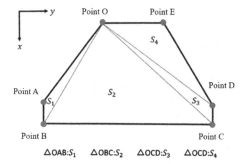

$\triangle$OAB:S_1 $\triangle$OBC:S_2 $\triangle$OCD:S_3 $\triangle$OCD:S_4

Fig. 8. Area calculation using four triangles.

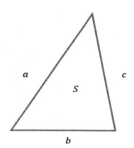

Fig. 9. Triangle (Heron's formula).

3 Experimental Result and Discussion

3.1 The Dynamic Base of Support Area

Based on the stride data obtained from the camera, the area of the BoS was divided into left and right for 4 steps (walking for 2 cycles). As the rhythm changes rapidly, the dynamic BoS tends to become wider (Fig. 10). This is because the sway of the center of gravity increases as the rhythm rises, and the area increases to prevent the center of gravity from falling out of the support base. In addition, Subject and camera are moving side by side. Therefore, although the camera is moving at a constant speed, it is necessary to examine the measurement error due to the camera deviation in the future. Next, based on the stride data of the inertial sensor motion analyzer, the area of the support base was divided into left and right for 4 steps (walking for 2 cycles). As in 1), the area of the dynamic support base tends to increase as the rhythm changes rapidly (Fig. 11). A tendency similar to the result calculated using the walking data measured by the camera was obtained from the calculation result using the stride data measured by the inertial sensor type motion analyzer. Therefore, it is considered possible to estimate the dynamic support base area to some extent without using a camera.

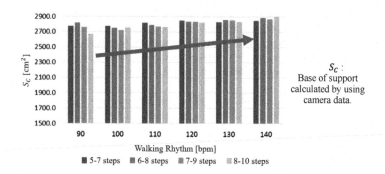

Fig. 10. Base of support of subject 1.

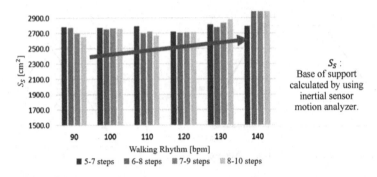

Fig. 11. Base of support of subject 1.

4   Conclusion

The purpose of this study is to measure and analyze human walking movements and to analyze dynamic changes in BoS. Currently, there is a lot of research on stumbling. However, there is few effective support equipment to prevent stumbling. For this reason, our final purpose of this study was to develop equipment that prevents accidents from stumbling. Thus, we focused on the base of support that is related to stumbling. In order to estimate the area of the dynamic change for BoS, the walking motion was measured and analyzed using a camera and a 3D motion analyzer, and the area was calculated from the obtained data. Therefore, the area of the BoS calculated from the image data, the area of the BoS calculated from the data of the inertial sensor type motion analysis device. In this study, we proposed a new index of dynamic stability of walking motion based on the proposal, estimation and consideration of the area of the supporting base during walking motion. It is necessary to verify the usefulness in the future.

References

1. Japan, Cabinet Office: Annual Report on the ageing society (2018). (https://www8.cao.go.jp/kourei/english/annualreport/2018/pdf/cover.pdf). Accessed 24 Oct 2019
2. Switzerland, World Health Organization: WHO global report on falls prevention in older age. https://www.who.int/ageing/publications/Falls_prevention7March.pdf. Accessed 24 Oct 2019
3. Japan, International Fire Service Information Center: Overview of the 2018 white paper on fire service. http://www.kaigai-shobo.jp/pdf/20190531_White_paper30_eng.pdf. Accessed 24 Oct 2019
4. BPAC better medicine: Falls in older people: causes and prevention. Accessed 24 2019
5. Murata, S., Tsuda, A.: Prevention of falls in the elderly. Kurume Univ. Psychol. Res. **5**, 91–104 (2006)
6. Suzukawa, M., Shimada, H., Makizako, H., Watanabe, S., Suzuki, T.: Incidence of falls and fractures in disabled elderly people utilizing long-term care insurance. Jpn. Geriatr. Soc. **46**(4), 334–340 (2009)

7. Schillings, A.M., Mulder, Th, Duysens, J.: Stumbling over obstacles in older adults compared to young adults. J. Neurophysiol. **92**(2), 1158–1168 (2005)
8. Robinovitch, S.N., et al.: Video capture of the circumstances of falls in elderly people residing in long-term care: an observational study. Lancet **381**(9860), 47–54 (2013)
9. Benda, B.J., Riley, P.O., Krebs, D.E.: Biomechanical relationship between center of gravity and center of pressure during standing. IEEE Trans. Rehabil. Eng. **2**(1), 3–10 (1994)

Leveraging Twitter Data to Explore the Feasibility of Detecting Negative Health Outcomes Related to Vaping

Erin Kasson[1], Lijuan Cao[1], Ming Huang[2] (iD), Dezhi Wu[3] (iD),
and Patricia A. Cavazos-Rehg[1(✉)] (iD)

[1] Department of Psychiatry, School of Medicine,
Washington University in St. Louis, St. Louis, MO 63110, USA
{erinmkasson,lcao24,pcavazos}@wustl.edu
[2] Department of Health Sciences Research, Mayo Clinic,
Rochester, MN 55905, USA
Huang.Ming@mayo.edu
[3] Department of Integrated Information Technology,
University of South Carolina, Columbia, SC 29208, USA
dezhiwu@cec.sc.edu

Abstract. Adverse health outcomes (e.g., respiratory infections, lung injury, death) related to vaping were reported at significantly higher rates in healthcare systems starting in the fall of 2019. This study seeks to leverage artificial intelligence (AI) techniques, such as latent dirichlet allocation (LDA) methods, to determine whether a signal of these negative health outcomes could have been detected by the frequency of Twitter content posted about vaping and these health outcomes prior to this increase. We utilized a random sample of 3,523 tweets from 2019 and performed LDA methods on this sample to cluster the tweets and identify latent topics. We then utilized keywords from within the health-related cluster (topic) to manually verify the frequency of these tweets across previous years to approximate topic trends. LDA methods resulted in 4 distinct topics of tweets, including a health-related topic. Keywords from this topic were found to increase slightly in 2017 and 2018, with a dramatic increase in 2019. Further, the highest performing keyword combination was found to increase most significantly beginning in August 2019. The results of this study support the feasibility of leveraging artificial intelligence techniques for surveillance of public health concerns such as vaping and adverse health outcomes reported in Twitter. Further research is needed into the development of such models, which could promote earlier detection of public health issues and timely outreach to those groups most at risk.

Keywords: Vaping · Social media · Twitter · Surveillance · Latent dirichlet allocation · LDA · GENSIM · Adverse health outcomes

C. Stephanidis et al. (Eds.): HCII 2020, CCIS 1294, pp. 464–468, 2020.
https://doi.org/10.1007/978-3-030-60703-6_60

1   Introduction

The use of vaping products (e.g., electronic nicotine delivery systems, e-cigarettes) has been increasing rapidly with in the past decade, dramatically changing the tobacco use and marketing landscape. Of concern, vaping products are especially popular among adolescents and young adults, with 25% reporting use in the past 30 days in 2019, possibly putting this group at risk for later chronic health conditions [1]. With limited information on the long-term effects of these products, health information provided in regards to vaping has been somewhat unclear about the associated risks: some sources claim vaping as a potential way to stop or reduce combustible smoking, while other sources suggest vaping has the same or increased health risks as combustible smoking [2, 3].

In the fall of 2019, adverse health outcomes related to vaping across the US increased at an alarming rate, including reports of lung injury, lung infections, respiratory issues, and even death [4]. Many of those who experienced these outcomes were adolescents and young adults due to the popularity of these products and the focus of marketing campaigns for vaping products toward this group. In addition to later health impacts, the surge in lung injury and health complications related to vaping in 2019 demonstrates acute and immediate risks associated with these products as well across those in all age groups.

Given that many individuals utilize social media to share and seek information regarding substance use and vaping products, especially adolescents and young adults with whom these products are popular, the content shared on these platforms could help to illustrate the frequency of adverse health outcomes experienced by those who vape and overall public sentiment toward vaping both before and after this drastic increase in later 2019. In this exploratory study, we aim to determine whether Twitter could be used as a means to conduct surveillance of public health concerns, such as the adverse health outcomes related to vaping, by detecting signals of these adverse outcomes early to provide timely and accurate health information to the public in order to subsequently prevent or decrease the number of negative outcomes experienced.

2   Methods

In this preliminary investigation, we utilized a random sample of tweets (N = 3,523) from 2019 using the broad terms vaping and vape. To pull this historic Twitter data, we used a Python module called Tweepy, which has been commonly used in social media studies leveraging computer science techniques [4]. Tweepy is an open-sourced library for accessing the Twitter API to gather a random sample of tweets with given keywords [5]. After collecting and cleaning this sample of data, we utilized latent dirichlet allocation (LDA), state-of-the-art topic modeling methods to group these tweets into topic clusters. LDA is a generative probabilistic model of a sample, where tweets are represented as random mixtures over latent topics, and where each topic is characterized by a distribution over words [6]. For this sample, we specifically used the LDA methods implemented in GENSIM package in Python for modeling topics in the

Twitter sample [7, 8]. The numbers of topic clusters were determined based on visual inspection of keyword similarities and clinical themes.

3 Results

3.1 Latent Dirichlet Allocation (LDA)

LDA methods used identified four distinct clusters with the following themes: (1) General vaping (N = 1, 503), (2) Method of use (N = 688), (3) Marketing (N = 451), and (4) Health (N = 881). Figure 1 outlines the number of tweets allocated to each topic cluster and examples of relevant keywords within each topic cluster. Within the health cluster, we reviewed the first 50 keywords pulled by the LDA in further detail for relevant clinical terms related to adverse health outcomes. We found a total of 11 health-specific keywords: *lung, ban, death, injury, popcorn (as in popcorn lung), illness, epidemic, doctors, cases, crisis, and disease.*

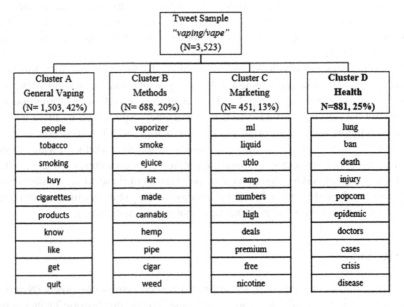

Fig. 1. Topic modeling results with examples of clinically relevant keywords from each topic cluster

3.2 Manual Validation Check

Utilizing these systematically identified keywords from 2019, we then went back into Twitter to visually check the number of the tweets containing these words and "vaping," "vape" across 2014–2019 to ensure they were in line with our research question and generated by unique Twitter users. The results of this validation check are shown below in Table 1. Of note, there was a slight increase found in health-related vaping tweets between years 2014–2017, with a steeper increase in 2018 for some terms. Further, nearly all health terms, when combined with "vaping" or "vape" returned too many results to be reliably counted by a human reviewer (i.e., 200+ tweets). We additionally took the highest performing combination, "lung"+"vaping," and checked the number of tweets month by month to gather a more fine-grained understanding on when the frequency of tweets containing these terms started to increase, which appeared to be around August 2019.

Table 1. Number of tweets by keyword combinations across years 2014–2019

Keywords	Year					
	2014	2015	2016	2017	2018	2019
vaping + lung	30	80	85	91	135	200+
vape + lung	40	56	80	76	120	200+
vaping + ban	70	122	69	74	91	200+
vape + ban	70	92	60	72	85	200+
vaping + death	55	88	77	100	65	200+
vape + death	60	57	80	48	59	200+
vaping + injury	16	36	44	42	48	200+
vaping + popcorn	30	61	60	64	63	165
vaping + illness	22	39	53	60	65	200+
vaping + epidemic	20	73	48	62	90	200+
vaping + doctors	53	123	90	92	105	200+
vaping + cases	75	108	105	100	165	200+
vaping + crisis	14	46	55	45	134	200+
vaping + disease	44	53	45	90	81	200+

2019 by Month								
Keywords	Jan	Feb	Mar	Apr	May	June	July	Aug	Sep
vaping + lung	110	110	110	120	110	120	75	200+	200+

4 Conclusions and Future Directions

The findings of this preliminary investigation support the utilization of artificial intelligence techniques for clustering themes and systematically generating clinically significant keywords to aid in the surveillance of vaping and adverse health outcomes on Twitter. Future studies could expand upon the exploratory investigation outlined above to leverage artificial intelligence techniques, such as (1) LDA methods or sentiment analyses year by year leading up to August 2019 to determine changes in the number of tweets specifically discussing adverse health outcomes related to vaping, (2) changes in sentiment related to vaping over time, and (3) the possible intersection of this sentiment with risk perception and continued use. Because of the complexity and dynamics of Twitter data, it is difficult to obtain and verify an entirely comprehensive sample of all tweets discussing vaping and its increasing adverse health outcomes over time. As such, it is crucial to develop more robust models of surveillance or detection associated with vaping adverse health outcomes, so we plan to use not only Twitter trend data but also advanced artificial intelligence and machine learning techniques, paired with human coding on tweet content, to achieve such goals. The development of such an algorithm has many important public health implications, as early detection of substance increases, and adverse health outcomes could lead to early problem recognition and policy change as well as outreach and treatment for individuals indicating substance use risk on social media. Given that the use of vaping products among adolescents and young adults has increased dramatically over the last decade to nearly 15% in 2018 [9, 10], and that the current COVID-19 pandemic places those who vape at a higher risk of infection and health complications [11], it is vital to develop and evaluate strategies to identify and prevent vaping, especially among this at-risk group.

Acknowledgements. Financial support for this investigation was provided by the National Institutes of Health (NIH), Grant #K02 DA043657 (PI: Patricia Cavazos-Rehg) and the University of South Carolina, Grant #80002838 (PI: Dezhi Wu). The content of this paper is solely the responsibility of the authors and does not necessarily represent the official views of the National Institutes of Health or the University of South Carolina.

References

1. Miech, R., Johnston, L., O'Malley, P.M., Bachman, J.G., Patrick, M.E.: Trends in adolescent vaping, 2017–2019. N. Engl. J. Med. **381**(15), 1490–1491 (2019)
2. Dulam, R.V.S., Murthy, M., Luo, J.: Seeing through the smoke: a world-wide comparative study of e-cigarette flavors, brands and markets using data from Reddit and Twitter. arXiv preprint arXiv:2002.01575 (2020)
3. Pepper, J.K., et al.: Impact of messages about scientific uncertainty on risk perceptions and intentions to use electronic vaping products. Addict. Behav. **91**, 136–140 (2019)
4. Evans, M.E., et al.: Update: interim guidance for health care professionals evaluating and caring for patients with suspected e-cigarette, or vap-ing, product use–associated lung injury and for reducing the risk for rehospitalization and death following hospital discharge— United States, December 2019. Morbidity and Mortality Weekly Report **68**(5152), 1189 (2020)
5. Asghari, M., Sierra-Sosa, D., Elmaghraby, A.: Trends on health in social media: analysis using Twitter topic modeling. In: 2018 IEEE International Symposium on Signal Processing and Information Technology (ISSPIT), pp. 558–563. IEEE (2018)
6. Roesslein, J.: Tweepy. Python programming language module (2015)
7. Blei, D.M., Ng, A.Y., Jordan, M.I.: Latent dirichlect allocation. J. Mach. Learn. Res. **3**, 993–1022 (2003)
8. Rehurek, R.: Genism: Topic Modeling for Humans, 19 June 2020. https://radimrehurek.com/gensim/index.html
9. Besaratinia, A., Tommasi, S.: Vaping epidemic: challenges and opportunities. Cancer Causes Control **31**(7), 663–667 (2020). https://doi.org/10.1007/s10552-020-01307-y
10. Al-Hamdani, M., Hopkins, D.B., Park, T.: Vaping among youth and young adults: a "red alert" state. J. Public Health Policy **41**(1), 63–69 (2020)
11. Volkow, N.D.: Collision of the COVID-19 and addiction epidemics. Ann. Int. Med. (2020). https://doi.org/10.7326/m20-1212

The Use of Human-Centered AI to Augment the Health of Older Adults

Ronit Kathuria[1] and Vinish Kathuria[2(✉)]

[1] The Shriram School, Gurgaon, India
[2] Indian Institute of Management, Lucknow, India
efpm014@iiml.ac.in

Abstract. The research studies the impact of Human-Centred Artificial Intelligence (HAI) to augment the health of older adults. The researchers are especially interested in looking at the impact of the decrease in the cognitive effort for users and an increase in the naturalness of Human-Machine interaction. A mobile application that uses Natural Language Processing to enable senior citizens to interpret doctors' handwriting is used as the mode of experimental study. The application consists of an optical character recognition program that leverages a Recurrent Neural Network and a data set of thousands of handwritten prescriptions. The interpreted information is linked to a personal calendar that automatically sets reminders to take the medicines. Voice is used as a medium of interaction with older adults to evaluate the role of naturalness in Human-Machine interaction. Initial results showcase a reduction in the amount of cognitive effort required to comprehend prescriptions and taking timely medication, while simultaneously making the elderly more aware and self-sufficient.

Keywords: Artificial intelligence · Human-machine interaction · Handwriting recognition · Voice interaction · Older adults

1 Introduction

Artificial intelligence is set to be the cornerstone of future technological development as experts expect it to add $15.7 trillion to the Global Economy in years to come. We now live in a time where AI-driven offerings ranging from Google Maps to Amazon's Alexa are nothing but ubiquitous. This ubiquity has led to a myriad of academic research focused on Primary Adopters - Adults, Youth, and Kids. However, an entire avenue of exploration that sheds light on the use of AI by Secondary Adopters such as Older Adults and Senior Citizens has been left almost untouched.

India, a country with 218 million citizens aged 50 years or older (Census India 2016), issues regarding the legibility of handwritten doctors' prescriptions are common. Such problems significantly increase the amount of cognitive effort required to interpret a prescription and older adults are often left helpless and dependent on local chemists to decipher the prescription for them. A study by MIT Age Lab (Lee 2014) showcases that when user experience and design aspects are tailored to provide a holistic framework that covers the needs of the elderly, technology can be used at the

© Springer Nature Switzerland AG 2020
C. Stephanidis et al. (Eds.): HCII 2020, CCIS 1294, pp. 469–477, 2020.
https://doi.org/10.1007/978-3-030-60703-6_61

center of strategies for effectively enabling adults to stay independent and healthy. The Media Naturalness Theory (Kock 2004) also suggests that the decrease in the degree of naturalness of a communication medium leads to increased cognitive effort for users.

The authors capitalize on the Human-Centred Artificial Intelligence (HAI) driven Automation framework combining natural human-machine interaction with personalization and service automation. Since computers are thought of as social actors, social rules from traditional human-to-human interactions apply to human-machine interactions. The framework builds upon the psychobiological model, media naturalness hypothesis and research in the fields of Human-Computer Interaction and Information Systems on handwriting systems.

2 Literature and Methodology

Older Adults' Technology Adoption. Technology is now regarded as the center of strategies for effectively enabling older adults to stay healthy, independent, safe and socially connected. Technological advancement, including processing power and transmission speeds, have made an abundance of relevant information available at our fingertips. Nimrod (2013) commented on the value of gerontographics in studies of internet use and successful aging. Jin et al. (2019) leveraged the Technology Acceptance theory and Social Cognitive theory to understand the everyday learning of older adults using mobile devices. A Finnish study (Vuori et al. 2005) leveraged the Life Stage Model of Healthy Indulging and Ailing Outgoing to understand older adults' acquaintance with technology. Kang et al. (2010) stipulated the desire of older adults for technology to help them live independently of others. A study by MIT Age Lab combined various related disciplines – human factors, behavioral science, information technology, consumer studies, computer science, gerontology, and more – to build conceptual and empirical models to describe how consumers and users accept and adopt innovations, technologies, and new products (Lee 2014). A study in China on mobile health services concluded that perceived value, attitude, perceived behavior control, technology anxiety, and self-actualization need positively affected the behavior intention of older users. (Deng et al. 2014).

Handwritten Text Recognition. Handwritten Text Recognition (HTR), is the ability of a computer to receive and interpret intelligible handwritten input from sources such as paper documents, photographs, touchscreens, and other devices. The difficulty of handwriting recognition can be attributed to the wide variety of writing styles. While traditional techniques focus on segmenting individual characters for recognition, modern techniques focus on recognizing all the characters in a segmented line of text. Particularly they focus on machine learning techniques that can learn visual features, avoiding the limiting feature engineering previously used. Deep learning has been widely used to recognize handwriting. Neural networks can learn features from analyzing a dataset, and then classify an unseen image based on weights. Features are extracted in the convolutional layers, where a kernel is passed over the image to extract a certain feature. State-of-the-art methods use Convolutional Neural Networks (CNN) to extract visual features over several overlapping windows of a text line image, which a Recurrent Neural Network (RNN) uses to produce character probabilities (Puigcerver 2017). An RNN is a class of artificial neural networks where connections between nodes form a directed graph along a temporal sequence. Derived from feed-forward neural networks, RNNs can use their internal state (memory) to process variable-length sequences of inputs and this makes them applicable to tasks such as unsegmented, connected handwriting recognition (Graves et al. 2009) or speech recognition (Li et al. 2014).

Furthermore, using neural networks on a database makes deep learning methods more resilient to changes in handwriting styles, and alleviates the challenges in feature extraction in classical methods. However, the output accuracy depends strongly on the quality and completeness of the dataset used in the training process. Early research in handwriting recognition was fuelled by the creation of the MNIST Database, which contains 70,000 handwritten digits, and has been used in deep learning since 1998. LeCun (1998) introduced the use of neural networks for handwriting. Ciresan (2011) leveraged a CNN to analyze handwriting, achieving a minuscule 0.27% error rate. Jayasundra et al. (2019) have introduced a method of producing new training samples from the existing samples, with realistic augmentations that reflect actual variations that are present in human handwriting.

Voice Interaction. People associate voice with communication with other people rather than with technology. Essentially, voice interaction is the ability to speak to your devices, have them proceed with your request and act upon whatever you're asking them. Voice interaction systems can significantly enhance the naturalness of human-machine interactions and ameliorate older adults' technological capabilities.

Voice interaction systems are dependent on speech recognition, an interdisciplinary subfield of computational linguistics that develops methodologies and technologies that enables the recognition and translation of spoken language into text by computers. Today, many aspects of speech recognition have been taken over by a deep learning method called Long short-term memory (LSTM), a recurrent neural network (Hochreiter and Schmidhuber 1997). In 2015, Google's speech recognition reportedly experienced a dramatic performance jump of 49% through CTC-trained LSTM, which is now available through Google Voice to all smartphone users (Sak et al. 2015).

Media Theories. Media theories have traditionally provided insights into the human aspect of content absorption and consumption and play a key role in driving the transition to naturalness in human-computer interaction. Kock's (2004) psychobiological model or Media Naturalness Theory, based on Darwin's theory of evolution, hypothesizes that face-to-face communication is the most "natural" method of communication, and a decrease in the degree of naturalness of a communication medium leads to increased cognitive effort for users. Overcompensation Principle states that individuals overcompensate for the cognitive obstacles they perceive to be associated with the lack of naturalness of the media (Kock 1998). Media Equation Theory (Nass et al. 1996) posits that computers are social actors and that social rules from traditional human-to-human interaction also apply to people's interaction with computer devices. The Media Equation theory claims that people tend to treat computers and other media as if they were either real people or real places.

Personalization. Research into personalization is multidisciplinary in nature, formed and influenced mainly by academic disciplines such as Artificial Intelligence (AI) and Machine Learning (ML), Human-Computer Interaction (HCI) and Information Systems (IS), and User Modelling based on (applied) social and cognitive psychology. Advances in ML/AI have made it necessary to reconsider traditional HCI approaches.

3 Research Objectives and Conceptual Framework

The underlying objective of the research is to investigate how Human-Centred Artificial Intelligence can be used to augment the health of older adults. The researchers are especially interested in looking at the impact of a decrease in the cognitive effort for users and an increase in the naturalness of Human-Machine interaction.

Traditional human-machine interfaces leave a lot to be desired and require a significant cognitive effort on part of older adults, which has been a reason for low self-efficacy. However, Artificial Intelligence is driving in a new age of automation and personalization on the machine end. Figure 1 presents a conceptual framework that underpins the discussion to be presented from this research. The framework showcases the role of Human-Centred Artificial Intelligence (HAI) driven automation and natural human-machine interaction in decreasing the effort and frustration for Older Adults' adoption of new-age technologies. The framework leverages the two basic goals of Human-Centered Artificial Intelligence - the AI system must continually improve by learning from humans while creating an effective and fulfilling human-robot interaction experience. The framework is meant to match the demand (of consumers) with supply (of information) in a seamless, natural manner to drive efficiency and accuracy in the system leading to high trust and repeat engagement.

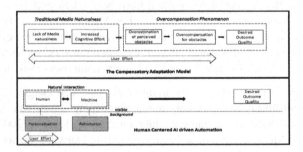

Fig. 1. Human-Centred Artificial Intelligence (HAI) driven automation framework

4 Study

The lives of a myriad of older adults are dependent on the timely and adequate consumption of medicines. However, the vast variety of types of medicines, dosages, and frequency of consumption can create significant frustration and even health issues. Today, tracking the time at which a certain medication must be taken, maintaining a medicine schedule and summarizing medicine intake for a health practitioner is either a memory-driven or manual system for most. The researchers are focused on this every day yet critical activity to see if the use of Artificial Intelligence technologies like Natural Language Processing (NLP) and Voice Interaction can decrease the effort and frustration of older adults while maintaining or improving the performance. A mobile application named Script+created by the researchers is used as a basis for the experimental study.

Design and Procedure. Script+ is an AI-driven mobile application that uses Machine Learning algorithms, Natural Language Processing and Voice Interaction Systems to accurately interpret handwritten doctors' prescriptions and actively remind users to take their medicines.

The Optical Character Recognition (OCR) system consists of a comprehensive neural network built using Python and TensorFlow that was trained on over 115,000 word-images from the IAM On-Line Handwriting Database (IAM-OnDB). The neural network consists of 5 Convolutional Neural Network (CNN) layers, 2 Recurrent Neural Network (RNN) Layers, and a final Connectionist Temporal Classification (CTC) layer. As the input image is fed into the CNN layers, a non-linear ReLU function is applied to extract relevant features from the image. The ReLU function is preferred due to the lower likelihood of a vanishing gradient (which arises when network parameters and hyperparameters are not properly set) relative to a sigmoid function. In the case of the RNN layers, the Long Short-Term Memory (LSTM) implementation is used due to its ability to propagate information through long distances. The CTC is given the RNN output matrix and the ground truth text to compute the loss value and the mean of the loss values of the batch elements is used to train the OCR system. This means is fed into an RMSProp optimizer which is focused on minimizing the loss, and it does so in a very robust manner. For inference, the CTC layer decodes the RNN output matrix into the final text. The OCR system reports an accuracy rate of 95.7% for the IAM Test Dataset, but this accuracy falls to 89.4% for unseen handwritten doctors' prescriptions.

The integration of the OCR system into the mobile application can be seen in Fig. 2. A 3rd party (user) scans the desired prescription using a smartphone camera. The neural network then utilizes NLP to extract relevant medicinal information and place it into 6 distinct categories: Medicine Name, Dosage, Frequency, Time, Start Date and End Date. The interpreted information is then displayed to the user for confirmation, post which the prescription data is automatically linked to a personal calendar where users can easily access medicine-specific details and track their intake. Due to the difficulties arising from the small font size of text notifications and low technological capabilities of older adults, coupled with the added benefit of eliminating the requirement to constantly check one's smartphone, Script+uses voice notifications to remind users to take their medicines. Through the incorporation of different languages and dialects, these personalized notifications can be tailored to meet the needs of the user and ameliorate Human-computer interaction while simultaneously reducing the amount of cognitive effort required to keep up with a medicine schedule.

The subjects' responses were recorded using Hart and Staveland's m (NASA-TLX), a subjective and multivariate assessment tool that rates perceived workload to assess a

Prescription Scanning   NLP Inference   Medicine Confirmation

Prescription Calendar   Reminder Notification   Voice Interaction

Fig. 2. Screens of the mobile application

task's effectiveness. The NASA-TLX divides the total workload into six subjective, and they together form a questionnaire that, in this study, was administered to subjects using a paper and pencil version. The paper and pencil version results in a reduced cognitive workload relative to processing information on a computer screen (Noyes 2007). The subscales include mental demand, physical demand, temporal demand, performance, effort and frustration, and providing descriptions for each measurement can be found to help participants answer accurately. The responses of the subjects are analyzed using Raw-TLX scores rather than weighted ones, as this reduces the time required to administer the TLX and leads to increased sensitivity and experimental validity (Hart 2006). The NASA-TLX has been psychometrically validated across multiple studies, ensuring that it measures what it intends to measure and generates consistent responses (Hart et al. 1988).

The sample-set consisted of users from across a myriad of locations, age groups, genders, professional roles, and technological competences. The experimental sessions for the study were conducted individually with each subject and a single session lasted between 10 and 15 min. Subjects were given an elaborate explanation of the functionality of the mobile application, following which they were requested to use the application for a short period to evaluate its usability and potential benefits. After having the opportunity to ask questions, subjects were asked to compare Script+ to how they usually meet their medicinal needs, including the interpretation of prescriptions and maintaining a medicine schedule.

5   Findings

The findings from the initial results shed light on thought-provoking aspects that can significantly improve Human-computer interaction, and more specifically the use of technology to augment the health of older adults. The results are summarised in Fig. 3, which showcases a comparison of the performance, effort, and frustration felt by subjects when using existing methods to track medicine intake and leveraging the mobile application Script+. The figures are based on Raw-TLX scores, and the lower the value recorded the more positive is the impact.

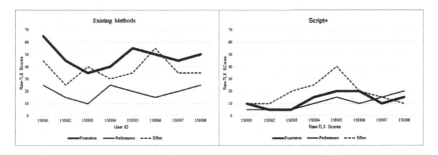

Fig. 3. Graphical representation of performance, frustration, and effort

Results indicate a significant drop in frustration and effort amongst the sample set while using the mobile application compared to existing manual processes. As per the NASA-TLX, frustration is defined as the combination of insecurity, discouragement, stress, and annoyance, whilst effort is the amount of mental and physical work required to achieve the desired level of performance. A decrease in frustration and effort has a positive impact on the quality of life and the findings reinforce the role of technology in improving the quality of life of older adults. The findings also show a negligible change in the performance or desired outcome quality, which is in line with expectations. As additional data points are collected and performance parameters additionally quantified (e.g., number of times one misses a timely medication), we expect quantifiable improvement in performance as well.

An interesting observation was the role of voice interaction. Most older adults and their caregivers had strong positive feedback on the simple but natural voice interaction system. In the current experiment, voice alerts were used as a means of reminders and for updating the post medicine consumption checks. Additional use cases of voice interactions may be looked into as research progress further.

6 Discussions and Implications

The research contributes to the evolving body of academic literature looking at fundamental scientific principles at the intersection of the sensing and actuating, cognitive and behavioral, communications, and computational fields to better predict the behavior of a service system with the human and their health at the center. The significant decrease in the level of frustration and effort, which is produced through the use of machine learning algorithms, NLP and voice interaction systems, is a portrayal of the potential that Human-Centred Artificial Intelligence has of ameliorating the Human-computer interaction of older adults. The decrease in cognitive effort generated by the mobile application, whilst maintaining performance levels, serves as a reminder of the fact that an increase in the naturalness of medicinal technology can remarkably augment the health of older adults. Therefore, as Human-Centered Artificial Intelligence takes center stage, it becomes critical to empirically study solutions that are designed with an awareness that solution is part of a larger ecosystem, including humans and the combination of user experience and technology creates a dyadic relationship where humans learn from machines and vice versa.

References

Census India (2016): SRS Report 2016, Census India

Ciresan, D., Meier, U., Gambardella, L., Schmidhuber, J.: Convolutional neural network committees for handwritten character classification. In: International Conference on Document Analysis and Recognition, Beijing, pp. 1135–1139 (2011)

Deng, Z., Xiuting, M., Shan, L.: Comparison of the middle-aged and older users' adoption of mobile health services in China. Int. J. Med. Inform. **83**(3), 210–224 (2014)

Graves, A., Liwicki, M., Fernandez, S., Bertolami, R., Bunke, H., Schmidhuber, J.: A novel connectionist system for improved unconstrained handwriting recognition. IEEE Trans. Pattern Anal. Mach. Intell. **31**(5), 855–868 (2009)

Hart, S., Staveland, L.: Development of NASA-TLX (Task Load Index): results of empirical and theoretical research. In: Advances in Psychology, Amsterdam, North-Holland, vol. 52, pp. 139–183 (1988)

Hart, S.: NASA-task load index (NASA-TLX); 20 years later. In: Proceedings of the Human Factors and Ergonomics Society Annual Meeting, vol. 50, no. 9, pp. 904–908 (2006)

Hochreiter, S., Schmidhuber, J.: Long short-term memory. Neural Comput. **9**(8), 1735–1780 (1997)

Jayasundara, V., Jayasekara, S., Jayasekara, H., Rajasegaran, J., Seneviratne, S., Rodrigo, R.: TextCaps: handwritten character recognition with very small datasets. In: IEEE Winter Conference on Applications of Computer Vision, pp. 254–262 (2019)

Jin, B., Kim, J., Baumgartner, L.: Informal learning of older adults in using mobile devices: a review of the literature. Adult Educ. Q. **69**(2), 120–141 (2019)

Kang, H., Mahoney, H., Hoenig, V., Hirth, P., Bonato, I., Lipsitz, A.: In situ monitoring of health in older adults: technologies and issues. J. Am. Geriatrics Soc. **58**(8), 1579–1586 (2010)

Kock, N.: Can communication medium limitations foster better group outcomes? An action research study. Inf. Manage. **34**(5), 295–305 (1998)

Kock, N.: The psychobiological model: towards a new theory of computer-mediated communication based on darwinian evolution. Org. Sci. **15**(3), 327–348 (2004)

Lecun, Y.: Gradient-based learning applied to document recognition. Proc. IEEE **86**(11), 2278–2324 (1998)

Lee, C.: User-centered system design in an aging society: an integrated study on technology adoption. Ph.D. Thesis, MIT Age Lab, Boston (2014)

Li, X., Wu, X.: Constructing long short-term memory based deep recurrent neural networks for large vocabulary speech recognition (2014)

Nass, C., Fogg, B., Moon, Y.: Can computers be teammates? Int. J. Hum. Comput. Studies **45**, 669–678 (1996)

Nimrod, G.: Applying gerontographics in the older internet users. J. Audience Reception Stud. **10**, 46–64 (2013)

Noyes, J., Bruneau, D.: A self-analysis of the NASA-TLX workload measure. Ergonomics **50**(4), 514–519 (2007)

Puigcerver, J.: Are multidimensional recurrent layers really necessary for handwritten text recognition? Document analysis and recognition (ICDAR). In: 14th IAPR International Conference, vol. 1 (2017)

Sak, H., Senior, A., Rao, K., Beaufays, F., Schalkwyk, J.: Google voice search: faster and more accurate. Wayback Machine (2015)

Vuori, S., Holmlund-Rytkönen, M.: 55+ people as internet users. Mark. Intell. Plann. **23**(1), 58–76 (2005)

Design and Application of Rehabilitation AIDS Based on User Experience

Yi Li[(✉)]

School of Design and Art, Beijing Institute of Technology, Zhuhai, People's Republic of China
34953291@qq.com

Abstract. Sports rehabilitation is an important branch of rehabilitation medicine and the most widely received project in the social security system. In the process of continuous improvement of rehabilitation services, the sports rehabilitation aids industry is developing towards product, industrialization and individuation. With the increasing number of rehabilitation patients and the development trend of the Internet, Traditional therapist-assisted training has been difficult to meet patients' rehabilitation needs, and more rehabilitation training equipment and service design are needed to meet modern technology and user experience. Modern rehabilitation training equipment has greatly improved the rehabilitation efficiency and curative effect than traditional methods, but it lacks the psychological and emotional satisfaction to the rehabilitation patients. This is also an important problem to be solved in the focus of rehabilitation auxiliary man-machine interface. Through the investigation and analysis of sports rehabilitation field, rehabilitation accessories industry and products, this paper clarifies the subject direction. The process of designing and developing rehabilitation accessory products based on user research is discussed in this paper. Under the guidance of the design concept, the design and development of rehabilitation accessory products and more humanized rehabilitation treatment service flow were carried out.

Keywords: User experience · Rehabilitation accessories · Human computer interaction

1 Introduction

Exercise rehabilitation is an important classification of rehabilitation medicine. Sports, health, medicine cross-disciplinary field. Exercise rehabilitation is a kind of therapy to promote the recovery of body function by guiding patients to carry out scientific and rigorous medical sports activities. Exercise rehabilitation plays an extremely important role in preventive medicine, clinical medicine and rehabilitation medicine. Under the guidance and care of the rehabilitation physician, the patient carries out physical sports therapy within the safe range with the help of the rehabilitation physician's manipulation or rehabilitation aids and other medical devices. The traditional sports rehabilitation training mainly relies on the rehabilitation doctor's technique and instruction, has the work task the disadvantages of large quantity, unstable intensity

© Springer Nature Switzerland AG 2020
C. Stephanidis et al. (Eds.): HCII 2020, CCIS 1294, pp. 478–485, 2020.
https://doi.org/10.1007/978-3-030-60703-6_62

and low efficiency. The core idea of the humanized design of rehabilitation aids is to pay more attention to human needs, to consider the dual needs of human beings in material and spiritual aspects [1], and to expand the functional connotation by using the advanced scientific knowledge at present. In the process of actual use [2], the pain points such as poor user experience, low utilization rate and poor therapeutic effect are exposed. The core of the problem is that many of these sports rehabilitation aids in the process of production, the design focus is still on the realization of technical functions but ignore the user research and product humanized design. Through the investigation and analysis of sports rehabilitation field, rehabilitation accessories industry and products, this paper clarifies the subject direction. The process of designing and developing rehabilitation accessory products based on user research is discussed. Under the guidance of user-centered design concept [3], the design and development of rehabilitation accessory products is carried out. The main elements include:

- To explore relevant background and current situation. Deeply understand the background and current situation of related fields and analyze related products. Identify the opportunities and challenges in the field of sports rehabilitation, understand the attributes, functions, industry characteristics of rehabilitation accessories and explore product design opportunities;
- Conduct user research and obtain user requirements. The product design and development process is applied to the development of rehabilitation equipment. Through the investigation of the users of rehabilitation equipment, the demand of the users is obtained in a strategic way;
- Transform user requirements into functional descriptions and analyze decision design elements [4]. Analysis of the user needs obtained, combined with the product survey of rehabilitation accessories, to obtain a list of functions and priority ranking. At the same time, it analyzes and clarifies the design elements of human-computer interaction flow [5], function, structure, modeling, CMF and so on, and provides the design decision basis for design practice;
- Design and development practice of rehabilitation accessory products. Through the function, the structure, the modelling, the interaction design implements the design decision to the product. Completed from investigation analysis, demand acquisition, design decision, design and development of rehabilitation accessories product development. User-centered user research, product design and development.

2   Industry Status, Development Opportunities and Challenges of Rehabilitation Accessories Products

One of the major Challenges in the field of health care today is the limited number of truly personalized care for a large number of patients in need of the service [6]. For example, when purchasing medical devices (usually hospital managers), they usually take into account factors such as hospital environment and work efficiency, so they are very concerned about the mobility, volume, shape, color and performance of the medical devices purchased; the users (usually hospital staff) are more concerned about the flexibility of use, the comfort of operation, the clarity of observation and the safety of the devices themselves; the recipients (usually hospital patients) are the main factors Consider the safety of medical device operation, the comfort of bearing and the effectiveness of the action. Therefore, the manufacturers of medical devices in the design of the corresponding medical devices, must take into account the purchase of personnel, users and users of the three needs, only in this way can improve the design level of medical devices in the real sense, reflect the care of human nature. HHC(Home Health Care Project) is a new type of medical service model advocated by the international medical community at present [7]. HHC model can not only reduce the medical burden of society and patients themselves to a great extent, but also can greatly improve the recovery process and health status of patients (Table 1. User requirements

Table 1. User requirements analysis.

User population	Product positioning	Humanistic care	Product Function
Mild cases	Short-term rehabilitation	Focus on physical recovery	Extensive adaptation
Moderate	Rehabilitation guidance and personalized services	Physical and psychological recovery	Easy for doctors and patients to use
Severe cases	Long-term use focus on experience	Development of rehabilitation plans Living Services	Mild cases, Functional diversity Easy to HHC Service more personal

analysis).

3 Development Process of Rehabilitation AIDS Based on User Experience

Conduct user research to obtain user requirements. The product design and development process is applied to the development of rehabilitation aids. Strategically, users of rehabilitation aids are studied to obtain user needs: first-hand user research information is obtained by interviewing doctors and patient use groups separately for each concerned user, as well as user behavior observation of rehabilitation use processes.

Through the interview survey summary, common ground: in the rehabilitation treatment process, because of the inconvenience caused by the physical condition, most patients need the care of relatives and friends [8]; most patients will try to find treatment materials through the network [9], and have the experience of finding friends to communicate, talk, and seek spiritual comfort. From the patient's point of view, it mainly includes: the inconvenience caused by the recovery period needs the family and friends around to take care of. Over time, guilt can easily happen in the heart. Because we do not know the correct rehabilitation treatment procedures, sometimes forget the guidance of the doctor, feel that they have recovered, premature termination of treatment or removal of accessories, resulting in The effect of rehabilitation treatment is not ideal. A lot of times I want to do rehabilitation. However, limited by the work, study and living environment [10], effective continuous rehabilitation training can not be carried out (Fig. 1. User itinerary map).

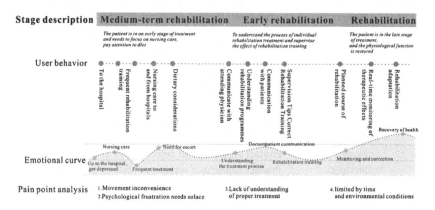

Fig. 1. User itinerary map

4 Transform User Requirements into Functional Descriptions and Analyze Decision Design Elements

Analysis of the user needs obtained, combined with the product survey of rehabilitation accessories, to obtain a list of functions and priority ranking. At the same time, it analyzes and clarifies the design elements of human-computer interaction flow, function, structure, modeling, CMF and so on, and provides the design decision basis for design practice [11]. Design team to understand market demand through survey and research focus. Detailed information on the activities in this phase includes the study of similar products on the market and their curability, and the definition of product availability, such as environmental conditions, user definitions and operational concept formation, and the final summary of sample construction: effective solution to the monotony of existing products, functional design operations are not friendly enough, due to the physical decline of rehabilitation patients, impaired physiological function reduces the ability to act and operate, the realization of the product's simple pursuit of function is not enough to pay attention to emotion, resulting in psychological rejection of rehabilitation appliances and the problem of low desire to use.

According to the development process classification of user experience, performance analysis is carried out from the aspects of modeling image, element application, value embodiment and attracting attention, as shown in Table 2.

Table 2. Function description and element analysis.

Modeling	Concise	Simple, neat shape
	Innovative	Unique, fashionable and novel style
	Visual integrity	The harmonious form has a unified coordination
Element	External contour	the externally visible contours have a unified whole, consistent with the formation principles (balance, proportion, prosody/rhythm, contrast and mixing) and the gestalt principles (proximity, similarity, closure, continuity and regularity)
	Dimensions	Define the quality of the external profile and sense the presence of the object (for example, the actual size of the object's appearance)
	Appearance Color	Hue, saturation and brightness displayed
Value	Design style	Product appearance to enhance user taste
	Product features	Product appearance represents product characteristics
	Popularity	Dynamic processes are widely welcomed by users
Attractive force	Semantic interpretation	Important Modeling Language
	Functional Orientation	Appearance shows a strong functional appeal
	Pleasantness	Styling brings pleasure to people

5 Design Practice of Rehabilitation Service System Based on User Experience

Design and development practice of rehabilitation accessory products. Through the function, the structure, the modeling, the interaction design implements the design decision to the product. With the help of artificial intelligence technology, the system design of rehabilitation accessory products from investigation and analysis, demand acquisition, design decision, design and development is completed.

Artificial intelligence is a powerful adjunct to rehabilitation medicine. With its inherent event prediction capabilities, AI has the potential to link patients to the right providers at the right time, thereby reducing inefficiencies and improving health status and overall patient experience. Forty-one percent of rehabilitation attending physicians expect AI to be the most effective technology in the near future, and many providers are already studying how to use it to expand services (see Fig. 2; Fig. 3).

Artificial intelligence brings precision to the field of medical discovery, enabling providers to quickly and accurately target the adoption of the right therapy at the right level of care, and to reduce unnecessary things later (see Fig. 4) machine learning in particular, will primarily enable health care to cover more patients than traditional health care settings (e.g. clinics and hospitals) through the use of remote patient

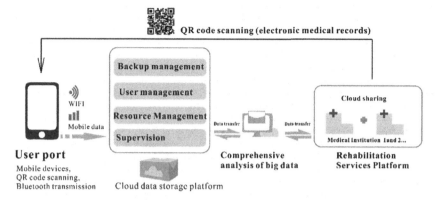

Fig. 2. Rehabilitation Medical Cloud Platform

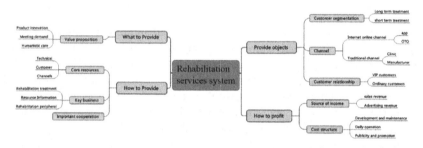

Fig. 3. Rehabilitation services system

monitoring (RPM). By the end of 2023, the RPM market is expected to reach $31.326 billion. The health care system collects data from patients through connected health care devices (the Medical Internet of Things) and uses it for information interaction to transform care into a winner dynamic and personalized, rather than passive and generic [12]. By doing so, if we are able to innovate in the right areas and issues, then AI unique function may be exactly what health care aspires to.

6   Conclusions and Recommendations

the user experience design method and how to solve the problem of rehabilitation accessories product design and development. It focuses on the user's thoughts, feelings, and behaviors in the process of use. This paper discusses the research and development and feasibility of user experience design in rehabilitation accessory products. extending to all aspects of the product use/service experience, the question of how to be perceived, learned, and used. Based on the psychological, physiological and social characteristics of users, according to the principles of usability, practicability and attractiveness of product design [13], the product is designed to meet the needs of users. A more rapid, effective and accurate service based on artificial intelligence

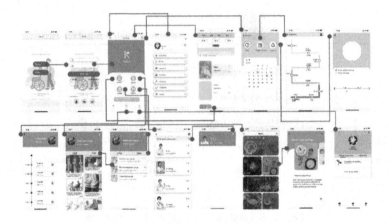

Fig. 4. AI Rehabilitation System interactive documentation

technology is discussed The potential for testing and future development is a more holistic, systematic and effective problem-solving tool. It makes rehabilitation easier to manage, more predictable and more personalized. Data can be used to identify high-risk disease early warning and high-risk time, and establish a much-needed credible relationship. these connected devices are able to reduce the cost per patient, break time and geographical environmental constraints, and identify pathology faster than ever before. Through the above practice, based on the user-centered design principles, it provides new methods and ideas for the application of user experience design methods and the research of rehabilitation aids, which is also the biggest highlight of the article. This It is of great value to the developing rehabilitation medical treatment.

References

1. Mace, R.: What is Universal Design. The Center for Universal Design at North Carolina State University, USA (1997)
2. Clarkson, P.J., et al.: Inclusive Design: Design for the Whole Population. Springer, London (2013). https://doi.org/10.1007/978-1-4471-0001-0
3. Du Ruize, C.: Research on hierarchical analysis (AHP) applied to sustainable product development strategy. Kaohsiung Normal Univ. J. Human. Arts (2006)
4. Erlandson, R.F.: Universal and Accessible Design for Products, Services, and Processes. CRC Press, Boca Raton (2007)
5. Fisk, A.D., et al.: Designing for Older Adults: Principles and Creative Human Factors Approaches. CRC Press, Boca Raton (2009)
6. Hogmanay, N.R., Kiyak, H.A.: Social Gerontology: A Multidisciplinary Perspective. Pearson Education, London (2008)
7. Righi, V., Sayago, S., Blat, J.: When we talk about older people in HCI, who are we talking about? Towards a 'turn to community' in the design of technologies for a growing ageing population. Int. J. Hum Comput Stud. **108**, 15–31 (2017)
8. Desmet, P.M., Pohlmeyer, A.E.: Positive design: an introduction to design for subjectivewell-being. Int. J. Des. **7**(3), 5–19 (2013)

9. Nejadi, F.: Investigation on integration of sustainable manufacturing and mathematical programming for technology selection and capacity planning. Ph.D. Dissertation, Brunel University (2016)
10. Katchasuwanmanee, K.: Investigation of the energy efficient sustainable manufacturing approach and its implementation perspectives. Ph.D. Dissertation, Brunel University (2016)
11. Evans, S., et al.: Business model innovation for sustainability: towards a unified perspective for creation of sustainable business models. Bus. Strategy Environ. **26–5**, 597–608 (2017)
12. Wang, S., Qui, Y., Chen, C., Chang, S.: A survey of sustainable design-centered integration for medical additive manufacturing. In: Advanced Materials Research, Special Volume: Advances in Materials and Processing Technologies, XVI, p. 635 (2015)
13. Daya, T.: Facilitating sustainable material decisions: a case study of 3D printing materials. Ph.D. Dissertation, U. C. Berkley (2017)

A Sleep State Detection and Intervention System

David Lin[1($\boxtimes$)], Gregory Warner[2], and Weijie Lin[3]

[1] Seven Lakes High School, Katy, TX 77494, USA
davidzwlin@gmail.com
[2] University of Houston-Downtown, Houston, TX 77002, USA
[3] Department of Medicine, Surgery, Pediatrics, Santa Clara Valley Medical
Center, Stanford University Hospitals, Santa Clara, CA 95128, USA

Abstract. We implemented an environment for daily physiological tracking using an FPGA DE10 board with integrated hand-made sensors made of an Micro:bit microprocessor. The system is capable of live streaming collected data, performing data processing and modeling, and exporting brain state to a mobile app for mental intervention. The FPGA microcomputer is capable of electroencephalogram (EEG) data preprocessing, feature extraction, and brain state classification using deep learning models. The data rendering software on the mobile phone simulates a professional medical interface through which the user is able to connect the EEG device to the phone, relay the EEG data to the FPGA board, and render the brain state curve on the phone. The mobile app runs a sleep inducing program which can help the user get into sleep more easily and deeply. The sleep-inducing technique takes advantage of Delta waves, which is proven to have the effect of deepening a person's sleep, when it is converted to sound wave and applied to the subject. Our system monitors the user's sleep state and adjusts the volume of Delta wave sounds, together with a user chosen background music, according to the user's sleep depth.

Keywords: Brain-computer interface · Sleep intervention · Machine learning

1 Introduction

Advanced sensor based wearable devices have shown to be successful in enhancing people's health levels. Low sleep quality, as a major health complaint in majority of age groups, especially the middle age group and the elders, recently gains more attention from the scientific and business groups. We built an electroencephalogram (EEG) based sleep enhancement system, with Delta wave and musical interventions, to decrease the frustration and dread associated with sleep complications. Data collected from users can be sent to a central server for brain state classifications and modeling. Our goal is to develop a light weight EEG system, with a biofeedback application, for convenient usage in a home environment. The system will have the capability for collecting physiological data, analyzing the data, and providing feedbacks.

The development of this system yields functional devices for users with sleep complications to increase their sleep qualities. Potential users include doctors,

© Springer Nature Switzerland AG 2020
C. Stephanidis et al. (Eds.): HCII 2020, CCIS 1294, pp. 486–492, 2020.
https://doi.org/10.1007/978-3-030-60703-6_63

researchers and complementary and alternative medicine focus groups. Users with low sleep quality will be places to explore and evaluate the use of the applications.

The challenges include effective EEG data collection and designing a portable yet computationally powerful device for data analysis and modeling. We investigate the potential of using a single channel EEG data to identify mental states. Using EEG data to monitor mental states normally involves multi-channel data. To overcome the difficulties of using single channel EEG data, proper positioning the EEG sensor, feature extraction, and choosing the right machine learning model become critical. Carefully choosing the target mental states is also very important. Research has found out that the forehead is a sensitive position in reflecting brain activities. As for the machine learning model, deep learning with neural network has been proven to be the most effective method.

A goal of biofeedback is to develop an increased awareness of relevant internal physiological functions, and establish control over these functions [1]. EEG analysis can help build applications that utilize mental control. For example, meditation is a method of lowering stress, and studies show that prayer and meditation significantly affect physiological data [2]. Skin conductivity and stress levels are lower in subjects after a meditation session.

Dry EEG sensors use Electrodermal activity (EDA), i.e., the human skin's ability to conduct electricity. The conductivity varies with the state of the sweat glands in the skin. This dermic response can be monitored by measuring the changes in skin resistance caused by the sweat [3]. With micro:bit, EEG is measured by placing two electrodes an inch apart on the skin. A small voltage is applied to the electrodes, a circuit is formed, and an electrical current will flow. The changes in the voltage are used to evaluate the stress level [4]. The forehead is one of the places on human body that have the greatest number of sweat glands [5]. This raises the potential of the EEG data to reflect brain activities.

2   Methodology

2.1   System Design

Existing physiological reading systems, e.g., those used in patient monitoring, are ineffective for daily practices. This project aims to simulate an environment for daily physiological tracking using a FPGA DE10 board with physiological sensors. On a single board computer, we implement an affordable, reusable, expandable, and wireless, machine that can monitor a user's electroencephalogram (EEG) brain waves. With the integrated sensors and coding, the device is capable of live streaming collected data, performing data processing and modeling, and exporting brain state data to a mobile app for mental intervention. Figure 1 shows the system architecture.

For the collection of EEG brain waves signals, a hand-made headset is connected to the mobile phone via a Bluetooth module. Data are collected from the EEG headset and sent to the FPGA board via the mobile phone. The design of the EEG headset is shown in Fig. 2.

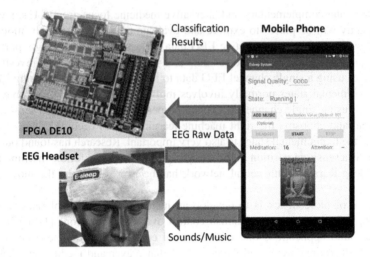

Fig. 1. System architecture

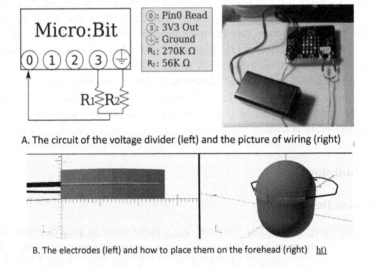

A. The circuit of the voltage divider (left) and the picture of wiring (right)

B. The electrodes (left) and how to place them on the forehead (right)   ht)

Fig. 2. EEG signal acquisition device

The FPGA microcomputer is made capable of configuring and programming the required python files for EEG data preprocessing, feature extraction, and brain state classification using a deep learning model (See Fig. 3 (Left) for the data processing and modeling flowchart). The data rendering software on the mobile phone simulates a professional medical interface through which the user is able to connect the EEG device to the phone, relay the EEG data to the FPGA board, and render the brain state curve on the phone (See Fig. 3 (Right) for the snapshot of the app).

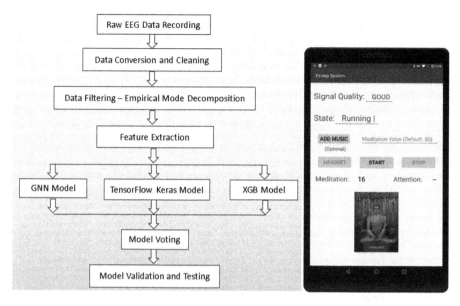

Fig. 3. EEG data processing flowchart (Left) and Sleep intervention app (Right)

The sleep inducing technique used in this project is taking the advantage of Delta waves. Scientists have proven that the 1 Hz Delta waves can be converted to sounds and those sounds have the effect of deepening a person's sleep. Our system monitors the user's sleep state and adjust the volume of Delta wave sounds together with a user chosen background music according to the user's sleep depth.

Our sleep mental intervention system can be used by general population who have a need for improved sleep quality, and patients in rehabilitation centers or hospitals who want to adopt a non-medication approach for sleep disorders and insomnia. This project aims to challenge the affordability and accessibility of existing healthcare oriented monitoring equipment. With the computational power provided by FPGA, such a system is able to diagnose the user's mental states based on the knowledge gathered with the machine learning power and the organized data collection and processing, and to render mind intervention activities based on the diagnosis of the user's mental state.

2.2   The FPGA Server

The FPGA DE10 board exerts its power in our system, especially in the stages of machine learning for brain state recognition and rendering of brain state information. FPGA DE10 enables a portable and onsite machine learning system while maintaining sufficient computational power to run machine learning algorithms. In particular, the data processing method, the ensemble empirical mode decomposition (EEMD), has high time and space complexity. Thereafter, our system extracts 20 features, including power spectral intensities (PSIs), relative intensity ratios PSIs (RIR PSIs), Petrosian Fractal Dimension, Higuchi Fractal Dimension, Hjorth Parameters, Spectral Entropy,

SDV Entropy, Fisher Information, Approximate Entropy, Detrended Fluctuation Analysis, and Hurst Exponent. FPGA is capable for implementing such an onsite real-time system with sufficient computational power.

Figure 4 illustrates a service log that shows the timestamps (in seconds) of the server's responses to EEG data uploading in every second. Our EEG acquisition device sends 128 samples of EEG reading every time to the server. It reads a sample whenever it detects voltage reading changes. While slow brain activities entails longer data collection time for 128 samples, statistically, it collects 128 samples in every second. Figure 4 indicates that the server's response time to data uploading allows real-time processing of input data.

"user_id": 10, "filename": "10_1560363446010.csv"}, {"id": 257, "state": "available", "filetype": "csv", "time": 1560363451,
"user_id": 10, "filename": "10_1560363447158.csv"}, {"id": 258, "state": "available", "filetype": "csv", "time": 1560363452,
"user_id": 10, "filename": "10_1560363448248.csv"}, {"id": 259, "state": "available", "filetype": "csv", "time": 1560363453,
"user_id": 10, "filename": "10_1560363449290.csv"}, {"id": 260, "state": "available", "filetype": "csv", "time": 1560363454,
"user_id": 10, "filename": "10_1560363450439.csv"}, {"id": 261, "state": "available", "filetype": "csv", "time": 1560363455,
"user_id": 10, "filename": "10_1560363451560.csv"}, {"id": 262, "state": "available", "filetype": "csv", "time": 1560363456,
"user_id": 10, "filename": "10_1560363452652.csv"}, {"id": 263, "state": "available", "filetype": "csv", "time": 1560363457,
"user_id": 10, "filename": "10_1560363453733.csv"}, {"id": 264, "state": "available", "filetype": "csv", "time": 1560363459,
"user_id": 10, "filename": "10_1560363454910.csv"}, {"id": 265, "state": "available", "filetype": "csv", "time": 1560363460,
"user_id": 10, "filename": "10_1560363456007.csv"}, {"id": 266, "state": "available", "filetype": "csv", "time": 1560363461,
"user_id": 10, "filename": "10_1560363457148.csv"}, {"id": 267, "state": "available", "filetype": "csv", "time": 1560363462,
"user_id": 10, "filename": "10_1560363458264.csv"}, {"id": 268, "state": "available", "filetype": "csv", "time": 1560363463,
"user_id": 10, "filename": "10_1560363459348.csv"}, {"id": 269, "state": "available", "filetype": "csv", "time": 1560363464,
"user_id": 10, "filename": "10_1560363460496.csv"}, {"id": 270, "state": "available", "filetype": "csv", "time": 1560363465,
"user_id": 10, "filename": "10_1560363461594.csv"}, {"id": 271, "state": "available", "filetype": "csv", "time": 1560363467,
"user_id": 10, "filename": "10_1560363462693.csv"}, {"id": 272, "state": "available", "filetype": "csv", "time": 1560363468,
"user_id": 10, "filename": "10_1560363463808.csv"}, {"id": 273, "state": "available", "filetype": "csv", "time": 1560363469,
"user_id": 10, "filename": "10_1560363465017.csv"}, {"id": 274, "state": "available", "filetype": "csv", "time": 1560363470,
"user_id": 10, "filename": "10_1560363466072.csv"}, {"id": 275, "state": "available", "filetype": "csv", "time": 1560363471,
"user_id": 10, "filename": "10_1560363467182.csv"}, {"id": 276, "state": "available", "filetype": "csv", "time": 1560363472,

Fig. 4. Server responses to EEG data uploading

2.3   EEG Data Processing and Analysis

This is the most challenging and time-consuming part of the system. For every 128-sample uploading, the FPGA board uses the procedure depicted in Fig. 3 to process the data and analyze the data to evaluate the sleep depth based on predictive machine learning models.

Empirical Mode Decomposition (EMD) transforms wave forms into a series of components called Intrinsic Mode Functions (IMFs). Some recording artifacts such as low frequency drift can be identified by examining the IMFs. Ensemble Empirical Mode Decomposition (EEMD) is a noise-assisted method to improve shifting and generate a better EEG data from a selected set of IMFs. Low frequency drift can be removed by eliminating IMFs that show consistent increasing/decreasing tendency. We then either compute the summary of remaining IMFs as the output of this process, or use the remaining IMFs directly as features in the steps onward.

Feature extraction is computed based on an open source Python module "PyEEG". Particularly, Fast Fourier transform was used to extract the PSI, such as delta (0.5–4 Hz), theta (4–7 Hz), alpha (8–12 Hz), beta (12–30 Hz), and gamma (30–100 Hz). RIR computed from PSIs were deltaRIR, thetaRIR, alphaRIR, betaRIR, and gammaRIR. Though Neurosky data also used Fast Fourier transformation to transform its data, the range of frequency is just in the interval [0.5 Hz, 50 Hz]. Other features also extracted were PFD, HFD, Hjorth Parameters, Spectral Entropy, SDV Entropy, Fisher Information, Approximate Entropy, Detrended Fluctuation Analysis, and Hurst Exponent.

The effectiveness of using EMD and features mentioned above has been proven in experiments. We compared the model accuracy across different combinations of data processing the feature extractions. Herein, we use term "filtered data" to refer to the data obtained by filtering the raw EEG data by EEMD, with the low frequency IMFs being eliminated and remaining IMFs combined; term "extracted data" the features extracted from either directly from the raw EEG data or filtered data after EEMD; "decomposed data" the data obtained by EEMD, with the low frequency IMFs being eliminated and remaining IMFs used individually (without combination) in the following process; "normalized data" the data or features normalized by the min-max normalization. We compared the results from 4 cases. In *case 1*, raw data were filtered, extracted, and normalized prior to being used to train the model; in *case 2*, raw data were extracted and normalized prior to being used to train the model; in *case 3*, raw data were decomposed and normalized prior to being used to train the model; in *case 4*, raw data were filtered and normalized before used to train the model. Figure 5 (left) shows the 4 cases of experiments and 9 (right) the accuracy of the predictions made by the models trained by different machine learning methods for each corresponding case.

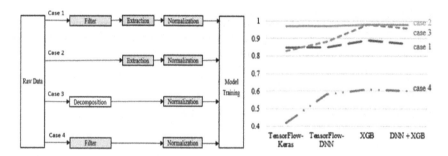

Fig. 5. Comparison of data processing and modeling methods

The experimental results support the importance of feature extraction in obtaining good performance from the model. Fourier Fast Transformation and other features such as PFD, HFD, Hjorth Parameters, Spectral Entropy, SDV Entropy, Fisher Information, Approximate Entropy, DFA, and Hurst Exponent all contribute to the very good performance of models. The results also verify that the low frequency drifts in the raw data affect the model accuracy. As part of the measuring artifacts, the low frequencies need to be removed from the input data, which is done after EEMD in our experiment. After removing low frequency drift, we can choose to combine the remaining IMFs to create filtered data, or use IMFs individually as processed data for further process and analysis. Our experiment supports that the latter derives better model performance.

3 Conclusion

We built a system for daily EEG tracking using a FPGA DE10 board with integrated hand-made sensors implemented using Micro:bit microprocessor. The system uses an FPGA microprocessor to perform data processing and modeling, and exporting brain state feedback to a mobile app for mental intervention. EEG data preprocessing consists of ensemble empirical mode decomposition and feature extraction in time and frequency domains. Brain state classification is done by deep learning models and XGBoost model. The mobile app simulates a professional medical interface through which a sleep inducing program helps the user get into sleep more easily and deeply. The sleep inducing technique takes the advantage of Delta waves, which are converted to sounds and those sounds have the effect of deepening a person's sleep. Our system monitors the user's sleep state and adjust the volume of Delta wave sounds together with a user chosen background music according to the user's sleep depth.

Our sleep mental intervention system can be used by general population who have a need for improved sleep quality, and patients in rehabilitation centers or hospitals who want to adopt a non-medication approach for sleep disorders and insomnia.

References

1. Ancoli, S., Peper, E., Quinn, M.: Mind/Body Integration. Plenum Press, New York (1983)
2. Das, I., Anand, H.: Effect of prayer and "OM" meditation in enhancing galvanic skin response. Psychol. Thought 5(2), 141–149 (2012)
3. Ramachandran, V., Blakeslee, S.: Phantoms in the Brain, p. 47. Fourth Estate, London (2012)
4. Schwartz, M., Andrasik, F.: Biofeedback: A Practitioner's Guide, p. 57. Guilford Press, New York (2016)
5. Bolis, L., Licinio, J., Govoni, S.: Handbook of the Autonomic Nervous System in Health and Disease, pp. 257–260. Marcel Dekker, New York (2003)

Faye: An Empathy Probe to Investigate Motivation Among Novice Runners

Daphne Menheere[1(✉)], Carine Lallemand[1,2], Mathias Funk[1],
and Steven Vos[1,3]

[1] Department of Industrial Design, Eindhoven University of Technology,
5600 MB Eindhoven, The Netherlands
d.s.menheere@tue.nl
[2] HCI Research Group, University of Luxembourg, 4365 Esch-sur-Alzette,
Luxembourg
[3] School of Sport Studies, Fontys University of Applied Sciences,
5644 Hz Eindhoven, The Netherlands

Abstract. The popularity of recreational sports such as running, has increased substantially due to its low threshold to start and it is attractive for a wide range of people. However, despite the growing popularity, running has a high drop-out rate due to injuries and motivational loss, especially among novice runners. To investigate factors influencing motivation among novice runners and design opportunities, we deployed an empathy probe at a women-only running event. Faye is a running shirt that reveals motivational feedback on the shirt, during the warm-up phase of the run. In this paper, we both inform on the impact of motivational feedback while warming up on running motivation and reflect on the use of an empathy probe to investigate motivational strategies among novice runners.

Keywords: Empathy probe · Recreational runners · Motivation strategies

1 Introduction

Running is a popular recreational sport due to its low threshold to start and it thus attracts a wide range of people [4, 12]. This has led to the development of a considerable number of running-related technologies to support and motivate runners in their training. Still we observe a high drop-out rate due to injuries and motivational loss, among novice and less experienced runners [2, 5, 13]. Moreover, wearable devices supporting running, such as sport watches, activity trackers and smartphone apps, tend to adopt a one-size-fits-all approach by motivating exercising through competition and performance strategies [9, 11]. Compared to quantified approaches, which focus on numbers (e.g. pace, heartrate, distance), we aim to investigate the use of a qualitative approach [7] as a motivation strategy for running.

We present and test a running shirt 'Faye' as an empathy design probe to investigate motivational strategies among novice runners (Fig. 1). Design probes as a method can support an empathic understanding of a person's needs and motivations [3]. Probes challenge traditional methods by acknowledging the role of subjectivity in

C. Stephanidis et al. (Eds.): HCII 2020, CCIS 1294, pp. 493–499, 2020.
https://doi.org/10.1007/978-3-030-60703-6_64

the design process in order to facilitate insights and ideas. By connecting knowledge and inspiration, design probes trigger designers' empathy [8] and intend to establish a dialogue between the design and the user [3]. Empathy probing has been introduced by Mattelmäki in the context of physical activity and well-being [8]. Thanks to their playfulness, individuality and design-orientation, empathy probes supported a better understanding of users' needs, emotions and motivations [8], which researchers in their study were unable to obtain via regular interviews or user tests.

Fig. 1. Faye, a running shirt revealing motivational feedback

In this paper, we first inform how novice runners of a women-only event known for its low-threshold character [14] perceived the empathy probe Faye, and how this affected their running motivation. Additionally, we reflect on the use of an empathy probe to further examine factors influencing their running experience, like motivation strategies and barriers. This paper contributes to offering future possibilities on the design of motivational feedback for novice runners.

2   Faye: An Empathy Probe

Faye is a running shirt, revealing motivational feedback on the shirt during the warm-up of the run (Fig. 1). We realized this with the use of thermochromic ink, an ink that disappears when it is warmed up to a specific temperature (depending on the tipping point) [10]. Due to the body heat of the runner, the thermochromic ink reacts and disappears, revealing a layer with textile ink beneath it (Fig. 2). This layer with textile ink exposes a motivational quote within the logo of the running event. For this quote we selected two options: "Don't Quit, Do It" or "Believe in Yourself, Be You" to boost motivation. As a design choice, this quote is presented upside down, so it can easily be read by the participant when looking from above. The technological component of Faye is relatively simple, relying on thermochromic ink only without expensive or complex electronics involved. This is in line with the principles for empathic methods defined by Koskinen [6]: these are user-centered, visual and tangible, cheap and low-tech to be easily adaptable, but also playful and pleasant in order to inspire users to imagine future experiences. Faye was designed as an exploration into how novice runners would perceive feedback while warming-up for a run. It probed their response as an engagement tool, in order to gain insight into how these runners think, feel and experience barriers to go running. Following the approach of empathic probing by Mattelmäki [8], we used a personal interview as an integral part of the process. We decided to postpone the data collection interview after the run, to not interfere with the moment and ritual of their running event.

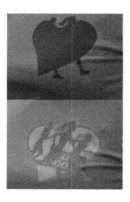

Fig. 2. Top image, thermochromic ink hiding the motivational message. Low image, thermochromic ink disappears revealing the quote "Don't Quit, Do It"

3   Method

We targeted a group of eight novice runners through deploying Faye at a women-only running event (average age $M = 32.6$, $Min = 21$, $Max = 48$) known for its low-threshold character [14]. Faye probed the responses as an engagement tool, in order to gain insight into how the participants think, feel and experience barriers to go running. Following the approach of empathic probing by Mattelmäki [8], we used a personal interview in combination with the probe shirt. Participants were recruited via the Facebook page of the event by inviting them to test an interactive running shirt, which they could keep afterwards. Out of the 120 respondents on Facebook, 15 runners were randomly chosen and handed out a shirt right before the event, to be worn during the race. They were not told that a motivational quote would appear.

Interviews were conducted with 8 participants in their home, within 3 weeks after the event, enabling the possibility of users wearing Faye in subsequent runs. The other participants were unavailable for logistics reasons (schedule conflicts, distance barrier). Each interview lasted approximately 30 min. The interview guide consisted of open-ended questions regarding the respondent's experiences with the design, as a starting point to explore running motivation. Beyond the probe, additional topics related to the theme were thus discussed, including running experience, running motivators and barriers, and the use of current motivation strategies. Interviews were recorded in Dutch, transcribed verbatim and translated in English. The transcriptions were manually coded based on a coding framework developed inductively.

4   Results

The eight participants were diverse in age, running experience, and the distance they ran during the event (Table 1). Both participants who have been runners for 5 years mentioned previous drop-outs due to physical reasons. Participants indicated their motivation to start running was to lose weight, stay fit or to feel better.

Table 1. Overview of the different participants, presenting their age, running experience, event distance, and if and when the participants observed the motivational quote

Participant	Age	Running experience	Distance	Quote observed	Timing
P1	32	5 years	10	Yes	During
P2	30	2 months	5	No	–
P3	35	6 months	5	Yes	During
P4	34	2 years	10	Yes	Before
P5	21	6 months	7.5	Yes	Before
P6	48	1.5 years	7.5	Yes	Before
P7	37	2 years	5	No	–
P8	24	5 years	7.5	Yes	Before

4.1   Empathy Probe

Upon wearing the shirt, the participants were not aware that Faye would change and reveal a motivational quote. Six participants noticed the motivational quote on Faye, while 2 did not (Table 1). When the quote became visible, the participants indicated that it served as an encouragement reminder: *"I thought it was nice, now and then I was looking at it and then I would see 'Don't Quit', so I was like: okay, let's go!" P3.* Notably, participants indicated these encouragements felt personally addressed to them, despite the quotes being quite generic: *"Well I thought that was kind of special, because you just expect it's visible to others. And I thought it was special it was visible for yourself." P1.* The placement of the quote and the way it was presented increased the personal relation to the message: *"It's an encouragement for yourself, like yes you can do it... and my friend was saying like, it is upside down, but the intention is of course that I'm able to read it" P4.* Once the participants knew the shirt could change yet without knowing which mechanism caused the change, some indicated to actively look at it during their run to see if it would change again. This added to the experience of being an encouragement: *"I like that it is on the shirt. And that it is not visible all the time but appears only sometimes" P4.*

Out of the six participants who saw the motivational quote, four indicated seeing it while warming-up for the run. This moment was considered as valuable for encouragement, also because it might be hard to notice the shirt changing for the first time while running: *"The timing was exactly right, this is why I was like 'Oh yes, we're going to do this'. I felt that was because if it would have just been black, during the race I wouldn't have seen it because you don't expect it, so I wouldn't have looked" P6.* Another runner explained that it would have been more motivating if it also showed during running: *"Well I thought it was a nice motivating factor, but it was a shame it wasn't showing during the race because we were running in the shades quite often…" P5.* Two participants indicated seeing the message at the end of the run, both explaining they were focused on the race: *"I thought I'm just going to run first and I'll have a closer look at the shirt later" P3.*

4.2 Personal Motivators and Barriers

Participants mentioned different strategies for personal motivation. Most participants do not run to be faster than others but focus on challenging themselves: *"I do it for me, there is nobody I have to do it for" P5.* Participants also used external mechanisms to motivate themselves. One common strategy was to buy oneself a gift after achieving a new goal or buy equipment as a trigger: *"Now I bought the shoes, so I have to start using them" P5.* Another external motivation strategy often mentioned was *social support,* experienced before the session: *"My partner often says: just do it, and that really helps" P2,* and throughout the run: *"I think it is really hard to run individually, to motivate myself" P6.*

Participants mentioned some barriers resulting in doubting to go running. A common barrier was planning: *"I really have to wait for 45 min after eating, otherwise it will really bother me while running" P1,* but also due to obligations after running *"I start working at 8am and sometimes I have to run beforehand, and when the alarm goes off, I'm like, pff no way" P2.* Other indicated barriers related to physical pain (e.g. hurting knees, back, being on a period) or that sometimes they were just not into it despite their positive intentions: *"If I plan it in advance, I can think rather quickly that I don't feel like it" P5.* This resulted in a drop-out for one participant: *"At some point I didn't feel like it. And then that lasts a bit longer than expected" P7.* Experiencing a lack of confidence was also explicitly mentioned as a barrier by two participants, affecting demotivating beforehand: *"Before running I start to think 'I hope I will persevere', well and then I don't" P6.*

5 Discussion and Conclusion

Using Faye, we gained insights on how female novice runners feel about motivational feedback within the preparation phase of the run by use of a wearable. The main insight of deploying the empathy probe, in line with previous findings [10] was that the message felt like a personal encouragement, due to its placement and visibility. The moment when the message became visible or seen was also deemed important. While some felt the message encouraged them during preparatory behavior, some participants did not notice it right away and appreciated getting a motivational quote during running. The timing of the motivational trigger in the designed artefact is thus a key factor to consider, as well as the potential issue of monotony once the trigger is revealed to the user.

The technology used for Faye (thermochromic ink) showed limitations both in the timing of the interaction and the impossibility to adapt or vary the message across time in order to keep the novelty level high. As an empathy probe, our aim was however not to achieve a perfect design but to start a conversation with the users. After the use of Faye, we could discuss more personal and sensitive topics during the interviews. We choose the empathy probe approach to create a dialogue with the users and facilitate more open and personal discussions on intimate experiences such as self-efficacy and demotivation. As stated by Mattelmäki [8, p. 61], *"probes prepare the users to give an account of their experiences, direct them to interesting issues, and facilitate their communication in interviews and observations"*. Interviewing users within 3 weeks after the event may have induced retrospection biases, in the way users remember experiencing the shirt. However, our purpose with this delayed interview was to let users reuse the shirt for following runs, thus collecting more experience and reflection.

Design probes are usually data collection tools allowing users' to actively record their experience. Here, Faye did not support self-documentation but acted as an experience prototype [1]. The empathic approach we used through the design of Faye, and the data collected, inspired us to rethink motivational feedback. Our results show that this is a promising direction, and we gained first insights into how to design this type of feedback to motivate no runners aiming to eventually help maintaining long-term running behavior.

In future work, we intend to design technology probes of similar or slightly higher complexity including sensing capabilities to further investigate how to support motivational strategies. These probes can then be deployed as technology probes, collecting data while being used. Through the use of Faye, an empathy probe, we succeeded to engage female novice runners to talk about their experiences, feelings, needs and values. Our findings go beyond the user test of Faye itself, fostering discussion on future possibilities of the design of motivational feedback for runners.

References

1. Buchenau, M., Fulton Suri, J.: Experience prototyping. In: Proceedings of the Conference on Designing Interactive Systems: Processes, Practices, Methods, and Techniques, DIS, pp. 424–433 (2000)
2. Fokkema, T., et al.: Reasons and predictors of discontinuation of running after a running program for novice runners. J. Sci. Med. Sport **22**(1), 106–111 (2019)
3. Gaver, W., Dunne, T., Pacenti, E.: Cultural Probes Interactions, pp. 21–29. ACM Press, New York (1999)
4. Janssen, M., Scheerder, J., Thibaut, E., Brombacher, A., Vos, S.: Who uses running apps and sports watches? Determinants and consumer profiles of event runners' usage of running-related smartphone applications and sports watches. PLoS ONE **12**(7), 1–17 (2017)
5. Kemler, E., Blokland, D., Backx, F., Huisstede, B.: Differences in injury risk and characteristics of injuries between novice and experienced runners over a 4-year period. Phys. Sportsmed. **00**(00), 1–7 (2018)
6. Koskinen, I., Battarbee K., Mattelmäki, T.: Empathic Design, pp. 7–12. IT press, Helsinki (2003)
7. Lockton, D., Ricketts, D., Chowdhury, S.A., Lee, C.H.: Exploring qualitative displays and interfaces. In: CHI Conference Extended Abstracts on Human Factors in Computing Systems, pp. 1844–1852 (2017)
8. Mattelmäki, T.: Design probes. Aalto University (2006)

9. Mauriello, M., Gubbels, M., Froehlich, J.E.: Social fabric fitness: the design and evaluation of wearable e-textile displays to support group running. In: Proceedings of the SIGCHI Conference on Human Factors in Computing Systems, pp. 2833–2842 (2014)
10. Menheere, D., Megens, C., van der Spek, E., Vos, S.: Encouraging physical activity and self-enhancement in women with breast cancer through a smart bra. In Proceedings of DRS: Design Research Society 2018. Design Research Society (2018)
11. Peeters, M. & Megens, C.: Experiential design landscapes: how to design for behaviour change, towards an active lifestyle. Ph.D. Thesis, University of Technology, Eindhoven (2014)
12. Scheerder, Jeroen., Breedveld, Koen, Borgers, Julie (eds.): Running across Europe. Palgrave Macmillan UK, London (2015). https://doi.org/10.1057/9781137446374
13. Vos, S., Janssen, M., Goudsmit, J., Lauwerijssen, C., Brombacher, A.: From problem to solution: developing a personalized smartphone application for recreational runners following a three-step design approach. Procedia Eng. **147**, 799–805 (2016)
14. Vos, S., Walravens, R., Hover, P., Borgers, J., Scheerder, J.: For fun or prestige? Typology of event runners [Voor de pret of de prestatie? Typologieen van Evenementen- loopsters.]. Vrijetijdsstudies, **32**(2), 19–34 (2014)

Diabetweets: Analysis of Tweets for Health-Related Information

Hamzah Osop[1]([⊠]) [iD], Rabiul Hasan[2], Chei Sian Lee[3],
Chee Yong Neo[3], Chee Kim Foo[3], and Ankit Saurabh[3]

[1] Agency of Science Technology and Research (A*STAR), IHPC, Singapore,
Singapore
hamzah_bin_osop@ihpc.a-star.edu.sg
[2] School of Computer Science, University of Sydney, Sydney, Australia
rabiul.hasan@sydney.edu.au
[3] WKWSCI, Nanyang Technological University, Singapore, Singapore
{W170002,CHEEKIM001,SAUR0004,leecs}@ntu.edu.sg

Abstract. Significant growth in health information sharing through Twitter is making it a compelling source for health-related information. Recent health research studies show Twitter data has been used for disease surveillance, health promotion, sentiment analysis, and perhaps has potential for clinical decision support. However, identifying health-related tweets in these massive Twitter datasets is challenging. With the increasing global prevalence of diabetes, user-generated health content in Twitter can be useful. Therefore, this preliminary study aims to classify diabetes-related tweets into meaningful health-related categories. Using an ensemble of neural network and stochastic gradient descent classifiers, we classified 13,667 diabetes-related tweets into five clusters. About 25.7% of the tweets were clustered as health-related, where 9.3% were classified as *Treatment & Medication*, 9.9% as *Preventive Measures* and 6.5% as *Symptoms & Causes*. More than 70% were clustered as *Others*. Analysing hashtags of tweets clustered in each of the categories showed significant relevance to health-related information.

Keywords: Health information sharing · Machine learning · Decision support

1 Introduction

Diabetes mellitus (DM), is one of the four major chronic diseases that have a huge global impact, and recently, has been described as "pandemic" [1]. By 2030, it is expected that the global diabetes prevalence will grow from 450 million to 578 million people [2]. Recent diabetes prevalence statistics of Singapore has shown that the prevalence had risen from 8.3% in 2010 to 8.6% in 2017 [3]. With the expectation for the prevalence to continue growing, it will be a worrying trend if diabetic patients do not receive proper treatments and increase their risk associated with diabetes.

The accessibility to information via the Internet has allowed stakeholders and consumers of health information to share health-related information online. Information sharing and seeking through social media tools like Facebook and Twitter are fast-

© Springer Nature Switzerland AG 2020
C. Stephanidis et al. (Eds.): HCII 2020, CCIS 1294, pp. 500–508, 2020.
https://doi.org/10.1007/978-3-030-60703-6_65

growing in significance. The term "information diffusion" has been used to describe the sharing of information amongst Twitter users [4]. Such activity contributes to a significant source of data on the Internet, encouraging users to engage in online health-related information search.

As the Internet becomes accessible and affordable to consumers, healthcare professionals, caregivers and patients are expected to use social media frequently. Searching for health-related information online provides an avenue for patients to find answers to their medical problems and help influence medical decisions. Healthcare organisations have also started utilising social media as part of their organisational strategy to improve patient care, expand medical education and advance medical research [5].

Therefore in this study, we will be classifying diabetes-related tweets into meaningful health-related categories that can be utilised by healthcare stakeholders when making decisions.

2 Literature Review

2.1 Health Information in Twitter

Information sharing and seeking through social media is fast growing in significance. Currently, Facebook (2414 million) and Twitter (336 million) have a combined total of more than two billion active users worldwide [6]. Daily, about 500 million tweets are generated [7].

Recent studies have shown that Twitter has been useful in health research. Twitter data has been purposefully used in disease surveillance, health promotion, network conversation analysis, sentiment analysis, and medical interventions [8–11]. As a platform, Twitter is used widely for patient engagement, recruitment, and as a biomedical research collaboration tool [5, 11].

For that reason, Twitter is becoming a significant source of health-related data for public health researchers due to its real-time nature of content and the ease of access to publicly available information [11]. [5] also shared that, Twitter users with medical accounts are more likely to share "general information for public health or new research about treatments and technology", for example, Mayo Clinic.

User-generated health content in Twitter, therefore, has the potential to contain meaningful and practical information. This can supplement healthcare decision-makers with vital patient-related details that can be utilised to improve patient-physician communication and clinical decision making. With the global diabetes prevalence, understanding how to support and manage the growing chronic population is essential.

2.2 Machine Learning Topic Modelling of Tweets

Tweets are frequently analysed to study the sentiments of its users. The most common approaches adopted to analyse tweets makes use of machine learning algorithms [12–14]. In such approaches, machine learning techniques have been used to classify or cluster tweets according to its significance or relevance with associated tweets.

[14] used an ensemble of Support Vector Machines (SVM) and adaboosted Decision Trees to classify user opinions into good, bad or neutral. The approach provided better accuracy than using machine learning techniques alone, resulting in an accuracy of 84%.

[13] used Twitter data to gather customers feedback regarding their sentiments on US airline services. Using seven different classifiers, namely Decision Tree, Random Forest, SVM, K-Nearest Neighbours, Logistic Regression, Naïve Bayes and Adaboost, the authors evaluated the accuracies of the classifiers in predicting if the sentiments were positive, negative or neutral. Using an ensemble of Adaboost and several other algorithms, the accuracy reached 84.5%.

However, other studies adopted the use of machine learning techniques beyond analysing sentiments alone. In a research study detecting dengue outbreak through Twitter content, the authors selected the use of supervised classification and unsupervised clustering using topic modelling. [15] trained the classifiers to achieve a prediction accuracy of 80% based on a training dataset of only 1000 tweets.

Hence, classification techniques using machine learning algorithms provide an avenue where health-related tweets can be efficiently identified from a massive dataset. This allows for health-related information to be easily extracted and consumed for future decision making.

3   Methodology

3.1   Data Collection

We used a corpus of 13,667 publicly available tweets, which were collected throughout 4 February to 14 February 2019. Due to the limitation set by the Twitter API, only two weeks' worth of tweets can be extracted at any point in time. All the tweets were retrieved using *tweepy*, a Twitter Streaming API. To search for the corpus, we used '#diabetes' as the search keyword. The collected tweet contained the full tweet details such as the full tweeted text, user information such as user details and geolocation, as well as the retweeted status.

3.2   Identifying Meaningful Health-Related Tweets

It is challenging to identify health-related tweets from the massive Twitter datasets. Classifying tweets into categories or themes by singling out tweets that may contain meaningful health-related information is essential. It is also vital that tweets which contain medical terms but otherwise not meaningfully health-related, be classified accordingly. We identified five categories of tweets that define our understanding of what is a health and non-health-related tweet. Three categories, i.e. *Preventive Measures (PM)*, *Symptoms & Causes (SC)*, and *Treatment & Medication (TM)*, are closely associated with health-related information that is routinely communicated during a patient visit. The remaining two, *News (NW)* and *Others (OT)*, are used to categorise tweets that are not meaningful in our context. A semi-supervised clustering technique is then adopted to cluster all tweets into relevant categories.

Manual Classification of Tweets as a Labelled Dataset. A semi-supervised clustering approach utilises both labelled and unlabeled data to classify datasets. Using Python's Scikit-learn library, we randomly generated a sample of 1048 tweets (7%) from the main corpus. The process of labelling is then done manually by five coders according to the predefined coding description, as shown in Table 1. An agreement index of at least 0.6 (3 out of 5 with the same label) was agreed upon to achieve label consensus, intercoder reliability and a high degree of consistency across coders. The result of the manual coding is as follows:

Table 1. Classification of tweets description

Categories	Description	Tweets	%
Preventive measures (PM)	Tweets containing measures that hinder or act as obstacles to diabetes	144	13.74%
Symptoms & causes (SC)	Tweets that contain features, both physical and mental that indicates signs of diabetes	107	10.21%
Treatment & medication (TM)	Tweets containing medical care rendered to patients, words associated with possible treatments (such as medication, therapy methods, etc.)	145	13.74%
News (NW)	Tweets containing news or regarding news shared on diabetes	63	6.01%
Others (OT)	Tweets that cannot be classified in all other categories (e.g. motivational, awareness, complaints)	589	56.20%

Data Preprocessing. Data preprocessing phase is required to clean the tweets before any machine learning algorithms can use it. Using Python's NLTK library (a Natural Language Processing package), the tweet corpus went through the process of cleansing.

The corpus was split into a 30:70 ratio and underwent the data preprocessing phase where stop words were removed. All texts were converted to lowercase and tokenised by stripping all the handles and stemming all the words. TF-IDF or term frequency-inverse document frequency was then used to calculate the statistical analysis of how a particular word or term is relevant in a given document [14].

Machine Learning Approach to Clustering Tweets. We narrowed down the following machine learning algorithms for our multi-class text classification; they are Logistic Regression (LR), Multinomial Naïve Bayes (NB), Support Vector Machine (SVM), Stochastic Gradient Descent (SGD) and Backward Propagation Neural Networks (NN).

The labelled data was split into training (30%) and testing dataset (70%) and used to evaluate the performance of each of the five machine learning algorithms using a cross-validation approach. The evaluation process was done using Python's Scikit-Learn library. The results showed that the NN algorithm performed the best amongst the rest at 73.8% accuracy with SGD coming closest at 72.4% accuracy. This was followed by SVM at 71.9%, LR at 64.5% and NB at 60.7%. The parameters for SGD and NN were then tuned further to identify the best model fitting that can result in further improved performance. A voting ensemble method was also implemented.

With the tuned parameters, both SGD and NN algorithms were tested for model fitting. SGD had an accuracy of 71.7% and NN at 70.4%. While an ensemble method, which is expected to improve the accuracy further, scored 72.7% accuracy rate. The model fit result is illustrated in Table 2. With that, the voting ensemble method was chosen to cluster the tweet corpus.

Table 2. Tuned parameters and ensemble method

Classifiers	Precision	Recall	f1-score	Accuracy (%)
Stochastic gradient descent	0.71	0.72	0.70	71.7%
Backward propagation neural network	0.7	0.7	0.69	70.4%
Voting ensemble method	0.73	0.73	0.71	72.7%

4   Analyses and Results

4.1   Machine Learning Classification Results

A total of 13,667 tweets were classified accordingly into five predetermined categories using the ensemble method. As a result, about 25.7% of the corpus were classified as meaningfully health-related. The proportion of tweets classified as *SC* was 6.5%, *TM* was 9.3%, and *PM* was 9.9%. Out of the 13,667 diabetes-related tweets, 1353 were classified as *PM*, 894 as *SC* and, 1265 as *TM*. On the other hand, a significant number of tweets were classified as *OT*, at 71.4%.

The results seemed to indicate that users were not sharing a substantial amount of health-related information through Twitter. For every 100 tweets associated with diabetes hashtag, one can only expect 25 tweets to be meaningfully health-related. This may seem insignificant because there is a need to sieve through an excessive amount of irrelevant tweets before getting to the relevant information.

However, when tweets are clustered as health-related, one can expect to get the majority of the information to be regarding *PM* and *TM*. This can be immensely useful to users, especially if they are healthcare decision-makers or caregivers.

4.2   Hashtags Analysis

The use of hashtags is useful in allowing users to follow topics they are interested in. To evaluate the relevance of the tweets, we analysed the hashtags used in tweets that were classified as health-related in *PM*, *SC*, and *TM* clusters. However, hashtags that contained descriptions such as "diabetes", "diabetic", "type1", "type2", "T1D" or "T2D" were excluded from the list as "diabetes" was the search term used to begin with. Including them in would be statistically not significant.

There were 3,512 tweets with a total of 5,802 hashtags in the health-related clusters. *PM* had 2,954 hashtags, *SC* with 1,188 hashtags and *TM* with 1,660 hashtags. A word cloud helped to visualise the frequent tags used for each cluster. However, it did not rank the frequency of words used (Fig. 1).

| Preventive Measures | Symptoms & Causes | Treatment & Medication |

Fig. 1. Hashtag word cloud associated with preventive measures, symptoms and causes and treatment clusters

A bar diagram was then used to illustrate the ranking of hashtags used in each cluster. The top 25 hashtags from each cluster were analysed and ranked according to its frequency of use.

We defined *PM* as tweets that contain measures that hinder or acts as obstacles to diabetes. As such, hashtags like "diet, weightloss, obesity, sugar, exercise, bloodsugar, fitness" seemed to suggest the actions that perhaps could help in the prevention of diabetes or reduce the impact of diabetes. Diet and food intake also appeared to be the general theme where hashtags like "nutrition, wholegrain, dietaryfiber, lowercarb, alcohol" could be implied as the need to look after food consumption.

"Insulin" was a frequently used hashtag for *TM*, which may not come as a surprise since the most common form of treatment for both type 1 and type 2 diabetes mellitus is insulin therapy. However, this may not necessarily be true as, according to [16], insulin therapy has the potential to increase the risk of cardiovascular risk and mortality in patients with type 2 diabetes. It was also interesting to notice that "estrogen" was also frequently used as a hashtag associated with diabetes. Coincidentally, there is a recent research study by [17] which investigates the protective role of estrogen and how its protective nature can be conferred to patients with diabetes mellitus. As we did not analyse the content of the tweet, we were not able to substantiate if indeed, the hashtags were about similar studies or findings by [17]. From the list of top hashtags, we found four other tags, such as "stemcells", "circadian", "immunotherapy" and "afrezza" that could probably be linked to current and future studies pertaining to the treatment or medication for the management of diabetes.

According to the definition by the National Institute of General Medical Science, circadian rhythms "are physical, mental and behavioural changes that follow a daily cycle, which primarily responds to light and darkness in the environment". According to the study by [18], circadian rhythms may impact sleep disturbance, that is linked to abnormal glucose metabolism and increased diabetes risk.

"Afrezza" is a powdered insulin that is administered via a breath-powered inhaler for patients with diabetes that require prandial insulin (rapid-acting), which is usually in injection-form (Fig. 2).

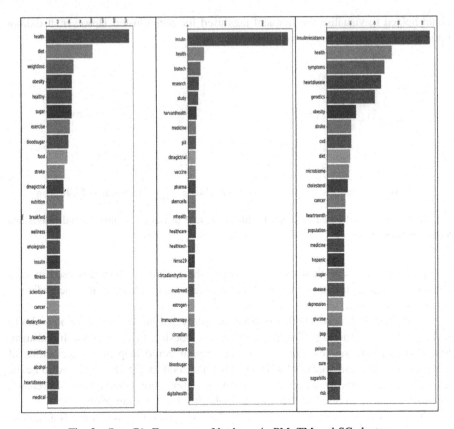

Fig. 2. (L to R): Frequency of hashtags in PM, TM and SC clusters

"Insulinresistance" was a highly used hashtag in *SC* cluster. Perhaps, the study by [16] could also explain the frequency of the word used. However, a study by [19], could better explain the link. In this study, the authors described the relationship between insulin resistance and metabolic disease that is associated with obesity, liver, pancreas and skeletal muscle. We also found a recent study that investigates how stem cells can be used to restore insulin production and cure diabetes by [20].

5   Discussion and Future Work

We implemented a machine learning approach that facilitated in the classification of tweets into health-related categories which could be meaningful to decision-makers such as healthcare professionals, caregivers and even patients themselves. From a collection of tweets related to diabetes, our approach clustered about 25% of the tweets into meaningful categories of *Preventive Measures*, *Symptoms & Causes*, and *Treatment & Medication*. While these clusters contain a small number of tweets, with an average number of tweets per day is 500 million tweets, the potential of curating information useful for decision support is intriguing. We believed that Twitter shows excellent promise in facilitating health information sharing, and thus, is a significant source for purposeful information. Based on our findings, a higher concentration of health-related tweets was clustered in *PM* and *TM*, which implied that Twitter users were more interested in sharing or finding out ways to prevent the onset of diabetes or treatments for the condition. Perhaps, it also had to do with diabetes mellitus being one of the four major chronic diseases prevalent globally; thus, such information is more rampant.

From the analysis of hashtags, we found significant keywords that were relevant to the three categories. In *PM* cluster, activities such as exercise and weight loss were evident as frequently used hashtags, suggesting actions that could be undertaken to prevent the onset of diabetes. Diet and food intake related hashtags could suggest ways how food consumption can have an impact on diabetes. Similarly, in clusters of *SC* and *TM*, hashtags for probable causes of diabetes mellitus, and current or latest treatments for diabetes management, recorded high recurrences.

Clinical decision making or decision making of any sort is a complex cognitive task that requires immense intellectual competencies. While software tools help to reduce the workload, it cannot be achieved without the availability of information to support decisions. In improving the usability and interaction between humans and computer systems, our approach has identified a viable avenue where practical information can be curated for use in supporting clinical decisions.

However, there are several limitations to the study. We only managed to collect a small number of tweets that spans two weeks. While our machine learning classifier was able to cluster tweets with reasonably high accuracy, more effort is required to optimise our algorithms further. As a preliminary study, we only managed analysed the hashtags to evaluate the relevance of tweets according to the categories the tweets were clustered in.

In our future works, besides using a significant number of tweets that span over one year or more, a deep learning model is proposed to analyse the full tweet text or information and its corresponding hyperlinked contents. Also, an improved data pre-processing approach to eliminate fake and malicious content will be implemented. A natural language approach can be adopted to find meaning in tweets so that more meaningful information can be extracted for use in a decision support system.

References

1. Hu, F.B., Satija, A., Manson, J.E.: Curbing the diabetes pandemic: the need for global policy solutions. JAMA **313**(23), 2319–2320 (2015)
2. Saeedi, P., et al.: Global and regional diabetes prevalence estimates for 2019 and projections for 2030 and 2045: results from the international diabetes federation diabetes atlas. Diabetes Res. Clin. Pract. **157**, 107843 (2019)
3. Data.gov.sg. Prevalence of hypertension, diabetes, high total cholesterol, obesity and daily smoking (2020). [cited 2020]. https://data.gov.sg/dataset/prevalence-of-hypertension-diabetes-high-total-cholesterol-obesity-and-daily-smoking?view_id=36a54ebf-3db6-48c8-84c8-c15e48ed5c0a&resource_id=c5f26f19-b6aa-4f4f-ae5b-ee62d840f8e7

4. Jung, A.-K., Mirbabaie, M., Ross, B., Stieglitz, S., Neuberger, C., Kapidzic, S. Information diffusion between Twitter and online media (2018)
5. Pershad, Y., Hangge, P.T., Albadawi, H., Oklu, R.: Social medicine: Twitter in healthcare. J. Clin. Med. **7**(6), 121 (2018)
6. Statista. Most popular social networks as of January 2020, ranked by number of active users (2020). https://www.statista.com/statistics/272014/global-social-networks-ranked-by-number-of-users/
7. Mention. Twitter engagement report 2018 (2018)
8. Finfgeld-Connett, D.: Twitter and health science research. West. J. Nurs. Res. **37**(10), 1269–1283 (2015)
9. Gabarron, E., Dorronzoro, E., Rivera-Romero, O., Wynn, R.: Diabetes on Twitter: a sentiment analysis. J Diab. Sci Technol. **13**(3), 439–444 (2019)
10. Sedrak, M.S., et al.: Examining public communication about kidney cancer on Twitter. JCO Clin. Cancer Inform. **3**, 1–6 (2019)
11. Sinnenberg, L., Buttenheim, A.M., Padrez, K., Mancheno, C., Ungar, L., Merchant, R.M.: Twitter as a tool for health research: a systematic review. Am. J. Public Health **107**(1), e1–e8 (2017)
12. Joyce, B., Deng, J.: Sentiment analysis of tweets for the 2016 US presidential election. In: 2017 IEEE MIT Undergraduate Research Technology Conference (URTC) (2017)
13. Rane, A., Kumar, A.: Sentiment classification system of Twitter data for US airline service analysis. In: 2018 IEEE 42nd Annual Computer Software and Applications Conference (COMPSAC) (2018)
14. Rathi, M., Malik, A., Varshney, D., Sharma, R., Mendiratta, S. Sentiment analysis of Tweets using machine learning approach. In: 2018 Eleventh International Conference on Contemporary Computing (IC3) (2018)
15. Missier, P., et al.: Tracking dengue epidemics using Twitter content classification and topic modelling. In: Casteleyn, S., Dolog, P., Pautasso, C. (eds.) ICWE 2016. LNCS, vol. 9881, pp. 80–92. Springer, Cham (2016). https://doi.org/10.1007/978-3-319-46963-8_7
16. Herman, M.E., O'Keefe, J.H., Bell, D.S.H., Schwartz, S.S.: Insulin therapy increases cardiovascular risk in type 2 diabetes. Prog. Cardiovasc. Dis. **60**(3), 422–434 (2017)
17. De Paoli, M., Werstuck, G.H.: Role of estrogen in type 1 and type 2 diabetes mellitus: a review of clinical and preclinical data. Can. J. Diab. **44**, 448–452 (2020)
18. Reutrakul, S., Van Cauter, E.: Interactions between sleep, circadian function, and glucose metabolism: implications for risk and severity of diabetes. Ann. N. Y. Acad. Sci. **1311**(1), 151–173 (2014)
19. Czech, M.P.: Insulin action and resistance in obesity and type 2 diabetes. Nat. Med. **23**(7), 804–814 (2017)
20. Sordi, V., et al.: Stem cells to restore insulin production and cure diabetes. Nutr. Metab. Cardiovasc. Dis. **27**(7), 583–600 (2017)

Development of a Non-Immersive VR Reminiscence Therapy Experience for Patients with Dementia

Angela Tabafunda[1], Shawn Matthews[1], Rabia Akhter[1],
Alvaro Uribe-Quevedo[1](✉) (iD), Winnie Sun[1], Sheri Horsburgh[2],
and Carmen LaFontaine[2]

[1] Ontario Tech University, Oshawa, ON, Canada
{angela.tabafunda,shawn.matthews,rabia.akhter}@ontariotechu.net
{alvaro.quevedo,winnie.sun}@ontariotechu.ca
[2] Ontario Shores, Whitby, ON, Canada
{horsburghs,lafontainec}@ontarioshores.ca

Abstract. The World Health Organization projects a continuous growth of the elderly population, causing a shift in the demographic distribution. With this shift, healthcare plays an important role when treating conditions such as dementia, which prominently afflicts the elderly and their families. Currently, reminiscence therapy helps support alleviation of dementia symptoms through memory recollection. However, the therapy relies on traditional printed media, including pictures shown to the patients that lack immersion. In this paper, we present a preliminary study from focus group and one-on-one interviews with patients, family members and care providers to gauge their interest and perception of two non-immersive or headset-less virtual reality scenes for complementing reminiscence therapy. One system features head tracking as an input to create shifting perspectives on the output display to provide a sense of depth, while the other system employs the Looking Glass, a holographic display providing horizontal depth perspective. The proposed non-immersive VR systems were deemed feasible for therapy purposes based on our preliminary data, with insights on challenges and opportunities for future development.

Keywords: Immersive · Non-immersive · Reminiscence therapy · Virtual reality

1 Introduction

The World Health Organization estimates that the elderly population will double by 2050 [11]. The growing ageing population will experience an increase of prominent health conditions associated with advancing age that affect both physical

Supported by Ontario Shores, the Ontario Tech University, and the Natural Sciences and Engineering Research Council of Canada in the form of a Discovery grant (RGPIN-2018-05917).

© Springer Nature Switzerland AG 2020
C. Stephanidis et al. (Eds.): HCII 2020, CCIS 1294, pp. 509–517, 2020.
https://doi.org/10.1007/978-3-030-60703-6_66

and mental capacity [13]. Amongst ageing conditions, dementia affects 5 8% of the worldwide population [12]. Dementia is caused by brain cell damage, and incites cognitive decline affecting memory, thinking, behaviour, and everyday activities. While there is no known cure for dementia, treatments include pharmacological and non-pharmacological interventions. Pharmacological treatments pose risks of side effects, therefore, the optimization of non-pharmacological interventions is important in the management of this condition [19]. For example, some non-pharmacological interventions include music therapy which has been studied to improve cognitive function as a first-line of non-pharmacological treatment [20], animal-assisted group therapy in boosting intervention adherence as a result of the engagement resulting from the interactions [10], the use of memories through reminiscence therapy [18], serious games for cognitive and psychomotor improvement [9], and sculpture-based art to improve well being [17] amongst others.

Reminiscence therapy (RT), one of these non-pharmacological interventions, is a psychosocial intervention technique used to support and improve the lives of dementia patients, caregivers, and families [18]. Defined by the American Psychological Association as the use of life histories delivered through written, oral, or both medium for the improvement of psychological well-being [1], in which RT helps individuals remember their past through recollection. RT therapy is usually facilitated in groups or individual sessions and aided with tangible articles such as photographs, objects, and music to trigger memories. Woods et al. [18] reviewed the effects of RT for dementia and caregivers concluding that the treatment briefly improves patient cognition immediately after treatment and reduces caregiver strain with the increased patient mood and communication.

Recently, a digital technology that has been gaining momentum is Virtual Reality (VR), as it allows to immerse users in environments with high levels of presence that can provide treatment and diagnostic benefits in the care of cognitive disorders [16]. Additionally, other areas of application include: i) VR experiences for the detection of dementia through user interactions [21], ii) exergames (i.e., games for eliciting physical activity) for improving and maintaining physical fitness [4], iii) diagnosing spatial navigation disorders [3], iv) memory rehabilitation [7], v) apathy reduction [2], vi) and training for fall prevention [8], amongst others. Regarding RT and VR, *Rendever* is a commercial Head-Mounted Displays (HMDs) driven solution that creates customized therapy and shared experiences[14]. However, VR equipment poses design and deployment challenges as patients at advanced stages of dementia may find total immersion confusing due to severe memory disturbance and behavioural changes, in which case, non-immersive or semi-immersive is more suitable. However, patients with mild and moderate stage of dementia may benefit from immersive VR as research continues to demonstrate promising potential in this area [15].

In this paper, we present a preliminary study focused on gauging the interest in using non-immersive virtual reality scenes for reminiscence therapy to increase immersion with 3D content by providing depth without VR headsets. We propose two non-immersive virtual reality systems; the first system employs a webcam-based head-tracking that creates shifting perspectives on a regular screen display, thus causing the effect on depth. The other system utilizes the Looking Glass, a holographic display that presents horizontal stereoscopic depth. Both systems use a custom narrative application, developed to create context and viability for reminiscence therapy purposes.

2 Development

The purpose of our application is to provide a platform to create personalized narrative for RT. The target users are the caregivers, who will build a narrative using digital media associated with the patient's past and placed in a virtual environment to trigger recollection. The completed narrative will be used for RT as the caregivers explore the experience with the patients, who will be able to view the scene from different perspectives through the non-immersive features.

We propose two non-immersive VR systems; the first system employs a webcam-based head-tracking that creates shifting perspectives on a regular screen display, thus causing the effect on depth. The visual perspective of this display will shift depending on the user's head position as illustrated in Fig. 1.

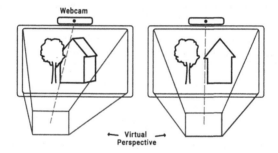

Fig. 1. Overview of the shifting perspective relative to head position approach.

The other system utilizes the Looking Glass, a holographic display that presents horizontal stereoscopic depth. Both systems use a custom narrative application to create context and viability for reminiscence therapy purposes to enable caregivers to customize the content being presented. The Looking Glass is a 3D holographic display, which creates the illusion of horizontal depth without requiring a HMD. Patients will experience the narrative during RT with increased immersion as the holographic display gives depth to the content. These components will work together to improve the VR experience with increased levels of immersion.

For developing the main application, the Unity game engine was chosen due to its cross-device compatibility that allowed us to develop the two proposed non-immersive systems. The development process followed user-centered design principles and was co-designed with the caregivers.

After conducting brainstorming sessions with our partners at the Ontario Shores Centre for Mental Health Sciences in Ontario, Canada, the application's functions were identified and separated into three different stages, each containing the following features: i) Media linking to allow caregivers to upload media that can be linked to objects within the scene (Fig. 2a), ii) create memory triggers that can be placed in the environment (Fig. 2a), and iii) create a path to navigate the objects in the environment (Fig. 2b). When the customization is completed, the caregivers can engage their patients in the reminiscence experience using narratives while navigating through the customized environment.

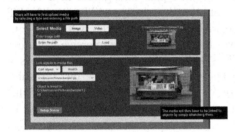 

(a) Media linking and trigger creation user interface. (b) Narrative path creation user interface.

Fig. 2. Non-immersive VR RT Content development stages.

2.1   Media Integration for Immersion

One of the features of our approach relies on adding content to enable the customization of the RT experience. Our initial development efforts were directed towards incorporating real locations in the narrative to aid patient recollection. Several tools such as mapping software development kits (SDKs) such as the Maps SDK for Unity[1], and extracted data from Google Earth along with other open-source tools such as Open Street Map[2] were explored to identify user-friendly, cost-effective options for the caregivers.

The workflow for obtaining the 3D meshes from real location requires to extract the information from map services such as Google Earth. For example, an extracted model from Google Earth using *RenderDoc*[3], a graphics debugger tool was imported into Unity to visualize its suitability for RT. However, this method was deemed ineffective, primarily due to the meshes' poor quality presented in Fig. 3b, which can affect immersion and engagement.

---

[1] https://developers.google.com/maps/documentation/gaming/overview_musk. Google. Accessed June 10, 2020.

[2] https://www.openstreetmap.org/. OpenStreetMap Foundation. Accessed June 10, 2020.

[3] https://renderdoc.org/. Karlsson, B. Accessed June 10, 2020.

Mapping SDKs from WRLD and Google Maps Platform presented a better alternative as this offered geographical freedom and fidelity that was ideal for narrative customization. However, during the co-design process, the healthcare partners indicated the lack of graphic fidelity as a possible shortcoming for immersion and engagement (see Fig. 3). The reason for striving for higher fidelity environments is needed for a visual representation to trigger familiarization, as otherwise, it may induce confusion rather than recollection to patients. Ultimately, feedback from co-design informed us to employ simplified environments that can convey more realism as these will likely provide a more relaxed environment for the patients.

(a) Google Earth mesh.   (b) WRLD mesh.

Fig. 3. Quality mesh comparison between *RenderDoc* and Mapping SDKs.

2.2   Looking Glass Non-Immersive Solution

Integrating the Looking Glass within the system requires using the manufacturer's SDK. Quilts of the scene were made to project the 3D depth on the device. Quilts are composed of tiled images of the scene from multiple viewing angles. A custom camera controlled the holographic properties was used in the application in place of Unity's built-in camera system. This custom camera generates the quilts in real-time, projecting the hologram based on user inputs. The camera has customizable view cone properties, which dictates the available number of viewing angles. While the Looking Glass supports a cone of 35°, a smaller view cone of 8.5° was used for the custom camera in order to reduce eye strain and improve visual resolution for finer details.

When caregivers are navigating the path, the patients will see content with depth as they watch the scene's triggering elements (see Fig. 4 for reference). Finer details like text and user interface elements are placed in the zero-parallax plane, a depth on the device's render volume where pixel representation across many views remains consistent and readable. It is worth noting that we are using the 8.3 inches Looking Glass that requires viewers to be 15 to 30 cm away from the device. At the time of writing this paper, the Looking Glass costs $599 USD and it is advancing towards positioning as a consumer-level solution with larger and more affordable displays.

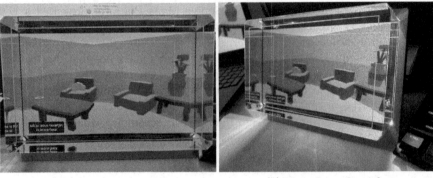

(a) View from center.   (b) View from the right.

Fig. 4. Looking Glass views within the cone.

2.3 Head Tracking Non-Immersive Solution

Head tracking was integrated by employing the OpenSeeFace toolkit [5]. This SDK provided us with pre-trained head tracking models, as well as a service that we could launch from Unity that would transmit the estimated translation, orientation, and marker points on the user. The most difficult issue we needed to overcome was the ability to determine the resolution of the capture device in a way that would not add complexity to the end-user. To do this, we used a Unity *WebCamTexture* and delayed the start of the head tracker until this texture could determine the capture device's dimensions and refresh rate (which were then fed into tracker initialization). As such, there is a short delay after starting the application before head tracking becomes available. We decided to use a web camera to minimize the entry barrier accessibility of the technology..

To provide the depth perception illusion, we added a calibration option that would set the origin transformation for the tracked object to the current head transformation, in order to have greater control over the position of the virtual camera in the scene. We then use the viewer's transformation relative to this origin to position the camera within the scene inspired by the projection matrix method made by Johnny Chuny Lee [6].

3 Preliminary Results

Due to the COVID-19 pandemic, we conducted one-on-one interviews with video demonstrations conducted by the Ontario Shores partners. Three participants were carefully selected under inclusion criteria with their respective caregivers (two in total) were invited to participate in the interview. Videos of the proposed systems were shown to patients and their caregivers for feedback. The caregivers who participated in the interview are informal carers who share a personal relationship with their patient (these are often family members, spouses, or friends). All participants were asked the same set of open-ended questions:

- What is your overall experience with the virtual reality training session? Do you think it would be a feasible intervention for dementia care?
- In your perspective, what would be the most effective way of virtual reality intervention (immersive/ non-immersive) in managing Behavioural and Psychological Symptoms of Dementia (BPSD)? Why?
- What approaches would you recommend most? Experiencing memories (e.g., home, neighborhood, favorite item) or experiencing natural environment (e.g., scenic beauty, oceans, greenery, etc.) on Virtual Reality? Why?
- What type of content do you think would be most effective - picture, videos, music, or a combination? If so, why?
- What do you think would be the challenges or barriers to using Virtual Reality in dementia care?

All three patients thought that the systems would be a feasible intervention for dementia care, stating interest in the overall experience. Experiencing memories through familiar places was favored over natural environments for the virtual environment approach. Patients also expressed concerns about vision difficulties when asked about the challenges that the immersive technology can have in dementia care. All of the caregivers have expressed similar responses but in greater detail with regards to the systems. Aside from vision difficulties, one of the caregivers mentioned wandering and attention loss as a barrier for VR in dementia care which can occur during therapy. A need for audio recollection materials is apparent within most responses, with one caregiver pointing out how their patient enjoys music, especially from their native language.

4   Conclusion

Here we have presented two non-immersive VR prototypes for complementing traditional Reminiscence Therapy. While VR poses great opportunities for elderly care, little has been explored in terms of non-immersive VR that provides depth perception without requiring a HMD. From our preliminary interview findings, we conclude that VR has a promising potential for complementing RT with immersive and engaging experiences. However, such novel approach presents several challenges to be addressed in terms of inclusive design, accessibility, and adherence as indicated by the participants.

Future work will focus on implementing audio features within the application to add further recollection cues, interactivity through simple gamified tasks related to the patient's experiences. Furthermore, additional user experience will be implemented to streamline the narrative creation, along with metrics analytics to customize the unique needs of each patient instead of having a one-size-fits-all solution.

References

1. Association, AP: APA dictionary of psychology. https://dictionary.apa.org/reminiscence-therapy

2. Brimelow, R.E., Dawe, B., Dissanayaka, N.: Preliminary research: virtual reality in residential aged care to reduce apathy and improve mood. Cyberpsychol. Behav. Soc. Netw. **23**(3), 165–170 (2020)
3. Cogné, M., et al.: The contribution of virtual reality to the diagnosis of spatial navigation disorders and to the study of the role of navigational aids: a systematic literature review. Ann. Phys. Rehabil. Med. **60**(3), 164–176 (2017)
4. Eisapour, M., Cao, S., Domenicucci, L., Boger, J.: Virtual reality exergames for people living with dementia based on exercise therapy best practices. In: Proceedings of the Human Factors and Ergonomics Society Annual Meeting,vol. 62, pp. 528–532. SAGE Publications Sage CA,Los Angeles (2018)
5. Emiliana, V.: Openseeface (2020). https://github.com/emilianavt/OpenSeeFace
6. Lee, J.C.: Head tracking for desktop VR displays using the wii remote, December 2007. http://johnnylee.net/projects/wii/
7. Mathews, M., Mitrovic, A., Ohlsson, S., Holland, J., McKinley, A.: A virtual reality environment for rehabilitation of prospective memory in stroke patients. In: KES, pp. 7–15 (2016)
8. Mirelman, A., Maidan, I., Shiratzky, S.S., Hausdorff, J.M.: Virtual reality training as an intervention to reduce falls. In: Montero-Odasso, M., Camicioli, R. (eds.) Falls and Cognition in Older Persons, pp. 309–321. Springer, Cham (2020). https://doi.org/10.1007/978-3-030-24233-6_18
9. Ning, H., Li, R., Ye, X., Zhang, Y., Liu, L.: A review on serious games for dementia care in ageing societies. IEEE J. Trans. Eng. Health Med. **8**, 1–11 (2020)
10. Olsen, C., Pedersen, I., Bergland, A., Enders-Slegers, M.J., Ihlebæk, C.: Engagement in elderly persons with dementia attending animal-assisted group activity. Dementia **18**(1), 245–261 (2019)
11. Organization, W.H.: Ageing and health. http://www.who.int/news-room/fact-sheets/detail/ageing-and-health
12. World Health Organization: Dementia. http://www.who.int/news-room/fact-sheets/detail/dementia
13. Pol, L.G.: Rapid growth in the elderly population of the world. In: Berhouma, M., Krolak-Salmon, P. (eds.) Brain and Spine Surgery in the Elderly, pp. 3–15. Springer, Cham (2017). https://doi.org/10.1007/978-3-319-40232-1_1
14. Rendever: Rendever is overcoming social isolation through the power of virtual reality and shared experiences https://rendever.com/
15. Rose, V., Stewart, I., Jenkins, K.G., Tabbaa, L., Ang, C.S., Matsangidou, M.: Bringing the outside. in: the feasibility of virtual reality with people with dementia in an inpatient psychiatric care setting. Dementia (2019). https://doi.org/10.1177/1471301219868036
16. Schiza, E., Matsangidou, M., Neokleous, K., Pattichis, C.S.: Virtual reality applications for neurological disease: a review. Front. Robot. AI **6**, 100 (2019)
17. Seifert, K., Spottke, A., Fliessbach, K.: Effects of sculpture based art therapy in dementia patients–a pilot study. Heliyon **3**(11), e00460 (2017)
18. Woods, B., Ophilbin, L., Farrell, E.M., Spector, A.E., Orrell, M.: Reminiscencetherapy for dementia. Cochrane Database Syst. Rev. (2018). DOIurl-https://doi.org/10.1002/14651858.cd001120.pub3
19. Zahirovic, I., Torisson, G., Wattmo, C., Londos, E.: Psychotropic and anti-dementia treatment in elderly persons with clinical signs of dementia with lewy bodies: a cross-sectional study in 40 nursing homes in Sweden. BMC Geriatrics **18**(1), 50 (2018)

20. Zhang, Y., et al.: Does music therapy enhance behavioral and cognitive function in elderly dementia patients? A systematic review and meta-analysis. Ageing Res. Rev. **35**, 1–11 (2017)
21. Zhong, Y., Tian, Y., Park, M., Yeom, S.: Exploring an application of virtual reality for early detection of dementia. arXiv preprint arXiv:2001.07546 (2020)

HCI in Mobility, Automotive
and Aviation

Neural Correlates of Mental Workload in Virtual Flight Simulation

Polina Andrievskaia$^{(\boxtimes)}$ ⓘ, Kathleen Van Benthem ⓘ,
and Chris M. Herdman ⓘ

Carleton University, Ottawa, ON K1S 5B6, Canada
polinaandrievskaia@cmail.carleton.ca,
kathy_vanbenthem@carleton.ca,
chrisherdman@cunet.carleton.ca

Abstract. Real-time monitoring of pilot mental workload has important applications in cognitive assessment and flight safety. Progress in wireless electroencephalography (EEG) and 3D flight simulation has provided novel opportunities to advance our understanding of adaptive levels of workload during flight. The present work examines neural correlates of mental workload evoked by ecologically valid flight tasks and furthers the application of human-computer interaction in aviation. Performance and EEG data were collected while 47 participants completed basic aviator tasks in a virtual reality environment where working memory load was manipulated. Analyses investigated event-related potentials (ERP) and spectral power density differences in moderate and high task load conditions across key brain regions. The subtle modulation of moderate to high workload did not reveal significant differences in frequency changes across parietal and frontal regions or participant performance; however, a frontal ERP showed a significant effect of workload. Classification by performance level showed better utility, where greater beta power was found in the parietal regions and increased delta activity was measured in the frontal regions. Results indicate that EEG analyses that exploit spectral data from the frontal and parietal regions may offer reliable approaches for classifying performance in high workload conditions in virtual aviation environments

Keywords: Aviation psychology · Encephalography · Workload · Virtual reality

1 Introduction

Recent advancements in virtual reality (VR) has expanded the applications of simulated flight environments in the aviation psychology domain. Visual cues available to pilots within VR flight simulation offer high relatability to the cues found in real flight [1]. Commercially available VR headsets and integrated flight simulation software hold promise for designing ideal environments where encephalography (EEG) systems can be used to objectively measure workload effects in real-time. In the present work, behavioural and EEG data were collected while participants (non-pilots) completed

© Springer Nature Switzerland AG 2020
C. Stephanidis et al. (Eds.): HCII 2020, CCIS 1294, pp. 521–528, 2020.
https://doi.org/10.1007/978-3-030-60703-6_67

basic aviator circuit tasks in a VR environment where working memory load was manipulated.

1.1 Measuring Workload

Mental workload is defined to be the relationship between the cognitive effort required to achieve a task, and the available mental processing capabilities [2]. Mental processing capabilities use working memory resources, and evidence has been presented supporting the correlation between the activation of anatomical regions and of different working memory systems. Work by Smith et al. [3] found that engaging in a verbal task activated the left parietal and frontal cortical regions, while engaging in a spatial task activated the right parietal and frontal regions. It has been suggested that visual and auditory tasks may compete for cognitive resources in working memory [4].

EEG as an Index of Workload. EEG systems have been found to be successful in predicting a person's cognitive workload [5]. EEG-slow waves have been categorized into four classes: delta (0.5–4 Hz), theta (4–7 Hz), alpha (8–12 Hz), and beta (13–30 Hz) waves [6]. These cortical oscillations are involved in numerous cognitive operations and top-down control of cognitive processes, such as visual and spatial processing and attentional changes [7]. For example, delta waves have been found to increase in the frontal lobe region during tasks requiring concentration, such as semantic processing and working memory tasks [8]. Theta wavelength activity has also been related to cognitive workload, where driving-related research has found theta band power to increase across the frontal cortex during increased workload [9]. Lastly, it has been generally stated that a decrease in alpha and beta power reflects working memory processing, as observed in power decreases across these frequencies after stimulus onset [10].

In this study, neuronal oscillations were also examined to identify levels of participant performance on working memory tasks during flight. Other researchers have also begun using EEG to investigate methods for classifying performance during complex tasks. For example, Yang et al. [11] used EEG data and a variety of brain-computer interface approaches to classify driver performance, and not workload states, on a vehicle following task.

ERPs have also been proposed as method for indexing cognitive workload. Previous work has found the N100 and P200 ERP components to have greater deflections for the easy task conditions than the difficult conditions [12]. In the present research it was expected that the ERPs would show a similar sensitivity to variations in workload.

Hypotheses. This study examined the effects of task demand and mental workload on participant performance across the frontal and parietal cortical regions. Performance effects on spectral data were also analyzed in the high workload condition to explore neural patterns of low and high performers. First, it was hypothesized that subtle differences in workload conditions would be evident in behavioural measures in our sample of non-pilots. It was also predicted that real-time EEG signals would demonstrate characteristic differences in moderate versus high workload states. Specifically, that the high workload condition would result in smaller ERPs (N100 and P200) in the frontal lobe due to higher levels of ongoing mental activity, and that spectral power across the slow wave frequencies would be associated with variations in workload and show sensitivity to low and high performance

2 Methods

2.1 Participants

Data was collected from 47 undergraduate students from (23 females). Age ranged from 16 to 43 years old ($M = 21.81$, $SD = 5.83$ years). Participants received course credit or refreshments as compensation. All subjects had normal-to-corrected vision

Measured Variables. The two flight conditions were categorized as moderate and high difficulty. The moderate workload condition required flying but no additional radio communication tasks, while both flying and radio call monitoring were required in the high workload condition. Participants were instructed to monitor the details of radio calls played during the high workload conditions, and their message recall accuracy was recorded as well. The number of hoops accurately flown through was used to calculate flight precision. Participants also completed a concurrent Peripheral Detection Task (PDT) wherein auditory tones were played every few seconds. Participants were instructed to press a button every time a tone was heard. Response time and accuracy were recorded for the PDT. Accuracy on the call sign task from the high workload condition was selected for further analysis, to establish whether participant performance could also be classified and serve as a reliable index of mental workload. Performance level (low or high) was determined by call sign accuracy. Performance for each call sign was first assessed on a 4-point scale, where a score of 1 indicated that the participant remembered none of the letters correctly, and a score of 4 indicated that they remembered all three letters of the call sign correctly. Twelve low performers (27.9%) were categorized to have received a score of 5 and below, and 31 high performers (72.1%) received a score of 6 or higher.

EEG Recording and Pre-processing. As shown in Fig. 1, the 14 channels of the Emotiv EPOC + headset reflected the International 10–20 system. EEG data was recorded at 2048 Hz and down-sampled to 256 Hz with Emotiv TestBench software [13]. Electrode impendences were kept within 10–20 kΩ. EEGLab [14] software was used to process the raw EEG data by applying a bandpass filter of 0.1–50 Hz. Independent Components Analysis isolated and removed noise artifacts from the epochs, such as eye blinks and eye movements. To create the ERSPs, the data between the onset of tones (3 s) was epoched and averaged, creating large sets of data that provided overall power variations across multiple frequencies. The data for the ERPs was further filtered from 0.1 to 12 Hz, and epoched 800 ms after the onset of the auditory stimulus. The Fast Fourier Transform process was applied to the remaining data to extract the absolute power densities for key frequencies at each channel.

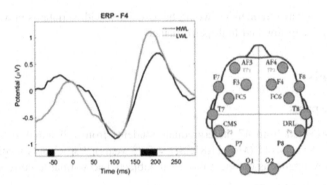

Fig. 1. ERP at F4 (left) and EMOTIV EPOC + electrode map (adapted from Emotiv [13]). (right). Black bars in ERP x-axis represent statistically significant differences between the workload conditions (p < 0.05).

3   Results

Due to the exploratory nature of this research, any effect of significance level $p < 0.1$ and $\eta p^2 > 0.1$ will be examined, as well as any non-overlapping means (per 1 SEM) on the data plots. To validate that the two workload conditions evoked different responses, responses to the PDT across the two conditions were assessed. The average hit rates across the two moderate workload conditions ($M = 93.42$, $SD = 8.09$) and the two high workload conditions ($M = 92.09$, $SD = 5.13$) were calculated. A paired samples t-test indicated a significant difference across the two workload states, where participants accurately responded to the tones significantly less in the high workload conditions, t $(28) = -2.32$, $p = .03$. Response times did not differ significantly across the two workload conditions

3.1   Event-Related Potentials and Event Related Spectral Perturbation (ERSP)

Twenty-eight participants met the criteria for full data and completed the four test circuits successfully.

Workload Effects. ERP responses to tones were analyzed in the frontal electrodes of both hemispheres. In the right frontal region (F4), a significant difference between workload conditions was found at the P200, where the positive deflection of the P200 was 0.6 μV for the high workload and 1.0 μV for the moderate workload condition (see Fig. 1).

A two-factor ANOVA was conducted to examine the effect of workload levels (moderate versus high) and brain regions (14 electrode sites) on spectral power (0–30 Hz) for several predetermined frequency bands. A significant main effect of the region across all frequencies was found, where $F(12,758) = 6.93$, $p < 0.001$, $\eta p^2 = 0.1$. No main effects or interactions with workload were found. Post hoc tests using the Bonferroni correction revealed that the both the P7 and P8 regions had significantly greater alpha frequency activity than the right frontal regions, $p = 0.001$. The left frontal region had significantly greater activity in the upper delta range and theta waves compared to the right frontal regions, $p = 0.012$.

Performance Effects. A series of two-factor ANOVAs were conducted to examine the effect of performance level on spectral power and to look for any interactions between performance level and brain regions (14 brain regions). A significant main effect of performance level $F(1, 364) = 13.66$, $p < 0.001$, $\eta p^2 = 0.04$ was found in the beta (13–15 Hz) regions, where low performing individuals have greater beta activation ($M = .27$, $SD = .71$), compared to high performers ($M = -.06$, $SD = 1.01$). Strongest effects were evident in the P8 electrode such that $F(1, 26) = 3.72$, $p = .0651$, $\eta p^2 = 0.13$, where the performance levels diverge with greater activation in the low performing group ($M = -.13$, $SD = .43$) compared to the high performing group ($M = -.73$, $SD = .92$). This is shown in Fig. 2. For the 2–4 Hz wave regions, a slight effect of performance level was found at electrode AF4, such that $F(1, 26) = 3.28$, $p = 0.08$, $\eta p^2 = 0.112$, where the low performing group ($M = -.25$, $SD = .71$) had slightly greater delta wave activity than the high performing group ($M = -0.82$, $SD = .84$). This main effect of performance and main effect of brain region was evident throughout 1–4 Hz.

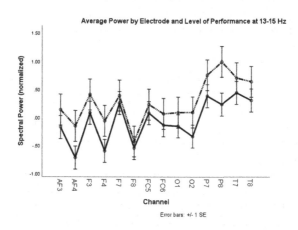

Fig. 2. Spectral power of the 13–15 Hz (beta) band as a function of the brain region and the participant performance level on the call sign tasks. Dotted bars represent the poorly performing individuals and the solid bars represent the high performing individuals. The P8 especially shows non-overlapping means between the two performance level groups.

4   Discussion

4.1   Event Related Potentials

The right F4 electrode showed evidence workload at later component latencies. This brain region was located over Brodmann's area (BA) 46 [15], a region associated with working memory [16]. This right frontocentral region showed a greater wave deflection in the moderate workload conditions, indicating that tone processing was somewhat inhibited when participants had to simultaneously process the call signs. It has been argued that the visual and auditory working memory systems contend for cognitive resources, therefore simultaneous processing of the auditory tasks may have led to overall power reduction in the right frontal region.

ERSP Differences Across Cortical Regions. Electrodes P7 and P8 are located at BA 37 [17] of the left and right parietal cortical regions, respectively. These parietal areas have been found to be associated with semantic function and visual perception [18]. Increase in verbal memory load has been associated with a decrease in alpha power in these regions [19]. In our results, frequency analyses revealed no main effect or interaction of workload within these regions. Post hoc analyses of participant performance found a main effect of performance level in the upper alpha and beta bands. At 12 Hz and above, the low performers experienced increased power activity compared to the high performers. As alpha and beta power decrease has been traditionally associated with increased working memory demands [10], greater beta power in the poorly performing participants can indicate weaker working memory performance, and high performing individuals exhibiting suppressed alpha and beta activity can be interpreted as more efficient information processing.

Electrode AF4 is located over BA 9 of the right frontotemporal region [20]. This region is part of the dorsolateral prefrontal cortex, an area associated with working memory and that has been found to show persistent levels of neuronal activation during delayed response tasks [21]. Delta wave power has been found to increase in this region during semantic processing and working memory tasks [8]. In this study, main effects of performance were found where the low performing group had higher delta power during the high work-load conditions in the right frontotemporal region, as compared to the high performers. Given that delta oscillations have been also reported to increase during fatigued states [22], an alternate argument can be made that the low performing individuals may have started their sessions more fatigued, or became fatigued faster over the course of the flights.

Due to the successful documentation of performance effects measured across select frontal and parietal regions, it is proposed that EEG systems are a valuable source of information when assessing individual differences in workload. Yang et al. [11] were also successful in classifying driver performance in a vehicle following task using EEG. The authors found that reasonable classification rates could be computed using a range of electrodes representing bilateral frontal and parietal brain regions and a focus on delta to beta frequency bandwidths from EEG data collected during the simulated driving task

5   Conclusion

In sum, the effect of workload was evident in the upper alpha and lower beta region, indicating that processing of the auditory task may be related more to the higher wavelength regions than the lower wavelengths. Workload effects on were also successfully measured in the right frontocentral hemisphere as evident in the differences of neural responses during the two workload conditions. Future research can explore differences across group performance in varying workload condition and include the higher bands of the frequency spectrum in analyses, to further understand how these factors influence task demands and workload measurement in aviation simulation.

References

1. Sparko, A., Burki-Cohen, J., Go, T.: Transfer of training from a full-flight simulator vs. a high-level flight-training device with a dynamic seat. In: AIAA Modeling and Simulation Technologies Conference, p. 8218 (2010)
2. Hart, S.G., Staveland, L.E.: Development of NASA-TLX (Task Load Index): results of empirical and theoretical research. In: Hancock, P.A., Meshkati, N. (eds.) Advances in Psychology, Human Mental Workload, North-Holland, pp. 139–183 (1998)
3. Smith, E., Jonides, J., Koeppe, R.: Dissociating verbal and spatial working memory using PET. Cereb. Cortex **6**, 11–20 (1996)
4. Saults, J., Cowan, N.: A central capacity limit to the simultaneous storage of visual and auditory arrays in working memory. J. Exp. Psychol. Gen. **136**, 663–684 (2007)
5. Gevins, A., Smith, M., Leong, H., McEvoy, L., Whitfield, S., Du, R., Rush, G.: Monitoring working memory load during computer-based tasks with EEG pattern recognition methods. Hum. Factors J. Hum. Factors Ergon. Soc. **40**, 79–91 (1998)
6. Nayak, C.S., Anilkumar, A.C.: EEG Normal Waveforms. In: StatPearls [Internet]. StatPearls Publishing (2019). Accessed 4 Apr 2020
7. Hanslmayr, S., Staudigl, T., Fellner, M.: Oscillatory power decreases and long-term memory: the information via desynchronization hypothesis. Front. Hum. Neurosci. **6**, 74 (2012)
8. Harmony, T.: The functional significance of delta oscillations in cognitive processing. Front. Integr. Neurosci. **7**, 83 (2013)
9. Lin, C., Chen, S., Chiu, T., Lin, H., Ko, L.: Spatial and temporal EEG dynamics of dual-task driving performance. J. NeuroEng. Rehabil. **8**, 11 (2011)
10. Palomäki, J., Kivikangas, M., Alafuzoff, A., Hakala, T., Krause, C.: Brain oscillatory 4–35 Hz EEG responses during an n-back task with complex visual stimuli. Neurosci. Lett. **516**, 141–145 (2012)
11. Yang, L., Ma, R., Zhang, H.M., Guan, W., Jiang, S.: Driving behavior recognition using EEG data from a simulated car-following experiment. Accid. Anal. Prev. **116**, 30–40 (2018)
12. Miller, M., Rietschel, J., McDonald, C., Hatfield, B.: A novel approach to the physiological measurement of mental workload. Int. J. Psychophysiol. **80**, 75–78 (2011)
13. EMOTIV EPOC + 14-Channel Wireless EEG Headset | EMOTIV. https://www.emotiv.com/epoc/. Accessed 14 Apr 2020
14. Delorme, A., Makeig, S.: EEGLAB: an open source toolbox for analysis of single-trial EEG dynamics. J. Neurosci. Methods **134**, 9–21 (2004)
15. Homan, R., Herman, J., Purdy, P.: Cerebral location of international 10–20 system electrode placement. Electroencephalogr. Clin. Neurophysiol. **66**, 376–382 (1987)
16. Courtney, S.: Attention and cognitive control as emergent properties of information representation in working memory. Cogn. Affect. Behav. Neurosci. **4**, 501–516 (2004)
17. Schlattner, I., Leydecker, A., Bießmann, F., Chen, Y., Fazli, S.: EEG-based neural decoding of Intelligence Questions. In: The 3rd International Winter Conference on Brain-Computer Interface, Sabuk, South Korea, 12–14 January 2015 (2015). https://doi.org/10.1109/IWW-BCI.2015.70730252015

18. Ardila, A., Bernal, B., Rosselli, M.: Language and visual perception associations: meta-analytic connectivity modeling of brodmann area 37. Behav. Neurol. **2015**, 1–14 (2015)
19. Stokić, M., Milovanović, D., Ljubisavljević, M.R., Nenadović, V., Čukić, M.: Memory load effect in auditory–verbal short-term memory task: EEG fractal and spectral analysis. Exp. Brain Res. **233**(10), 3023–3038 (2015). https://doi.org/10.1007/s00221-015-4372-z
20. Vieira, S., et al.: Industrial designers problem-solving and designing: an EEG study. In: Research & Education in Design: People & Processes & Products & Philosophy: Proceedings of the 1st International Conference on Research and Education in Design (REDES 2019), Lisbon, Portugal, 14–15 November 2019, p. 211. CRC Press (2019)
21. Curtis, C., D'Esposito, M.: Persistent activity in the prefrontal cortex during working memory. Trends Cogn. Sci. **7**, 415–423 (2003)
22. Knyazev, G.: EEG delta oscillations as a correlate of basic homeostatic and motivational processes. Neurosci. Biobehav. Rev. **36**, 677–695 (2012)

Plane-Gazing Agorá: Design for Building a Community at The Airport Observation Deck Through Photography Activities

Shun Arima[1(✉)], Chihiro Sato[1(✉)], and Masato Yamanouchi[1,2]

[1] Keio University Graduate School of Media Design, Yokohama, Japan
{arima-shun,chihiro,masato-y}kmd.keio.ac.jp
[2] Professional University of Information and Management for Innovation,
Tokyo, Japan
masato-y@i-u.ac.jp

Abstract. This paper discusses Plane-Gazing Agorá, a cyber-physical environment at the airport observation deck that stimulates taking and sharing photos of airplanes. Since airports worldwide are on intense competition, airport operators are recognizing the need for differentiating themselves. Our research spotlights the airport observation deck; focusing on the customers' activities on taking and sharing photos of airplanes. The experience at the observation deck is site-specific and unique, hence we see the potential to contribute to the need for differentiating themselves.

Plane-Gazing Agorá consists of the following 2 phases. (1) Photo-taking support by interactive displays installed in various spots on the deck and app. These display information about the upcoming aircraft and suitable shooting locations. The dedicated app provides congestion information and weather forecast for the deck. (2) Photo-sharing support by a public screen and app. Photos displayed on a large public screen are selected from photos posted by customers. The airplane photographers can post these photos from a dedicated app. This paper seeks a community centered on the observation deck that shall be formed by the experience design of the hybrid of cyber-physical space.

Keywords: Airport · Community · Photography · Media sharing · Experience design.

1 Introduction

A legendary American band in the 1960 s called *The Grateful Dead* is not just known for its music but also for its avant-garde marketing style; allowing the audience to record and shoot their performances by providing a "taper section" as a physical space for the audience to record with profound sound quality. This led their fans network to exchange their individual recordings, which became an environment that turned current customers into evangelists and creates new fans. As a result of their progressive efforts, they have continued to grow their fans around the world for decades, with commercial success [21].

© Springer Nature Switzerland AG 2020
C. Stephanidis et al. (Eds.): HCII 2020, CCIS 1294, pp. 529–537, 2020.
https://doi.org/10.1007/978-3-030-60703-6_68

This paper explores a similar challenge of turning current customers into fans but in the context of an airport. We propose a digital-physical space for the airplane-lover community to share photos taken at the observation deck (Fig.1). By transforming the airport environment into a meaningful "place"—rather than just a functional 'space for customers getting on and off the plane [25]—we aim to eventually increase the loyalty of airport fans and contribute as part of the airport branding strategy.

Fig. 1. An airport observation deck.

Since airports worldwide are on the intense competition for both travelers and cargo [8], airport operators are recognizing the need for differentiating themselves [4], and have strived to pursue profits [28]. However, the airport is a "multipoint service provider firm," not only passengers but a broader group of target customers are targeted [11]. Therefore, direct marketing to passengers is too complicated, and airport operators are working to enhance the customer experience through branding [2,4,24]. Branding is considered as one approach to increase airport awareness and enhance customer loyalty [27].

In addition, competition is intensifying not only at airports but also at airlines, and research is being conducted to design the experience within the cabin of an aircraft in order to improve the passenger experience [29]. However, passenger experience includes not only cabin experience but also airport experience. The findings of this research will contribute not only to airport branding but also to airline experience design.

Our research spotlights the airport observation deck; focusing on the customers' activities on taking and sharing photos of airplanes at runways or parked at gates. The viewing experience at the airport observation deck (airplanes, runway, etc.) is site-specific and unique enough that photography-lovers are spotted at the airport observation deck every day.

This is based on our team's ethnographic survey series conducted at major airports in Japan in 2019, which built on the existing idea that airport customers include not only passengers [4,9], but we also identified whom and where the non-passengers are. Thus, we highlight the airport observation deck as a place to turn airport customers into fans.

We propose Plane-Gazing Agorá, a cyber-physical environment at the airport observation deck that stimulates taking and sharing photos. The interaction of sharing photos and reacting to them shall bond the communities [19]. This design provides not only the moment-based experience deriving from the real-time measures of instant utility, but also memory-based experience accepting user's retrospective evaluations [12], which shall reflect on the ongoing relationship between airports and customers, and contribute to airport branding method.

2   Literature Review

The airport environment is divided into primary services (services aimed at promoting travelers from check-in to boarding) and secondary services consisting of shopping [18]. Aggressive efforts have been made to integrate the secondary services of entertainment—cinemas, casinos, skating rinks, golf courses, etc.—and restaurants and shopping malls into the airport environment [3,7,17].It should be noted that each of these approaches focuses on designing a real-time experience [12]. In building a brand, it is important to create fans and increase loyalty [27]. Loyalty comes from the frequency of interaction [13].

There are some research cases where digital and physical installations in public spaces provide pedestrians with the opportunity to stop and interact among each other [5,23]. In particular, public libraries are space similar to an airport are responsible for building social capital as a place to meet others—different ages, classes, ethnicities, and genders—and interact in the same physical space [1].

On the other hand, the widespread of camera-equipped smartphones enabled many individuals to casually take photos on any occasion, where photography has created a variety of social connections and visual communications [22]. Even before the advent of SNS, the desire to exhibit rare photos not only to family and friends but also to a wide audience existed [6]. In today's world, uploading photos to SNS is a public act that is no different from public viewing [16]. Posting a photo to a public screen can be a means of communication and can be done without resistance. The projection of the photos on the screen can stimulate the reminiscence process [10]. Image sharing on social media creates interactions not only between businesses and consumers, but also between consumers. And that leads to business branding[20].

Presenting and sharing photos in the same place has long been important in people's daily lives, which has led to personal self-understanding and the establishment and maintenance of community relationships [26], and we can stimulate photo sharing by designing people's interactions in the same place [14]. In addition, displaying photos on public displays can increase community interaction and improve relationships [15]. Our study attempts to apply these findings to the airport observation deck.

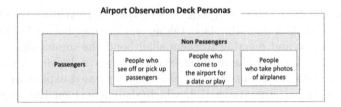

Fig. 2. Airport observation deck personas

3   Design

We conducted a series of in-field ethnographic research throughout the terminals of airports in Japan. Our focus in particular were on areas before boarding and after landing, because we wanted to spotlight airport customers that are not just passengers, but a more broader perspective. It will induce a visit to the airport other than to fly, creating a continuous relationship between the airport and customers. By observing 310 different individuals in 5 different locations within the terminal (departing lobby, arriving lobby, shopping and dining area, entertainment area, and the observation deck), our study has shown that there are four types of personas for customers on the observation deck. Passengers and non-passengers are of three types: "people who see off or pick up passengers", "people who come to the airport for a date or play", and "people who take photos of airplanes" (Fig.2).

Many of airport customers are the person of passengers. They may come to the observation deck to the free time before boarding the airplane. The observation deck allows passengers to see many airplanes that inspire passengers' curiosity, and the large space around it is a reason for parents and children to visit. There are also cafes, tables, and benches on the observation deck, so passengers may visit to take a break or work while passengers are free.

The persona of people who see off or pick up passengers have few opportunities to visit the airport's observation deck (because they often leave the airport as soon as they see off or pick up the person). There may be times when they suddenly need to kill time at the airport, such as when the person's flight is delayed. At that time, the observation deck is a good place to spend time easily because they don't have to worry about fee or time.

The persona of people who come to the airport for a date or play can be seen more often when the airport is equipped with substantial commercial facilities. Especially at night, the observation deck is illuminated by some airports, and the scenery is beautiful, making it a romantic place. They often take pictures on the observation deck as a record of their visits.

The persona of people who take photos of airplanes is there are many more huge airport. They get information from magazines, the internet, their community in advance, come to the airport with well-equipped photography equipment, and take pictures of the plane. When visiting as a group, they sometimes take pictures while communicating with each other, but there are few cases where individual groups or individuals communicate with each other.

Table 1. Example of behaviors on the observation deck of each personas

Personas	Examples of behaviors
Passengers	• Chatting with friends while watching the scenery • Looking at the plane • Sitting on a bench and reading a book • taking a picture • A running child and a father chasing it
People who see off or pick up Passengers	• taking a picture • Pointing at an airplane and frolicking
People who come to the airport For a date or play	• Watching the plane together • Pointing at an airplane and frolicking • taking a picture
People who take photos of airplanes	• Holding the camera and taking a picture

Plane-Gazing Agorá focuses on these persona features and their behaviors (Table 1), which all include taking pictures of the plane and talking while watching the plane and stimulates the photo-taking and photo-sharing activities at the observation deck. It consists of four components; two per activity including one on-site and one mobile (Fig.3). This integration supports the non-passebgers to take and share photos, and nurture a plane-gazing community at the airport observation deck.

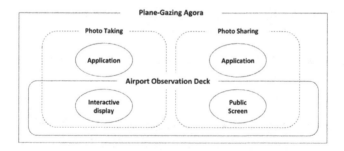

Fig. 3. Components of Plane-Gazing Agorá.

3.1 Photo Taking Support Design

Any photo-lovers—professionals or beginners—are welcomed. Interactive displays are installed in various spots on the observation deck (Left of Fig.4). These display information about the upcoming aircraft taking off and landing (airline, model, paint, etc.). It also shows information about suitable shooting locations, generated considering the weather, wind direction, and runway used by the airplane (Center of Fig. 4). Based on our research survey, we learned that determining a suitable situation for the shooting is important for photographers.

The dedicated mobile application provides congestion information and weather forecast for the observation deck and traffic information to the airport (right of Fig. 4).

Fig. 4. Left:An interactive display at observation deck Center:Example of airplane information Right:Photo taking support application UI

3.2   Photo Sharing Support Design

All customers, even those that do not photograph themselves, can enjoy it. Photos displayed on a large public screen are selected from photos posted by customers. The displayed photos change every half a minute like a screen saver (Left of Fig. 5). The airplane photographers can post these photos from a dedicated app. In addition to posting photos to the public screen, this app allows them to react to photos (post comments, press the like button, etc.) just like any other existing SNS (Right of Fig. 5) since viewer feedback plays an important role in motivating new photos to post on the app [6].

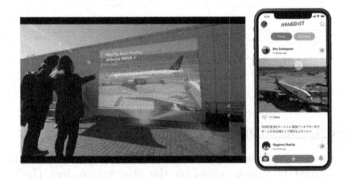

Fig. 5. Left:Public screen Right:Photo sharing application UI

3.3   Values for Customers

With these designs, "people who see off or pick up passengers" can enjoy their pocket of time on the observation deck by taking photos or seeing public screen photos. While "people who come to the airport for a date or play" can enjoy taking photos airplanes with their companion and enjoy the photos displayed on the screen. Finally, "people who take photos of airplanes" can take better photos and get the opportunity to share their photos with others, and communicate with other people with similar interests. We seek for a fan community centered on the observation deck shall be formed by the experience design of the hybrid of cyber-physical space.

4   Future Works

A concrete implementation and a proof-of-concept of this design concept are yet to come. Forming a plane-gazing community centered on the airport shall enable various fan events for fans gathered on-site (photo competitions, exchange events, workshops, etc.), which can lead to creating new services targeting them (such as the provision of photography equipment information, equipment rental services, and discounts at shops in airports). Such efforts are already being undertaken by various corporate brands, resulting in the expansion of the fan community and economic benefits [13]. We will also strive for the development of these aspects.

Acknowledgements. We thank DSInnovation which provided funding this research and all the volunteers, publications support and staffs.

References

1. Bilandzic, M., Johnson, D.: Hybrid placemaking in the library: designing digital technology to enhance users' on-site experience. Australian Library J. **62**(4), 258–271 (2013)
2. Castro, R., Lohmann, G.: Airport branding: content analysis of vision statements. Res. Transp. Bus. Manag. **10**, 4–14 (2014)
3. Farahani, A.F., Törmä, E.: Assessment of customers' service quality expectations: testing the'hierarchical structure for airport service quality expectations' in a swedish context (2010)
4. Figueiredo, T., Castro, R.: Passengers perceptions of airport branding strategies: the case of tom jobim international airport-riogaleão, brazil. J. Air Transp. Manag. **74**, 13–19 (2019)
5. Fredericks, J.: From smart city to smart engagement: exploring digital and physical interactions for playful city-making. In: Nijholt, A. (ed.) Making Smart Cities More Playable. GMSE, pp. 107–128. Springer, Singapore (2020). https://doi.org/10.1007/978-981-13-9765-3_6
6. Frohlich, D., Kuchinsky, A., Pering, C., Don, A., Ariss, S.: Requirements for photoware. In: Proceedings of the 2002 ACM conference on Computer supported cooperative work, pp. 166–175 (2002)

7. Fuerst, F., Gross, S., Klose, U.: The sky is the limit? the determinants and constraints of European airports commercial revenues. J. Air Transp. Manag. **17**(5), 278–283 (2011)
8. Gitto, S., Mancuso, P.: Brand perceptions of airports using social networks. J. Air Transp. Manag. **75**, 153–163 (2019)
9. Halpern, N., Graham, A.: Airport Marketing. Routledge, Abingdon (2013)
10. Jansen, M., van den Hoven, E., Frohlich, D.: Pearl: living media enabled by interactive photo projection. Pers. Ubiquit. Comput. **18**(5), 1259–1275 (2013). https://doi.org/10.1007/s00779-013-0691-x
11. Jarach, D.: The evolution of airport management practices: towards a multi-point, multi-service, marketing-driven firm. J. Air Transp. Manag. **7**(2), 119–125 (2001)
12. Kahneman, D., Kahneman, D., Tversky, A., et al.: Experienced utility and objective happiness: a moment-based approach. Psychol. Econ. Decisions **1**, 187–208 (2003)
13. Keller, K.L., Parameswaran, M., Jacob, I.: Strategic brand management: Building, measuring, and managing brand equity. Pearson Education India (2011)
14. Lucero, A., Holopainen, J., Jokela, T.: Pass-them-around: collaborative use of mobile phones for photo sharing. In: Proceedings of the SIGCHI conference on human factors in computing systems, pp. 1787–1796 (2011)
15. McCarthy, J.F., Congleton, B., Harper, F.M.: The context, content & community collage: sharing personal digital media in the physical workplace. In: Proceedings of the 2008 ACM conference on Computer supported cooperative work, pp. 97–106 (2008)
16. Miller, A.D., Edwards, W.K.: Give and take: a study of consumer photo-sharing culture and practice. In: Proceedings of the SIGCHI conference on Human factors in computing systems, pp. 347–356 (2007)
17. Peneda, M.J.A., Reis, V.D., Macário, M.D.R.M.: Critical factors for development of airport cities. Transp. Res. Record **2214**(1), 1–9 (2011)
18. Potgieter, M., Saayman, M., Du Plessis, L.: Key success factors in managing a visitors' experience at a south African international airport. J. Contemp. Manag. **11**(1), 510–533 (2014)
19. Putnam, R.D., et al.: Bowling alone: The collapse and revival of American community. Simon and schuster, New York (2000)
20. Pauzie, A.: Head up display in automotive: a new reality for the driver. In: Marcus, A. (ed.) DUXU 2015. LNCS, vol. 9188, pp. 505–516. Springer, Cham (2015). https://doi.org/10.1007/978-3-319-20889-3_47
21. Scott, D.M., Halligan, B.: Marketing lessons from the Grateful Dead: What every business can learn from the most iconic band in history. Wiley, New york (2010)
22. Serafinelli, E.: Analysis of photo sharing and visual social relationships: instagram as a case study. Photographies **10**(1), 91–111 (2017)
23. Tomitsch, M., Ackad, C., Dawson, O., Hespanhol, L., Kay, J.: Who cares about the content? an analysis of playful behaviour at a public display. In: Proceedings of The International Symposium on Pervasive Displays, pp. 160–165 (2014)
24. Tse, I.A.: An empirical study of airport branding at selected Canadian international airports. Master's thesis, University of Calgary (2007)
25. Tuan, Y.F.: Space and Place: The Perspective of Experience. U of Minnesota Press, Minneapolis (1977)
26. Van House, N.A.: Collocated photo sharing, story-telling, and the performance of self. Int. J. Hum Comput Stud. **67**(12), 1073–1086 (2009)
27. Wheeler, A.: Designing Brand Identity: An Essential Guide for the Wholebranding Team. Wiley, Hoboken (2017)

28. Wiltshire, J.: Airport competition: reality or myth? J. Air Transp. Manag. **67**, 241–248 (2018)
29. Zhong, X., Han, T.: Passenger experience revisited: in commercial aircraft cabin design and operations' sights. In: Stephanidis, C., Antona, M. (eds.) HCII 2019. CCIS, vol. 1088, pp. 453–462. Springer, Cham (2019). https://doi.org/10.1007/978-3-030-30712-7_56

Development of a Driver-State Adaptive Co-Driver as Enabler for Shared Control and Arbitration

Andrea Castellano[1(✉)], Giuseppe Carbonara[1], Sergio Diaz[2],
Mauricio Marcano[2], Fabio Tango[3], and Roberto Montanari[1]

[1] RE:Lab Srl, Reggio Emilia 42122, Italy
andrea.castellano@re-lab.it
[2] Fundación Tecnalia Research and Innovation, Parque Científico y Tecnológico de
Bizkaia, Derio, BI, Spain
[3] Centro Ricerche Fiat, Strada Torino, Orbassano, Italy

Abstract. For automated and partially automated cars, there are new
crucial questions to answer: "When should the driver or the automated
system take control of the vehicle?" ; and also: "Can both control the
vehicle together at the same time, or can this create potential conflicts?"
. These are non-trivial issues because they depend on different conditions, such as the environment, driver's state, vehicle capabilities, and
fault tolerance, among others. This paper will describe a human-machine
cooperation approach for collaborative driving maneuvers, developed in
the EU funded project PRYSTINE. In particular, this study presents the
work-in-progress and will focus attention on the proposed architecture
design and the corresponding use case for testing.

Keywords: Shared control · Arbitration · Highly automated vehicles ·
Human-machine cooperation.

1 Introduction

The primary aim of this exploratory study is to present a collaborative driving
framework for a partially automated driving system based on a combination of
external (through the monitoring of a simulated environment outside the vehicle) and in-vehicle data, generated through the tracking of the human driver
behavior to measure his/her fitness to drive. This framework considers an arbitration system to manage the transitions of control authority between driver and
automation when both are active driving agents.

Arbitration, in vehicle automation, is a concept that concerns the strategical
and tactical level of driving task. Nowadays, many systems consider separately

PRYSTINE has received funding within the Electronic Components and Systems for
European Leadership Joint Undertaking (ECSEL JU) in collaboration with the European Union's H2020 Framework Programme and National Authorities, under grant
agreement No. 783190.

specific aspects of driving: in this paper we describe the data-fusion process of driver's behaviors and external conditions to enable the development of a co-driver model able to assist the driver in manual and automated mode.

To achieve that, we are developing a trajectory planner based on a Nonlinear Model Predictive Control (NMPC) approach [2]. The detection of driver's condition is performed merging the classification of the cognitive (e.g., distraction and drowsiness), and behavioral state (what s/he is doing), using Deep Neural Networks approach from images and sounds inside the vehicle. The arbitration module that manages the decisional process makes use of Fuzzy Inference Systems (FIS), and FIS applications using neural networks (ANFIS), to re-plan in real-time the Level of Authority; following the classification and the assessment, the control system tracks the optimal trajectory.

The originality of our study lies on a hybrid approach of redundant systems for driving inattention integrated by an arbitration and shared control system based on FIS techniques. The system will take into account the state of the driver, the system, and the external environment, to assess the level of control and responsibility that each decision-maker should have and to delegate or retrieve control smoothly toward the ADS or the human driver. This development is part of the ongoing work in the PRYSTINE (Programmable Systems for Intelligence in Automobiles) project [6].

2   Research Context

As long as vehicle technology will not provide full automation, their design should always take into consideration a combination of both vehicle and human driver capabilities, cooperating during decision-making, and specifically sharing the driving task at the control level (humans and machines drive together).

In current concepts and early implementations of semi-automated vehicles, the human remains the primary driver and the vehicle intervenes only in a dangerous situation. However, the trend is to convey more authority to the machine agent, allowing the driver to temporarily turn away the attention from the driving task which becomes secondary. This means that drivers do not have to constantly monitor the traffic anymore, but to take back the control in case of danger, for example in case of system limitations.

Given the necessity of bringing the driver into the loop whenever necessary, a constant driver distraction monitoring is crucial to allow a smooth and safe transition between the human and the autonomous driving, to retrieve control from the driver in case of high distraction level, or to perform a successful takeover in case of ADS failure and geofence area limits.

2.1   Inattentive Driving State

Dong et al. [2] proposed a categorization of inattention in two groups of inattentive driving behaviors: **distraction** defined as "a diversion of attention away from activities critical for safe driving toward a competing activity" and **fatigue** which refers to a combination of symptoms such as impaired performance and a subjective feeling of drowsiness.

Distraction: Distraction may be characterized as any activity that takes the driver's attention away from the task of driving and can cause or contribute to crashes. Thus, it needs to be monitored during the driving task or in takeover requests (e.g., when the ADS is unable to proceed in autonomous mode).

Fatigue: Regarding fatigue, the European Transport Safety Council (ETSC) states that "concerns the inability or disinclination to continue an activity generally because the activity has been going on for too long" . It is possible to identify different types of fatigue. The most dangerous mental state for driving behavior is the central nervous fatigue which leads to drowsiness and sleepiness and may increase the probability of accident and failure in the driver takeover control process. The state of drowsiness is progressive and variable, but the ETSC defines four levels of sleepiness which indicate a diverse amount of drowsiness, each level can last for a certain lapse of time and precede the onset of sleep as followed [1]:

- Completely awake;
- Moderate sleepiness;
- Severe sleepiness;
- Sleep.

2.2   Inattention Monitoring Methodologies

In the literature different methodologies for driver inattention detection are present. In general, they can be summarized in five categories [2,3]:

- **Subjective report measures:** consist of a self-reported questionnaire of evaluation of the mental state or workload while driving.
- **Biological measures:** these methodologies have been used to detect driving inattention and include EEG, ECG, EOG, and sEMG; these signals are collected through electrodes in contact with the skin of the driver.
- **Physical measures:** head-position, head-pose, eyes-movement, and respiratory signal of the driver are commonly used for distraction detection.
- **Driving performance measures:** A change in the mental state often induce a change in driving performance.
- **Hybrid measures:** integration of multiple of the above methods to provide more reliable solutions

3   Our Approach: System Architecture and Implementation

In this paper, we present the data-fusion approach of driver's behaviors and external conditions data to enable the development of a co-driver agent, which will be able to cooperate and interact with the human driver in manual and auto-mated modalities. The detection of driver's condition will be performed merging the classification of the cognitive (distraction and drowsiness) and behavioral state (what s/he is doing), using Deep Neural Networks approach to analyze the images inside the vehicle and the driving performance data. The arbitration mod-ule that manages the decisional process, based on FIS and ANFIS techniques, will re-plan in real-time the Level of Authority to provide optimal trajectories (based on a trajectory planner with human compatible patterns).

The system will be tested on a simulator equipped with all the modules described above. The architecture of the demonstrator is illustrated in Fig. 2.

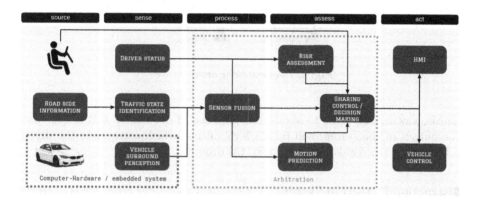

Fig. 1. Proposed system conceptual architecture

To achieve so, we will equip a driving simulator with three different sys-tems for inattention detection, able to detect the overall driver's fitness to drive; with an optimal trajectory planner based Nonlinear Model Predictive Control (NMPC) [4] and an arbitration system that will integrate all these data to dis-tribute in real-time the authority to each agent. Finally, a user-centered HMI, based on visual, acoustic, and haptic feedback, will be developed to ensure ade-quate communication, user acceptance, and cooperation between the parts.

3.1 Driver Inattention Monitoring

Drowsiness Detection System. The drowsiness monitoring system encom-passes an IR HD camera and a Class 1 laser-pattern directly projected on the driver's chest [7]. The objective is that analyzing the pattern projected by the laser, the infrared camera will be able to follow that cloud of points, track them, and extract the trajectory of these points that are describing the breathing.

The respiratory effort extracted from the video signal is analyzed in real-time with algorithms searching for patterns directly related to sleep onset stages in driving performance situations. The algorithm able to extract the drowsiness from the breathing signal is the TEDD algorithm [5]. We will track episodes as

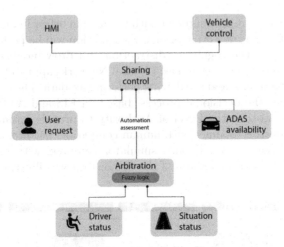

Fig. 2. Demonstrator architecture

apneas, yawns, and sight to assure the presence of drowsiness if it is the case. The output of the system will be a 3 level output which categorizes the driver in the states: (1) Awake, (2) Fatigued, (3) drowsy.

Distraction Detection System. As explained above, our approach is to create a reliable ADS based on redundant data in order to guarantee a Fail-operational systems. Two different methods of driver distraction detection are here applied: physical monitoring and driving performance monitoring.

Physical Monitoring. On the one hand, we will infer the driver distraction through physical data monitoring. This system will exploit a regular HD camera positioned in the driving cabin in front of the driver and pointed at both the driver head and the steering wheel. This system will be able to detect both visual distraction (when the driver takes his/her eyes off the road) and manual distraction (when the driver takes his/her hands off the wheel).

Driving Performance Monitoring. With regards to the distraction monitoring method based on driving performance, our algorithm will process the signals collected through both the Control Area Network (CAN) bus and the simulation environment. These will include the standard deviation of the steering wheel angle and the pedals pressure, as well as the position of the vehicle respect to the external environment as the Lane position variability (SDLP).

3.2 Arbitration and Shared Control System

Our arbitration and shared control system will integrate the state of the vehicle with the driver's fitness to drive (distraction and drowsiness) constantly for any driving situation in a comprehensive ADS system which will function as information, warning, and intervention manager.

The optimal functionality of a semi-autonomous vehicle hypothesized in this study involves two main decision-makers: the driver and the automation. Hence, the arbitration system will determine the level of authority for each at any time, and will allow smooth transitions between the different automation levels.

The real-time estimation of the driver's state and, at the same time, the evaluation of the driving-related risk factors, are the parameters on which the system assesses if it is necessary to intervene because of risky driver actions. If the driver is not enabled to drive, then the automated system takes full control.

3.3   Visual, Acoustic and Haptic HMI

The information, after been processed by the arbitration system, will be communicated to the driver if it is necessary to warn them or if an action is required from them (e.i., a takeover request). The system will provide visual, acoustic, and haptic feedback depending on the ongoing specific case. The visual feedback will be delivered through a screen mounted on the simulator which will function as vehicle's dashboard, some warnings (depending on their urgency) will be accompanied by an acoustic signal (e.i. a hard takeover request or an emergency stop). In case of intervention's need, as the arbitration control retrieves some authority from the driver to change the vehicle trajectory, active force feedback will be applied on the wheel as torque and will allow linking the message directly at the action that needs to be performed (e.i. turn slightly to the right or left).

Fig. 3. System's HMI visual prototype

3.4   Integrated ADS

In terms of the ADS which has the capability to take vehicle control to correct or improve the driver response, the system provides a global control system that allows a combination of longitudinal and lateral control actions. For example, the system can provide when required or needed: lane-keeping assistance and blind-spot detection/ lane change assistance as lateral control; as well as Adaptive Cruise Control and Automatic Emergency Braking as longitudinal controls.

4   Use Case for Testing

In terms of the ADS, which can take vehicle control to correct or improve the driver response, the system provides a global control system that allows a combination of longitudinal and lateral control actions. For example, the system can provide when required or needed: lane-keeping assistance and blind-spot detection/ lane change assistance, as lateral control; as well as Adaptive Cruise Control and Automatic Emergency Braking as longitudinal controls.

References

1. National Highway Traffic Safety Administration, "Crash factors in intersection-related crashes: An on-scene perspective," Nat. Center Stat. Anal., National Highway Traffic Safety Administration, Washington, DC, USA, Technical Report DOT HS 811366 (2010). http://www-nrd.nhtsa.dot.gov/Pubs/811366.pdf
2. Dong, Y., Hu, Z., Uchimura, K., Murayama, N.: Driver inattention monitoring system for intelligent vehicles: a review. IEEE Trans. Intell. Transp. Syst. 12(2), 596–614 (2010)
3. Yusoff, N.M., Ahmad, R.F., Guillet, C., Malik, A.S., Saad, N.M., Mérienne, F.: Selection of measurement method for detection of driver visual cognitive distraction: a review. IEEE Access 5, 22844–22854 (2017)
4. Gutjahr, B., Gröll, L., Werling, M.: Lateral vehicle trajectory optimization using constrained linear time-varying MPC. IEEE Trans. Intell. Transp. Syst. 18(6), 1586–1595 (2016)
5. Rodríguez-Ibíez, N., García-González, M. A., Fernández-Chimeno, M., Ramos-Castro, J: Drowsiness detection by thoracic effort signal analysis in real driving environments. In 2011 Annual International Conference of the IEEE Engineering in Medicine and Biology Society, pp. 6055–6058. IEEE August 2011
6. Druml, N., et al.: PRYSTINE-technical progress after year 1. In: 22nd Euromicro Conference on Digital System Design (DSD), pp. 389–398 (2019)
7. Ficosa International SA. https://www.ficosa.com/es/productos/adas/somnoalert

User Vocabulary Choices of the Voice Commands for Controlling In-Vehicle Navigation Systems

An-Che Chen[✉], Meng-Syuan Li, Chih-Ying Lin, and Min-Cian Li

Ming Chi University of Technology, 24301 New Taipei City, Taiwan
anche@mail.mcut.edu.tw

Abstract. Voice control is becoming a popular technology for in-vehicle user interactions. One of the primary design issues of voice control systems is the accuracy of voice recognition. Providing a limited vocabulary set for user-system interactions is known to be a viable strategy for enhancing the system usability and user experience in voice interactions. From the human factors perspective, the development of such a vocabulary set of voice commands for system controls should be based on user intuitions rather than technical specifications. Previous researches were mostly focusing on the recognition of specifying trip destinations, less attention has been allocated on the overall interface controls of in-vehicle navigation systems.

This study aims to preliminarily explore potential patterns of the vocabulary choices of voice commands for in-vehicle navigation systems from the users' perspective. Through a comprehensive market research, a set of 17 control functions, such as map orientation, zooming, navigation-related information, and general interface operations, of user interface interactions commonly used in modern in-vehicle navigation systems was instrumented for our experiments. Video clips showing the transitions of before-and-after scenario images for every control function were presented and prompted to experimental participants for their intuitions of the voice command vocabulary. All the intuitive voice commands collected for each control function were sorted in patterns of word cloud for further analysis. Post-experiment interviews were conducted for the subjective evaluation of the easiness of prompting voice commands and the possible reasons behind.

A total of 30 Mandarin-speaking subjects (19 males and 11 females) in Taiwan with at least 2 years of driving experience voluntarily participated in our experiment. A great discrepancy in the variety of vocabulary choices among control functions was demonstrated in our analysis. As our data indicated, for example, volume control functions (volume-up/-down/mute) are with the vocabulary choices with the most consistent results among participants, while the control functions regarding presenting detailed navigational information, such as real-time traffic situations and nearby POIs, were the poorest. Subjective preferences showed a slightly different pattern to the objective data in vocabulary choices. Recommendations to the voice interface design for in-vehicle navigation systems and future research venues are further discussed.

Keywords: Human factors · Command vocabulary · Voice control · In-Vehicle navigation

© Springer Nature Switzerland AG 2020
C. Stephanidis et al. (Eds.): HCII 2020, CCIS 1294, pp. 545–552, 2020.
https://doi.org/10.1007/978-3-030-60703-6_70

1 Introduction

For better driving experiences and safety, voice control has become a popular technology for in-vehicle user interactions. Despite voice control systems have some advantages over the traditional visual-manual interfaces (Tijerina et al. 1998; Carter and Graham 2000; Shutko et al. 2009), they still raise certain skeptical concerns (Tijerina 2016). Most concerns of using an in-vehicle voice control system are toward driving performance (Lee et al. 2001; Barón and Green 2006) and cognitive workload or distraction (Engström et al. 2005; Garay-Vega et al. 2010; Strayer et al. 2013a, b; Cooper et al. 2014; Niezgoda et al. 2015; Chang et al. 2017; and Simmons et al. 2017).

Voice control navigations can be error-prone tasks to drivers (Wu et al. 2015). Recognition errors in voice control systems may interfere with driving performance (Gellatly and Dingus 1998; McCallum et al. 2004; Kun et al. 2007). Low speech recognition accuracy can induce greater variation in manual control performance in driving (Kun et al. 2007). Delayed system response along with poor recognition accuracy can be harmful to the driver's cognitive resources (Gellatly and Dingus 1998; Kun et al. 2007; Chang et al. 2017).

One of the primary design issues of such speech technology is the accuracy of voice recognition (Savchenko and Savchenko 2015; Errattahi et al. 2018). Providing a limited keyword/vocabulary set with semantic relevance for user-system interactions is known to be a viable strategy for enhancing the recognition accuracy (Wang and Sim 2013) and the system reliability in speech interactions (Kou et al. 2010). From the human factors perspective, the development of such a vocabulary set of voice commands for system controls is better to be based on user intuitions rather than technical specifications. Previous researches were mostly focusing on the recognition of specifying trip destinations (e.g., Wu et al. 2015; Chang et al. 2017; Simmons et al. 2017), less attention has been allocated on the interface controls of in-vehicle navigation systems. Therefore, for a better user experience, it is important to understand user choices of command vocabulary for voice control navigation systems.

2 Method

This study aims to preliminarily explore potential patterns of the vocabulary choices of voice commands for in-vehicle navigation systems from the users' perspective. Through a comprehensive market research, a set of 17 control functions, such as map orientation (e.g., North-up vs. Heading-up), zooming, navigation-related information (e.g., time/distance to destination or nearby POIs) and general interface operations (e.g., volume or brightness control), of user interface interactions commonly used in modern in-vehicle navigation systems was instrumented for our experiments.

In order not to mislead possible semantic intuitions of voice commands elicited by experiment participants, text and oral instruction regarding the functionality of tested controls were avoided. Instead, video clips showing the transitions of before-and-after scenario images for every control function were presented and prompted to experimental participants for their intuitions of the voice command vocabulary. Figure 1 shows examples of the transition images used in our experiment.

Fig. 1. Examples of transition images for prompting voice commands

The trials of all 17 control functions are repeated randomly for each participant to minimize possible misunderstandings on the functionality illustrated. All the intuitive voice commands collected for each control function on the second trial were sorted by the words prompted and their frequencies. A popular tag cloud application – Word Art – was then used for result demonstration and further analysis. Post-experiment interviews were conducted for subjective evaluation of the easiness in prompting voice commands and the possible reasons behind.

3   Results and Discussion

A total of 30 Mandarin-speaking subjects (19 males and 11 females) in Taiwan with at least 2 years of driving experience voluntarily participated in our experiment. Their ages ranged from 21 to 55 and with the driving experience positively correlated.

Figure 2 shows the comparisons in the convergences of voice command phrases used by experimental subjects in both trials. The quantitative measures of the horizontal axis in the figure indicate the convergences of command phrasing, which are calculated as the cumulative percentages of the top three command phrases used for the specific control function. As shown in Fig. 2, the agreement in the command phrases used in trial 2 is equal to or slightly higher than that of trial 1 for most of the voice control functions in our experiment. It is interpreted as the better representative data in trial two by this tendency of mild improvement in phrasing convergence between trials.

As Fig. 2 indicates, a great variance in phrase convergence was found among the voice control functions in our experiment. It is obvious that the volume control functions, i.e., volume-up, volume-down, and mute, are with the vocabulary choices with the highest convergent results among control functions, all with the 3 main phrases covered 100% cases at the second trials. For the control functions regarding presenting pop-up detailed navigational information, such as 3D view of interchange ramps, nearby points-of-interest (POIs), and the real-time traffic conditions, were the poorest in terms of phrasing convergence, only 56% coverage by the top three phrases reported.

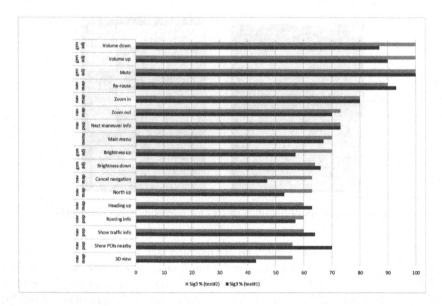

Fig. 2. Convergences in voice command between subjects in two trials: the percentages of the top 3 command phrases specified to all.

The analysis of subjective evaluation to the easiness of phrasing voice commands showed that 60% of experimental participants rated the volume control functions (i.e., volume-up/-down/mute) as the easiest, followed by map zooming functions (i.e., zoom-in/-out) with 24% of ratings. The most difficult control functions to phrase a voice command were map orientation controls (i.e., north-up/heading-up) rated by approximately one-third of our subjects, and the function of showing the 3D view of interchange ramps was next (10%). These subjective results showed only a slightly different pattern to the objective data in vocabulary choices of actual experimental trials.

These collected voice command phrases were further tokenized into "keywords", which are typically as assemblies of two or three Chinese characters. These keywords can be the vocabulary foundations for voice recognition. For each control function, these tokenized keywords were processed through Word Art to visualize the formation of vocabulary choices and their respective frequencies. For example, Fig. 3a, 3b, and 3c are the Word Art results of the voice control functions of volume-down, volume-up, and mute, respectively. These three control functions are the top three functions with the most consistent vocabulary choices among experimental participants, as shown in Fig. 2. The word cloud results in Fig. 3 show similar patterns of keyword organization with great concentrations. It is also obvious that Volume-up and Volume-down shared the same major keyword "音量" (volume) for the voice commands in Mandarin, but not with the function of Mute. Furthermore, when we put all the keywords choices of these three control functions altogether into one word cloud, as shown in Fig. 4, a collective vocabulary choice pattern with great concentration was also revealed for this functionality category of volume controls.

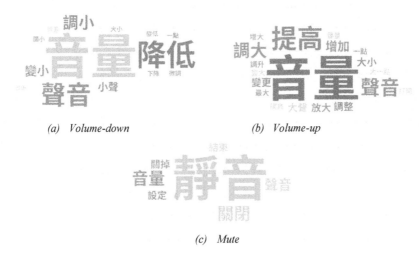

(a) Volume-down   *(b) Volume-up*

(c) Mute

Fig. 3. The Word Art results for the keyword choices of the voice commands for volume controls.

Fig. 4. The collective Word Art results for the three volume-control functions in Fig. 3.

The equivalent cloud patterns of Show-traffic-info, Show-routing-info, and Show-nearby-POIs, which are the control functions with great variations in vocabulary choices in our study, are demonstrated in Fig. 5 for comparison. Similarly, Fig. 6 shows the collective results of the three control functions in Fig. 5 since these three functions are all under the functionality category of "detailed navigational information pop-ups". These cloud patterns show more diversity in vocabulary choices in individual and collective results.

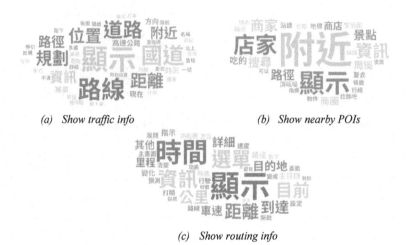

(a) *Show traffic info*   (b) *Show nearby POIs*

(c) *Show routing info*

Fig. 5. The Word Art results for the keyword choices of the voice commands for the three control functions with great vocabulary diversity.

Fig. 6. The collective Word Art results for the three control functions in Fig. 5.

4   Conclusions

The primary purpose of this study is to preliminarily explore potential patterns of the vocabulary choices of voice commands for in-vehicle navigation systems from the users' perspective. Through a set of lab experiments by eliciting intuitive voice commands from subjects for the scenarios of controlling a navigational interface, a great discrepancy in vocabulary choices among different control functions was revealed in our analysis results. It is found that the volume control functions are with the vocabulary choices with the highest convergent results among control functions, while the control functions regarding presenting pop-up detailed navigational information were the poorest in terms of phrasing convergence. The analysis of word cloud presentations further demonstrates the details in vocabulary choice patterns for each individual control function and the collective category. Subjective preferences showed a slightly different pattern to the objective data in vocabulary choices.

The analysis scheme proposed in this study can provide a feasible methodology for establishing preliminary vocabulary sets of voice commands of in-vehicle navigation systems for a better user experience and system usability. It is also recommended that future research efforts can be directed to the investigation on the learning effects regarding instructions for vocabulary suggestion/training as well as the influences of individual differences induced by system experiences.

References

Barón, A., Green, P.: Safety and usability of speech interfaces for in-vehicle tasks while driving: A brief literature review (Techical report. No. UMTRI-2006-5). University of Michigan Transportation Research Institute, Ann Arbor, MI (2006)

Carter, C., Graham, R.: Experimental comparison of manual and voice controls for the operation of in-vehicle systems. In: Proceedings of the Human Factors and Ergonomics Society Annual Meeting, vol. 44, pp. 3-286–3-289 (2000)

Chang, C.C., Boyle, L.N., Lee, J.D., Jenness, J.: Using tactile detection response tasks to assess in-vehicle voice control interactions. Transp. Res Part F: Traffic Psychol. Behav. 51, 38–46 (2017)

Cooper, J.M., Ingebretsen, H., Strayer, D.L.: Mental Workload of Common Voice-Based Vehicle Interactions across Six Different Vehicle Systems. AAA Foundation for Traffic Safety, Washington, DC (2014)

Engström, J., Johansson, E., Östlund, J.: Effects of visual and cognitive load in real and simulated motorway driving. Transp. Res. Part F: Traff. Psychol. Behav. 8, 97–120 (2005)

Garay-Vega, L., et al.: Evaluation of different speech and touch interfaces to in-vehicle music retrieval systems. Accid. Anal. Prev. 42(3), 913–920 (2010)

Gellatly, A.W., Dingus, T.A.: Speech recognition and automotive applications: using speech to perform in-vehicle tasks. In: Proceedings of the Human Factors and Ergonomics Society Annual Meeting, vol. 42, pp. 1247–1251. SAGE Publications (1998)

Kou, X.Y., Xue, S.K., Tan, S.T.: Knowledge-guided inference for voice-enabled CAD. Comput. Aided Des. 42(6), 545–557 (2010)

Kun, A.L., Paek, T., Medenica, Z.: The effect of speech interface accuracy on driving performance. In: INTERSPEECH, pp. 1326–1329 (2007)

Labiale, G.: In-car road information: Comparisons of auditory and visual presentations. In: Proceedings of the Human Factors Society Annual Meeting, vol. 34, No. 9, pp. 623–627. SAGE Publications, Los Angeles, October 1990

Labiale, G., Ouadou, K., David, B.T.: A software system for designing and evaluating in-car information system interfaces. In: Analysis, Design and Evaluation of Man-Machine Systems 1992, pp. 257–262. Pergamon (1993)

Lee, J.D., Caven, B., Haake, S., Brown, T.L.: Speech-based interaction with in-vehicle computers: the effect of speech-based e-mail on drivers' attention to the roadway. Hum. Factors 43(4), 631–640 (2001)

McCallum, M., Campbell, J., Richman, J., Brown, J., Wiese, E.: Speech recognition and in-vehicle telematics devices: potential reductions in driver distraction. Int. J. Speech Technol. 7, 25–33 (2004)

Niezgoda, M., Tarnowski, A., Kruszewski, M., Kamiński, T.: Towards testing auditory–vocal interfaces and detecting distraction while driving: a comparison of eye-movement measures in the assessment of cognitive workload. Transp. Res. Part F: Traff. Psychol. Behav. 32, 23–34 (2015)

Putze, F., Schultz, T.: Cognitive dialog systems for dynamic environments: progress and challenges. In: Hansen, J., Boyraz, P., Takeda, K., Abut, H. (eds.) Digital Signal Processing for In-Vehicle Systems and Safety. Springer, New York (2012)

Savchenko, A.V., Savchenko, L.V.: Towards the creation of reliable voice control system based on a fuzzy approach. Pattern Recogn. Lett. **65**, 145–151 (2015)

Shutko, J., Mayer, K., Lansoo, E., Tijerina, L.: Driver workload effects of cell phone music player, and text messaging tasks with the Ford SYNC voice interface versus hand-held visual-manual interfaces (Paper No. 2009-01-0786). Society of Automotive Engineering (2009)

Simmons, S.M., Caird, J.K., Steel, P.: A meta-analysis of in-vehicle and nomadic voice-recognition system interaction and driving performance. Accid. Anal. Prev. **106**, 31–43 (2017)

Strayer, D.L., Cooper, J.M., Turrill, J., Coleman, J., Medeiros-Ward, N., Biondi, F.: Measuring cognitive distraction in the automobile (2013a)

Strayer, D.L., Cooper, J.M., Turrill, J., Coleman, J., Medeiros-Ward, N., Biondi, F.: Measuring Cognitive Distraction in the Automobile. AAA Foundation for Traffic Safety, Washington, DC (2013b)

Tijerina, L.: Driver distraction and road safety. In: Smiley, A. (ed.) Human Factors in Traffic Safety, 3rd edn., pp. 219–276. Lawyers and Judges Publishing, Tuscon, AZ (2016)

Tijerina, L., Parmer, E., Goodman, M.J.: Driver workload assessment of route guidance system destination entry while driving: a test track study. In: Proceedings of the 5th World Congress on Intelligent Transport Systems [CD-ROM], Washington, DC: ITSA (1998)

Wang, G., Sim, K.C.: Context dependent acoustic keyword spotting using deep neural network. In: 2013 Asia-Pacific Signal and Information Processing Association Annual Summit and Conference, pp. 1–10. IEEE (2013)

Wu, J., Chang, C.-C., Boyle, L.N., Jenness, J.: Impact of in-vehicle voice control systems on driver distraction insights from contextual interviews. Proc. Hum. Factors Ergon. Soc. Ann. Meeting **59**, 1583–1587 (2015)

Augmented Berthing Support for Maritime Pilots Using a Shore-Based Sensor Infrastructure

Michael Falk[1][(✉)], Marcel Saager[1], Marie-Christin Harre[1],
and Sebastian Feuerstack[2]

[1] Humatects GmbH, Marie-Curie Str. 1, 26129 Oldenburg, Germany
{falk,saager,harre}@humatects.de
[2] OFFIS, Escherweg 2, 26121 Oldenburg, Germany
sebastian.feuerstack@offis.de

Abstract. In harbor navigation and berthing, maritime pilots are facing today many challenges such as high dense traffic, changing environmental conditions and a lack of accurate information. In order to better handle this situation, systems are needed that offer improved situation awareness. This paper presents an Augmented Reality design concept for Smart Glasses to support maritime pilots in berthing and port navigation. Unlike other approaches, the extended docking support does not depend on ship-specific sensors, but benefits from a land-based infrastructure. To design the augmented berthing support for maritime pilots, the Konect method is applied. Finally, preliminary designs which serve as a basis for further research are provided in this paper.

Keywords: Augmented reality · Situation awareness · Support system

1 Introduction

Harbors are dense maritime traffic areas including ferries, large container vessels and pleasure crafts. Therefore, extensive navigation skills and specific knowledge about local navigation habits and constraints given by the environment (e.g. tide dependent port access) or the infrastructure are required. Navigational decisions often need to be taken in high workload situations caused by surrounding traffic, obstacles or a limited view (i.e. fog). Maritime pilots support shipmasters to navigate safely in such areas. While bulk carriers tend to become continuously larger [9], their maneuvering get even more challenging [7]. Specifically, maritime pilots need to adapt quickly to different vessel behaviors and changing environmental conditions such as currents, wind, tidal changes, and surrounding traffic.

This paper presents an Augmented Reality design concept for Smart Glasses to support maritime port pilots to increase situational awareness for berthing and port navigation in narrow passage situations. Different to other approaches

© Springer Nature Switzerland AG 2020
C. Stephanidis et al. (Eds.): HCII 2020, CCIS 1294, pp. 553–559, 2020.
https://doi.org/10.1007/978-3-030-60703-6_71

the concept is vessel-agnostic and benefits from a shore-based sensor infrastructure instead of interfacing with vessel specific sensors. While the state-of-the-art depends on tablet-based Portable Pilot Units (PPU) requiring pilots to focus on a screen instead of observing the immediate ship environment [8], Smart Glasses augment information within their current work context. We report about interviews we did with the pilots from German harbors and a hierarchical task analysis that we used to extract the most relevant information to derive the initial design concept.

2   Related Work

In maritime sector, situation awareness is a key element to ensure safety in safety-critical environments. Support systems for navigation safety control can reduce human errors and support operators, e.g. maritime pilots, to assess dangerous situations and to apply the right navigational decisions [11]. The usage of Portable Pilot Units as a portable, mostly tablet-based system for maritime pilots is state-of-the-art and well-accepted. A PPU shows a sea chart with an updated position of the vessel and the movements of other vessels via an AIS interface which enhances the awareness in the maritime domain [1,13]. However, AIS lacks availability and ships not moving faster than 3 kn only receive updates every 3 min [10]. For berthing support, where there is the need of high-accuracy and real-time information, the AIS information is not enough. Therefore, maritime pilots are relying mostly on their experiences. However, studies have shown that most accidents are caused by decision errors which include the lack of situation awareness, e.g. caused by poor visibility [2]. They also have shown that there is a high demand for support systems to reduce human errors [3].

Smart Glasses have been recently reported to support pilots' situational awareness by presenting relevant ship information retrieved from AIS data by Wnorowski et al. [14]. Augmented Reality design concepts as proposed by Ostendorp et al. [5] presented initial ideas for berthing support through the usage of Smart Glasses. However, these approaches depend on ship specific sensor systems that introduce high technical barriers as standards and ship interfaces are often missing or proprietary. The AR approach, we are presenting in this paper, is using a shore-based sensor system which is installed in the harbor infrastructure and aggregated by sensor fusion in order to be used by our Smart Glass application. The advantage is that the system is vessel-agnostic and the maritime pilots get the information needed for berthing directly inside their work context.

3   Design Approach

In the following section, the approach to design the AR berthing support as well as a description of the design itself is provided.

3.1   Methodology

To design the augmented berthing support for maritime pilots, we applied the Konect method [4,6]. The Konect method offers a systematic procedure to derive information visualizations optimized for fast and accurate perception of critical system states in the safety-critical domain. Here, the Konect method offers special support to design user interfaces for monitoring tasks in which fast and accurate perception of critical system states is necessary. The method offers a procedure with 4 steps: The first step is the *Information Determination*. In this step, the information to be shown on the user interface should be specified systematically. Therefore, interviews with actual users can be conducted to specify their tasks and to establish which information is needed to perform these tasks. As soon as the tasks and the information to be shown on the interface are specified, the Konect idea box should be specified in the second step (*Idea Box Specification*). In this idea box, the designer has to further specify why the user needs an information (this is the so-called *insight*) e.g. does the user wants an information as a quantitative value or does he or she just need to know that the value is within the permitted limits and is not critical. Based on this insight the Konect method offers different efficiency rankings of possible visualizations e.g. to perceive a quantitative value a length is the most efficient visualization while a color is most efficient for recognizing if a value is ok and not critical. In the third step (*Glyph Sketching*), this idea box is used to sketch glyphs for the user interface. In this regard, a glyph is a combined visual form integrating several visual attributes in one visualization. The last step is the *design composition*. In this step, the overall design is composed following specific rules. Details about all steps and how these were applied to design the augmented berthing support are described in the following subsections.

3.2   Information Determination

In the first step, we conducted two different interviews with maritime pilots. These pilots came from two different Northern German ports: Cuxhaven and Hamburg. They were interviewed on their work utilizing a semi-structured interview guide. The guide was divided into "general activity", "sensor based information" and "possible scenarios with augmented reality".
Based on the interviews, we specified a hierarchical task analysis (HTA). This task analysis is shown in Fig. 1. A task analysis consists of an overall task that is broken down into individual subtasks. It is important to ensure that the fulfillment of the individual subtasks together fulfill their overall task [12].

The task model deals with the berthing maneuver from the point of view of the harbor pilot. T1, preparing the maneuver, is disregarded, as the focus is on T2, executing the maneuver. Part of this task is on the one hand to observe the vessel (T2.1) and on the other hand to keep an eye on the environmental conditions (T2.2). Part of the ship observation is monitoring the speed (T.2.1.1), the distance to the quay wall (T.2.1.2) and the current position (T2.1.3). Especially for the speed and the distance to the quay wall, changes and absolute values

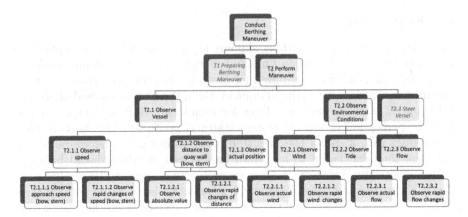

Fig. 1. The task analysis.

are of importance. For the observation of environmental conditions (T2.2), wind (T2.2.1), tide and current were identified as relevant information. Again, the current value and changes are particularly relevant.

3.3 Idea Box

The information to be shown on the user interface for the berthing support can be found on the lowest level of the previously described HTA (see Fig. 1). The information is further specified in the Konect idea box shown in Fig. 2. After specifying the insight for each information, Konect suggests different efficiency rankings. The efficiency ranking acts as a basis for the derivation of a design for the glyphs.

For information *rapid changes of approach speed, distance to quay wall, wind* and *flow* as well as *absolute approach speed* from bow and stern, the *distance to quay*, the *absolute wind* and the *absolute flow* with the insight *perceive if value is ok fast*, color hue is the most efficient visualization. According to the fast perception of the quantitative values for these parameters, a length is the most efficient visual attribute. Lastly the *direction of wind, flow and apporach* should be perceived as direction which is a pattern or structure. Edges/depth or orientation at multiple scales are possible for visualizing this kind of information most efficiently. The last column offers possibilities on how to combine the visual attributes in one integrated visual form (a glyph). This is based on the gestalt laws [6].

3.4 Glyph Sketching

Based on the idea box described in the previous subsection, we derived a design for the glyphs. This is shown in Fig. 3. The design consists of two glyphs to cluster the different information. While Glyph (a) shows all information related

Information	Insight	Efficiency Ranking	Combination
rapid changes of approach speed (bow, stern), distance to quay wall (bow, stern), wind, flow	perceive if value is ok fast	color hue(1) shape (2) length (3) slope (4) volume (5)	
rapid changes of approach speed (bow, stern), distance to quay wall (bow, stern), wind, flow	perceive quantitative value fast	length (1) slope (2) volume (3) color hue (4)	Symmetry Figure and Ground Spatial Proximity Connectedness
absolute approach speed (bow, stern), distance to quay wall (bow, stern), absolute wind (relative to vessel), absolute flow (relative to vessel)	perceive if value is ok fast	color hue(1) shape (2) length (3) slope (4) volume (5)	Continuity Closure Relative Size Similarity
absolute approach speed (bow, stern), distance to quay wall (bow, stern), absolute wind (relative to vessel), absolute flow (relative to vessel)	perceive quantitative value fast	length (1) slope (2) volume (3) color hue (4)	Mental Model
direction of wind, flow, approach	perceive pattern (distribution, trends, frequency, structure)	edges/depth/orientation at multiple scales (1) size/location (2) categorical relation (3) coordinate relation (4)	

Fig. 2. The Konect idea box.

to the docking, glyph (b) shows all environmental information. Each line shows a unique parameter with its absolute value on the left side and rapid change on the right side. The color red acts as a warning that a value changed rapidly so that the pilot can react fast to these critical changes. In the glyph for the docking information, the first two parameters are the approach speed from bow and stern, the last two parameters are the distance from bow and stern to the quay wall. In the glyph for the environmental information, the first parameter is the wind with wind speed, rapid change of wind speed and the direction of the wind shown by the arrow. The second parameter is the flow with speed, rapid change and direction as well.

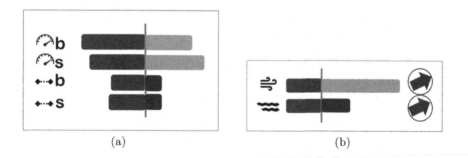

(a)   (b)

Fig. 3. Glyph Sketching

Fig. 4. The Konect AR design.

3.5   Design Composition

The last step is the design composition. The Konect method offers three guidelines to ensure that the overall design is fast and accurate perceivable and that different visualizations do not interfere with each other. These guidelines are:

1. Consistency Use the same visual attribute for the same kind of insight for similar important information elements.

2.1 Simplicity in shapes Choose simple shapes and visual forms, choose non-accidental visual forms with regard to orientation.

2.2 Simplicity in colors Reduce colors that do not carry any information besides structuring the interface.

For the design of the interface in step 3 (see Fig. 4), we followed these guidelines (e.g. used bars as consistent and simple shape) and reduced colors to the neutral color of dark blue for all elements. Furthermore, we composed the glyphs to the left and right top of the field of view so that the lower part is not occluded and the maritime pilot is still able to assess his environment. For further work, we also see the opportunity to integrate 3D objects, e.g. arrows, inside the environment of the ship as shown in Fig. 4.

4   Conclusion

In the underlying paper, we presented an AR design approach for the berthing support of maritime pilots. We derived the design by applying the Konect method. As part of the method, we conducted interviews with different pilots, specified a hierarchical task analysis based on the interview results and derived a first design. In the next steps, we will involve the maritime pilots again to validate how far this design meets the requirements of the pilots.

Acknowledgments. The research received funding from the project SmartKai which is funded by the German Federal Ministry of Transport and Digital Infrastructure.

References

1. Alexander, L., Casey, M.: Use of portable piloting units by maritime pilots (01 2008)
2. Chauvin, C., Lardjane, S., Morel, G., Clostermann, J.P., Langard, B.: Human and organisational factors in maritime accidents: analysis of collisions at sea using the HFACS. Accid. Anal. Prevent. **59**, 26–37 (2013).http://www.sciencedirect.com/science/article/pii/S0001457513001978
3. Gruenefeld, U., Stratmann, T., Brueck, Y., Hahn, A., Boll, S., Heuten, W.: Investigations on container ship berthing from the pilot's perspective: accident analysis, ethnographic study, and online survey. TransNav: Int. J. Mar. Navig. Safe. Sea Transp. **12** (2018)
4. Harre, M.-C., Feuerstack, S., Wortelen, B.: A method for optimizing complex graphical interfaces for fast and correct perception of system states. In: Bogdan, C., Kuusinen, K., Lárusdóttir, M.K., Palanque, P., Winckler, M. (eds.) HCSE 2018. LNCS, vol. 11262, pp. 65–87. Springer, Cham (2019). https://doi.org/10.1007/978-3-030-05909-5_5
5. Harre, M.C., Lenk, J., Lüdtke, A.: Smart glasses to support maritime pilots in harbor maneuvers. Proc. Manufact. **3**, 2840–2847 (2015)
6. Harre, M., Hahn, A., Lüdtke, A., Baumann, M.: Supporting Supervisory Control of Safety-Critical Systems with Rationally Justified Information Visualizations. BIS der Universität Oldenburg (2019). https://books.google.de/books?id=lE1AzQEACAAJ
7. Hockey, G., Healey, A., Crawshaw, M., Wastell, D., Sauer, J.: Cognitive demands of collision avoidance in simulated ship control. Hum. Factors **45**, 252–65 (2003)
8. Holder, E., Pecota, S.: Maritime head-up display: a preliminary evaluation. J. Navig. **64**, 573–594 (2011)
9. Rodrigue, J.P., Comtois, C., Slack, B.: The geography of transport systems (2016)
10. Series, M.: Technical characteristics for an automatic identification system using time-division multiple access in the VHF maritime mobile band (2010)
11. Smirnova, O.: Situation awareness for navigation safety control. TransNav Int. J. Mar. Navig. Safe. Sea Transp. **12**, 383–388 (2018)
12. Stanton, N.: Hierarchical task analysis: developments, applications, and extensions. Appl. Ergon. **37**, 55–79 (2006)
13. Tetreault, B.J.: Use of the automatic identification system (AIS) for maritime domain awareness (MDA). In: Proceedings of OCEANS 2005 MTS/IEEE, pp. 1590–1594. IEEE (2005)
14. Wnorowski, J., Łebkowski, A.: Ship information systems using smartglasses technology. Sci. J. Silesian Univ. Technol. Ser. Transp. **100**, 211–222 (2018)

Designing Ride Access Points for Shared Automated Vehicles

An Early Stage Prototype Evaluation

Fabian Hub[(⊠)], Marc Wilbrink, Carmen Kettwich, and Michael Oehl

German Aerospace Center (DLR), Lilienthalplatz 7, 38108 Brunswick, Germany
{fabian.hub,marc.wilbrink,carmen.kettwich,
michael.oehl}@dlr.de

Abstract. Future oriented mobility solutions, based on digital technologies, emphasize the need for digital and flexible urban infrastructure to give guidance to users. In the case of automated mobility on-demand (AMoD) services high user experience (UX) is essential for user acceptance. One of the main challenges is to enhance the user's competence and information supply to overcome the physical meeting problem of user and shared automated vehicle (SAV). Hence, the need for the new concept of defined virtual ride access points (RAP) derives. The objective of this study is to evaluate a first human-centered RAP design prototype regarding usability and intuitiveness. By remotely interviewing 18 participants of young age, residing in urban areas and with experience in using ride-sharing services the authors show that already a first RAP prototype was positively rated with regard to usability and intuitiveness. So the mere existence of RAP presented with means of augmented reality has the potential to improve UX of new urban mobility services. With his article the authors seek to conceive guidelines for future digital human-centered AMoD infrastructure.

Keywords: Shared automated vehicle · Mobility on demand · Ride access point · User experience

1 Introduction

In times of an ever present discussion concerning climate change and metropolization, a call for disruption towards more flexible and individual solutions for urban mobility is more present than ever. Conventional forms of individual transportation show inefficiencies and reach their limits in terms of resource use, traffic congestions and air pollution. With the use of digital technologies more sustainable forms of individual urban mobility emerge, including demand responsive transport (DRT) services [1]. Future DRT solutions also emphasize the need for flexible and digital traffic hubs and infrastructure, utilized by both private and public mobility providers in order to give guidance to users [2]. The objective of this study is to evaluate an early stage human-centered ride access point (RAP) design prototype and to conceive design guidelines for digital human-centered DRT infrastructure.

© Springer Nature Switzerland AG 2020
C. Stephanidis et al. (Eds.): HCII 2020, CCIS 1294, pp. 560–567, 2020.
https://doi.org/10.1007/978-3-030-60703-6_72

Dynamic ride-sharing services, like ride-hailing (in operation such as Uber) and ride-pooling (in operation such as ViaVan) concepts, are likely to play a crucial role in future urban mobility [3, 4]. On-demand transportation services have the ability to decrease traffic and environmental impact. Especially in urban, densely populated areas they leverage their potential due to higher contact rates which increases the overall effectiveness of matching driver and rider [5, 6]. The projected impact of automated vehicles (AV; SAE levels 4 & 5) is widely discussed and could increase both scope and positive impact of on-demand mobility services [7–9].

Distler et al. [10] investigate user acceptance of automated mobility on-demand (AMoD) and show the importance of positive perception and experienced effectiveness of the service. Another key factor is the user's need for important information in order to feel competent with the shared automated vehicle (SAV). Especially information regarding safety is crucial to the user but the pragmatic quality is considered essential for high user experience (UX) [10, 11].

We assume that for AMoD not only the vehicle itself but also the accessibility of the SAV might be an important factor for user acceptance and adaption. At present, the user is given rather rudimental information about shuttle (e.g., plate number, vehicle type), pick-up time and navigates to his/her pick-up location with a map-based solution. When arrived near the pick-up location the user is awaiting the shuttle and making himself/herself noticed by the driver to get on board. Hansen et al. [12] point out the importance of defined RAPs to face a physical meeting problem for rider and driver when sharing a ride. Especially in the case of SAV this meeting problem could intensify and decrease pragmatic quality of AMoD. Accordingly, the need to support the user in identifying the exact pick-up location and corresponding SAV in chaotic urban environment can be derived. With the use of state of the art technology, like augmented reality (AR) solutions for smartphones, we try to overcome this meeting problem by enhancing users' competence, increase information supply and maximize UX of AMoD.

In this paper the authors want to provide the reader with the first impressions on how RAPs might be designed from a human-centered perspective, aiming to decrease uncertainty and trigger positive experiences with a dynamic SAV service.

2   Method

This present paper is based on a qualitative research approach, enriched with quantitative measurement methods. Research shows that the target group to most likely use SAV and on-demand mobility services are young adults in urban areas. This is mainly rooted in their experience with technology and their relationship with an individual modality style [11]. To evaluate the prototype by the target group, participants were preselected in this user-centered study. Participants ought to be between the ages of 20 to 40 years and have experience with the use of ride-sharing services. The sample consists of eleven male and seven female participants (N = 18), between the ages of 21 and 36 years (M = 27.67; SD = 4.41). As 72% of the participants live in Berlin, 11% in Hamburg and 16% in other large German cities, all reside in urban areas. All except one participant are in possession of a driving license and all have experience in using on-demand ride-sharing services. All of the participants stated to use ride-sharing for private reasons and 39% for job-related reasons. The most used ride-pooling service was Berlin's BerlKönig (80%; joint venture of Mercedes-Benz and ViaVan), followed by Clevershuttle (37%; operates in Berlin, Munich, Leipzig and Dresden) and Volkswagen's Moia (13%; operates in Hamburg and Hannover). Other used ride-pooling services where AllygatorShuttle (7%) in Berlin and EcoBus (3%) (pilot project in rural areas in Central Germany). Additionally, the participants mentioned to have used ride-hailing services like Uber (33%), FreeNow (17%), Lyft (3%) and Grab (3%) before. Overall, on-demand ride-sharing services are used not very frequently (more than a couple of times a year, $M = 2.77$; $SD = 0.81$; using a 5-point Likert scale from 1 = "once" to 5 = "daily") and none of the participants stated a daily use. All participants knew AVs from the media and four participants have ridden in an AV before. Nevertheless, overall interest in AVs was high ($M = 4.00$; $SD = 0.68$; using a 5-point Likert scale from 1 = "not interested at all" to 5 = "highly interested"). The majority of participants had at least some experience with virtual reality (VR) technology (77%), 61% experienced AR technology before and 11% had experienced neither. Technology affinity of the participants can overall be described as high ($M = 4.36$; $SD = 1.12$) using the standardized ATI questionnaire (six-point scale from "completely disagree" to "completely agree") [13].

A structured interview method was used to gain insights from on-demand ride-sharing users about their information need when interacting with AMoD. Due to the Covid-19 pandemic interviews were conducted online via video conferencing software, enabling the participants to share their screen in order to control for standardized procedure. Participants were able to follow the interview guideline, answers were directly transcribed by the interviewer and interviews were recorded. The objective of the interviews was to test and evaluate the early stage RAP design prototype regarding usability, informational content and intuitiveness. This first prototype of a user-centered design process was created by vehicle human-machine interface (HMI) experts during a first brainstorming and design session at the German Aerospace Center, Braunschweig, Germany. The aim of the brainstorming was to approximate how RAPs could meet the users' usability needs and hence promote UX of AMoD. The developed RAP concept should provide users with the essential and meaningful information and intuitiveness so that usability of SAVs can be maximized.

In the first step of the interviews, participants were introduced to the research objective. After an open conversation about their typical use of on-demand ride-sharing services they were told to imagine themselves into a concrete situation of utilizing AMoD (using a SAV from a German large city main railway station to the city airport). For immersive reasons the participants were presented with a video prototype, displaying them a possible AR solution of a RAP. The video prototype shows the RAP AR-design concept on a sidewalk in an urban environment, put in place with video editing software. After the video experience a picture of the RAP prototype was presented to the participants, showing the same RAP AR-design concept in an urban VR environment (Fig. 1). After demonstrating the design concept, the RAP prototype was explained in detail to the participants, followed by an intuitiveness check for each component. Measuring comprehensibility a 5-Point Likert Scale (from 1 = "not comprehensible at all" to 5 = "very comprehensible") was used. The RAP components are: 1) *flagpole*, 2) *waiting area*, 3) *light beam*, 4) *shuttle identification*. The first component with the information "*H*" (referencing a German bus stop sign), "*552*", "*In 2 Min*" and "*nach Flughafen*" (to the airport) covers the RAP with a shuttle number, countdown for pick-up and destination. The second component shows a safe space and the designated area to wait (green rectangle on the floor). The third component shows a simulated light beam to associate the RAP with the corresponding shuttle. Fourth, a green rectangle above the shuttle serves as identification and displays the shuttle number ("*552*") and destination ("*Ziel: Flughafen*" – destination airport).

Fig. 1. RAP prototype evaluated by participants.

Subsequently, participants were asked to fill in the standardized user experience questionnaire (UEQ) with 26 randomized items to evaluate the design concept regarding UX [14]. The overall user experience is divided into six subscales. *Attractiveness* gives an overall impression and measures whether users like or dislike the product. *Perspicuity*, *Efficiency* and *Dependability* evaluate the pragmatic (goal-oriented) quality of a product. *Perspicuity* indicates how easy it is to get familiar with a product. Whether users can solve their tasks easily is shown in the *Efficiency* scale. *Dependability* indicates whether the user feels in control of the interaction with the product. In contrast, hedonic (not goal-oriented) quality can be evaluated by *Stimulation*, which measures whether the use of a product is exciting, and *Novelty*, which indicates the creativeness and whether the product catches users' interest. In order to evaluate the RAP-prototype by positive and negative impact on UX, each of the 26 UEQ-items was transformed so that scales range from −3 (= horribly bad) to +3 (= extremely good). Scale values from −0.8 to 0.8 are considered neutral.

3   Results

As the participants stated to use ride-sharing largely in private circumstances, the most frequent use case in this survey was going to or coming home from leisure activities (e.g., cultural events, meeting with friends) during the evening or at night (n = 11).

Mainly a poor connection of public transportation (PT) (especially during the late hours; n = 10), convenience (n = 5) and a faster travel time in comparison to PT (n = 5) are the reasons for using an on-demand ride-sharing service. Six participants favor on-demand ride-sharing over traditional taxi service because of lower fares for similar travel time. Four participants preferably use on-demand ride-sharing when travelling with friends as a group. Two participants stated to use ride-sharing due to feeling unsafe when using PT at night.

Overall, participants stated a positive understandability of the RAP prototype (see Table 1). All components were evaluated positively and received "very comprehensible" rating at least once. Especially component 2 (*waiting area*; M = 4.56; SD = 0.92) and component 4 (*shuttle identification*; M = 4.67; SD = 0.77) received very high ratings in terms of comprehensibility. Component 1 (*flagpole*; M = 4.47; SD = 0.79) did not receive any negative ratings (Min = 3). Although component 3 (*light beam*; M = 4.11; SD = 1.13) was on average comprehensible for the users, it was rated "not comprehensible at all" by one participant. The prototype overall shows a high mean rating in comprehensibility (M = 4.45; SD = 0.24), indicating high intuitiveness for the participants, hence potential improvement of UX when using AMoD.

Table 1. Comprehensibility of RAP Prototype (1 = "not comprehensible at all" to 5 = "very comprehensible")

Component	Comprehensibility			
	Min	Max	M	SD
1) Flagpole	3	5	4.47	0.79
2) Waiting area	2	5	4.56	0.92
3) Light beam	1	5	4.11	1.13
4) Shuttle identification	2	5	4.67	0.77
Overall prototype			4.45	0.24

Before analyzing the results of the UEQ [14] participants' answers were analyzed for inconsistencies. If a participant shows 3 scales in which answer distributions of items differ >3 between the best and the worst, it can be suggested that participants did not answer all items seriously. Analysis shows that none of the 18 participants' answers indicate inconsistencies.

Analysis of Cronbach's Alpha for internal consistency of the used scales shows that *Attractiveness* (α = 0.83), *Stimulation* (α = 0.90), *Novelty* (α = 0.95) and *Perspicuity* (α = 0.76) are acceptable to very consistent and hence can be interpreted. Low values of internal consistency can be seen in *Dependability* (α = 0.36) and *Efficiency* (α = 0.28). One reason for the low alpha values can be the small sample size (N = 18). The most probable reason for these inconsistencies might be that the items belonging to these scales were not fully referable to the shown prototype. Both *Dependability* and *Efficiency* capture goal related data, e.g., whether the users can solve their tasks without unnecessary effort. In this present case the users had no specific task to solve but rather an observing experience with the prototype. *Efficiency* shows four participants with outliers in their answer distribution. In particular item no. 9 (*slow/fast*; M = 1.06; SD = 1.26) shows inconsistencies as nine participants rated it either highly positive or highly negative, indicating that the item was confusing to some participants. Additionally, other items of *Efficiency* were rated significantly more positive (mean values ranging from 1.61 to 2.11). *Dependability* shows three participants with outliers. Hence scales *Efficiency* and *Dependability*, and overall pragmatic quality of the prototype should be interpreted carefully.

Figure 2 shows the results of each scale of the UEQ with error bars at the 95%-probability confidence interval.

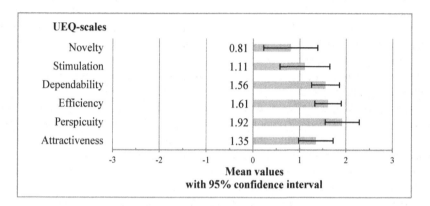

Fig. 2. Participants' mean ratings regarding the user experience questionnaire (UEQ) scales.

Overall, the results show that the RAP prototype gives a good initial impression to the participants (*Attractiveness*: M = 1.35; SD = 0.81). Users seem to like the prototype even though it is still an early stage design concept in the development process of a RAP. Especially the pragmatic quality (score = 1.69; SD = 0.19) of the prototype seems already to meet the users' information needs and requirements regarding conciseness very well. Although limited in their significance, *Efficiency* (M = 1.61; SD = 0.62) and *Dependability* (M = 1.56; SD = 0.65) show positive results and indicate that uncertainty is reduced and users are not overwhelmed. *Perspicuity* (M = 1.92; SD = 0.79) shows very positive results which leads to the conclusion that the design concept is very easy to understand and gives orientation to the user. The hedonic quality (score = 0.96; SD = 0.22) on the other hand shows room for improvement of the prototype. *Stimulation* (M = 1.11; SD = 1.16) was evaluated positively, which shows that the users are excited using the prototype. In terms of creativity and innovativeness the RAP design achieves a neutral score as *Novelty* (M = 0.81; SD = 1.26) indicates.

4 Conclusion

The results of the prototype evaluation show that the first RAP design concept already enhances the user's competence and gives useful support overcoming the meeting problem when accessing SAVs. Especially its good pragmatic quality reveals the RAPs potential to increase UX and acceptance of AMoD. These results build on prior studies [10]. The improved information supply with means of AR-technology and high intuitiveness of the RAP concept are strong indicators that future research should investigate a broader AMoD experience and not only focus on the AV itself. Low scores in hedonic quality of the prototype are acceptable at this early stage of development because an appealing design was not the goal of this study. Nevertheless, as hedonic quality contributes to overall UX this part shouldn't be left out in future research. In order to achieve a more valid understanding of the prototype's UX a larger sample size is required. Another limitation of this study is the low fidelity of this first prototype. Nevertheless, in terms of intuitiveness it can be noticed that the presented early stage prototype already received very good ratings. Noticeably, *flagpole*, *waiting area* and *shuttle identification* can be considered as the core components, giving the user most guidance. The *light beam* component shows room for improvement despite good comprehensibility. These results could serve as a starting point for further RAP design concepts. Concluding, the presented prototype provides a good basis for further HMI design research in the field of digital AMoD infrastructure.

Introducing the mere concept of RAPs for DRT services to users led to curiosity and positive feedback regarding acceptance. With these findings, further research to enhance the user's information supply with virtual infrastructure for mobility services is identified. This first investigation of a RAP design was conducted with users who are considered early adopters. Future research should involve other user groups, e.g., elderly, to give perspective on requirements for intuitiveness and UX. Putting the results into a nutshell, this study succeeds in giving first guidelines about how to design digital AMoD infrastructure with a human-centered approach.

Acknowledgements. This Project has received funding from the German Federal Ministry of Transport and Digital Infrastructure.

References

1. Ryley, T.J., Stanley, P.A., Enoch, M.P., Zanni, A.M., Quddus, M.A.: Investigating the contribution of demand responsive transport to a sustainable local public transport system. Res. Transp. Econ. **48**, 364–372 (2014). https://doi.org/10.1016/j.retrec.2014.09.064
2. Hahn, A., Pakusch, C., Stevens, G.: Die Zukunft der Bushaltestelle vor dem Hintergrund von Mobility-as-a-Service – Eine qualitative Betrachtung des öffentlichen Personennahverkehrs in Deutschland. HMD **57**(2), 348–365 (2020). https://doi.org/10.1365/s40702-020-00589-9
3. Alonso-González, M.J., van Oort, N., Cats, O., Hoogendoorn-Lanser, S., Hoogendoorn, S.: Value of time and reliability for urban pooled on-demand services. Transp. Res. Part C Emerg. Technol. **115**, 102621 (2020). https://doi.org/10.1016/j.trc.2020.102621

4. Shaheen, S., Cohen, A.: Shared ride services in North America: definitions, impacts, and the future of pooling. Transp. Rev. **39**(4), 427–442 (2018). https://doi.org/10.1080/01441647.2018.1497728

5. Lokhandwala, M., Cai, H.: Dynamic ride sharing using traditional taxis and shared autonomous taxis: a case study of NYC. Transp. Res. Part C Emerg. Technol. **97**, 45–60 (2018). https://doi.org/10.1016/j.trc.2018.10.007

6. Alonso-Mora, J., Samaranayake, S., Wallar, A., Frazzoli, E., Rus, D.: On-demand high-capacity ride-sharing via dynamic trip-vehicle assignment. Proc. Natl. Acad. Sci. U.S.A. **114**(3), 462–467 (2017). https://doi.org/10.1073/pnas.1611675114

7. Martinez, L.M., Viegas, J.M.: Assessing the impacts of deploying a shared self-driving urban mobility system: an agent-based model applied to the city of Lisbon, Portugal. Int. J. Transp. Sci. Technol. **6**(1), 13–27 (2017). https://doi.org/10.1016/j.ijtst.2017.05.005

8. Fagnant, D.J., Kockelman, K.: Preparing a nation for autonomous vehicles: opportunities, barriers and policy recommendations. Transp. Res. Part A Policy Pract. **77**, 167–181 (2015). https://doi.org/10.1016/j.tra.2015.04.003

9. Herminghaus, S.: Mean field theory of demand responsive ride pooling systems. Transp. Res. Part A Policy Pract. **119**, 15–28 (2019). https://doi.org/10.1016/j.tra.2018.10.028

10. Distler, V., Lallemand, C., Bellet, T.: Acceptability and acceptance of autonomous mobility on demand. In: Mandryk, R., Hancock, M., Perry, M., Cox, A. (eds.) The 2018 CHI Conference, Montreal QC, Canada, pp. 1–10 (2018). https://doi.org/10.1145/3173574.3174186

11. Krueger, R., Rashidi, T.H., Rose, J.M.: Preferences for shared autonomous vehicles. Transp. Res. Part C Emerg. Technol. **69**, 343–355 (2016). https://doi.org/10.1016/j.trc.2016.06.015

12. Hansen, E.G., Gomm, M.L., Bullinger, A.C., Moslein, K.M.: A community-based toolkit for designing ride-sharing services: the case of a virtual network of ride access points in Germany. IJISD **5**(1), 80–99 (2010). https://doi.org/10.1504/ijisd.2010.034559

13. Franke, T., Attig, C., Wessel, D.: A personal resource for technology interaction: development and validation of the affinity for technology interaction (ATI) scale. Int. J. Hum.-Comput. Interact. **35**(6), 456–467 (2018). https://doi.org/10.1080/10447318.2018.1456150

14. Laugwitz, B., Held, T., Schrepp, M.: Construction and evaluation of a user experience questionnaire. In: Holzinger, A. (ed.) USAB 2008. LNCS, vol. 5298, pp. 63–76. Springer, Heidelberg (2008). https://doi.org/10.1007/978-3-540-89350-9_6

Cooperative Work Analysis in Case of Aerodrome Flight Information Services

Satoru Inoue[1]([⊠]) and Taro Kanno[2]

[1] Electronic Navigation Research Institute, 7-42-23 Jindaiji-higashi-machi, Chofu, Tokyo 182-0012, Japan
s-inoue@enri.go.jp
[2] The University of Tokyo, 7-3-1 Hongo, Bunkyo-ku, Tokyo 113-8656, Japan
kanno@sys.t.u-tokyo.ac.jp

Abstract. Cooperation is a key in the group or team work to accomplish a mission successfully.

It is a critical factor to establish good relationships between humans and artefact systems as a group or team. In other words, cooperative work is one of important part to design current complex systems. It is important to understand the details of the basic functions, roles and their tasks in the system, in order to design more reliable interfaces and training programs for team cooperative work. Distributed cognition is an effective approach for understanding the interactions across the cooperative condition in a system.

In this research, we attempted to apply a method based on distributed cognition to analyze the activity that takes place in cooperative work. Distributed cognition analysis makes explicit the dependencies between humans and artefacts by examining the transformation and propagation of information through various forms of representations. We focus on aerodrome operators' work (aerodrome flight information services) as a case study of cooperative work.

Keywords: Cooperative work · Distributed cognition · Human modeling

1 Introduction

There are various forms of cooperative work, such as human-human or human-machines. Therefore, it can be said that "cooperation" is an important interactive perspective that should be considered in most situations in order to achieve goals in the system of modern society. In other words, good team cooperation can improve system performance, reliability and stability of it. However, it has not yet been understood well compared with individual cognitive processes. Because, these are complex and have complicated information flow. Analyzing interaction in a team and formalizing the cooperative processes and relations must be useful for designing systems that required high reliability and safety. Therefore, in this research, we tried to analyze interactive process of the system and formalizing the process of cooperation based on distributed cognition. As a case study, we analyzed a remote aerodrome flight information services for a small airport.

© Springer Nature Switzerland AG 2020
C. Stephanidis et al. (Eds.): HCII 2020, CCIS 1294, pp. 568–574, 2020.
https://doi.org/10.1007/978-3-030-60703-6_73

2 Approach of Distributed Cognition

In order to analyze cooperative work, it is necessary to focus on the interactive activity between human and artefacts in the team. Distributed cognition is a method of analysis that serves as a framework for understanding interactions between humans and artefacts such as machines in order to instruct the design of interactive systems [1]. Distributed cognition is an effective approach for analyzing cooperative work process from a cognitive perspective. The interaction of individuals with different levels of knowledge and skills, as well as artefacts within the system, allows them to come together as a single resource to accomplish their assigned tasks.

Distributed cognition analysis reveals dependencies between human actors and artefacts by examining the transformation and propagation of information through various forms of representation. Distributed cognition is based on the idea that the concept of cognition is not limited to individuals, but can be applied to an ensemble of distributed individuals and artefacts [2]. The interaction of individuals with different levels of knowledge and skills, and artefacts in the system allows them to come together as a single resource to accomplish their assigned tasks. The concept applied to cognition is the same as for distributed cognition, but it covers the interactions between a large number of individuals and technological devices, or "agents." Cognitive systems can be described using different units of analysis, allowing some systems to subsume others. This enables the examination of different interacting elements: from an individual with a single set of tools, to groups of individuals interacting with each other and a number of tools [3]. Information is represented by media of the cognitive system, including internal representations (personal memory) and external representations. A cognitive activity within a system are considered computationally, which are possible through the propagation and/or transformation of representational state of information between agents between different media. These propagations form a traceable trajectory of information from the initial input to the system to the final output. Assuming these trajectories form a stable pattern, an observable and modifiable "cognitive architecture" is revealed. In other words, the focus in distributed cognition is on how information is represented, transformed, and distributed through the individual and represented forms. The main advantage of adopting a distributed cognition approach is that information processing within the system of interacting individuals and artefacts can be directly observable. Through observation, we can deepen our understanding of information processing, which may lead to more effective system design. This ability to observe information processing differs from the traditional view of cognition.

3 Case Study

3.1 Domain

In this study, we considered how to apply for analyzing the cooperative work process in the remote Aerodrome Flight Information Service (AFIS) as a case study. Remote AFIS is a kind of air traffic service for providing information that is needed to fly aircraft such as weather information, delivering departure clearance, approach clearance, and so on at the small airport. In the remote AFIS operation, an operator provides flight information to the pilot from the Flight Service Centre (FSC) remotely. Remote operation is expected to make up service level more efficiently. However, current systems also have traffic volume limitation from safety perspective. To improve traffic capacity and applying this service to larger size airport which has more traffic volume while keeping safety and efficiency as for future systems, the systems need to be more optimized for operators' working position.

In remote AFIS operation, it is necessary to understand the role and the character of operators as users for modelling team cooperative process initially to design a future system.

3.2   Setting of Remote AFIS Work

Here we show the observation of Remote AIFS work. We observed that there are some specific features in the work of Remote AFIS, in particular, the basis of work is prediction and instruction to secure and maintain a safe traffic situation. An AIFS operator normally provides information to the aircraft pilot for taking off or landing airport, and to coordinate clearance information with air traffic controllers. In remote AFIS operation, an operator gives information to the pilots from FSC through radio communication. An operator normally use the remote AFIS systems which consist of radar (Aircraft Position Display Unit: APDU), weather information, airport monitoring remote control camera, flight information display. He/she decides an appropriate timing to send advisory information to the aircraft pilot by the system. An operator usually checks the condition of airport and monitoring traffic situation. When aircraft is taking off or landing, he/she provides appropriate information to the aircraft for keeping safety traffic condition. Their work process is typically working process. However, it needs to provide interactively among an operator, aircraft pilots and adjacent air traffic controllers in the appropriate timing. Therefore, it can be said "cooperative".

Current Japanese remote AFIS systems are consisted of some functions such as weather information including wind, radar display, radio communication, Pan-Tilt-Zoom camera, flight plan list, airport information and so on (Fig. 1). The operator handles those system functions for providing information.

As cooperative process, an AFIS operator frequently monitor displays of supporting systems, and carry out tasks while exchanging information with them. The context of situation is analyzed based on the activity data which were recorded. Therefore, we think analysis of distributed cognition is an effective method to understand the behaviour of actors, environmental conditions of workplaces, and information flow including interaction in collaborative work from cognitive systems perspective [4].

3.3   Analyzing Interaction with Aircraft Pilots

AFIS operator's work consists of verbal communication with pilots and air traffic controllers and interaction with the tools of the support system to acquire information which need for operational work. The operator can acquire necessary information by

Fig. 1. Operator's working position in Remote AFIS.

doing physical interaction with the work support system according to the situation, and by monitoring the situation of the system. In addition, the system is used as well as when an operator carries out tasks in accordance with the situation/event in takeoff or landing phases. On the other hand, when an operator carries out his/her tasks, initial contact from the pilot can be an event-trigger for a series of task processes from the analysis. For example, when an airplane contacts for landing, the operator starts tasks to provide information of runway conditions, weather and situation of traffic information which are needed for landing. In case of takeoff situation, although the content of the task is different from the case of landing, we confirmed that "initial contact" triggered the task execution in the series of tasks. In that sense, it is important in the cooperative process to correctly understand the contents of the verbal communication, and to collect information according to the situation in order to be carried out the task properly. We can understood that AFIS operator is constantly monitoring and using the support system to prepare for task execution so as to keep the operational work process even if the frequent verbal communication occurs.

3.4   Analyzing Interaction with Cooperative Systems/Functions

We recognized that the current system displayed lots of information on the screens and update most of information automatically. The operator advised airport information such a weather and airport condition to the aircraft pilot. The procedure of providing information to aircraft for taking off or landing is defined typical and fixed work process. Especially, the task of camera controlling is important in their working process due to check the airport condition.

Figure 2 shows the details of current system structure. The system interfaces consists of 5 displays mainly. An operator normally check aircraft flight schedule on the Flight Information Handling Systems: FIHS panel. He/she also inputs actual landing or departure time to the FIHS. ITV (Industrial Television) monitor provides the view of airport instead of airport tower. ITV provides zoom-up view instead of binocular and panorama view on the screen. Weather Receiving Unit: WRU shows the weather information. This system indicates wind direction and force information. An operator sends those wind parameters to the aircraft pilot. Aircraft Positioning Display Unit: APDU displays radar information. Radar system provides flying aircraft position around the airport. MPID is multi-purpose information display that can provide documentation or static information such as air route, airport map, and so on.

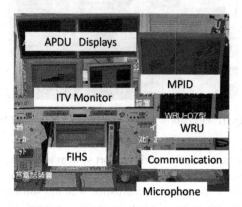

Fig. 2. Current Interface Component of Remote AFIS in Japan

Table 1. Frequency of Touch-usage (physical interaction)

Functions name	Numbers of use	
	Arrival	Departure
FIHS	86	59
ITV	57	71
WRU	1	10
APDU	1	8
MPID	6	0

From the observation of real operational work, Table 1 shows the frequency of the usage of interfaces during 80 min in operator working position. From the analysis, we considered these 5 displays were divided into 2 types. One is mainly existing physically interaction to the system interfaces for inputting and change functions. These interaction are shown in FIHS and ITV from analysis. Another is mainly monitoring activity to get information and rare occurring physical interactions to the system interfaces. On the other hand, we could understand the displays which mainly monitoring usages have also key roles in their work. For example, an operator uses the ITV monitor to estimate the timing of next activity from observing the aircraft situation. In that case, if he/she could see "passenger boarding" through the ITV display, an operator can expect to contact from pilot for staring taking off preparation from the monitoring task.

As described above, the analysis shows that two characteristics exist in the system. One is a system function with many physical interactions, and the other is a function which is often used only for monitoring. For example, when considering a layout design, such results are useful for integrating interfaces and optimizing functional layout for a system having a lot of physical interactions and a system in which monitoring is mainly used.

Further, as shown in Fig. 3, by analyzing the interaction, it is possible to represent the network connection and the relation between the agents with operator. The thickness of the connecting line represents the frequency of interaction. From this figure, all of artefacts in this figure interact only with the operator. It can also be seen that the structure of the information flow of the system is simple. Because, there is no network between other agents except for connection with the operator. On the other hand, if various agents interact with each other are occurred, the relationship between agents and the strength of the connection can be represented in a network diagram. It is an effective description technique for considering the relationship in a cooperative system. For example, it is useful for understanding the structure of interactions in tasks process of cooperative work.

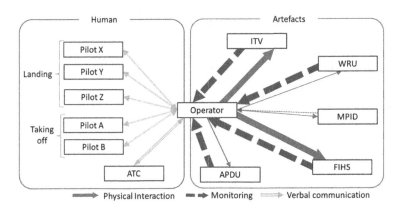

Fig. 3. Agent network of interaction

4   Summary

We introduced the idea of a practical technique based on distribute cognition to understand cooperative work. Distributed cognition is a useful perspective to adopt when analyzing the interaction among a team of individuals and artefacts. We showed a case study of analysis as a simple cooperative process. However, the approach generates significant levels of data, which require a substantial amount of time to analyze. We will continue to develop framework for understanding the complex cooperative work as a future work.

References

1. Hollan, J., Hutchins, E., Kirsh, D.: Distributed cognition: toward a new foundation for human-computer interaction research. ACM Trans. Comput.-Hum. Interact. 7(2), 174–196 (2000)
2. Hutchins, E.L., Klausen, T.: Distributed cognition in an airline cockpit. In: Engström, Y., Middleton, D. (eds.) Cognition and Communication at Work. Cambridge University Press, Cambridge (1996)
3. Furniss, D., Blandford, A.: DiCoT Modeling: From Analysis to Design. In: Computer Human Interaction 2010, Atlanta, Georgia, USA (2010)
4. Furniss, D., Blandford, A.: Understanding emergency medical dispatch in terms of distributed cognition: a case study. Ergon. J. 49(12/13), 1174–1203 (2006)

Evaluating Global Integrated Transportation Application for Mega Event: Role of Trust and Exchanging Personal Information in Mobility as a Service (MaaS)

Soyoung Jung[1]([⊠]), Hyejin Hannah Kum-Biocca[2], Frank Biocca[3], SungMu Hong[4], Mincheol Shin[5], and Hongchao Hu[1]

[1] Department of Communications, Renmin University of China, Beijing, China
soyoungjungs@gmail.com
[2] M.I.N.D. Labs International, College of Architecture and Design,
New Jersey Institute of Technology, Newark, NJ, USA
[3] Department of Informatics, New Jersey Institute of Technology,
Newark, NJ, USA
[4] Korea Telecom, Seoul, South Korea
[5] Department of Media and Communication, HYU Media Big Data Research,
Seoul, South Korea

Abstract. By evaluating user experience (UX) with an integrated transportation mobile application, called GoPyeongChang, which was developed for 2018 Winter Olympic and Paralympic Winter Games in South Korea (see Fig. 1), this study aims to provide insights into how the advanced networked technology could be utilized for future, global, mega events. The GoPyeongChang mobile application was primarily designed to help users from different nationalities navigate through the public transportation services they could opt for while attending the mega sports event. This mobile application integrated transportation information to provide international users the ability to navigate Korea using any combination of available transportation systems information (e.g., a shared car system, public transportations information) in four languages (i.e., Korean, English, Chinese, and Japanese). The application allowing users to purchase tickets using the in-app payment system. However, challenges integrating with local based mobile application services, (e.g., phone number-based identification system) was inevitable, and foreign visitors had to suffer from difficulties in using the application due to unfamiliarity with local services and the applications UI hierarchy. Despite these difficulties, this case study surprisingly found that the GoPyeoungChang has contributed to forging global users' positive attitude toward the site and the mega sports event through the mediating role of trust. This effect extended to the positive evaluation of the image of host country. Based on the findings, we attempted to provide an explanation for the experiential process through which the integrated transportation application was successfully adopted by non-local users who attended the mega sport event.

Keywords: User experience · Mobile as a service · Transportation interface first section

© Springer Nature Switzerland AG 2020
C. Stephanidis et al. (Eds.): HCII 2020, CCIS 1294, pp. 575–584, 2020.
https://doi.org/10.1007/978-3-030-60703-6_74

1 Introduction

This study investigated the factors that could lead international travelers and users to adopt an integrated transportation system (i.e., the GoPyeoungChang mobile application). Such systems are also known as Mobility as a Service (MaaS) [1–3]. MaaS has emerged as a term for denoting mobility information technology as it integrates various information technologies such as transportation services, infrastructures for traffic, and passenger information based on cloud computing and networks. Currently, the MaaS Alliance, which is formed in Finland and being used in the UK provides integrated transportation information services. This service considers itself as "a public-private partnership to creating a common approach to MaaS [4]".

The MaaS Alliance is aimed at building a single integrated mobility service application by providing diverse transportation options through a single payment channel and by connecting users with infrastructures, drivers, vehicles, transport service providers, and mobility service providers. Similar to the MaaS Alliance, the GoPyeongChang Winter Olympic Official application integrated transportation infrastructures (e.g., the high-speed train called, KTX; road/rail networks; sharing car system) with multiple public transport service providers (e.g., bus companies, subway, taxis) to provide easier access via integrated digital services. The GoPyeungChang app services include the road construction/pavements, road/rail networks, and the departure/destination information. All different services were gathered by a platform. The vendor provides the Application Programming Interface (API) platform services and directions from Location A (departure) to B (destination). Through this service, the several available modes of transportation can be calculated and provided. They also provide a distance matrix API, which computes the travel distances and durations between multiple departures and destinations, by collecting information from available transportation modes (e.g., bus, train, taxi, carpool, shuttle bus, rental car, and driving). Also, the MaaS connects each different level of service platforms. It may create usability problems.

1.1 Determinants of MaaS Acceptance

Within the information communication technology (ICT) scholarship the Technology Acceptance Model (TAM) is Participants used widely to explain possible determinants that could influence the acceptance of emerging technologies [5, 6]. While much attention has been previously paid to the role of Perceived Ease of Use (PEOU) and Perceived Usefulness (PU) [7]. Habib et al. suggest that perceived trust could play a critical role as a new facilitator in the context of cloud computing systems [8].

Guided by the extended technology acceptance model [9], this study examines how perceived trust, together with PEOU and PU, will play a role in affecting MaaS acceptance. In addition, this study examines how trust might extend to more favorable attitudes toward South Korea and the Winter Olympic game, considering that trust is interconnected with attributes of brand image improvement [10].

Fig. 1. GoPyeongChang App: The official transport app for the PyeongChang 2018 Olympic and Paralympic Winter Games (Left) Developed Persona for this case study: Sean hasn't been in S.Korea nor Olympic games before but interested in K pop and culture. (Right)

Previously, the extended TAM has been applied to seek out other determinants of technology acceptance, i.e., trust, prior experience, attitude [9], context [9, 11], computer playfulness and perceived enjoyment [12]. Similar studies have suggested other possible factors that could play a role as determinants of the acceptance of emerging technologies, such as speed, navigability, content, interactivity, response time, personalization, intuitiveness, and attractive visual interface elements [12]. Given that individual differences in technology usage (e.g., prior technology experiences, topic relevance), may moderate the acceptance of a technology [13], this study measured and statistically controlled for all three different prior experiences such as technology usage, and pre-existing attitude toward the S. Korea and Olympic Games [9]. Generally, ICT scholarship demonstrates the vital relationship between the technological attributes of the services and consumer trust in e-vendor [9]. Specifically, Gefen et al. examined the role of trust in e-commerce because consumers are often reluctant to provide their transaction information and personal data to e-vendors, i.e., cloud computing infrastructure. [6, 9, 14]. The interactivity and download speed are the keys to increasing trust in technology. These factors could increase the intention to accept the technology.

Attitudes and Perception Improvement with Trust in Technology. Trust is an antecedent that plays a dominant role in influencing consumer behaviors, especially in online shopping contexts [15]. The usage of cloud computing service and the purchase of online shopping are based on virtual network and virtual online shopping mall, which are all digitized. In this respect, trust can be the most decisive factor that could influence consumers' intention to purchase an item or use online services. Gefen et al., examined the association between trust and technology acceptance in an e-commerce context, while reviewing the conceptualization and the operationalizations of trust, and measuring how it emerges in e-commerce contexts [9]. Based on related work in commerce and trust studies, they suggested that trust is comprised of four different elements: 1) a set of specific beliefs: integrity, benevolence, and ability; 2) a general belief, also known as trusting intentions; 3) affect related trust; 4) a combination of three elements. In the same research, they adopted the notion of "a set of specific beliefs," which are known as "integrity," "benevolence," and "ability," This notion separates trust and actual behavioral intentions, which is consistent with the theoretical foundation of TAM.

According to McKnight et al., the structural assurances could be the cues of safety nets and guarantees: the Better Business Bureau's seal (http://www.bbb.com/), explicit privacy policy statements, a 1–800 number, or affiliations with respected companies [16]. Such an application of warranting cues in the e-commerce setting can increase perceived feeling of trust. To put it clearly, such cues might motivate users to build trust on services in e-commerce. Therefore, the integration between public transportation, commerce rental car company, and individual transportation networks can potentially interplay in enhancing the structural and institution-based trust and this may eventually contribute to the formation of trust on the MaaS.

2 Method

2.1 Participants

In order to control for users' previous experiences, the UX with GoPyeongChang, the integrated services as a one app was evaluated by US population who had not previously attended Olympic games or experienced Naver Maps (i.e., the dominant map service app in S. Korea). A total of 26 participants (male = 5 and female = 21) were recruited at a University located on the West Coast in the U.S. Most of the participants reported previous experiences with mobile transportation applications such as Uber and/or Lyft. All participants' first language was English. In addition, all participants were experience in the use of the Google Map mobile application, which provides geographical information for navigation.

2.2 Procedure

Before participants experience the GoPyeongChang application, we had them finish the pre-survey questionnaire which asked their attitude toward the Winter Olympic, brand image towards Korea, Korean culture, and products of S. Korea. The main usability test included 5 tasks (See Table 1) Detailed instruction for each of the five tasks were provided during the experiment. After completing the 7 tasks (see left), a post-survey was given to the participants.

2.3 Measurement

The items from Media Technology Usage and Attitude scale (MTUAs) were used to measure users' app usage behavior. To control for participants' attitude toward the Winter Olympics, which can be another predictor of TAM, we developed some items to check their attitude toward the Olympics. For scales of PEOU, PU, attitudes of the system, evaluation of the technology, and behavioral intention, we adopted the items from the TAM measurement, including Trust. The pre and post-attitude toward S. Korea, as well as familiarity with and intention to visit S. Korea, were also measured. All the information in regard to the descriptive statistics, internal consistency reliability of measures, are presented in Table 1. The Cronbach's alpha was used to check the internal consistency reliability. Most of the measurements' reliability was 0.6 or higher, which is an acceptable level.

Data Analysis. The individual data were recorded and analyzed using the Morae software which is automated usability test tool. The behavioral data were analyzed with other coders.

Table 1. Tasks for MaaS usability test.

Tasks	Content
1. Check the daily event schedule	Find today's competition and look for the place and the time for figure skating game *Able to find the page that has the schedule? Able to identify the place the game will be held?
2. Set the destination and departure	Set your current location as "Shinhan Museum" and destination location as "Pyeongchang Olympic Stadium." Select your departure time as February 27 at 11 am. *Able to find the "direction" without help? Able to differentiate current location and destination
3. Find the route	With Public transportation, choose the route that uses least amount of time to reach the destination or choose the route cost least amount of money. *Able to make route change? Able to change transportation option freely?
4. Reserve a train ticket	For the same route that was given, find the designated route that allows you to reserve a train ticket. *Able to find the reservation button for the train?
5. Use the Naver map navigation	Click on the Naver map button and use the same route that was given. Observe the route and start the route. *Able to head back to the main page easily

3 Results

FINDINGS 1: UI Design Problem Found from UX Usability Test
The behavioral data commonly showed the following results:

- User guide was difficult to find
- The main screen has overloaded information and hidden the features e.g., two menus (see Fig. 3)
- Participants could not tell that grayed out buttons were clickable (see Fig. 4)
- There was no beginning tutorial to help one get comfortable with the system, resulting in confusion and annoyance (see Fig. 4)

The results of usability test were in line with the behavioral data. Users have reported that GoPyeongChang is not comfortable to use and it was hard to complete the tasks (see Fig. 5 and 6) (Fig. 2).

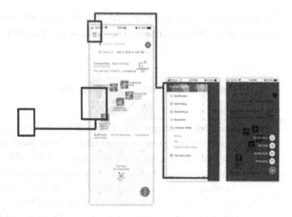

Fig. 2. Problem Found: The duplicated menu was embedded in the main page.

Fig. 3. Possible solutions for UI Design (1) Having the user guide pop up the first time the app is downloaded would be immensely helpful to everyone using the app and (2) Any buttons that are not clickable should be any color other than gray.

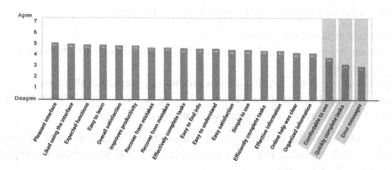

Fig. 4. Survey Responses-Averaged number of users describing how they feel on a scale of 1 to 7

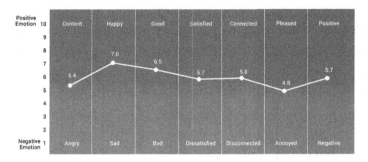

Fig. 5. Visualized Emotional Response from average number of users rating the emotions they felt on a scale of 1 to 10

FINDINGS 2: MaaS Acceptance While Comparing Attitude Change and Survey Data analysis the path model has suggested that while the foreign participants evaluated Go PyeongChang's user experience as causing some confusion and hard to learn, the app might induce positive user perceptions on S. Korea. The usability evaluation of app was relatively low (See Fig. 4, most of the average points) while the emotion report shows relevantly better, mostly above 5 points (See Fig. 5). After comparing the results from pre-and post-survey, the path model has suggested that while the foreign participants evaluated Go PyeongChang's user experience as causing some confusion and hard to learn, the app might induce positive user perceptions on S. Korea.

4   Discussion

The mega sport event is a chance to show host country's technological advancement. The current case study found that the experiencing integrated transportation app, GoPyeongChang may improves the users' attitude towards a country, in this case S. Korea. In addition, the government driven technology improves users' trust of the technology including app and system. This government context makes users feel secure enough to share their credit card information and willing to use the application, even if they evaluate the app UX negatively and feel uncomfortable to use the app. As a result of the case study, we identified the problems of user interfaces which creates confusion and difficulties thus, we suggested possible UI solution. Also, the survey results show that the integration of a private and public transportation and transaction system, which relate with trust by showing government logo or Olympic signage, is appealing to the users and increases the intention to make the transaction through MaaS Application. A number of trust antecedents have been identified, namely: cognition-based [17], knowledge-based [9], and institution-based trust [18]. MaaS and the extended TAM with trust can be based on cognition-based and institution-based trust. Cognition-based trust is formed through categorization [19]. The categorization progress occurs while accessing a person's trustworthiness based on the stereotypes or without first-hand

information [20]. Generally, a different form of trust is built on first impressions [21]
With high-quality information, e.g., completeness of design, helps to reduce the
uncertainty and risk regarding the transaction.

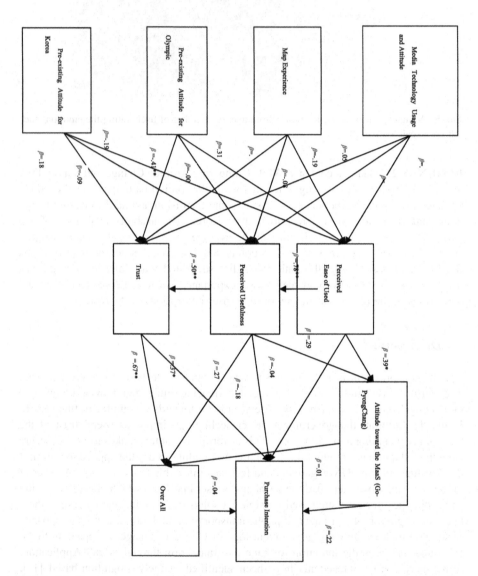

Fig. 6. MaaS acceptance mediating trust: the ease of used doesn't lead to purchase intention but
the trust leads to purchase intention. (PLS analysis was used to validate the proposed model. We
used the WarpPLS 6.0 software for the validation of our model. PLS analysis allows the testing
of the causal relationship between variables and also allows the assessment of the combined
hypotheses in one operation model with several hypotheses. In addition, this method also allows
to test the validity of constructs in latent variables (Chin 1998, Gefen et al. 2000). The reliability
and validity of the measurement were assessed with the SPSS software. Finally, the combined
hypothesis with one path model was assessed using the WarpPLS 6.0 software.)

At a global level, loyalty to a brand, service, or product is known as an important factor that predicts the formation trust on brand [22]. Loyalty is closely related to purchasing behaviors [23]. When the service provides transaction service through technology (e.g., e-commerce), trust in technology can be understood as an attribute of loyalty, and this could also lead to purchasing behaviors. Institution-based trust affects a buyer's perception, which is in-effect for "third-party institutional mechanism" [9].

Limitation. This study has some limitations while the path modeling shows many potential implications with trust and technology acceptance tendency by controlling preexisting conditions. The data were acquired from college students in USA. Thus, to extend this study the population should be expanded. Also, the path model is needed to be tested several times to show generalizability. For the future study, we need to choose other MaaS type of services and test with larger population.

Implication. A practical implication of this study is that emphasizing structural- and institution-based trust on MaaS type of service can increase the penetration rate of the technology, e.g., emphasizing cues of government driven or networks between public transportation and trustworthy private corporations or emphasizing on embedded high technology of constructs in latent variables (Chin 1998, Gefen et al. 2000).

References

1. Goodall, W., Dovey, T., Bornstein, J., Bonthron, B.: The rise of mobility as a service. Deloitte Rev. **20**, 112–129 (2017)
2. Sochor, J., Karlsson, I.M., Strömberg, H.: Trying out mobility as a service: experiences from a field trial and implications for understanding demand. Transp. Res. Rec. **2542**(1), 57–64 (2016)
3. Sochor, J., Strömberg, H., Karlsson, I.M.: Implementing mobility as a service: challenges in integrating user, commercial, and societal perspectives. Transp. Res. Rec. **2536**(1), 1–9 (2015)
4. Mobility as a Service Alliance—MAAS-Alliance. https://maas-alliance.eu/. Accessed 16 Oct 2019
5. Gefen, D., Benbasat, I., Pavlou, P.: A research agenda for trust in online experiments. J. Manag. Inf. Syst. **24**, 275–286 (2008)
6. Flanagin, A.J., Metzger, M.J.: The role of site features, user attributes, and information verification behaviors on the perceived credibility of web-based information. New Media Soc. **9**(2), 319–342 (2007)
7. Davis, F.D.: Perceived usefulness, perceived ease of use, and user acceptance of information technology. MIS Q. **13**, 319–340 (1989)
8. Habib, S.M., Hauke, S., Ries, S., Mühlhäuser, M.: Trust as a facilitator in cloud computing: a survey. J. Cloud Comput. Adv. Syst. Appl. **1**(1), 19 (2012)
9. Gefen, D., Karahanna, E., Straub, D.W.: Trust and TAM in online shopping: an integrated model. MIS Q. **27**(1), 51–90 (2003). https://doi.org/10.2307/30036519
10. Chaudhuri, A., Holbrook, M.B.: The chain of effects from brand trust and brand affect to brand performance: the role of brand loyalty. J. Mark. **65**(2), 81–93 (2001)
11. Rosa, M.J., Seymour, B.: Decoding the matrix: benefits and limitations of applying machine learning algorithms to pain neuroimaging. Pain **155**(5), 864–867 (2014)

12. Park, E., Kim, K.J.: Driver acceptance of car navigation systems: integration of locational accuracy, processing speed, and service and display quality with technology acceptance model. Pers. Ubiq. Comput. **18**(3), 503–513 (2013). https://doi.org/10.1007/s00779-013-0670-2

13. Venkatesh, V., Davis, F.D.: A theoretical extension of the technology acceptance model: Four longitudinal field studies. Manag. Sci. **46**(2), 186–204 (2000)

14. Flanagin, A.J., Metzger, M.J.: The perceived credibility of personal Web page information as influenced by the sex of the source. Comput. Hum. Behav. **19**(6), 683–701 (2003)

15. Reichheld, F.F., Schefter, P.: E-loyalty: your secret weapon on the web. Harv. Bus. Rev. **78**(4), 105–113 (2000)

16. McKnight, D.H., Chervany, N.L.: What is trust? a conceptual analysis and an interdisciplinary model. In: AMCIS 2000 Proceedings, p. 382 (2000)

17. Doney, P.M., Cannon, J.P., Mullen, M.R.: Understanding the influence of national culture on the development of trust. Acad. Manag. Rev. **23**(3), 601–620 (1998)

18. Pavlou, P.A., Gefen, D.: Building effective online marketplaces with institution-based trust. Inf. Syst. Res. **15**(1), 37–59 (2004)

19. Vance, A., Elie-Dit-Cosaque, C., Straub, D.W.: Google 학술 검색 (2008). https://scholar.google.co.kr/scholar?hl=ko&as_sdt=0%2C5&as_vis=1&q=+Vance%2C+Elie-Dit-Cosaque%2C+%26+Straub%2C+2008&btnG+. Accessed 16 Oct 2019

20. Langer, E.J.: The illusion of control. J. Pers. Soc. Psychol. **32**(2), 311 (1975)

21. Meyerson, D., Weick, K.E., Kramer, R.M.: Google 학술 검색 (1996). https://scholar.google.co.kr/scholar?hl=ko&as_sdt=0%2C5&as_vis=1&q=Meyerson%2C+Weick%2C+%26+Kramer%2C+1996%29&btnG=. Accessed 16 Oct 2019

22. Jevons, C., Gabbott, M.: Trust, brand equity and brand reality in internet business relationships: an interdisciplinary approach. J. Mark. Manag. **16**(6), 619–634 (2000)

23. Heide, J.B., John, G.: Alliances in industrial purchasing: the determinants of joint action in buyer-supplier relationships. J. Mark. Res. **27**(1), 24–36 (1990)

Users' Internal HMI Information Requirements for Highly Automated Driving

Merle Lau[✉], Marc Wilbrink, Janki Dodiya, and Michael Oehl

German Aerospace Center (DLR), Lilienthalplatz 7, 38108 Brunswick, Germany
{merle.lau, marc.wilbrink, janki.dodiya,
michael.oehl}@dlr.de

Abstract. The introduction of highly and fully automated vehicles (SAE levels 4 and 5) will change the drivers' role from an active driver to a more passive on-board user. Due to this shift of control, secondary tasks may become primary tasks. The question that arises is how much information needs to be conveyed via an internal Human-Machine Interface (iHMI) to fulfill users' information requirements. Previous research on iHMI regarding lower automation levels has shown that user require different information respectively. The present study focuses on how users' information requirements change for highly automated driving (SAE level 4) when the on-board user is distracted with a secondary task opposed to when the user is non-distracted. Twelve participants experienced different driving conditions and were asked to rate their attention distributions to other traffic participants. Results show clearly that users rated their attention distribution to other traffic participants significantly lower in automated distracted mode compared to automated non-distracted mode and manual driving. Furthermore, the question of users' information requirements was translated into iHMI design preferences. For this purpose, four different iHMI prototypes based on a 360° LED light-band communicating via color-coded interaction design, which proved to work well for lower levels, were evaluated regarding the information richness level sufficient for users for highly automated driving (SAE level 4). Results show that the sufficient information richness level is conditional upon gender. Implications for future research and applied issues will be discussed.

Keywords: Highly automated driving · Internal HMI · Intelligent HMI · User-centered design

1 Introduction

The development of automated vehicles (AV) will change the roads of tomorrow and will shift the drivers' role from an active driver to a more passive on-board user [1]. In conditional automation (SAE level 3), the driver needs to be able to take control over the vehicle as soon as the driving system reaches its limits, whereas in higher automation levels (SAE level 4 & 5), the on-board user will be more or less decoupled from the driving task [2]. Due to this shift of control, the task of vehicle control will become increasingly irrelevant for the on-board user and secondary tasks may become primary tasks [3]. Therefore, possible consequences for the on-board user needs to be

---

The original version of this chapter was revised: minor error in figure 2 was corrected. The correction to this chapter is available at https://doi.org/10.1007/978-3-030-60703-6_84

considered, e.g., the increasing allowance to execute non-driving related activities (NDRA) [4].

The question that arises is how much information needs to be transmitted by a vehicle's on-board or so-called internal Human-Machine Interface (iHMI) to meet users' information requirements. An iHMI serves as communication channel between the vehicle and the on-board user ensuring a well-working collaboration by transmitting sufficient information about the vehicle's behaviors (e.g., driving mode) playing a key role for the driver's trust in automation [3, 5]. Latest research on iHMI design focusing on lower automation levels (until SAE level 3) has shown that information supporting the monitoring process becomes more relevant compared to information that is necessary for executing the driving task [6]. So far, there has been little research as to what extent the on-board users' information requirements will change in terms of higher automation levels (SAE level 4 & 5). Therefore, the present study focuses especially on the change of on-board users' information requirements for highly automated driving (SAE level 4).

When translating users' information requirements into design preferences in terms of iHMI, former research shows promising results by using the peripheral vision of the driver as iHMI modality. The presentation of information via a LED light-band showed great potential even in lower levels of automation [7–9]. However, since the tasks of the driver and her or his information requirements in higher automation level, the interaction strategies need to change as well. Even if no driving related task remains at the on-board user, the interaction between her or him and the AV stays important since the information communicated by the iHMI plays a key role regarding acceptance and trust in AV [10]. Since the on-board user does not need to perform any safety critical system interventions, a certain level of unobtrusive information could be enough to gain the transparency of the AV. Therefore, besides the investigation of users' information requirements for highly automated driving, the present study focuses on the desired information richness levels for a LED light-band iHMI design.

2   Users' Information Requirements (Part 1)

In part 1, the present study investigates the on-board users' information requirements for highly automated driving (SAE level 4). Therefore, the attention distributions to interacting traffic participants when driving in different levels of automation, i.e., manual and highly automated driving (SAE level 0 & SAE level 4) is in focus. Furthermore, the study investigates the changes in attention distributions when the on-board user of a highly automated vehicle is distracted and occupied with NDRA opposed to when the user is non-distracted.

2.1   Method

A qualitative in-depth interview using a within-subject design was conducted by twelve participants (six female) with ages between 23 and 75 years (M = 48.00; SD = 23.90). In a fixed-base driving simulator, all participants experienced three driving conditions (manual driving, highly automated driving being non-distracted, highly automated driving being distracted) in an urban left-turn scenario. The selected scenario was a video recording of a partially signalized left-turn intersection at Kastanienallee in Braunschweig, Lower Saxony (Germany). All participants possessed a valid German driver's license and were familiar with the selected scenario since they had experienced the exact intersection in real life before. The participants' affinity for technology was rated M = 4.75 (SD = 0.80) on a 6-point scale (from "completely disagree" to "completely agree") with the ATI questionnaire [11]. The participants received an expense allowance of 10 € per hour. The complete experiment was recorded on video for later reference with participants' consents.

The purpose of the study was explained and consent forms were signed by the participants. The participants were asked to take a seat in a fixed-based driving simulator consisting of two projection displays positioned in front and on the left of the on-board user. A 360° LED light-band was in the interior of the driving simulator communicating via a color-coded interaction design. A blue LED light-band means the car is driving in a highly automated mode and white LED light-band means the car is in manual mode. Firstly, the participants saw a pre-recorded video from the driver's perspective of the left-turn scenario for one minute. During the video, the participants were instructed to keep their hands on the wheel to imagine manual driving. After this, the participants were provided with a snapshot of the left-turn scenario based on a segmentation approach [12] and were asked to rate their attention distribution to other traffic participants on a 7-point Likert scale (from 0 = "not important" to 7 = "important"). After this, to experience highly automated driving, the participants drove in highly automated mode on a preselected route in a virtual environment two times. The first run was non-distracted. The second run was distracted, which means the participant performed a secondary task, i.e., reading a magazine while driving in the AV. After both simulation runs, the participants were provided again with the snapshot of the left-turn scenario based on a segmentation approach [12]. They were asked to imagine driving in an AV for both runs (being non-distracted vs. being distracted) and to rate their attention distribution to other traffic participants on a 7-point Likert scale (from 0 = "not important" to 7 = "important").

2.2 Results

The participants' attention distributions given to other traffic participants were categorized into three types:

- **Type 1:** Other traffic participants with direct interaction
- **Type 2:** Other traffic participants with indirect interaction
- **Type 3:** Environment surrounding the traffic situation

In Fig. 1, the mean attention for type 1 to 3 for all three driving conditions (manual driving, highly automated driving being non-distracted, highly automated driving being distracted) are shown.

For manual driving, type 1 traffic was rated highest, i.e., vehicles M = 6.75 (SD = 0.62) and cyclists M = 6.61 (SD = 0.88). Moreover, type 2 traffic was rated with M = 4.27 (SD = 0.70). Type 3 was rated as not important. During highly automated driving being non-distracted, type 1 vehicles were rated M = 1.83 (SD = 0.65)

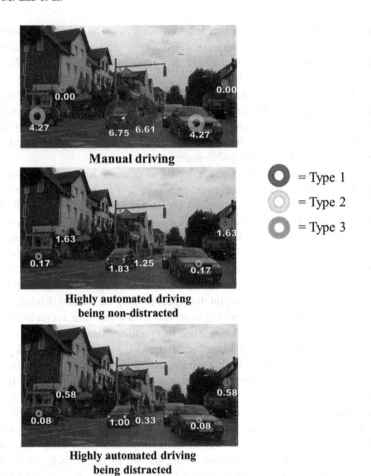

Fig. 1. Driver's subjectively rated (0–7) mean attention given to other traffic participants for manual driving (at the top) vs. automated driving being non-distracted (mid) vs. automated driving being distracted (bottom).

and type 1 cyclists with M = 1.25 (SD = 0.51). Type 2 traffic scored M = 1.63 (SD = 0.66). Type 3 was rated with M = 0.17 (SD = 0.17). Moreover, for highly automated driving being distracted, type 1 vehicles scored M = 1.00 (SD = 1.28) and type 1 cyclists were rated with M = 0.33 (SD = 0.65). Type 2 traffic was rated M = 0.08 (SD = 0.29) and type 3 M = 0.58 (SD = 0.39).

Non-parametric Friedman tests were used for analyzing the data due to violated normal distributions. Results show that the mean attention differ significantly between the three driving conditions for type 1, i.e., for vehicles ($\chi^2(2) = 22.29$, p = .00) and cyclists ($\chi^2(2) = 21.33$, p = .00) and type 2 traffic ($\chi^2(2) = 15.94$, p= .00). Post-hoc Dunn-Bonferroni tests showed that the mean attention for type 1 vehicles is significantly higher for manual driving compared to highly automated driving being non-distracted (z = 4.19, p = .00) and highly automated driving being distracted (z = 3.16, p = .01) with showing the highest attention for manual driving and the lowest attention for highly automated driving being distracted. The same effect is found for type 1 cyclists and type 2 traffic (p < .05).

3   Internal HMI Design Evaluation (Part 2)

In part 2, the users' information requirements were translated into design preferences in terms of an iHMI. Therefore, four paper-pencil iHMI prototypes using a 360° LED light-band as key modality for human-machine interaction were presented and evaluated focusing on the users' desired information richness levels.

3.1   Method

Participants experienced the second part of the study right after the first part on the same day. Therefore, the same sample as in part 1 was used (see Sect. 2.1). Four different iHMI prototypes (paper-pencil) using a 360° LED light-band were presented on a computer screen to the participants. The iHMI prototypes describe different levels of information richness with a color-coded interaction design (Fig. 2).

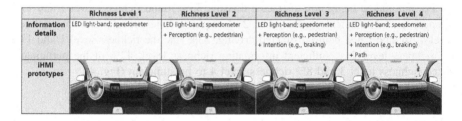

Fig. 2.   Different information richness levels for an AV's LED light-band iHMI design.

Richness level 1 consists of head-down-display (HDD) including speedometer and the LED light-band giving information about the actual driving mode (automated vs. not automated). The dark blue colored LED light-band indicates that the AV is in highly automated mode (SAE level 4). The information available to the user increases with higher information richness levels. *Richness level 2* consists of the richness level 1 information plus the perception of other traffic participants by the AV (e.g., pedestrian in the direct path of the vehicle). An additional light blue colored bar on the LED light-band (directly under the object in the environment) states that a traffic participant was detected, e.g., a pedestrian. Additional to the previous described information, *richness level 3* includes the intention of the AV, i.e., the next maneuver (e.g., braking) which is displayed via a red colored bar on the LED light-band. Additionally, *richness level 4* consists of the path, i.e., the next trajectory of the AV which is conveyed via a green colored bar on the LED light-band. After the presentation of the iHMI prototypes, participants were asked to state the sufficient information richness level for iHMI LED light-band regarding automated non-distracted and automated distracted mode so that they feel well-informed.

3.2   Results

For the iHMI design evaluation, four different information richness levels for a LED light-band were evaluated regarding the information richness level sufficient for users (see Fig. 3).

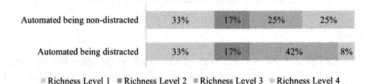

Fig. 3. For users sufficient information richness level for iHMI LED light-band (automated being non-distracted vs. automated being distracted).

For automated being non-distracted driving, 33% found richness level 1 and 17% richness level 2 sufficient. Furthermore, 25% require richness level 3 and 25% richness level 4. In automated being distracted driving, 33% rate the richness level 1 and 17% the richness level 2 as sufficient information richness level. 42% of the participants stated richness level 3 and 8% richness level 4 to be sufficient (Fig. 4).

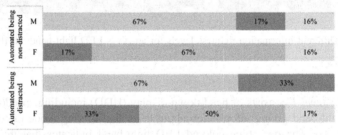

Fig. 4. Sufficient information richness level for male (M) and female (F) participants for iHMI LED light-band (automated being non-distracted vs. automated being distracted).

4   Discussion

In this study a qualitative in-depth interview was conducted to get a deeper insight into on-board users' information requirements for highly automated driving (SAE level 4). Regarding the users' attention distributions to other traffic participants, results show clearly that users rated their attention distribution to other traffic participants significantly lower during distracted mode opposed to not being distracted and especially in comparison with manual driving. It becomes evident that traffic participants in direct and indirect interaction that were given a high rating during manual driving are no longer as important for the user during highly automated driving being distracted. The results are consistent with previous findings for lower automation levels (until SAE level 3) which show that users require different information regarding different automation level [7]. Based on individual statements by the participants, it was noted that children and to some extend cyclists are of great importance due to their sometimes unpredictable behavior especially during manual driving. Due to the fact that children are not included in the stimulus material of this study, it is necessary to particularly consider other road users, e.g., children, requiring special attention in further research.

Referring to the users' desired information in terms of an LED light-band iHMI, results show that when driving highly automated, 33% of the participants found the lowest information level to be sufficient that just indicates automated driving mode being active in terms of ensuring the user's mode awareness. 17% found level 2 in both conditions (non-distracted vs. distracted) sufficient. But in the distracted scenario, 42% of the participants require a higher information richness level 3 compared to 25% (non-distracted). Only 8% of the participants required the highest information richness level 4 (distracted) vs. 25% (non-distracted). So they did not want to be informed about the AV's path in the distracted condition. Here participants stated that they just want to be well-informed in case of any critical interaction so that they quickly can gain a minimum of situation awareness. A closer look shows that users' desired information richness levels are especially conditional upon gender. Whereas male preferences were towards lower information richness levels, i.e., 67% found just level 1 sufficient for both conditions, female preferences were towards higher information richness levels so that they felt well-informed by the automation. This might be discussed in terms of trust in automation. So maybe a longer contact of female participants might have created higher trust in automation. The use of paper-pencil prototypes can be seen as a limitation and therefore, more realistic prototypes and simulations with the possibility to experience the AV's driving dynamics providing additional information to the user should be used in future research. Overall, the findings can be seen as a first outlook on how users' on-board information requirements will change during highly automated driving (SAE level 4) and how these information requirements can be translated into design preferences in terms of an iHMI LED light-band.

References

1. Meyer, G., Deix, S.: Research and innovation for automated driving in Germany and Europe. In: Meyer, G., Beiker, S. (eds.) Road Vehicle Automation. LNM, pp. 71–81. Springer, Cham (2014). https://doi.org/10.1007/978-3-319-05990-7_7
2. Society of Automotive Engineers: Taxonomy and definitions for terms related to driving automation systems for on-road motor vehicles. SAE, Michigan (J3016_201806) (2018)
3. Carsten, O., Martens, M.H.: How can humans understand their automated cars? HMI principles, problems and solutions. Cogn. Technol. Work **21**(1), 3–20 (2018). https://doi.org/10.1007/s10111-018-0484-0

4. Kun, A.L., Boll, S., Schmidt, A.: Shifting gears: user interfaces in the age of autonomous driving. IEEE Pervasive Comput. **15**(1), 32–38 (2016). https://doi.org/10.1109/MPRV.2016.14

5. Bengler, K., Rettenmaier, M., Fritz, N., Feierle, A.: From HMI to HMIs: towards an HMI framework for automated driving. Information **11**(2), 61 (2020). https://doi.org/10.3390/info11020061

6. Beggiato, M., Hartwich, F., Schleinitz, K., Krems, J., Othersen, I., Petermann-Stock, I.: What would drivers like to know during automated driving? Information needs at different levels of automation. In: 7th Conference on Driver Assistance (2015). https://doi.org/10.13140/rg.2.1.2462.6007

7. Dziennus, M., Kelsch, J., Schieben, A.: Ambient light – an integrative, LED based interaction concept or different levels of automation. In: 32. VDI/VW Gemeinschaftstagung Fahrerassistenzsysteme, Wolfsburg, 8–9 November 2016, pp. 103–110 (2016)

8. Dziennus, M., Kelsch, J., Schieben, A.: Ambient light based interaction concept for an integrative driver assistance system: a driving simulator study. In: de Waard, D., et al. (eds.) Proceedings of the Human Factors and Ergonomics Society Europe Chapter 2015 Annual Conference, Groningen, NL, pp. 171–182 (2016)

9. Pfromm, M., Cieler, S., Bruder, R.: Driver assistance via optical information with spatial reference. In: 16th International IEEE Conference on Intelligent Transportation Systems (ITSC 2013) (2013)

10. Wilbrink, M., Schieben, A., Oehl, M.: Reflecting the automated vehicle's perception and intention. In: IUI 2020: 25th International Conference on Intelligent User Interfaces, Cagliari Italy, pp. 105–107 (2020). https://doi.org/10.1145/3379336.3381502

11. Franke, T., Attig, C., Wessel, D.: A personal resource for technology interaction: development and validation of the affinity for technology interaction (ATI) scale. Int. J. Hum.-Comput. Interact. **35**(6), 456–467 (2018). https://doi.org/10.1080/10447318.2018.1456150

12. Fastenmeier, W., Gstalter, H.: Contribution of psychological models and methods for the evaluation of driver assistance systems. Zeitschrift für Arbeitswissenschaft (ZfA) **62**, 15–24 (2008)

Automotive eHMI Development in Virtual Reality: Lessons Learned from Current Studies

Duc Hai Le[(⊠)], Gerald Temme, and Michael Oehl

German Aerospace Center (DLR), Lilienthalplatz 7, 38108 Brunswick, Germany
{duc.le,gerald.temme,michael.oehl}@dlr.de

Abstract. More and more studies in automotive research and development are conducting user-centered development in the emerging field of external human-machine interfaces (eHMI) in virtual reality (VR). As time, cost and risk are decreasing with progressively affordable sophisticated VR technologies, researchers have shifted to virtual testing. Within this context, they use a variety of methods and technologies to develop new designs but so far little examination has been done towards validity of virtualization and description of the technical setup. As level of immersion is one of the current pillars in VR and technology evolves rapidly, study setups differ a lot in recent years, resulting in poorer comparability. In this paper, our goal is to review the current generation of VR studies in automotive eHMI development and extract in the sense of a lessons-learned approach best practices with regard to their VR setup. For that, we assessed a total of six current studies published between 2017 and April 2020 in automotive eHMI development to extract lessons learned from study designs and virtualization setups. We took a look at hardware and software used as well as study procedure. The results allow us to find useful conclusions on automotive eHMI development practices in VR.

Keywords: Virtual Reality (VR) · external Human-Machine Interface (eHMI) · Review · User-centered design · HMI development

1 Introduction

Towards multi-modal user-centered human-machine interfaces (HMI) in automotive research and development, it is essential to consider the user in early stages. Multi-modality includes visual, auditive and haptic stimuli during development.

These HMIs are designed, e.g. to direct and enable users to understand important information faster and act properly in relevant situations. A good HMI conveys confidence and trust to the user, therefore needs comprehensive testing to be used on a larger scale. However, testing is a resourceful component as well as time, money and labor consuming. Adding the higher risks of testing on open roads and the difficulty to replicate trials, industry and science has shifted to more advanced and safer ways to build experiments.

Within this context, virtual reality (VR) has been a common tool in the automotive sector to design, develop and evaluate new external HMI (eHMI) since the 1990s with Cave Automatic Virtual Environment (CAVE) [1]. Since then, designers and test

© Springer Nature Switzerland AG 2020
C. Stephanidis et al. (Eds.): HCII 2020, CCIS 1294, pp. 593–600, 2020.
https://doi.org/10.1007/978-3-030-60703-6_76

architects have been able to test human-centered user interaction in a risk-free environment while showing prototypes in early development stages. Today's hardware with advanced and fast multi-processors is able to output high-resolution stereoscopic 3D-rendered images on small head-mounted display (HMD) with additional auditive and haptic feedback. These components help bringing a more immersive experience to the user and setting up a new environment detached from the physical world while being more efficient, smaller and less expensive than its predecessor.

Using VR reduces development time and cost but also comes with new challenges to build real-world-like scenarios. Instead of creating a potentially dangerous situation and compromising safety, users may sit in a laboratory perceiving auditive signals to immerse into an virtual world. Different approaches have been described to conduct automotive eHMI development in such environments but with little analysis of the overall setup.

To extract important key points and common practices, we are going to take a closer look at automotive eHMI development procedures in VR and compare experimental hands-on practices. Our analysis is based on the implementation and execution of the evaluations published in each paper. For that, we are going to take a closer look in our paper on VR simulation key points that need to be taken into account.

2 Concept of Immersion and Interactivity

To foster authentic feedback in VR, an environment has to be created to trigger realistic user perception and reaction. Walsh and Pawlowski [2] worked out a set of dimensions for VR user experience (UX) in information system research based on cumulative literature review. With multiple studies supporting the same pillars [2, 4], we will use this as our concept reference and concentrate on immersion and interactivity as being largely responsible for VR experience and the well-being of users [3]. The two dimensions will be our main focus when assessing the studies to point out strengths and weaknesses.

Immersion is the degree of isolation from the real world, i.e., from multi-modal stimuli according to Slater and Wilbur [5]. Unlike the subjective feel of presence inside VR, immersion corresponds to the objective stimuli put onto the users' sense to generate the degree of immersion. The more we are disconnected from the real world the more we feel immersed into the virtual world. The level of immersion is a product of visual, audio and haptic input or output. In 1992, Steuer assessed the field of immersion and placed breadth (varieties of sense, i.e., visual, audio, haptics) and depth (e.g., frequency, resolution, field of view (FOV), detail) as the key factor for an immersive experience [6]. Common practices uses devices to shield physical environmental input and overlay virtual ones [6]. To assess the objective stimuli onto study participants, we are going to take a look at the hardware setup and 3D environment contributing to the immersion.

Interactivity refers to how the user can modify and interact with the objects and environments of VR. Interaction can be done using a variety of input devices like hand-held motion controller, steering wheel or other sensor inputs. On one hand, it enables user interaction and direct feedback while on the other hand it amplifies the feel of presence. To map interactivity to HMI development, we assess the tools used to generate such interactivity.

3 Automotive HMI Development in VR

Previous studies addressed the concept of driver simulation and its design for near-realistic UX, giving recommendations when creating a virtual automotive study [7–9], i.e., high-fidelity setups and multi-modality for better immersion. Most studies agree on the advantages of VR over conventional testing environments like risk reduction and reproducibility and encourage to use VR for automotive development and early prototyping [7, 9–11].

In 2019, Colley et al. [12] investigated seven automotive studies in VR using simulation criteria derived from the discussion paper by Winter et al. [9]. They concluded that the usage of HMD should be limited below one hour. Furthermore, the researchers suggested more motion opportunities like actual walking and the presentation of questionnaires within VR. They also pointed out to consider the design of urban environment regarding sociocultural differences in VR to vary experimental outcome. The conclusion will be taken into consideration while assessing our findings in this review.

Hock et al. [13] proposed a checklist of eight points to consider in a driver simulation study. Considering our scope immersion and interactivity for eHMI, i.e., the view point of traffic participants, we concentrate on two out of the eight points: 1) *simulator sickness* (i.e., low motion speed, short VR exposure, for better readability we will refer to this as *continuous immersion*) and 2) *simulator training* (some form of familiarization for participants to get accustomed).

After defining our criteria to assess the goal of our study, the upcoming sections will cover the study selection.

4 Paper Selection

To focus on more recent and more affordable HMD technology used, we considered for a better comparison current studies from 2017 to currently April 2020. We identified a total of six studies on automotive eHMI prototype evaluation in VR from our database search (ACM Digital Library, IEEE, Scopus, Springer Verlag). Considering the emerging field of research both of automotive eHMI in automated vehicles (AV) and HMDs, The selected studies are only about eHMI development using modern HMDs and study design in VR. The criteria allow us to give a valid and focused view for comparison between all reviewed studies.

For the sake of simplicity, we assume that all studies used VR-ready hardware to back up the computational power. Because of that, variations on computational hardware will be neglected unless feedbacks reported some lag or technical issues. A more detailed list of the study setup is shown in Table 1.

Table 1. Setup and procedure of eHMI development studies in VR

[15]	Headphones used	HTC VIVE @2160 × 1200 px, 90 Hz, 110° FOV, near-realistic vehicle and world physics, detailed 3D world	n/a	Yes, one test run for each task	30–40 min.	n/a
[16]	Background and vehicle sound	Oculus Rift CVI @2160 × 1200 px, 90 Hz, 110° FOV, detailed 3D world	Button controller	n/a	30 min., divided in 5 blocks with 2 min. breaks in between	Increasing discomfort but low, no abortion
[17]	n/a	n/a	Gesture recognition	Yes	n/a	Technical issue
[18]	Integrated headphones	HTC VIVE Pro @2880 × 1200, 90 Hz, 110° FOV, detailed 3D world	n/a	Yes, baseline run	n/a	n/a
[19]	n/a	HTC VIVE @2160 × 1200 px, 90 Hz, 110° FOV, detailed 3D world	Motion tracker	Yes, multi-staged virtual lobby	40 min.	No abortion, no reported discomfort

5   Results

Now that we have our identified studies accumulated, we can assess the studies against the background of VR dimensions [2] and simulation criteria [13].

Immersion: In terms of resolution and detail, the level of immersion created by the 3D engine and displayed onto the HMDs is mostly similar as depicted in all studies. The studies showed a typical western urban environment from a pedestrian's point of view showing at least all relevant characteristics of a street (i.e., sideways, lane markings) and some building structures. The lack of descripted devices used in [17] in addition to an unspecified hardware failure makes this study in terms of hardware specification difficult to compare. Aligned with user feedback across all studies, the immersive experience can be described as positive. Since setups are not fully described in detail (as shown in Table 1), we are summarizing the approximated setup as sufficient in terms of FOV, refresh rate, resolution and level of detail. Sound was implemented by [14, 16, 17] using audio environment with dynamical changes depending on vehicle speed and distance. Two studies [15, 18] reported using headphones which can be attributed to the integrated headphones of the HMD and may imply a sound environment. In the after-study questionnaire by [14], participants attributed increased immersion due to the combination of visualization and sound which is align with prior research [5, 20]. Due to insufficient description, we cannot make a statement regarding the sound environment in the other studies. Questionnaires are administered before and after studies and therefore are not presented during VR sessions as suggested by [13]. However, considering the short duration of VR experience for users, we did not find any immersion drawbacks or need to implement within-VR questionnaires.

Interactivity: Regarding locomotion, [14] allowed for a 9×3 m^2, [19] for a 4×7 m^2 area, resembling a road section where participants could move. Controllers were used in [15, 16] to determine a movement decision by pressing a button on the motion controller. In the study by [17], participants used gestures to signal the AV to stop. However, an unspecified technical problem occurred during the recognition which limits the results. [18] did not offer any interactivity as the participants had to fill out a survey to report their experience.

Simulator sickness: Questionnaires measuring the user's well-being help researchers to evaluate potential discomfort during their study. Conducted questionnaires to assess level of immersion and simulation sickness showed little to no discomfort in user feedbacks [14, 16, 19]. Some participants experienced increased discomfort [16] but no abortions were documented [14, 17, 19]. The time spent in the VR was documented between 20 and 40 min which is within the recommended limits stated by [13]. Differences in duration showed no significant changes across all identified studies.

Simulator training: Familiarization or warm-up period was given in almost every study. So most researchers do practice some kind of user acclimation to the VR. [15] suggested no longer than 30 min experiencing VR at a time, [19] conducted their study within 40 min per participant and [16] recommended taking a break every 5 min. It is shown that the learning curve helped users to get familiar and comfortable within VR. Feedback on the VR experience and level of immersion therefore was reported positively and is in line with prior research.

Overall, all researchers concluded a positive experience with their VR setup, praising the safe execution over real-life scenarios and confirmed to use it again. Although slightly different in setup constellation, studies share similar HMD specifications. All setups provided a visual environment with currently common 3D engines like Unity or Unreal Engine, providing potentially high-resolution images for the HMD [15–19]. Conference Name: ACM Woodstock conference Conference Short Name: WOODSTOCK'18 Conference Location: El Paso, Texas USA.

6 Discussion

Our goal was to assess studies in automotive eHMI development in VR to understand and filter for common applications. The studies had some descriptive gaps, making it difficult to understand certain setup structures as well as having a comprehensive view on the study design. The lack of multi-modal immersive stimuli in [15, 17–19] makes it challenging to compare immersion factors to other studies, especially when the differences in hardware use can be neglected. To our surprise, little effort was done to stimulate more senses, i.e., embodiment or locomotion for a better feel of presence in VR.

Besides multimodality, the analyzed studies seem to focus on ready-made and easy-to-use hardware and software solutions. Since hardware and software available on the market is still in an early product phase, it is hard to create a multimodal experience. However, as described in Sects. 2 and 3, we would still suggest to take more senses into consideration than just visual immersion to allow more reliable results and stable user well-being during the assessment. Overall, we tackled different aspects of VR and simulation structures and found frequent similarities between implementation and theory.

We do understand the lack of necessity to provide virtual interaction as studies often concentrate on the premise of observing the decision-making of traffic participants choosing to cross a street or not. Because of that, most studies disabled locomotion or even a virtual body representation. This is align with the conclusion [13] came to in their review study. Even without the need to take any action inside the VR, based on studies like [16], we encourage more interactivity to increase participants' UX and give them a sense of presence through, e.g., walking or hand movement.

Regarding the simulation criteria, we found little to no drawback. Most studies introduced a warm-up phase to get familiar with the VR. The extended familiarization period presented in [19] showed a rewarding effort to lower feel of uncertainty and discomfort which we believed can help inexperienced users in VR. The consideration of sample was difficult to conclude as little was reported to show heterogeneity and overall user profiles. As for our examination, we believe this might not be as relevant for our paper as this study dimension has not produced abnormal study results and participants were mostly selected randomly.

Considering our challenge to show eHMI evaluation done in VR, we came across multiple limitations in our study: Firstly, it is important to point out that the automotive eHMI studies found and considered in our review are mostly of visual nature, making the perception of eHMIs highly dependent on visual input while auditive, haptic and interactive factors mainly serve the purpose to increase level of immersion. Depending on the assessing eHMI, auditive, haptic or interactive elements might be highlighted more. In general, we would suggest future studies to further take multi-modal stimuli into consideration to not only increase the feel of presence within a virtual situation but also to emphasize genuine reaction. Secondly, most study designs were methods to evaluate a specific eHMI design. Therefore, the validity is difficult to confirm or disprove by just criticizing the VR setup. Furthermore, as new technological devices reach the market, they become more accessible. Advanced VR interaction tools like VR gloves or gait recognition are still limited in their usage and need more time to be tested to reliably enhance virtual interactivity.

7   Conclusion

We assessed six different eHMI development VR setups against the background of VR dimensions and simulation criteria recommended in research to gain a comprehensive immersive experience for user studies. The scenarios built and setups made an overall immersive and profound baseline to evaluate new eHMI designs and test users in near-realistic environments. Towards our attempt to extract ideas and lessons learned, we distilled the following recommendations:

- Let the user get familiar with the system and observe the user's well-being during the study to ensure reliable results;
- Build a near-realistic visual VR environment, backed up by a multi-modal environment to enable better interactivity and proprioception within VR;
- Decide to use immersion factors depending on the evaluating eHMI;
- Document setup description precisely and mention factors contributing to the VR experience of the user (i.e., hardware specification and study procedure).

Overall, all studies in our review support the usage of VR as a promising addition to early prototyping and they advocate the advantages of immersive virtual environments. Further studies are needed to provide a more in-depth look into eHMI-specific traits when building a virtual test environment for participants. The results suggest a high potential in future automotive eHMI development studies in VR with higher immersion and better multi-hardware setups.

References

1. Cruz-Neira, C., Sandin, D., Defant, T., et al.: The cave-audio visual experience virtual environment. Commun. ACM – CACM, 65–72 (1992). https://doi.org/10.1145/129888. 129892
2. Walsh, K.R., Pawlowski, S.D.: Virtual reality: a technology in need of is research. CAIS **8**, 297–313 (2002). https://doi.org/10.17705/1CAIS.00820
3. Mütterlein, J., Hess, T.: Immersion, Presence, Interactivity: Towards a Joint Understanding of Factors Influencing Virtual Reality Acceptance and Use (2017)
4. Ryan, M.: Narrative as Virtual Reality. Immersion and Interactivity in Literature and Electronic Media. Parallax: Re-visions of Culture and Society. The Johns Hopkins University Press, Baltimore (2015)
5. Slater, M., Wilbur, S.: A framework for immersive virtual environments five: speculations on the role of presence in virtual environments. Presence Teleoperators Virtual Environ. **6** (6), 603–616 (1997). https://doi.org/10.1162/pres.1997.6.6.603
6. Steuer, J.: Defining virtual reality: dimensions determining telepresence. J. Commun. **42**(4), 73–93 (1992). https://doi.org/10.1111/j.1460-2466.1992.tb00812.x
7. Lhemedu-Steinke, Q., Meixner, G., Weber, M.: Comparing VR Display with Conventional Displays for User Evaluation Experiences, pp. 583–584 (2018). https://doi.org/10.1109/vr. 2018.8446076
8. Weidner, F., Hoesch, A., Poeschl, S., et al.: Comparing VR and non-VR driving simulations: an experimental user study. In: 2017 IEEE Virtual Reality (VR), pp. 281–282 (2017). https:// doi.org/10.1109/vr.2017.7892286
9. de Winter, J., Leeuwen, P.M., Happee, R.: Advantages and Disadvantages of Driving Simulators: A Discussion, pp. 47–50 (2012)
10. Buchholz, C., Vorsatz, T., Kind, S., et al.: SHPbench – a smart hybrid prototyping based environment for early testing, verification and (user based) validation of advanced driver assistant systems of cars. Procedia CIRP **60**, 139–144 (2017). https://doi.org/10.1016/j. procir.2017.02.025
11. Ihemedu-Steinke, Q.C., Erbach, R., Halady, P., Meixner, G., Weber, M.: Virtual reality driving simulator based on head-mounted displays. In: Meixner, G., Müller, C. (eds.) Automotive User Interfaces. HIS, pp. 401–428. Springer, Cham (2017). https://doi.org/10. 1007/978-3-319-49448-7_15
12. Colley, M., Walch, M., Rukzio, E.: For a better (simulated) world: considerations for VR in external communication research. In: Proceedings of the 11th International Conference on Automotive User Interfaces and Interactive Vehicular Applications: Adjunct Proceedings, pp. 442–449. Association for Computing Machinery, New York (2019). https://doi.org/10. 1145/3349263.3351523

13. Hock, P., Kraus, J., Babel, F., et al.: How to design valid simulator studies for investigating user experience in automated driving: review and hands-on considerations. In: Proceedings of the 10th International Conference on Automotive User Interfaces and Interactive Vehicular Applications, pp. 105–117. Association for Computing Machinery, New York (2018). https://doi.org/10.1145/3239060.3239066

14. Böckle, M., Pernestål, A., Klingegård, M., et al.: SAV2P: exploring the impact of an interface for shared automated vehicles on pedestrians' experience, pp. 136–140 (2017). https://doi.org/10.1145/3131726.3131765

15. Chang, C., Toda, K., Sakamoto, D., et al.: Eyes on a car: an interface design for communication between an autonomous car and a pedestrian, pp. 65–73 (2017). https://doi.org/10.1145/3122986.3122989

16. de Clercq, K., Dietrich, A., Velasco, N., Pablo, J., et al.: External human-machine interfaces on automated vehicles: effects on pedestrian crossing decisions. Hum. Factors 61(8), 1353–1370 (2019). https://doi.org/10.1177/0018720819836343

17. Gruenefeld, U., Wei, S., Löcken, A., et al.: VRoad: gesture-based interaction between pedestrians and automated vehicles in virtual reality. In: Proceedings of the 11th International Conference on Automotive User Interfaces and Interactive Vehicular Applications: Adjunct Proceedings, pp. 399–404. Association for Computing Machinery, New York (2019). https://doi.org/10.1145/3349263.3351511

18. Kettwich, C., Dodiya, J., Wilbrink, M., et al.: Gestaltung der Interaktion von Fußgängern mit automatisierten Fahrzeugen - Ergebnisse einer Virtual-Reality-Studie. In: 10. VDI-Tagung Mensch-Maschine-Mobilität 2019, Deutschland, Braunschweig (2019)

19. Deb, S., Carruth, D.W., Hudson, C.R.: How communicating features can help pedestrian safety in the presence of self-driving vehicles: virtual reality experiment. IEEE Trans. Hum.-Mach. Syst. 50(2), 176–186 (2020). https://doi.org/10.1109/THMS.2019.2960517

20. Cummings, J., Bailenson, J.: How immersive is enough? A meta-analysis of the effect of immersive technology on user presence. Media Psychol. 19, 1–38 (2015). https://doi.org/10.1080/15213269.2015.1015740

Delineating Clusters of Learners for Driver Assistance Technologies

John Lenneman[1(✉)], Laura Mangus[2], James Jenness[2],
and Elizabeth Petraglia[2]

[1] Toyota Motor North America, Ann Arbor, MI 48105, USA
john.lenneman@toyota.com
[2] Westat, Rockville, MD 20850, USA

Abstract. Driver assistance (DA) technologies pose challenges to the formation and maintenance of drivers' mental models (i.e., understanding) of their operation. The challenges can be overcome through consumer education, training methods, and interface design strategies, but an understanding of how mental models for DA technologies form and evolve is needed. Therefore, we studied drivers' experiences under extended real-world driving conditions for the purpose of delineating their mental models of DA technologies. Participants (n = 52) who recently purchased a vehicle with at least two DA technologies were interviewed for approximately six months. Cluster analyses (hierarchical and k-means) of data elements extracted from the interviews (e.g., ratings of mental model complexity, accuracy of technology understanding, trust, perceived usefulness, satisfaction) revealed five different types of learners of DA technologies: expert, skilled, moderate, uninformed, and misinformed. This paper reviews how mental model formation and evolution of DA technologies vary across the five learner types. The results indicate that facilitating efficient and appropriate mental model development could be enhanced by incorporating variations in mental model formation and evolution in future consumer education and design approaches.

Keywords: Drivers · Mental models · ADAS · Naturalistic · Consumer education · HMI · Automated driving · Driver assistance

1 Introduction

Driver assistance (DA) technologies such as lane keeping assistance, adaptive cruise control, and blind spot monitoring are becoming prevalent in newer vehicle models. However, these systems might pose challenges to the formation and maintenance of a drivers' mental model (MM) of their operation. Potential challenges can be overcome through consumer education, training methods, and interface design strategies, but a deeper awareness of how MMs of DA technologies form and evolve may be an important step in facilitating consumer apperception. In the current research we broadly define a MM as a driver's conceptualization of his or her vehicle's systems, including one's understanding of the functional capabilities and limitations, one's emotional valence towards the systems, and one's perceptions about the usefulness and reliability of these systems.

We conducted a series of longitudinal interviews for the purpose of delineating drivers' MMs of DA technologies. We hoped to identify and define the variations in mental model formation and evolvement as drivers' experience with the systems increased. Note, while the findings presented herein are preliminary, we believe they illustrate the breadth of variation in how users learn about their DA technologies and could be used as inspiration for the execution of future research and analyses.

2 Method

Fifty-two participants who purchased a 2018–2019 vehicle with at least two DA technologies (and who had never owned a vehicle with DA technologies before) participated in the longitudinal study. Forty-seven participants enrolled within the first month after purchasing their vehicle. Forty completed 9 interviews over the course of their first 6–7 months of ownership while seven completed 5 interviews over approximately 3 months. The remaining 5 participants enrolled when they had already owned their vehicle from 8–60 weeks. They completed three interviews over the course of approximately 4–7 weeks.

Every participant completed in-person interviews at the beginning and end of the study. All other interviews were phone-based and occurred approximately every two weeks. All interviews were recorded for later analysis. Intake questionnaires including the Hoyle Brief Sensation Seeking Scale (assesses thrill-seeking and general disinhibition), the Driver Behavior Questionnaire (assesses driving risk, errors, lapses, and violations), and the Rotter Locus of Control (assesses internal vs. external locus of control) were completed at the first interview [1–3]. During the last interview participants completed an outtake questionnaire that assessed confidence in their knowledge of their vehicle's DA technologies, their feelings of importance in understanding how the system works, perceptions of system intuitiveness/difficulty, and how much they trusted their vehicle's DA technologies.

The Van Der Laan Scale of System Acceptance was completed at the first and last interview as a means to gain insight into participant's perceived satisfaction and usefulness of their vehicle's DA technologies [4]. Additional data extracted from both the first and last interviews included researchers' ratings (i.e., interpreted variables) that were reduced using pre-defined criteria. For example, functional accuracy of capabilities (see below) was rated high if participants had multiple correct statements, no incorrect statements, and stated at least one limitation to system operation. In contrast, functional accuracy was rated low if multiple incorrect statements, guesses, and vague descriptions were provided. Interpreted ratings for the variables were analyzed for interrater reliability, with the final set of interpreted variables all having an interclass correlation of $r = .6$ or greater. The final six interpreted variables are considered to be critical elements of drivers' MMs and include:

- MM complexity (e.g., number of systems mentioned, detail and specificity provided in descriptions)

- Accuracy of technology understanding (e.g., types of sensors of technologies present, how those systems work, details of interface, system logic)
- Functional accuracy of capabilities (e.g., systems capabilities and limitations, enabling conditions)
- Emotional valence (e.g., overall emotional response to their safety system)
- Level of anthropomorphic orientation (e.g., extent that the participant describes vehicle or safety assist system having human-like characteristics, emotion, mood, or intellect)
- Level of mechanical orientation (e.g., extent that the participant describes their vehicle or safety assist system as a machine or computer)

MM complexity, technology understanding, and functional accuracy were rated on a 3-point scale of low, medium, and high. Emotional valence was assessed on a 5-point scale from very negative to very positive. Anthropomorphic orientation and mechanical orientation of the participants' descriptions were rated on a 3-point scale of none, low, and high.

For data collected at the first and last interviews only, a hierarchal cluster analysis using the `hclust` function in R was used to determine the initial number of plausible clusters: based on the clustering diagnostics, 5 clusters appeared to be the optimal choice. A k-means cluster analysis (using the `kmeans` function in R) was then run to divide participants into exactly 5 groups. For this analysis, two observations with missing last interview data were dropped.

3   Results

Execution of the k-means cluster analysis resulted in clusters we labeled as expert, skilled, moderate, uninformed, and misinformed learners (see Table 1). A description of each learner type is provided below.

Table 1. Number of participants by learner/cluster type.

Learner Type	N
Expert	10
Skilled	21
Moderate	9
Uninformed	7
Misinformed	5

3.1   Experts

Expert learners exhibited a stable, highly complex mental model over time. In their first interview, all experts were rated as having a high level of MM complexity, 90% had high accuracy of technology understanding, and 70% had high functional accuracy. By the last interview, 100% of participants in this cluster were rated as high in all three categories (see Table 2).

Table 2. Percentages of summary variables ratings within each cluster for the first and last interviews.

Summary Variable	Expert		Skilled		Moderate		Uninformed		Misinformed	
	First	Last	First	Last	First	Last	First	Last	First	Last
Complexity: High	100	100	43	62	11	22	0	14	20	60
Complexity: Medium	0	0	57	33	78	78	14	14	20	0
Complexity: Low	0	0	0	5	11	0	86	71	60	40
Accuracy of Technology: High	90	100	5	19	0	11	14	0	0	20
Accuracy of Technology: Medium	10	0	57	57	89	78	0	71	80	60
Accuracy of Technology: Low	0	0	38	24	11	11	86	29	20	20
Functional Accuracy: High	70	100	14	52	44	44	0	14	40	60
Functional Accuracy: Medium	30	0	86	48	56	56	43	71	60	20
Functional Accuracy: Low	0	0	0	0	0	0	57	41	0	20
Emotional Valence: Very Positive	60	50	76	71	11	0	14	14	20	0
Emotional Valence: Somewhat Positive	40	50	24	29	89	89	29	57	80	80
Emotional Valence: Neutral	0	0	0	0	0	11	43	29	0	0
Emotional Valence: Somewhat Negative	0	0	0	0	0	0	14	0	0	20
Emotional Valence: Very Negative	0	0	0	0	0	0	0	0	0	0
Anthropomorphic: High	40	50	14	24	33	22	43	0	20	20
Anthropomorphic: Low	40	40	71	71	56	44	29	86	80	60
Anthropomorphic: None	20	10	14	5	11	33	29	14	0	20
Mechanical: High	80	90	0	10	0	0	0	29	0	20
Mechanical: Low	20	10	33	57	22	33	43	43	40	0
Mechanical: None	0	0	67	33	78	67	57	29	60	80

Further, in their first and last interviews experts had the highest ratings of mechanical orientation (80% and 90% respectively). Finally, experts self-reported a high level of trust in their system (M = 8.8; see Fig. 1).

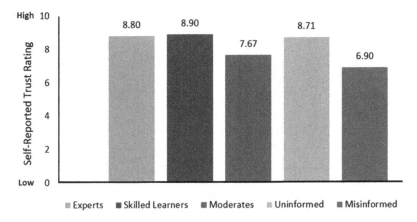

Fig. 1. Final Interview: Mean self-reported trust in safety system ratings by cluster.

3.2   Skilled Learners

57% of skilled learners were rated as a having medium and 43% were rated as high levels of MM complexity in the first interview. In the last interview, 33% of skilled learners had medium while 62% had high MM complexity, which demonstrates this cluster's ability to learn over the course of the study. Similarly, high rating for function accuracy of DA technology increased by 38% from first to last interview (see Table 1). Finally, skilled learners had the highest ratings of satisfaction and usefulness for their vehicle's DA technologies at the last interview (see Figs. 2 and 3).

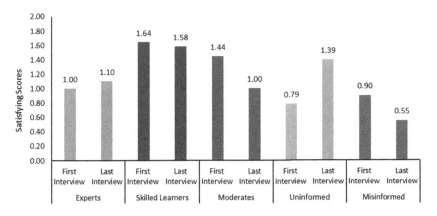

Fig. 2. Van Der Laan Scale: Change in mean satisfying scores by cluster between first and last interviews.

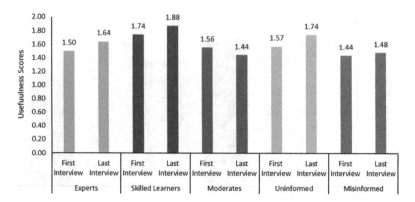

Fig. 3. Van Der Laan Scale: Change in mean usefulness scores by cluster between first and last interviews.

3.3   Moderate Learners

Moderate learners displayed mostly medium ratings for MM complexity and accuracy of technology understanding in both the first and last interviews. Functional accuracy was rated as either medium (44%) or high (56%). Overall, there was little change between the first and last interview for the interpreted variables (see Table 1). No one in this cluster was rated as high for level of mechanical orientation in either interview. Moderate learners self-reported a decrease (from 1.44 to 1.00) in DA technology satisfaction from the first to the last interview (see Fig. 2). Finally, most moderate learners (78%) did not feel confident that they understood everything there is to know about their safety system (see Fig. 4).

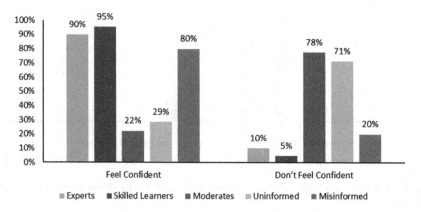

Fig. 4. Final Interview: Percent response of self-reported confidence in understanding everything participant needs to know about their vehicles driver assist systems by cluster

3.4 Uninformed Learners

In the first interview, uninformed learners were rated as having the lowest MM complexity (86%), lowest level of accuracy of technology understanding (86%), and lowest functional accuracy (57%). This group continued to display low ratings of complexity mental model by the last interview (71%). There was some learning for accuracy of technology understanding and functional accuracy (see Table 1).

Uninformed learners are the only cluster to display a somewhat negative or neutral emotional valence in the first interview (14% and 43% respectively), though they rated higher in emotional valence at the last interview. 71% of uninformed learners reported that they were not confident in their understanding of DA technologies at the last interview. Finally, 43% of uninformed learners self-reported that they did not find their safety system to be simple and intuitive.

3.5 Misinformed Learners

Misinformed learners generally had incorrect DA technology knowledge in their first interview as 60% were rated as having low MM complexity while 80% had medium accuracy of technology understanding. The percentage of misinformed learners with high MM complexity increased by the last interview, and there were slight improvements as a group for functional and technical accuracy (see Table 1). Misinformed learners self-reported the lowest levels of trust in their DA technologies (see Fig. 1), self-reported the lowest satisfaction with their DA technologies (see Fig. 2), and by the last interview they were the only type to rate as having a "somewhat negative" emotional valence towards their system (see Table 1). Interestingly, this cluster also self-reported the highest level of knowledge about their DA technologies (see Fig. 5) with a high amount of confidence (see Fig. 4).

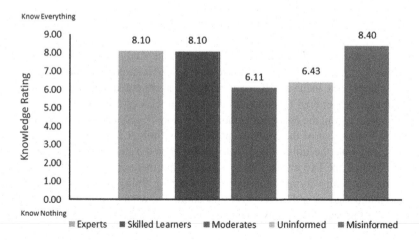

Fig. 5. Final Interview: Self-reported rating of how well participants know the capabilities and limitations of their driver assist systems by cluster.

4 Discussion

Inspection of the differences between clusters enabled the identification of five types of learners of DA technologies and highlighted key differences between them across a number of different attributes. We believe that the delineated differences between learner types can be utilized to tailor design and consumer education approaches to improve users' understanding and subjective experience with their vehicle. For example, the results revealed that a group of learners (we labeled misinformed) had inaccurate and incomplete MMs of ADAS technologies and associated low levels of trust and satisfaction. However, they also self-reported the highest levels of knowledge in DA technology capabilities and limitations and had high levels of confidence in their knowledge. Thus, misinformed learners could benefit from consumer education programs that are designed to break down barriers and overcome internal biases about one's own knowledge about system operation so that actual knowledge and self-perceived knowledge are more accurately calibrated.

Further, uniformed learners, who scored lowest in many of the mental model categories but displayed some ability to refine their MMs over time, could benefit from additional trainings over the first year or two of vehicle ownership. Finally, the results revealed a group of learners (we labeled experts) had relatively refined MMs even at the first interview which were, in general, maintained over time. Developing ways to predict which consumers are expert learners may prove useful since additional training could be better allocated to other consumers. More strategic allocation of consumer education resources could prevent misuse, non-use, or over-reliance of DA technologies by other learner types and in turn, lead to increases in trust, perceived utility, and satisfaction.

5 Limitations and Future Research

In the current study we were able to delineate five clusters using an extensive and varied set of data. Yet, while we feel confident that these clusters are representative of real-world learner types, we should acknowledge that our inclusion of drivers who owned their vehicle 8–60 weeks prior to entering the study (i.e., experienced drivers with relatively longer exposure to their vehicle's DA technologies) could influence the analysis. Simply, the inclusion of "experienced" drivers could have introduced a small set of subjects who weren't as naïve to the technologies as the other drivers; thus, we are planning to re-run the analysis excluding the more "experienced" drivers. However, it is worth noting that of the 5 experienced drivers, only 1 fell into the expert learner cluster (3 fell into the uninformed learner cluster and 1 fell into the skilled learner cluster). Further, the five clusters make sense in that there are essentially three logical groups: drivers with varying knowledge and varying ability to learn, drivers with no substantial knowledge, and drivers with inaccurate knowledge. The number of clusters identified in the analysis simply identifies and clusters the range of variance within these clusters.

Additional planned analyses include a more detailed inspection of MM evolution. In this paper, we reviewed differences in MMs between the first and last interviews relative to the 5 learner types identified. However, as stated previously, we interviewed subjects approximately every two weeks while they were in the study. Many of the insights presented herein were also gleaned during the intermediate phone interviews. Thus, more detailed analysis of changes in MMs, and in the information that influence MM formation and evolution, has begun and will be released at a later date.

Further, we noted previously that a number of different personality and driving behavior questionnaires were completed at the beginning of the study. Sample findings from a preliminary analysis include misinformed learners self-reported the highest scores in driving lapses, errors, and overall risk in comparison to the other drivers, uninformed learners self-reported high ratings in risky driving behaviors and associated aggressive violations, and expert learners self-reported generally low ratings in risky driving behaviors. Future analyses will also include a more detailed inspection of the intersection between personality, driving behavior, and formation and evolution of MMs of DA technologies.

Finally, it is worth noting that conducting research on this topic in a natural setting is important as it affords information to the driver and opportunities for the researcher to observe behaviors that cannot be replicated in a driving simulator. The information and experiences by the driver could have impacts on the formation and evolution of MMs. To date, this study is one of only a few that study the formation and evolution of MMs of DA technology in a naturalistic setting [e.g., 5]. Thus, our hope is that this research can inspire more studies like this.

6 Conclusion

The current research provides insight into the formation and evolution of MMs of DA technologies, specifically with regard to the variation in various learner types. Understanding of mental model components, different learner types, and external factors associated with these leaner types can provide vital information about which driver assist systems are most frequently misunderstood, the types of training that are needed, and if different consumer populations require tailored trainings. Facilitating efficient and appropriate mental model development could be enhanced by incorporating variations in mental model formation and evolution in future consumer education and design approaches. Finally, while the findings herein are insightful, additional research is necessary in order to confirm and more fully capture the variation in ways drivers develop their understanding of DA technologies.

References

1. Hoyle, R., et al.: Reliability and validity of a brief measure of sensation seeking. Personality Individ. Differ. **32**, 401–414 (2002)
2. Reason, J., Manstead, A., Stradling, S., Baxter, J., Campbell, K.: Errors and violations on the roads: a real distinction? Ergonomics **33**, 1315–1332 (1990)
3. Rotter, J.: Generalized expectancies for internal versus external control of reinforcement. Psychol. Monogr. **80**, 1–28 (1966)

4. Van der Laan, J., Heino, A., De Waard, D.: A simple procedure for the assessment of acceptance of advanced transport telematics. Transp. Res. Part C Emerg. Technol. **5**, 1–10 (1997)
5. Fridman, L., et al.: MIT advanced vehicle technology study: large-scale naturalistic driving study of driver behavior and interaction with automation. IEEE Access **7**, 102021–102038 (2019)

Multi Remote Tower - Challenge or Chance? An Empirical Study of Air Traffic Controllers Performance

Maximilian Peukert[✉], Lothar Meyer, and Billy Josefsson

Luftfartsverket LFV, Research and Innovation, Hospitalsgatan 30, 602 27
Norrköping, Sweden
{maximilian.peukert,lothar.meyer,
billy.josefsson}@lfv.se

Abstract. The purpose of this study was to investigate the effect of shifting among and updating of mental models in multi remote tower operations.

Background. Within the development of the future workplace for air traffic controllers (ATCO), innovation shifts to multi remote tower operations. Multi remote tower means, that an ATCO serves air traffic control services for more than one airport at a time from one physically remote located workplace. This change requires adjustments in the way how the ATCO works, as multiple mental models need to be updated constantly. Frequent shifting between airports and mental models respectively is necessary. Updating and shifting are cognitive cost sensitive, as they affect workload and situational awareness negatively. In contrast, higher workload could be beneficial for alertness which could act as a countermeasure in turn.

Method. Four 90-min lasting remote tower Human-In-The-Loop simulation runs with traffic and weather were performed by eight conventional tower experienced ATCOs. Each ATCO completed two runs in multi- and two runs in single-mode. Situational awareness, workload and alertness was measured via self-reports before, during and after each run.

Results. No differences between both modes with respect to situational awareness and alertness could be found. However, significant workload differences could be found during the simulation runs at two times, due to a simulated snowstorm.

Conclusion. The findings indicate no negative effect of shifting among and updating of mental models in multi remote tower. A possible explanation could be, that a common hybrid mental model for in multi-mode is internally developed so that shifting among mental models is perhaps not necessary.

Keywords: Multi remote tower · Air traffic control · Mental models · Situational awareness · Workload · Alertness

1 Introduction

A recent major development in air traffic control is the change from the conventional tower to remote tower services. The conventional tower workplace is characterized through a direct view on the airport operational surfaces, runway and the airspace

© Springer Nature Switzerland AG 2020
C. Stephanidis et al. (Eds.): HCII 2020, CCIS 1294, pp. 611–618, 2020.
https://doi.org/10.1007/978-3-030-60703-6_78

surrounding. In remote tower operations air traffic control services for a single airport are performed from a physically remote located control center workplace (single-mode). Since there is no direct view of the airport surface, real-time video cameras are positioned at the airfield, which provide an image on screens at the remote tower workplace in the tower [1].

The interest to serve multiple airports from a limited number of workplaces in the remote tower center is increasing. Here, the upcoming step is providing multi remote airport service, meaning, that more than one airport is controlled from one air traffic controller (ATCO) at one workplace at the same time (multi-mode). While technological feasibility is already given, the impact on mental models of the ATCO is not yet fully understood. The aim of this study was to investigate the effects of updating of and shifting among mental models in multi remote tower. The chosen approach comprises a Human-In-The-Loop simulation that shall allow a comparison of human performance measures in single and multi-mode.

2 Theoretical Background

2.1 Multi Remote Tower as a Safety Challenge?

Multi remote tower is considered as a fundamental change for ATCOs, since it influences how, which and when tasks are done. Presumably, visual scanning and task patterns require modifications [2]. From a cognitive perspective, the impact on ATCO workload in multi-mode must be considered. A relevant aspect that influences workload is the increased traffic volume in multi-mode [3]. In a simulation study by Moehlenbrink et al. this influence was investigated and a significant increase in workload in multi-mode in comparison to single-mode was shown [4]. A further aspect is the constant updating of the respective mental models for all controlled airports by the ATCO [2, 3]. Mental models contain mental representations of airspace, aircraft as well as air traffic control (ATC) procedures and technical systems. These models support the development of situational awareness [5]. Since multi-mode is characterized by a higher degree of dynamic changes, it is considered to be more complex than single-mode, which seems to be associated with reduced situational awareness [6]. Updating of mental models is accompanied by the monitoring and coding of external information and requires replacing of outdated information, which is affecting workload [7]. In order to update all mental models, a frequent cognitive shifting among the models is also necessary, affecting workload as well [8]. For shifting, attention is practically relocated from on to the other airport. Updating and shifting are executive functions that are considered as causing cognitive costs [9]. This influence of shifting among and updating of mental models on workload and situational awareness in multi-mode has not yet been investigated. Increased workload and reduced situational awareness pose a potential challenge for multi-mode, since safety could be decreased.

2.2 Multi Remote Tower as a Safety Chance?

Multi remote tower is of special interest for airports that feature low traffic volumes. In the conventional tower, a low traffic volume can cause working conditions that promote low workload (underload). Underload can lead to monotony and decreased vigilance, which could impair performance, alertness and safety in air traffic control [10]. Moreover, Straussberger and Schaefer [11] showed a link between monotony and increased sleepiness in ATCOs. In the multi remote tower, a safety benefit is expected by the lower exposure of the ATCO to monotony which is, combined with a demand for high alertness, a known stressor [12].

To compare, the radar workplace in air traffic control allows changes of the controlled area (sector) size, based on traffic load and time of day. The idea behind this procedure is, to avoid overload within peak hours (decreased sector size) and underload during nighttime (increased sector size). The multi remote tower enables a similar flexibility of balancing workload, which could be a key to adapt to human demands. Hence, adjusting the workload by increasing or decreasing the number of airports and aircrafts provides the scope to respond to monotonous working conditions.

For multi-mode, it could be interesting if shifting among and updating of several mental models is workload sensitive. Besides the higher amount of traffic in multi-mode, the increase in workload could support ATCO alertness. Increased alertness shows a potential chance for the multi-mode, since this could improve safety and working conditions.

2.3 Research Aim and Hypotheses

Research activities undertaken so far show an ambiguous picture on the expected effects of multi-mode to ATCO performance and related safety. The central aim of this study is to gain a better understanding of mental models and executive functions in multi remote tower.

Firstly, we hypothesize, that the ATCO develops a separate mental model for each airport in multi-mode. As the monitoring of multiple airports requires the shifting among and updating of the various mental models, we secondly hypothesize an increased ATCO workload in multi-mode. Thirdly, we hypothesize, that this increased workload causes reduced situational awareness, which can be regarded as 'shift costs'. Finally, we hypothesize that higher workload increases alertness, as there is less exposure of the ATCO to monotony.

3   Methods

Our approach bases on a Human-In-The-Loop simulation study that was chosen for gaining empirical evidence by observations and subjective questionnaires. A pivotal element of the simulation is to keep the traffic volume at an equal load across the single and multi-scenarios. This is to exclude any secondary variance induced by an added traffic load on workload and situational awareness.

3.1 Sample Characteristics

In the study, $n = 8$ licensed Swedish ATCOs (1 female) with a mean age of 48,8 years ($SD = 8,5$) and a mean work experience of 24,2 years ($SD = 8,1$) participated.

3.2 Apparatus

We conducted the study in the ATC research lab at the Area Control Centre in Malmö. The platform based on the NARSIM simulator that featured a high-fidelity simulation of a remote tower workplace. Video presentation of 14 simulated cameras was shown on six 55" wide-screen screens. A smaller, pan-tilt-zoom camera was shown in a picture in picture view for each airport. The pan-tilt-zoom camera could be operated by means of a control stick and buttons for pre-defined zoom levels and camera directions (Fig. 1).

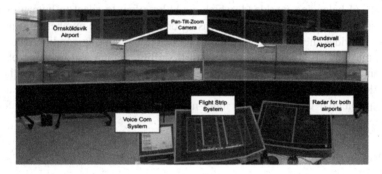

Fig. 1. Workplace during multi-mode, including left-right-split for outside view and screens.

3.3 Test Design and Scenarios

Within the study, participants controlled air traffic across two scenarios in four simulation runs; each run had a duration of 90 min. All runs followed a crossover-design for counter balancing confounding factors and to provide a design for within-subject comparison. The scenario set consisted of two runs in single- and two in multi-mode as independent variables. All scenarios shared the same amount of flights, weather figures and ground movements. Simulated flights compromised scheduled Instrument Flights (IFR) and non-scheduled Visual Flights (VFR). VFR-Flights performed touch-and-go and circling exercises. In multi-mode, traffic movements were split fairly over both airports, while in single-mode the traffic was handled at one airport. Calls of the adjoining control sector and from the meteorological department were simulated as well. Two pseudo pilots and one simulation operator ensured a realistic radio communication and aircraft behaviour during every run.

Prior to the first simulation run, a 90 min training run was conducted to ensure sufficient system knowledge and confidence. Before and after each experimental run, participants completed questionnaires.

3.4   Measured Variables

Situational Awareness was measured by means of the Situation Assessment Rating Technique (SART) [13], applied after each run. Workload was measured during and after every run. During simulation, the Instantaneous Self-Assessment (ISA) [14] was administered. It had to be completed every three minutes (indicated by a tone) and represents a workload self-rating. After the run, participants completed the NASA Task Load Index (NASA-TLX) [15]. Alertness was measured using the Karolinska Sleepiness Scale (KSS) [16] before and after each run.

4   Results

Pre-analysis of the data characteristics revealed a lack of normality (significant Kolmogorov-Smirnov-Test) and variance equality (significant Levene-Test). Mann-Whitney U-Tests were applied to analyse the data obtained from SART, ISA, NASA-TLX Raw and KSS.

4.1   Situational Awareness

Analysis of SART data revealed no differences between single- and multi-mode (global score, $U = 93.0$, $Z = -1.07$, $p = .283$; $U = 103.5$, $Z = -.658$, $p = .510$; supply, $U = 73.0$, $Z = -1.88$, $p = .060$; understanding, $U = 111.0$, $Z = -.362$, $p = .718$).

4.2   Workload

During each run, workload was measured every 3 min through ISA queries. Figure 2 shows the mean values with respect to both modes. The analysis revealed significant ($p < .05$) higher ratings in multi-mode in comparison to single-mode for $ISA_{Minute\ 48}$ ($U = 72.0$, $Z = -2.14$, $p = .033$) and $ISA_{Minute\ 51}$ ($U = 75.0$, $Z = -2.18$, $p = .029$).

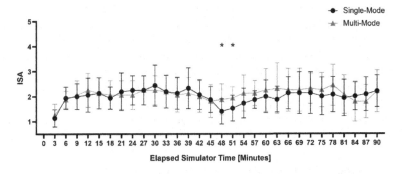

Fig. 2. Mean results of ISA values. Error bars represent standard deviation. *$p < .05$

Analysis of NASA-TLX Raw data revealed no significant difference between single- and multi-mode ($U = 95.5$, $Z = -.969$, $p = .338$).

4.3   Alertness

The analysis of KSS data indicated no differences between both groups in pre- and post-measurements (pre, $U = 103.5$, $Z = -.987$, $p = .324$; post, $U = 126.0$, $Z = -.059$, $p = .953$). In order to analyse for any changes over the time of the scenarios, a Wilcoxon-Signal Rank test was conducted. Analysis within every group revealed for single- and multi-mode no differences between pre and post measurements (single, $Z = -1.35$, $p = .177$; multi, $Z = -.302$, $p = .763$).

5   Discussion

The present study investigated the effects of shifting among and updating of mental models in single and multi-remote tower. Simulations with experienced ATCOs were conducted. Measures for situational awareness, workload and alertness were applied.

The results revealed no differences for workload and situational awareness between single and multi-mode. Shifting among and updating of two mental models in multi-mode did not lead to reduced situational awareness and increased workload. While this result is contrary to our hypothesis, this means nevertheless no additional risk for multi-mode. ATCOs were able to control a high traffic volume across both modes with good performance. The initial assumption, that multiple mental models are developed, needs to be rejected. Instead of developing two independent mental models for two airports, the ATCO is perhaps developing a common, hybrid mental model for both airports at a time, including a clear distinction between both airports. Since ATCOs are trained to work in high traffic situations, the participants had probably sufficient remaining cognitive capacity to handle traffic on both airports parallel and update a single mental model accordingly. Furthermore, as multi-mode featured the same traffic amount across two airports, less of control advices are necessary to keep traffic safely separated. This concerns especially the runway and airspace whose capacity was doubled in multi-mode on the expense of time separation between simultaneous landings. The added separation may lead to a reduced demand for situational awareness in multi-mode. A probable aspect to consider is behavioural adaption of the participants that may feel uncertain in multi-mode due to its novelty beyond the familiar working environment. This may hide any effects, which perhaps become evident on the long-run. Through a possible subjective feeling of a higher situational instability in multi-mode, participants may have checked more the surrounding area and concentrated more.

The hypothesis, that multi-mode increased workload which in turn leads to higher alertness cannot be confirmed. The shift costs per se was concludingly not a pivotal factor for workload. However, traffic amount and characteristics are dominant factors as demonstrated by the workload diagram during the snowstorm.

5.1   Conclusion: Safety Challenge or Safety Chance?

Based on the data gathered, shifting among und updating of mental models in multi remote tower should not be considered as a safety challenge. Shifting among mental models is, if existing, not as workload demanding, and hence situational awareness reducing and alertness increasing, as expected.

The indicated, workload is rather associated with traffic characteristics and volume. Multi remote tower will feature increased traffic volumes, that will have an effect on workload subsequently. While overload could lead to reduced situational awareness, slightly increased workload could act as a countermeasure for monotony, supporting alertness in turn [17]. Additionally, we did not measure long-term effects of working in both modes. This is from a great interest, since the hypothetical optimum of ATCO workload is dynamic and changes over time due to workload and shift work factors [18]. Moreover, a long-lasting strain due to constant shifting is associated with cognitive fatigue [19]. Taking together, a well-balanced mixture between under- and overload seems to be a key for safety and for operational implementation of multi remote tower. Here, a follow-up study to compare realistic traffic volumes in single- and multi-mode should be striven for.

Finally, we conclude, that multi remote tower still accommodates 'challenges' and further research should be performed to answer remaining questions. The 'chance' to overcome monotony and promote alertness by multi-mode is evident, however, it requires a careful workload management, that takes margins for individual variations and overload peaks due to emergencies into account.

References

1. Fürstenau, N., et al.: Steps towards the virtual tower: remote airport traffic control center (RAiCe). In: Proceedings EnRI International Workshop on ATM/CNS (2009)
2. Meyer, L., Peukert, M., Josefsson, B., Lundberg, J.: Validation of an empiric method for safety assessment of multi remote tower. In: Proceedings ATM2019 (2019)
3. Meyer, L., Fricke, H.: Validation of an empiric method for safety assessment of multi remote tower investigating the safety-relevance of limited distinctive features on a multi remote tower-working position. In: Proceedings ATM2016 (2016)
4. Moehlenbrink, C., Papenfuss, A., Jakobi, J.: The role of workload for work organization in a remote tower control center. Air Traffic Control Q. 20(1), 5–26 (2012)
5. Mogford, R.H.: Mental models and situation awareness in air traffic control. Int. J. Aviat. Psychol. 7(4), 331–341 (1997)
6. Kaber, D., Zhang, Y., Jin, S., Mosaly, P., Garner, M.: Effects of hazard exposure and roadway complexity on young and older driver situation awareness and performance. Transp. Res. Part F Traffic Psychol. Behav. 15(5), 600–611 (2012)
7. Morris, N., Jones, D.M.: Memory updating in working memory: the role of the central executive. Br. J. Psychol. 81(2), 111–121 (1990)
8. Oehme, A., Leitner, R., Wittbrodt, N.: Challenges of multiple airport control. Aviat. Psychol. Appl. Hum. Factors 3, 1–8 (2013)
9. Miyake, A., Friedman, N.P., Emerson, M.J., Witzki, A.H., Howerter, A., Wager, T.D.: The unity and diversity of executive functions and their contributions to complex "frontal lobe" tasks: a latent variable analysis. Cogn. Psychol. 41(1), 49–100 (2000)
10. Thackray, R.I., Bailey, J.P., Touchstone, R.M.: Physiological, subjective, and performance correlates of reported boredom and monotony while performing a simulated radar control task. In: Mackie, R.R. (ed.) Vigilance, pp. 203–215. Springer, Boston (1977). https://doi.org/10.1007/978-1-4684-2529-1_12

618 M. Peukert et al.

11. Straussberger, S., Schaefer, D.: Monotony in air traffic control. Air Traffic Control Q. 15(3), 183–207 (2007)
12. Thackray, R.I.: The stress of boredom and monotony: a consideration of the evidence. Psychosom. Med. 43(2), 165–176 (1981)
13. Taylor, R.M.: Situational awareness rating technique (SART): the development of a tool for aircrew systems design. In: Situational Awareness, pp. 111–128. Routledge (2017)
14. Jordan, C.S., Brennen, S.D.: Instantaneous Self-Assessment of Workload Technique (ISA). Defence Research Agency, Portsmouth (1992)
15. Hart, S.G., Staveland, L.E.: Development of NASA-TLX (Task Load Index): results of empirical and theoretical research. Adv. Psychol. 52, 139–183 (1988)
16. Åkerstedt, T., Gillberg, M.: Subjective and objective sleepiness in the active individual. Int. J. Neurosci. 52, 29–37 (1990)
17. Endsley, M.R.: Situation awareness in aviation systems. In: Garland, D.J., Wise, J.A., Hopkin, V.D. (eds.) Handbook of Aviation Human Factors, pp. 257–275. Lawrence Erlbaum Associates, Mahwah, NJ (1999)
18. Grech, M.R., Neal, A., Yeo, G., Humphreys, M., Smith, S.: An examination of the relationship between workload and fatigue within and across consecutive days of work: is the relationship static or dynamic? J. Occup. Health Psychol. 14(3), 231 (2009)
19. Matthews, G., Desmond, P.A.: Task-induced fatigue states and simulated driving performance. Q. J. Exp. Psychol. Sect. A 55(2), 659–686 (2002)

Communicating Issues in Automated Driving to Surrounding Traffic

How Should an Automated Vehicle Communicate a Minimum Risk Maneuver via eHMI and/or dHMI?

Julian Schindler[(✉)], Domenic Lysander Herbig, Merle Lau,
and Michael Oehl

German Aerospace Center (DLR), Lilienthalplatz 7, 38108 Brunswick, Germany
{julian.schindler,domenic.herbig,merle.lau,
michael.oehl}@dlr.de

Abstract. Cooperative automated vehicles (CAV) are not able to drive automated in all situations. Each vehicle has or is going to have its own operational design domain (ODD), which exactly specifies which situations can be handled, and which cannot. Vehicles of higher levels of automation according to SAE J3016 will try to take the driver back into the control loop if the vehicle approaches the border of its ODD by issuing a transition of control (ToC). If the driver is not responding, the vehicle will perform a minimum risk maneuver (MRM), where the CAV is stopping. Instead of looking at the internal HMI of single CAVs, the H2020 project TransAID focusses on the effects of automation limitations on traffic efficiency and safety. Besides helping the CAV to reduce negative impacts of such situations by infrastructure measures, also informing the surrounding vehicles about a CAV's current issues and about its plans to solve them will most likely improve such situations. To approach this assumption, DLR conducted a first virtual reality study, where e.g. a 360° externally mounted LED light-band as external HMI (eHMI) of a CAV and specific vehicle movements as dynamic HMI (dHMI) are used in case it needs to perform an MRM. In the study, ten participants tested different variants and combinations. Preliminary results show that the use of an eHMI is a useful and informative approach.

Keywords: Cooperative automated vehicles · Transition of control · Minimum risk maneuver · External HMI · Exploratory study

1 Introduction

Cooperative automated vehicles (CAV) will be introduced into so called mixed traffic environments, e.g., interacting in traffic with other manually driven vehicles, cyclists or pedestrians, and therefore CAVs must be able to communicate with other traffic participants (TP) [1]. Whereas in SAE level 1 or 2 [2], the driver is still required to intervene if the operational design domain (ODD) is malfunctioning, in SAE level 3 and beyond, the driver becomes more and more decoupled from the manual driving

© Springer Nature Switzerland AG 2020
C. Stephanidis et al. (Eds.): HCII 2020, CCIS 1294, pp. 619–626, 2020.
https://doi.org/10.1007/978-3-030-60703-6_79

task and more demanding actions need to be made if a transition of control (ToC) is needed due to system failure [2]. If there is no response by the driver during a ToC, the vehicle automation will (in level 3 optionally, in level 4 and above mandatory) stop the CAV due to safety reasons executing a so called Minimum Risk Maneuver (MRM) [2]. If this MRM is not communicated to other TP, an MRM has fatal consequences in terms of traffic efficiency as well as safety issues, esp. when the vehicle is simply stopping on the driving lane [3]. Therefore, this information needs to be communicated to the surrounding traffic environment in order to achieve a safe and sound collaboration of all TP.

To ensure this, external and dynamic Human-Machine Interfaces (HMI) represent promising approaches [4]. An external Human-Machine Interface (eHMI) serves as a communication tool to transmit implicit and explicit signals to its surrounding traffic environment [4, 5] (Fig. 1).

Fig. 1. External LED light-band on a CAV as eHMI used in the EU project interACT [6].

Apart from the communication of MRMs, recent research developed several eHMI designs to face the challenge of technological progress while taking traffic communication patterns into account, e.g., light-strips on the surface of a vehicle, displays and laser projections [5, 7]. As one example, displays positioned on the vehicle's front mostly use symbols or text in order to communicate with other TP [8]. Furthermore, laser projections are suggested that project information about the CAV's status and willingness to cooperate with other TP on the road surface [9]. One promising approach within this context are light-strips on a CAV's surface that can transmit information about the CAV's behavior through different light patterns, e.g., flashing and pulsing [1, 10]. In the EU H2020 project interACT, a 360° LED light-band eHMI with color-coded interaction design was developed that is able to transmit information about the CAV's perception (i.e., the detection of other TPs) and the CAV's intention (i.e., next maneuver) to other TPs. Results show that the LED light-band works well for the interaction between CAV and pedestrians or CAV and manually driven cars in urban scenarios [6].

Another way of communication used by a CAV to transmit implicit signals to its traffic environment is a dynamic Human-Machine Interface (dHMI), i.e. the CAV communicates with its surrounding environment via the vehicles' motion patterns in terms of translatory and rotational dynamics [5]. A study by Beggiato et al. [12] focusing on the interaction between CAV and pedestrians showed that motion parameters (i.e., deceleration rate) can influence the gap acceptance. Latest research on lane changing and merging processes emphasize the consideration of motion patterns showing that other drivers need to be informed about the CAV's behavior and intention to cooperate and to perform a safe maneuver [13].

So far, eHMI and dHMI communication designs in terms of critical traffic situations, e.g., MRM, have not been sufficiently studied. Therefore, the present study focuses on the consideration of different communication strategies, i.e., eHMI and/or dHMI, in the case of a MRM. Within this context, this study follows an exploratory approach to shed some light on the design of eHMI/dHMI for MRM and it can be seen as a first step in the user-centered design process investigating CAV's possibilities of different communication strategies for transmitting information to other TPs when an MRM needs to be executed by the CAV.

2 Method

The sample included in total N = 10 participants (4 male; 6 female). All of them were between 19 and 35 years old (M = 23.2; SD = 5.5). All participants possessed a valid German driver's license. 80% of the participants had an annual mileage of at least 7,000 km per year, half of them more than 15,000 km per year (M = 14,350 km; SD = 9,928 km; Min = 4,000 km; Max = 35,000 km). All participants were interested in automated driving, with the largest proportion of the sample indicating a very strong interest (M = 5.7; SD = 1.7) on a Likert scale from 1 = 'not at all' to 6 = 'very much'. Only two participants had previous experiences with similar studies before. 80% of the participants had experiences with gaming and VR systems. The participants received an expense allowance of 10 € per hour.

Following a within subject design, participants experienced in a randomized order six different scenarios in virtual environment using VR glasses, being the driver of a manually driven car following a CAV until the CAV performed an MRM (Fig. 2).

Each scenario presents a different communication strategy to the driver (Table 1). Scenario 1 was used as baseline condition in which no information was provided to the driver. In scenario 2, the driver was informed by the CAV showing hazard warning lights as a kind of traditional eHMI. In scenario 3, the CAV transmitted information via an LED light band eHMI which flashed constantly. In scenario 4, a dHMI was used transmitting information by the CAV driving waving lines in the street. Scenario 5 was a combination of hazard warning lights (scenario 2) and the dHMI (Scenario 4). Moreover, scenario 6 combined the LED light-band eHMI (Scenario 3) and the dHMI (Scenario 4).

Fig. 2. Use case of the present study in virtual environment.

Table 1. Driving scenarios presented to the participants focusing on the CAV's different communication strategies.

Scenario	Communication strategy	Description
1	Baseline	CAV does not inform
2	eHMI 1 (traditional)	CAV informs by hazard warning lights
3	eHMI 2 (new)	CAV informs by the LED light-band constantly flashing
4	dHMI	CAV informs by driving waving lines
5	Combination eHMI 1 + dHMI	CAV informs by hazard warning lights + driving waving lines
6	Combination eHMI 2 + dHMI	CAV informs by LED light-band constantly flashing + driving waving lines

In Fig. 3, examples of the communication strategies in the presented scenarios above are displayed. After each run, the participants were asked to rate the usability of the six communication strategies. This was assessed by the Van der Laan acceptance scale [14] and items out of the standardized UEQ [15]. For the subscale 'usefulness' of the acceptance scale the values range between −2 and 2. For the perceived information content, we used items of the UEQ ranging from −3 to +3. A higher score represented that the participant assessed the scenario (or better the communication strategy) as more useful or informing respectively. In addition to that, the participants were asked at the end of the experiment to rank all communication strategies according to their preference.

Fig. 3. Communication strategies in scenario 1 (top left), scenario 2 (top right), scenario 3 (bottom left), and scenario 6 (bottom right).

3 Results

In the following, the results of the ratings of the acceptance scale's subscale 'usefulness' and the perceived information content for all six communication strategies (scenarios) are reported. The descriptive results and the participants' preference rankings of all communication strategies are presented (Table 2).

For the participants rated 'usefulness' of the communication strategies for conveying an MRM highest ratings were obtained by the both eHMI versions. Lowest ratings obtained baseline and dHMI. Participants were rather indecisive for both combinations of eHMI and dHMI. However, for all six different communication strategies standard deviations were quite high indicating larger variability of participants' ratings for each communication type. Non-parametric Friedman tests were used for analyzing the data due to violated normal distributions. Results showed that the participants' mean acceptance ratings for 'usefulness' differed significantly between the communication strategies ($\chi^2(5) = 24.6$, p = .00). Post-hoc Dunn-Bonferroni tests show that the mean acceptance rating for 'usefulness' differ significantly for scenario 1 compared to scenario 2 (z = −3.2, p = .02) and scenario 3 (z = −3.0, p = .04), with showing the highest rating for scenario 2 (M = 1.0; SD = 0.7). Furthermore, post-hoc tests show significant differences for scenario 4 compared to scenario 2 (z = 3.6, p = .00) and scenario 3 (z = 3.5, p = .01), with presenting the highest rating for scenario 2. All other comparisons showed no significant differences (n.s.).

Regarding the mean perceived information, content ratings of the communication strategies for conveying an MRM, highest ratings were obtained by both eHMI versions, especially eHMI 2 (new). Lowest ratings obtained baseline and dHMI. Again, participants were rather indecisive for both combinations of eHMI and dHMI. These ratings are in line with the 'usefulness' ratings. Moreover, again for all six different communication strategies standard deviations were quite high again indicating larger variability of participants' ratings for each communication type. Non-parametric Friedman tests showed significant differences between the communication strategies ($\chi^2(5) = 23.4$, p = .00). Post-hoc Dunn-Bonferroni tests show that the mean perceived information content differ significantly for scenario 3 compared to scenario 1 ($z = -3.7, p = .00$) and scenario 4 ($z = 3.8, p = .00$) with the highest rating for scenario 3 (M = 1.5; SD = 1.2). All other comparisons showed no significant differences (n.s.).

Finally, with regard to the forced choice preference rankings of the six different communication strategies we found the same pattern again as before in the other ratings. Here the results indicated that both eHMI strategies (eHMI 2 as best and eHMI 1 as second best) were placed first and second best according to their mean ranks, whereas the baseline and dHMI were ranked as lowest. The combinations of both eHMI and dHMI were ranked third and fourth.

Table 2. Participants' mean ratings (M; SD) for acceptance (usefulness), perceived information content and preference ranking of the scenarios/communication strategies.

Scenario	Communication strategy	U		I		Rank
		M	SD	M	SD	
1	Baseline	−1.1	0.8	−1.7	1.5	5.3
2	eHMI 1 (traditional)	1.0	0.7	1.0	1.5	2.2
3	eHMI 2 (new)	0.8	0.9	1.5	1.2	2.1
4	dHMI	−0.9	0.8	−1.6	1.6	5.3
5	Combination eHMI 1 + dHMI	−0.1	1.2	0.1	1.9	2.9
6	Combination eHMI 2 + dHMI	0.3	1.3	0.5	1.5	3.2

Note. U = Usefulness (−2 to +2), I = Information Content (−3 to +3), Rank of preference (1 = best to 6 = worst)

4   Conclusion

The question how a CAV could communicate a MRM to other traffic participants via eHMI and/or dHMI is hardly studied yet. Within this context, this study follows an exploratory approach to shed some light on the design of eHMI/dHMI for MRM and it aimed at making a first step in the user-centered design process towards a CAV's possible communication strategies for transmitting information to other TPs when an MRM needs to be executed by the CAV.

With regard to the preference rankings the study showed that participants prefer eHMI communication strategies, especially the new eHMI 2, over not having any eHMI. The same pattern was found for the acceptance scale 'usefulness' as well as for the rated information content of the presented communication strategies. Here, the both eHMI (eHMI 1, eHMI 2) communication strategies were ranked significantly higher compared to the baseline, i.e., having no eHMI or dHMI. In summary, compared with all other presented communication strategies the LED light-band as new eHMI 2 was rated highest by participants.

Nevertheless, all ratings included high standard deviations resulting from participants' heterogeneous answers. This is an indication that more research and especially more participants are required in this area probably combined with qualitative research to grasp this variance. In terms of eHMI, this research should also include lane changes when performing MRMs, e.g., when the vehicle is not simply stopping on the lane but changing to a safe spot position or the emergency lane. In this case the usage of hazard warning lights (eHMI 1) prohibits the direction indication of the vehicle which is using the same lights for all emergency issues. Here, LED light-bands (eHMI 2) may enable their full potential when used properly, e.g., in combination with standard direction indication using indicator lights, or in an animated way.

Furthermore, the appropriate color, brightness and pattern (e.g., pulsing, flashing, dynamically animated) of the LED light-band are important factors. While in the study a pulsing bright orange-red has been chosen for the MRM, this may be confused with the strobe lights of emergency vehicles in some countries.

Equally, dHMI needs to be composed and parametrized in a very careful and tentative way. In case of this study, the dHMI has been designed using the simple pattern of driving in waving lines. Here, both the amplitude and the frequency of the waves will have large impact on visibility and perceived criticality. In addition, the impact of driving in waving lines in already complex situations needs to be investigated in terms of safety. This applies as well for the complex interplay of both dHMI and eHMI.

Therefore, as the present study follows a first exploratory approach, the results can be identified as first outlook on how a CAV could communicate a performed minimum risk maneuver.

 Acknowledgements. The TransAID project has received funding from the European Union's Horizon 2020 research and innovation programme under grant agreement No 723390.

References

1. Habibovic, A., et al.: Communicating intent of automated vehicles to pedestrians. Front. Psychol. **9**, 1336 (2018). https://doi.org/10.3389/fpsyg.2018.01336
2. Society of Automotive Engineers: Taxonomy and definitions for terms related to driving automation systems for on-road motor vehicles. SAE, Michigan (J3016_201806) (2018)
3. Maerivoet, S., et al.: TransAID deliverable 4.2 - preliminary simulation and assessment of enhanced traffic management measures (2019)
4. Schieben, A., Wilbrink, M., Kettwich, C., Madigan, R., Louw, T., Merat, N.: Designing the interaction of automated vehicles with other traffic participants: design considerations based on human needs and expectations. Cogn. Technol. Work **21**(1), 69–85 (2018). https://doi.org/10.1007/s10111-018-0521-z
5. Bengler, K., Rettenmaier, M., Fritz, N., Feierle, A.: From HMI to HMIs: towards an HMI framework for automated driving. Information **11**(2), 61 (2020). https://doi.org/10.3390/info11020061

6. Schieben, A., et al.: Testing external HMI designs for automated vehicles - an overview on user study results from the EU project interACT, vol. 9. Tagung Automatisiertes Fahren, Munich, Germany (2019)
7. Bazilinskyy, P., Dodou, D., de Winter, J.: Survey on eHMI concepts: the effect of text, color, and perspective. Transp. Res. Part F Traffic Psychol. Behav. **67**, 175–194 (2019). https://doi.org/10.1016/j.trf.2019.10.013
8. Clamann, M., Aubert, M., Cummings, M.L.: Evaluation of vehicle-to-pedestrian communication displays for autonomous vehicles. In: 96th Annual Research Board Meeting, Washington, D.C., pp. 6–12 (2017)
9. Dietrich, A., Willrodt, J.-H., Wagner, K., Bengler, K.: Projection-based external human machine interfaces-enabling interaction between automated vehicles and pedestrians. In: Proceedings of the DSC 2018 Europe VR, Antibes, France (2018)
10. Sorokin, L., Chadowitz, R., Kauffmann, N.: A change of perspective. In: Brewster, F., et al. (ed.) Proceedings of the CHI Conference 2019, pp. 1–8, Glasgow, Scottland (2019)
11. Habibovic, A., Andersson, J., Nilsson, M., Lundgren, V.M., Nilsson, J.: Evaluating interactions with non-existing automated vehicles: three Wizard of Oz approaches. In: IEEE Intelligent Vehicles Symposium, pp. 32–37 (2016)
12. Beggiato, M., Hartwich, F., Schleinitz, K., Krems, J., Othersen, I., Petermann-Stock, I.: What would drivers like to know during automated driving? Information needs at different levels of automation. In: 7th Conference on Driver assistance, Munich, Germany (2017)
13. Kauffmann, N., Winkler, F., Naujoks, F., Vollrath, M.: "What makes a cooperative driver?" Identifying parameters of implicit and explicit forms of communication in a lane change scenario. Transp. Res. Part F Traffic Psychol. Behav. **58**, 1031–1042 (2018). https://doi.org/10.1016/j.trf.2018.07.019
14. Van der Laan, J.D., Heino, A., De Waard, D.: A simple procedure for the assessment of acceptance of advanced transport telematics. Transp. Res. Part C **5**(1), 1–10 (1997)
15. Laugwitz, B., Held, T., Schrepp, M.: Construction and evaluation of a user experience questionnaire. In: Holzinger, A. (ed.) USAB 2008. LNCS, vol. 5298, pp. 63–76. Springer, Heidelberg (2008). https://doi.org/10.1007/978-3-540-89350-9_6

Analysis of Human Factors in Satellite Control Operation During Equipment Failure

Huiyun Wang[1,2], Mo Wu[1,2,3], and Jingyu Zhang[1(✉)]

[1] Institute of Psychology, CAS Key Laboratory of Behavioral Science,
16 Lincui Road, Chaoyang District, Beijing 100101, China
zhangjingyu@psych.ac.cn
[2] Department of Psychology, University of the Chinese Academy of Sciences,
19 Yuquan Road, Shijingshan District, Beijing 100049, China
[3] Beijing Satellite Navigation Center, Beijing, China

Abstract. The satellite navigation system provides continuous, timely, and precise temporal-spatial information signals to users all over the world. Although modern satellite systems, such as GPS and Beidou, are highly autonomous, human supervision and control still play an important role in the normal functioning of the system, especially when certain parts of the system break down. Therefore, it is vital for improving the response and disposal efficiency of equipment failures. This study used real documents to examine how human factors affected the recovery process of the system. The actual data of this study came from the log files of a ground control center of the Beidou satellite navigation system. In total, 169 records of the fault handling process of an uplink equipment were of particular interest in the present study. We collected the malfunction information, including the technical description of the failure, the time it took place, the information of the team on shift, and the task completion times of two different stages (fault judgment and recovery operation). We then transformed this information into task complexity, time of day, shift handover period, and operator team skill composition as the independent variables, while the judgment time and operation time were used as the dependent variables. Multiple regression analysis showed that task complexity is the most significant predictor of the two completion times. More complex tasks took longer time to finish. Moreover, it took more time to finish the recovery operation when the time was 16:00–18:00, and when the most adept team member on shift lacked relevant expertise. Based on the results, we made corresponding suggestions for both management and interface design.

Keywords: Satellite navigation system · Human factors · Fault handling

1 Introduction

Satellite navigation system (SNS) is important for a modern society for it can provide continuous, timely, and precise timing, position, and navigation service to users all over the world [1]. Like many other complex systems, SNS is already highly automatic, yet human supervision is still vital, especially when certain equipment failure occurs.

© Springer Nature Switzerland AG 2020
C. Stephanidis et al. (Eds.): HCII 2020, CCIS 1294, pp. 627–632, 2020.
https://doi.org/10.1007/978-3-030-60703-6_80

When a certain instrument, among the many thousands on a satellite, has a failure, quick discovery and recovery are key for the system's effectiveness.

Previous studies have found many human factors may influence the fault handling process of operators. However, most studies used data from either pre-operation evaluation or self-reported measurement [2, 3], except for a few [1]. In this study, we aimed to expand a previous study [1] using log file data to investigate how task complexity, time of day, shift period, and team expertise may influence the fault handling process of the Beidou satellite.

The Chinese Beidou satellite navigation system (BDS) is one of the four SNSs in the world, in addition to US-owned GPS, EU-owned GALILEO, and Russia-owned GLONASS. We collected 169 records from the ground control center of the Beidou satellite navigation system on the fault handling process of a particular type of equipment to understand the underline human factors that may influence the Satellite Control Operation during equipment failure.

The operational control of BDS is managed by the navigation service control center (NSCC) and the satellite platform control center (SPCC). The two centers have different functions but work together in a sequential and dependant manner. In case of an equipment failure, the operators at NSCC will first receive the alarm and have to check the alarm, conduct an early diagnosis to figure out the location of the failure, and report it to the operators at SPCC. This process is called the failure judgment stage. Receiving the notification from NSCC, the operators at SPCC will then conduct further diagnosis and manual operations to recover the onboard equipment, which is called the onboard diagnosis and recovery stage. In certain circumstances, the operators and SPCC will further ask NSCC operators to do some software reinitiation (which is not relevant in the current study, for details, see [1]). In this study, we collected the log files of NSCC, in which the two completion times (T1 for the first stage and T2 for the second stage) are recorded in addition to the technical details of the failure, the time the incidents happened, and the team composition of NSCC operators on shift. In this way, such data can be used to identify the possible influential human factors.

2   Method

2.1   The Nature of the Equipment Failure

In this study, we focused on the failures of a particular type of uplink equipment. For confidential reasons, the specificity of the equipment was not revealed, but such equipment is vital for the normal functioning of the satellite. Indeed, the fault of this equipment is not quite difficult to handle, but it should be done in a timely manner, so correct early diagnosis (by NSCC operators) is important, which may also have a certain carryon effect on the operation of SPCC operators. We collected 169 cases of these failures, which accounted for 26.2% of all faults (639 records), suggesting such failure is also quite common.

2.2 Dependent Variables

The judgment time (T1) and the operation time (T2) were used as the dependent variables. T1 referred to the length of time from the operator in the NSCC detected the alarm sound to the time when the operator sent the request to the SPCC operators. T2 referred to the length of time from the SPCC received the notification from NSCC until the satellite platform was fully recovered.

2.3 Independent Variables

Task complexity. Through expert interviews and analysis of fault recovery process and operation steps, the task complexity was determined by two factors: the number of fault modules and the location of the satellite when the fault occurs [4]. According to the above two factors, the task complexity of navigation fault handling was divided into three levels:

Level 1. Only module A fails, and the satellite was within the visual range of navigation service control center.

Level 2. Module A and module B failed at the same time, and the satellite was in the visible range. Or only module A was faulty, and the satellite was out of the visible range.

Level 3. Both module A and module B fail at the same time, and the satellite was beyond the visual range of navigation service control center.

Time of Day. In our study, the time of day was analyzed by examining the differences among the 12 two-hour time periods in a whole day, starting from 0:00–2:00 to 22:00–24:00. Using the time period 8:00–10:00 as the reference, eleven dummy variables were created and used in the regression analysis.

Shift Handover Period. The shift handover period was coded as "1" if it fell into the specified period (30 min before or after the shift handover time at 8:30 and 16:30, that is, 8:00–9:00 and 16:00–17:00, respectively) and as "0" if it was another time. We assumed that when an unexpected fault occurs during the shift handover, the processing time would be prolonged.

Highest Skill Level in the Shift Team. All on-shift operators' skill levels were evaluated on the three-point scale from Level 1 to Level 3 based on their major and past experience in relation to performing the diagnosis of this particular equipment. An operator is score level 1 if his major was not relevant and had not much direct experience, while scored level 3 if his major was very relevant and had often been in charge of similar situations. As a previous study has found the skill level of the most adept team member was the best predictor of the completion time, we used the highest value of the shift team in our further analysis.

3   Result

3.1   Differences of T1 and T2 Across Three Task Complexity Levels

We first conducted an one-way ANOVA to examine the difference of T1 and T2 across the three Task Complexity levels. It was found that higher task complexity level was linked with longer T1 (Judgement time) (F (2,166) = 7.988, p < .001), and longer T2 (Operation time), F (2,166) = 10.943, p < .001), respectively. The post-hoc test showed that for T1, the differences between level 1 and level 3 (M_D = −3.47, p < .001) and between level2 and level 3(M_D = - 3.32, p < .001) reached significance. For T2, the differences between level1 and level2 (M_D = - 8.52, p < .001), level 1 and level 3 (M_D = −11.94, p < .001) reached significance.

3.2   Regression Analysis

To synthesize the findings and adequately control possible confounding variables, hierarchical regression analyses were conducted, and the results were shown in Table 1.

Table 1. The difference between the time and level

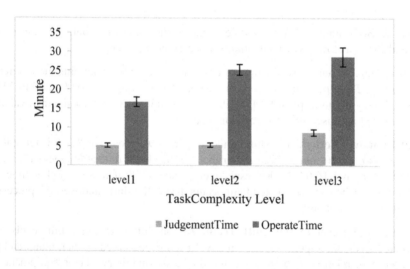

In predicting T1, the whole model was non-significant, but task complexity can significantly predict T1 (β = .25, p < .001). In predicting T2, the whole model was significant, F (14, 154) = 3.44, p < .001, and all variables accounted for 24% of the total variance of the operating time. It was found task complexity was a significant predictor of T2 (β = .34, p < .001). In addition, it was found that more time was spent when the breakdown happened between 16:00–18:00 as compared with 8:00–10:00

(β = .24, p < .05). Finally, if the most adept operator in NSCC had higher skill level, the operation time at SPCC could be reduced (β = $-.19$, p < .05) (Table 2).

Table 2. The regression analyses of the two stages

Independent variables	T1 (Judgement time)	T2 (Operation time)
1. Task Complexity	$.25^{**}$	$.34^{***}$
2. Shift handover Period$^+$	.02	$-.02$
3. Highest team skill level	$-.07$	$-.19^*$
Time of day		
4. 0:00–2:00	$-.14$	$-.02$
5. 2:00–4:00	.04	.08
6. 4:00–6:00	$-.06$	.05
7. 6:00–8:00	$-.00$	.06
8. 8:00–10:00++	–	–
9. 10:00–12:00	.05	.11
10. 12:00–14:00	$-.07$	$-.14$
11. 14:00–16:00	$-.08$	$-.03$
12. 16:00–18:00	$-.08$	$.24^*$
13. 18:00–20:00	$-.05$	.01
14. 20:00–22:00	$-.16$	.14
15. 22:00–24:00	$-.04$	$-.07$
R^2	.11	.24
F	1.35	3.44^{***}

* Significant at .05 level, ** Significant at .01 level, *** Significant at .001 level + Shift handover Period was coded as 1 when the time is 30 min within shift handover, as 0 if it is out of this period; ++ referenced category

4 Conclusion and Discussion

The purpose of this study is to explore the influence of task complexity, shift period, time of day, and team skill composition on the fault handling and recovery process of the Beidou satellite navigation system. Based on the 169 records from log files of a ground control center, we found that task complexity was the most significant predictor of the judgment time (T1) and the operation time (T2). The more complex the task, the longer time to conduct the work, regardless of the stage. In addition, we found the operation time (T2) can be influenced by time of day; it is interesting to note the longest operation occurred during 16:00–18:00. One possible explanation is that this is the most tiring period of the day shift, plus it was close to supper. Moreover, another more interesting finding was that the highest skill level of NSCC could predict the operation time of SPCC. Such carry-over effect suggested that there is a high level interdependency among the two centers and the failure of early diagnosis caused by non-proficient teams (rather than the response time of the first stage) may result in troubles for later operations.

This research expands previous studies and has implications in several ways. First, we replicated the findings that task complexity plays an important role. Since task complexity is the strongest predictor of fault processing time, it is necessary to reduce task complexity from the aspects of simplifying operation process, improving interface availability of instruments and equipment, etc. Second, we found the time period may have certain effects, but further studies are needed to understand the underline mechanisms. Finally, the carry-over effect we found in our study has two implications. On the one hand, the expertise composition of personnel on duty is important, so the team must be carefully trained and arranged. Rotational training might be useful. On the other hand, since the performance of the two centers are highly correlated, a more careful communication system and performance evaluation system are needed.

References

1. Wu, M., Zhang, L., Li, W.-C., Wan, L., Lu, N., Zhang, J.: Human performance analysis of processes for retrieving Beidou satellite navigation system during breakdown. Front. Psychol. **11** (2020). https://doi.org/10.3389/fpsyg.2020.00292
2. Littlepage, G.E., Hein, M.B., Moffett, R.G., Craig, P.A., Georgiou, A.M.: Team training for dynamic cross-functional teams in aviation. Hum. Fact. J. Human Fact. Ergon. Soc. **58**(8), 1275–1288 (2016)
3. Wang, Y., et al.: BDS and GPS stand-alone and integrated attitude dilution of precision definition and comparison. Adv. Space Res. **63**(9), 2972–2981 (2019)
4. Martin, K., et al.: The impact of environmental stress on cognitive performance: a systematic review. Human Fact. J. Human Fact. Ergon. Soc. (2019), https://doi.org/10.1177/0018720819839817

Design and Development of an Integrated Development Environment for the Driving Simulation Software Mave

Andreas Weisenburg[✉], Arthur Barz[✉], and Jan Conrad

HCI2B Group, Facility of Computer Science and Micro Systems Technology,
Hochschule Kaiserslautern – University of Applied Sciences,
Zweibruecken, Germany
{andreas.weisenburg,arthur.barz,jan.conrad}@hs-kl.de

Abstract. At the University of Applied Sciences Kaiserslautern, empirical user interface studies in the automotive sector are being conducted at the driving simulation environment K3F. To improve the workflow, the driving simulation software Mave is being developed specifically designed for the setup of empirical automotive studies. A major problem is the use of different technologies for the realization of the different study components. Driving tasks are implemented via scripts; user interfaces are based on Web UI components and virtual environments are defined by several geographic data formats. The sum of these technologies is difficult to handle if a user does not have in-depth technical knowledge. The goal of this contribution is to design and develop an integrated development environment that makes it easier for new users to get started with each of these elements and to make further work more efficient. An easier start is possible by providing many example scenarios that solve different tasks. Working on own scenarios is simplified through an integrated documentation and context-aware code completion. In addition, error sources are reduced by a syntactic validation of code.

Keywords: Integrated development environment · Driving simulation · Scripting

1 Introduction

The steadily increasing use of driving simulations for the implementation of empirical user studies is coupled with increasing possibilities of software solutions. Depending on the study question to be addressed, the software must be capable of creating very different driving tasks. However, this increases the complexity of the software and its user interface. An automotive study contains one or more driving tasks including their own sequences and events like changing the lane on a highway with heavy traffic. The addressed study question may require to adapt these very accurately to the requirements of the study. The virtual vehicle used by the test persons for the driving tasks may have to be customized for the respective purpose. In some cases, the virtual environment is also predefined. Simulation software may provide tools for this as well. Optionally, graphical user interface elements such as study menus or special visual control

© Springer Nature Switzerland AG 2020
C. Stephanidis et al. (Eds.): HCII 2020, CCIS 1294, pp. 633–638, 2020.
https://doi.org/10.1007/978-3-030-60703-6_81

elements can be created. They are used, for example, to display information to the subject or to organize several driving sessions of a study.

Allowing the flexible customization of all these components in a driving simulation software results in an increasingly complex usability for the study setup. This requires the development of a specially designed study development and setup environment.

2 Driving Simulation Framework Mave

The driving simulation framework Mave is part of the driving simulation project K3F [2] and is based on Unreal Engine 4, which was originally designed as a framework for the development of video games. Due to its performance and functionality, it is increasingly used as a platform for interactive 3D real-time applications including driving simulation [3, 5]. The framework is based on the programming language C++ and for the development of own software usually an API for this language is used. Alternatively, a visualized type of programming language called Blueprints is offered. Much of the functionality of the Unreal Engine can be accessed in a blueprint editor using visualized functional blocks. Mave provides a plug-in API that can be used to implement studies via blueprints, but this approach requires in-depth knowledge of computer graphics and the Unreal Engine itself. For this reason, an additional interface is offered to make the implementation of studies more efficient.

2.1 Study Scripting

Primarily the creation of a study scenario is done via a scripting interface. The scripting language Lua mainly developed by Roberto Ierusalimschy of the University of Rio de Janeiro is used for this purpose. This language is straightforward and has an easy to read syntax. It is also technically well suited because it is designed to be embedded and extended in other applications [4]. Inside Mave, the language is extended with functionalities that are specifically designed for use in driving simulation studies.

A study scenario in Mave consists of at least one script file. Project name, version and similar meta information are defined in this file. Subsequently, various elements such as courses, events, input and data collection of a study are specified. Initial instructions, such as loading files and creating environments and vehicles, are given at the start in the *OnStart* entry point. Repeated instructions can be made in the *Update* function. Triggers in the virtual environment can be used to define additional functions that are executed when certain conditions occur. Optionally, functionality can be moved to multiple script files. Figure 1 illustrates a driving task scenario utilizing these functionalities.

Other components of driving simulations are also implemented or controlled by means of scripting. Vehicles are provided with characteristics that are relevant to the study question. Virtual environments are created with the help of procedural generation using geographic data that can be edited by the user [1].

Fig. 1. Screenshot of a driving task including lane ideal line highlighting within Mave

2.2 Web Based Graphical User Interfaces

The creation of study scenarios may require the integration of graphical user interfaces into the study. Possible examples include study menus that coordinate the execution of several study sessions, displays in three-dimensional space such as head-up displays, or various information displays for test subjects. These are not solved with Lua scripts like other functionalities. The creation of any graphical user interface requires extensive and complex tools. In order to keep the initial effort low, it is therefore offered to create these interfaces with the help of Web UI frameworks and then display them in the simulation. This provides the user with a large selection of tools and sufficient documentation.

3 Integrated Development Environment

Integrated Development Environments (IDE) help developers create software using tools such as an editor for graphical user interfaces or debugging and testing written code. The framework Mave combines several technologies where a user is supported by a specialized, domain specific IDE. A simplified and assisted workflow shall guarantee an efficient creation of studies.

3.1 Project Setup

All files required for a driving simulation study are included in a project setup. Within the IDE, different files can be created and arranged in a folder structure. An overview of the project files is displayed in a tree view. Several files can be opened for editing at the same time and are listed in a tab view in the workspace. Tabs are highlighted in color when changes have been made to the corresponding file. Documentation including a manual, tutorials and code reference can be displayed optionally next to the workspace and is thus visible at any time during work. Shortcuts for common functions have been implemented for faster operation. Default settings can be modified as required or supplemented with your own shortcuts. Figure 2 provides a screenshot of the entire application.

Fig. 2. Screenshot of full Mave IDE

3.2 Code Editor

Most of the work for creating a study in Mave is done in the code editor. Many different text files, such as Lua, HTML, CSS and JavaScript, are modified in this editor. To assist the work with these different files, the editor provides functionality to avoid errors in the code and improve navigation and clarity.

- Search and Replace: A search function allows the user to search for terms within a file and replace them as required. Regular expressions can be used in this contex.
- Go to File: Using a dialog allows the user to search for a file in the project in order to open it directly. This accelerates the navigation in larger projects.
- Help on Mouse Over: If the mouse cursor is placed over an element, information such as the structure of the symbol, function signatures and documentation of the is displayed. The corresponding documentation can also be opened via shortcut.
- Context Sensitive Autocompletion: While users are entering code, the editor provides suggestions for automatic completion based on their input. Keywords, functions and custom symbols can be edited more efficiently and less error-prone due to automatic syntax completion. Figure 3 illustrates an example of context sensitive autocompletion.
- Code Snippets: When entering certain keywords, the editor offers the possibility to insert code snippets for the corresponding keyword. The input of variable elements of the code snippets is guided by an assistant.

Together with the documentation, these functionalities should ensure that users without programming knowledge have a quick start into the creation of driving simulation studies in Mave.

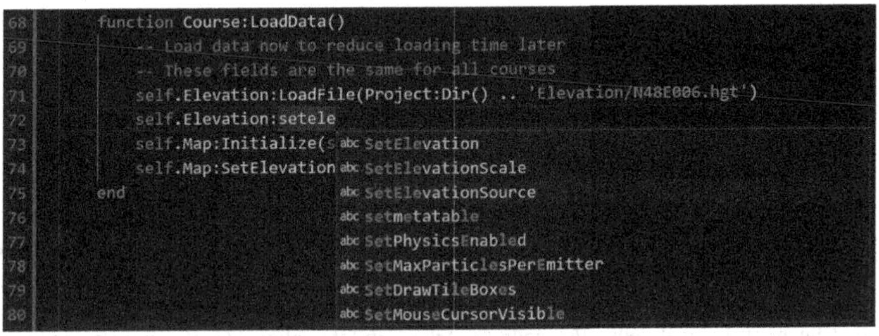

```lua
68    function Course:LoadData()
69        -- Load data now to reduce loading time later
70        -- These fields are the same for all courses
71        self.Elevation:LoadFile(Project:Dir() .. 'Elevation/N48E006.hgt')
72        self.Elevation:setele
73        self.Map:Initialize(s  abc SetElevation
74        self.Map:SetElevation abc SetElevationScale
75    end                       abc SetElevationSource
76                              abc setmetatable
77                              abc SetPhysicsEnabled
78                              abc SetMaxParticlesPerEmitter
79                              abc SetDrawTileBoxes
80                              abc SetMouseCursorVisible
```

Fig. 3. Code completion in mave

The development environment offers the possibility to start a test run of the simulation at any time. This way, study processes can be evaluated and iteratively improved after each modification. Test runs are started in a separate process, ensuring that the IDE is not affected if errors occur in the simulation.

3.3   Used Technology

The integrated development environment is implemented as a project in the Mave framework. The graphical user interface of the editor is based on the Web UI framework Angular. This enables the integration into Mave comparable to a study menu. Lua scripts with the same command set as driving simulation studies are used to implement parts of the application logic allowing seamless communication between the development environment and the scenarios created in it. At the same time, this approach enhances the functional scope and stability of the framework.

The core of the IDE is the Code Editor Monaco developed by Microsoft. It is also used in Visual Studio Code and provides many of the usual functionalities of a modern code editor. It is also designed for integration in Web applications.

4   Conclusion and Upcoming Features

The developed IDE already provides an improved workflow for the creation of study scenarios, but some aspects of the software are still incomplete. To provide a better user experience, more features will be added to the editor in upcoming releases. Code assist will be further improved and provided for all required languages. Monaco already provides this functionality for the languages TypeScript, JavaScript, CSS and HTML. The code assist capabilities for Lua scripting including the added functionality of Mave will be further improved. In order to further reduce programming errors during the editing of study code, scripts will be continuously checked for syntactical errors. Findings are highlighted in color and suggestions for possible corrections are offered. These will be provided with additional explanations to help users get accustomed to working with Mave. The number of incorrect test runs will also be reduced.

For an improved workflow during creation of graphical user interface elements with HTML files a live preview will be displayed. Errors are to be recognized and avoided as early as possible.

References

1. Barz, A., Conrad, J., Wallach, D.: Advantages of using runtime procedural generation of virtual environments based on real world data for conducting empirical automotive research. In: HCII 2020, Late Braking Papers (2020)
2. Conrad, J., Wallach, D., Barz, A., et al.: Concept simulator K3F. In: Janssen, C.P., Donker, S. F., Chuang, L.L., et al. (eds.) Proceedings of the 11th International Conference on Automotive User Interfaces and Interactive Vehicular Applications. Adjunct Proceedings, pp. 498–501. ACM, New York (2019)
3. Dosovitskiy, A., Ros, G., Codevilla, F., et al.: CARLA: An Open Urban Driving Simulator (2017)
4. Ierusalimschy, R., Figueiredo, L.H., de Filho, W.C.: Lua—an extensible extension language. Softw. Pract. Exper. **26**(6), 635–652 (1996)
5. Müller, M., Casser, V., Lahoud, J., Smith, N., Ghanem, B.: Sim4CV: a photo-realistic simulator for computer vision applications. Int. J. Comput. Vision **126**(9), 902–919 (2018). https://doi.org/10.1007/s11263-018-1073-7

A Language-Oriented Analysis of Situation Awareness in Pilots in High-Fidelity Flight Simulation

Alexia Ziccardi$^{(\boxtimes)}$ ⓘ, Kathleen Van Benthem ⓘ,
and Chris M. Herdman ⓘ

Carleton University, Ottawa, ON K1S 5B6, Canada
alexiaziccardi@cmail.carleton.ca, {kathyvanbenthem,
chrisherdman}@carleton.ca

Abstract. Situation awareness is needed to build dynamic mental models of the environment and contributes to safety during flight. Radio communications are key sources of information used by pilots to construct situation models. The present research investigated linguistic features of messages received during flight to understand aging effects on situation awareness. Fifty licensed pilots (age 17 to 71 years) flew a 60-min flight in a Cessna 172 simulator. Situation awareness was objectively measured throughout the flight. EEG was collected using a 14-channel wireless system and produced event-related and spectral indices of mental activity at key brain regions. Linguistic features of radio messages during flight were analyzed. Results showed significant deleterious effects of age on situation awareness. The linguistic features of messages, such as their pitch and intensity, were also associated with specific segments of the messages. EEG results supported the linguistic findings and indicate that age may impact later stages of the language processing pipeline. This research is important for informing efforts, such as the development of cockpit technologies to improve communication, that address older pilot safety.

Keywords: Linguistics · General aviation · Human-Computer Interaction · Neuroscience · Cognition · Aging

1 Introduction and Background

Situation awareness (SA) is a critical cognitive function employed by pilots for building mental models of the environment they are flying in. SA is the ability to acknowledge elements within an environment and their projections in the near future [1]. Maintaining up-to-date and accurate mental models is a key cognitive factor associated with flight safety. Radio communications among pilots provide important information required to build and add to their mental models regarding the location of other aircraft.

Most cognitive functions show typical age-related decline in pilot populations [2] and this decline is extended to SA [3]. Flight simulation studies find that older age is associated with lower levels of SA, for all three levels, as characterized by Endsley [1, 4]. Lower levels of SA (integrating auditory information) are also linked to increased

© Springer Nature Switzerland AG 2020
C. Stephanidis et al. (Eds.): HCII 2020, CCIS 1294, pp. 639–646, 2020.
https://doi.org/10.1007/978-3-030-60703-6_82

risk for critical incidents [4]. Negative effects of age on processing aurally presented information was found by Morrow et al. [5], who showed that air traffic controller information to pilots was reported back with less accuracy in older, as compared to younger pilots.

Of interest for this research was the process by which pilots perceive auditory information, encode its features into representations, and further recode it into mental maps. Specifically, this study investigated whether there were age-related issues at two key points in the auditory processing pipeline that may cause less robust mental models: namely, at the message feature level (pitch and intensity) and during middle to late neural encoding phases in the brain.

2 Methods

2.1 Participants

Licensed pilots were recruited from local flying schools and clubs, and via pilot associations. Participants were divided into a younger (n = 32, 17–54) and an older group (n = 18, 55–71). Pilots provided written informed consent and received refreshments and paid parking as compensation for their participation.

2.2 Procedure

Pilots flew an FTD-6 equivalent Cessna 172 simulator. The 60-min flight scenarios included circuit patterns, low-level flight over hilly terrain, and cross-country flight. Pilots were briefed with written and verbal instructions before the flight and at the half-way point. Pilots wore an EEG headset throughout the flight (see Fig. 1).

Radio calls from other aircraft were communicated throughout the flight path. There were 14 radio messages which contained information about other aircraft flying simultaneously (e.g., other pilot's aircraft type, call sign, location and intention). In addition, there were tones frequently presented randomly at intervals of 4–7-s throughout the flight, that were amplified from the two speakers, at the back of the aircraft. Pilots were instructed to pay attention to the radio messages, as well as to press a button on the yoke when they heard the tones. At the end of each leg, pilots were asked to indicate other aircraft locations on a map and report on the other details of the radio messages heard, including aircraft call sign, type (make or model), and intention (their planned future location).

Linguistic Analyses. Each communicated message was separated into its common components. These message segments included the call sign (of the addressing aircraft, n = 15), type (the make or model of the aircraft, n = 6), location (current position, n = 13) and the intention (planned actions, n = 14). The total number of cases in these analyses was 48. Linguistic variables included the average situation awareness scores based on the accuracy of recalled information pertaining to the call sign, type, location, and intention. Two other variables were created using Praat (an open source software package [6]) to investigate the overall pitch and intensity associated with each message segment. The Praat software decomposed the radio call spectrograms to extract the

Fig. 1. Participant in the Cessna 172 simulator with the 14-channel wireless EMOTIV EPOC + EEG headset.

average pitch as well as the average intensity (mean-energy intensity) for each segment of each radio call.

Electroencephalography Recording and Processing. The 14 electrodes were located in accord with the 10–20 international system (see Fig. 1). Electrodes P3 and P4 were the reference locations. The EEG recordings were collected at 2048 Hz and down-sampled to 256 Hz. Data was transmitted via proprietary Bluetooth technology to an iMac desktop computer. EMOTIV TestBench acquisition software enabled the recordings and signal quality monitoring to ensure that impedance levels were within the 10–20 kΩ range. The EEG acquisition software applied a bandwidth filter of .2 to 45 Hz before further processing was undertaken with the open source EEGLAB [7] software (run on MATLAB v. 2016). Independent component analysis (ICA) decomposed the raw EEG data to determine 14 independent components. Non-brain noise components, such as muscle and eye artifacts were removed from the data. The remaining data was used to conduct a source analysis using the Dipfit v 2.3. plugin for EEGLAB.

Event-related Potential (ERP) and Event-related Spectral Perturbation (ERSP) Analyses. During the recording, markers (triggers) were inserted into the EEG data via a stimulus presentation software (Psychopy 3.0) to mark the onset of the auditory tones. Epochs based on the onset of the tones were created at −2000 to +2000 ms. For 21 datasets with good ERPs, the Study function in EEGLAB created a grand average of the ERPs across all participants at selected electrode sites. Average ERSPs were created using fast-Fourier time-frequency transformation to determine the spectral power across the tone epoch for the 2–40 Hz frequency bands. Datasets were grouped according to age of participant (split at age 50-years) to permit the examination of age effects on neural responses to the tones (Fig. 2).

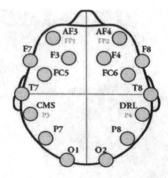

Fig. 2. The configuration of the EMOTIV EPOC+ EEG headset used for data collection in the Cessna 172 simulator [8].

3   Results

The first results presented are the situation awareness and linguistic analyses as related to the message segment factor. The outcome variables for this first section are the mean situation awareness scores for older and younger pilots for each of the radio call segments from the 14 radio messages and the mean pitch (perceived frequency) and intensity (perceived loudness) values for each of these message segments (N = 48) . The second section of the results examined the neural responses to the repeated tone stimuli which were presented while the pilots were simultaneously engaged in the flight tasks, including listening to the radio messages.

3.1   Situation Awareness Task

Univariate ANOVAs were conducted on the mean situation awareness scores corresponding to recall measures of each message segment for each age group. As shown in Fig. 3, in the younger group, there was a main effect of the message segment on the mean performance, $F(3, 47) = 26.883$, $p < 0.001$, $\eta_p^2 = 0.647$. Posthoc comparisons (Bonferroni) found that the main effect of the message segment was driven by significant differences between Call Sign (M = 0.74) and Type (M = 1.18) with Location (M = 1.64), $p < 0.05$. There was no significant difference between Intention (M = 1.16) and Type, $p > 0.1$. Also shown in Fig. 3, there were similar effects of the message segment in the older age group. In the older group, there was a main effect of the message segment on the mean performance, $F(3, 47) = 30.249$, $p < 0.001$, $\eta_p^2 = 0.673$. Posthoc comparisons (Bonferroni) found that the main effect of the message segment was driven by significant differences between Call Sign (M = 0.59) and Type (M = 0.78) with Location (M = 1.37), as well as Call Sign with Intention (M = 1.15), $p < 0.05$. There was no significant difference between Intention and Location, nor with Type and Call Sign, $p > 0.1$

For each message segment, paired t-tests were conducted to examine the effect of age on SA. The strongest effect of age was seen for Type, such that lower SA scores were seen in the older (M = 0.78) as compared to younger participants (M = 1.18),

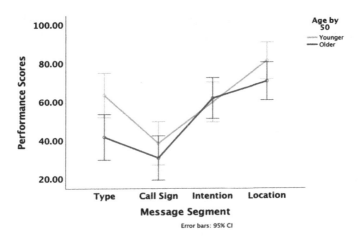

Fig. 3. Mean situation awareness performance

$t(5) = 9.83$, $p < .001$. Similar negative effects of age were seen for Call Sign and Location, $p < 0.05$. In contrast, there was no significant effect of age for intention $p > .1$.

3.2 Linguistic Analyses

Pitch. A Univariate ANOVA revealed an overall effect of the message segment on the average pitch, $F(3, 47) = 2.894$, $p < 0.046$, $\eta_p^2 = 0.165$. Posthoc analyses (Bonferroni) revealed that the average pitch of Type (M = 39 Hz) was significantly higher than that of Call Sign (M = 21 Hz), $p = 0.043$. Similarly, the average pitch for Type was higher than that of Location (M = 24.21), $p = 0.08$.

Intensity. A Univariate ANOVA revealed an overall marginal effect of the message segment on the average intensity, $F(3, 47) = 2.473$, $p < 0.074$, $\eta_p^2 = 0.144$. Posthoc analyses (Bonferroni) revealed that this effect was produced by greater intensity for Call Sign (M = 30.93 dB) as compared to Intention (M = 18 dB), $p = 0.076$.

3.3 ERP Analyses

The neural responses to repeated tone stimuli were investigated to understand how age affects the processing of auditory information during flight. An ERP analysis examined the allocation of neural resources for earlier auditory processing in older and younger pilots in the primary auditory cortices. The ERSP, using an ICA dipole fitting method, investigated tone-related perturbation in the parietal regions.

Auditory Cortex Tone Processing. Figure 4 illustrates the average ERP linked to the onset of the tones for both age groups in the left and right primary auditory cortex. In the left primary auditory cortex, there was no significant difference in the processing of the tone at any latency. We also see that in the right primary auditory cortex, there is a significant (p < 0.05) difference in the processing of the tone at the P200 such that older pilots have greater neural responses at this point at this stage in processing.

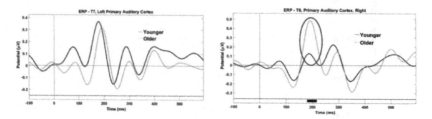

Fig. 4. Auditory cortex ERPs in the left (left ERP) and right cortex (right ERP).

ERSP. The ICA dipole fitting found there to be clusters of activity in the left parietal region. In Fig. 5. we see that around 250–300 ms there is greater neural activity in the younger participants that is greater than that of the older participants. This points to later-tonal processing along the auditory processing pipeline. The younger participants (see Fig. 5), in the beta range (20–25) show dedicated energy being put in tonal processing in which we do not see as intense in the aging group's data.

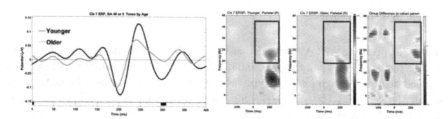

Fig. 5. ERP (left image) and ERSP (right image) at the left parietal region. The far-right image illustrates areas where age differences in the ERSP were observed (red cells are $p < 0.05$).

4   Discussion

The present research investigated age-effects of linguistic processing on situation awareness in pilots. It was hypothesized that older pilots would have lower situation awareness scores than younger pilots. Additionally, higher pitch was predicted to have a negative effect on pilot performance. Finally, tone-processing was expected to produce greater neuronal activation in earlier than in later cognitive auditory processing.

The first hypothesis, that older pilots would perform worse on SA tasks, was supported by the findings. These results are consistent with the aging literature. Bolstad [5] found that SA performance scores, in non-aviation related tasks, were lower for older individuals. In a similar analysis, Van Benthem, Enouy, and Herdman [9] also found that mental models based on auditory information were less robust in older aviators, although this age effect was attenuated by having greater recent flight hours.

Significant effects of the message segment were found on SA performance in both age groups, such that the Type and Call Sign scores were significantly lower than scores for Location. Linguistic analyses supported the second hypothesis, in that the message segment, Type, had a strikingly higher overall pitch than the other segments and illustrated the greatest differentiating performance results between pilot age groups. The impact of pitch suggests that message segments with higher pitch may disadvantage older pilots, since higher pitch is known to reduce auditory processing in older adults.

The ERP analyses showed that in the left primary auditory cortex, there were no significant differences in processing of tones. However, in the right primary auditory cortex there was a significant difference between groups at P200 such that older pilots showed greater neural responses at this stage of processing. These results could be associated with hemispheric lateralization of speech versus tone processing in the auditory cortex [10]. The ERSP analysis showed clusters of activity in the left parietal region in the younger participants that was greater than the activity of the older participants, pointing to age-related alterations in later stages of the auditory processing pipeline.

5   Conclusion

The results of this study suggest that there can be processing issues in the auditory processing pipeline. These processing issues can lead to critical issues related to processing radio messages and transforming these messages into aspects of mental models. The greatest effect seemed to be that higher pitch was linked with less accurate SA in older pilots. The findings of this research contribute to efforts investigating the role of aging in flight performance. Ideally, the findings can inform the development of technology and resources to address pilot safety

References

1. Endsley, M.: Design and evaluation for situation awareness enhancement. Proc. Hum. Factors Soc. Annual Meeting **32**, 97–101 (1988). https://doi.org/10.1177/154193128803200221
2. Hardy, D., Parasuraman, R.: Cognition and flight performance in older pilots. J. Exp. Psychol. Appl. **3**, 313–348 (1997). https://doi.org/10.1037/1076-898X.3.4.313
3. Bolstad, C.: Situation awareness: does it change with age? Proc. Hum. Factors Ergon. Soci. Ann. Meeting **45**, 272–276 (2001). https://doi.org/10.1177/154193120104500401
4. Van Benthem, K., Herdman, C.M.: A model of pilot risk: predicting critical incidents with situation awareness, prospective memory, and pilot attributes. Safety Science (2020, in press). https://doi.org/10.1016/j.ssci.2020
5. Morrow, D.G., Menard, W.E., Ridolfo, H.E., Stine-Morrow, E.A.L., Teller, T., Bryant, D.: Expertise, cognitive ability, and age effects on pilot communication. Int. J. Aviation Psychol. **13**(4), 345–371 (2003). https://doi.org/10.1207/S15327108IJAP1304_02
6. Boersma, P., Weenink, D.: Praat: doing phonetics by computer. http://www.praat.org/ (2018). Accessed 10 June 2020

7. Delorme, A., Makeig, S.: EEGLAB: an open source toolbox for analysis of single-trial EEG dynamics including independent component analysis. J. Neurosci. Methods **134**, 9–21 (2004)
8. EMOTIV.: Emotiv Epoc+ User Manual. https://emotiv.gitbook.io/epoc-user-manual/ (2018). Accessed 10 June 2020
9. Van Benthem, K., Enouy, S., Herdman, C.M.: The effects of recent pilot-in-command hours on situation awareness and critical incidents for pilots across the lifespan. In: Proceedings of CASI AERO 2019 (2019)
10. Tervaniemi, M., Hugdahl, K.: Lateralization of auditory-cortex functions. Brain Res. Rev. **43**, 231–246 (2003). https://doi.org/10.1016/j.brainresrev.2003.08.004
11. Schvartz-Leyzac, K., Chatterjee, M.: Fundamental-frequency discrimination using noise-band-vocoded harmonic complexes in older listeners with normal hearing. J. Acoust. Soc. Am. **138**, 1687–1695 (2015). https://doi.org/10.1121/1.4929938
12. He, N., Mills, J., Ahlstrom, J., Dubno, J.: Age-related differences in the temporal modulation transfer function with pure-tone carriers. J. Acoustical. Soc. Am. **124**, 3841–3849 (2008). https://doi.org/10.1121/1.2998779
13. Rosen, S.: Temporal information in speech: acoustic, auditory and linguistic aspects. Philos. Trans. Roy. Soc. Lond. Series B Biol. Sci. **336**, 367–373 (1992). https://doi.org/10.1098/rstb.1992.0070
14. Van Benthem, K., Herdman, C.M., Tolton, R.G., Barr, A.: Working memory, age, and experience influences on simulated critical incidents for general aviation pilots. Presentation at the 22nd Annual Meeting of the Canadian Society for Brain, Behaviour and Cognitive Science, University of Waterloo, Ontario, 7–9 June 2012 (2012)

Correction to: Meta-Analysis of Children's Learning Outcomes in Block-Based Programming Courses

Jen-I Chiu and Mengping Tsuei

Correction to:
Chapter "Meta-Analysis of Children's Learning Outcomes in Block-Based Programming Courses" in: C. Stephanidis et al. (Eds.): *HCI International 2020 – Late Breaking Posters*, CCIS 1294, https://doi.org/10.1007/978-3-030-60703-6_33

The originally published version of the chapter 33 contained a typesetting error in the Table 1. This has been corrected.

The updated version of this chapter can be found at
https://doi.org/10.1007/978-3-030-60703-6_33

Correction to: Users' Internal HMI Information Requirements for Highly Automated Driving

Merle Lau, Marc Wilbrink, Janki Dodiya, and Michael Oehl

Correction to:
Chapter "Users' Internal HMI Information Requirements
for Highly Automated Driving" in: C. Stephanidis et al. (Eds.):
HCI International 2020 – Late Breaking Posters, **CCIS 1294,**
https://doi.org/10.1007/978-3-030-60703-6_75

In an older version of this paper, there was error in figure 2. This has been corrected.

The updated original version of this chapter can be found at
https://doi.org/10.1007/978-3-030-60703-6_75

Author Index

Printed in the United States
by Baker & Taylor Publisher Services